GETTING BEYOND THE FACTS

STUDIES IN THE
POSTMODERN THEORY OF EDUCATION

Joe L. Kincheloe and Shirley R. Steinberg
General Editors

Vol. 100

PETER LANG
New York • Washington, D.C./Baltimore • Bern
Frankfurt am Main • Berlin • Brussels • Vienna • Oxford

Joe L. Kincheloe

GETTING BEYOND THE FACTS

Teaching Social Studies/Social Sciences in the Twenty-first Century

SECOND EDITION

PETER LANG
New York • Washington, D.C./Baltimore • Bern
Frankfurt am Main • Berlin • Brussels • Vienna • Oxford

Library of Congress Cataloging-in-Publication Data

Kincheloe, Joe.
Getting beyond the facts: teaching social studies/social sciences
in the twenty-first century / by Joe L. Kincheloe
p. cm. — (Counterpoints; vol. 100)
Includes bibliographical references and index.
1. Social sciences—Study and teaching—United States. I. Title.
II. Counterpoints (New York, N.Y.); vol. 100.
H62.5.U5 K56   300'.71'073—dc21   2001037141
ISBN 0-8204-4162-7
ISSN 1058-1634

Die Deutsche Bibliothek-CIP-Einheitsaufnahme

Kincheloe, Joe:
Getting beyond the facts: teaching social studies/social sciences
in the twenty-first century / by Joe L. Kincheloe –New York;
Washington, D.C./Baltimore; Bern; Frankfurt am Main; Berlin;
Brussels; Vienna; Oxford: Lang.
(Counterpoints; vol. 100)
ISBN 0-8204-4162-7

Cover design by Joni Holst

The paper in this book meets the guidelines for permanence and durability
of the Committee on Production Guidelines for Book Longevity
of the Council of Library Resources.

Printed in the United States of America

To Clint Allison on his
retirement from the University of Tennessee.

After all these years I have yet to find a
better teacher or scholar.

Table of Contents

PART I

The Foundations of
the Social Studies

Chapter 1

Is There a Cure for the Twenty-First Century Social Studies Blues? Problems and Hopes

Social studies education is not healthy. The discipline has endured 40 years of confusion marked by the rise and fall of the "new social studies," the attempt to elevate the skills of decision making and reflective inquiry, a brief obsession with relevance, a crusade for moral education and values clarification, a sordid affair with competency-based instruction and the back to basics movement, and, most recently, a crusade for standards.

The result of these trends and fads has been quite harmful on a number of levels. First, the confusion has destroyed much of the credibility of social studies educators with the public well as with many public school teachers. Many people, as evidenced by the call for technical content standards, have come to the conclusion that academicians in the social studies are incompetent bunglers susceptible to every fad which appears. Also lamentable is the perception of social studies theorists by public school teachers. The relationship between theorists and practitioners has always been strained, but the confusion of the last four decades has contributed to the uncertainty about both the definition of social studies and how best to teach it. Despite the millions of dollars spent and volumes of literature written, many practitioners are more confused than ever about what the term, social studies, actually means. As theoreticians have flitted from fad to fad and practitioners have faced frustration and confusion resulting often in lack of interest, students have reflected the confusions and lack of interest in the subject.

To this stark school-based reality must be added a larger social context in which deep social, political, cultural, economic, and even civic understandings are hard to find. Over the last forty or so years a dramatic change has occurred in U.S. society. The culture has moved from a so called modernist era into "something different," something even in the early years of the twenty-first century we cannot even name. Some people have referred to this time period as the postmodern era or postmodernity. Numerous analysts have argued that this designation is not satisfactory. Others disagree over the meaning of the term, postmodern, and argue it simultaneously means everything and thus means nothing.

Whether or not there is a postmodern condition is a debate best saved for another book. For our purposes here, it is important to understand that something has changed in the culture of North American society since the 1950s that profoundly affects our social, cultural, political, economic, and civic consciousness—something that changes the relationship among the individual, the larger society, and the community. And anything that shapes such dynamics affects social studies education because these are the areas that constitute the concerns of the discipline. In this so-called postmodern condition—let's use the term while keeping in mind its limitations—individuals have lost touch with traditional notions of time, self, and history. New structures of cultural space and time generated by bombarding electronic images from local, national, and international locations shake our personal sense of place. Postmodernity has seen the emergence of a social vertigo.

Electronic transmissions from radio, TV, popular music, movies, video, e-mail, and Internet engulf us in nonlinear encounters with the world. Some refer to this new world as hyperreality—a place with so much input that we have difficulty finding meaning or making sense of the chaos of the data we encounter. If nothing makes sense, then what in this twenty-first century postmodern condition merits commitment? Raised in hyperreality, individuals (though they are often unable to name it) reflect the emotions (or lack of such) that postmodernity engenders. To understand the "twenty-first century social studies blues" and to begin the process of rethinking what social studies can become, the brilliance it can produce, and the hope and insight it can provide, it is important to delve a little deeper into the nature of this social reality. In this manner we will begin to "get beyond the facts" and to appreciate what it might mean to teach social studies in a way that changes our own and our students' lives in the twenty-first century.

FORTY YEARS ON THE FRONTIER

Change has changed in the last forty years. The beginnings of this social alteration can be traced to the period of a major rupture in American social and political life: the 1960s (maybe, more specifically, 1965–1975). The United States did change in this decade and the way we interpret that modification in the first decade of the twenty-first century has much to do with the way we make sense of our civic lives and our relationship to the world. Those who characterize themselves as conservative, with their concerns with order, hierarchy, the protection of property, custom, and convention, and the superiority of Western values, are uncomfortable with the many things that happened in the 1960s. Mythologizing the decade, and possibly exaggerating its importance, many twenty-first century conservatives demarcate the '60s as a time of national decline in the United States (Dionne, 1991).

The hippie counterculture movement with its drugs and rock music, as well as popular culture, the sexual revolution, the civil rights movement, women's and gay rights movements, and the nation's inability to win the Vietnam War, all are markers of American decline in this era. The emergence of these social dynamics corresponds with and shapes what might be referred to as the postmodern frontier. It is amazing that 40 years after these issues emerged, and we began our negotiation of the postmodern frontier, they still have the power to shape the way we feel about social and political life in the United States (Grossberg, 1992). This feeling or affective aspect of our private and public lives is central not only to American politics but to the social studies as well. Any attempt to engage teachers and educational leaders in a discussion of contemporary social studies education without an understanding of the postmodern frontier and our feelings about it will not provide an authentic picture of the issue.

In the context of our feeling toward the postmodern frontier, Aaron Gresson (1995, 2000) has written several books on how such dynamics have shaped American social, cultural, political, and educational life since the 1960s. Gresson, in *The Recovery of Race in America* and *America's Atonement*, maintains that, since the 1960s, American politics has engaged in an unending debate over recovering what was perceived to be lost in the various social movements of the 1960s. In particular, white men have felt the need to reestablish their sense of power, weakened, many of them believe, by the African American civil rights movement, Native American and indigenous peoples' struggle for social justice, women's liberation, and the gay pride movement. Of course, from an empirical standpoint, white males still overwhelmingly dominate social, economic, and political institutions—so much so that one is hard-pressed to understand their sense of a threat.

Nevertheless, the perception of the need for recovery is real, and such a feeling places such white men in a particular relationship to the postmodern frontier. America needs, they argue, to go back to a time—before the 1960s and the appearance of the postmodern divide—when the nation was great, high moral standards were intact, and people "knew their place." As Republican Congressman Henry Hyde implied after President Bill Clinton was found innocent in his Senate impeachment trial in 1998: "Here's just another example of the damage the '60s gener-ation and their immoral behavior has inflicted on our nation." Hyde cer-tainly knew where he stood in relation to the postmodern divide.

In the lives of many Americans, the feelings evoked by the events of the 1960s produced a type of cynicism. Such cynicism has shaped the way Americans approached their country, their citizenship, and (impor-tant in the concerns of this book) the study of the social, political, eco-nomic, and civic—social studies—education. Many conservatives label this feeling of cynicism a form of moral relativism, meaning that they believe many Americans have lost their ability to distinguish between right and wrong. Those often labeled liberals have given in to cynicism, in that they no longer believe that positive social and political change is possible, and have retreated from the civic realm. Whatever the reaction, this affective feature is powerful since it shapes the political and social identities of many Americans.

A central theme of *Getting Beyond the Facts: Teaching Social Studies in the Twenty-First Century* will involve how individuals who believe in and teach about the possibilities of democracy will deal with the postmodern frontier and the feelings that surround it. Throughout the book, I will integrate the relationship between the teaching of social studies and the lessons of the larger social, cultural, and political domain. One of the problems, I believe, of contemporary social studies education is that we often attempt to make sense of social studies teaching outside the context of contemporary society. How, for example, can we understand social studies education outside the context of the postmodern frontier and the feelings it generates about participation in civic life? I don't think we can. Indeed, this book is grounded on the interaction between social studies education and the oscillations of public life in the dynamic global society of the twenty-first century. If we are to change American society for the better, to realize the dream of democracy, and to put into practice the ideals of justice and equality that we talk about, these dynamics must be understood and acted upon.

THE CONTEMPORARY DIVIDE

It is fascinating to note how many people in the United States are shaped by the postmodern divide. One large group actively opposes the logic of the postmodern condition even as they live within it: the new conservatives, with their advocacy of a cultural war against the heathens, involving family values, the restoration of social order and discipline, the regulation of sexuality and desire, and a discomfort with the pursuit of pleasure. Another sizable group is comfortable in their surrender to the logic of the postmodern condition. Because conservative advocates have set the tone of the political conversation since about 1975, with their language of recovery of white male power and Judeo-Christian definitions of morality and virtue, members of the second group may often feel emotionally uncomfortable with their affective relationship to public life and to the pleasure they might have derived from sex, drugs, and rock 'n' roll. Such individuals find it difficult to speak about their affective investments in the world shaped by the conservative recovery of the post-1975 cosmos. Those from this second group who teach social studies often find their lives filled with emotional turmoil precipitated by their inability to express their perspectives in the school culture so profoundly shaped by the conservative restoration. Prozac finds a huge targeted market in this group.

In this divided cultural context, the right-wing political victories of the last 25 years have depended on the conservatives' ability to widen the polarization between the two groups and to exacerbate cynicism. In every domain—political, social, educational, and even moral—right-wing activists remind Americans of how the world is going to hell. The reason, they tell the nation over and over again, is the "moral relativism," "secular humanism," "permissivism," "anti-patriotic, anti-Americanism," and "multiculturalism" that emerged in the 1960s. The politics that emerges from this construction teaches a social studies and civics curriculum with two main lessons: 1) maintain a cynical stance toward the possibility of making meaning of, or changing, the public sphere: give up politics—it's a nasty realm of activity; and 2) make the center of your life the private domain. Live out your moral commitments with your family, religion, and consumption.

In such a context, how could social studies education with its public and civic focus be important? Is it surprising that many elementary curricula ignore it, and, in secondary schools, it is often relegated to those teachers with little background in the subject area? Indeed, social studies in the first decade of the twenty-first century rests at the nexus of our cynicism. Issues of improving the public sphere or social progress in areas of justice and the extension of democracy are portrayed as irrelevant in the conservative politics of cynicism; so why bother with them? Such a politics articulates positions along the boundaries of the postmodern divide, associating itself with the conservative restoration in private life while deploying cynicism toward the notion that anything can be improved in public life (Grossberg, 1992; Kincheloe, 1995).

Here rests one of the most important political and social studies-related understandings in recent American history: the colonization of the postmodern divide with its dismissal of the public and its hostility toward social improvement is part of a successful political strategy to kill politics. The more Americans hate politics, see its workings as crass and distasteful, and perceive it as a futile waste of time, the less impediments exist to impede power wielders from shaping the society and the world in their own interests. Social studies education is caught right in the middle of this sociopolitical and cultural vortex. The teaching of social studies, with its focus on improving the public sphere, producing active citizens, evoking social criticism, and exploring social problems, does not fit the privatized global order. It is a curricular dinosaur.

On the postmodern frontier, with its privatization and centralization of information, conservative guardians of power view the role of a public government as negative. "Government interference" becomes a far more common phrase than "government protection." In this context, the only choices available become the destruction of government or the replacement of public government with a private government: Attempts are being made to accomplish both of these choices in the first decade of the twenty-first century. In this situation, the functions of the democratically elected government are being reduced, while the control over everyday life by an unelected, privatized government in the form of multinational corporations and unaccountable conglomerates increases. This holds profound consequences for the future of democracy, as individuals hold less and less power to shape their destinies. Such dynamics are infrequently discussed in the literature of mainstream social studies.

The point of this analysis on the negative positioning of government on the postmodern frontier is not to argue naively for a position of always supporting government. Of course, governments do bad things, and social studies educators need to be ever vigilant about the possible tyranny of government. But such a responsibility does not address the issue at hand. A vigilant stance about the abuses of government is very different than the right-wing war on the concept of the public, democratically elected state. The war on the state in the postmodern world is premised on the dangerous assertion that the public activity of a democratically elected government is always inferior to private undertaking. Not only is this not true but it operates to transfer power into the hands of those who already possess it in the private sector. Private tyranny is just as possible—if not more so—than governmental tyranny.

This sea change of political sentiment over the last 40 years has taken place more along the postmodern frontier of feeling as opposed to some form of logical policy analysis. A theme that will run throughout *Getting Beyond the Facts* is the notion that the new terrain on which political opinions are shaped is not the political sphere as much as it is the cultural arena. Thus, in a form of pretzel logic, the cultural has become the primary political playing ground. This means that areas that we once considered mere "entertainment" are now used for profound political impact. Social studies educators need to understand that television, movies, popular music, video games, the Internet, web sites, and virtual realities are not simply cultural but are the most important political sites along the postmodern divide. In this new political context the passive notion of consumer has replaced the active concept of citizen (Davis & Fernlund, 1995; Hursch & Ross, 2000; Dionne, 1991; Kincheloe, 1999; Grossberg, 1992; Steinberg, 2000).

KEEP THE DIVIDE WIDE

Using the cultural domain to promote cynicism, rewriting history to "prove" the failure of democratic government, returning to the same divisive issues of a previous era, power wielders have managed to undermine public conversation, pull the plug on a critical civics education, and create a climate generally hostile to political analysis. In such a hostile context, power wielders have justified a policy of doing nothing about the public problems we face. As they often contend, just throwing money at social problems will not make them go away. Of course, doing nothing will not solve such problems either. A political-economic philosophy of letting the free market have its way was inserted into the vacuum left by the antigovernment cynicism. This non-policy has worked effectively to make the wealthy much wealthier while leaving the poor poorer. It has also allowed public services and infrastructures to deteriorate in the midst of the creation of great private wealth and individual fortunes. The postmodern divide widens the cultural and the economic gap between different Americans.

Electoral politics generally fails to address such divisions, as it degenerates into an orgy of posturing. As candidates scramble to defend particular symbols: "I love the flag;" "God bless America;" "I will defend the family;" "We need to bring morality back to our nation," the public's cynicism grows. Rarely does the defense of such symbols result in action; sometimes, the only public action taken operates to undermine the symbols referenced. Issues dealing with race become especially effective in "keeping the divide wide," as racial hatreds and fears are deployed in the politics of the postmodern frontier. Any possibility that the "have nots"—African Americans, Latinos, American Indians, and poor white people—might form alliances to fight power wielders is quickly squashed. Right-wing politicians have become adept at dividing such potential allies by convincing whites that the cause of many of their problems can be traced to "immoral, lazy, criminal, stupid" nonwhites. Such racial politics work expertly to maintain the unequal distribution of power along the postmodern divide.

In addition to race, power wielders have used gender to separate Americans. An important aspect of right-wing cultural politics involves the vilification of women who have embraced the egalitarian politics of feminism. It is not unusual to observe movies and TV shows that subliminally inscribe a hatred of strong women and/or attempt to blame them for the "decline of the nation" beginning in the 1960s. In a recent book on the cultural politics of the family and child rearing, *Kinderculture: The Corporate Construction of Childhood*, Shirley Steinberg and I traced the portrayal of women in a few segments of popular culture. In my chapter on the *Home Alone* movies of the early 1990s, I traced the depiction of Kevin's mother in both *Home Alone* and *Home Alone 2: Lost in New York*. Kevin's mother, played by Catherine O'Hara, internalizes the right-wing blame of "liberated" mothers for family pathology. The screenplays leave no doubt who is to blame for leaving Macauley Culkin's Kevin character home alone.

As I quote from the first *Home Alone* movie in that chapter, Kevin has just been unfairly banished to the attic during a family gathering because he is perceived as a nuisance:

KEVIN: Everyone in this family hates me.
MOTHER: Then maybe you should ask Santa for a new family.
KEVIN: I don't want a new family. I don't want any family. Families suck.
MOTHER: Just stay up there. I don't want to see you again for the rest of the night.
KEVIN: I don't want to see you again for the rest of my whole life. And I don't want to see anyone else, either.
MOTHER: I hope you don't mean that. You'd be pretty sad if you woke up tomorrow morning and you didn't have a family.
KEVIN: No I wouldn't.
MOTHER: Then say it again. Maybe it'll happen.
KEVIN: I hope I never see any of you again.

The mother is the one who sets up the possibility that Kevin will be left behind as the family flies to Paris for Christmas. She pushes Kevin to wish for a new family, to tempt fate by wanting never to see them again. In *Home Alone* and countless other movies, it is clear that child care is the mother's sole responsibility. John Heard's father character in the movie is a virtual nonentity. He is uninterested in Kevin, often condescending, and even hostile. He knows (along with the audience) that he is not responsible for Kevin's abandonment even though he was present throughout the entire episode. Heard's character has no reason to be upset or guilty; this is the mother's domain.

The mother accepts all culpability for Kevin spending Christmas home alone. She rides in the back of a U-Haul trailer with a polka band to get back to her son in *Home Alone*. She runs hysterically through the mean nighttime streets of New York, calling for her son, in *Home Alone 2*. Her penitence, her quest for forgiveness, includes a larger social blame of feminist women for their changing perspective on parenting as a shared responsibility of both genders. The right-wing males' blame of such women for the problems of the family, however, is grotesquely distorted, insinuating, as it does, that divisions of strong but tender men are struggling with their wives to let them take charge of child rearing—not exactly (Paul, 1994; Rapping, 1994). Thus, the *Home Alone* movies move out of the realm of "mere entertainment" (Steinberg and Kincheloe, 1997). They, and countless productions like them, form the terrain on which political consciousness is constructed in postmodernity. Racial and gender issues are only a couple of the numerous areas addressed in this media/popular culture-based social studies curriculum of the contemporary era. In postmodernity, the realm that we call social studies has significantly expanded.

LEARNING FROM CONTEXT: MAKING SENSE OF SOCIAL STUDIES ON THE CONTEMPORARY FRONTIER

I admit it: Times are tough for those of us interested in teaching social studies. It is hard sometimes to escape those twenty-first century social studies blues. But despite the problems, hope persists. We must be rigorously aware of the impediments we face; in these understandings, we can find opportunities for change. Social studies teachers must be cognizant of the cultural hostility to their subject. They must be sensitive to their students' lack of knowledge in the area (Davis and Fernlund, 1995). Why should students in the first decade of the twenty-first century understand historical, social, cultural, and political concepts? They have been taught by the larger culture's curriculum not to value such knowledge. In addition, few social or educational sites exist that help young people (or adults) make sense of the socio-political reality they encounter. Most of the high school and middle school students I speak to do not possess the conceptual tools needed to organize social information.

At the same time, most of the students I talk to in middle and high school and the undergraduate social studies education students I teach, have a basic sense of the values of freedom, justice, and equality. They want to be fair in their dealings with other people in the world. What they often don't have is the experience connecting their personal values to the public sphere. Talented and knowledgeable social studies teachers can help them make that all-important connection. A central feature of this book will involve helping social studies students develop conceptual schemas for making sense of the knowledge of twenty-first century social, cultural, political, historical, economic, and civic affairs. Students and their teachers must get beyond factual memorization and develop the ability to interpret the world they confront daily. They must understand the hidden agendas that move events, structures of power that undermine the quest for democracy, and the subtle working of oppression in its various expressions.

These are difficult tasks. Their accomplishment challenges teachers, students, teacher educators, and educational and political leaders alike. I believe they are worth the effort in a postmodern hyperreality that threatens the very foundations of democratic self-government in the United States. Indeed, these tasks constitute some of the most important work in American political history. What we are dealing with here is understanding and formulating action to counter threats to the democratic process. The social studies education proposed here fights against the abuse of the poorest and most vulnerable people in the world and the tyranny of the most powerful. It explores the ethical requirements of citizenship in the globalized society of the twenty-first century with its sweatshops, dire poverty, disease, and famine in the midst of the greatest wealth created in human history (Pang, Gay, & Stanley, 1995). It is perplexed by the image of a stock market falling on the news that some of the lowest wageworkers among us are receiving a few cents higher pay.

The social studies education envisioned in *Getting Beyond the Facts* is grounded in an appreciation of the interconnectedness of all inhabitants on the planet. On this foundation, it attempts to develop new conceptions of citizenship and social action. In order to keep hope alive and to accomplish the goals delineated here, the social studies education promoted in *Getting Beyond the Facts* is grounded in a rigorous notion of scholarship. We must understand the knowledge and conceptual aspects of the various disciplines that make up the social studies. At the same time, we must understand the limitations of these sometimes fragmenting disciplines and understand social reality in multi- and trans-disciplinary ways. We will explore these dynamics in more detail later in the book.

In this scholarly context, one of the most important features of the rigorous social studies proposed here involves teachers and students performing meaningful research (Puk, 1994). Schools must be sufficiently democratic to allow teachers and students to do their own social studies research, to interpret their findings in the way they deem best, and to become knowledge workers who understand the implicit values and interests embedded in all social information. Such abilities empower teachers and students to become full participants not only in the educational but the political process as well. A truly democratic society does not simply allow such behavior but encourages it for all students.

As social studies students conduct research and create knowledge, we must listen carefully to what they tell us (Metzger & Bryant, 1993). They are often experts on the knowledge production of the postmodern condition. From their participation in the products of popular culture, they often bring a visceral understanding of the cultural curriculum to the classroom. Thus, a democratic social studies gives voice to students and jealously protects the importance of student insights in a classroom setting. This jealous protection does not mean, however, simply validating anything students say or bring to class. It means granting students enough respect to engage with their knowledge, exploring problems and oppressive tendencies within it. Does it further the civic goal of connecting people around the globe? Does their knowledge inspire new forms of human interaction and human possibility? Or does it oppress or silence individuals from disempowered groups?

These are just a few of the questions social studies teachers need to bring to the exploration of their students' knowledge (Darder, 1991). Social studies education, as conceptualized in *Getting Beyond the Facts*, does not claim neutrality on the social, cultural, and political questions of the day. I profess a view of social studies and other forms of knowledge that assumes its historical, social, economic, political, and cultural formation. This means that information is always produced from someone's perspective and value assumption. As a result, I have abandoned the quest for some form of absolute or certain knowledge and seek only information and concepts about social studies topics that I know are limited by where, when, and by whom they were produced. Believing this, I assume that all information is open to question, research, criticism, and exposure of the assumptions embedded within it.

Making this argument, I'm not simply speaking of my students' information or information garnered from textbooks but my own information as well. I hope that you will question, research, criticize, and expose the assumptions embedded in *Getting Beyond the Facts*. It is not presented to you as the final truth about social studies. Not at all. It is submitted as my speculations at this point. It is your duty to question it. In the process of your interaction with this information, you will emerge as a more informed social studies teacher, regardless of whether or not you accept its validity. In a democratic society, individuals have the right to accept or reject the information presented them. Making wise judgments of information is a central goal of a democratic social studies and a critical notion of citizenship. Not only is it a central theme of this book but it is becoming more and more of a survival skill with the information saturation of the postmodern hyperreality.

Chapter

We Hate Social Studies: Traditions, Failures, and the Social Studies Methods Course—Beginning the Reform

Over the past 40 years, study after study has indicated that social studies, as taught in the elementary, middle, and secondary schools, is not in good standing (Owens, 1997). While there are many examples of individual teacher success, the field in general is viewed negatively. The following is an overview of the findings of studies of the state of social studies over the last four decades.

THE FINDINGS: DELINEATING THE PROBLEMS

1. STUDENTS ARE LEARNING LITTLE. Students in contemporary social studies classes are learning less than ever before and disliking it more. Most students have only a superficial understanding of American government and American history and lack an integrated understanding of the subject areas. In economics, it is hard to argue that students even have a superficial knowledge base. In reference to social studies skills and attitudes, the researchers found more bad news. While most students can identify sources of information and can read simple graphs, most cannot interpret complex graphs and tables, make reasonable inferences from information, or identify the main idea of a speaker or a discussion group. In reference to political attitudes, the researchers

found that most students grant verbal support to basic democratic values, but little proof of student behavior reflecting these values was discovered. Most students have negative experiences with social studies and express unqualified dislike for it. In addition, they see it as quite irrelevant to their lives. Students of all grade levels found social studies less useful and less important to their future needs than other subjects.

2. LACK OF VARIETY OF TEACHING METHODS AND EVALUATION; INATTEN-TION TO THE BENEFITS OF EDUCATIONAL RESEARCH. Social studies teachers, analysts have found, rely on textbooks because the books helps organize the various bodies of knowledge they teach. They often refuse to expand the resources and the range of classroom learning activities because they argue that such expansion will make the management of the classroom too difficult. Social studies teachers pay little attention to educational theorists and researchers because teachers often hold the perception that such "innovators" live in ivory towers and do not understand the realities of everyday practice. Most social studies teachers like to play it safe, for they realize that innovative practices may jeopardize their working relationship with peers, students, administrators, and parents.

3. SOCIAL STUDIES CURRICULUM DOES NOT HELP STUDENTS UNDERSTAND AND PARTICIPATE IN THE CURRENT AND FUTURE SOCIAL WORLD. The social studies curriculum that is generally taught in the nation's classrooms is typically based on traditional factual history and grants little attention to the developmental characteristics of students or the social context in which they live. Social studies programs repeat state, United States, and world history about five times and are organized around the teaching of facts taken from disciplinary structures and geographical places, rather than around ideas, problems, or skills that students need. When contemporary advocates of technical, top-down content standards argue that social studies teachers need to teach history-based factual knowledge to students, they don't acknowledge this is exactly what too many of them have been doing.

4. THE SAD STATE OF SOCIAL STUDIES AS A PROFESSION. Elementary and secondary teaching, the research contends, is an isolated activity where teachers and students work alone. There is little interaction

among those people who are involved in the different levels of social studies teaching and research; there are limited opportunities for personal growth for teachers; and there is much confusion about the role social studies should play in the educational process. Secondary and elementary teachers view college teacher educators with mistrust and suspicion. The reason for this seems to involve the existence of hierarchical subcultures, with elementary teaching at the bottom and graduate teaching at the top. The suspicions among the various groups outweigh any common concern for social studies teaching, and, as a result, the profession is divided into cliques. While these characteristics may be true of teaching in all subject areas, research seems to indicate that social studies is affected more than any other discipline. Because of this intradisciplinary alienation, confusion reigns over the field's basic goals and direction and there are too few effective avenues of communication between members.

5. A SCHOOL CULTURE HOSTILE TO LEARNING. Most of the energy of teachers, the report asserted, is directed toward classroom management and control rather than toward the teaching process. The central objective of many school personnel is often student socialization, and this concern frequently conflicts with the creation of a context for learning. Academic activities are not designed with the goals of learning in mind; rather, they are conceived for purposes of controlling student behavior. An example of such an activity is in-class student chapter reading and end-of-the-chapter question answering. Other aspects of school culture that reduce the chances of learning, include the size of modern schools, their fragmented time schedules, testing and grading systems, and extracurricular activities. The subcultures, which seem to develop in most large schools, succeed in alienating one group of students from another, while imposing walls between teachers and all groups of students. Thus, the large school becomes increasingly alienated and depersonalized, as communication between people is destroyed.

6. LACK OF PUBLIC AWARENESS OF THE IMPORTANCE OF SOCIAL STUDIES. The general public sees social studies as being less useful than English, math, commercial courses, shop, or even extracurricular activities. The public perceives the most important function of social studies to take place on the secondary level in the development of

patriotic citizens. There is little public understanding of the social studies goals of conceptual thinking, social studies skill development, knowledge work in the social studies, the subject's emphasis on contemporary issues or decision making. Indeed, there seems to be growing support for mandating competencies that can be used to measure a narrowly defined comprehension of civic responsibility and free enterprise. When the curriculum is mandated from the top-down, as in many of the technical reforms of the last thirty years, less time is given to elementary social studies. In some districts, elementary social studies is actually fighting for its existence. Research seems to indicate that one reason public support for social studies is so low is the low perception many people have of their own social studies experiences. In most American schools, social studies has never played an important role in the elementary curriculum. On the secondary level, most citizens have seen social studies as only a factual drill in American history and government—subjects, deemed by many students and former students to possess little relevance to their present or future lives. In light of these concerns, the social studies profession has attempted little action to edify the public. No awareness campaigns have been planned or implemented, as social studies educators have tended to ignore popular conceptions of the field.

7. CONFUSION OVER WHAT CONSTITUTES THE SOCIAL STUDIES. Numerous individuals, both inside and outside of the educational establishment, are unable to define exactly what is signified by the term "social studies" (Owens, 1997). In a recent hiring of a social studies professor in a university where I taught, I was amazed at the differing and conflicting conceptions of what constituted the social studies and what should be considered an adequate scholarly background for a social studies education professor. After the search committee, on which I was serving, unanimously selected our top candidate for the position, the department refused to hire her because her sociology and cultural studies background was not deemed appropriate for a social studies professor. Although social studies educators on the search committee argued that professionals in the field come from many different subject areas and that there is not one single background deemed necessary for becoming a professor, scholars from other fields refused to accept such explanations. The department refused to hire the candidate, citing, even after the social studies professors' protests, her inadequate preparation.

ANALYZING THE SOCIAL STUDIES METHODS CLASS IN LIGHT OF THE DISCIPLINE'S PROBLEMS

In light of such problems, let us turn our attention to the social studies methods class. What is typically taught in social studies methods classes? The answer to such a question, of course, depends upon the professor in question. Under the title of social studies methods, students experience courses ranging from simplistic, rote-based exercises to sophisticated thinking adventures in the discipline. While scores of sophisticated, creative teachers introduce elementary and secondary teacher education students to the world of social studies teaching, explorations have found too many professors who offer a nonconceptual, technical view of social studies teaching.

These nonconceptual classes were consistently marked by an absence of analytical questions about and critical examination of the nature of the social studies curriculum. Questions concerning the origins of practices, the implicit assumptions underlying certain language used in the discipline, the connections between social studies teaching and larger socio-political issues, and the general purposes of social studies methods classes in a democratic society were almost always ignored. The composition of textbooks now in use in many social studies methods classes often dictate the topics covered in these nonconceptual classes. While many of the textbooks may attempt to provide a conceptual context for the topics they cover, this context is often overlooked by the nonconceptual methods course.

There is a tendency for these nonconceptual classes to assume a rather common format. The subject matter of many of the methods textbooks probably contributes to this uniformity. In every social studies methods textbook I surveyed, the following topics were examined with varying degrees of sophistication: lesson planning, behavioral objectives, evaluation, values, social studies materials, current events, and alternative strategies/inquiry. In every methods class labeled as nonconceptual, these same topics were emphasized. The argument here is not that topics are not valid—not at all. Given an analytical context, such topics can be developed conceptually and quite productively. The attempt here is simply to describe what often occurs in the nonconceptual methods class in an attempt to move to more scholarly and sensitive understandings of the field.

The Teaching of the Seven Common Topics

1. LESSON PLANNING. The nonconceptual social studies methods courses and the methods texts almost always delineate the types of plans
   used in the schools: unit plans, short-range plans focused on a central topic, and daily plans. Components of a lesson plan are then listed. Though they may vary from author to author and teacher to
   teacher, the format is generally the same: title for lesson, statement
   of objectives, introduction, sequence of learning activities, evaluation, and a list of materials to be used. Tests in such classes often ask
   students to list these components of a lesson plan.

   Again, note that lesson planning is extremely important. The salient
   question becomes: How does one best teach such skills? Teaching the
   skills in contextual isolation, as do the nonconceptual courses, does not
   work. If one of the most important goals of a methods class is to teach
   prospective social studies teachers to think analytically about the discipline, then such an isolated approach fails. Lesson planning should be
   learned in the context of putting a real class together. The substance of
   planning should take precedence over form, as prospective teachers grapple with the problem of determining what is significant about a body of
   information as it relates to a certain group of students.

   Little attention is granted to the ways in which larger educational
   purposes may influence or determine the types of lesson plans utilized or
   the content of the plans. Such nonconceptual methods of teaching fail
   to engage the student in the magic of the discipline of social studies, for
   they strip methodology from the subject matter of social studies. The reasons individuals are attracted to history, geography, political science,
   sociology, cultural studies, anthropology, or economics are buried under
   a preoccupation with lesson plan format.

2. BEHAVIORAL OBJECTIVES. In our nonconceptual methods classes, lesson planning is often followed by a study of behavioral objectives.
   The key element in the examination involves precision of the statement of objectives. Such clarity, it is argued, will lead to purposeful
   and meaningful activities in the classroom. Great effort is given to
   the task of teaching prospective teachers the proper language of
   behavioral objective writing. Methods students often are asked at
   this point to memorize infinitives, such as "to name," "to locate," "to

choose," "to provide examples"; students are taught that infinitives, such as "to understand," "to believe," "to enjoy," "to appreciate" are to be avoided.

Again, the concrete concern with format is overemphasized and the goal of learning factual data instead of producing and interpreting information is embraced. The nonconceptual methods teacher typically misses an excellent opportunity at this point to explore the culture of the classroom. What are the objectives of an exciting social studies class? What happens when learning outcomes are specified in a behavioral manner? Is conceptualization compatible with such a specific format? What are the assumptions which underlie social studies classes taught in American schools today? Is there a dominant ideological orientation which directs the nature of social studies teaching?

3. EVALUATION. The study of evaluation in the nonconceptual methods class often degenerates into a listing of testing methods. An idea common to most methods classrooms involves the recognition that a variety of testing procedures should be used by the teacher. After pencil and paper tests (both objective and subjective), evaluation strategies, such as group discussion, observation, checklists, teacher-student conferences, anecdotal records, work samples, and student attitude scales, are commonly mentioned. It is important to understand that such evaluation techniques exist, but much more understanding is needed.

Prospective social studies teachers need to understand the biases and assumptions underlying the use of the various evaluation strategies. Certain evaluation strategies are specifically tied to certain perspectives on the nature of knowledge and the goals and purposes of social studies. Walter Parker and John Jarolimek (1997) in their popular text, *Social Studies in Elementary Education*, do a good job of addressing the biases of standardized minimum competency tests used in the social studies. Such tests, they contend, do not encourage a balanced assessment of student skills, knowledge, or abilities. Their use often results in fragmented fact-based social studies teaching by intimidated instructors who cover themselves by directly teaching the test.

Discussions based on the type of information that Parker and Jarolimek present rarely find their way into the nonconceptual methods class. In the race to provide students with so-called "practical" skills, the analysis of the origins and larger meanings of such evaluative practices as minimum competency testing is sacrificed. The social, political, and philosophical contexts which give birth to such educational strategies are neglected. It is this type of understanding that builds the analytical ability necessary to the professionalization of social studies teachers. Without it, social studies teachers are reduced to mere technicians condemned to a work life marked by an attempt to follow the top-down rules and survive day to day.

4. VALUES. The teaching of values in the social studies is undoubtedly one of the most complex and ambiguous aspects of the discipline. For this very reason, the subject is often ignored in the nonconceptual classroom. Because of its complexity and ambiguity, the teaching of values reflects the spirit and essence of the social studies better than almost any other topic. Accordingly, an analysis of values teaching should occupy a central position in social studies methods.

The topics that can be examined under the values umbrella are numerous. The debate over moral reasoning by Kohlberg and his detractors, authoritarian values versus relative values as illustrated by New Right textbook and curriculum controversies, and teaching personal values via values clarification and all of the accompanying arguments this topic has elicited are just a few values-related social studies topics. How can a social studies methods class ignore an examination of democratic values and an accompanying reading of John Dewey on the nature of democracy and the role of social studies education in a democratic society? The nonconceptual methods class seems to ignore the fact that value choices determine what goes on in a social studies class. Values are real, either consciously or unconsciously, they determine our approach to the subject. Social studies teachers need to understand the impact of tacit or unexplained values on the way social studies is taught.

5. SOCIAL STUDIES MATERIALS. In the nonconceptual social studies methods classes I observed, the study of materials usually involves a survey of the different categories of materials available. Sometimes, examples of materials are brought to the classroom where displays of films or supplemental paperback texts are presented. The purpose of the lessons on materials merely involves exposing prospective teach-

ers to the materials. Analysis of the materials is consistently neglected. Evaluative statements typically involve indications of personal preference for one book or film over another.

Most nonconceptual methods course lessons covered the following materials: textbooks, encyclopedias, supplementary books and references, pictures, films, filmstrips, slides, overhead projectors, maps, auditory aids, TV, bulletin boards, and computers. Classroom discussions of such materials offer an excellent opportunity to explore some basic questions about social studies. While the point was often made that knowledge of a variety of materials was helpful because not all children learn in the same way and that students remember better when more than one sensory system is involved in the learning process, the discussion often ended with these points.

Analysis of these materials can help social studies teachers approach the issues which make social studies what it has become. If research tells us that most elementary and secondary social studies teachers rely heavily on the textbook, then textbook content certainly determines much of what goes on in social studies classrooms around the country. Observers can thus determine what is often taught in social studies via textbook content decisions. On what basis are textbook content decisions made? The attempt to answer such a question opens a new world for the prospective social studies teacher. Literature such as Frances Fitzgerald's *America Revised* provides great insight into the process by which social studies texts are produced. Methods students soon learn from Fitzgerald that marketing considerations, and pressure from special interest and political power groups exert very important influences on textbook writers. Armed with such information, social studies teachers approach materials with a greater degree of sophistication.

Such sophistication might involve the realization that much of what textbooks present as fact is simply not true or is, at best, mere speculation. Nonconceptual, uncritical methods texts and elementary and secondary social studies book publishers are afraid to admit that there is far less certainty about the validity of the information in their materials than has been traditionally believed. If they are not aware of the problematic nature of social studies materials, social studies teachers can develop sophisticated secondary research-based teaching methods and still fail their students. All that such inquiry methods may accomplish, if teachers are not aware of textbook content, is leading students on little more than futile exercises of shuffling different publishers' social and historical myths. Various producers of social studies materials have devoted so much time to sanitizing the social, historical, and the political features of their texts that students and teachers often fail to understand the complex, messy, and uncertain nature of social studies knowledge. This recognition of complexity is a basic insight in a democratic social studies (Puk, 1994).

Television in the nonconceptual methods class is often viewed only in the context of its direct use in the classroom. TV discussions revolve around what shows may be valuable for social studies classes or how VCR's may open new vistas for classroom TV use. Rarely are the sociopolitical effects of TV examined. What an excellent opportunity for a study of how TV often shapes the way teachers and students approach social studies. This medium is part of a curriculum that shapes our view of the world, current events, what it means to be informed politically, the nature of our modern political system, our study habits, and our attention spans. In the last few years, more and more methods classes have examined the use of the Internet in the classroom. In the uncritical classes studied here, the Internet and cyberspace are simply reduced to one more resource in the social studies educator's bag of tricks. The implications of these sources in relation to the politics of knowledge production, their potential to further democratic activity, and questions of source validity and are too often ignored. Such absences are particularly disturbing in this era of endangered democracy.

6. CURRENT EVENTS. As with other topics, the nonconceptual approach to teaching about current events in the social studies involves the listing of various means of transmitting unexamined subject matter. Such classes minimize the effort to examine the role current events play in achieving the goals of the social studies. The study of current events in the nonconceptual methods classes typically revolves around the use of newspaper, student publications (including classroom newspapers), listings of information sources, current events days, and news bulletin boards. Of course, all of these vehicles for current events can be used with great effectiveness. The point here is that awareness of the existence of such vehicles and how to set them up in the classroom is merely a first step. Social studies teachers need to understand how to relate current events knowledge to other aspects of the social studies curriculum.

A thoughtful social studies teacher must be ready to connect current events to any phase of a social studies program. Current events must be an ever present laboratory of information that can be used to illustrate any social studies concept. Current events must be a living part of the curriculum—not an isolated curricular fragment addressed on Friday afternoons at 1:15–1:30. Rigorous democratic teachers must possess an ethic which moves them to be well-informed. Indeed, they must be familiar with the publications of various ideological perspectives, so that they are ready to set up situations where students can compare and contrast differing viewpoints on current events.

Given these understandings, a news-bulletin board or a student newspaper becomes something special. Students no longer pick stories at random but select topics which evoke debate. Such news stories tend to be the ones with long-range significance and, as such, are well-suited to facilitate the development of a world view. Few topics present a better opportunity to facilitate analytical thinking than do current events.

7. ALTERNATIVE STRATEGIES: INQUIRY. One of the most important means of developing analytical thinking among prospective social studies teachers and their future students involves an understanding of inquiry methodology. In the nonconceptual methods class, the examination of inquiry often receives little attention. One reason for such neglect is that social studies students in both the elementary and even secondary education programs have little opportunity in their teacher education courses or their liberal arts classes to study research methodology. Probably the shortest route to teaching a prospective teacher how to administer an inquiry-based social studies program is to provide a basic familiarity with research. For this reason, we feel that it is important for social studies teachers to engage in both primary and secondary social science research.

Many social studies methods texts point out that inquiry-based teaching rests on the assumption that social studies is not concerned only with the accumulation of knowledge but with both the accumulation and the application of knowledge. Such a concept is a good starting place for an analysis of inquiry methodology. Once this concept is discussed, attention can be directed to specific examples of how inquiry-generated knowledge can be applied. Social studies knowledge is thus connected to the lived world in such a way that students understand its meaning in their own lives. Unfortunately, the nonconceptual methods class fails to take advantage of this opportunity.

Instead of exploring the infinite possibilities offered by an analysis of the application of social studies knowledge to social problems, the nonconceptual class often turns its attention to a brief look at "thinking development" and "finding information." Inquiry is valuable as an alternative strategy, the argument goes, because it fosters thinking. Thinking, the argument continues, must be viewed as a process that is divided into subskills. Of course, this is true, but actual practice in specific forms of primary research and interpretation, with concurrent attention to the types of thinking utilized in the process, would be more valuable for prospective teachers. Typically, the examination of thinking subskills in uncritical methods classes amounts to little more than a rote listing of given categories. The approach to "finding information" rarely transcends a listing of social studies information sources.

Social studies methods teaching must get beyond the nonconceptual approach. It is such an approach that gives methods classes a bad name. Few courses in the university have a better opportunity to foster analytical thinking than does the teacher education methods class. To examine the various purposes analysts have devised for social studies, while at the same time taking the subject matter of the social sciences and searching for concrete and practical strategies of classroom implementation, is a very sophisticated task. Until a critical mass of social studies professionals can accomplish this task, the problems that plague the discipline will intensify and students will continue to hate social studies. A brief perusal of the history of the social studies provides further insight into the nature of these problems.

The Origins of Social Studies

The traditional way many historians of the discipline of social studies have chronicled its origins has been to evoke the work of the National Education Association's Committee on Social Studies in 1916. Here, they maintain, rest the origins of the field. Like so many historical "facts," this one is ambiguous. Other historians locate the discipline's beginnings in the late nineteenth century when the country was experiencing a transition from a rural and agrarian to an urban and industrialized society. Social commentators, such as John Dewey, argued in this era that the role of citizenship and education needed to be rethought in light of the profound social and political changes taking place. Whether in the 1890s, the 1910s, or the first decade of the twenty-first century, social studies has always been shaped by the political forces operating within the larger society. It always has and always will (Ross, 1997; Brady & Barth, 1995).

What we choose to teach about our political system, our history, and our society will always be a political issue, a subject of debate. The educational conversation about how these tasks should be performed will always be a power struggle. For example, in the 1890s, during the attempt to come to terms with the sociopolitical, cultural, and economic changes of the era, individual analysts offered differing opinions about the proper role of a good citizen. Citizenship education thus was inseparable from how one made sense of the politics of the period. Those who embraced a populist political perspective at the end of the nineteenth century, for example, were very uncomfortable with the definition of good citizenship promoted by corporate leaders and bankers. A good citizen, populists argued, was an individual who participated in mass movements designed to challenge the power of organized wealth. Unfortunately, the populists lost the argument, as corporate leaders turned back their challenge and formed a corporate-dominated state. Citizenship in this new context was defined as loyalty to the status quo. One can trace the process by which this perspective came to dominate the elementary and secondary social studies curriculum.

In the early conflicts over the nature of the emerging social studies curriculum, other divisive issues arose. Educators argued about whether social studies should be based primarily on history or if it should be a multidisciplinary subject. Scholars debated whether the primary goal of social studies was to pass along information produced by the academic social sciences or to help students engage in social improvement. Still others tangled over whether the social studies curriculum should be formulated by a centralized group of experts and taught the same way everywhere or whether individual teachers should be able to develop their own social studies curriculum. Arguing against the tyranny of centralization, John Dewey contended that, if students didn't learn centralized knowledge in the context of particular, local situations, the information would hold little meaning for them.

Dewey's call for local curriculum development and teacher empowerment is one of the most important ideas in the history of democratic social studies education. Unfortunately, however, his perspective rarely met with general approval. When social studies was formally incorporated into the educational system, after the National Education Association's recommendation in 1916, the political Progressive Era was coming to a close. Unlike populism, progressivism was not concerned as much with the redistribution of power as it was with good government. It is ironic that Dewey's concept of activist citizenship and participatory community building were much more populist than progressive, for it is the term, "progressive" (as in progressive education"), that is associated with his work.

The populist spirit is reflected in the desire of democratic social studies teachers to produce empowered citizens to engage with official version of the truth. We can see it expressing itself periodically throughout twentieth century social studies with efforts to rethink and reconstruct the American democratic experience. And, of course, it is present in *Getting Beyond the Facts* in the attempt here to rethink social studies in the postmodern, twenty-first century context in which we find ourselves. But the populist impulse has not been the dominant orientation toward social studies, as one can discern in previous references to the problems of the field and the nonconceptual methods course. By the late 1940s and 1950s, Dewey's ideas were out of favor: They were seen as inappropriate in an expanding post-WWII economy where many conservative analysts believed that there was general satisfaction with the way things were.

The year 1958 stands as an important moment in social studies education, as the Soviet launch of Sputnik motivated the United States to pass the National Defense Education Act. Attempting to keep up with the superior Soviet educational system, the legislation called for disciplinary specialists to construct new curricula for the schools. These new courses in the social studies came to be known as the New Social Studies. This innovation addressed many of the debates that had been a part of the discipline since its inception. Knowledge for the social studies would come from the academic disciplines of social sciences. Experts presented a top-down centralized body of lessons for teachers to implement. There was a definite hierarchy, with experts as curriculum developers on top and teachers and students on the bottom. Social studies teacher education involved helping teachers carefully use the expert materials in the "proper" manner (McCall, 1996; Ross, 1997; Brady and Barth, 1995).

Expected to know their place, teachers were not viewed as equal partners in the New Social Studies. Because of this relegation of teachers to the margins and, many would argue, the centralization of the process, the New Social Studies failed. After the fall of the New Social Studies, the discipline has found itself influenced by the push and pull of the liberation movements of the 1960s and the subsequent efforts to "recover" from them. Is social studies a force that promotes critical reflection about issues of justice, equality, democracy in the United States and its relationship to the peoples of the world? Or, is social studies a discipline that rallies Americans around the flag, encourages loyalty and obedience, considers American democracy a project already completed, and views the rest of the world as an inferior domain that doesn't meet the standards of mainstream America? Such questions shaped social studies in the last three decades of the twentieth century and continue to move the discipline in the first decade of the twenty-first. As we move into a globalized society, with all of its high-tech and virtual features, it is time to reassess the discipline and its goals for the future.

CURRENT HISTORY: THE NECESSITY OF SOCIAL STUDIES TEACHERS AS SCHOLARS IN THE TWENTY-FIRST CENTURY

Just as the populists were faced with challenges to American democracy at the end of the nineteenth century in the move from an agrarian to an industrial society, we are challenged in the twenty-first century by the move from industrialism to a form of international technocapitalism. The new conditions, new problems, and new possibilities that confront us in this period of history are daunting. If we are to make a difference as a profession, we must understand these new conditions and develop a vision of what a good society, prosperous economy, vibrant culture, just democracy, and a new form of human consciousness might look like. To accomplish such a task, social studies teachers must be scholars who are capable of conducting research and engaging their students in knowledge production and knowledge analysis.

John Dewey, as usual, recognized this dynamic, arguing, early in the twentieth century, that one of the most important impediments to democratic educational reform was the scholarly subservience of teachers. This must be overcome, Dewey maintained, and the right of teachers to act on their own initiative must be protected. When teachers are mandated to teach an "expert-produced" set of methods and judged on their fidelity to the procedures, reforms are destined to fail. Thus, reform in the social studies is contingent on the professional development of social studies teachers. Unfortunately, in many of the expressions of the late twentieth and early twenty-first century standards movement, this lesson is forgotten. Yet again, the expert-produced curriculum is viewed as the most important piece of the social studies reform puzzle. The concept of teachers as curriculum developers and respected professionals is rejected for a more subservient, passive, and deskilled role. Current social studies history repeats itself (Yeager & Wilson, 1997; Barth & Brady, 1995; Ross, 1997).

Scholarly social studies teachers move far beyond the expectations of the nonconceptual methods courses or the failing field portrayed by the various research studies. They understand that the accumulation of social, political, and historical knowledge is only one feature of professional preparation and, while necessary, does not by itself lead to a more sophisticated teaching of the social studies. A key ability of the scholarly democratic teacher promoted here involves not simply the accumulation of knowledge but what a social studies teacher does with that knowledge. Thus, as previously mentioned, the purpose of *Getting Beyond the Facts* is to argue for and help produce social studies teacher-scholars who are knowledge workers.

Several years ago, I was teaching in a small college in Louisiana and living in a working-class section of town. All of my neighbors were humble working-class people; many were employed at the local General Motors plant until it was shut down and moved to Mexico. I was an object of fascination for many of the neighborhood kids, since I went to the university with a briefcase, not a lunchbox, like all the other fathers in the area. I was bombarded by questions about the briefcase: What was it? What was in it? Where did I keep my lunch? One child, David, at the time struggling to make it through the eighth grade, was especially interested in my work.

"You say you teach social studies teachers?" he asked time and again. As I explained my work to him, he was fascinated with my educational background. I told him that I had majored in history and had both a B.A. and M.A. in the subject. After explaining what college degrees were, I answered David's questions about my history degrees. "But, why would you spend all that time studying history?" he asked. I tried to explain. "But, after you know all the facts in the book, what else would there be to do?" It was obvious how David had been taught to think about the nature and purpose of social studies. To his teachers and himself, social studies involved little more than the memorization of meaningless data in a book. "How could anyone be interested in that?" David asked me incredulously. What kind of weird geek was I?

I understood exactly where he was standing in the web of reality. No one had ever explained to him the importance or usefulness of such material, and he was unable to understand why anyone would devote any time to it. What David needed was a scholarly social studies teacher to engage him in exploring his work in relation to the larger concepts of the discipline. I learned the same lesson with my own children in their elementary and high school years. Excited to help them when they asked me about sixth- or tenth-grade social studies reports, I found relevant books and articles on the historical, political, or sociological aspects of the topic. I talked to my kids ad nauseam about different schools of thought and different perspectives on the topic and the nature of knowledge production about the area.

Though they learned a little about the nature of knowledge production in the social studies, they quickly learned to ignore my social studies advice. When they turned in their multiple-source, interpretive reports to their teachers, their work was judged to be "totally inappropriate" for the assignment. Tired of low grades, they learned to provide the teachers with what they wanted: a "legally plagiarized" synopsis of a short piece from the *World Book Encyclopedia*, or, in keeping with the new millenium, a cut and paste web paper. The designation of legal plagiarism comes from the way students were expected to use the encyclopedia. All of the concepts and perspectives from the entry were retained without question; students merely copied the data and changed a few words here and there. "Big" became "enormous" and "little" was changed to "small." Too many of us recognize this procedure.

Unfortunately, these types of stories are not uncommon. In research that involved students other than my own children, I found countless similar cases. Teachers and their social studies students are too often unfamiliar with the concept of social science research and knowledge work. In no way do I want to blame or demonize these teachers. They are victims of a system that too infrequently challenged them to think about the purposes and scholarly demands of high quality social studies teaching and never raised the question of what it means to be a knowledge worker. Paulo Freire, the great Brazilian educator, helps us understand where we might begin to conceptualize how social studies teachers become democratic knowledge workers. Though the nature of such work is very complex, the first steps we take to engage in it are quite simple.

BEGINNING THE PROCESS: BECOMING RESEARCHERS AND KNOWLEDGE WORKERS WHO MAKE A DIFFERENCE

Taking our cue from Freire (1970, 1985) we start our education as knowledge workers by learning to criticize ourselves, to question our own beliefs and opinions, to reflect on the knowledge we produce, and to avoid proclaiming that we have found the final answer. In this admission of our fallibility to ourselves, colleagues, and students, we are taking a risk. We are leaving ourselves open in an expert and macho culture to charges of not being authoritative; we put ourselves in an emotionally vulnerable position. If we are strong enough to withstand the criticism that will come from some quarters, such a move will be worth the risk. Even as we give up the notion of absolute authority, we become active agents who take control of our personal lives, professional lives, and our knowledge production. Social studies teachers, starting with this humble but empowered orientation, can use their abilities to change a battered discipline into a curriculum that makes a positive difference in the world (Freire & Faundez, 1989).

When social studies teachers and their students become knowledge workers, they not only explore new information but new and better ways of life. Such teachers are not looking for a blueprint or all the answers to what constitutes a better way of living, but they are searching for good questions about the notion. Democratic social studies teachers as knowledge producers are looking for new modes of "human being," better forms of social interaction, improved democratic formats, and more sophisticated forms of intelligence. I am excited by such possibilities and use my excitement to generate not only this book but my activities in everyday life. The social studies I imagine is not merely an analysis of the wisdom, insights, and failures of the past—although this is extremely important—but it includes unlimited discovery, new constructions of social, political, civic, and psychological insight, and the great wide open of human potential.

Our students will gain more from the questions that motivate us than the disciplinary data we pass along to them. Don't get me wrong: The disciplinary information and the meanings we make from it are essential to social studies rigor and excellence. The point here is that there is more to the process: the expansion of human consciousness and the journey to a new and better world. And this is where democratic social studies teachers engage students at the affective level, around their desires, passions, hopes, dreams, and fears. Our role is to connect the disciplines of the social sciences and humanities as well as the individual and social problems of the day to these dynamics. It takes profound knowledge, research abilities, and the capacity for interpretation and analysis to accomplish such tasks. As students learn to exercise power over their own lives and to dream of what could be, social studies education becomes what Dewey envisioned: a place where citizens are produced who can build a new democratic order (Butler, 1998; Prettyman, 1998; Fried, 1995).

Such a democratic order is not grounded on some formal and intractable blueprint but draws upon the lived forms of empowerment in the everyday world. Adept social studies teachers will connect ever evolving democratic principles and the dream of new forms of human being to concrete student experience. What does equality mean in a classroom arrangement? What is democracy in the everyday experience of play? What does civic participation mean in the effort to address an injustice in the community? What do we need to know to answer these questions and act accordingly? The democratic order that our social studies seeks envisions citizens who govern rather than those who passively submit to being governed. The nonconceptual social studies education described earlier, I'm afraid, too often teaches both teachers and students to be governed.

Social studies for a new democratic order produces teachers and student as researchers and knowledge workers who take control and set the direction of the learning process (Steinberg & Kincheloe, 1998). They refuse to be controlled by some top-down blueprint or pre-developed mode of teaching and learning. As they learn about issues of importance to their everyday lives, democratic social studies teachers and students connect such concerns to various knowledge bases and develop essential intellectual skills such as reading, writing, interpreting, and communicating. In this educational context, they begin to develop awareness of themselves as social players—citizens who are shaped by social, cultural, and political forces and who have a role in molding the social sphere. They are of the social sphere; not apart from it. They produce knowledge themselves and interpret what has already been produced; they do not relegate this task to the experts (King and Darder, 1991).

As students educated in this context leave schools and move into the workforce, they become workers who demand democratic and learning-centered workplaces (Kincheloe, 1995, 1999). Such democratic workers explore the way power operates to shape their consciousness and, their

understanding of their role in the workplace. As they research the political, economic, and social forces that shape the way their jobs are
defined, democratic workers begin to see themselves in relation to the
work around them and to understand the workplace as part of a larger
political economy of power and privilege. Exploring these power relations, they begin to understand that, oftentimes, they are reduced to
objects of administration defined by prevailing conceptions of what it
means to be merely a worker. They find out that, instead of being driven
by a logic of democracy, the workplace is shaped by a logic of capital:
questions of production and profit take precedence over questions of justice and humanity. They often come to realize that their democratic
vision of empowered workers who can evaluate a job in terms of its social
significance or moral effects becomes, from the prospective of management, the talk of an impractical and annoying group of workers. In this
context, they use their knowledge skills to help them determine how to
resist such antidemocratic forces.

Democratic Social Studies: Questions Lead to Inquiry

A central knowledge skill of empowered workers, such as these and other
civic agents, involves their ability to ask kinetic questions that can initiate action. Paulo Freire always maintained that the origins of any educational activity involved curiosity that led to informed questions (Freire
& Faundez, 1989). Indeed, the first thing anyone who is planning to
teach should learn, he argued, is the art of asking questions. The questions that come out of everyday life are the most important because that
is where the most important issues of life reside. Conventional social
studies teaching often ignores everyday life, opting instead for inert formal knowledges and low-level cognitive operations. Democratic social
studies teachers learn to ask both their students and themselves the type
of questions that stimulate the society and the people around them.
Learning to conduct research itself starts with learning to ask compelling
questions. If social studies teachers are tyrannized with top-down prescribed curricula, they will have been stripped of one of their greatest
teaching tools: questioning that manifests creativity, inspires curiosity,
and engages students in the adventure of learning.

If questions are the most important scholarly instruments known to
humans, then we should not only teach social studies teachers about the
art of questioning but, maybe, such an art should rest at the foundation

of the elementary, middle, secondary, and college social studies curriculum. Social studies teachers from the first to the twelfth grade engage their students in asking questions of the world around them. Social studies students learn to interview, ask how, and ask why. Elementary students can ask individuals in their communities about topics being explored in social studies classes. Students can then analyze their data; all this means is that students learn to ask new questions of the different answers they obtained from their questions to community members. As they compare different answers, students can ask even further questions about why people see the world differently. What, they might inquire, does this tell us? There is no reason elementary students can't successfully engage in this activity. Obviously, this is research and students at all grade levels can engage in it (Postman, 1995; Marker, 1993).

John Dewey had these types of ideas in mind when he argued for a form of education that engaged students in the world so they could reflect on and ask questions about it. When he suggested that students cultivate gardens, it was not for the purpose of making them future gardeners. Dewey used the experience of gardening to induce students to think about the role farming and horticulture have played in human affairs. Immersed in the experience of gardening, students would become more disposed to think about the social, cultural, political, and economic aspects of farming. At the same as time they were dealing with such social studies issues, students could be thinking about physical scientific concepts such as the chemistry of the soil, photosynthesis, the ecological balance of life, etc. Students in this learning context would appreciate the interconnectedness of the social studies as well as the physical sciences and the necessity of viewing them in relation to one another. The experience of gardening would grant students insights into asking questions about and researching these dynamics (King, 1990).

There is no boundary demarcating where social studies teachers can or cannot teach research skills. Kathleen Berry (1998) maintains that teacher/student research sites can include unlikely places in the school itself: hallways, gymnasiums, lunchrooms, bathrooms, and playgrounds. She induces students to ask questions about play activities: Why do only the boys play soccer and baseball? Why are the restroom doors labeled "men" and "girls?" Why do all the murals and posters include pictures of men and not women? Such questions raised about gender can generate lessons, units, and research projects in class. In addition, teachers and students can use the community to generate research topics: sources of pollution, the history of particular communities, the origins of certain institutions, and the reasons for homelessness. Making use of community resources and community members not involved in schooling can change one's teaching life. Because many people in the community come from a different world and mind-set than teachers, they often provide a fresh perspective on possible research topics.

In my own experience, I have asked local construction workers or food service workers about possible student research projects and received numerous topics and insights that I had never considered. Such interactions were both humbling and insightful. Of course, the community and other out-of-school sites are brimming with possibilities for teacher and student research. The postmodern hyperreality has brought us new out-of-school resources such as TV, videos, computers, the Internet, virtual realities, databases, etc. and as we have discussed, teachers and students must develop a sophisticated ability to use these resources. But there were out-of-school information sources long before the advent of postmodernity. Some people argue that contemporary sources of information make school obsolete; democratic social studies teachers argue just the opposite. With the overload of information, disciplines, research abilities, and, especially, interpretive skills to make sense of the surfeit of data, become more important than ever. Good teachers teach these skills (Horton & Freire, 1990; Postman, 1995).

As social studies teachers ask questions that lead to inquiry and move their students into a curriculum based on an understanding of secondary and primary research, they establish a social studies for social change. Action emerges from the knowledge obtained and produced. In the all-important process, academic skills are sharpened, awareness is enhanced, consciousness is reconstructed, and real, live needs in the community are met. Myles Horton—a fellow Tennessean and founder/director of the Highlander School that helped prepare the leaders of the Civil Rights Movement—argued that teacher and student research that did not lead to social action of one type or another was not very helpful. As Horton's students surveyed the local East Tennessee community in an effort to understand standards of living and working conditions, they not only worked for social improvement but used their research to ask new questions, uncover unseen problems, and reflect on new ways of perceiving (Preskill, 1991).

It is a shame that social studies teachers in the first decade of the twenty-first century often have to fight to engage in this type of teaching. Reared educationally in a system that often denigrates such approaches, social studies teachers can have difficulty understanding the social and educational vision behind such research-based teaching. But, once a teacher is attuned to the concepts behind such approaches, changing one's curriculum orientation is not extremely difficult. One can call on the help of more experienced colleagues for help, possibly arranging for a joint research project by two different classes. Or, a teacher engaging in collaborative student research for the first time could ask for help from community members who conduct research as part of their job. Often, teachers ask me how they might grade student research projects. How do you write an objective test to measure what they know? Such questions indicate that they are struck in paradigmatic limbo. They still understand the purpose of social studies to involve the memorization of externally-mandated knowledge. Of course, an objective form of test would not fit into the research-based social studies described here. Our purpose is to produce knowledge, to understand it in relation to data produced by other researchers, to gain research and interpretive skills, and to be able to use the knowledge produced in the solution of social problems.

Students get amazingly excited when they produce knowledge that has an audience in the school or community. Later in this book, you will read a chapter about a research project a social studies methods class of mine conducted in Louisiana. Their research made the front page headlines in the local newspaper and the lead story on three network affiliates' 6 and 11 p.m. news programs. From elementary to graduate school, student research can result in book or pamphlet writing. In a graduate class I taught on "whiteness" a few years ago at Penn State, I threw out the syllabus after the second night of class and told my very sophisticated students to "go write a book on the subject." The students were so amazing that two books (*White Reign: Deploying Whiteness in America*, Eds., Kincheloe, Steinberg, Rodriguez, & Ron Chennault; and *Dismantling White Privilege*, Eds., Rodriguez & Villaverde) were the results.

Obviously, elementary and secondary social studies teachers and students don't need to get a book published to have successful research and writing projects. It is important, however, to seek audiences for student research findings; it is a great motivator for anyone to have his or her writing read. Teachers can put student research in the school library

Chapter

Beyond Mere Execution: Controlling the Conceptualization of Teaching

As a book examines social studies, its problems, and its goals, it must strive to place the analysis in social context. One of the great failures of methodological teaching in American education involves its lack of sociopolitical context. Too often, teaching methods are taught in contextual isolation, thus ignoring the very factors which give meaning to a subject. Would we want to teach reading methods unmindful of the reading habits displayed by many Americans? Would we want to teach physical education methods unmindful of the exercise habits displayed by many Americans? Would we want to teach math methods unmindful of the math anxiety harbored by many of us?

Thus, would we want to teach social studies methods without regard to the social climate which confronts postmodern Americans? As society has changed, education has been subjected to new challenges and demands. The changes have resulted from many factors, not the least of which is technology. One way to examine the nature of this technological change involves an awareness of the so-called information environment that surrounds the contemporary social studies classroom. What must social studies teachers do to make their teaching responsive to the new realities created by the postmodern information environment?

Before we confront such questions, let us define and examine the information environment of the postmodern era.

Contextualizing the Contemporary Information Environment

The information environment is formed by the interaction connecting information systems, codes, message networks, and the media of communication. These components set and maintain the parameters of thought and learning within a culture. The manner in which people pass information among themselves creates an environment just as important and influential as their geographic environment. In the same manner that the physical environment influences what we wear and the type of work we perform, the information environment advances the particular modes of thinking, social attitudes, predispositions toward knowledge, particular definitions of intelligence and purposes of education.

The information environment that confronts us in the twenty-first century, many analysts argue, is changing the nature of human thought. Students of the social consequences of technology argue that particular technological innovations are taking over more and more of the situations where human thought was once required. This could have positive outcomes as computers and other technologies are designed to relieve human beings of the drudgery of certain types of low-level thought. Unfortunately, we have not reached the point where human beings, freed from rote-based thought, are encouraged to delve into higher-level, analytical thought processes.

Thus, many power wielders make use of information and other technologies in a way that serves to "deskill" workers, students, and even teachers. Technically defined, deskilling involves taking complex tasks and breaking them down into highly specified actions that can be performed by low-skill workers. Such a process takes place in contemporary workplaces and schools. The concept of deskilling can be extended to include not only specific job performance but the nature of thinking itself. Cognitive deskilling, therefore, is a way of thinking that views particular forms of rational thinking as superior to all other forms of thought: the emotional, the intuitive, the spiritual or the interconnected. The point here is not to throw out rational thought—far from it. What democratic social studies attempts to do is to improve rationality by connecting it to other types of thinking produced in different times and cultures. The improvement of rationality involves globalizing our thinking by learning from African insights, Asian intellectual and theological traditions, and the ways of seeing of indigenous peoples. The rationality that dominates our schools is a European-based system of logic. The mistake often made in Western societies such as the United States is that this system is used exclusively; it rejects the possible contributions of other cultural systems. In its isolation it undermines self-critique and the possibility of reaching new, unconsidered ways of thinking.

One of many outcomes of this Eurocentric form of thinking is deskilling. In this cognitive context, humans come to concern themselves primarily with the execution of their vocations; they are less concerned with the conceptualization of work. Theory is thus separated from practice, and the attempt to understand contextually what we do is lost. Unable to take control of the conceptualization of their tasks, deskilled workers, students, and teachers find themselves subservient to instead of in charge of technologies. This is often referred to as "technicalization." The implications of this dynamic for social studies education are profound on a couple of levels. First, like everyone else, social studies teachers and students are deskilled. Second, social studies teachers and students should delegate special attention to social influences, and the postmodern information environment is one of the most important social influences in human history.

One of the most important aspects of this postmodern information environment over the last fifty-some years has been television. The technology of TV plays a very important role in determining the nature of communications and, thus, thought in postmodern society. Though the influence of television is now interacting with the influence of cyberspace, the Internet, and interactive virtual media, TV still plays a dramatic role in shaping our ways of thinking in the postmodern information environment. TV's cultural landscape has separated us from traditional notions of time, community, self, and history: central social studies concerns. New structures of space and time generated by bombarding electronic images from local, national, and international locations shake our personal sense of who we are and from where we come. The world is not brought into our homes by TV, as much as TV brings viewers to a quasi-fictional locale: postmodern hyperreality. Our contact with this bizarre information environment diminishes our ability to find meaning or generate passion for commitment. To some degree we are lost in cyberspace.

Our sense of being lost is enhanced by the postmodern information environment's status as a domain of manipulation. In this environment, power wielders attempt to persuade individuals to operate in ways that serve the interests of power: to buy certain products, to vote for particular candidates, to hold particular views of the economic system, to embrace particular purposes of schooling, and/or to accept particular views of success. Modernist European science has produced the manipulative strategies of the advertising industry, which in turn has revolutionized the nature of political campaigns. The culture of marketing has dramatically altered the discourse of politics, relegating traditional forms of ethical and political thinking to the cloisters of academia far away from the public sphere.

While the intent of the advertising-directed politics of the postmodern is manipulative, progressive impulses are salvaged by a myriad of contradictory readings. No one can predict the outcome of the media capture of campaigning. Many of those who view ads fall victim to the manipulative intent of the producers; others, while recognizing the manipulation, become discouraged and turn off any involvement in a corrupt and degraded political system; still others, who recognize the manipulation, are inspired to fight it by organizing community groups dedicated to authentic public conversation.

Obviously, as discussed in Chapter 1, this postmodern or contemporary information environment is complex and so are its effects on individuals. Nevertheless, a climate of manipulation continues to exist in the first decade of the twenty-first century. Though the process is subtle and ambiguous, those who possess the financial resources to control various information media are the most important social studies educators of our time. These individuals and groups are amazingly adept at shaping consumption habits and patterns of taste. The postmodern information environment is fueled by globally expanding technocapitalism that seeks to colonize everything from outer space to inner consciousness. In this bizarre context, questions of power, information, and education become more important than ever before. In the first decade of the twenty-first century, for example, concentrated power's control over information continues to expand. In book publishing two percent of publishers control 75 percent of the books published in the United States. Corporate images have become more and more important, not simply for marketing purposes but also for capital raising, mergers, gaining the competitive edge in the production of knowledge, the effort to influence government policy, the attempt to privatize education, and the goal of advancing particular social and cultural values (Kincheloe, 1993, 1995, 1999).

THE CLASSROOM ENVIRONMENT IN THE CLIMATE OF MANIPULATION AND DESKILLING

All of these forces of the postmodern condition intersect in some way with the concerns of social studies in general and the everyday life of schooling in particular. Indeed, there are numerous connections between the manipulative information environment and the practices that occur in postmodern classrooms. The use of management techniques often reek of the manipulative intent of the modern media. Students are not viewed as active agents with minds and values of their own but as passive entities to be directed. The goals of the learning process in this behavioristic situation are not determined by an interactive negotiation among individuals in the society at large, students, and teachers; goals are dictated by groups and individuals far away from the classroom and then imposed by teachers using manipulative strategies. Such a model is antidemocratic and tends to ignore the active role of students in the determination of the nature of their learning situation.

Maybe, the most important connection between manipulative elements of the information environment and contemporary American education focuses on our concern with the influence of technology. We have previously referred to the process of deskilling, which seems to be taking place as a result of the postmodern American information environment. In the workplace, the deskilling process seems to correspond to the attempt of management to exercise more, yet more subtle, control over workers. For this reason and many others, the same deskilling process seems to be taking place in contemporary education. We will first examine the deskilling process in the workplace and then extend the analysis into the social studies classroom.

There are three types of control used in the workplace to extract more work from employees: simple, bureaucratic, and technical. Simple control is obvious: You tell a worker what you have decided he or she should do and overtly make him or her do it. Bureaucratic control is very important in extracting labor since it establishes a social structure that dictates interpersonal relations and job descriptions. Bureaucratic control uses established policy and procedures to grant rewards and punishments that control worker motivation and behavior. Technical control and deskilling are intimately intertwined. As stated earlier, technical control involves hyperrationalization: taking a complex task with a high level of skill and decision-making and fragmenting it into specific actions so simple that even unskilled workers can perform them.

In this context, it is important to understand a key theme of this book: the critique and exposé of hyperrationalization in the society in general and social studies education in particular. As we think about technical control and deskilling in the social studies, it is important to briefly explore the nature and influences of hyperrationality. As one of the dark sides of Western science, hyperrationality stands as a marker of where unexamined Western values have taken us over the last three and one-half centuries (Barton & Rittenhouse, 1998). It is important for social studies teachers and their students to think about their relationship to Western science and how it has shaped their consciousness and ways of thinking about the purposes of schooling. My purpose is not to reject Western reason or the concept of rationality. Instead, the point is to acknowledge the limits of reason and the dangers of its excesses: the possibility of irrationality in rationality.

Understanding such limits, our democratic social studies searches for alternative rationalities in the diversity of different cultures' modes of thinking and in the constructions of unique individuals. Later in this book, I will introduce you to Shirley Steinberg's and my concept of postformal thinking which is designed to push the boundaries of Western rationalities and imagine new orders of cognition and ways of being human. Postformalism rebels against the tyranny of Eurocentric rationality and the rationalized managerial approach to social studies that it has supported. E. Wayne Ross (1997), describes the contemporary version of this hyperrationalized social studies as an approach to the discipline that works

> to define curricular goals: design assessment tasks based on these goals; set standards for the content of subject matter areas and grade level; and test students and report the results to the public. The intent is to establish standards for content and student performance levels (p. 15).

On the surface, observers may sense no problem with such procedures. A closer examination, however, reveals the rationalization process at work. Ross and many others understand that such an approach focuses on the teaching of social studies where method is reduced to an isolated concern with matching techniques of instruction to prearranged outcomes. In such an arrangement there is no concern with the context in which social studies takes place or any room for analyzing the ideological imprints on prearranged purposes for social studies teaching. The purpose of social studies education in this context is, thus, rationalized; the objective becomes not analysis, but a form of compliance with dictates issued far away from the classroom. Rationalization is achieved when all effort is expended meeting dictates; not teaching students and producing relevant knowledge. Information in this context is reduced to a form of decontextualized data stolen away from the social and disciplinary contexts that give it meaning. The rationalization process has rendered social studies teaching irrational (Thornton, 1997).

The complexity and idiosyncrasy of the everyday classroom is lost in this rationalization and technicalization. The night preceding the day I wrote this chapter, I spoke with a teacher in Brooklyn who taught in a high school that was shut down because of its failure to comply with New York state standards. Of course, it is in a very poor neighborhood with a large immigrant population. No one in an official capacity ever acknowledged the heroic individual teachers who were, year after year, coming to this school, engaging students in community research, helping them learn to write and publish their work, and inspiring them to read a wide variety of literature. Because such pedagogical brilliance did not fit within the rationalized boundaries of prearranged standards, it was ignored as something outside the domain of "good professional practice." It was irrelevant. The passion, validation, love of learning, life transformation it provided students was lost on educational leaders. Rationalization is important because it directly affects human lives.

As rationalization separates means (instruction) from ends (the purpose of social studies), teachers are reduced to mere implementers of expert curricula: information deliverers. What the rationalizers seem to miss is that teachers—no matter how much they may be deskilled—always make influential decisions that shape what happens in the classroom. What teachers know and believe about the purposes and curriculum of social studies, and the way they view "proper" modes of instruction and classroom management, profoundly shape, what happens in the everyday life of the social studies classroom. The curriculum provided teachers can be rationalized and specified down to the last detail, but the background, beliefs, personality, concerns, anxieties, passions, pathologies of the individual teacher in the particular classroom will still make a difference on what actually happens in social studies education. Thus, social studies education must not simply focus on developing standards documents and master curricula but must deal with every teacher's ability to understand the various purposes and content and to engage students in making sense of these issues and connecting them to their lives. Any reform that leaves out this teacher-based concern is doomed to failure (Ross, 1997).

Indeed, democratic teachers should engage their students in a study of this rationalization process and its effect not only on the education they receive but on the arrangement of the workplace, medical care, social services, business, and a myriad of other domains. This rationalization impulse is one of the most important dynamics in the nineteenth, twentieth, and, now twenty-first century social world. That would make it, I believe, an apt topic for social studies analysis. Such a study would begin with an analysis of the birth of modernity with the scientific revolution of the seventeenth and eighteenth centuries. We will focus on this sociohistorical mega-event later in this book. Social studies and other school subjects have traditionally ignored some of the most powerful forces that have shaped the way we see ourselves and the world around us.

To understand rationalization, we must discern our relationship to science, dissect the power and effects of Western science, and discern how it constructs our consciousness. As we escape the rationalization of a prearranged social studies curriculum and mandated objectives, we find that our lives as social studies teachers begin to change. In a rationalized educational world, we often watch students learn to comply with dictates. Such obedience is often at odds with higher orders of analysis and original work enthusiastically produced. Thus, we teach the same data, the same compliance skills, over and over with little lasting effect. Rationalization cannot tolerate unique students such as Albert Einstein, with amazing, even unfathomable, genius (Kincheloe, Steinberg, and Tippins, 1999). They don't fit the narrow rationalized picture of what constitutes intelligence and high student performance. Rationalization's fragmentation of reality destroys teacher and student understanding of how schooling connects to their lives. As a result, their interest and passion about learning is fragmented to such a degree that the flame of curiosity is snuffed out.

When jobs are rationalized, broken into components, and simplified, the conception of the overall process of production is lost on the workers. Of course, someone must understand the production process, and that someone is management. With this knowledge, management can separate conceptualization of the job from execution of the job. In control of the conceptualization of jobs in the workplace, management gains a technical form of control over its workers, as individuals at the top of the hierarchy plan precisely the schedules of their laborers and arrange the workplace in a way more conducive to short-term productivity. The arrangements that serve to foster short-term productivity may not necessarily be in the best interest of worker welfare. Such arrangements typically do not foster a situation where worker understandings of the process of production is valued. In other words, the labor force which suits managerial needs best is a deskilled group of workers.

The workplace of teaching, traditionally, has been a place where teachers have been relatively free from administrative control of classroom practice. In most places, teachers could close their doors and remain fairly undisturbed. Only in the last few decades, has this relative teacher autonomy begun to change to any significant degree. As the information environment legitimizes certain forms of manipulation, the school and its teachers and students become more vulnerable. As technical control becomes a more and more common device used in scientific management of individuals in institutions, such forms of control begin to seep into the management of the educational "workers." Thus, this process of separating job conception from job execution becomes a part of teaching. Such a development undermines the professionalism of teachers as it trivializes the profession. Let us examine how this educational technicalization works.

One of the best examples of the deskilling of teachers involves the growth of packaged curricular materials in the last few years. These standardized materials usually come in an attractive package, which includes: objectives, all "necessary" curricular content, prespecified teacher behavior and "appropriate" student responses, and evaluation materials. In many of these prepackaged programs, even the exact words the teacher is to say are specified. Traditional teaching skills are not necessary in this situation, for all the conceptualization and planning goes on far away from the school and the unique students it houses. If all components of teaching are to be prespecified (even down to the teacher's conversation with the students), then our educational system's protestation of concern for the uniqueness and individuality of each child is a sham.

As teachers are deskilled, a new, albeit less sophisticated, set of skills is provided to them. These new skills are taught in some education courses, in-service workshops, teacher journals, methods textbooks, and the curricular materials themselves. The old skills involved understanding child development, mastery of subject matter content, the understanding of the larger aims of education, and an appreciation for the social context in which education takes place. We do not mean here to romanticize past teacher education. It is apparent that many teachers in the past did not walk into their classrooms with these types of skills. The difference between the past and present situation is that many of those in educational leadership positions in days gone past by at least wanted teachers to possess these traditional teaching skills. The new skills are based on the assumption that teachers should be the executors not the conceptualizers of educational policy. The skilled teacher of the technicalized era would possess: a desire to work smoothly and efficiently with administrators and fellow teachers, an appreciation of behavioristic psychological models, a positive attitude toward the workplace and children, a familiarity with a variety of curriculum packages; and an ability to implement scientific classroom management strategies—skills and attitudes often taught in so called "practical" methods classes.

The importance of the emerging technical control of education revolves around its ability to integrate what are perceived to be unrelated concerns. The first concern involves the manpower goals of many American businesses. Many corporate leaders want the job market of the twenty-first century to be flooded with high school graduates with the proper personality traits and minimum literacy skills for entry-level jobs and with college-trained, highly qualified scientists and engineers—sci-tech workers. The schools and social studies programs that will result from the application of technical control, the business community believes, will be far better equipped to turn out graduates who are better adapted to the needs of business. The second concern entails the need for teacher accountability that has grown out of the widespread public perception of teacher incompetence. A school system that is staffed by teachers who have standardized materials and which, in the first decade of the new century, is shaped by technocratic top-down curriculum standards that direct efforts toward standardized outcomes is deemed superior to a "haphazard," teacher-directed educational program. With content and teaching technique controlled, teachers can be held far more accountable. The third concern involves the need for administrators to control their workplace and their personnel. Like their industrial counterparts, educational managers (principals, supervisors, and curriculum directors) realize that a deskilled teaching force, controlled by technical means, is more easily manageable. Teacher resistance to administrative demands is reduced by technical control.

The fourth concern is related to the fact that the education which results from technical control is far more standardized and thus more measurable. Curriculum packets accompanied by highly centralized school administrative control accentuate the standardized arrangement of teaching. Not only do all students study the same materials at the same time, different teachers teach their classes in a uniform manner. Standardized test scores improve in this situation because they become the focus of attention, the raison d'être of schooling. The institutional arrangement is thus legitimized, as "objective" proof exists to substantiate the curricular organization. The fifth concern pertains to the true needs of teachers to have something practical to use with their students. Unique, creative materials are important to all teachers, regardless of their ability. In a job with far too many demands and far too many students, prepackaged materials are viewed by teachers as a labor saving device. Teachers who see 160 students five days a week do not typically think about the loss of control of curricular conception that such materials bring about; like most anybody in their circumstances, they think about survival.

EDUCATION UNDER TECHNICAL CONTROL: THE ALTERED, RATIONALIZED SCHOOL

Thus, everybody's needs are ostensibly served by the technical control of teaching. The deskilling that results is rarely a matter of discussion, for it is too subtle a process. Who would recognize it? Not the news media; it is too concerned with the short, attention-grabbing story. The information environment does not encourage in-depth analysis of such "academic" issues. Not teachers themselves; they are too busy surviving in their educational bunkers. Not technically oriented nonconceptual social studies methods professors, they are too busy teaching technique and practical skills. Technical control thus proceeds unimpeded, leaving in its wake a permanently altered school system.

This altered school system is marked by several characteristics:

1. Teachers relinquish control of their curricula and teaching technique to large publishing houses and those "experts" who devise social studies standards.

2. Students are inundated with worksheets and other "individualized" activities. The use of these types of prepackaged materials creates a situation where students work more and more in isolation, rarely needing to interact with the teacher or other students.

3. Students become "fact collectors" not knowledge workers who can conduct research and interpret data. Intelligence is defined in a narrow way that excludes those qualities that make individuals agents of positive social change. The use of such a limited definition may leave students with unique characteristics unrewarded and unaware of their potential achievements.

4. The teacher becomes more and more like a foreman, a factory supervisor. Like a foreman, the teacher merely oversees the workers (students) as they carry out plans someone else has conceived.

5. As the teacher becomes a blue-collar worker, talented individuals considering a career in teaching are put off by a job with decreasing autonomy and a reduced need for creativity. Thus, the profession tends to attract less and less capable individuals.

6. There is less need for interaction between teachers. Economists have noted that, as labor is divided and controlled, the social atmosphere of the workplace is altered. So is the case in school. As educational planning is separated from execution, teachers have less to discuss than before. Teachers become detached individuals.

7. This detachment comes to permeate the educational workplace as teachers grow not only isolated from one another but from the spirit of their work as well. Just as industrialization with its division of labor alienated workers from the meaning of their work, teachers with little investment in the conception of their teaching grow alienated from the purposes and meaning of education. As such alienation intensifies, teachers, like workers, feel an increased need to organize in order to regain some control over their professional lives.

8. Unfortunately, it is not just teachers who suffer from the changes wrought by educational technicalization and deskilling. Students are also subjected to more control and confined within narrower bound-

aries of acceptable academic behavior. Like teacher behaviors, student responses are becoming more prespecified. Thus, original and creative thinking becomes less desirable, for such thought is unanticipated in the prearranged learning packet. As a result, creativity becomes an annoyance, an impediment to an efficient, orderly, preplanned classroom. As student creativity is undermined, students become deskilled.

9. A good student becomes one who possesses a large quantity of competencies and skills which serve the technical interests of society. An educated person becomes one who has collected technical skills and atomistic bits of knowledge which can be measured on a competency test. The relationship of one fact to another, the connection between what one learns and how such knowledge might affect his or her fellow human beings, the kinship between the school curriculum and what constitutes a good society, are modes of student thinking discouraged by the information environment, the technicalized school, and the deskilled teacher.

As we examine social studies education in this larger socioeducational context, a few points become uncomfortably clear. The attempt to incorporate analytical thinking into social studies education is thwarted not by student laziness or teacher incompetence. Such neglect is entwined in a social complex that reflects postmodern civilization and its information environment. Economic and cognitive deskilling affects the very fabric of society and when combined with television culture and modern advertising, it even permeates the contemporary social studies classroom. To reform the social studies, professionals must connect it to the world in which it takes shape.

GETTING TO THE CONCEPTUAL REALM: MULTIDISCIPLINARITY AND THE QUEST FOR SELF-DIRECTION

Connecting social studies to the world is an extremely important aspect of the reforms advocated in this book. While knowledge of the various social studies disciplines—history, sociology, anthropology, cultural studies, economics, and geography—is necessary to this task, it is not enough. Too often, the way these disciplines are arranged involves a fragmented view of the world around us and the problems that confront us. No one domain of knowledge explains our connection to the world, the ways our identity is shaped by sociohistorical forces, or how we might exercise more insight into the ways we are inextricably intertwined with that which surrounds us. The task of understanding these relationships is a complex one—just like most of the important concerns of social studies. What we are referring to here involves the ability of social studies teachers and students to understand how these connections have shaped their consciousness and view of themselves and how they might act on such understandings in democratic, socially just, and equitable ways. This is the challenge of a democratic social studies that recognizes both complexity and the need for civic action (Parker, 1997b; Pang, Gay, & Stanley, 1995).

Add another ingredient to this complex recipe: You guessed it—our contemporary condition. The confusion, loss of meaning, and information overload of postmodernity's hyperreality reduces our ability to mount a resistance to the social conditions that shape our lives. In this context, the complexity of social studies is exacerbated, and we are further intimidated. The disciplines that ground social studies, especially as they are taught in elementary, secondary, and, too often, college social science courses and social studies methods classes, are not sufficient for this complex task of making sense of our connection to the world and the ways it shapes who we are. If such courses do not address such issues, of what use are they? Why bother with them?

Who we are is always influenced by the location in the web of reality from which life is experienced and understood. We all stand or are placed somewhere in this complex web: some of us are African American females from upper-middle-class backgrounds who attend the Catholic Church. Others of us are urban white males from lower/working-class backgrounds who are Jewish but do not attend a synagogue. Depending on such infinite possibilities of places to stand in the web, many of us see the world in very different ways. Sometimes, those of us who come from very similar locations in the web see the world and its impact on us in surprisingly dissimilar ways. Whatever our viewpoint, it is limited by what we have experienced, and the information about the world we have encountered. None of us has the whole story or has the ability to see from a God-like perspective. Such a realization should make us humble and aware of the limitations of our insights.

In light of such understandings, especially in the postmodern hyperreality, power wielders play a profound role in filtering the ways all of us come to see and make sense of the world, ourselves, and our relationship to it. Thus, many of the ways of thinking that we claim as our own are heavily influenced by information that is produced by particular groups who stand to benefit from large numbers of people coming to view the world and themselves in particular ways. They spend countless billions of dollars every year to convince us of their concern for our best interests, their dedication to our good health, popularity, sexual attractiveness, and achievement of success.

Such information producers tell us that issues, such as fighting pollution, depend on our individual behavior as consumers and our dedication to recycling. Not to reject the importance of individual behaviors, the point here is what is not being said: the biggest polluters are the industries that produce a variety of products and their culpability in environmental destruction is erased in such media representations. National and international pollution policies are not the solution according to corporate information producers; the modification of individual behavior is. How one sees the world, one's relation to it, one's political perspective, and one's view of the purposes of social studies, are all profoundly shaped by how one makes sense of such information. To appreciate the profound complexity of this information and its effects we must explore analytical tools and ways of interpreting meaning that are not to be found in one isolated discipline (Grossberg, 1992).

The capacity to produce information that saturates us is one of the most important ways that power over the individual and the social and political system is accumulated in the first decade of the twenty-first century. The only problem is that those who study the ways power is obtained and deployed to the detriment of individuals in particular and society as a whole are often deemed "dangerous radicals," and "the people your parents warned you about." What *Getting Beyond the Facts* is urging you to do—to reestablish democracy by confronting those information controlling power wielders who have subverted it—is a dangerous mission. If you choose to accept it, please understand that you will not always be rewarded for your actions as a power-sniffing social studies teacher. As social studies educator Theodore Kaltsounis (1997) describes the concerns of some social studies professionals with power: "with friends like [these] who needs enemies" (p. 19)?

MULTIDISCIPLINARITY, CONNECTEDNESS, AND KNOWLEDGE PRODUCTION

Understanding its dangerous mission, a democratic social studies attempts to get beyond the limitations of disciplinary fragmentation and connect the disciplines to the lived world. As referenced in these first three chapters, a social studies that is connected to the world and that is always aware of contemporary threats to democracy can focus on its task of producing well-informed, highly skilled citizens for a democracy. My advocacy of a multidisciplinary approach to social studies does not mean that we abandon the knowledge of the disciplines—far from it. It means that we understand history, sociology, cultural studies, anthropology, political science, and economics as discourses. This means that democratic social studies teachers examine the hidden rules that regulate what can and cannot be said, who can speak with the blessing of authority and who must listen, whose social science constructions are scientific and valid and whose are unscientific and unimportant.

In the everyday world of social science, legitimized discourses insidiously tell social studies teachers what books may be read by students, what instructional methods may be utilized, and what belief systems, views of citizenship, and definitions of success may be taught. Indeed, the point is that democratic social studies teachers should understand the disciplines and the assumptions that shape them better than do those who work in them. Too often, social scientists are blind to the tacit rules of the game, the discourse in which they are operating. The knowledge they produce bears the imprint of such rules. It is shaped in ways that reflect certain social and political values and not others. Thus, it is biased in ways that those who do not understand the discursive rules do not understand. Without these understandings, the work of the social scientists that ultimately makes its way into college, secondary, and elementary textbooks will be viewed as objective truth. This is the basis of the concern of democratic social studies teachers who pride themselves as professional knowledge workers.

The multidisciplinarity promoted here attempts to engage teachers and other social science professionals in an awareness of the discursive limitations of the disciplines in a way that helps them produce and distribute more informed and compelling knowledge. This "complex mulidisciplinarity" in the social studies asserts that something can't be understood by merely reducing it to smaller units. Racism can't be understood as simply a sociological issue, but as a historical, cultural, psychological, psychoanalytic, economic, and political dynamic. Racism, and other issues like it, can only be understood as an integrated whole. This complex multidisciplinarity is the opposite of reductionism. A character in a novel, for example, cannot be understood until she is appreciated as part of a larger context, a network of interactions. The novel is a process that helps provide meaning for its individual parts, its characters.

The notions of reality assumed by many modernist knowledge producers in the social sciences fail to account for the holistic, interconnected, web-like nature of reality. They fail to account for the ways a knowledge producer's own placement in the web shapes the way reality is perceived. Democratic social studies teachers work diligently to understand the strengths and weaknesses of the social sciences and where they stand or are placed in the web of reality. They work throughout their lives to understand how that placement in the web of reality constantly shapes the way they see the world. Thus, democratic social studies teachers make a lifetime commitment to study themselves—not because of some narcissistic impulse but because they know that the multiple contexts in which they have operated have shaped the way they see the world, as teachers, and the goals of social studies. Once they understand these dynamics, they are better equipped to analyze and discern, after being exposed to a variety of perspectives, how they want to position themselves in a conscious manner.

Understanding these connections, this holism, advocates of a complex multidisciplinarity seek diverse ways of producing knowledge and making meaning, including the scientific method, indigenous and multicultural ways of knowing, intuition, subjective experience, empathetic insights, the hermeneutic (the art of interpreting reality) tradition, and many others. In other words, Shirley Steinberg and I study the concept of *bricolage*, where we get down to the nuts and bolts of multidisciplinarity. As we erase the artificial divisions between disciplines, we bring philosophical concepts, literary forms of analysis, artistic/aesthetic criticism, musical understandings, theatrical and dramatic ways of bringing meaning to bear on the social sciences and the social studies. In this way, we move beyond the blinds of particular disciplines and peer through a conceptual window to a new world of research and knowledge production. Teachers with such knowledge work skills and possess sophisticated curricular and instructional insights can never allow the social studies to remain a boring corner of the educational universe. They will never allow themselves to be deskilled and give up the conceptualization process to faraway experts.

DEMOCRATIC SOCIAL STUDIES EDUCATORS UNDERSTAND THE EFFECTS OF KNOWLEDGE PRODUCTION AND INTERPRETATION

Democratic social studies educators learn quickly that human beings neither see the world nor act in it in totally individualistic ways. Their insights and actions are always constrained by the cultural, historical, political, and economic contexts in which they exist. Thus, if a purpose of social studies is to understand and operate ethically and effectively in the world, it is important to understand the specific nature of these constraints. What moves us to action? What shapes our perceptions? Does state or corporate control over the distribution of information play a role in the decisions we make? Human beings are shaped by social and cultural practices; they do not exist independent of their contexts. Power, especially in the postmodern era of information saturation, plays an exaggerated role in shaping who we become. There is no "pure" human nature that exists outside of time or space. All human beings involve an intersection between the social/cultural and the biological.

The form humanity takes is always contested, always a matter of struggle over competing perspectives. This is why social studies is so important, why it deserves a spot at center stage as it studies who and what we might become. The democratic social studies advocated here understands that social context does not determine human behavior. Instead, it is interested in how individuals operate in their daily lives in relation to forces and structures about which they are uninformed. What happens when individuals gain an awareness of such invisible forces and structures? Democratic social studies educators believe that this is the first step in their empowerment, and their ability to take conscious steps to live their lives in more humane, just, and democratic ways. They can do this because external forces and structures do not determine their life tracks. They still have agency: the ability to shape the direction of their lives.

Human agency is more powerful than the forces of history. While humans are not simply free to do what they want—they must always negotiate these forces and structures—they can significantly increase their self-determination with consciousness. Though we can never escape history, we can reflect on our experiences and learn in ways that change our own and other people's lives. In this context, social studies educators learn how context shapes people. Historical and social forces oppress and dominate individuals, but conscious individuals are far more capable of resistance. We come to understand the historical, social, political, economic, and civic world much better when we appreciate the fact that human lives and institutions are shaped by unequal resources of the economic, political, and cultural variety. Social studies teachers and students with these insights grasp individual actions in a far more nuanced and complex manner. Such knowledge is very important in their quest for transformative civic action (Grossberg, 1992; Hinchey, 1998).

Understanding these dynamics becomes, like so many other features of social studies, more important in the postmodern hyperreality. The information-saturated society operates to hide social forces in ways previously unimagined. Thus, the struggle for civic empowerment becomes more difficult than it has ever been before. We are more confused as to the way the sociopolitical world operates than we were previously. In the media-influenced context of hyperreality, social problems are rearticulated to the personal/individual level. For example, the fact that huge numbers of children live in poverty is not a result of social and economic structures and forces but is simply caused by bad parenting. In this and countless other situations, the public comes to believe there is no political solution to such a problem. "There's nothing we can do—just forgedaboudit." Thus, a kind of cynical conservatism has emerged in hyperreality that assumes a debilitated public space capable of positive social action. It becomes silly and even distasteful to speak of the possibility of political action in the social conversations of the contemporary era. Indeed, the subject matter of social studies is inappropriate party talk.

It's a tough time for the discipline of social studies. Social studies teachers have many hurdles to jump in order to help their students make sense of themselves in relation to the world. To accomplish this difficult task, teachers must understand the subject matter of the social sciences and its weaknesses, the way power operates in the contemporary social context to shape an out-of-school social studies curriculum, the goals of a democratic social studies, curriculum development and instructional practices that draw upon and integrate these understandings, and how to integrate student experiences into everyday classroom activities.

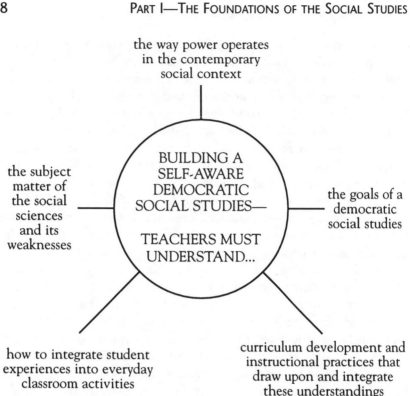

the way power operates
in the contemporary
social context

the subject
matter of
the social
sciences
and its
weaknesses

BUILDING A
SELF-AWARE
DEMOCRATIC
SOCIAL STUDIES—

TEACHERS MUST
UNDERSTAND...

the goals of a
democratic
social studies

how to integrate student
experiences into everyday
classroom activities

curriculum development and
instructional practices that
draw upon and integrate
these understandings

Social studies teachers need to learn a million ways to connect a variety of knowledges to diverse students' experiences. The ability to accomplish this task seamlessly and with flair is a wonderful process to observe. Some social studies teachers make it a veritable art form. As they assist students in gaining particular conceptual understandings, these adept teachers help these students help other students. They convert their classrooms to cooperative, happy think tanks where everyone becomes a learner, researcher, knowledge analyst, and democratic activist. The concept is not difficult. When students or anyone else sees how a body of knowledge, concepts, and skills is central to the way they live their lives, they will become far more motivated to learn. The possibilities of what we can accomplish with these notions in mind are unlimited.

Chapter

Connecting Social Studies to the Lived World: Naming the Contemporary Social Condition and Confronting its Social Studies Curriculum

This book consistently attempts to discuss issues in a context that encourages students, teachers, parents, and supervisors to connect social studies practice to the world outside the classroom. This would seem to be merely a commonsense approach, but, as Project SPAN (Social Studies Priorities and Needs) and scores of other researchers have pointed out, it is too infrequently the reality in contemporary social studies classrooms. Examining social studies classes, the teaching strategies, course content, and the literature and materials used in the courses, I too often find that the attempt to bring the world of the social studies classroom and the world outside the classroom closer together is deemed unimportant. There is little attempt to connect past with present, as knowledge is reduced to measurable pieces. Rather than being presented as an interconnected set of ever powerful, ever evolving ideas, knowledge assumes the rationalistic character of a commodity: cheap merchandise that holds value only as long as it can be used on a test. From the perspective of economics, knowledge in this type of classroom is ultimately elastic, for its value varies with the market created by the test. In other words, knowledge has no permanent inelastic value which transcends the evaluation process.

With knowledge viewed in this condescending manner, it is not surprising that social studies textbooks and materials for elementary and secondary schools have a relatively minor concern with portraying the lived world. Textbook publishers are infrequently concerned with the dangerous task of helping students find out where their personal worldviews and ideas originate. From the text, students get little sense that anyone is really interested in helping them understand why they believe the things they do, and most students have little idea that such exploration is even a major role of the social studies. Academicians in the social sciences have traditionally invested little in elementary and secondary textbooks, and rarely are the books read by specialists in the field or reviewed by academic journals. Most social studies textbooks are unchecked for intellectual quality or accuracy. When we examine the list of priorities of textbook publishing companies, an accurate portrayal of the world is near the bottom. Thus, social studies textbooks are often not written to explore the world but merely to instruct—to let children know a safe but mythological body of facts agreed to be inoffensive.

As fundamentalist Christian and right-wing pressure groups continue to challenge textbooks that approach controversial issues, textbook publishers become more and more timid. Take, for example, the social-studies-textbook treatment of religion. Studies indicate that publishers often skip over the vital role that religion has played in the development of human history and institutions. Such deletions render social studies textbooks bland and soulless. For example, textbook treatment of the Renaissance as a period of rebirth of classical learning is anti-Christian, right-wing analysts argue. A truly Christian account of the Renaissance, they argue, must indicate that the movement glorified mankind above God. Unwilling to offend more moderate perspectives on the subject, textbook publishers refuse to present such an interpretation. They compromise: Print as little as possible about the Renaissance and maybe no one will be offended. Choosing safety over conceptual understanding textbook publishers strive to keep their markets happy or at least unruffled.

Such textbooks are safe in the sense that they rarely examine ideas which move events—most of which are controversial in someone's eyes. Too often, students are only exposed to a superficial calendar of occurrences that rarely deals with the spirit of the beliefs that have shaped America and grants us an understanding of the foundation on which the sociopolitical life the nation rests. No wonder social studies is perceived to be so unimportant, for so often it is presented as if it has no power to shape people's lives. Frances Fitzgerald (1979) argues that because of the textbooks and the weak state of teacher education, social studies becomes a bland fiction, propagated for the purpose of creating good citizens. As a result, she says, social studies courses may in fact achieve the exact opposite: actually inhibiting the cultivation of good citizenship by painting a misleading, simplistic picture of the world and not providing young people with a warning of the dangers ahead. Fitzgerald concludes that the major aim of much that passes for social studies education is to gain as much control over children as possible. Instead of freeing children to explore ideas wherever such insights might take them, social studies educators often feel compelled to manipulate the ideas of children to meet a predetermined model of conformity. One reason that ideas moving events are so rarely studied is because these ideas are so powerful. Once students have examined and reflected upon such ideas, it becomes harder for teachers to control student belief systems. Thus, social studies teachers cannot let students get too close to the lived world, for, once exposed, there is no telling where young learners might end up.

If we accept this critique of the discomfort of many contemporary social studies educators in allowing their students to confront the real world, then we are faced with a number of unpleasant implications, the most important of which involves the undemocratic nature of social studies education in contemporary schooling. In a democracy, it is not the main business of school to condition students to accept certain beliefs and values. (Of course, this would be the case in an authoritarian society.) Rather, one of the most important goals of education in a democracy is to help provide students critical distance between themselves and their society—to let them stand back and examine the world from new perspectives. Another important goal of social studies education in a democracy is to help children and young people gain the capacity for interpretation and critique by examining the beliefs which are imposed upon them by their environment.

In the process of examining the world from a distance, students have an opportunity to think about what makes for a good and just society. As they analyze such a question, they may encounter doubts and uncertainties, and, before profound learning in the social studies takes place, some of these doubts may be necessary. Indeed, it may be the case that social studies programs are democratic to the degree to which they allow for doubt and uncertainty concerning the prevailing sociopolitical belief systems. The basic difference between democratic and totalitarian social studies education is that democratic social studies allows students to step back and examine social assumptions. Unfortunately, many social studies programs in postmodern America provide students little opportunity for uncertainty. If social progress and empowerment are possible, we must get beyond this discomfort with uncertainty.

Naming the Condition In Which Social Studies Teachers Must Operate

As alluded to in Chapter 1, the postmodern condition is difficult to understand and must be carefully clarified, especially for those unfamiliar with the concept. If social studies teachers are to connect social studies to the lived world of the first decade of the twenty-first century, they must understand that world. Understanding of that world demands clear insight into the postmodern condition. The following list is a concise (and simplified) description of the main characteristics of the postmodern condition:

1. The increased importance of the sign—the image—in moving everyday life and the sociopolitical sphere.

2. An exaggeration of the power of those who hold power and its use of information to colonize human consciousness.

3. The fragmentation of meaning and the subsequent production of social vertigo—the depoliticization of perception.

4. The growth of cynicism in a climate of deceit.

5. The celebration of surface meanings; the validation of shallowness.

6. The substitution of fascination for analysis; the age of spectacle.

7. The reorganization of capital/economic power in a global context—technocapitalism is supported by a new social Darwinism.

8. The change of change: everything is different or at least feels that way.

1. THE INCREASED IMPORTANCE OF THE SIGN—THE IMAGE—IN MOVING
   EVERYDAY LIFE AND THE SOCIOPOLITICAL SPHERE. The increased
   importance of the sign or the signifier (e.g., McDonald's golden arch-
   es or Nike's "swoosh") in the postmodern condition exerts tremendous influence on moving the actions of individuals. Understanding
   the fragility of meaning in hyperreality, media advisors realize that
   their goal is to produce comforting signs of common values for a postmodern gaggle of mobile citizens who are unsure of what it all means.
   If successful, these media operatives will induce citizens to emotionally bond to the images in ways that benefit the product, candidate,
   or whatever else is being sold. Often the rational content of the product or candidate's message is less important than the signs/signifiers
   chosen by the media expert.

Over the last 25 years, for example, right-wing movements have
taken advantage of this postmodern confusion and increased power of the
sign and image to connect signifiers of the European cultural heritage, the
true Americanness of a laissez-faire economics, the knowledge of the traditional Western canon, and the values of a heterosexual nuclear family
life to their organizations and political candidates. Such strategies have
worked successfully to help win electoral victories, polarize Americans,
and evoke hostility on those who fall outside the group brought together
by such appeals. What seem at times to be passing images and signs exert
a profound political effect. Those media specialists who design these
image campaigns have carefully studied the complex relationship between
image and reality and have developed sophisticated strategies to deploy
signs for particular purposes (Feuer, 1995).

Because of such success, the culture of postmodern hyperreality celebrates the look and the sign. This communal image promotes a form of
social amnesia that turns us away from a knowledge of the historical shaping of our consciousness as it engulfs us in a white-water river of signs: a
torrent of changing images that dull our senses. Unlike many analysts of
contemporary information culture, critical postmodern analysts recognize
a political dimension in these seemingly random signs. For example, while
advertisers claim that advertising is predominantly informative, careful
study indicates that it is grounded on image. Also, these images do not
simply attempt to market products by connecting them to desirable traits;
they sell an accompanying ideology, a system of values that further an
individual's identification with a culture of consumerism. Once again the

curriculum of a democratic social studies has been undermined. Through the "sign curriculum" of hyperreality, students and other individuals are further removed from recognizing the significance of the civic domain, the public space, the political sphere. As social studies teachers, we have to work that much harder to engage them.

Indeed, the democratic social studies envisioned here attacks this depoliticizing tendency head-on. A twenty-first century social studies teaches students to interpret how images are constructed, how they shape our consciousness, and what they mean in different situations. Such an approach to social studies education uses interpretive and analytical strategies to understand the power of the sign and image in electronic media. We begin to deconstruct the forms of thinking embedded in contemporary television. In so doing, we find that linear forms of Cartesian-Newtonian logic have little to do with the construction of political media campaigns or television advertising. Traditional attempts to distinguish between true or false advertising claims are misguided in their assumption that such claims are couched in the language of logical propositions. If such a language is discarded, advertising cannot be analyzed under the same ground rules applied to other forms of communications. Advertisers on television appeal to a domain of symbols that cannot be validated or refuted (Postman, 1985, 1995; Kellner, 1995).

Like so many other aspects of our rigorous and democratic social studies, we employ a knowledge of research to study and make sense of the power of the sign and image as they are used by the architects of TV, radio, popular music, video games, computers, databases, and web sites. Studying and learning to use semiotics, film analysis, and ethnography, social studies teachers can teach elementary, middle, secondary, and college students to research the ways signs and images work in our everyday lives. How do they shape the way we receive information? How do they contribute to our attempts to make sense of the world? Such research fits into a larger category of knowledge work—a necessary vocational and civic survival skill in the first decade of the twenty-first century. Neil Postman (1985) argues that such knowledge work should involve not only contemporary analysis of information forms but a historical understanding of the origins and uses of ideograph writing, the origins and sociopolitical consequences of the alphabet, the development and impact of the printing press, newspapers, and magazines, the technological origins of the computer and its present effects, and so on. Postman's point is clear: media should be made problematic to our students in a way that causes them to assess the impact of information, signs, and images in their lives (Semali & Pailliotet, 1999; McLaren, Hammer, Reilly, & Shole, 1995; Kellner, 1995).

2. AN EXAGGERATION OF THE POWER OF THOSE WHO HOLD POWER AND THE USE OF INFORMATION TO COLONIZE HUMAN CONSCIOUSNESS. Obviously, the conditions under which knowledge is produced have changed dramatically over the past 40 years. With the construction of a global network of communications and its effect on the generation of information, those who hold power and economic resources have found an unprecedented ability to control what is heard, viewed, and received by the peoples of the world. Thus, the power of power is exacerbated and the possibility of shaping human consciousness in ways that may not serve people's interest is greater than ever before. Though the way people interpret and make sense of this power-generated information is always open and never pre-determined, observers in the twenty-first century contend that never before have the viewpoints of so many members of the working class matched the self-interests of those with the most power.

In their attempt to make meaning of postmodern hyperreality, democratic social studies teachers focus on the relationships connecting power, technology, and information. As information technology evolved in the late twentieth century, fingerprints on information became harder and harder to identify. By the first decade of the twenty-first century, few individuals who have access to mass media are speaking about the relationship between power and information. This is why power wielders can enjoy such dominance in contemporary life. In hyperreality, power seems to require coproduction by those who generate electronic information and by those who consume it. Those who produce information must seduce the consumptive public into collaboration. The production and dispersion of seductive images requires so many financial resources that it can only be accomplished by extremely large firms and industries. In this context, class and racial inequalities are perpetuated by new technologies and, at the same time, rendered more impervious to exposure by the removal of those with limited access to information from those who produce it. In hyperreality, television viewers are continuously baffled by the nebulous "they" who control information in the process exercising some mysterious form of control over their lives (Luke, 1991).

This postmodern knowledge production is viewed most clearly outside of schools in the various mass media, but it is also making its mark in schools. In universities, power wielders pay for projects that support their political and economic interests. This process has become so profound that students of higher education are looking at the present era as a time when the university has been privatized, its knowledge production capabilities sold to the only bidder that can pay its bills: private corporations. The knowledge produced in colleges and universities trickles down to elementary and secondary schools as time passes. As democratic social studies educators begin to understand the relationship between knowledge and power, they realize that taken-for-granted assumptions about the information delivered in schools begin to crumble.

What comes to be known as objective knowledge or truth is not some disinterested, pristine body of information. The "truth" of the official social studies curriculum is information that has won a long series of political struggles concerning what ideas best serves the interests of the powerful. A quick look at James Loewen's, *Lies My Teacher Told Me* (1995) and *Lies Across America: What Our Historical Sites Get Wrong* (1999) can help one's understanding of this dynamic. Democratic social studies teachers, as part of their everyday work, uncover the power hierarchies that travel in disguise, producing a bogus but believable notion of higher truth. Though known to everyone, these power hierarchies mask their shady backgrounds of political conflict. If we did not dig below the surface, we would never have known the fights, the multitude of perspectives, the silencing, the unseemly deals, that took place before the winners proclaimed a unitary, seamless, unproblematic truth.

Despite these conflicts over public knowledge, democratic social studies teachers know that the information of TV, radio, newspapers, magazines, and web sites has never been adequately addressed by schooling. In the twenty-first century, it is still difficult to find rigorous media literacy components in elementary or secondary schools. With the development of cyberspace and virtual knowledges in the last couple of decades, we can easily perceive how primitive many schools are in terms of understanding the interaction of power, technology, and knowledge. This lack of knowledge persists, no matter how important it may be in making sense of ourselves and global society in contemporary life. Those social studies students who do have some insights into these matters typically learn them on non-school time. While many of their insights and abilities often border on genius, there are still many aspects of the contemporary technoelectronic landscape that are missed by such students. Nevertheless, the technological abilities obtained by such students—typically economically privileged with access to computer equipment at home—exacerbates the gulf between the haves and have-nots in alarming ways. Nonconceptual forms of social studies that emphasize memorization of data are devised as if we are still living in an oral culture. The cognitive and pedagogical processes required by such decontextualized social studies teaching hearken back to medieval schooling where students memorized texts because there was so little literature in print.

Knowledge work in a democratic social studies engages teachers and students in an appreciation of the complexity of the relationship connecting power, technology, and information. Such social knowledge workers understand historically how this relationship has shaped human thinking across the centuries to the present. The printing press, for example, made texts far more available and changed our relationship with information. The information revolution made possible by personal computers and hypertext modifies our interaction with knowledge even further. Albert Einstein understood this informational dynamic in the second decade of the twentieth century. When he stepped off the ship on his first trip to the United States, he was bombarded with questions by reporters anxious to engage the genius who had just won the Nobel Prize in physics. One blurted out the question: "Dr. Einstein, what is the speed of sound?" Einstein humbly admitted that he didn't know. Perplexed, the reporter followed up: "You're the smartest man in the world. How could you not know the speed of sound?" Einstein replied, "If I ever need to know it, I'll look it up." The great physicist understood his relation to information in an era with an abundance of printed literature. In electronic reality, democratic social studies teachers must rethink and continue to analyze the nature of our relations with data and its implications for pedagogy, cognition, and human consciousness.

In the context of cyberspace, we possess less and less knowledge of the cultural location, the human contributions, the sociopolitical and economic interests that shape information. In those few classrooms where students are asked who produced the data they downloaded off the Internet the night before, they are often at a loss to answer. They have never considered such a question or its multidimensional implications. Information in such situations has lost its borders; it moves and flows in the nonlinear and instantaneous ways that human thought operates. Traditional forms of knowledge, organized in books and official interpretations are undermined in this new context. A subversive element implicitly operates, challenging the informational status quo but at the same time allowing power wielders who control informational pipelines to covertly promote data that serves their economic, social, and political interests. Obviously, such a dangerous reality demands new forms of knowledge work, social studies education, and cognition. In an era when the power of economic institutions, especially in relation to control of information, has risen to unprecedented heights, the development of our ability to delineate the hidden interests of the knowledge cybertechnology provides us so abundantly is crucial to the future of democracy.

3. THE FRAGMENTATION OF MEANING AND THE SUBSEQUENT PRODUCTION OF SOCIAL VERTIGO: THE DEPOLITICIZATION OF PERCEPTION. Analysts of contemporary society observe a changing world, a hyperreality marked by a social vertigo. The situation is in many ways analogous to the modernist industrial changes John Dewey documented at the end of the nineteenth century and beginning of the twentieth century. When Dewey called for new ways of thinking and new modes of analysis to better understand the new aspects of the society emerging a century ago, he did not argue that there was no continuity between mid-nineteenth century America and the world emerging in the early twentieth. His focus, understandably, was on the new, as he attempted to convince the public of the need to address the challenge presented by new problems. The democratic social studies advocated here is similar to Dewey's, only a century later and with a new set of problems. As we have maintained, constructions of time and cultural space are changing in relation to bombarding electronic images from local, national, and international locations. Social dislocations result in such a process. Given the informational focus of many of these changes, meaning is fragmented. With so much information bombarding our senses, many lose faith that they can make sense of anything. The social vertigo resulting in this context induces us to explore the process of its production, directing our attention again to the relationship between information, technology, and power.

As meaning is destabilized, as more happens in a given period of time, we begin to lose touch with what came before the instant. A time dislocation undermines our personal and social histories, in the process, decontextualizing our identities and institutions. This atrophy of memory or social amnesia produces profound consequences, for, as the past is forgotten, its power over the present is obscured. The amnesia makes "what is" seem as if "it had to be"; for example, "There's nothing we can do to help the poor."

When this erasure-of-memory process is replaced by informational campaigns to create new memories, social vertigo is exacerbated. Many of us are familiar with the Dean Witter ads where a grainy, "antiqued" film quality is used to convey a historical depiction, an origin myth of a bespeckled 1930s-esque Dean Witter (?) telling his staff of their sacred obligation to the individual needs of the customer. Many people I've interviewed are shocked to discover that these ads are not authentic. A recent McDonald's ad campaign also creates memory by presenting a nostalgic, sentimentalized, and conflict-free American family pictorial history. The purpose of the ad is to create a true-blue American historical role for McDonald's where there was none before. You can almost hear in your imagination the male voice-over: "Though we didn't yet exist, we were there to do it all for you—McDonald's then, McDonald's now." As hyperreality produces such pseudo-memories our ability to find meaning, to engender the passion necessary to commitment, is undermined. In this context, Americans are increasingly oblivious to politics, even as they have become increasingly sensitive to culture—popular culture in particular. Questions of power, justice, income distribution, control of information are ignored by most Americans.

The attempt to raise such issues in hyperreality is greeted with boredom and even anger (Grossberg, 1992). Television, which was supposed to increase citizen knowledge and political participation, has been so manipulated by power wielders that it has decreased people's desire to participate in the political realm. Many argue that the corporate control of the medium has contributed to the production of a privatized, consumer society at the expense of civic interest. News programs provide detailed coverage of mainstream figures while neglecting the ideas of groups and individuals critical of existing cultural arrangements. TV advertisements construct a world where commodity consumption solves social and political problems—the stress of contemporary life signified by "you deserve a break today" can be eased by a Big Mac and fries. The corporate advertisement's "we" induces consumers to align their interests and identities with the impersonal power wielders—interests that would include support on political issues to help "us" create good business climates with lower corporate taxes and state, local, and national incentives for locating in "our" communities. Although highly political, the sign community is represented in a manner which removes it from the political domain. It may be where we find personal and familial pleasure, but it has nothing to do with the political. The political is represented as that unpleasant realm where elections take place and unseemly deals are made (Airaksinen, 1992; Kellner, 1990).

Corporations over the last few decades have successfully contributed to the undermining of the society's understanding of what constitutes the political. Terms, such as "ideological," "domination," and "hegemonic" are not known nor do they seem appropriate in contemporary society. (I will discuss these terms later in this book.) The corporate ads tell us there are two realms in the world: the cultural and the material (the political economic). Never will the realms intersect with one another, for one's likes and dislikes in relation to commodities have nothing to do with the political world. Marc Cooper (1998, March 23) provides an excellent example of this depoliticization process in contemporary free-marketeered, corporatized Chile. Having worked in Chile in the late sixties during the Allende regime, Cooper was fascinated by the society's political passion around issues of social justice and the public good. Returning to the postmodernized corporatized Chile in 1998, Cooper painfully documented the expanding influence of national and international corporations. Especially interested in the change in public consciousness, Cooper writes of a social vertigo, a social amnesia, an embrace of free-market values, an obsession with social mobility and bourgeoisie status at any costs, and a breakdown of community solidarity in favor of privatized citizenship. The once politically well-informed Chilean society is not even a distant memory, as citizens operate in the alleged nonpolitical realm of consumer capitalism. It may be easier for Americans to recognize the sociopolitical dynamics when they occur outside the familiarity of their own society (Goldman & Papson, 1996).

The neglected realm of politics, of political literacy as it relates to everyday life, to the workplace and the economic domain, and to race and gender, becomes more important than ever in an era of depoliticization. Any democratic social studies must take on the responsibility of making sure that students and citizens are politically literate. Any attempt to study the nature of social justice must be grounded in a familiarity with the political, that domain of social studies that analyzes the way power is produced and distributed. Nonconceptual social studies, in the name of democracy, actually subverts democracy with its whitewash of social antagonisms and conflicts. Mainstream media take the same evasive action with their reduction of social conflict in the United States to electoral politics among Democrats, Republicans and the Perot-financed Reform Party, and sometimes between liberals and conservatives. Such battles are often little more than catfights within the power bloc and have relatively little to do with questions of depoliticization, the politics of information, and contemporary social vertigo. A democratic social studies makes sure that students understand, as a part of the curriculum of political literacy, that Western societies are terrains of sociopolitical struggle that involve not only the production of knowledge but the purpose of the social studies curriculum they are studying.

Democratic social studies teachers need to engage their students in an analysis of their own feelings about politics. So often, when I ask students to express words that come to mind when they think of politics, words such as "dirty," "corrupt," "distasteful," "boring," "irrelevant," "stupid," and "obnoxious" come out. While there is much corruption and stupidity in American politics, what is of concern here is that students and other American citizens in this depoliticized era feel that politics is intrinsically that way. There's nothing we can do about it, they reason; it's always been that way; it'll always be that way. This is where I begin to question how their consciousness has been constructed. I show them how the media represents political participation as distasteful. To be concerned with issues of democracy and justice is to appear socially immature and out of step with the times. The curriculum of depoliticization is quite powerful.

4. THE GROWTH OF CYNICISM IN A CLIMATE OF DECEIT. In light of this loss of meaning and depoliticization, cynicism has reached crisis levels at the end of the century. As postmodern icon, David Letterman's hip humor insinuates: "I may be stupid and uninformed, but, at least, I'm not going to be duped by some phony TV or advertising promotion. My fans and I know what you (power wielders) are up to. We don't believe doing anything about it will help, but we're not your dupes." The Lettermanesque brand of cynicism is easy to understand in a context where particular beliefs or values are exploited by companies for their sign value. The typical process involves advertisers using such signifiers so often that they squeeze much of the meaning out of them. For example, companies have used family values and the love

between family members to the point that such promotions have lost some of their emotional impact. When such a loss is perceived, companies drop the ad campaigns and wait until the family signifiers regain some of their meaning. In some ways, however, the process has longlasting effects. When family love has been used to sell tires, some of the sanctity slips away. Such a climate of deceit is a terrarium for the growth of cynicism.

Such cynicism undermines belief structures without providing alternative ways of meaning making. Individuals in this context are often left with little to believe in. As a result, bizarre ways of seeing arise—from zealous fundamentalist religious sects and racial hate groups, to occultism—attracting people with nothing left to lose. "Now that you're castrated, Bob, get your Nikes on, we're going to catch the comet." A key aspect of this postmodern cynicism involves a division of human intellect and emotion, a bifurcation that results in a sociopsychological schizophrenia. Such metaphorical schizophrenia manifests itself in our personal relationships, international affairs, human relationships with nature, and our ability to create meaning. It is exacerbated by hyperreality's proliferation of images and information that bombard us from every angle. In this hypercontext, meaning and emotional affect are rent asunder, as signifier and signified are separated in a Diesel jeans advertisement or a Benneton billboard. No matter what, we must consume; no matter how boring our jobs may be, we must make more money to get the products available to us (McLaren, Hammer, Reilly & Scholle, 1995; Bohm & Edwards, 1991).

In the human brain, the emotions and the intellect are in a constant relationship with one another in a way not fully understood. While we must be careful of grandiose pronouncements, it is safe to say that, together, they harmonize with and synergize one another. Both modernist scientific and postmodernist social impulses, however, have disturbed this bimodal coherence. The effects of this disturbance are profound and multidimensional. In the modernist context, a logocentrism (reason-centeredness) began to develop with the scientific revolution (the Age of Reason) in the seventeenth and eighteenth centuries that considered intuition and emotion incompatible with male-centered logic. This logocentric masculinization of thinking negated the potential insight derived from the body, feeling, and subjective personal experience. Western logocentrism has viewed higher-order thinking as a facility with abstract principles, thus denigrating emotional investments and the wisdom gained through feeling (Carlson, 1991). Thus, Western education over the last three centuries has tended to upset the balance between emotion and intellect. As the postmodern condition has developed, with its technology-driven bombardment of images and information, a very different cognitive impulse has emerged that has torn apart meaning and affect. As advertisers and politicians have bypassed reason on their way to the seduction of human desire, they have undermined the role of reason in the public conversation. Such sociopsychological dynamics have created a dualistic phenomenon that manifests itself in a schooling that devalues feeling and emotion and a public culture that subverts rationality. Neither sphere provides a space where the relationship between logic and emotion can be studied and cultivated in a psychologically, cognitively, and socially productive manner.

A democratic social studies is concerned with this division of logic and emotion and the cynicism and hopelessness that comes out of it. Such teachers view emotion as a mode of perception, a sense similar to sight, touch, or hearing. In this context, emotion is viewed actively, like the other senses, as a human function, as something people do. Indeed, the manner in which we deal with situations is not approached in isolation from feelings but is constituted by them. Emotion plays an extraordinary role in life situations, providing the self with instantaneous feedback on what is happening in relation to what we anticipated. Having provided such data, emotion then prepares us to take appropriate action. In a research context, for example, such information is invaluable in making sense of a cultural/educational phenomenon. But according to the dictates of Western modernist science such data are disallowed since they constitute a corruption of objective research methodology. From a democratic perspective, emotion is one of many ways we know the world; thus, it is not the antithesis of reason. The relationship is one of partnerships, not antagonism. Emotion can connect us to the world in ways that reason cannot, and vice versa. The Western, modernist, scientific association of emotion with irrationality reflects a masculine fear of connection more than a well-considered theory of cognition. No doubt, unfiltered feeling may deform sensibility and subvert analysis, but the dismissal of emotion promises the same effect (Ferguson, 1984).

In a culture beset by the splitting of intellect and emotion and characterized by the deceit of power wielders, cynical young people no longer look to school or to work as venues in which the creative spirit can be developed. Instead, they endure school, and they find slots in the work-place where they can insert their labor. Once in place in the economic machine, they confront boredom, the requirements of technological devices, and faceless supervisors (Borgmann, 1992). The concept of rewarding work becomes a source of ironic humor, nothing more. Jobs are not big enough for the human spirit, so workers emotionally withdraw from their labor. Students learn this behavior early in their school lives, moving through the day without affect, staring straight ahead at nothing in particular (Terkel, 1972). They see no larger purpose to school. No one has provided a convincing account of the meaning of education; they discern no direction in their everyday activities. They quickly learn that school has nothing to do with their passions; indeed, their emotional health is irrelevant.

A crisis of motivation accompanies the loss of meaning in the postmodern condition. Both work and schools are characterized by evidence of a malaise: low quality work, absenteeism, sullen hostility, waste, alcohol and drug abuse. Americans don't like to talk about malaise. Jimmy Carter became an object of ridicule for broaching the subject. Ronald Reagan built a political career by denying its existence. There is no concerted effort to address this postmodern crisis of motivation in the public conversation; it doesn't even have a name. It doesn't take much, however, to evoke an understanding that the problem exists. When I discuss the situation with my students, they quickly grasp the concept and, within minutes, are providing examples of the crisis in their personal lives and their lives as students and workers. They can all empathize with my description of the classroom of students with their heads on their desks as the teacher drones on. We want to be good workers and good students, they tell me, but they are so unmotivated by the nature of their jobs and their classes (Kellner, 1989; Wirth, 1983; Zunker, 1986). Democratic social studies teachers confront this cynicism and motivational crisis, and identify it as one of the most important sociopolitical issues of the first decade of the twenty-first century.

5. THE CELEBRATION OF SURFACE MEANINGS—THE VALIDATION OF SHALLOWNESS. Within what is referred to as the postmodern condition, there exists a tendency to focus on the surface, a refusal to go beyond the shallow. We see this in many social, cultural, and political domains where individuals have neither the ability nor the disposition to challenge the literalness of the visual or to see behind the

visual or media images. This tendency is very much a part of non-conceptual social studies since curriculum developers and educational leaders avoid directing teachers and students to penetrate the social surface. As a result, concepts of interest to a democratic social studies such as power, interpretation, threats to democracy, and meaning making—all of which are not instantly accessible to the senses—are erased from educational and public awareness. We can also view this tendency in the politics of postmodernism with its surface explanations of complex phenomena. Any effort to go beyond the surface in the political domain will be punished swiftly with the sting of electoral defeat.

TV news programming represents another example of this postmodern shallowness. In recent years there has been a marked decrease in coverage of macropolitical issues in lieu of personal pieces on interesting, often quirky individuals. Such a postmodern depthlessness can be clearly observed on the morning news programs: *Good Morning America*, *The Early Show*, and *The Today Show*. *The Today Show*, for example, has programmed less and less hard news and more entertainment-oriented fluff pieces over the last three decades. Understanding that postmodern audiences don't want in-depth stories about the political, social, and cultural domains, network executives have focused more attention on promoting entertaining hosts (Matt Lauer and Katie Courec) and less on investigative reporting and political analysis. Hard news programming doesn't work—doesn't get high ratings—in the first decade of the twenty-first century.

As life speeds up and intensifies in hyperreality, fashions, products, and even values and ideologies quickly come and go. Don't dig too deep into today's cultural dispositions; they'll be gone tomorrow. The value of the instant—a fast food chain is called Hot 'n' Now—the shallow, and the throwaway penetrate all dimensions of postmodern life. Such instantaneity and disposability have to do with more than fast food and paper plates, as values, lifestyles, and relationships become obsolete. Meaning is destabilized, as more happens in a given period of time than those who lived in the modernist era could imagine. Recently, while I was fixing my morning coffee, I watched my teenage daughter standing impatiently in front of the microwave oven. Speaking to no one in particular, she suddenly exclaimed, "Ahhh, this microwave takes forever!" Something profound was embedded in this "whine." Prior perceptions of time, I realized, had been undermined, and a new sense of duration had emerged. This new sense of time—hypertime—has little patience for depth, for time-consuming attempts to dig below the surface. The entire culture is affected by ADD (Attention Deficit Disorder). What psychologists don't seem to understand as they designate certain children as ADD is that this is not a pathological but a perfectly reasonable response to the depthless culture of hyperreality.

In an era where time has intensified and time for depth is lost, meaning and commitment have been undermined; thus, the emergence of the previously discussed depoliticization, social vertigo, and cynicism. What can one do in such an intense cultural situation to find meaning in the depths of shallowness? Over the last few decades, a phenomenon has appeared that, for the absence of a better word, might be called hyper-motivation. Individuals who are hypermotivated exhibit a nervous restlessness, a narrow and shallow focus on the world, and an intolerance of more mellow men and women. The stereotype of the hypermotivated individual is the workaholic careerist with his or her consumerist concerns. Maybe an even better prototype would be the true-believing Amway salesperson, since the Amway image implies a wild enthusiasm for nothing in particular save enthusiasm itself (Lash, 1990). Give me something to believe in, to be passionate about—anything. High-fee motivational consultants travel from business to business: "When I give the signal," they tell their audiences, "stand and cheer yourselves!" "Motivate yourselves. . . you can do it. . . today is the first day of the rest of your lives," motivators preach. They save souls, and win converts for technocapitalism and its depthlessness.

Postmodern citizens are mobilized to a state of hypermotivation. When meaning has faded, then affect must become a jihad. Warriors in this postmodern jihad come to see the less than hypermotivated in condescending terms: loafers and welfare cheats. In their own lives, the warriors degrade relaxation and quiet contemplation, interrupting their long tours of duty by intense interludes of exotic recreation and manufactured fun at Disneyland or on a Carnival Cruise: "If you could see me now." Japan is the quintessential hypermotivated society, the envy of techno-capitalist leaders. Global competitiveness is the overt goal of the hyper-active society. Its pursuit holds dramatic but infrequently discussed repercussions that involve the subversion of civility in the single-minded pursuit of success. *Homo economicus* becomes *Homo hyper-economicus* and schools become the breeding ground for the terminally hypermotivated.

The motivational techniques that worked so well with businesses and industries are adapted for high school, middle school, and elementary school use (Borgmann, 1992). Youth corps in the technocapitalist jihad cheer themselves wildly, hug their schools, sell more magazines than their rival middle school, and get McDonald's Big Macs for good grades. They are caught in a jihad without a cause, a celebration of surface affect.

Democratic social studies educators can avoid the shallowness of hypermotivation by seeking deeper meanings based on social and economic justice, egalitarianism, and a democracy that appreciates various forms of difference between people, culture, religion, and philosophy. In this context I have called for new forms of thinking, an alternate consciousness that moves us beyond the shallowness and depoliticization of both Cartesian scientific thinking and the postmodern condition. Utilizing recent advances in social and educational theory, we have attempted to construct a sociopolitical form of thinking that understands the way our consciousness, and our subjectivity is shaped by the world around us. Such a perspective grants us a new conception of what "being smart," or being a good student might entail. This postformal view of higher order thinking induces psychologists and educators to recognize the politicization of cognition in a manner that allows them to desocialize themselves and others from Cartesian psychology's and nonconceptual school-based pronouncements of who is intelligent and who is not. Postformalism is concerned with questions of justice, democracy, meaning, self-awareness, and the nature and function of the social context: the depth of human and social existence. In this manner, postformalism grapples with purpose, devoting attention to issues of human dignity, freedom, power, authority, domination, and social responsibility.

The point being made here involves the recognition that the postformal vision is not only about revealing the way consciousness is shaped by the social domain but also about creating new forms of human being and imagining better ways of life. A democratic social studies informed by postformalism involves the political struggle to reshape schooling in the service of progressive values. As they lurk in the shadows of pseudo-objectivity, educational psychology and mainstream social studies deny their political complicity. In contrast, postformalism embraces its own politics and imagines what the world could become. As Gaile Cannella (1999) puts it, human possibility is enhanced when the tyranny of dominant ideology, formalist reason, and Cartesian-Newtonian science is removed. Moving into the conversation from another philosophical locale, Aostre Johnson (1999) contends that Cartesian-based schooling undermines the expression of human multidimensionality by excluding spiritual dimensions of being. It subverts our vision of human possibility, she maintains, by proclaiming the individual rational mind as the central organizing dynamic in cognition and action.

The new forms of democratic living that postformalism attempts to make possible are indelibly linked to an alternative rationality. Contrary to the claims of some critics, postformalism does not seek to embrace irrationalism or to reject the entire enterprise of empirical research. I borrow the phrase, "alternative rationality," from Stanley Aronowitz (1988), whose critique of mainstream science helps shape our vision of postformalism. In this schemata, new rationalities employ forms of analysis sensitive to the signs and symbols of postmodern shallowness, the power of context in relation to thinking, the role of emotion and feeling in human activity, and the value of the psychoanalytical process as it taps into the recesses of (un)consciousness. The effort to develop a postformal democratic social studies extends Aronowitz's powerful alternatives by asking ethnical questions of cognition and action. Such inquiries induce social studies and other scholars to study issues of purpose, meaning, and, ultimately, worth. Do certain forms of thinking undermine the quest for justice? Do certain forms of research cause observers to view ways of seeing as problematic if they deny their complicity with power and privilege (Shotter, 1993; Usher & Edwards, 1994; Cannella, 1997; Schleifer, Davis, & Mergler, 1992)?

Mainstream social studies has simply never encouraged a serious conversation about the impact of the postmodern condition, about the reasons humans engage in certain behavior, about the purposes of so-called higher order thinking, or about the social role of schooling in a democratic society. For the most part the discipline has never considered the implications that Paulo Freire's notion of "conscientizacion" holds for the work of practitioners. What happens in the realm of cognition when individuals begin to gain a new consciousness via the process of: 1) transforming themselves through changing their reality; 2) grasping an awareness of the mechanisms of oppression; and 3) reclaiming their historical memory in order to gain an awareness of their social construction, their social identity (Freire, 1970)? In an era where meaning is subverted and shallowness celebrated, the need for conscientizacion is profound. Understanding the implications of such concerns, Phillip Wexler (1997) describes an alternative rationality that involves the effort to move beyond the limitations imposed by the discipline of psychology. In recent scholarship on the ethnography of being, alternate rationalities emerge as analysts study altered states of consciousness.

In such moments of transcendence, individuals gain insight into the constructed nature of what is labeled normal Western consciousness, an insight that allows for a reframing of experience in exciting new ways. A democratic postformal social studies struggling with the postmodern shallowness has much to learn from Wexler's work, since it brings together questions of knowledge (epistemology) with questions of being (ontology). Such a synthesis moves scholars to consider rigorous democratic analyses of power's role in shaping consciousness vis-à-vis the effort to live more fully—Wexler calls it the process of enlivenment. In the synergistic fusion of these compelling considerations, a democratic postformal social studies opens new paths to human development and insight. Subsequent chapters will clarify this postformalism and its specific relationship to a democratic social studies. Suffice it to say at this point that, in the cynical shallowness of the postmodern condition, we must reinvent ourselves and imagine new forms of human being. There are more compelling forms of motivation than mere hypermotivation.

6. THE SUBSTITUTION OF FASCINATION FOR ANALYSIS—THE AGE OF THE SPECTACLE. In the context of the preceding discussion of postmodern shallowness and the substitution of fascination for analysis, a recent Diet Coke ad extends our understanding of the postmodern condition: "Some people live their life as an exclamation, not an explanation." Here resides a powerful philosophical—more specifically, an epistemological (having to do with the nature of knowledge and questions of truth)—revolution. What good does the philosopher's traditional need to explain the world do us, it asks. To hell with reason, with analysis, for, as Diet Coke puts it: "You get to taste it all." There's no need for reflection here. Why think about the social, cultural, political, economic, and moral aspects of the world around us? The stimulation of the senses—entertainment-value is the core value of the postmodern condition—is the name of the game. Corporations, political machines, businesses, and their higher education hired hands are focused on the development of new ways to amuse the public, and to colonize human desire/libidinal energy. They know that the possession of such an ability is the most effective pathway to economic and political power. Not a new concept for

sure—remember the Roman bread and circuses—but one that, combined with contemporary electronic communication technologies, penetrates the most geographically distant reaches of the globe and the most private mind spaces of the individual.

As postmodernity substitutes fascination for insight, creating a culture of entertainment, we can understand why the political domain is seen as boring to so many. At the same time, politics is boring, culture is fascinating and almost everyone attends to it. How many of us do not know something about Diana and Dodi, Frank and Kathie Lee, O. J. Simpson, Tonya and Nancy, Amy Fischer and Joey Buttafuco, the Menendez brothers, Monica Lewinsky and cigars, Dennis Rodman and dresses, and cola wars? Billy Joel could write a song out of this material. It is extremely difficult for Americans to understand that culture is the location of where consent or political allegiance is won. The postmodern condition is characterized by fascination and the spectacle. And, it is this spectacular domain of entertainment that is the new political terrain. The spectacle is not simply about entertainment; it is also very much about politics.

Controlling the government may, in hyperreality, no longer even be necessary for corporate leaders to win political battles. On many levels, such a statement may not make sense—and this is the point. Logical and rational argument may have less to do with winning public consent in this age of the spectacle than it did 50 years ago. This does not mean that the politics of corporate-produced entertainment does not want governmental power, but it does mean that the world of the twenty-first century has changed. The politics of the corporate spectacle, in other words, does not attain power by making the most persuasive political argument; it attains power by restructuring our public lives and our feelings and emotions at the level of our private experience (Grossberg, 1992). It entertains us.

Here rests the secret of political power in the postmodern condition. With its ability to fascinate and thus gain access to people's private, everyday lives, postmodern power is able to help shape our identities and, consequently, the ways we make sense of our experiences. Our consent to be governed is structured not only through political messages but through pleasure and feeling derived by way of popular forms of television, music, dance, movies, and so on—the spectacles. For example, when individuals experience self-expression through consumption and consumption-related practices, TV commercials may structure political meanings and dispositions through the pleasure these experiences provide. A consumer enjoys car ownership and the image such a purchase projects to the world; thus, the effect of a Corvette commercial may be experienced on many levels. The ability of corporate advertisers to create imagery that connects and extends the consumer's pleasure produces a variety of effects. Consumers may identify the present economic arrangement as the one best designed to provide them with the pleasure the Corvette accords. They may have to adjust their life within the boundaries of particular social conventions to make the money required to purchase the Corvette and the pleasures it provides. Engaging in such practices privileges certain political orientations, in this case making for a conservative identification with the maintenance of the status quo. It is important to note at this point that similar circumstances may produce very different effects in different individuals, but power strives to shape the effects in ways that serve its interests.

Students of power have traditionally failed to understand that people make sense of reality with both the mind and the heart/body. Corporate leaders, however, understood this notion long ago, designing their commercial advertisements not around a logical appeal to the buyer's rationality but around the regulation and reshaping of the consumer's desire and emotions. In their attempt to uncover the workings of contemporary power, democratic social studies educators must understand what people know, how they come to know it, and how such knowledge and the process of obtaining it shape their consent to the powerful. Adding analysis to their fascination with the spectacle, democratic social studies teachers help their students understand the way contemporary corporate power wielders employ media technology to shape public feeling and, thus, opinion around the world. Social studies educators must be students of this process. They must be able to point out the ways that fascination with the spectacles of our era undermine rigorous social and political analysis of the public sphere.

7. THE REORGANIZATION OF CAPITAL/ECONOMIC POWER IN A GLOBAL CONTEXT—TECHNOCAPITALISM SUPPORTED BY A NEOSOCIAL DARWINISM. The change in corporate behavior in the late twentieth and early twenty-first centuries is a study of contrast and continuity. Even though new technologies, modes of knowledge production, and sign systems have developed, the twenty-first century free enterprise

system still reflects particular characteristics of its nineteenth century take-off phrase:

a. It is growth-oriented. It is only by way of growth that profits can be guaranteed. Under this growth imperative, managers have sought to achieve expansion no matter what the human, social, geopolitical, or ecological consequences are.

b. Growth has traditionally required that workers be exploited. This doesn't mean that labor gets nothing, but it does mean that growth is based on the differences between what workers create and what they get.

c. The free enterprise system places great emphasis on technological and organizational innovation. Competition demands that entrepreneurs constantly search for an edge over their business rivals (Harvey, 1989)

The changes in capital accumulation resulting in a savage new economic order have changed and are continuing to change Western culture. Technocapitalism, as Doug Kellner (1989) describes it, becomes increasingly multinational as new technologies, such as satellite TV and computers, carry forms of mass consumer culture throughout the world, colonizing previously private spaces. Making use of these new technologies, technocapitalism moves money, ideas information, images, technologies, and goods and services quickly from one country to another. If the "business climate" is not good enough in one place, a corporation will move, or at least threaten to move, to a more profitable venue. Such threats can facilitate a corporation's attempt to consolidate power, as it effectively undercuts a locale's attempt to levy a corporate tax or a group of workers' attempt to gain benefits or improve their wages.

As we have observed, postmodern technocapitalism uses consumer goods, film, TV, mass images, and computerized information to shape desires and consciousness throughout both the developed and the developing world. In the first decade of the twenty-first century, this multinational technocapitalism is helping to shape a worldwide cultural change that dramatically enhances the power of those connected to the administration of these nomadic corporations. One of the most important points here involves the increasing difficulty for individuals to identify the reality of this growing power. Unlike power in the past, it is not administered with an iron hand but more with a velvet glove. Perpetually disguised, postmodern power has extended its influence so subtly that most people are unaware of the insidious oppression at work in their own lives. This is, of course, why the work of democratic social studies teachers is so important at this point in history. Citizens of the United States and the world must come to understand the relationship between technopower and the future of democracy.

The social studies curriculum taught by technocapitalism is the social studies curriculum of the twenty-first century. It teaches a plethora of social and political lessons to "students" who are not aware they are learning—by the most powerful and effective way to teach, that is, indoctrination. Those who "make it" in the new globalized culture are those who operate on the basis of their self-interests. The concept of a larger social good, conceived outside of a cynical corporate representation of it for good image building, begins to fade from the public radar screen. The seductive corporate commodified images of individual choice, privatized lifestyles, and commercial interests share little space with collective needs. Even when the social good is addressed by corporations, what emerges can be quite misleading. In a recent book on power and McDonald's (*The Sign of the Burger: McDonald's and the Culture of Power*, 2001) I explore the way the company represents itself as a firm very concerned with the environment. In numerous ads, it publicizes itself as the world's biggest recycler of waste. What is not mentioned is that the company produces more trash than any other organization in the world. In addition, McDonald's pamphlets and school materials stress the nutritional value of its food. Warnings from the medical community concerning the dangerously high levels of fat and calories in the restaurant's food are missing. The company presents itself as a model employer with happy and contented workers. Erased, of course, are statistics on pay, turnover, and union-busting activity that positions McDonald's as an enemy of labor around the world (Deetz, 1993; Manning & Cullum-Swan, 1994). The knowledge the company produces about these social issues is quite misleading, because it shapes the public's view of the social effects of corporate activity.

Thus, social studies education in the postmodern out-of-school public arena becomes the domain of powerful groups who use it as a means of solving social problems in a way that serves their own interests. These same groups are concurrently attempting to replace public education with a system of privatized, for-profit schools that will further promote the politics of the free market to the detriment of the public space and civic concerns. Pushed and pulled by such groups and their threat of privatization, contemporary schools are often not moved by educational and political visions—like the one offered here—that value the human spirit, egalitarianism, democratic institutions, and human possibility. The promotion of school privatization under the public relations label, "school choice," is a dangerous threat to the values of a democratic social studies and a free society.

Technocapitalism's social studies curriculum rests on a new version of nineteenth century social Darwinism: society should operate on the basis of the laws of nature and allow the fittest to survive and the weak to die. Students, teachers, and workers must submit to the law of the jungle. This neosocial Darwinism is inherently naïve, because it fails to question the forces that privilege certain groups and impede others. Thus, success is founded not simply on one's resourcefulness but on one's initial acquaintance (often attained through socioeconomic background) with the forms of knowledge, the attitudes, and the skills required for success, often called "cultural capital." This cultural capital is a very important concept, because both schools and workplaces reward individuals who possess the cultural capital of the dominant culture. Few employers or teachers recognize that individuals' cultural capital is shaped by where they grow up and what socioeconomic class they fall into (McLaren, 1994a). When cultural capital intersects with social Darwinism, tracking in schools and undemocratic hierarchical work arrangements are the result. The most damaging aspect of this unholy fusion is that it causes us to view these human hierarchies not as inhumane and unjust but as natural and just. And when we view oppression, race, class, and gender discrimination as natural and just, democracy dies.

8. THE CHANGE OF CHANGE—EVERYTHING IS DIFFERENT OR AT LEAST FEELS THAT WAY. The world is a very different place than it was just a few years ago. Throughout my children's childhoods and adolescences I have often imagined them attempting to interact with my parents at the same ages. They would have trouble communicating, I think, separated by different concerns, values, interests, and level of acquaintance with the world of adulthood. My children at the age of twelve knew so much more about what used to be the secret knowledge of adults than my parents did at twelve. Not only has the world changed dramatically, but change itself has changed. Postmodernity, as much as anything else, represents the change of change. Contrary to traditional modernist scientific beliefs, change is a nonrational,

often an irrational, process. Change viewed in postmodern terms, forces us to reexamine the concept of self and social transformation from new perspectives. Because the self is not viewed as an entity which is shaped in a rational, linear, and predictable way, the post-modern shift allows us to see the multidimensional forces that often interact with our desires to create erratic personal, and, thus, erratic social, development.

For example, sexual impulses, guided by identifications with popular cultural imagery, move us in directions unimagined by our ancestors in their pre-electronic folk culture. The way individuals construct cate-gories of meaning within the competing *Zeitgeist* (spirit of the times) of the postmodern culture shape how they respond to sociopolitical events. Teachers negotiate their professional roles around the interrelationship among their categories of meaning, the postmodern culture, and the dis-course of teaching. When empowered, these teachers come to under-stand their student's response to school knowledge in the same process that they come to understand their own response to the role of teacher. This process involves an appreciation of the dynamics of change in a postmodern cosmos; it involves understanding the sites and social prac-tices that shape experiences and through which individuals construct their identities. The sites and social practices may vary—they might include the church, gospel music, Boy Scouts, and Disneyland; or anar-chist youth culture, skateboarding, and industrial music; or, more com-monly, the combination of some of the above. The sites of the postmodern curriculum that are imbued with power will, of course, pro-vide the most powerful lessons.

In this technopower-driven change of change everyone feels that he or she and everyone around them is going crazy—"We're all Bozos on this bus." The everyday is frightening and, many argue, we would all be a lot better off if we didn't know the truth. The *X-Files* TV show fits this post-modern sentiment well, as Muldar and Scully constantly seek a terrifying hidden truth about the way the world operates. "We both are crazy, Dana," Fox frequently tells his partner, knowing that horror and terror lurk around every corner. Politics and political participation are absurdi-ties in the postmodern *X-Files* universe; the government is controlled by small cadres of angry and seemingly irrational men.

In such a world, one can't take anything too seriously; it would drive you crazy. The postmodern side of the frontier is the insane one where nothing ever makes total sense. Everything is different than before. "What a long strange trip it's been," the Grateful Dead told us as they watched the postmodern condition unfold around them. There is a self-consciousness to all of this, and television producers and moviemakers know that we are amused, or at least entertained, by the terror of it all. The popular entertainment of contemporary twenty-first century society is on another side of the postmodern divide. In its self-conscious cynicism and social vertigo, it laughs at our confusion and lack of understanding of the world around us.

One of Jay Leno's pet routines on *The Tonight Show* is to ask people about current events, political figures, or geography. The purpose of the sketches is to derive humor from the social studies ignorance of those (typically young) that he asks. The audience and Leno laugh uproariously as a college student or young worker fails to know that Ontario is a province in Canada or that Mexico is in North America. Our alienation from and fear of the world is a source of entertainment. David Letterman has made a career on feigning total ignorance of and astonishment about the affairs of the day. He even mocks the very notion of understanding current events with his fastest growing game show sensation on TV, "Know Your Current Events." In postmodernity, Letterman has ingeniously commodified our ignorance. Something has changed.

Chapter

Separating Method and Subject Matter in the Name of Practicality: Modernism and its Fragmented World

Understanding Chapter 4's delineation of the postmodern condition is necessary knowledge in the effort to construct a democratic social studies. As you now understand, one of the main purposes of this book involves inducing social studies teachers to step back and examine the uncertainty of the lived world. Indeed, democratic empowerment may only be possible when we grasp this understanding and free ourselves from the "truth" claims, the certainty of traditional forms of schooling. Such freedom allows us the chance to embrace the uncertainty that stimulates reflection on who we are as individuals and as a society. As we understand power, contemporary technopower and its sociopolitical influences, we begin to realize the inadequacy of existing social studies teacher education in colleges and universities and the teaching of social studies in elementary and secondary schools. One of my purposes here is to open a new debate in social studies education.

FALSE DICHOTOMIES: THE FRAGMENTATION OF RATIONALIZATION

The old categories of debate within social studies education have not only created false dichotomies but have contributed to the alienation between academicians and public school practitioners. Practitioners are tired of arguments over matters that seem to have little importance in the context of their classrooms. Often, traditional debates have centered around controversies concerning the emphasis of subject matter over method or a delineated scope and sequence as opposed to a less rigid, possibly a problem-centered, curriculum. Can social studies education not be both a problem-based curriculum and a subject-based curriculum? Don't social studies professors in colleges of education want students to acquaint themselves with both content and method? It seems that the conflicts deemed inherent are not conflicts at all. This book asserts that there is no distinction between method and subject matter; indeed, subject matter is method and method is subject matter. To deal with either of the two outside of the context of the other is inherently misleading.

With these ideas in mind, it is our contention that social studies education must stop separating method and subject matter. Until social studies educators reunite these two entities, they will neither gain respect in the academic community nor educate teachers effectively. This book consistently attempts to examine method in the context of subject matter. Method should presuppose a knowledge of a certain body of content, not that we accept the "truth" of such information. The way we approach that content, massage it for effective transmission to a targeted group, decide what is important about it, determine how it relates to other content and other ideas, and ascertain the ways it affects our lives and the lives of others are the concerns of educational methodology. Such tasks cannot be accomplished when method is separated from content. Though the argument over the attempt to unite method and subject matter is as old as social studies itself, social studies educators have too infrequently designed effective strategies for uniting the two. Moreover, when we examine the professionalization of social studies teachers, we must accompany our discussions of method with actual methodological approaches to specific subject matter. This book challenges social studies educators to develop programs that operate within this context.

The irony of this tendency to divorce methodology from subject matter is that it is accomplished in the name of practicality. The quest for the immediately applicable has cursed colleges of education and social studies education in particular. The perception that teachers must have their teaching behaviors specifically delineated before they enter the classroom has demeaned the role of the teacher. First, it has restricted the professional autonomy of the practitioner, implying that classroom teaching is not a professional role marked by complex independent diagnosis and decision making in ever changing situations. It assumes that teaching is merely the application of a set of prearranged packages to a set of standardized students. Second, it has demeaned the role of students, stealing their autonomy and blurring their uniqueness, as it views them as entities to be manipulated.

Teacher training strategies that attempt to provide teachers with a set of prearranged behaviors assume that learning outcomes are measurable and predictable. Honest, spontaneous (i.e. human) interaction between teacher and student with subtle benefits such as inspiration, raised consciousness of possibilities and alternatives, and increased happiness for all parties is deemed insignificant and irrelevant. We reject the rationalized view of teaching as a set of prearranged behaviors. From our perspective, the well-prepared teacher is not one who enters the classroom with a set of prearranged lessons but is a professional with a thorough knowledge of subject, a knowledge of what is happening in the world, an awareness of children and students, an understanding of educational goals and purposes, and an appreciation of the teacher's role in the attainment of certain educational outcomes. None of these understandings can be reproduced in a list of specific competencies; they are too diverse and nebulous to be reduced in such a crudely practical way.

Until we discard dehumanizing strategies that attempt to manipulate individuals rather than celebrate their uniqueness, we will make little progress in social studies education. Contemporary teachers often harbor a vague sense of discomfort with the mentality that views learning in terms of competencies and content standards. Practicing teachers often resent professional preparation programs that are based on narrow scientific and behavioral assumptions. They are troubled by education curricula and in-service programs that are constructed around the assumption that teachers are incapable of understanding the foundations on which certain strategies are based. These teachers know that something is wrong when they watch "experts" evaluate their teaching ability and their school programs on the basis of lesson plans and other written goals, sometimes without ever observing their classroom teaching. The anger resulting from such experiences is understandable, indeed it is justified; but it is often not channeled into positive outcomes. Teachers sometimes sense that individuals with ears sympathetic to their frustrations do not exist, especially not in colleges of education. It is very important that social studies experts in higher education listen to the concerns of practicing teachers and learn from their frustrations. Until such learning takes place, social studies education is destined to languish, a victim of interdisciplinary alienation.

Maxine Greene (1988, 1995) writes about teaching young people to reach out as participants. Probably no one single social studies principle is as important as this one, as we work to connect social studies with the lived world. It is only as participants in the world that we can see the need to learn about it. Hence, it becomes essential, that as we teach our students, we treat them as people who are participating in the world around them and who plan to participate even more in the future. If we hold such a goal in mind as we prepare our lessons, it should help us transcend, for example, the inert study of the form of government and move political science to a study of how that form relates to everyday life with all of its power relations and irrationality. Legal questions of fairness, potential problems with the political system, specific benefits that come from a just and responsive government add meaning to such political study. History helps us answer questions about why the things around us happened to develop into their present form, who we are, and what it means to be human. Sociology helps to explain differences between people that often lead to misunderstanding, distrust, and hatred. Geography grants us a sense of the effects of the physical environment on our occupations and values, and thus, through that understanding, gives us more control over our lives. Cultural studies helps us understand the limitations of traditional disciplinary structures and the way culture shapes all aspects of our lives, even the scholarly tools we use to study ourselves and the world.

A study of social studies with students viewed as participants in the lived world is quite different from social studies that sees students as passive receptors in a fact-based, memory game. As we prepare to become democratic social studies teachers, it is important to study why it is that method, subject matter, and the lived world should be torn asunder in social studies classes. What is surprising about this fragmentation is that it doesn't just happen but is the consequence of a specific set of social and historical set of circumstances. In this chapter we will explore this amazing historical context, and its effect on the social studies and our everyday lives. We begin with the birth of modernism in seventeenth and eighteenth century Western Europe. It is here that we see the origins of the rationalized fragmentation, the rational irrationality of twentieth and twenty-first century social studies.

THE BIRTH OF MODERNISM:
THE ENLIGHTENMENT AND THE SCIENTIFIC REVOLUTION

During the Middle Ages, what Europeans thought of as science was grounded on a Thomist-Aristotelian synthesis of faith and reason. The main goal of the synthesis was to understand the nature of natural phenomena. But when the Black Death swept across Europe, killing about one-fourth of the population, many realized that the medieval way of seeing was inadequate. Under the pressure of such catastrophic sickness, Western scholars began contemplating a new way of perceiving the natural world—a way that would enable them to understand and control the outside world (Fosnot, 1988; Kincheloe, Steinberg, & Tippins, 1999; Leshan & Margenau, 1982).

With the coming of the Scientific Revolution, or the Age of Reason, in the sixteenth and seventeenth centuries, nature was to be controlled, "bound into service and made a slave" (Capra, 1982). The basis of this control was founded on the epistemological (the branch of philosophy that pertains to the study of knowledge) separation of knower and known. This bifurcation legitimates the assumption that the human perceiver occupies no space in the known cosmos; existing outside of history, the knower knows the world objectively. Thus, knowers are untainted by the world of opinions, perspectives, or values. Operating objectively (without bias), the knower sets out on the neutral mission of science: the application of abstract reasoning to the understanding of the natural environment. Reason told the pioneers of science that complex phenomena of the world can be the best understood by reducing them to their constituent parts and then piecing these elements back together according to laws of cause and effect. Here rests an important clue in our effort to understand the separation of method, subject matter, and the lived world in traditional social studies education. Such an isolated approach reflected a larger fragmentation tendency in Cartesian reasoning.

Rene Descartes' separation of mind and matter, his Cognito, ergo sum (I think, therefore, I am) is central to our story. This view led to a conception of the world as a mechanical system divided into two distinct realms: an internal world of sensation, and an objective world composed of natural phenomena. Building on the Cartesian dualism, scientists argued that laws of physical and social systems could be uncovered objectively by researchers operating in isolation from human perception with no connection to the act of perceiving. The internal world of mind and the physical world, Descartes theorized, were forever separate and one could never be shown to be a form of the other (Lavine, 1984; Lowe, 1982; Kincheloe, 1991). We understand now, but could not have understood then, that this division of mind and matter had profound and unfortunate consequences. The culture's ability to address problems like the Bubonic Plague undoubtedly improved, as our power to control the "outside" world advanced. At the same time, however, Western society accomplished very little in the attempt to comprehend our own consciousness, our "inner experience" (Leshan & Margenau, 1982).

Sir Isaac Newton extended Descartes' theories with his description of space and time as absolute, regardless of context. Clarifying the concept of cause and effect, Newton established modernism's tenet that the future of any aspect of a system could be predicted with absolute certainty if its condition were understood in precise detail and the appropriate tools of measurement were employed. Thus, the Cartesian-Newtonian concept of scientific modernism was established with its centralization, concentration, accumulation, efficiency, and fragmentation. Bigger became better, as the dualistic way of seeing reinforced a rationalistic, patriarchal, expansionist, social and political order, welded to the desire for power and conquest. Such a way of seeing served to despiritualize and dehumanize, as it focused attention on concerns other than the sanctity of humanity (Fosnot, 1988).

Along with Sir Francis Bacon, who established the supremacy of reason over imagination, Descartes and Newton laid a foundation that allowed science and technology to change the world. Commerce increased, nationalism grew, human labor was measured in terms of productivity, nature was dominated, and European civilization gained the power to conquer in a way previously unimagined. The rise of modernist science was closely followed by a decline in the importance of religion and spirituality. An obsession with progress supplied new objectives and values to fill the vacuum left by the loss of religious faith. Even familial ties were severed as the new order shifted its allegiance to the impersonal concerns of commerce, industry, and bureaucracy (Aronowitz & Giroux, 1991; Bohm & Peat, 1987). Rationality was deified, and, around the scientific pantheon, the credo of modernity was developed. The world is rational (logocentric), and there is only one meaning of the term. All natural phenomena can be painted within the frame of this monolithic rationality, whether we are studying gunpowder, engines, dreams, politics, or learning.

This modernist view of knowledge, this one-truth epistemology affected all aspects of Western life, all institutions. Education was no exception. Since knowledge (like a child's conception of pre-Columbian North America) is predefined, waiting to be discovered, "out there," what use is it to teach speculative and interpretive strategies? Schools of the post-Enlightenment era emphasized not the production of knowledge but the learning of that which had already been defined as knowledge. Students of modernism's one-truth epistemology are treated like one-trick ponies, rewarded only for short-term retention of certified truths. Social studies teachers learn in their "educational science" courses that knowledge is acquired in a linear skill or subskill process. Pre-identified in the context of adult logic, the linear process is imposed on children in a manner that focuses teacher/parent attention away from the child's constructions of reality, away from the child's point of view. Thus, children's answers are often "wrong," when actually, given their point of view, the wrong answer may indicate ingenuity. We see this modernist view of knowledge embedded in the nonconceptual social studies methods class and expert-developed social studies content standards used around the country in the first decade of the twenty-first century. Obviously, even in a postmodern global society this modernist view of knowledge still prevails.

Seduced by its claim to neutrality, scientists and educators employ Cartesian-Newtonian epistemology in their quest for the higher ground of unbiased truth. The ideal modernist educator becomes the detached practitioner, an independent operator who rises above the values of special interests. The detached practitioner occupies a secure position immune from critique. He or she has, after all, employed the correct methodology in reaching his or her position. If pursued "correctly," there is no questioning the authority of the scientific method. Thus, the educational status quo is protected from critics, such as John Dewey, Paulo Freire, or Maxine Greene, with their "agendas" and value judgements. Their critiques are not deemed scientific; they are "mere opinions" (Codd, 1984; Harris, 1984; Brooks, 1984; Kincheloe, Steinberg, & Villaverde, 1999).

The Reagan-Bush-Clinton era of the last decades of the twentieth century witnessed a reconfirmation of modernism's one-truth epistemology. Reacting to the threats of social change and the critique of those concerned with the underside of modernism, mainstream conservative and liberal educators sought educational solutions within

Cartesian-Newtonian boundaries. Spurred by the Reagan-Bush-Clinton reforms, state after state adopted technocratic reform packages emphasizing modernist scientific testing and evaluation procedures and standardized curricula.

As the century turned, these various technocratic reforms came together under the flag of the standards movement. Many democratic educators opposed the standards movement not because they were against high quality education and rigorous standards but because of the Cartesian standardization, rationalization, and fragmentation of the curriculum it required. There seems to be a consistency to the reforms that revolves around the assumption that teaching, learning, and thinking are generic, that, like polyester stretch pants, one style, one size fits all. Teaching practices that are not teacher-directed, or do not hold knowledge transference as a primary goal, do not fit into the reform schemes. Social studies teachers who are concerned with improving student thinking skills, who attempt to connect schooling with life, who value the knowledge that students bring with them to school, or who take seriously the cultivation of civic courage and citizenship cannot be evaluated until they conform to the vision of teaching tacitly embedded in the reform proposals. Only learning outcomes that can be measured by standardized tests or teacher behaviors that lend themselves to quantification, such as time-on-task measurements, count in the assessment of a teacher. Pedagogical dimensions, such as a teacher's knowledge of content or a teacher's understanding of the knowledge that is produced when student experience collides with the concerns of the subject matter disciplines, are irrelevant, inadmissible evidence in the teacher's attempt to prove self-worth as a professional.

This technical Cartesian reform fails to understand the complexity of the teaching act because it requires not only direct instruction by the teacher but a narrow academic focus, drill and recitation, little student choice of activities and materials, large group as opposed to small group instruction, truncated exploration of conceptual knowledge, and an emphasis on convergent questions with short correct answers. Such strategies privilege a fragmented, unconnected form of thinking that tends to match Jean Piaget's description of concrete cognition. Undoubtedly, it is easy to measure whether students have "mastered" this type of thinking, and it is hard for school leaders to resist the facile, commonsense justifications that play so well in the media and the political arena. The only problem with such an education is that it does not challenge students with anything significant; it trivializes education, rendering it a meaningless game, a fatuous rite of passage into adulthood (Jones & Cooper, 1987).

QUESTIONING CARTESIANISM: DEVELOPING A NEW CONVERSATION IN SOCIAL STUDIES

Individuals and groups from all political and cultural corners have expressed some discomfort with this modernist one-truth epistemology and the education it supports. From religious fundamentalists, to those advocating a counter-Cartesianism, the continuum of antimodernists takes in a variety of assumptions and perspectives. Fundamentalists attack modernism from a premodernist perspective, asserting that the one-truth epistemology of science has excluded God and religious ways of knowing. Democratic social studies educators question the modernist view of what constitutes knowledge, where it comes from, and the nature of the human role in its production. Many educators assert that what I am preparing to describe now, the postmodern critique, is very complex and confusing. It may be complex, but, in many ways, it is easy to understand its importance. This democratic social studies critique of Cartesian modernism is sometimes labeled a "postmodern perspective."

Since we have already discussed the postmodern condition, it is important to carefully distinguish the postmodern condition from a postmodern perspective. This postmodern perspective (or, as I will refer to it subsequently in this book, "counter-Cartesianism") analyzes social, philosophical, and educational forms previously shielded by the authority of modernist science. It does not attempt to throw out Western science but to understand its limitations and the underside of its application. It is a global perspective, since it admits to the conversation previously forbidden evidence derived from questions asked by previously excluded voices. Postmodern thinkers challenge hierarchical structures of knowledge and the power which promote "experts" above the "masses," as they seek new ways of knowing that transcend empirically verified facts and "reasonable," linear arguments deployed in the quest for certainty (Greene, 1988; Hebridge, 1989).

When postmodern analysis is grounded on a democratic system of meaning that is concerned with questioning knowledge for the purpose of understanding more critically oneself and one's relation to society, naming, and then changing, social situations that impede the development of egalitarian, democratic communities marked by a commitment to economic and social justice, and contextualizing historically how world views and self-concepts come to be constructed, counter-Cartesianism becomes a powerful tool for progressive social studies education and transformative political action. In this context, we can begin to bring back together that which modernist educational perspectives fragmented. Our democratic counter-Cartesian social studies connects method, subject matter, social problems, and the lived world in a way that transforms social studies into something that matters in the lives of students.

Please allow me to be redundant for the purpose of clarity. Do not confuse what I have just described, postmodernism as philosophical perspective, from Chapter 4's delineation of the postmodern condition. Though the two are intimately connected, this is the point where many individuals become lost on the postmodern linguistic landscape. Jean-Francois Lyotard uses postmodernism to refer to the general condition of contemporary Western civilization. The "grand narratives of legitimation" (i.e., all-encompassing explanations of history, like the Enlightenment story of the inevitable victory of reason and freedom) in the postmodern world are no longer believable. They fail to understand their own construction by social and historical forces. Reason is undermined because of it's co-option by those in power who speak with the authority of a science not subjected to introspection, to self-analysis, or to cultural critique. Thus, the postmodern condition has arisen from a world created by modernism; the postmodern critique attempts to take us beyond the nihilism of the modern world, the deadening routine of the traditional school and social studies.

A postmodern counter-Cartesian analysis will be analysis that will be applied to social studies education throughout this book. Part of my task will be to employ postmodern modes of deconstruction to expose the caricature of certainty offered by modernist institutions, education in particular. Contemporary visions of education and educational reform often employ a Cartesian-Newtonian conception of linear, cause-effect logic. Thinking and the teaching act are viewed as an English sentence, subject acting on object. Postmodernism denies this simplistic view of reality, contending that, often in a classroom (and in life), numerous events act on one another simultaneously. It is this notion I am referring to when I write about an understanding of complexity or a social studies of complexity—later in this book, an epistemology of complexity. For example, consider a fight between two fourth-grade students. Teachers know that it is often impossible to determine who instigated the fight, that is, to determine linear cause-effect. Another common experience of nonlinearity is dreaming. Our dreams may consist of a plethora of images appearing to us simultaneously, but in our telling we transform them into lines of narrative sequence. Such a sequence represents a distortion of the "truth" of the dream. The tendency is common in our lived world, as we struggle to align our world with Cartesian ways of thinking.

Here we confront a significant aspect of the postmodern critique of language as a reservoir of unexamined cultural and political assumptions. Indo-European languages, for example, confine us to particular ways of thinking. They often fragment experience by devaluing relationship—a key concern in this chapter. Because of their subject-predicate matrix, these languages induce us to consider the world in terms of linear cause-effect. Trapped in the view of language as a neutral medium of communication, modernist thinkers have found it hard to talk (or think) about subjects such as quantum physics, the nature of consciousness, higher orders of cognition, political socialization, or any other concept without identifiable boundaries, specified beginnings and ends, and a clear delineation of then and now. The postmodern critique attempts to denaturalize the modernist universalization of Indo-European linguistics. Pointing to the fact that events in nature often have simultaneous multiple causes, postmodernists argue that not all human languages have difficulty with nonlinearity. Hopi and Chinese, for example, speak nonlinearily. Westerners from ancient Greece to contemporary America say "the light flashed" even if the light and the flash are inseparable. If we spoke Hopi, we would simply say, "Reh-pi," meaning "flash" (Ferguson, 1980). No linearity, no cause nor effect, is implied.

Postmodern perspectives offer an alternative to Cartesian modernism, a starting place in our attempt to formulate new forms of social studies education that draw upon the great thinking of people from around the world: Africans, Asians, Latin Americans, African Americans, Native American Indians, a variety of indigenous peoples and suppressed European thinkers. In other words, postmodern counter-Cartesianism reexamines and derives insight from forms of cognition, manifestations of genius, and cultural insights now eclipsed by the European modernist moon. One of the most important points to be made in this analysis and critique of Cartesian modernism and its impact on contemporary social studies education involves the insidious ways that such modes of seeing have shaped our consciousness and identity.

Without us knowing it, this Cartesian epistemology has helped make us who we are. Thus, it is even more important to understand its nature and influence because it is a part of us.

THE MODERNIST RATIONALIZATION OF TEACHING

These Cartesian modernist mind-sets have shaped schooling in the U.S. from Horace Mann's common school crusade in Massachusetts in the 1840s to the technicist content standards movement of the present. Cartesian modernist concerns with the development of a rationalized and controlled social order have influenced the nature and purpose of civic education and, after 1915, what came to be called social studies education. One of the main purposes of education in general and social education in particular was to create a culture of regulation that would influence students—poor and "culturally different" (non-WASP) students in particular. Thus, throughout Cartesian modernist-based American education, there has been an inherent conflict between a rhetoric of democracy and opportunity versus a white-dominated, class-based set of educational assumptions (Nasaw, 1979).

The common school movement in Massachusetts has traditionally been considered important because it was the first public school campaign in the United States. What has traditionally been missed has involved the modernist concern for order and social control. Mann's effort was initially supported, not as much by common people as by the developing industrial interests in the state. These interests recognized the common school as an efficient means of maintaining a skilled and docile labor pool, soon the very buttress of capitalism (Tyack & Hansot, 1982). School taxes became a sort of property insurance, a way of preserving the power of corporate capital (Nasaw, 1979). Immigrants would be educated and assimilated, and radical (that is to say, "foreign") ideas regarding the rights of labor would be extinguished. A common school would ensure that children were properly prepared for the needs of industry. Efforts to understand the origins of state-supported public education in America cannot succeed without appreciation of these industrial needs and the impact of economic forces on American schooling.

Thus, modernist rationalization interacted with the economic interests of the industrial owners to drive the first movement for public education. Before the Industrial Revolution, which began in the United States in the 1820s, 19 of every 20 Americans lived and worked on a farm. A nation populated by rural dwellers needed practical agricultural knowledge to make a living; reading and writing could be taught in the home after work. After the 1820s with the beginnings of the Industrial Revolution, many Americans, especially the new urban dwellers, began to sense that the country was changing. At first, Massachusetts was influenced by the socioeconomic effects of industrialization more than any other state, and the economic changes there would create the context for Mann's great idea: the first state-supported compulsory school system in America.

Industrialists found it difficult to adapt agrarian males to the demands of unskilled factory work. Consequently, New England mill owners hired women, children, and the inmates of charitable institutions as laborers. When Irish Catholics began to immigrate in larger numbers, industrialists hired them to replace American-born workers. They soon saw the value in developing "proper" industrial attitudes among both the immigrants and future generations of Americans. This realization led them naturally to consider the role of schools in "attitude adjustment." Thus, the industrialists' support of public education did not reflect a concern for either an empowered, educated citizenry or the economic welfare of American citizens; it reflected their economic self-interest, and specifically, a pool of workers with attitudes conducive to industrial productivity and "right" ways of thinking.

Social studies educators need to understand these ideas in order to appreciate the notion that all education is social education—schools always attempt to paint a particular picture of the social, political, and economic world and the "proper" way for students and teachers to fit into it. Democratic social studies teachers understand that all educational decisions are also social and political decisions, since they concern questions of power and its distribution among different interest groups. In the postmodern condition in particular, Americans have had difficulty understanding the dynamics of political questions. Too often, we restrict the adjective "political" to the sphere of political parties, candidates, and elections, and we thereby miss the power-related aspects of politics. As a result, we could miss the significance of the political dimensions of Horace Mann's common school crusade and its relevance for social studies educators. Engaging questions of power with the understanding that power elites possess inordinate influence in the shaping of school policy can help educators appreciate how schools work, as well as their personal roles in the larger, sociopolitically driven educational process.

Mann worked hard to sell the public schools to his Massachusetts contemporaries. In his conversations with powerful industrialists and business leaders in his home state, he addressed their fear of social disharmony. Made anxious by the growing dissatisfaction of workers with the tedium, danger, long hours and low pay of industrial jobs, factory owners sought ways to ensure social stability and order. When Mann talked of schools producing a "common core of values," the industrialists inferred that such values would support and promote industrial development. The common schools, Mann said, would turn out factory workers who were docile, easily administered and likely to avoid strikes and working-class violence. Schooling would reduce the poor people's hostility toward the wealthy. These implications were music to the ears of industrial leaders, far more concerned, as they were, with orderly and docile workers than with well-educated and inventive workers, particularly those workers already discussing "working men's associations" designed to protect their interests against the power of factory owners. One finds a fear of worker organization or revolt perpetually preoccupying the minds of factory owners.

An important question arises in this context: Where in a mid-nineteenth century Massachusetts textile mill would a worker need to exercise creativity or employ a refined ability to analyze and interpret? As far as the owners were concerned, such traits could lead only to labor trouble. As with most educational reform initiatives, the political dimension of the common school movement involved its alliance with monied interests. Although Mann's vision of public schooling went far beyond providing malleable workers, the movement would never have succeeded had the commercial banking and manufacturing interests not believed that schools would yield long-term financial benefits. The key element in the political coalition that brought universal, compulsory, state-supported education to America was the expectation among the power elite that public schools would inculcate a core of values that would prepare students to accept the inherent indignities of industrial life.

THE UNDERSIDE OF CARTESIANISM: RATIONALIZATION, ORDER, AND SOCIAL REGULATION

Thus, the origins of American public education cannot be understood outside the quest for order: political and economic regulation, for sure, but also an ordering of human thinking and spirit. The needs of such a psychic regulation, of course, were met by modernist strategies of hyper-rationalization that evolved with the birth of the social and behavioral sciences in the latter nineteenth century. The great leap forward in hyperrationalization was effected by Frederick W. Taylor's development of scientific management around the turn of the twentieth century. As immigrants from Eastern and Southern Europe poured into America in the 1890s and the first decade of the twentieth century with what were seen as alien and anti-American belief systems, political leaders and educators sensed the need for drastic action. Schools were the central weapon in the battle to Americanize these dangerous foreigners. Thus, a new social education was unleashed, designed to rid these Jews, Poles, Italians, and Greeks of their foreignness.

Scientific management influenced schooling to such an extent that power relations between administrators, teachers, and students were profoundly affected. When behavioral psychology was added to the pedagogical recipe, teachers, as well as students, began to be seen more and more as entities to be controlled and manipulated. In the spirit of the times, Edward Thorndike announced that the human mind is an exacting instrument, given to precise measurement. Teachers, he concluded, are not capable of such measurement, and, therefore, the formulation of instructional strategies and curriculum development should be left to experienced psychologists. It is no surprise that the behaviorists soon won the battle for the soul of the school, shaping its ambience with their control of instructional design (Popkewitz, 1987).

Though subsequent decades have witnessed an evolving sophistication of their strategies, the forces of efficiency, productivity, and scientific management unleashed by Taylor and Thorndike helped shape the twentieth century. Efficiency, productivity, science, and technology achieved almost godlike status on the twentieth-century modernist landscape. The daily lives of educators attest to the power of these forces, as teachers teach subject matter that has been broken into an ordered sequence of separate tasks and "factoids." Trained to follow a pretest, drill work, posttest instructional model, well-socialized teachers efficiently deliver a scientific pedagogy that has insidiously embedded itself as part of their cultural logic—a logic which serves to tame their pedagogical imagination. No thought is necessary; it's just common sense to assume that, if one wants to teach somebody something, you simply break the information into separate pieces, go over the pieces until the learner has mastered them, then test him or her to make sure the pieces have been "learned" (Goodman, 1986).

Here rests the power of Cartesian modernism: It becomes so much a part of our daily lives that it becomes naturalized, common sense. In other words, teachers have internalized, as common sense, a professional approach that breaks the complex task of teaching into a series of simple steps that even unskilled laborers can perform. As I characterized this rationalization process earlier, teachers (and students) become deskilled. As scientific manager Frederick W. Taylor put it to one of his workers: "[You're] not supposed to think; there are other people paid for thinking around here" (Wirth, 1983, p. 12). The need for the judgment of the worker would be eliminated in Taylor's system. The deskilling of teaching was thus rationalized; the conception of the pedagogical act was separated from its execution. Teachers did not need to learn the intricacies of subject matter, nor did they need to understand the sociohistorical context in which the knowledge to be taught was produced. All they needed to do was to identify the subject matter to be transferred to the learner, break it into components, present it to the student, and test him or her on it. It was a method as right as rain, so commonsensical it defied the need for justification.

The scientific management of social education in general, and social studies education in particular, with its accompanying deskilling, has initiated a vicious circle of harm to the profession. As teachers were deskilled, they lost more and more autonomy. As they became accustomed to the loss of autonomy, it was argued that they were incapable of self-direction. While in no way meaning to romanticize work conditions for nineteenth- and early twentieth-century teachers, social studies teachers in the first decade of the twenty-first century are subjected to forms of control unimagined by older teachers. Teacher education often serves to enculturate social studies teachers into their deskilled role. Prospective teachers learn to be supervised in courses that teach them to meticulously write behavioral objectives and lesson plans in the "correct" format. Many of us have been subjected to this deadening routine of rationalized professional education

Enculturated into an academic culture of passivity, teachers find themselves in workplaces that impose both teaching objectives and testing and evaluation procedures. As a result, teachers have little input into what to teach, how to teach it, or how to judge the outcome. Such a system is an insult to teacher dignity, since it assumes that teachers are too ignorant, dumb, and/or lazy to be permitted to decide such matters. Teachers become the pawns in a cult of expertise—just as Thorndike envisioned it—taking orders from experts conversant with the language of efficiency and scientific management. In such a system, some teachers do grow lazy and apathetic. But, are we surprised, when they have suckled at the breast of passivity and grown up professionally in a bureaucratic system that discourages initiative? Critical and responsible teachers find themselves too often as pariahs, outsiders who are banished because of their "bad attitudes" and their reluctance to become "team players" (Kamii, 1981; Hinchey, 1998).

Underlying these barricades to autonomous, freethinking educational professionals is a functionalist social education that views schooling as the organ of society responsible for the transmission of culture in a manner that perpetuates the social system's equilibrium; in other words, schooling that upholds the status quo of power relations. Despite protestations to the contrary—protestations issued in the language of democracy promising important decision-making roles for teachers—teachers are relegated to the role of spectators who receive the directives of their superiors (Britzman, 1991). Students will continue to suffer from their contact with teachers whose intellect and autonomy are not respected. Students who struggle to survive within the existing school framework will especially suffer. So often, they need a nurturing teacher with a creative approach to learning to release them from a cycle of failure. In the schools envisioned by the Reagan-Bush-Clinton-(Dubya)Bush-era reformers, however, these students find themselves with constrained teachers who exercise little control over the curriculum, are vulnerable to harassment for their creative approaches, and are chained to the conventional instruction demanded by top-down standards and standardized tests. Unfortunately, these students slip through the cracks of the system uneducated. Indeed, most students find the school to be more of a sorting and labeling machine and less of a vehicle for intellectual and personal growth (Bullough and Gitlin, 1991). The social educational goals articulated in Massachusetts in 1840 were and still are being achieved.

Social studies students will continue to find schools intellectually irrelevant as long as political and educational leaders succumb to the blinders of imbedded functionalism and the deadening mechanical routines of the modernist Cartesian school. The standardization, the social regulation, and the dull uniformity of the modernist school becomes a cognitive anaesthetic, a psychotropic hidden curriculum that numbs teacher and student curiosity. Democratic social studies teachers issue a call for pedagogical audacity, a manner of teaching that refuses to swallow the anaesthetic of modernism and that goes "cold turkey" in a postmodern context. I have been amazed during my years of teaching social studies teachers by the almost total lack of acquaintance with any of these ideas, any critique of modernist Cartesianism, my students bring to class.

The vast majority of my students are very smart and dedicated to the profession of teaching. Their lack of acquaintance with these perspectives is not attributable to their being dumb—far from it. The school and cultural curricula they have experienced have virtually nothing to say about different viewpoints. Even students I teach who were schooled in the former Soviet Union often have more acquaintance with a variety of social opinions than contemporary U.S. students. As I discuss these issues with my students, engaging them in an analysis of how such concepts have shaped them, and their view of teaching, and their understanding of social studies, they express great difficulty in believing that schooling could be organized in ways that harmed particular people. Such a concept runs against the grain of everything they have been led to believe. They tell me over and over again, year after year, that they just can't imagine this possibility. With their incredulity in mind, it is important to examine the conceptual backbone of Cartesian modernism and delve a little deeper into its effects on all of us.

THE EPISTEMOLOGY OF CARTESIAN MODERNISM: POSITIVISM

Do not be frightened by the word "epistemology". As mentioned earlier, epistemology is the branch of philosophy that studies the nature of knowledge. Contrary to the belief of some, it is not the study of urinary tract infections. Epistemology is not simply an academic word that is meaningful only for philosophy majors. My argument in *Getting Beyond the Facts* (an epistemological title by the way) is that epistemology has shaped not only social studies education but the way we think, the way we see the world, even our self-concept. Epistemology matters because it shapes us and the world around us. Epistemological questions might include: How do we know? Is that true? Is this an objective test? Why do you believe that? Is history based on fact or interpretation? The epistemological position of Cartesian modernism is known as positivism. Few philosophical orientations have been so influential on the way we live our lives and construct education as modernist positivism. Yet, concurrently, few philosophical orientations have been so little understood.

From a technical perspective, the term "positivism" began to be used widely in the nineteenth century. French philosopher August Comte popularized the concept, maintaining that human thought had evolved through three states: the theological stage, where truth rested on God's revelation; the metaphysical stage, where truth derived from abstract reasoning and argument; and the positivistic stage, where truth arises from scientifically produced knowledge. Comte sought to discredit the legitimacy of nonscientific thinking that failed to take "sense knowledge" (knowledge obtained through the senses and empirically verifiable) into account (Kneller, 1984; Smith, 1983). He saw no difference between the ways knowledge should be produced in the physical sciences and in the human sciences, and he believed one should study sociology just like biology. This had a dramatic impact on the way we would approach the social studies. Social knowledge and information about humans would be subjected to the same decontextualizing forces as the study of rocks. Social and behavioral scientists would pull people out of their cultural setting and study them in laboratory-like conditions.

Society, like nature, Comte argued, is nothing more than a body of neutral facts governed by immutable laws. Therefore, social actions should proceed with lawlike predictability (Held, 1980). In a context such as Comte's, education would also be governed by unchanging laws; the role of the educator would be to uncover these laws and then act in accordance with them. For example, educational laws would include universal statements regarding how students learn and how they should be taught. The positivist educator, in other words, sees only one correct way to teach, and scientific study can reveal these methods if we search for them diligently.

The following ten characteristics of positivism help us understand the impact of epistemology on our consciousness, the larger society, and social studies education in particular.

1. ALL KNOWLEDGE IS SCIENTIFIC KNOWLEDGE. First, positivism insists that only scientifically produced information should be regarded as authentic human knowledge. Scientific knowledge can be verified and proven. It is knowledge about which we are positive; hence the name "positivism." When Newton formulated the theory of gravity, he told us that the apple *always* falls to the ground and that what goes

up must come down. No exceptions to these scientific generalizations exist. Scientific knowledge is not merely one form of knowledge, the positivists maintain, for knowledge can *only* be produced by science. Positivists hold nonscience in disdain, and they dismiss ways of knowing through religion, interpretation, metaphysics and intuition as unverifiable nonsense. This might help us to understand why indigenous and native people were thought by European colonizers to be ignorant savages.

The positivist view of the world exerts a dramatic impact on all of us, social studies teachers in particular. If expert-produced scientific knowledge constitutes the only valuable information about education, then schooling should be organized so that experts and administrators simply tell teachers how to perform their jobs. In this situation experts do all of the thinking, and teachers merely execute plans. Any thought about the purposes of education and the daily work of the classroom remain separate. The positive context denies teachers their skills (as in our discussion of deskilling), and the teaching act and classroom practice are torn apart. Once deskilled, teachers are provided with teacher-proof materials and must simply implement lessons prepared in advance by textbook companies, computer programs, or state and district supervisors. The teacher then functions as a proctor in an ACT, SAT, or GRE testing session by reading instructions, distributing materials, regulating time, monitoring for cheating, and answering questions.

Teacherproof curriculum materials assume that teachers are incapable of making instructional decisions and must be guided through their daily work. Examples of teacherproof materials include scripted lessons that teachers actually read to their classes:

> The teacher says, "OK, class, take out your social studies books and turn to page 23. Do not proceed until all books are on desk and open to the appropriate page." Then the teacher says to a selected student: "Read the first sentence on flax production in Brazil, Karen."

Unfortunately, this scenario is becoming all too familiar. But efforts continue to secure or restore teacher empowerment in democratic workplaces where they are viewed as self-directed and reflective professionals rather than monitors. The political implications of teacherproof materials and the logic behind them disaffects those of us who value democracy; thus we challenge this first premise of positivism: All knowledge is scientific.

2. ALL SCIENTIFIC KNOWLEDGE IS EMPIRICALLY VERIFIABLE. Second, positivism assumes that, when we use the phrase "scientific knowledge," we are referring to knowledge that can be verified empirically (through the senses). What the eye sees, what the ear hears, what we can count, what we can express mathematically—these things constitute empirical knowledge. But, we contend that many aspects of education, social studies education in particular, resist empirical validation. These invisible factors might include ways of seeing or sets of assumptions. They might include a student's feelings of hurt or humiliation or the self-esteem of an abused child or the value positions that move people to join a political revolution; such human dynamics do not lend themselves to quantification or empirical verification. Indeed, the existence of positivism itself as a force that shapes what we "see" cannot be empirically verified. In other words, positivism cannot study its own assumptions because they are not empirically verifiable.

When we encounter educational knowledge that uses such an epistemological base exclusively, we find it limited in what it can tell us about schooling and the learning process. Indeed, when social studies education students learn from materials produced by such a positivist science, they tend to find that the most important aspects of education are left out or distorted. To become the best possible teacher, one should understand the epistemological dynamics of knowledge production. Knowledge about the world, and about the educational cosmos in particular, is never neutral. It is always based on an entire set of values and assumptions about the nature of the world and the people who live in it. These epistemological dynamics shape beliefs about the purposes of education.

3. ONE MUST USE THE SAME METHODS TO STUDY THE PHYSICAL WORLD AS ONE USES TO STUDY THE SOCIAL AND EDUCATIONAL WORLDS. Serious problems result when one applies physical science methods to the study of the social world or education. A key aspect of positivistic research in the physical sciences involves the attempt to predict and control natural phenomena. When applied in social education, phys-

ical science methods then apply social knowledge as a tool to control human beings. Thus, students come to be viewed, understood, used, and controlled just like any other thing. Positivism loses sight of the idea that the objects of social research—humans—possess a special complexity that sets them apart from other objects of study.

Positivist social-educational scientists fail to understand that the physical scientists they emulate impose their observations on the objects under observation. Physical scientists do not have to consider the consciousness of their objects of study or their history and sociocultural contexts. Neither need they consider their own consciousness and assumptions. This makes research on humans different from the study of, say, sulfuric acid or field mice. If we fail to understand this difference, we miss the very elements that make us human, that shape us or restrict our freedom.

Here rests one of the key points in our discussion of modernism in general and positivism in particular: Modernism and its positivist epistemology lead to a devaluation of human beings and a depersonalization of our institutions. People become merely more variables in a larger social equation; our sacredness as spiritual beings disappears. Think of how degraded we feel when we are being processed by large institutions— insurance companies, welfare agencies, university business offices, the court system—that see us as just a social security number or case five on the docket. Impersonal positivism promotes this kind of treatment. If for no other reason, anything that exerts this much impact on the social world deserves attention in the social studies curriculum.

4. IF KNOWLEDGE EXISTS, IT EXISTS IN SOME DEFINITE, MEASURABLE QUANTITY. Positivism teaches that we can express knowledge in mathematical terms. If something exists, positivists argue, we can measure how much of it exists. Indeed, we can express the generalizations, principles, and theories derived from positivistic data in mathematical language (Beed, 1991; Garrison, 1989). Positivists define systematic observation that produces valid knowledge in terms of mathematical experiments. In this context, researchers look for mathematical relations between variables. If such mathematical relations emerge, they generalize the relationships to produce a universal law.

Many of us who call for democratic social studies education and democratic research methods, however, find ourselves uncomfortable with the positivist assumption that "to be is to be measurable" and that human endeavor can be expressed in mathematical terms. Much of what education researchers want to study does not lend itself to measurability or even direct observation. To address this problem, positivists developed what they call "reduction sentences," which are characteristics that summarize statements in a way that makes them more observable and measurable. A hard-to-measure concept such as hunger becomes "20 percent loss of original body weight" for a mature man or woman. Since weight is a measurable concept, hunger can be expressed in terms of weight. Behavioral psychologists who operate within a positivistic context label such reduction sentences "operational or working definitions." Thus, we develop operational definitions for concepts such as intelligence (what one scores on an IQ test) or productivity (output by workers per hour). Indeed, positivists argue, even concepts such as love or creativity can be operationally defined and measured.

These operational definitions may or may not help us understand the phenomena under investigation. But such an orientation often focuses our attention on merely the symptoms of larger issues or ideas, that is, on the consequences rather than the causes. Thus, a belief in the measurability of everything actually distorts our understanding of reality because it hides the assumptions often made in the production of knowledge. For example, what mental characteristics do questions on an IQ (intelligence quotient) test really address? Short-term memory? The ability to store and call up a wide range of factual data? Certainly, IQ tests cannot measure an ability to see connections between ostensibly unrelated concepts or the skill to apply such understandings to the identification and solution of problems. IQ tests deemphasize such difficult-to-measure but important abilities, while easy-to-measure but trivial abilities gain center stage. Education is thus undermined, reduced to memorization, computation, and busywork with little purpose or connection to the passions and complexities of human beings. In such a context learning becomes a mindless game, the trivial pursuit of abstract and inert information.

5. NATURE IS UNIFORM AND WHATEVER IS STUDIED REMAINS CONSISTENT IN ITS EXISTENCE AND BEHAVIOR. Positivists assume that the objects they study will remain constant. They believe in an underlying natural order in the way both the physical and the social worlds behave.

These regularities, or social laws, positivists argue, are best expressed through quantitative analysis using propositional language and mathematics. The goal for educational research within this tradition, therefore, is to develop theories that regularize human expression and make it predictable.

Democratic, counter-Cartesian social studies teachers believe, by contrast, that human beings are much less regular and predictable than the positivists portray them to be. As humans exhibit their irregularities and unpredictabilities—their diversity—counter-Cartesians make the case that men and women defy positivist attempts to reduce their behavior to measurable quantities. Teachers and students, for example, are hardly uniform, predictable, and consistent in their personalities, actions, psychologies and responses. Contrary to positivist opinions, humans are not machines whose behavior can be easily broken down into separate parts. Thank goodness that researchers cannot yet provide full and final explanations of the human dynamic. These should be central issues in social studies education because we are talking about how the social/human world is studied and known. When we find a statistical correlation between social dynamics, we still have not asked what exactly the correlation means. Different observers may interpret the correlations very differently. What criteria do we use to determine the validity of different interpretations? And, since human beings are constantly changing and evolving entities, is the interpretation we offered last week of the correlation between particular social features still valid this week? At the very least, democratic social studies educators recognize a complexity in these matters that modernist positivists often miss.

6. THE FACTORS THAT CAUSE THINGS TO HAPPEN ARE LIMITED AND KNOWABLE, AND, IN EMPIRICAL STUDIES, THESE FACTORS CAN BE CONTROLLED. Positivists believe that variables can be isolated and studied independently to determine specific causes for individual events. Following Newton's laws of the physical universe, they believe that for every action there is an opposite and equal reaction and that these actions and reactions can be identified and measured. Positivists refuse to acknowledge the complexity of the world, especially the world of human beings. The world, they believe, is neat and tidy, and the noise and confusion foisted on it by the humanness of human beings makes positivists edgy. Research would be so much

easier if researchers and the researched could only avoid this untidy world and the imprecise medium of verbal language.

Positivists dream of a spick-and-span social science in which all researchers are identical, unbiased, infallible, measuring instruments. Modernist positivism accepts a cause-and-effect linearity that works like a machine. For example, when the human body breaks down, doctors may reliably identify one certain factor immediately contributing to the illness. But, in reality, the causes are always multiple. Some are environmental, some psychological, and some physical. Diet, stress, chemicals, exercise, emotions, heredity and viruses all affect the health of the human body, and these multiple causes rarely function in a simple, easily traced manner. Life processes, like social processes, are rarely neat and tidy; we must view them in the context that shapes them if want to make sense of the way they operate.

As we think about the positivistic assumption that causative factors are limited and knowable, imagine the way we study classroom management or, as some call it, discipline. Hundreds of researchers have studied classroom discipline in the last 30 years. In addition to problems of sample size and the relationship between what gets defined as good discipline and desirable educational achievements, the control of variables in discipline research presents several other special difficulties. Literally thousands of unmentioned factors can significantly influence what happens in any classroom (Fiske & Schweder, 1986; Barrow, 1984). One student may respond to a specific teacher's discipline one way, but not because of the discipline at home. For example, a student raised in a permissive home may interpret a subtle, mildly coercive, noncorporal disciplinary act quite differently from a student raised in a strict home where punishment is physical. To the first student, it reveals the teacher's weakness.

Another student reacts differently to the subtle, mildly coercive discipline because of the nature of his or her relationship with the teacher. One student, whose parents are long-time acquaintances of the teacher, may know the teacher as a trusted friend. When confronted with corrective action of any kind, this student may feel uncomfortable because he or she is unaccustomed to conflict in his or her relationship with the teacher. What appears to the observer to be a mild admonishment provides a great deal of embarrassment to the student. Another student is affected by the presence of an outside observer and reacts in a way that is inconsistent with prior behavior. Still another student's behavior may be triggered by Tourettes's syndrome or some other physical condition that may or may not be diagnosed or known to the teacher. A researcher can hardly account for all the possible variables that may affect what is being observed (Barrow, 1984). Veteran teachers recognize this. When a supervisor or observer enters the classroom, the atmosphere changes dramatically. Students who are usually well behaved and who participate actively may suddenly become disrespectful or inattentive.

So, the various facets of a student's or a teacher's nature, of every individual's background, of every context and of all the interrelationships and combinations of factors may be individually, or in conjunction, the key elements in explaining what happens in a classroom. This is sometimes called "chaos theory" or "complexity theory." These crucial elements elude positivist researchers. In this context, an education that provides you with five scientifically validated surefire methods to discipline students, no matter who they are, or where they come from, is probably worthless. Unless the methods are contextualized by attention to the teacher's philosophical assumptions, the purposes of education he or she embraces, and the ethnic, class, socioeconomic, religious, cultural, racial, and gender backgrounds of the students, such methods generally will lead you astray. In fact, they often can keep you from connecting with students in a way that motivates, validates, and inspires them.

7. CERTAINTY IS POSSIBLE, AND WHEN WE PRODUCE ENOUGH RESEARCH, WE WILL UNDERSTAND REALITY WELL ENOUGH TO FORGO FURTHER RESEARCH. The goal of positivist social science research involves the quest for answers to human questions, and such a quest implies a definite end point. But, because we cannot control all variables, as we just saw, because the factors that cause variable behaviors are unlimited, the quest for positivist certainty is futile and quixotic. If we learn anything definite from positivist science, it is that our ideas about the world change with new revelations and that they will continue to change, probably for all time. The chance of arriving at some juncture in human history where research becomes unnecessary because we all understand the nature of reality is slight.

Better, then, to abandon the quest for absolutes that focuses our attention on the trivial—on only those things we can easily measure. One of the reasons history tests often emphasize dates, people, places, and battles is that teachers find it easy to measure whether students have "learned" this kind of information. They find it much harder to evaluate an essay test, with its potential ambiguity and complexity. In fact, the quest for absolute certainty in testing and evaluation encourages the lowest form of thinking (rote memorization) and dismisses higher-level thinking (analysis, interpretation, contextualization and application).

For these and many other reasons, democratic social studies educators often view with skepticism the certainty with which positivists make so-called valid arguments. We are generally inclined to take a more humble and limited perspective. Indeed, it seems safe to predict that educational researchers will never determine the five best ways to teach economics, the five steps to teaching excellence, or the eight steps to teacher popularity. There are as many good ways to teach as there are good teachers, and some of them conflict. Believe it or not (ha!) there are great social studies teachers who disagree with every word of *Getting Beyond the Facts*. I am always humbled when I watch some of these teachers teach and find that they are brilliant at what they do. Though I disagree with their conclusions and many of the decisions they make, I still would argue that they are great teachers who inspire many of the students that may find me boring and even offensive. Indeed, what we do successfully in one context may fail in another. The best teachers adjust lessons and adapt to changing classroom environment.

Discuss this concept with an experienced teacher in a departmentalized school who teaches five periods of social studies every day, and he or she will tell you that, even though the lesson plans may be identical, each period proceeds differently. The teacher may gain an insight in the first period that is applicable in the next four periods. A student in the second period may ask a question that alters the structure of the lesson. Students in each class ask different questions, have different personalities, have unique learning styles and learning needs and respond differently because of the time of day, weather conditions, events in the school schedule, and so forth. A uniform lesson plan for all five sections of the class may be possible, but, because of the complexity teachers cannot control, uniform lessons are not. In fact, even if teachers could control every lesson, such control would hinder learning. The best teachers are comfortable with the variety of social interpretations, political perspectives, and historical analyses their social studies students bring to class.

8. FACTS AND VALUES CAN BE KEPT SEPARATE, AND OBJECTIVITY IS ALWAYS POSSIBLE. Unlike positivists, I do not consider scientific

research a value-free activity. The popular image of science reflects the belief that the only parameters that limit a scientist's activities are intellect and curiosity. This belief is misleading because values and power dynamics continually shape research. If educational researchers operate in a college of education dominated, for example, by positivist assumptions about the nature of research, they might lose such career benefits as tenure if they attempt to conduct research that deviates from the rules of positivist methods. More important, because financial grants from government and private foundations often determine the type of research that takes place, funded inquiries typically reflect the values and interests of funding agencies. A brief survey of accepted and rejected grants will illuminate the political values that drive knowledge production in education and elsewhere.

Nevertheless, positivist educators continue to insist that researchers suppress their value judgments, convictions, beliefs, and opinions (Beed, 1991). They insist that empirical inquiry should remain value-free and objective and that values are tainted because they are subjective. Thus, the proclamations issued from the positivist pulpit project the illusion of political and moral neutrality. Accordingly, the wizard must be exposed, and the epistemological rules that dictate exactly what we can and cannot count as facts, must be uncovered (Garrison, 1989).

The implicit rules that actually guide our generation of social studies data almost always reflect specific worldviews, values, religious and political perspectives and definitions of intelligence. Research can never really be nonpartisan, for we have to choose the rules that guide our research. Inquiry rules focus our attention on certain aspects of education and deflect it from others. Positivism, for example, focuses our attention on education as a technical act. When we measure certain aspects of education to determine how well school systems or particular schools or particular teachers are doing, we cannot separate this question from the political issue of what schools should be doing. Therefore, if positivist research has established the criteria, by way of research instruments, that measure how well we are doing, it has also established what we should be doing. Positivism, thus, becomes a political instrument of social control, even while its adherents proclaim their neutrality, their disinterestedness, and their disdain for mixing politics and education (Bowers, 1982).

For example, if researchers describe students' readiness for work as the ability to follow orders, respect authority, and function as team players, the schools with good evaluations teach these skills. The "objective" process of defining work readiness conceals some very specific values: From a variety of ways to define work readiness, the researchers choose the definition closest to their political and economic beliefs. They want to prepare a society of compliant workers who obey orders without raising questions or challenging authority. Having made a value-driven choice, the researchers are no longer political innocents.

The same holds true for the teacher who gives a multiple-choice test. The test appears to be an objective, value-free instrument of evaluation, but closer examination reveals a set of hidden value assumptions. In constructing the test, the teacher had already chosen the textbook on which the test material was based, a value choice that prioritized one book over several others. The teacher had also considered particular material from the book more important than other material, a value choice of some facts over others. The teacher had chosen a multiple-choice format over other formats, a value choice that advanced certain forms of learning (fact memorization) over others (for example, analysis, interpretation and application in an essay or a series of short written answers). Such value choices are inherent in teaching and living. Although we can hardly avoid them, we should understand that we are making them. This awareness is a key goal of a democratic education in general and a democratic social studies in particular. With this understanding, we can change the world of education. Such recognitions ground a democratic form of social studies education and constitute a cardinal aspect of higher-order thinking.

9. THERE IS ONE TRUE REALITY, AND THE PURPOSE OF EDUCATION IS TO CONVEY THAT REALITY TO STUDENTS. Positivists generally contend that one best way to accomplish a task exists somewhere. For example, given one undisputed best way (best method) to teach, the purpose of the positivist professor of social studies teacher education is to pass that method along to students. Educational science grounded in positivist research assumes that the laws of society and the knowledge of human existence are verified and immutable and ought to be inserted directly into the minds of children. Operating on this assumption, educational "engineers" devise curricula and organizational strategies for schools as if no ambiguities or uncertainties in

the social and educational worlds exist. Nothing is problematic: "Columbus discovered America." "The Indians were an impediment to Westward expansion, but by the turn of the century this hindrance had been removed." "After the Mexican War ended, and land disputes had been resolved, the size of the United States increased." Pass the facts along to students; don't ask too many questions about the values and assumptions embedded within them.

Contemporary culture teaches us to revere science and the scientific method and, interestingly enough, to accept its primacy on faith, which is to say, unscientifically. The authoritarian voice of positivist science silences our language of intuition, aesthetics, spirituality, and insight. The view of science that regards the aesthetic and subjective as soft, effeminate, impressionistic, and nonscientific devalues such language. Cowed by the authority of positivist science, we accede to its demands and allow it to define teachers as mere practitioners (Aronowitz, 1983; Koller, 1981; Eisner, 1984).

In his studies of the street-corner culture in Toronto's Jane-Finch Corridor, Peter McLaren found students from lower socioeconomic classes questioning the school's view of themselves as passive recipients of sacred and official facts. The teachers less frequently questioned their own passive position in relation to the expert producers of knowledge (McLaren, 1989). When positivists control knowledge and student-teacher evaluations, we find the range of behaviors considered to be good teaching considerably narrowed. Many positivistic social studies supervisors find it easy to label creative lessons that fail to follow the "one best method" unsatisfactory. Thus, teachers earn rewards less for their sophisticated notions of competence and creativity and more for their adherence to a prescribed format. Like workers on a factory assembly line, teachers in positivist school systems become rule followers with little influence over how the rules are made. They become the executors of managerial strategies for keeping students on the task. Even among the best teachers, the passion for creativity and engagement slowly erodes as positivistic science becomes ever more deeply entrenched in our schools and society. Blind faith in positivism may be one of the great tragedies of our era. But along with many critical researchers and postmodern scholars, we are trying to reverse its philosophical dominance.

10. TEACHERS BECOME "INFORMATION DELIVERERS," NOT KNOWLEDGE-PRODUCING PROFESSIONALS OR EMPOWERED CULTURAL WORKERS. In such a positivist context, we wonder why society should bother with teacher education programs. If teachers are merely information deliverers, we need hire only those with the abilities to read the scripted teacherproof material and intimidate and control students. In the corporate for-profit schools emerging in the twenty-first century, managers are calling for exactly these types of teachers. In such a context, the idea of a scholarly teacher with interpretive and analytical abilities becomes irrelevant. School is simply a memory game in which the more creative teachers make memorization palatable by creating contests and mnemonic devices designed to ease role learning. Only a desire to compete or to please their teachers or parents can motivate students in such an educational purgatory. Education has no intrinsic value, no connection to the lived world of human beings.

Indeed, knowledge-producing social studies teachers who understand the tenets of positivism can be viewed as dangerous undesirables in unreflective modernist schools. In my own teaching experience, I have been viewed by administrators as a subversive who exerted a negative influence on my students. When I was teaching geography and history in high school, my principal told me after observing a geography class: "Why don't you get rid of all that interpretation and analysis crap and just give the students the facts they need to know. They'll be happier and I'll be happier." I couldn't do it. I had to get behind and beyond "the facts" and find out why it had to be these facts and not others. My view of social studies teaching transcended mindless, positivistic information delivery. If I had wanted to be a deliverer, I could have gone to work for Domino's. In a positivist system I would have probably be better off there. Certainly, my administrators and supervisors would have been happier with my career decision.

Chapter 6

Situating the Critical: What Is an Emancipatory Social Studies in the Twenty-First Century?

As students search as participants for meaning in the study of social studies, come to understand the social and political dislocations of the postmodern condition, and grasp the impact of Cartesian modernism in shaping their schooling, they have embarked on a critical democratic journey to take control of their lives. Democratic social studies teachers view students as participants in the lived world and help them achieve an internal locus of control over their lives. Such social studies teachers help their students use such control to become active members of the civic community. Too often in the postmodern world, the locus of an individual's control over his life is external, as both personal and impersonal forces work to reduce human autonomy. The most serious form of external control occurs when the individual is unaware that he or she is not in control. In this context, a democratic social studies program can become an extremely powerful force, as it alerts students to their loss of autonomy and suggests creative strategies for regaining it.

The first step in the attempt to control one's own destiny is to understand those forces that limit control. One measure of a successful social studies program revolves around its ability to address those forces and to engage students in a personal examination of their lives in light of those forces. Of course this is what we have been doing in the first five chapters of this book. In Chapter 6 we name our actions, illustrating how they reflect the notion of critical theory. As we attempt to encourage teachers to treat students as participants in the real world—to exploit the power of social studies to help students control their own lives—we are actually proposing that teachers operate from a critical perspective. We are suggesting that teachers transcend the confines of a one-dimensional view of social studies and analyze not only the subject but, at the same time, analyze the elements which give meaning to the subject.

As Neil Postman (1979) puts it, "one learns to talk about the subject, but also learns to talk about the talk . . ." In other words, social studies teachers need to operate from a perspective where they can step back from their teaching and look at and analyze the forces that shape it. Teachers need to see themselves from another perspective—from the eyes of individuals from different locations in the web of reality. In this way, they can understand and analyze the assumptions of their language and their teaching. They can ascertain when they are imposing their values on their students, and where the values come from. Now, they can consider the hidden messages that their lessons and interactions with students are transmitting. In the process of operating from such a meta-educational perspective, they will not only become better teachers but they will also know themselves better. An examination of this critical approach to social studies is in order.

THE MEANING OF CRITICAL: DEFINING CRITICAL THEORY AND ITS RELATIONSHIP TO A DEMOCRATIC SOCIAL STUDIES

The term "critical," as we are using it here, comes from the concept of critical theory. The term refers to the social analysis tradition developed by the Frankfurt School, a group of writers connected to the Institute of Social Research at the University of Frankfurt. However, none of the Frankfurt school theorists ever claimed to have developed a unified approach to cultural criticism. In its beginnings, Max Horkheimer, Theodor Adorno, and Herbert Marcuse initiated a conversation with the German tradition of philosophical and social thought, especially that of Marx, Kant, Hegel, and Weber. From the vantage point of these critical theorists, whose political sensibilities were influenced by the devastations of World War I, postwar Germany, with its economic depression marked by inflation and unemployment, and the failed strikes and protests in Germany and Central Europe in this same period, the social world was in urgent need of reinterpretation. From this perspective, they defied Marxist orthodoxy while deepening their belief that injustice and subjugation shaped the lived world (Bottomore, 984; Gibson, 1986; Held, 1980; Jay, 1973). Focusing their attention on the changing nature of capitalism, the early critical theorists analyzed the mutating forms of domination that accompanied the change.

Only a decade after the Frankfurt school was established, the Nazis controlled Germany. The danger posed to the Jewish membership of the Frankfurt school convinced Horkheimer, Adorno, and Marcuse to leave Germany. Eventually locating themselves in California, these critical theorists were shocked by American culture. Offended by the taken-for-granted positivistic empirical practices of American social science researchers, Horkheimer, Adorno, and Marcuse were challenged to respond to the social science establishment's positivist belief that their research could describe and accurately measure any dimension of human behavior. Piqued by the contradictions between progressive American rhetoric of egalitarianism and the reality of racial and class discrimination, these theorists produced their major work while residing in the United States. In 1953, Horkheimer and Adorno returned to Germany and reestablished the Institute of Social Research. Significantly, Herbert Marcuse stayed in the United States, where he would find a new audience for his work in social theory. Much to his own surprise, Marcuse skyrocketed to fame as the philosopher of the student movements of the 1960s. Critical theory, especially the emotionally and sexually liberating work of Marcuse, provided the philosophical voice of the New Left. Concerned with the politics of psychological and cultural revolution, the New Left preached a Marcusian sermon of political emancipation (Gibson, 1986; Hinchey, 1998; Kincheloe & Steinberg, 1997; Surber, 1998; Wexler, 1991, 1996).

Many academicians who had come of age in the politically charged atmosphere of the 1960s focused their scholarly attention on critical theory. Frustrated by forms of domination emerging from a post-Enlightenment culture nurtured by positivism and capitalism, these scholars saw in critical theory a method of temporarily freeing academic work from these forms of power. Impressed by critical theory's approach to the social construction of experience, they came to view their disciplines as manifestations of the discourses and power relations of the social and historical contexts that produced them. The "discourse of possibility" implicit within the constructed nature of social experience suggested to these scholars that a reconstruction of the social science could eventually lead to a more egalitarian and democratic social order.

New conceptualizations of human agency and their promise that men and women can, at least partly, determine their own existence offered new hope for emancipatory forms of social research and social action when compared with orthodox Marxism's assertion of the iron laws of history, the irrevocable evil of capitalism, and the proletariat as the privileged subject and agent of social transformation. For example, when critical educators criticized the argument made by Marxist scholars Samuel Bowles and Herbert Gintis (1976)—that schools are intractable capitalist agencies of social, economic, cultural, and bureaucratic control—they contrasted the deterministic perspectives of Bowles and Gintis with the idea that schools, as venues of hope, could become sites of resistance and democratic possibility through concerted efforts among teachers and students to work within a democratic pedagogical framework. Many critical social studies educators maintained that schools can become institutions where forms of knowledge, values, and social relations are taught for the purpose of educating young people for critical empowerment rather than subjugation.

In this context I offer my take on the features of a twenty-first century critical theory and its relationship to a democratic social studies. This new critical theory questions the assumption that societies such as the United States, Canada, Australia, New Zealand, and the nations in the European Union, for example, are unproblematically democratic and free. Over the twentieth century, especially since the early 1960s, individuals in these societies have been acculturated to feel comfortable in relations of domination and subordination rather than equality and independence. Given the social and technological changes of the last half of the century that led to new forms of information production and access, critical theorists argued that questions of self-direction and democratic egalitarianism should be reassessed. And considering the changing social and informational conditions of late-twentieth-century media-saturated Western culture, critical theorists needed new ways of researching and analyzing the construction of individuals. The following points briefly delineate my interpretation of a critical theory for the new millennium.

It is important to note that we understand a social theory as a map or a guide to the social sphere. In social studies education it does not determine how we see the world but helps us devise questions and strategies for exploring it. Critical theory is concerned in particular with issues of power and justice and the ways that the economy, matters of race, class, and gender, ideologies, discourses, education, religion and other social institutions, and cultural dynamics interact to construct the social systems that construct our consciousnesses.

1. CRITICAL ENLIGHTENMENT. In this context, critical theory analyzes competing power interests among groups and individuals within a society, identifying who gains and who loses in specific situations. Privileged groups, critical analysts argue, often have an interest in supporting the status quo to protect their advantages; the dynamics of such efforts often become a central focus of critical study. Such examinations of privilege often revolve around issues of race, class, gender, and sexuality. In this context, to seek critical enlightenment is to uncover the winners and losers in particular social arrangements and the processes by which such power plays operate. We may find that, in some situations, particular individuals have access to social power, while, in other contexts, the very same individuals do not. The analysis of power interests is, at the least, always complex. Also, very importantly, critical enlightenment does not mean that we finally see the truth or a picture of true reality. Critical analysts understand that the social world is too complex for such an arrogant proclamation.

Critical enlightenment is grounded on understanding the ways human consciousness is tied to history. Indeed, one of the goals of teaching history in a democratic social studies involves the exploration of the way history shapes who we are. Critical enlightenment in this social studies context always directs awareness to the relationship between teacher's, student's, and administrator's consciousness and the sociohistorical contexts in which they operate. In this way, the critical enlightenment helps us open the door to the analysis of the personal: how our private selves have been shaped by historical forces. Guided by this search, we expose those buried parts of ourselves that we hold in common with our brothers and sisters; such solidarity allows us to overcome impediments to self-direction together. The bonds between consciousness and history reveal a new form of knowledge to the social studies teacher: the self-understanding and possible empowerment that comes from the uncovering of the ways that one's psyche has been constructed by historical gender roles (Westkott, 1982). Guided by such concerns, teachers inspired by the search for critical enlightenment seek to expose what constitutes reality for themselves and for the participants in educational situations. How do these participants, critical social studies teachers ask, come to construct their views of educational reality?

Thus, from the very beginning of their work, critical theorists engage with the nature and effects of power. Critical enlightenment cannot be grasped outside of this concern with the imprint of historical power on ourselves, our consciousness, our education, and the world around us. Another feature of critical enlightenment involves an individual's efforts to disengage him- or herself from power's norms and ideological expectations—the tyranny of the normal. The term "ideology" involves the way power defines reality, the way things work, in a way that helps maintain existing power structures. Dominant ideology reifies (makes appear natural) inequality as the inevitable outcome of power's superior talent and effort. The term becomes extremely important in the conceptual vocabulary of democratic social studies teachers because most of the curriculum guides, standards, and textbooks of contemporary social studies reflect dominant ideology.

Thus, as democratic social studies teachers seek critical enlightenment, they seek to expose these manifestations of dominant ideology and their effects. In this precise way they move far beyond traditional nonconceptual social studies thinking and move to a new level of cognition: a critical consciousness. At this level of critical consciousness, social studies teachers and students grapple with questions concerning their life purposes, attending, in this process, to questions of human dignity, freedom, authority, and social responsibility (Kegan, 1982). Critical enlightenment demands attention to the construction of a system of meaning that can be used to guide teaching, cognitive activity, and knowledge production. Never content with what they have constructed, never certain of the system's appropriateness, always concerned with the expansion of self-awareness and consciousness, a critical social studies teacher engages in a running metadialogue, a constant conversation with self, a perpetual reconceptualization of his or her system of meaning.

Such a critically enlightening dialogue focuses the democratic social studies teacher's attention on the process of question formulation, as opposed to Cartesian modernism/positivism's concern with question answering or problem solving. This question-formulating, problem-posing stage, Albert Einstein argued, is more important than the answer to the question or the solution to the problem. Critical social studies teachers are question formulators, problem posers. When such teachers set up a problem, they select and name those things they will notice. Thus, problem posing is a form of world making; how we select the problems and construct our worlds is based on the system of meaning we employ.

Without a system of meaning, teachers and administrators learn how to construct schools but not how to determine what types of schools to construct. In other words, social studies teachers, school leaders, and teacher educators need to realize that school and classroom problems are not generic or innate. They are constructed and uncovered by insightful educators who possess the ability to ask questions never before asked, questions that lead to innovations that promote student insight, sophisticated thinking, and social justice (Schon, 1987; Ponizo, 1985). If the genius of, say, an Einstein revolved around his ability to see problems in the physical universe that no one else had ever seen, then the genius of a democratic social studies teacher revolves around his or her ability to see social and educational problems that no one else has ever seen. The application of such skills by social studies teachers moves learning to a level unimagined by those trapped within the Cartesian tradition. Not only is such educational orientation grounded on a democratic conception of teacher empowerment but it serves to expose previously hidden forces that shape the consequences of the educational process.

Thus, critical enlightenment seeks practical ways to study, to tease out the effects of power. Confronted by the undemocratic features of the postmodern condition, social studies teachers on the path to critical enlightenment become agents of democracy on a power-saturated landscape. They recognize growing corporate control over information flow, as fewer and fewer corporations control more and more of the production of information. They discover that the contemporary corporation frequently regards the advertising of products as secondary to the promotion of a positive corporate image. Controlling information in this way enhances the corporation's power, as it engages the public in relating positively to the goals and the "mission" of the corporation. In this way, corporations can better shape government policy, control public images of labor-management relations, and portray workers in a way that enhances the self-interest of management.

As a result, corporate taxes are minimized, wages are lowered, mergers are deregulated, corporate leaders are lionized, and managerial motives are unquestioned. The poor are punished and the wealthy, especially in the booming economy of the early twenty-first century, are rewarded with unprecedented returns on their invested money. How can these huge profits remain exclusively in the hands of those already blessed with money, critical theorists ask. Such issues of power are directly related to critical enlightenment.

Understanding critical enlightenment and its concern with power and knowledge, democratic social studies teachers observe a corporately controlled mass communications industry that profoundly shapes the way we look at socio-political and economic issues and exerts increasing domination of individuals of all stripes. The notion of knowledge has become a source of power in this society because power is often acquired by those who, via their economic position or their professional status, announce just what is to be considered knowledge. Professionals in various fields determine "healthy" child-rearing procedures, "proper" family life, the nature of social deviance, and the form that schooling and work will take. Knowledge, which must be certified by professionals, results in antidemocratic tendencies as it renders individuals dependent upon experts.

Based on these observations, many social scientists have become more and more attracted to social visions grounded in critical theory. These critical social inquirers are interested in questioning the dominant assumptions in modern industrialized societies, rejecting earlier constructions of meaning and value structures, and embarking on a quest for new meanings and practices. Ever concerned with the centrality of the individual and the powerfulness of individual endeavor, critical analysts refuse to see the individual as a puppet of wider forces. We must protect the creative, active, meaning-seeking aspects of humans; social scientists, in particular, must see men and women as potentially free and marked by the capacity to set and achieve their own goals. Thus, the forces which preclude this human agency must be exposed and changed. A social science, for example, which deifies the social scientist as expert and purveyor of truth must be confronted.

Personal authority has been undermined by the authority of professional experts who gain unquestioned knowledge through rigorous (methodologically exacting) social scientific research. The family, for example, is subject to state determination of its competence. Parents have little authority over those experts in the legitimized institutions who make pronouncements about normal child rearing. The family's dependence on the professional is representative of a larger pattern of dependence in modern industrialized, bureaucratized societies. Individuals depend on organizations, citizens depend on the state, workers depend on managers, and, of course, parents depend on the "helping professions." A professional oligarchy of doctors, psychiatrists, welfare workers, civil servants, and social science researchers exert significant influence on the governance of the state and on the "knowledge industry."

The professional assault on the autonomy of the family and its members, as well as on other institutions and individuals, must be viewed in light of its historical moment. The advent of industrialization and its companion, monopoly or corporate capitalism, set the stage for the rest of the experts. As the family was being assaulted by the expert, the advertising industry was persuading people that store-bought goods were superior to homemade items. The growth of scientific management of industry and the expansion of the expert both represent new forms of control within an industrialized, corporate state. The struggle against the destruction of personal authority necessitates a struggle against the general authoritarian trends of the industrialized, corporate state. Individuals cannot protect their personal autonomy unless they regain their voice in the workplace and demand a role in the production of the knowledge on which the modern state and its experts ground their authority. In this context, critical democratic social studies teachers call for individuals to take the solution of their problems into their own hands. The goal of arresting the erosion of competence will be accomplished, they argue, by students and ordinary citizens who create their own "communities of competence." Thus, teachers, students, and parents must participate in critical enlightenment. They must help determine what is designated social studies knowledge.

When social studies teachers are critically enlightened, they engage in what John Dewey referred to as a reconstruction of their previous experiences. They begin to remake their world of practice in a way which reveals the deep structures that have determined their professional lives; they gain what can be labeled "reflexive awareness." It may seem insignificant to those trapped in the culture of positivism and corporate power, but the critical ability to step back from the world as we are accustomed to perceiving it and to see the ways our perception is constructed through linguistic codes, cultural signs, and embedded ideology is a giant step in learning to research, to teach, indeed, to think. Critical teachers are required to construct our perception of the world anew, not just in a random way, but in a manner which rethinks what appears natural, which opens to question that which seems real.

We ask questions of how that which is came to be, whose interests do particular institutional arrangements serve, and from whence do our own frames of reference come. In other words, we are engaging in a critical construction of the world and our relation to it. In this way, social studies teachers can remake their professional lives around the asking and answering of such questions. Facts are no longer simply "what they are;" the truth of beliefs is not simply testable by its correspondence to these facts. Professional knowledge does not rest on the foundation of the proven. To engage in critical enlightenment is to take part in a process of world making. To remake, to rename, our world, we seek guidance from our system of meaning, our emancipatory, democratic source of authority (Slaughter, 1989; Shon, 1987). Social studies teaching in this critical democratic context moves to a new dimension. It can never be the same again.

2. Critical emancipation/empowerment. Those who seek emancipation attempt to gain the power to control their own lives in solidarity with a justice-oriented community. Here, a democratic social studies attempts to expose the forces that prevent individuals and groups from shaping the decisions that crucially affect their lives. In this way, greater degrees of autonomy and human agency can be achieved. At the beginning of the new century, we are cautious in our use of the term "emancipation" because, as many critics have pointed out, no one is ever completely emancipated from the sociopolitical context that has produced him or her. Also, many have questioned the arrogance that may accompany efforts to emancipate others. These are important criticisms and must be carefully taken into account by critical teachers. Thus, as critical social studies teachers who search for those forces that insidiously shape who we are, we respect those who reach different conclusions in their personal journeys.

It is hard to distinguish the concept of emancipation from empowerment in the critical lexicon. Emancipation implies an empowerment to act that comes from critical enlightenment—an awareness of the sociocultural, political, and economic forces that shape our consciousness and identity. Action is a key concept in the attempt to understand the meaning of critical emancipation/empowerment. Emancipation/empowerment occurs when students gain the power of self-direction. A pedagogy of empowerment cultivates cognitive, intrapersonal, dispositional, and motivational changes that enable students to gain greater control over the quality of their present and future lives. Such a social studies education grants students a sense of possibility, a sense that positive change can take place. Empowered students look for the footprints of power and domination not only in the construction of their own consciousness but also in the literature and curricula of social studies education.

They question inequity, asking why some positions confer more status than others. Acting on their empowerment, they weigh existing social institutions against their own claims of integrity and democracy. Do social institutions pursue policies that insure the realization of different abilities, or do they inhibit their accomplishment? Simply put, do social institutions work to expand what it means to be human? As a critical emancipatory education expands the possibilities of "humanness," it joins with other critical social agencies (unions, worker councils, churches, women's organizations, racial organizations, and so forth) to coordinate and supplement its justice-related social action.

A critical emancipatory/empowering social studies engages students in social projects. For example, social studies students in such a critical context join with vocational education students and help restore homes in poor neighborhoods, provide large-scale food distribution for the homeless, or participate in an ethnography on the unemployed in the local community. In all of these projects, such work is accompanied by detailed research on housing for the poor, the causes of homelessness, and ways to reduce unemployment. Taking a cue from William Heard Kilpatrick's democratic progressive "project method," devised in the second decade of the twentieth century, critical emancipatory teachers construct research-based experiences for students. Instead of teaching random skills and facts, Kilpatrick argued that classrooms should be organized around the purposeful activity of a project. Although the project method is undermined by several flaws, it holds great potential when reconceptualized within the framework of a critical emancipation/empowerment. The central feature around which this critical project method is constructed involves the notion of student as researcher and interpreter of reality. The ability to make sense, to uncover meaning, to interpret, and to produce knowledge about the social world becomes the guiding goal of the critical project method (Spring, 1994; Kliebard, 1987).

A key feature of an emancipatory social studies involves teachers engaging students in the recognition of the way class, racial, ethnic, and gender biases operate in education. Students on the road to emancipation and empowerment understand the subtle and hidden ways such biases filter into both the school and cultural curriculum and how they might act in response to such discrimination. Schools, media, religious groups and politicians often maintain that Western capitalist societies are lands of wealth and opportunity open to all who are willing to work. Lessons are taught daily that former communist nations in Eastern Europe and Third World societies in Africa, Asia and Latin America are stricken by poverty and its concurrent social problems, but that Western societies are above such pathology. Indeed, countries like the United States, Britain, Canada, Australia and New Zealand constantly use their expertise to repair the problems of other, less developed, nations. Implicitly embedded in such a curriculum is the notion that Western societies are at their essence white and middle-class nations. They are populated by upwardly mobile white men who are the smartest, most industrious people in the world. Their main concern is to make a prosperous life for themselves and their families, an objective that operates in the best interests of everyone on the planet.

In the mainstream social studies curriculum, the poor are rarely studied. In elementary and secondary social studies curricula, the contributions of workers are erased, as textbooks and curriculum guides depict a world where factory and business owners and politicians do all the work. At an implicit, subtextual level, such teaching inscribes irrelevancy on the lives of the working classes. The study of the past is an examination of "the lives of the rich and famous." One can almost hear Robin Leach's grating voice uncritically enshrining and ennobling the behaviors of the privileged, especially when they are engaged in morally reprehensible practices, such as slavery, conquest of indigenous peoples, political and economic colonization, and sweatshop management. Such activities are often presented unambiguously as heroic acts of "progress" that brought honor and wealth to the motherland. The brutal, often genocidal, features of these practices are too often ignored. Students and citizens involved in critical emancipation and empowerment gain the ability to expose features of the class-biased curriculum that operate daily in their lives (Swartz, 1993; Sleeter & Grant, 1994).

Again, everyone benefits, the poor in particular, from an understanding of the way power works and poverty develops. Such knowledge empowers the poor not only to escape such forces themselves but to initiate public, institutional, and private conversations about the relationship between poverty and wealth. Such knowledge empowers the poor to "call" media commentators and political leaders on the superficial and misleading pronouncements that pass for an analysis of the causes of poverty (Jones, 1992). Western peoples—Americans in particular—have yet to discuss the social, political, and economic aspects of privilege vis-à-vis deprivation. In this context, students and citizens will learn that the polarization of wealth and the economic perspectives that allowed it to happen have created a situation where our society's economic machine no longer needs young inexperienced people.

Adolescence as a preparatory stage for adulthood is obsolete. It has become a corral for unneeded young people drifting in a socioeconomic purgatory (for more information on these changing conditions of youth in the late twentieth century, see Steinberg and Kincheloe, 1997). Demographers report that elderly men have the highest suicide rate. Perceived by society and themselves as socially superfluous, old men are removed from the workforce, stripped of a future, and left to wait for death. Over the past quarter century, the group that witnessed the fastest growing suicide rate was males aged fifteen to nineteen (Gaines, 1990). Stripped of their hopes for socioeconomic mobility and burdened with the masculine expectation for self-sufficiency, these young men reflect the Western social dilemma. An emancipatory/empowering social studies must provide a voice of hope, an avenue of participation, for students and citizens victimized by contemporary economic strategies, youth policies, and racial class bias.

At the very core of a critical democratic social studies rests the emancipatory/empowering concern with helping marginalized students use social knowledge to help escape poverty. Marginalized students must understand the impediments to social and economic mobility and the specifics of how one gets around such social, cultural, psychological, and educational roadblocks. As a rigorous multidimensional course of study, the social studies empowerment curriculum views men and women in more than simply egoistic, self-centered, and rationalist terms. Individuals, especially poor ones, need help making meaning in their lives, developing a sense of purpose, constructing a positive identity, and cultivating self-worth. Unlike previous forms of social studies education, the pedagogy of emancipation and empowerment would address these issues, using the dynamics covered in this book as the program's conceptual basis.

Understanding socioeconomic class and race in the larger context of historical power relations, students would understand that poverty is not simply a reflection of bad character or incompetence. In this context, social studies students would appreciate the organizational dynamics necessary to the effort to "pull oneself up by one's bootstraps"—an undertaking often referenced but infrequently explained. The empowerment curriculum would help poor individuals develop strategies to take control of schools, social agencies, health organizations, and economic institutions. Understanding how these organizations work to undermine the interests of the marginalized, with their narrow and often positivistically produced definitions of normality, intelligence, family stability, etc., the curriculum helps students devise strategies to resist the imposition of policies grounded on such definitions (Ellwood, 1988; Jennings, 1992; West, 1992).

The social studies empowerment curriculum begins with the personal experiences of marginalized students but moves to understandings far beyond them; teachers constantly relate what is being learned back to student experience. Concepts and information about the world are integrated into what students already know. Such data are then analyzed in the light of questions of economic justice, environmental/ecological connections to class bias and racism, and understanding of modernist Cartesian ways of seeing the world and the needs of democracy. Such understandings help create a critical consciousness grounded on an appreciation of both the way ideology works to convince the marginalized of their own inferiority and how empowered people are capable of generating democratic change. Students with a critical consciousness are able to point out the ways power enforces its dominance and how, in the electronic world of postmodernity, the process takes on new degrees of impact and complexity. Empowered students who possess a critical consciousness draw upon the reality of everyday conflict in their lives, their recognition of the gap between the premise of democracy and the despair they have experienced as members of the lower socioeconomic class, to illustrate the stark reality of injustice. In this emotional connection of lived experience to larger conceptual understanding, students and teachers begin to get in touch with their passion, the lived impact of their encounter with an emancipatory social studies (Sleeter & Grant, 1994; Britzman & Pitt, 1996).

With such insights, social studies students are ready to formulate forms of resistance to power's disabling features. When marginalized students come to the conclusion—and most of them eventually do—that education is set up to reward the values of the already successful, those whose culture most accurately reflects the mainstream, they have to negotiate how they react to this realization. Most lower-socioeconomic class and racially marginalized students are, understandably, confused and dislocated because of this reality. An emancipatory/empowering social studies is devoted to helping marginalized students make sense of this reality and facilitating the formulation of the resistance to it. A central lesson for angry marginalized students involves developing an awareness of the costs of various forms of resistance. Rejection of middle class propriety often expresses itself as an abrasive classroom behavior antithetical to mutual respect and focused analysis.

Democratic social studies teachers believe that the outcome of marginalized student resistance does not have to be disempowerment. To formulate an emancipatory form of resistance, I draw upon the work of cultural analyst John Fiske (1993). Fiske argues that marginalized peoples comprise localized power groups who typically produce popular forms of knowledge. Such knowledge forms are powerful and can be drawn upon for psychic protection from the ideological teachings of the power bloc. Marginalized knowledge forms or subjugated knowledges allow the oppressed to make sense of their social and educational experiences from a unique vantage point and, in the process, to reconstruct their identities. Social studies teachers concerned with emancipation both study these knowledge forms and encourage their students to explore their origins and effects. Without such understanding and encouragement, we fear that lower socioeconomic class and racial anger over unfairness and oppression can turn violent.

Violence has begun in many places. But what Americans have observed so far may simply represent only the beginning. Marginalized peoples become violent when they are not heard. Obviously, racial and class violence has a plethora of causes, but one of the most important involves the fact that power wielders often do not listen to nonwhite or poor people. In this context, studies indicate that, while violence can be observed at all socioeconomic levels, it is concentrated among males from poor backgrounds. As the disparity of wealth increases, the impulse for violence also grows. We can see such an impulse quite clearly in a variety of popular cultural forms consumed by working-class men and women, young males in particular, including heavy metal music, violent movies and professional wrestling (Gaines, 1990; Fiske, 1993; Gresson,

1997). To avoid the escalation of violence among the oppressed, issues of social and economic justice will have to be taken seriously by individuals from various social sectors. Constructive, nonviolent strategies of resistance must be carefully studied in the coming years.

Resistant, democratic action is grounded in a set of empowered, emancipatory abilities that democratic social studies teachers can work to develop:

a. Empowered individuals on the road to emancipation have achieved an analytical distance between themselves and their lives. They have developed a "metaperspective," meaning that they have gone beyond personal experience and have reached a location with a vantage point that allows them to view their lives in new contexts. From this perspective, they can free themselves from the limitations of egocentric concerns to the degree that they can see more clearly the forces that have shaped them. Without this perspective, individuals merely act; they have little consciousness of what constitutes their values and aims.

b. Once this metaperspective is achieved, individuals are ready to assume power by controlling the decision-making process in their lives. The empowered individuals rely not only on the dictates of others or on the expectations of convention but assume responsibility of their own lives. Decisions are made via a process which consciously attempts to coordinate daily actions with larger political visions and ethical values.

c. Such coordination cannot take place until the individuals recognize the unity between social values and individual actions. This sense of unity must be extended to various portions of life. Politically, philosophically, and ethically informed action is a result of a critically examined and ideologically disembedded struggle.

d. It is difficult to critically examine one's life and fail to see it in relation to the world. Empowered individuals are acutely conscious of their social responsibilities; they cannot fail to recognize the power of ideas on the way they live their lives. Ideas from the perspectives of such individuals are not inert. Ideas are action-evoking, moving individuals to attempt the unattempted and to free others from the shackles of manipulation.

e. One reason that individuals on the road to emancipation are moved to action is that they can envision alternatives. Action cannot take place before one envisions a more desirable state of affairs; it is this vision of a better order which motivates our most noble instincts. Critical theorists referred to this notion as "eminent critique," the ability to imagine what could be. This facility is a central feature of critical emancipation.

f. Through their understanding of context, critically empowered individuals grow more understanding and, thus, more comfortable with diversity. They come to realize that ideas are not spontaneously generated. With this knowledge, they can appreciate the fact that certain beliefs have emerged from the interplay of specific, social, economic, historical, and cultural forces. Differences between people are not to be hated; they are to be understood, learned from, and celebrated.

g. One of the most important characteristics of individuals seeking emancipation, and the one that a democratic social studies is well-suited to provide, involves the ability to teach oneself. The philosopher Gilbert Ryle has argued that learning does not actually begin until people learn to teach themselves. Indeed, the desire for emancipation cannot begin until individuals learn to teach themselves. As long as social studies teachers fail to make self-teaching a primary goal, nonconceptual forms of teaching, with the accompanying uninspiring rote-learning of a curriculum promoting a dominant ideology, will continue unchallenged.

Capable of teaching themselves, empowered social studies teachers working toward emancipation don't need to be told what and how to teach. They have no need for a nonconceptual methods class. Donaldo Macedo (1994) understands this dynamic and has argued that an emancipatory education is always an "antimethod pedagogy." This means that democratic social studies teachers do not require a nonconceptual methods course to provide them specific directions for running their classrooms. Drawing upon the poetry of Antonio Machado, Macedo maintains that empowered social studies teachers will "make their road as they walk."

Social studies teachers caught in a Cartesian modernist program are required by supervisors to force students to memorize, as fact, problematic information and then measure their "mastery" with specific evaluation tools. In such situations, teachers are disempowered as they and their students are denied intellectual responsibility for selecting materials, producing the knowledge, and evaluating what they have learned in the process. Teachers and their students, just like anyone else, rise to the occasion when they are respected and given the responsibility to shape their own practice. Protecting the professional responsibility and self-direction of social studies teachers is a critical emancipatory act.

3. THE REJECTION OF ECONOMIC DETERMINISM. A caveat of critical theory involves the insistence that the tradition does not accept the orthodox Marxist notion that "base" determines "superstructure"—meaning that economic factors dictate the nature of all other aspects of human existence. Critical theorists understand, in the twenty-first century, that there are multiple forms of power, including racial, gender, sexual axes of domination, as well as class. In issuing this caveat, however, critical theory in no way attempts to argue that economic factors are unimportant in the shaping of everyday life. Economic factors can never be separated from other axes of oppression. This traditional Marxist economistic notion focuses attention on merely one form of oppression (the economic) as more important than any other. As the economic takes precedence over all other modes of subjugation, lost is an understanding of the diversity of oppression, especially in different historical times and different cultural contexts.

Democratic social studies teachers, informed by critical theory, understand the Cartesian assumptions of traditional Marxism. Appreciating the existence of multiple frames of reference and the many ways to approach a social event, democratic social studies teachers understand that the world can be viewed in many different contexts. Traditional Marxism argued in its own deterministic way that humans see only what their conceptual lenses allowed them to see, and that they understood what their context for understanding permitted. In the spirit of hope, possibility, and antideterminism, critical theory-informed teachers seek to liberate themselves from such determinism by taking control of our perceptual abilities by transcending what one context permits. In this way, we emancipate ourselves from the constraints of the Cartesianism and the structural forces that limit our ability to see the world from outside our restricted vantage point. In this trans-Cartesian spirit, democratic social studies teachers are constantly searching for new ways of seeing, new research methods, and new forms of intelligence with which to explore the ways oppression takes place and democracy is undermined. The understanding derived from this appreciation of social complexity helps teachers and students formulate specific social action.

Though the study of the social world and the oppression that operates within it is very complex, the critical theoretical concept discussed here is very simple. Racial, gender, sexual, and class oppression can be understood only in relation to one another and in the context of larger social structures. This means, for example, that gender bias plays itself out on the terrain of economic and patriarchal macrostructures. An economic macrostructure might involve white male domination of the highest salary brackets in American economic life. A patriarchal macrostructure might involve the small percentage of upper level corporate managers who are women or, in a domestic context, the high rate of spousal abuse perpetrated by American males. Differences in men's and women's lives in general, and economic opportunities in particular, revolve around inequalities of power. For example, African American women, Latinas, Asian American women and Native American women experience gender as one aspect of a grander pattern of unequal social relations. Indeed, the way one experiences race, class, and gender is contingent on one's intersection with other hierarchies of inequality—other hierarchies in which the privileges of some individuals grow out of the oppression of others (Amott & Matthaei, 1991; Zinn, 1994; Zinn & Dill, 1994).

Let us focus for a moment on the ways in which gender intersects with race and class. Some intersections create privilege. For example, if a woman marries a man from the upper class, gender and class intersect to create privileged opportunities for her. On the other hand, however, if a woman is Haitian American, forms of racial prejudice will exacerbate the ways in which she experiences gender bias. Thus, whether it be through subordination or privilege, race, class, and gender dynamics affect everyone, not just those at the bottom of the status hierarchy. The problem is that those at the top of the race, class, and gender hierarchies often do not understand the ways the intersections of the various axes affect them. The economic divisions of class serve to structure the ways race and gender manifest themselves. Though we understand that connections between race, class, and gender exist, we never know how to predict the effects of the interactions. Racial and gender hostilities, of course, can subvert class solidarity. Class solidarity can undermine gender-grounded networks. Working-class women, for example, have rarely felt a close affinity to the middle- and upper-middle-class feminist movement (Amott, 1993; Zinn, 1994).

As these race, class, and gender forces interact, sometimes in complementary and sometimes in contradictory ways, school experience cannot be viewed simply as an uncomplicated reflection of social power. The school experience is exceedingly complex, and, while there are general patterns of subjugation that occur, such patterns play out in unpredictable ways with particular individuals. Cameron McCarthy and Michael Apple (1988) maintain that school mediates rather than imposes its power upon students. This means that students from lower socioeconomic class backgrounds are not simply classified and relegated to low status classes and ultimately to low status jobs; instead, forces of race, class, and gender create a multilevel playing field on which students gain a sense of their options and negotiate their educational and economic possibilities. Race, class, and gender dynamics combine to create a larger playing field with more options for some and a smaller, more limited field for others. In these contexts students struggle to make sense of and deal with triple or more divisions of the social gridiron: here, they wrestle with fractious social classes, genders, and racial and ethnic groups.

As it integrates and connects the study of race, class, and gender to the nature of consciousness construction, knowledge production, and modes of oppression, a critical democratic social studies embraces a social vision that moves beyond the particular concerns of specific social groups. While these concerns are important and must be addressed in a critical education, we ultimately embrace a democratic politics that emphasizes difference within unity. The unity among different racial, ethnic, class, and gendered groups can be constructed around a well-delineated notion of social justice and democratic community. Within this critical context the need for separatist, integrationist, and pluralist moments are appreciated. Indeed, there is a time for African Americans to study Afrocentrism, women to study feminism, and working people to study labor's continuing struggle for economic justice. Concurrently, there is a need for such groups to join together in the mutual struggle for democracy and empowerment. Democratic social studies teachers seek a way of making sense of the world that understands the specific nature of difference but appreciates our mutual embrace of principles of equality and justice. This system of meaning cannot embrace one axis of oppression as more important than, or taking precedence over, others. This is a central tenet of critical theory.

The critical theoretical movement from one-dimensional views of social reality to complex multiple readings of the lived world alerts social studies teachers not only to new ways of understanding oppression but to the world in general. Democratic social studies teachers cannot accept economic determinism or any other one-dimensional, simple, reductionistic, linear, positivistic view of reality. The trans-Cartesian understanding of complexity demands recognition of multiple causations and the possibility of various vantage points in the web of reality. The machine has functioned as the dominant metaphor of the linear positivist reality. The positivist analyst assumes that, when machine-like social reality malfunctions, a link in the cause-effect chain of parts has been broken. The job of the researcher is to identify the link and make the repair. But reality just doesn't work this way. For example, when the human body breaks down, doctors may identify a certain factor, but the cause of the illness is always multiple. Living entities are always composed of a multitude of feedback loops—a cardinal concept in chaos theory.

A home furnace is one of the most familiar forms of a simple feedback loop. We all know that when a room cools down below the temperature set on the thermostat, the thermostat responds by switching on the furnace. As the furnace heats up the room to a point above the second temperature set on the thermostat, the furnace automatically shuts off. The ear-splitting screeches produced when a microphone is placed close to a speaker, feedback, is another example of a feedback loop. Output from the amplifier is detected by the microphone and looped back into the amplifier. The chaotic sounds which result are the consequence of a feedback loop where the output of one stage turns into the input of another. Because human beings are composed of so many feedback loops (e.g., the transformation of food into energy, the increase in heart-rate in the presence of danger, etc.), the attempt to study them takes on far more complexity than traditional conceptions of cause-effect linearity could imagine (Lincoln & Guba, 1985; Briggs & Peat, 1989; Kincheloe, Steinberg, & Hinchey, 1999). On this recognition of complexity rests the future of a democratic social studies.

4. THE CRITIQUE OF INSTRUMENTAL OR TECHNICAL RATIONALITY. As discussed in Chapter 5, instrumental rationality is a key aspect of modern positivism. Critical theory sees instrumental/technology rationality as one of the most oppressive features of contemporary society. Such a form of "hyperreason" involves an obsession with means in preference to ends. Critical theorists claim that instrumental/technical rationality is more interested in method and efficiency than in purpose. It delimits its questions to "how to" instead of 'why should." In an educational context, critical theorists claim that many rationalistic scholars become so obsessed with issues of technique, procedure, and correct method that they forget its humanistic purpose. Instrumental/technical rationality often separates fact from value in its obsession with "proper" method, losing in the process an understanding of the value choices always involved in the production of so-called facts.

Questions of the purposes of social studies education in a democratic society are subservient to the provision of specific methods of delivering information in an instrumentally rational classroom. When social studies teachers separate purpose from teaching methods, the tendency to break learning into discrete pieces considered in isolation is perpetuated. In the instrumental rationality of teaching to behavioral objectives or to expert-produced content standards, positivist educators have assumed that teaching and learning were never more than the sum of their parts. Houses from these perspectives are no more than the nails and lumber that go into them, and education is no more than the average number of objectives mastered. Many educators have referred to this fragmentation process as "bitting." It is not hard to imagine a social studies classroom caught in the bitting process. Students copy historical information from chalkboards and overhead projectors and skim textbooks to find information fragments that would answer both the questions in the study guides and the multiple-choice tests. Children listen (when they're not talking); they respond when called upon; they read fragments of the textbook; they write short responses to questions provided on worksheets.

They rarely plan or initiate anything of length or conceptualize their own projects. They rarely even write essays. They are learning to be deskilled, to be passive, to be citizens who are governed, not citizens who govern. They are being taught not to seek deep structures that move events but to examine only the surface level of appearance. They will not understand the concept of consciousness construction or the subtlety of the process of domination. Ideology will remain a foreign abstraction in their eyes. Those students who will transcend such blindnesses will make their emancipatory journey in spite of their classroom experiences, finding analytic inspiration outside the school context. Instrumentally rational education serves to perpetuate the most pernicious effects of bureaucratized school practices (Bracy, 1987; Hinchey, 1998).

Just as positivism negates our view of how instruction and evaluation might take place in particular contexts, it also shapes our view of how social studies teachers might relate to the act of knowledge production. In a positivistic, instrumentally rational context, we know that research produces theories that are applied to achieve specific goals. Positivistic research sets up a context where the factory model division of labor is reproduced: the researcher conceptualizes the teaching act and produces theory; the practitioner executes the directives of the researcher and applies theory. The teacher is alerted to some weak component of his or her subjective theory of education by the researcher's comparison of it to a research-grounded scientific theory. The researcher provides the teacher with a choice of scientifically validated teaching strategies. The teacher exercises his or her professional autonomy by selecting, applying, and then practicing a strategy in a supervised training session where contextual variables have been controlled.

All phases of such a process depend on an instrumentally rational concern with the measurable results of particular strategies. Does the strategy serve to raise social studies test scores? No questions are asked of issues such as: the worth of raising the scores, the tacit view of politics embedded in them, the educational and social side effects of viewing their improvement as the primary goal of teaching. Value dimensions, ideological dimensions of human practice, escape the vision of instrumental rationality. No room for uncertainty or spontaneous innovation exists; instrumental rationality demands that research cannot begin until agreement exists on all definitions and that a well-formed problem has been established. Research, and thus teaching, will proceed in line with the dictates of the well-formed problem—in contemporary schools, the improvement of test scores often constitutes the problem. Research is reduced to the attempt to find relationships between specific teaching skills and test score improvement. "Remarkable" findings are produced that are passed along to teacher education students; for example, the more time students study their social studies text, the greater the possibility that they will raise their test scores. Such a logocentrism, an embrace of reason accompanied by the exclusion of the affective, the emotional aspects of learning and knowing, forces us to focus on the least important aspects of social studies education—aspects which are inevitably the most measurable (Kroath, 1989; Eisner, 1984; Schon, 1987; Kincheloe, Slattery, & Steinberg, 2000).

A medical analogy might be in order. In the instrumentally rational world of positivistic medicine, doctors are subjected to some of the same forces as teachers. Technological innovation in medicine has produced machines which inexorably fix the attention of both doctor and patient on those aspects of an illness which are measurable. Human dimensions of the illness, which are at least of equal importance, are neglected. Doctors must rebel if they are to serve their patients effectively; they must not allow a science of measurability to dictate what techniques they use, no matter how effective the technique might be in addressing the particular variable measured by the high-tech equipment purchased at great cost by the hospital administrators. The doctor must never lose sight of the patient as a human being with unmeasureable, but yet important, feelings, insights, pains, and anxieties (Wiggins, 1989). In education, the technology of the standardized tests often moves us to forget that students are human beings with unmeasurable but yet important characteristics.

We cannot suppress the concept that science is more than merely a method. Indeed, it is a philosophy. Moreover, reason embraces a corpus of qualities which transcend mere calculation; it cannot, in other words, be reduced to a formula for problem solving. Positivistic researchers, their opponents argue, focus on the rigor (commitment to the established rules for conducting inquiry) of research at the expense of touching the lived world. William James captured this idea almost one hundred years ago when he chided scientists of his day about their excessive love of method. Science, he wrote, "has fallen so deeply in love with method that . . . she has ceased to care of truth by itself at all." Anticipating one of the central tenets in the critique of instrumental rationality, James argued that scientists pursued their technically verifiable truth with such a vengeance that they forgot their "duty to mankind," i.e., technical means took precedence over human ends. Human passions, he concluded, are more powerful than technical rules, as the heart understands that which reason cannot comprehend.

Social studies teaching ensnared in the fishnet of instrumental/technical rationality fails to comprehend the importance of the complex existential conditions in which learning takes shape. As a result, the cognition emerging from such a pedagogy is reduced and deformed. As top-down lessons focus on the technical, learning is fragmented and loses sight of any holistic sense of how concepts fit together, where ideas come from and who produced them, and the way the interpretation of this social studies information was formulated. By following the dictates of the positivistic technocrats to spend more time on task and to identify beforehand the competencies that students will master during class, teachers may indeed increase the amount of social studies knowledge inserted into each student's mind. Questions concerning the worth of such knowledge and whose interests it serves, however, are irrelevant to the process. Instrumentally rational evaluators, focusing on a quantitative measurement of the knowledge component of such a classroom, might ignore the very essence of the educational experience. The relationship of the knowledge to the existential worlds of the students is a question that is infrequently asked in an instrumentally rational context.

When they overlook the lived context of teaching, positivistic experts acquire a very thin view of the nature of the democratic social studies process. In asking a question about, say, the causes of student learning in a classroom, a far more in-depth understanding would be necessary if the experts were to suggest policy changes on the basis of the understanding gained through research. This use of thin knowledge of education to support policy changes and methodological changes often reflects modern educational practice. Modern empirical investigations often eventuate in a set of rules for pedagogical planning and management of a classroom. These rules are often cited as inviolate because of their hard scientific basis. Not only are there research methodological questions about the efficacy of such rules but there are also questions about the general relationship between research findings and the process by which rules for practice are developed. If we fail to ask these questions, positivistic researchers may transform value-laden issues of policy into merely technical issues which can be resolved empirically (Macmillan & Garrison, 1984; Donmoyer, 1985).

The effect, then, of expert knowledge production based on instrumental rationality is a social studies curriculum marked by an emphasis on control and conformity. Researchers strive to understand systems of causal laws and the ways the variables relate to one another. Such understandings lead to a perspective that assumes certain variables may be manipulated to achieve certain outcomes. Control, and thus conformity, are deemed desirable and rendered possible by such research orientations.

Unfortunately, social studies teachers are profoundly affected by such a positivistic process. They are taught to accept passively and to apply empirical knowledge gathered by professional researchers. Manageable bits of facts are the building blocks of knowledge, and these pieces of knowledge can be efficiently transmitted to students. Most of the educational reform movements of the last 30 years have been grounded in instrumentally rational research. Teachers have curricular choices only when their decisions contribute to a more efficient and controllable system. Science is geared toward the administration of human beings. The moral implications of goals, such as control and efficiency, are eliminated from consideration. Social studies practitioners, grounding their actions on this research base, act upon the belief that the laws of social life are well-known and devoid of ambiguity (Baldwin, 1987; Steinberg & Kincheloe, 1993). Critical theory wants everyone to understand how this instrumental/technical rationality works to promote the interests of power wielders in the larger society. This, critical theorists maintain, is a basic feature of a democratic citizen's political education.

5. THE IMPACT OF DESIRE. Critical theory appreciates poststructuralist (poststructuralism is a postmodern way of seeing that understands the complexity of causation and asserts that social structures cannot determine human consciousness and behavior in some type of cause-effect rational process) psychoanalysis as an important resource in pursuing an emancipatory education. In this context, critical researchers are empowered to dig more deeply into the complexity of the construction of the human psyche. Such a psychoanalysis helps critical researchers discern the unconscious processes that create resistance to progressive change and induce self-destructive behavior. A poststructural psychoanalysis, in its rejection of traditional psychoanalysis's tendency to view individuals as rational and autonomous beings, allows critical researchers new tools to rethink the interplay amount the various axes of power: identity, libido, rationality, and emotion. In this configuration, the psychic is no longer separated from the sociopolitical realm; indeed, desire can be socially constructed and used by power wielders for destructive and oppressive outcomes. On the other hand, critical theorists can help

mobilize desire for progressive and emancipatory projects. Taking their lead from feminist theory, critical researchers are aware of the patriarchal inscriptions within traditional psychoanalysis and work to avoid its bourgeois, ethnocentric, and misogynist practices. Freed from these blinders, poststructural psychoanalysis helps researchers gain a new sensitivity to the role of fantasy and imagination and the structures of sociocultural and psychological meaning they reference.

As democratic social studies teachers understand the politics of the postmodern condition, they come to appreciate that individuals make sense of the world with both their minds and their hearts. Especially in light of our discussions of affect in postmodernity in earlier chapters, social studies teachers recognize the political importance of the quest to "colonize desire." Power wielders in the corporate world have long understood this notion, designing their commercial advertisements not around a logical appeal to the buyer's rationality but around the regulation and reshaping of the consumer's desire. In their efforts to study the workings of twenty-first century politics, democratic social studies teachers must understand what people know, how they come to know it, how they feel about it, and how such knowledge and feelings and the process of obtaining them shape their relationship to the powerful. In such an analytical process, social studies teachers begin to understand the ways technopower regulates the society, the ways popular culture undermines human potential, and the ways it helps construct human possibility for self-direction and empowerment.

Democratic social studies teachers, taking their cue from critical theory's concern with desire, study the ways they themselves, citizens in general, and their students in particular invest their libidinal energies (desire) in popular culture. This postmodern "politics of pleasure" involves the way individuals identify with particular cultural forms and the ideologies they imply by the pleasures they provide. We miss the point when the assumption is made that popular culture simply manipulates its audience. The relation an audience develops with a cultural form is always complex and ambiguous. Social studies attempting to trace the production of desire in the cultural forms of hyperreality and its political impact quickly realize the complexity of the task.

The fact that it takes place so much outside the boundaries of rationality, in the realm of desire, makes it extremely difficult for traditional researchers to comprehend the process. For example, we can libidinally invest in and enjoy a music video even though we may rationally recognize its inherent sexism. The interaction between listener/watcher and video may produce unanticipated political effects (Giroux & Simon, 1989). Never able to dominate in some incontestable manner, along the lines of these contradictions are openings for emancipatory change. Larry Grossberg (1995) argues that, since power never gets all that it wants, there are always opportunities for challenging its authority. Democratic social studies teachers must stand ready to seize these opportunities when they present themselves.

A few years ago, Shirley Steinberg and I, operating in a critical theoretical context concerned with the politics of desire, set out to study the impact of power's production of pleasure on children. Honestly, we uncovered more than we had bargained for since we found that power and pleasure had not simply affected childhood in postmodernity but had irrevocably changed it. The boundary between childhood and adulthood had blurred, as power had granted children access to information that was once the private property of adulthood. The childhood cultural dynamic produced by corporate power, we labeled "kinderculture." In postmodernity, power does not simply repress democratic expressions of children but is most effective in shaping young people when it produces pleasure for them.

If power were always expressed by "just saying no" to children's desire, it would gain little authority in their eyes. The power of Disney, Mattel, Hasbro, Warner Brothers, and McDonald's is never greater than when it produces pleasure, stimulates the desire of consumers. Recent cultural studies of consumption link it to the identity formation of the consumer, meaning to some degree that we are what we consume. Status in one's subculture, individual creations of style, knowledge of cultural texts, role in the community of consumers, emulation of fictional characters, internalization of values promoted by popular cultural expressions, all contribute to our personal identities. Popular culture provides children with intense libidinal experiences often unmatched in any other phase of their lives. It is not surprising that such energy and intensity exert powerful influences on self-definition and on the ways children choose to organize their lives (Warde, 1994; Steinberg & Kincheloe, 1997).

Obviously, power mixed with desire produces an explosive cocktail; the colonization of desire, however, is not the end of the story. Social studies educators drawing upon critical theory understand how power enfolds into consciousness and the unconsciousness in a way that, no doubt, evokes desire but also guilt and anxiety. The intensity of the guilt and anxiety children may experience as a result of their brush with power is inseparable from the cultural context in which they live. Desire, in many cases, may take a back seat to the repression of desire in the construction of child consciousness/unconsciousness and the production of identity (Donald, 1993). The cocktail's effects may be longer-lasting than first assumed, because expression of the repression may reveal itself in bizarre and unpredictable ways.

To make this observation about the relationship among power, desire, and the repression of desire and the way it expresses itself at the psychological level is not a denial of human agency (self-direction). Although power has successfully commodified kinderculture, democratic social studies teachers know both adults and children can successfully deflect its repressive elements. The role of the elementary social studies teacher involves helping students develop what John Fiske (1993) calls the affective moments of power evasion. Using their abilities to "reread" Disney films along the fault lines of gender or to reincode Barbie and Ken in a satirical mode, children take their first steps toward self-asserting and power resistance—key democratic social studies skills. Such effective moments of power evasion don't constitute the ultimate expression of critical resistance to power's colonization of desire, but they do provide a space around which more significant forms of critical consciousness and civic action can be developed.

6. FOCUSING ON THE RELATIONSHIPS AMONG CULTURE, POWER, AND DOM-
    INATION—"HABITUS" AND THE CONSTRUCTION OF CONSCIOUSNESS.
    From our previous analysis of the postmodern condition and power,
    we have learned how culture has taken on a new importance in the
    effort to understand the political realm and issues of domination. As
    stated earlier, democratic social studies teachers, operating with an
    understanding of critical theory, know that culture is a domain of
    struggle where the production and transmission of knowledge is
    always a contested process. Dominant and subordinate cultures
    deploy differing systems of meaning based on the forms of knowledge
    produced in their cultural domain. Recognizing that popular culture
    is not a trivial domain but has become the primary location in hyper-
    reality for the construction of political consciousness, students of cul-
    tural studies (we will explore its relationship to a democratic social

studies in Chapter 27) examine not only the popular domain but the hidden rules that shape cultural production in general.

Arguing that the development of mass media has changed the way the culture operates, cultural studies researchers maintain that cultural epistemologies (concerning ways of thinking about and producing knowledge that are taught tacitly via participation in everyday cultural activities) in the first decade of the twenty-first century are quite different than those of only a few decades ago. New forms of culture and cultural domination are produced as the distinction between the real and the simulated is blurred. Understanding these dislocations, democratic social studies teachers work to develop teaching strategies that involve:

a.　the ability to link the production of representations, images, and signs of hyperreality to power in the political economy; and

b.　the capacity, once this linkage is exposed and described, to delineate the highly complex effects of the reception of these images and signs on individuals located at various race, class, gender, and sexual coordinates in the web of reality.

Critical theorists assert that all cognitive activity is connected to power relations. If teachers' and students' perspectives are always shaped by power, then one of the key roles of a democratic social studies teacher involves the effort to illustrate the nature of this influence to their fellow teachers and their students. French social analyst Pierre Bourdieu used the term, "habitus" to describe the situation in which a student or anyone else is culturally located. Habitus is an important critical theoretical concept as it exposes the embodied culture that shapes styles of knowing, learning, and relating to the world. Students embody their habitus as they walk into social studies classrooms in the ways they conceptualize the role of social studies in their lives, their disposition toward learning the skills and concepts that make up the curriculum. A sensitive social studies teacher can sense quickly the ways this embodied culture positions different students to the issues in question.

Indeed, habitus is personally felt and experienced, but it is the product of history, socioeconomic structures, and enculturation. Habitus is internalized culture that helps an individual make sense of the world. It works within large structures of power to maintain patterns of socialization. For example, working-class students are predisposed by their socialization to enter manual vacations. Such young people learn through their body—"Stand up straight;" "Don't hold your knife in your left hand"—an entire way of life, a mode of being (Mostern, 1994; Robbins, 1992; Gibson, 1986).

A democratic social studies is focused on this habitus, the way of seeing that students bring to class (McLaren et al., 1995). It is concerned with helping high school students understand that their view of school and their career choices have had more to do with their habitus—for example, with embodied notions of their gender role—than with a decision carefully and freely made from a range of possible vocational choices. Indeed, young working-class women, training for dental hygienist and paralegal jobs instead of choosing to become dentists or lawyers, may have been moved by an embodied sense of working-class gender expectations. Critical democratic social studies teachers help everyone in the school culture understand the effect of habitus on these and other social dynamics and how human possibility may be subverted in the process.

Thus, culture, power, and domination work in complex ways to shape our consciousness. As you now understand, critical theory is devoted to tracing the specific ways this process works to create both oppressive and emancipatory ways of viewing self and world. If democratic social studies teachers are to understand power's construction of consciousness, how it affects students in various social and educational settings, and how they might incorporate these understandings into their teaching, they must become researchers of students, culture/popular culture, communities, subcultures, the stated and unstated/hidden social curriculum of schools, and themselves. This is not something social studies teachers will do next semester or next year. It is a lifelong process that is never ending. Hopefully, as our lives progress, we gain more and more insights that inform our teaching.

Every time I walk into a classroom, I am thinking about these dynamics, this intersection of culture, power, and domination and the ways they shape the consciousness of the marginalized and the privileged. The book *White Reign: Deploying Whiteness in America* (1998) reflected the type of critical theoretical work described here, as it examined the sociocultural forces working to shape white consciousness at the end of the twentieth century. Our effort was to explore the ways the privilege of whiteness shaped the consciousness and actions of white people and how such individuals could reshape their identities in ways that were antiracist, egalitarian, and just. This is exactly what I am writing about here. Critical theory asks all of us to rethink our perspectives in light of an analysis of our self-production by forces of culture, power, and domination so that we might act in democratic ways. This is what critically informed social studies teachers do,

7. Strengthening democracy: building communities of solidarity. Critical theory is always concerned about the nature of democracy, the way it is subverted in the name of democracy, and the relationship between democracy and community. Critical democratic social studies teachers understand that, in the United States, democracy and community have been consistently subverted by the distortions of power and the inability of dominant culture to deal with power difference—racial, gender, religious, and sexual difference in particular. To establish a working democracy, critical theorists make use of voices and perspectives that have been traditionally excluded. Such viewpoints help social studies educators clarify cultural, political, and economic values, an exercise that keeps power elites from using dominant ideologies as modes of control. With these subjugated perspectives, critical social studies teachers tell suppressed stories: the marginalized perspectives on race, Native American perspectives on the Westward Movement, and women's viewpoints from their location in the socioeconomic order.

Cartesian modernist social scientists have long contended that the foundation of democratic thinking has rested on a close-knit community with a common set of precepts. Sharon Welch (1991) has challenged that perception, arguing from a critical perspective that heterogeneous communities with differing principles may better contribute to the cultivation of critical thinking and moral reasoning. A homogeneous community is often unable to criticize the injustice and exclusionary practices that afflict a social setting. Criticism and reform of cultural pathology often come from the recognition of difference—from interaction with communities that do not suffer the same social injustices or that have dealt with them in different ways. We always profit in some way from a confrontation with another system of defining that which is important. Consciousness itself is spurred by difference, in that our first awareness of who we are occurs only when we become aware that we exist independently of another or another's way.

Welch has maintained that the concept of solidarity is more inclusive and transformative than the concept of consensus. Even if we perceive consensus as involving a common recognition of social pathology and the belief that we must work together to find a cure, we first have to accept the value of solidarity. For Welch, the ethic of solidarity: a) grants social groups enough respect to listen to their ideas and to use them to consider existing social values; and b) realizes that the lives of individuals in differing groups are interconnected to the point that everyone is accountable to everyone else. No assumption of uniformity exists here—just the commitment to work together to bring about democratic, mutually beneficial social change. In the social studies classroom, this valuing of difference, and its political and cognitive benefits, exhibits itself in a dialogical sharing of perspective. Students come to see their own social and political points of view as one particular sociohistorically constructed way of perceiving. As the classroom develops, students are exposed to more and more diverse voices in various texts and discussions, a process that engages them in other ways of seeing and knowing. Thus, the democratic circle of understanding is widened, as difference expands their social imagination, their emancipatory vision of what could be. Social studies students begin to realize that, because they can imagine a strengthened democracy and democratic action, they are possible.

Social studies teachers and students, grounded in a foundation of democratic solidarity in difference, learn to question social and educational perspectives that do not value difference and don't view diversity as a positive feature of a democratic community. Understanding that the notion of interconnectedness is a central but undervalued feature of social life, critical democratic social studies students and teachers explore the ways identity and consciousness are shaped in interaction. Are we exposed only to one social, religious, or political perspective? What might we need to do if we find ourselves in this situation? Democratic social studies teachers scramble to open themselves, their colleagues, and their students to a variety of perspectives. They work to illustrate that, in a democratic global society marked by the values of solidarity and interconnectedness, the pain and hardships of any individual or group negatively affects us all (Pang, Gay, & Stanley, 1995; Stanley, 2000).

In critical theoretical appreciation of a community of difference, social studies teachers and students push the envelope of their social and political imaginations. Often, power wielders consider teachers and students who have developed such imaginations dangerous, since they refuse to unquestioningly do their bidding. Such teachers and students have become members of a valued community, united as participants in the democratic political arena. As knowledge producers who develop counternarratives to power's ideologies, these teachers and students challenge established networks of dominance. Buoyed by these critical orientations, social studies teachers begin to redefine learning in the critical democratic community. In Cartesian social studies, of course, learning has typically involved the acquisition of specific unchallenged information that lends itself to quantitative measurement. Success in this context is individually-oriented and is evaluated on the basis of short-term results (Marsick, 1989). The teacher-student community, established by critical theory's notion of democracy, is baptized in dialogue and dedicated to thinking together. Social studies teachers and students analyze patterns of interaction that sabotage learning and keep them from working together toward common goals.

They learn together like members of a think tank, producing knowledge about particular social issues. These teachers and students establish strong links with a variety of workers and citizens to help them work toward their objectives. Though they are guided by democratic principals of solidarity and equality of all community members, students, and teachers, they refuse to work toward a final goal, some predetermined state of community emancipation. A critical perspective is not a commodity that is peddled like snake oil. Students do not leave class saying, "I have finally achieved universal consciousness. I am everywhere and nowhere. I am emancipated." A critical, theoretically informed social studies seeks to produce a democratic community of learners that struggles to counter traditions, prejudices, positivist rationality, and other dominant forces that undermine democratic action. One of the most important ways to ensure the success of this work to strengthen democracy involves helping teachers, students, and community members to become researchers, knowledge workers. Knowing that knowledge is always tied to power, critical teachers set out to produce their own (Alvesson & Willmott, 1992; Kincheloe, 1991, 1993; Murray & Ozanne, 1991).

Grounded by the critical theoretical concern with democratic communities of solidarity, social studies teachers direct research toward the exploration of dangerous memory and subjugated knowledge. As students explore the specific ways consciousness is constructed and the social world operates, they make the notion of critical emancipation and the world of schooling accessible to marginalized members of the local community. They develop radical modes of resistance to power-produced alienation and dehumanization. In this process, they construct a foundation on which hope is built. Democratic social studies teachers view community building as a form of critical civics. This emancipatory citizenship education makes its commitments clear from the outset; it envisions a politically savvy society with active citizens who are rigorously educated as researchers and knowledge analysts, capable of reestablishing a working democracy and making the world a better place to live.

Interestingly, over the last three or four decades, this effort to build democratic communities and establish a critical civics has become increasingly difficult. The ideological climate that took shape in the 1970s positioned not only government but the political process itself as the enemy. In this ideological context, any effort to use government to accomplish socially beneficial goals was perceived as favoring big government or governmental interference in our lives. Time and again over the last 30 years, when I have spoken about social justice and building democratic community, I have been interrupted by those who object to these traditional American goals with cries of "No more big government." Nothing within this project necessitates large, intractable government bureaucracies; indeed, such organization models should be avoided. There are other ways to govern other than through large, rationalized, unchangeable bureaucracies.

Key to building the diverse communities of solidarity advocated by critical theorists is the notion of decentralization and dispersed notions of community control. This is a central step in the attempt to restore democracy. In this spirit, critical analysts believe that individual social studies teachers should have the prerogative to adjust the curriculum to the diverse needs of their students and the concerns of the local community. This degree of self-determination is necessary if top-down rationalization, teacher deskilling, and antidemocratic centralized control of schooling is to be avoided. Without an understanding of the connection linking democracy, community building, civil liberty, and economic security, much of our talk about empowerment and solidarity is empty (Noffke, 2000; Dionne, 1991). There is no way we can speak of political rights, critical theorists remind us, outside of the context of economic democracy. In many ways, social studies curricula that ignore this economic dynamic in the study of democratic political science, government, and civics are presenting a misleading body of knowledge. We will discuss this issue throughout this book.

8. A POLITICS OF SKEPTICISM THAT METAMORPHISIZES INTO A PEDAGOGY
    OF HOPE. A critically grounded social studies is dedicated to chal-
    lenging comfortable assumptions about politics, culture, psychology,
    human potential, economics, and society. What are the conse-
    quences of schooling? Is the United States really a democratic socie-
    ty? Can everyone who works hard succeed? Is intelligence genetically
    determined? These are only a few of the questions that emerge from
    a critical politics of skepticism. Operating within such a political
    framework, democratic social studies teachers encourage students to
    question the information delivered to them as fact, research and ana-
    lyze alternative perspectives, develop their political imagination to
    develop new alternatives, and make ethical and democratic choices.
    Critical theorists understand that the information we are presented
    about the world is partial, incomplete, and shaped by social, politi-
    cal, and economic interests. Such power dynamics produce
    inequities in the ability of students (and everyone else) to discern,
    delineate, and realize their own best interests, as well as the best
    interests of the larger society. As we act on our politics of skepticism,
    we gain enlightenment, that is, a knowledge of whose interests are
    being served in particular social arrangements. Such knowledge pro-
    vides us the ability to act in empowering ways that were previously
    impossible.

What we are talking about here is understanding ideological mysti-
fications of the world so that we can challenge the power brokers who
frame things to serve their interests, not those of the democratic community. It is fascinating, in the first years of the twenty-first century, to
examine information providers, such as the cable financial/business
networks. Based on an obsession with short-term stock market profits,
business reports on CNBC, CNNFN, Bloomberg TV, etc. promote ways
of viewing the political economy that further these goals. Because of
the rise of the market, more and more viewers are watching such programs. As a social studies curriculum, the networks assume a political
stance that maintains any governmental investment in helping the
most needy will harm the economy. Indeed, almost anything that helps
the poor will harm the stock market. For example, when the hourly
wages of the lowest paid workers go up—even by a few pennies—the
stock market moves down. When corporate managers' salaries and
wealth increase from, say, $60 million per year to $95million dollars a

year, the market rises. Twenty-first century critical theorists are not comfortable with this reality.

Thus, a critically grounded social studies urges teachers, students, and citizens to be skeptical of such media-produced information, to expose many of the assumptions on which such pronouncements are grounded, to explore the effects of such reporting on the political consciousness of the people watching around the world. The tragedy that I have often observed in the nonconceptual social studies high school and elementary classes and the social studies methods courses in the teacher education curriculum involves the cognitive and political passivity that is often promoted in these contexts. Such passivity is an important milestone on the path to the loss of political freedom and the breakdown of democracy. If instruction involves simply providing information that is intended to improve standardized test scores or mandated social studies content standards, the thinking that results from the intent of such instruction will hold little meaning for the student or the teacher (Ross, 2000). Indeed, such instruction may be viewed by some social studies scholars as ineffective, but, at least, politically neutral, since it passes along the truths of earlier generations to contemporary students. Skepticism in regard to such official knowledge is punished, and its political dimension is hidden. As students are subjected to such instruction, they are tied to the whipping post of tradition.

Rewarded for uncritical acceptance of the social and political canon, students remain victims of the restraints of earlier generations. Critical thought is not the province of the school; it takes place on the students' own time, on a very different terrain of culture. Ironically, it is not the school that encourages such analysis but aspects of the world of countercultural music, TV, and film. Unfortunately, the two worlds often remain unconnected because students come to see the cold, concrete, disembodied school experience as no place for critical, analytical thought. Thinking in the Cartesian social studies for both student and teacher often is rewarded for the degree to which it reflects the dominant ideology of mainstream courtesy, marked by a conception of dissent as distasteful, and the status quo power relations implied by an acceptance of laissez-faire capitalism. Thus, a form of politically passive conformity is cultivated that views good students and teachers as obedient to externally imposed ways of thinking and rules that possess little personal meaning. In such a context, neither students nor teachers are encouraged to construct new ways of seeing when beset with an unanticipated contradictory situation. Piaget labeled this process "accommodation," the reshaping of cognitive structures to accommodate unique aspects of what is being perceived in new contexts. In other words, through our knowledge of a variety of comparable social contexts, we begin to understand their similarities and differences, and we learn from our comparison of the different contexts.

Employing critical theory to push Piaget one more cognitive step, a more critical notion of accommodation is offered. Understanding the socially constructed nature of our comprehension of reality, critical accommodation involves the attempt to disembed ourselves from the pictures of the world painted by power. For example, a teacher's construction of intelligence would typically be molded (assimilated) by a powerful scientific discourse that equated intelligence with scores on intelligence tests. The teacher would critically accommodate the concept as she or he began to examine students who had been labeled by the scientific discourse as unintelligent, but, upon a second look, exhibited characteristics that, in an unconventional way, seemed sophisticated. The teacher would then critically accommodate (or integrate) this recognition of exception into a definition of intelligence that challenged the dominant discourse. Thus empowered to move beyond the confines of the socially constructed ways of seeing intelligence, the teacher could discover unique forms of intelligence among his or her students: students who, under the domination of the Cartesian scientific discourse of intelligence testing, would have been overlooked and relegated to the junk heap of the school. In a sense, this process of critical accommodation is what Howard Gardner (1983) employed when he conceived his theory of multiple intelligences. This is the kind of thinking that allows us to escape the gravitational pull of modernist passivity with its cognitively deadening, uninterrupted inculcation of tradition.

In a postmodern hyperreality, saturated as it is by endless data and media imagery, critical social studies educators are faced with a difficult, but not impossible, task in their attempt to unmask the hidden political dimensions of thinking. Democratic social studies teachers must capture the image of what it means to be a teacher, to be a thoughtful, politically educated person. We must become a part of the struggle to name the ideology produced on CNBC and the larger social terrain, as we induce our students to develop a skeptical stance toward the information and images constructed by power. And a dangerous act it is. Whenever we talk of challenging the tacit political dimensions of mainstream thinking, of advocating a pedagogy that admits to its political allegiances, we open ourselves to attack on our alleged attempt to indoctrinate our students. Even in these days of qualitative meta-analysis of educational research and educational policy that has exposed the pseudo-objectivity of so-called value-free and politically neutral positions, many technicist Cartesian educators continue to charge indoctrination when analyzing critical democratic social studies.

We must keep politics out of education, many Cartesian educators argue, not understanding the inseparability of political and educational questions. Critical social studies educators suggest that educators should be made more political, that we should expose the hidden politics of neutrality. Of course, this admission of political interest is represented as the advocacy of indoctrination as the goal of social studies education. Critical theorists maintain that one can hold a political position without using it to indoctrinate one's students, recognizing that education is never neutral. Indeed, when we attempt to remain neutral, like many churches in Nazi Germany, we give our political support to the prevailing power structure. A critical politics of skepticism that recognizes the political inscriptions on information and the political implications of specific modes of thinking suggests that social studies teachers have the obligation to reveal their political commitments to their students. Having done this, critical analysts contend, they, by no stretch of the imagination, have the right to impose these positions on students.

I want to make this point very clear. It is not critical social studies teachers who are typically guilty of indoctrination, of imposing their beliefs on students (Kincheloe, 1991; Giroux, 1988; Hinchey, 1998). More common is social and political indoctrination by ostensibly neutral, mainstream, Cartesian educators. When mainstream opponents of critical teaching promote the reductionist notion that all political behavior that opposes the dominant ideology is a form of cultural imposition, they forget how experience is constructed within a social context marked by an inequitable distribution of power. To refuse to name the structural sources of human suffering and exploitation is to take a position that supports oppression and the power relations that sustain it. The mainstream argument that any oppositional way of seeing represents an imposition of one's views on somebody else is similar to the nineteenth-century ruling-class idea that raising one's voice, struggling politically, or engaging in social criticism violated a gentlemanly code of civility. Who's indoctrinating whom? In the name of neutrality, the mainstream promotes particular forms of decontextualized thinking: the irony of objectivity. When someone tells me that he or she is "simply giving me the facts," I guard my wallet. The importance of a critical politics of skepticism is never greater.

Such a politics of skepticism pushes critical social studies educators to expand the boundaries of cognitive activity and human possibility. Human beings in general, and our social studies teachers and students in particular, are capable of so much more than what is expected of them at this historical juncture. A key theme emerges as we discuss the critical theoretical interplay of skepticism and hope: There's got to be more than this. We merely stand at the beginning of an attempt to become smarter and to develop new forms of consciousness, more democratic and equitable social organizations, and new creative and humane forms of social action. *Getting Beyond the Facts* means that we get behind the ideological curtain of modernism. In this sociocognitive domain, we begin to discover, rediscover, and create new possibilities for humanity. A critical democratic social studies is an education of hope.

As we go behind the Cartesian curtain, we find that we have been taught to view non-European, lower socioeconomic class, and women's ways of thinking as inferior (Kohli, 2000). Some of the greatest expressions of human thought have been summarily dismissed from consideration by Western education. This is one of many great tragedies constructed by dominant forms of Eurocentric reason. Cognition, as we maintained earlier, is just as much a political domain as an election campaign. The group that typically holds power has gained the prerogative to label their own cognitive styles as reason. Since Westerners have been in colonial power positions over the past few centuries, they have long possessed this right. Critical social studies educators exercise skepticism about this cognitive ethnocentrism and seek new insights from non-Western and other traditionally marginalized sources.

No matter what the grade-level, democratic social studies teachers can compare Western and non-Western classification schemas in ways that evoke new cognitive insights and visions. Such intercultural dialogues tap into the benefits to be derived from cognitive diversity and the insights into an unimagined future such diversity provides. For example, people living in different circumstances—whether it be climatic, political, religious, cosmological, epistemological, economic, or whatever—devote more attention to the features of their environment that are central to them. Such mindfulness motivates them to produce more precise knowledge about phenomena they consider central to their lives. After scores of generations have devoted close attention to a particular feature of their environment, the knowledge possessed by the cultural group about it is detailed and profound. When such data is viewed in relation to Western scientific knowledge on the topic, the comparative insights that emerge can help uncover cultural assumptions previously unknown by Western peoples. Knowledge of such assumptions can play a profound role in the critical social studies effort to change consciousness, to expand the Western cognitive envelope.

Key to this critical effort is an understanding of specific types of non-Cartesian Western ways of knowing—indigenous knowledges (Semali & Kincheloe, 1999). Indigenous peoples include Native Americans, Australian Aboriginals, various African peoples, and many other groups around the world. Indigeneity is an ambiguous term that can be easily misused, but the power of indigenous knowledge is sufficiently compelling to merit further study. While it is difficult to precisely define indigenous knowledge, it involves the ways in which local residents of an area have come to understand themselves in relation to their natural environment and how they organize specific knowledges of flora and fauna, cultural beliefs, social connectivity, and history to enhance their lives. Democratic social studies teachers see, within indigenous knowledges, great insights into both the weaknesses of Cartesianism and new possibilities for human redefinition. Indigenous knowledge offers great hope in the critical effort to develop innovative social organizations and new and better ways to be human.

The effort to use indigenous knowledges to induce cognitive change and to rethink modernist social studies will be a difficult struggle. Western modernist psychology has consistently been dismissive of non-Western cognitive abilities and cultural expressions. In the United States, the school curriculum has typically consisted of Western literature, Western history, Western economic theory, and Western religious value, all grounded on a Cartesian epistemology of disciplinary fragmentation and scientific "truth." Teacher education programs don't often study this epistemological dynamic, not to mention indigenous knowledges and cognitive strategies. Since indigenous knowledge is unknown to many Western educators, democratic social studies teachers and critically grounded psychologists will have to become researchers of indigenous knowledges—cognitive detectives. In addition to researching indigenous knowledge and the sociocognitive issues that surround it in general, democratic social studies teachers must seek out and analyze the indigenous knowledges surrounding their schools.

As democratic social studies educators engage students in the historical development of ideas in any field of study, they can bring in indigenous perspectives to show students that ways of understanding particular phenomena can be different, that intellectual progress can take diverse directions, and that different perspectives can create a critical consciousness that single perspectives cannot. Such a consciousness can change university, secondary, and elementary social studies curricula in unprecedented ways. Indigenously informed curricula and cognitive theories not only can change education at the macrolevel, but they hold profound implications at the microlevel of everyday social studies teaching practice as well. An awareness of these indigenous dynamics helps teachers adapt programs to the special needs of local cultural settings or specific students. Social studies educators operating in this manner become far more aware of the relationships between the purposes of their teaching and the interests, needs, problems, and unique cognitive talents of their local community. Such an awareness allows for educational innovations and cognitive growth unthought of by most professional educators and educational psychologists.

New emancipatory forms of cognition and consciousness are formed by the critical juxtapositioning of indigenous ways of seeing with Western logic. The relationship between these different traditions holds profound cognitive and educational insights. A democratic social studies deploys the notion of relationship not only in this context but in a plethora of settings to gain new insights into critical thinking and higher-order ways of seeing. In an ontological (having to do with what it means to be human, to exist) sense indigenously informed critical social studies teachers understand that life itself may have less to do with the parts of a living thing than with patterns of information, the "dance" of the living process, the "no-thing" of the relationship between the parts. In this framework, "human being" is connected to relationships between the internal parts of humanness, between humans and the physical universe, between men and women and the social and political context, and between individuals and other human beings (O'Sullivan, 1999). In this ontology of relationship, a critical democratic concept of human connectedness opens previously unimaginable cognitive possibilities. Our politics of skepticism metamorphisizes into an education and a psychology of hope.

THE POWER OF A CRITICALLY GUIDED SOCIAL STUDIES

These critical theoretical dynamics are powerful. They can be used by democratic social studies teachers to change their understanding of the purpose of schools in a democratic society in general and the teaching of social studies in particular. Before anyone argues that social studies students have enough trouble learning the relatively simple basics of social studies (whatever they may be, I'm not sure) without adding the complexity of critical theory, a few points are in order. Over the past few decades, I have observed countless students who, according to their teachers, were unable to learn even the most basic educational skills. I have watched these students struggle in social studies class, unable to finish simple assignment or answer the most obvious rote-based questions. Once they left school, however, they seemed to morph into different beings. In out-of-school activities in which they were interested, they performed sophisticated and creative tasks that far and away surpassed the cognitive skills required by simple social studies drill-and-recite lessons.

The point here is that we need to tap into these interests. There is no reason why the field of social studies should not be one of the most exciting and provocative domains of a student's life. Our charge as critical democratic social studies teachers is to understand the critical principles laid out here and connect them to the lives and passions of students. It is absolutely amazing what motivated social studies students with a democratic vision and a critical sense of purpose can accomplish. Included in this accomplishment is an improved ability in important basic skills of reading, writing, and thinking. In addition to these necessary skills students will gain a sophisticated view of the purpose of social studies.

Without this critical perspective, teachers and students are often rudderless, operating without the guidance of any purpose, holding no larger understanding of their respective roles, and merely surviving a day-to-day battle between adversaries. Tests become battlefields where students play the memory game, attempting to succeed by outflanking their teachers by whatever method necessary. The idea that the value of learning may transcend such models of conflict is rarely discussed. The existence of alternative ways of approaching learning is rarely imagined. Those alternative ways of conceptualizing what social studies can become is what I am interested in stimulating in *Getting Beyond the Facts*. I hope you can find that it speaks to your passions and personal goals.

Chapter  7

Developing a Twenty-First Century Democratic Social Education: Critical Tradition, Cultural Pedagogy, and the Construction of Identity

Most of us by now understand that we live in a new era. Many of you will probably agree that this new era—the postmodern condition, hyperreality—demands a new form of social studies education. In Chapter 7 I will use the term "social education." I do not mean to confuse the reader with this term; indeed, it intersects at almost every point with social studies education. As I am using it here, social education is a more general term that involves the overarching relationship between the social domain and the life of the individual. In this context, social studies education is a more specific branch of social education, typically designating consciously designed in-school and larger cultural pedagogies. Social education refers more to the always present relationship between the social and individual. In the critical democratic version of social studies presented in *Getting Beyond the Facts*, social education is always an important concern of social studies teachers.

Drawing on the work of social analysts, Heinz Sünker and Philip Wexler, Chapter 7 maintains that understanding this relationship between the social domain and the life of the individual is necessary to social action, civic contribution, and successful teaching of a critical democratic social studies. In order to begin a rigorous analysis of social education—the social, the individual, and the relationship that connects them—an appreciation of the realms of critical social and educational theoretical traditions, culture and the forces that are changing it, and identity and the increasingly complex ways in which it is being shaped is necessary.

The attempt to make sense of contemporary culture and identity formation is enhanced by an appreciation of the critical social theoretical tradition as delineated in Chapter 6. Such an analytic, systematic approach has been too often missing in previous analyses of social education and social studies education. My goal here is to conceive a social education that cultivates a profound intellectual ability to acquire, analyze, and produce both self-knowledge and social knowledge. Grounded by such knowledge and scholarly facility, individuals would be equipped to participate in the democratic process as committed and informed citizens. A basic assumption in this civic context involves the belief that, in terms of a democratic social education, Western public life and public education have failed. As maintained earlier, corporations and other power wielders have gained increasing control over the production and flow of information. Here, public consciousness is aligned in a complex and never completely successful process with the interests of power.

One of the most important goals of public life over the last few decades has been the cultivation of more and more social obedience and less democracy. The effort to win the consent of the public (hegemony), via appeals to both logic and affect, for privatization projects that may not be in the public's best interests has been frightenly successful. In the same context, and driven by many of the same forces of power, public schooling has failed to promote a rigorous, democratic social education. Operating in the shadow of Frankfurt School critical social theorist, Theodor Adorno, we reference his notion of "half-education" in which he described the way mainstream education perpetuates students' alienation from knowledge of the social and the self. In this process, the possibility of agency, of self-direction, is lost in a sea of social confusion (Sünker, 1994b). To confront this alienation, social analysts must provide specific examples of formal and informal educational programs that promote a progressive social education that fights alienation. Understanding the affective dimensions of these programs, social educators/social studies teachers analyze why students and other individuals are emotionally invested in specific programs, why energy is produced and absorbed by participants, and why the disposition to imagine and create new projects is cultivated in some programs and not in others.

THE FAILURE OF SCHOOL-BASED SOCIAL EDUCATION

The assumption that much school-based social education has failed involves the understanding that few schools conceive of their role as a training ground for democratic citizenship. The public role of social education in many schools has been undermined by a private corporate view of the role of education. In addition to its role as supplier of regulated labor to the economy, schools in this privatized view have come to be seen as commodities, subject to the dictates of the free market. In this milieu, students are transformed from citizens into consumers, capable of being bought and sold. The logic of this right-wing social reeducation involves the replacement of government service agencies with private corporate services, the redistribution of wealth from the poor to the wealthy, and the construction of a private market system that promotes the values of isolated individualism, self-help, corporate management, and consumerism in lieu of public ethics and economic democracy. Thus, the new social education being taught in Western schools often involves a sanctification of the private sphere in a way that helps consolidate the power of corporations. In this context, the freedom of the corporation to redefine social and educational life in ways that serve its financial interests is expanded.

This conservative reeducation project has been difficult for progressive social educators to counter because it has been adeptly couched in the language of public improvement and democratic virtue. The public sphere has failed, the apostles of privatization proclaim. The private market is a much more effective mechanism in the effort to achieve socioeconomic improvement. Since market forces govern the world, students, citizens, and social education itself must learn to adapt to this reality. A key element of this conservative social education involves this adaptation, the attempt to promote a market philosophy. Corporations now sponsor schools or enter into school-business partnerships. Upon analysis, one begins to perceive a pattern in the lessons taught to students in these corporate curricula of privatized social education. The new social education is grounded on a set of free market goals. Schools are expected to graduate students who will help corporations: 1) increase worker output for the same wages; 2) reduce labor turnover; 3) decrease conflict between management and workers; 4) convince citizens that labor and management share the same goals; and 5) create a workforce loyal to the company. I enter the conversation about social education with these realities in mind.

This political process of privatization is a universal social education taking place on a daily basis in the information environment of twenty-first century Western society (Sünker, 1994b). In contemporary Western societies, social education occurs both in and outside of schools in a variety of social and cultural venues. Thus, our notion of social education takes into account the changing social conditions of an electronically mediated society, especially the new conditions under which information is produced. In this context, an imaginative social education analyzes the fact that it transpires at the intersection of the political economy and the culture. Understanding these dynamics, an important aspect of a democratic social education is its analytic project, a mapping of the ways political meanings are made in both schools and the social locales previously referenced. Here social educational analysis begins the important task of interpreting how domination takes place on the contemporary political economic, informational landscape (Sünker, 1994b). In an interpretive sense, our analytical social education becomes a holographic (a dynamic where the whole is contained in all of its parts) hermeneutics (the art of interpretation) that analyzes the ways the ideologies produced by sociopolitical structures (the whole) embed themselves in the individual (the part). What is the relationship between macropower and the subjectivity of individual human beings?

SOCIAL EDUCATION:
THE RELATIONSHIP BETWEEN THE INDIVIDUAL AND SOCIETY

This intersection of the social and the individual is key to my conception of a critical social education. Indeed, as critical social educational analysis reintegrates the political, the economic, and the cultural on the new historical plane of the globalized society of the twenty-first century, we work to rethink and reassert the importance of subjectivity (pertaining to the domain of personhood, consciousness) in this context. In many ways, such a move is controversial in the critical tradition, as numerous social analysts criticize—often for good reason—the contemporary concern with individualism, self-actualization, and identity politics. Understanding the problems inherent within these obsessions, I still believe that there are emancipatory possibilities embedded within this emphasis on self-development. Drawing upon the work of Philip

Wexler (1997), a key dynamic in this context involves the effort to extract such possibilities and use them to inform a democratic concept of social education.

Since social education takes place in a variety of domains, study is demanded of not only the social (macro-) level and the individual (micro-) level but the institutional (meso-) level as well. In this integrative approach, the interactions of these three levels in the process of social education, the ways they operate in the construction of the social and individual, are significant. In such analysis, these multilevel concerns induce social/social studies educators to avoid one-sided approaches of any variety to social education. For example, I am concerned with not only the social construction of the individual's knowledge but also with the individual's responsibility for his or her actions. This attention to individual volition is often missing from some articulations of social education—much to their detriment. This notion of individual volition must be carefully reconsidered in light of liberal celebrations of individual freedom and deterministic (Marxist, for example) laments of a totalized domination (Grossberg, 1992, 1995). Individuals frequently defeat the power of capital, white supremacy, and patriarchy; at the same time, however, the structures of oppression too often induce individuals to acquiesce to dominant power's ways of viewing the world.

Obviously, there is nothing simplistic about social education. How does one get across an understanding of the complementarity of the self-directed (autonomous) and the social individual? Such a complementarity refuses the collapse of the social and the collapse of the individual, as it seeks a third way. This third-way social education, rather than avoiding, embraces the complexity of the topic. It addresses head-on the contradictions inherent in the interaction of autonomy and belonging. The essence of this notion of social education involves the nature of the relationship between independence and interaction. The sociability of the individual within this complex relationship involves much more than just understanding the social context. While an appreciation of context is necessary, this articulation of social education involves the development of individual human senses. In this context, Wexler's concept of "revitalization," emanating from the concern with spirituality in contemporary society, is added to the critical theoretical mix. A critical democratic social education takes Wexler's revitalization seriously, analyzing its problems and potentialities in relation to our larger concerns with equity and justice. The possibilities for social change and self-transformation offered by revitalization are compelling in this context.

APPROACHING SOCIAL EDUCATION FROM THREE DIRECTIONS

The reconceptualized social education offered here can be drawn on by critical democratic social studies teachers. Informed by the critical tradition as articulated by German social analyst Heinz Sünker, the reconstruction of individual identity as developed by Philip Wexler, and my own concerns with cultural pedagogy, a new concept of social education for hyperreality emerges.

Tradition

Heinz Sünker (1994a, 1994b, 1998) maintains that education is one social practice connected to and mediated by other social practices; in this context, he asks what is good in a good upbringing of youth. Utilizing German theorists from the Frankfurt School as well as Haydorn and Theunissen, a critical canon of social education is constructed. This body of work takes seriously one's contribution to the good life as a member of society, a contribution based on an awareness of the nature of the social construction of both consciousness and the social fabric. Such a canon understands the importance of intersubjectivity (relations of various individuals, interpersonal interaction) in the construction of subjectivity. In this context, historical educational efforts to act on such understandings are analyzed. Questions are asked about the reasons for their failures and successes and their relevance for contemporary practice. To better answer these questions Sünker (1994b) introduces Heydorn's articulation of Bildung, focusing on its concern with emancipation, maturity, and self-determination.

The tradition of Bildung is especially important to social education in its interest in the production of subjectivity in the context of intersubjective relations. Sünker advocates the relevance of Bildung to contemporary social education via his emphasis of two dimensions: 1) the mediating processes between the individual and society; and 2) the processes involved with the construction of the subjectivity of the individual. In this way, Bildung transcends education's effort to normalize the individual so as to adjust him or her to the existing social order. Rejecting bourgeois liberalism's effort to form the individual without referencing extant social conditions, *Bildung* is interested in individual development in the context of relational consciousness and the development of social competencies. In this context, *Bildung* mediates materialist (political economic) understandings of the world and concerns with everyday life—in the process, connecting the macro to the micro. In this theoretical context, learning is conceived as an activity taking place with one eye on education and the other on democracy. The concept of *Bildung* insists that learning in a social education always be a part of a larger democratic struggle.

With our social education canon firmly grounded on a knowledge of *Bildung*, we move to other traditions for insights into our conception. Our transformative model of social education is also informed by Philip Wexler's efforts to reclaim ancient knowledges abandoned since the European Enlightenment and the birth of Cartesianism in the seventeenth and eighteenth centuries. If the modern era is ending (or at least changing), the problems we are called on to solve are mutating as well. As these social/cultural/political changes have occurred, Wexler points out the way religion has returned to the forefront of social practice and cultural consciousness. Moving in different directions simultaneously, religion moves backward, before modernity, and forward, past postmodernity, to provide differing grounds for ways of seeing and acting. Wexler warns progressives and critical theorists not to reject precipitously such religious insights in a materialist knee-jerk presumption of religion as merely dominant ideology. Through the theological window, social educators can explore premodern modes of sacralization and mystical insights. Carefully avoiding commodified and distorted "New Age" articulations of these traditions, Wexler views them through the lenses of an exacting and rigorous critical sociological tradition. In his hands, new applications for such knowledge emerge.

Picking up on Wexler's theoretical move, I contribute to the canon of a transformative social education by bringing subjugated and indigenous knowledges to the pedagogical table. Derived from dangerous memories of history that have been suppressed and information that has been disqualified by social and academic gatekeepers, subjugated knowledges play an important role in a transformative social education. Through the conscious cultivation of these low-ranking knowledges, alternative democratic and emancipatory visions of society, politics, cognition, and social education are possible. The subjugated knowledge of Africans, indigenous peoples from around the world, working-class people and many other groups have contested the dominant culture's view of reality. At the very least, subjugated knowledges induce students operating within mainstream schools and society that there are multiple perspectives on all issues. A social education that includes subjugated ways of seeing teaches a lesson on the complexities of knowledge production and how this process shapes our view of ourselves and the world around us.

Individuals from dominant social formations have rarely understood (or cared to understand) how they look to marginalized others. As a result, women often make sense of men's image of women better than men understand women's view of men; individuals from Africa, or with African heritages, understand the motivations of white people better than the reverse; and low-status workers figure out how they are seen by their managers more clearly than the managers understand how they appear to workers. Obviously, such insights provide social educators and their students with a very different view of the world and the processes that shape it. Social educators who employ such subjugated viewpoints become transformative agents who alert the community to its hidden features, its submerged memories, and in the process, help specific individuals to name their oppression or possibly understand their complicity in oppression.

In this context, transformative social educators search out specific forms of subjugated insights, such as indigenous knowledges. Indigenous knowledges are special forms of subjugated knowledges that are local, life-experience-based and non–Western-science-produced. Such knowledges are transmitted over time by individuals from a particular geographical or cultural locality. Only now at the beginning of the new millennium, are European peoples just starting to appreciate the value of indigenous knowledges about health, medicine, agriculture, philosophy, ecology, and education. Traditionally, these have been the very types of knowledges Western social education tried to discredit and eradicate. A transformative social education works hard to save such knowledges, which are, unfortunately, rapidly disappearing from the face of the earth. Democratic social studies teachers have much to learn from this feature of social education.

Culture

This section focuses on the expanding role of the cultural realm in the production of social education in the first decade of the twenty-first century. If a new era is dawning, then social educators must search for the new places in which new ways that social education is taking place. The emergence of a new role, an expanded political and educational function, for culture is a cardinal feature of the new social condition. The contemporary era confronts social educators with new contradictions, new ways of thwarting emancipation. As previously discussed, in this new era, cultural capital has reorganized itself in ways that make it more flexible, innovative, and powerful. New technological and organizational developments have allowed capital greater access to both the world at large and human consciousness in particular. Reorganized capital has embraced an aesthetic that celebrates difference, ephemerality, spectacle, and fashion. In this observation, we uncover the central concern of the cultural realm in this chapter: this new flexible aesthetic of capital gains its hegemonic force from its ability to commodify the cultural realm. Thus, the cultural domain emerges as a central political venue, a place where ideological consciousness is constructed, a new locale for social education.

Thus, an indispensable lesson is learned by contemporary critical social educators: everyday life takes place on a new ideological template—a semiotic (concerned with signs, signifiers, and symbols that shape meaning making) matrix shaped in part by corporate-produced images. A new social education is produced by capital that is designed to regulate the population, as affectively charged consumers operating in a privatized domain lose consciousness of what used to be called the public sphere. This privatized domain is both globalized and decentralized/localized at the same time, distorting traditional concepts of space and time. The past is commodified, turning public memory into Disney's Frontierland—a powerful social educational venue, I might add. In this context, time is rearticulated and everyday life becomes an eternal present. Without critical intervention, the public space deteriorates and critical consciousness is erased. The disorientation the informational overload of the new cultural condition induces moves individuals to seek more expert help, more therapeutic involvement, in their everyday affairs. In the HBO series, *The Sopranos*, for example, Tony, the Mafioso leader, is so distraught and confused by changing cultural conditions that he seeks psychological therapy and is prescribed Prozac™ for his depression. The same theme is found in the movie *Analyze This*, as mobster Robert DeNiro seeks counseling from psychologist Billy Crystal.

Even those who pride themselves as self-sufficient outlaws cannot escape the effects of cultural disequalibrium. Working in the realm of information control and the production of pleasure, capital embeds pos-itive images of itself at the deepest levels of our subconscious. Many come to associate the "good things of life" and happiness with the priva-tized realm of consumption. As powerful as crime boss Tony Soprano may be, for example, he cannot get his own son's attention while the boy plays his Nintendo video game. Indeed, pleasure is a powerful social edu-cator, and the pleasure produced by capital teaches a very conservative political (social educational) lesson: since corporations produce pleasure we should align our interests with them. In this way our a "affect" is organized in the service of capital: lower corporate taxes, better business climates, equation of the corporate bottom line with social well-being, larger executive salaries, lower labor costs, fewer environmental regula-tions, to name just a few. Hegemony in this new context operates where affect and politics intersect: the cultural realm (Grossberg, 1992, 1995). The revolutionary feature of this repressive, capital-driven social educa-tion is that culture shapes the political. Progressives have failed to appre-ciate the reality, not to mention its dramatic impact on the shaping of political consciousness.

Thus, transformative social educators must understand the new affective dynamics at work in the production of subjectivity. When we speak of the cultural realm, of course, a central feature of this domain involves popular culture and its relationship to power. Popular culture involves TV, movies, video games, music, Internet, shopping malls, theme parks, etc. These are the sites of a contemporary cultural pedagogy of commodification that meets people where they exist in their affective fields. As it provides fun, pleasure, good feelings, passion, and emotion, this capital-inscribed social education connects ideology to these affec-tive dynamics. In contemporary society, ideologies are effective to the degree that they can be articulated along the affective plane. Affect is complex to the degree that both pleasure and displeasure are affective responses. One's affective dislike, for example, of rap music can be inscribed ideologically with particular meanings about youth with African heritages around the world. Though complex, the power pro-duced and deployed along this affective plane is profound in its ability to shape subjectivity and ways of seeing the world.

Our vision of a transformative social education recognizes these con-temporary politico-cultural dynamics and analyzes their consequences at both the macro- and micro-levels (Sünker, 1994b). One of the most important effects of this corporate colonization of affect has involved, of course, the phenomenon of depoliticization. At the heart of this phenomenon exists a paradoxical reality: while many Westerners have invested affectively in the emerging privatization of the social order, they do not rationally buy into the political-economic policies of conservatism. In this bizarre context, individuals remain politically uncommitted and civicly inactive. Except for a significant minority of citizens on the Right, individuals have removed themselves from the political realm. I don't want to discount the importance of janitors' struggles for economic justice and protests against the World Trade Organization, but these actions are still the exceptions. In addition, the depoliticization process has produced a staggering illiteracy around political language and concepts, especially among the young. This social educational dynamic is so important that social studies teachers simply cannot do their jobs if they don't understand it.

In the electronic, mediated culture of the early twenty-first century, youth are no longer shielded from the esoteric knowledge of adulthood. Young people, in a sense, know too much to retain the idealism traditionally associated with this phase of life. In their knowledge of the world they have become jaded to the point that they know of nothing worthy of their faith outside of the intrinsic value of pleasure and affect in and of themselves. In their unshockability, many young people become emotional only about emotion—certainly not about some complex political issue. In such a culture-driven context, political discourse is reduced to "gut-level" emotion, to affective investments directly tied to self-interest. Politics becomes successful only when it is represented as "not politics." Questions of racial justice become important only when many white citizens perceive that Blacks and government leaders, via affirmative action, are taking their jobs away. Issues of social policy and public morality are irrelevant in this context: "Non-whites, aided by big government, are stealing 'our' jobs." Rational political debate is irrelevant; affirmative action is an affective issue. Effective TV campaign advertisements do not make a rational case for ending affirmative action; they depict a black hand taking a job application away from a working-class white hand. Professional political consultants chant their mantras: "Keep it on the affective plane, stupid." A transformative social education in this media-saturated context can never be the same.

Identity

After having established a canon (the critical theoretical tradition) for a transformative social education and explored the changing cultural conditions of early twenty-first century society, attention needs to be focused on questions of identity and the production of the individual. In this context, Philip Wexler (1997) maintains that the affect-centeredness of electronically mediated reality contains within it a decentered social movement that offers possibilities for emancipatory social education. There is, he contends, a mysticism that often operates affectively to revitalize those caught in the commodified information environment of the present. Just as affective measures can be used by power to hegemonize individuals and social groups, they can also be deployed by individuals to make certain things matter in ways that assert their self-direction and group solidarity by using the positive productive ability of power. Picking up on this dynamic, Wexler moves to take critical advantage of what is available on the contemporary cultural landscape. If the self is the locus of historical change in the twenty-first century, then a transformative social education must seize the opportunity to produce meaningful selves.

Aware of the politico-cultural dimensions described previously, transformative social educators study the various ways individuals protect their identities from the power flows of capital. In such defensive actions, individuals not only shield themselves from the social earthquakes shaking the cultural terrain on which they live but forge new forms of collective alliances. Examples of such actions can be found on the Internet, as individuals morph their identities and connect with a wide range of similar web surfers. In such virtual lives, traditional boundaries of self are blurred in the interactions of dematerialized beings. In the electronic informational cosmos, Wexler's recognition of a retreat to a defensive inner world becomes a central understanding of the transformative social educator. The revolution of social being is grounded on the possibilities offered by such an inward turn and the effort to reshape consciousness that accompanies it. At this important point, Sünker's *Bildung*-grounded assertion that consciousness is the central element of the educational process, new cultural technologies of consciousness construction, and Wexler's analysis of the consequences of an opportunities provided by the "inner turn" converge. In this intersection, the new social education finds its purpose and the possibility for the construction of a new critical ontology (an emancipatory way of being human). Central to this synthetic dynamic, however, is Wexler's understanding of the potentialities of neomysticism and enlivenment in the emancipatory reconstruction of consciousness and identity.

One aspect of the electronic informational culture of the contemporary era involves the emergence of a new concern with the worldview and methods of classical mysticism. Even though this mediated culture has often served to shatter identities, Wexler identifies a new power in people's minds. Moving past the Cartesian Enlightenment, the new consciousness of social being emerges around a resacralization of culture codes, the globalizing synthesis of cultural expressions that exposes the ethnocentrism of European science and epistemology, and a new historicism that reengages the premodern, the ancient, and the archaic. Revitalization of the self and the new identities it encourages take shape in this synthetic context. Directly responding to the fragmenting effects of informational hyperculture, revitalization uses imaginative power to protect the self from threats posed by informationalism in hyperreality. Fueled by these recognitions and an understanding of the traditions of critical theory and cultural studies, Wexler conceptualizes the synergy between a resacralized self-realization and a critical social education.

The emancipatory power of this synergy hinges on the articulation of these conceptual intersections and the consciousness, agency, and praxis (informed action) that emerge therein. Wexler understands that self-realization, in both its bodily and psychic expression, must transcend its roots in narcissism and plant itself firmly in the transcendent or the cosmological (pertaining to the nature of the universe as a whole) to be of benefit to a transformative social education. Employed at the sacred level, self-realization, a'la revitalization, provides a compelling strategic grounding in the struggle against the alienation of commodification and rationalization. As it embraces desire and vitality in everyday life and discerns how to use them in an emancipatory and not a manipulative way, self-realization reexamines the relationship between self and environment. A transformative social education takes advantage of this conceptual opening, drawing upon the vitality of this new individualism and connecting it to Sünker's canon and my own cultural concerns. Here self engages other in a strong union that constructs a vision for a reinvigorated critical practice.

CENTRAL FEATURES OF A NEW SOCIAL EDUCATION

In a contemporary culture that finds it increasingly difficult to mobilize itself for political action, a transformative social education must take place on uncharted social and cultural territory. In the complexity and high-speed change of hyperreality, efforts to address alienation and oppression seem somehow outside the spirit of the times. Our transformative social education must be not only conceptually compelling but sufficiently contextually aware to operate on the bizarre sociocultural landscape that confronts us in the twenty-first century. The central features of our new social education include:

1. THE DEVELOPMENT OF A SOCIO-INDIVIDUAL IMAGINATION. At the basis of our transformative social education rests the ability to imagine new forms of self-realization and social collaboration that lead to emancipatory consequences. An important aspect of these emancipatory consequences involves the rethinking of educational practice, knowledge production, and engaged forms of citizenship. These dynamics interact to help us imagine new forms of consciousness and cognition grounded on creative images of a changing life. These new forms of consciousness cannot be separated from the educational realm and the democratic effort to reframe learning as part of the struggle against multiple forms of domination. Framed in this manner, a critical social studies education plays a central role in the development of our socio-individual imagination, as it induces individuals to rethink their subjectivities in order to emphasize the role of democratic community and social justice in the process of human development. An education for socio-individual imagination becomes increasingly more important in a society torn asunder by commodified informationalism (McLaren, 1994).

2. THE RECONSTITUTION OF THE INDIVIDUAL OUTSIDE THE BOUNDARIES OF ABSTRACT INDIVIDUALISM. The reconstitution of the individual that is connected to our social education's celebration of self-realization must be articulated carefully in light of the use of the concept of individualism in the Western tradition. Our notion of self-realization is a corrective of both a critical tradition that rejects the possibilities of an authentic individuality and a market-based individualism that rejects the importance of social context. In critical communitarian-

ism, the importance of the community consistently takes precedence over the interests of the individual—a position that poses great danger to the health of the democratic impulse. In the market context, egocentrism is equated with action for the common good—in the process, creating powerful forms of regulatory power that ultimately destroy the social fabric. When our social education expresses its concern for individualism, by no means should this be interpreted as a naïve acceptance of the Cartesian notion of the "abstract individual." This individual subject is removed from the effects of complex power relations and endowed with abstract political rights that mean little when disconnected from the regulatory and disciplinary aspects of economic, social, and cultural forces.

3. THE UNDERSTANDING OF POWER AND THE ABILITY TO INTERPRET ITS EFFECTS ON THE SOCIAL AND THE INDIVIDUAL. One of the most important horizons within which social educators analyze the world and its actors involves the context of power. Transformative social educators are interested in both how power operates in the social order and the ways it works to produce subjectivity. In this context they focus on the nature of ideology and the process by which it imprints itself on consciousness, the ways hegemonic forces mobilize desire in the effort to win the public's consent to the authority of various power blocs, the means by which discursive powers shape thinking and behavior via the presences and absences of different words and concepts, and the ways that disciplines of knowledge are used to regulate individuals through a process of normalization. In this context, of course, social education studies the methods individuals and groups use to assert their agency and self-direction in relation to such power plays. The new social education is especially concerned with the complex relationship connecting individuals, groups, and power. Such an interaction never occurs around a single axis of power, and the ambiguity of the subjectivity that is produced never lends itself to simple description or facile prediction of ways of seeing or behaving. Mainstream forms of social/social studies education have consistently ignored this effort, trivializing, in the process, the role of social analysis.

4. THE PROVISION OF ALTERNATIVES TO THE ALIENATION OF THE INDIVIDUALS. A central concern of a transformative social education

involves providing an alternative to social and educational alienation. Individuals in contemporary society experience social reality mainly as a world of consumerism and not as the possibility of human relations. In a consumerist hyperreality, both young people and adults are alienated from daily life and cultural and educational capital. Such an alienation affects individuals from different social locations in divergent ways. Men and women from more dominant locales suffer an informational alienation that erases issues of power, justice, and privilege. Those from less dominant locales are denied access to institutions that provide tickets to social mobility by the use of a rhetoric of standards, excellence, and values. Via the deployment of such discursive strategies and regulatory forms, less privileged individuals are induced to blame themselves for their lack of access to various forms of capital. Such a reality can be described as a form of "second degree alienation," a state that is unconscious of the existence of alienation. In this alienated circumstance, the possibility of self-direction fades. In this context, our social education, drawing on the *Bildung* tradition, provides individuals alternatives to their alienation. Here the concepts of resacralization and enlivenment become central to the generation of empowering alternatives.

5. THE CULTIVATION OF A CRITICAL CONSCIOUSNESS THAT IS AWARE OF THE SOCIAL CONSTRUCTION OF SUBJECTIVITY. A transformative social education produces conscious individuals who are aware of their self-production and the social conditions under which they live. With this in mind, our social education is concerned not just with how individuals experience social reality but how they often operate in circumstances that they don't understand. A critical consciousness is aware of these dynamics, as it appreciates the complexity of social practices and their relationships with other practices and structures. Indeed, our social education promotes a critical consciousness of self-production that not only understands the many planes of history on which an individual operates but how subjectivity is specifically colonized on these various planes. In this context, questions of the social construction of identity are viewed through the lenses of affect and emotion. Empowered by such knowledge, individuals with a critical consciousness are able to use their insights to overcome alienation and construct social and individual relations with other social actors. If democracy is to succeed, then large numbers of individuals

need to reflect on the effects of the social on the individual. Via this consciousness-producing activity, the public space/political cultural is reconstructed (Sünker, 1994a; Wexler, 1997; Grossberg, 1992).

6. THE CONSTRUCTION OF A DEMOCRATIC COMMUNITY—BUILDING RELATIONSHIPS BETWEEN INDIVIDUALS. The development of the individual coupled with the construction of a democratic community is central to a transformative social education. Embracing a critical alterity (an awareness of difference) involving responsiveness to others, the new social education works to cultivate an intersubjectivity that develops both social consciousness and individual agency. The notion of an individual's relational existence becomes extremely important in this context as we focus attention on the power of difference in social education. Utilizing its understanding of how power relations shape individual subjectivity, a critical social education explores the power-inscribed nature of group difference. In this context, students learn how power shapes lives of privilege and oppression in ways that tear the social fabric and deny community. Students, workers, and other citizens who belong to diverse socioeconomic, racial, ethnic, and gender groups can learn much from one another if provided the space to exchange ideas and analyze mutual difficulties. As such a powerful force, difference must not simply be tolerated but cultivated as a spark to human creativity. Thus, relational existence is not only intrinsically important in a democratic society, it also holds cognitive and educational benefits for self-development. Understandings derived from the perspective of the excluded, or the culturally different, allow for an appreciation of the nature of justice, the invisibility of the process of oppression, and the difference that highlights our own social construction as human beings.

7. THE RECONCEPTUALIZATION OF REASON—UNDERSTANDING THAT RELATIONAL EXISTENCE APPLIES NOT ONLY TO HUMAN BEINGS BUT CONCEPTS AS WELL. Drawing upon its critical roots, the new social education understands the irrationality of what has sometimes passed for reason in the post-Enlightenment history of Western societies. Thus, an important aspect of our social education involves the reconstruction of reason. Such a process begins with the formulation of a relational reason. A relational reason understands conventional reason's propensity for conceptual fragmentation and narrow focus

on abstraction outside of a lived context. The point here is not to reject rationality but to appreciate the limits of its conventional articulation in light of its relationship to power. Such a turn investigates various rationalities from the subjugated to the ancient, as it analyzes the importance of the irrational and arational in social affairs. Such alternative ways of thinking are reappropriated via the realization of conventional decontextualization: individuals are separated from the culture, schools from society, and abstract rights from power. Our transformative social education critiques Cartesian Enlightenment reason's tendency to view an entity as a thing-in-itself. All things are a part of a larger interactive dynamics, interrelationships that provide meaning when brought to the analytical table. Indeed, our social education finds this relational reason so important, so potentially transformative, that we see the interaction between concepts as a living process. These relational dynamics permeate all aspects of not only our social education but critical consciousness itself.

8. THE PRODUCTION OF SOCIAL SKILLS NECESSARY TO ACTIVE PARTICIPATION IN THE DEMOCRATIC COMMUNITY. As a result of a transformational social education, social studies students will gain the ability to act in the role of democratic citizens. Studying the political in relation to self-development, socially educated individuals begin to conceptualize the activities of social life. Viewing their social actions through the lenses of not only the political but the economic, the cultural, and the psychological, individuals (not just students) analyze the forces that produce apathy and passivity. In this manner, the new social education comes to embody the process of democratization, the continuing effort to have input into civic life. As individuals of all stripes, ages, and backgrounds in contemporary hyperreality search for an identity, social education provides them an affective social and individual vision in which to invest. Making connections between the political, the economic, the cultural, the psychological, and the educational, individuals gain insight into what is and what could be as well as the disposition to act. Thus, as political agency is cultivated, our social education turns pedagogy into a democratic social politics. Once again, social consciousness and the valorization of the individual come together to produce an emancipatory synergy.

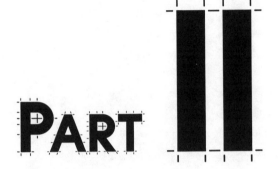

PART II

Social Studies Reform: Epistemology and Knowledge Work

Chapter

Social Studies Teachers as Scholars: From the Rationalized Methods Class to the Epistemology of Complexity

The long maligned methods course has served as a symbol of the shallowness of teacher education in the minds of critics of colleges of education both past and present. This chapter contends that, if the methods course is to gain respectability, it must contribute to the scholarly study of education. It must transcend the limitations imposed by an exclusive preoccupation with "how-to-ism." It must reach for the higher values of analysis and synthesis in relating the Great Questions of Education to the important questions of "how to."

Methods-dominated teacher education is perceived to lack an intellectual tradition. The accusation is tragically unfair to the best and brightest methodologists who offer stimulating and creative experiences for prospective teachers. Too often, however, the indictment accurately hits the mark. In these unfortunate cases, the quest to challenge teacher education students to think and to study systematically the complexities of the educational process takes a back seat to the attempt to fit the students to the mundane expectations of the teaching workplace—so-called "practical" vocational teacher training.

The burden of the methods class is to provoke prospective teachers to think in terms of the larger purpose of a specific subject matter, to contemplate a body of knowledge as it relates to the logic of the curriculum, to consider what aspects of a discipline speak to the needs of a particular student, to analyze the relationship of the topics covered to the concerns of the social context in which one's teaching takes place, and to formulate ways that such knowledge and skills may be effectively imparted. No simple task, we all agree?! An effective social studies methods teacher is certainly a valuable and special scholar. As we examine the culture of many schools and the nature of formal and informal in-service teacher education, it becomes apparent that the methods class may be the last opportunity many social studies teachers have to analyze the teaching process in these ways. The formal and informal modes of in-service teacher education offer numerous opportunities to review curricular materials, to consider classroom management strategies, and to size up various teaching techniques. Questions of purpose or contextual analysis of teacher education are infrequently studied in on-the-job learning situations.

THE MEANING OF METHOD

We have never clarified what exactly we mean by the word "method" in teacher education. Method can be used to refer to two different processes: 1) method as information delivery and 2) method as information approach. Method as information delivery refers to techniques and strategies of imparting knowledge and skills to students; method as information approach refers to ways of understanding, interpreting or making sense of a body of knowledge. A teacher must understand the significance of a body of information before he or she can intelligently impart it to students. Thus, both method as information delivery and method as information approach are necessary components in the study of educational methods. An examination of the distinction between these two meanings of method is needed.

When we use the words "scientific method," "historical method," "quantitative" or "qualitative method," we are referring to method as information approach. Method as information approach, in other words, concerns the way we go about exploring the world. It is our map in the search for knowledge. Method as information approach involves the set of logical steps that directs an inquiry. In different situations, different methods of inquiry will be used. As Aristotle put it, what we are trying to find out determines how we make the attempt (Sherman, Webb, & Andrews, 1984). Thus, when we use the phrase "method as information approach" we are referring to how we organize our attempt to find out something.

As we employ our method of information approach, we not only discover bits of data but we organize them, order them, note the connections between them, and ascertain their significance in our attempt to understand ourselves and the world. As we subject data to such analysis we make it "teachable." In other words, our method of information approach is necessary first step to the critical democratic teaching process. We do not merely accept data handed to us; teaching is a more critical process.

Method as information delivery involves transmitting knowledge to individuals in a manner appropriate to their needs and their backgrounds. We often begin our study of method as information delivery with an examination of standard procedures recognized as valid. Next, we ask questions why such recognized methods of delivering information to students work or don't work. Knowledge of these standard procedures and their applications constitutes the study of what could be called the general method of information delivery. Contrary to what has often been the case in the teaching methods of information delivery, there is an important distinction between a general method and a prescribed rule. A prescribed rule is an exact guide; a general method is inexact. A general method demands no specified action; it serves merely to inform one about the nature of the means and ends of teaching. In other words, a general method seeks to make an individual more intelligent about the teaching task. A prescribed rule attempts to induce conformity to orders externally imposed. Social studies teacher educators, especially administrators involved with in-service teacher education, need to take note of this distinction. As John Dewey wrote in 1916: "General methods are worth or of harm as they make a teacher's reaction more intelligent or as they induce a person to dispense with exercise of his own judgment" (p. 172).

To be effective, teachers must understand both types of method. The critical democratic social studies teacher must possess the ability to produce and arrange subject matter in a manner meaningful and contextually significant for the learner. He or she must be able to employ a specific body of knowledge for a specific end or goal. The great teachers of the past have based their actions on understanding both meanings of method. It is essential that contemporary social studies methods courses adopt this bidimensional approach.

ISOLATED TECHNIQUE

In order to teach method as both information delivery and information approach, methods professors must concern themselves with the ability to analyze subject matter and produce knowledge. How can we possibly study ways of approaching information and delivering information if we don't possess a sophisticated grounding in the production of the information involved? Methods classes must never be guilty of teaching isolated technique at the expense of a systematic study of the educational process. The separation of method from subject matter begins as we watch how a child learns. We gradually isolate the special conditions which seem to promote the most productive learning. We then attempt to recreate those same conditions for other children; this constitutes our new method of teaching. Too often, we take this new method and apply it to different children with different backgrounds and interests who are learning different subjects for different purposes. We soon discover that the method may hold little relevance in these new situations.

When we teach our method to prospective teachers, we remove it from the context in which it worked. Successful methods must be based around concrete experiences of particular teachers with their particular personalities and strengths teaching a particular subject matter to students with particular needs and interests. General observation of what works can be viewed as experiences to be studied and considered but not as authoritative guidelines. Teachers must develop their own methods based on their own intelligent observations of their particular circumstances. Only then, do methods relate to the lived world; only then, can method and subject matter remain unified; only then, can methods avoid being reduced to mechanical routine.

To escape modernist teacher training as mere mechanical techniques of information delivery, methods classes must avoid the trap of contextual isolation. To be meaningful methods of information delivery and information approach must be studied within a social context. Isolate method from subject matter and teaching context, and, presto, we have the nonconceptual methods class discussed in Chapter 2. It is the nonconceptual methods class that is subjected to endless vilification by the critics of colleges of education. Marked by an absence of analysis and conceptualism, such classes present easy targets for critics of teacher education. Indeed, analytical questions about the nature of the curriculum are rarely posed in such classes. Questions concerning origins of practices, the implicit assumptions underlying certain language used in the discipline, the connections between teaching and larger sociopolitical issues, and the purposes of education in a democratic society are almost always ignored.

Many critics of modern teacher education argue that when this non-conceptual teacher education is combined with the structure of the modern bureaucratic, accountability-based school, teachers have less opportunity to control the planning of their own work (Apple, 1983). As previously discussed, teachers, more and more, are becoming the mere executors, not the conceptualizers, of teaching. In many situations, teacher administrators and supervisors, along with the authors of textbooks and curriculum guides, devise educational plans; teachers merely see that these plans are carried out to specifications. In this situation, teachers often come to internalize their reduced role. They begin to demand teacher education classes and in-service programs that are crudely practical and nonconceptual. Such teachers attempt to avoid what they call "theory," as they seek out materials which can be plugged into their classes on Monday morning. They adopt a nonconceptual ethic which glorifies paint-by-numbers education and denigrates and even ridicules those who seek to understand method in relation to educational purpose as "impractical."

Teacher educators are under great pressure to cater to those teachers who have internalized their role as the mere executors of someone else's plans. Methods professors who refuse to offer instant recipes for how to operate a classroom (we might call it TV-dinner pedagogy) are rarely winners of professional popularity contests. Education courses and in-service programs are often judged by the sheer bulk of the materials teachers can cart away, not by the conceptual base they help teachers build. The teacher, as mere executor, expects the teacher educator to set up his or her classroom and supply all necessary equipment. Teaching from this perspective is viewed as similar to running a Pizza Hut. Learn the standardized managerial system and count on executives to provide the recipe, the dough, the olive oil, tomato sauce, toppings, mozzarella cheese, and pizza ovens. Now we're ready to make pizzas; and we'll make them the same way whether we're in South Philadelphia, Grand Forks, or Baton Rouge. We're not chefs—we're laborers.

This TV-dinner methods pedagogy is just one aspect of technically oriented, rationalized, modernist teacher education. Course work that does not impart "how to" information is deemed impractical, superfluous, or too theoretical. Schools-as-they-are, are taken as natural; the role of teacher education is simply to fit the neophytes to them. Explorations of inscribed political meanings, even in social studies methods classes designed to teach teachers how to teach political science, are deemed irrelevant. The social education concerns of the relation of individual to larger social domain discussed in Chapter 7 are out of place in the rationalized methods course. Indeed, rarely considered in the first decade of the twenty-first century are buzz phrases such as "high standards," "educational excellence," or "quality education." Upon interrogation, for example, we often find that such terms have definite class and race dimensions, as poor or minority-dominated schools are rarely deemed excellent. Without such forms of analysis, teachers too often are taught to simply follow orders, to unquestioningly take a predetermined body of information and transfer it to students via a variety of strategies (Ross, 1988; Britzman, 1991; Greene, 1986, 1995; Weil & Anderson, 2000; Hursh & Ross, 2000).

It is particularly disturbing that many teacher education programs maintain a virtual silence on the influence of the sociocultural patterns that shape the thinking of teachers. Because Cartesian-Newtonian lenses focus only on the explicit level of school life—that which can be observed and measured—the less obvious cultural dimensions are ignored (Bowers & Flinders, 1990). What is interesting in this context is the unabashed rejection by some technical educators of the importance of studying the cultural dynamics of education. Daniel Duke (1979) argues, for example, that cultural contextualization is not simply superfluous to the education of teachers, it is actually dangerous. When we attempt to explain social behavior in terms of cultural influences, he contends, we depersonalize blame. Individual students guilty of misbehavior are released from responsibility for their actions by those who value culturally grounded analysis. Duke concludes that teacher professionalism would be better protected by dismissing context and recognizing the supremacy of individualism.

Such a naïve view ignores the ways individual identity is structured. Our subjectivities are formed by the cultural forces of race, class, gender, and place; the influence of such factors is difficult to address as they construct boundaries and possibilities in our various relations. They help shape the kinds of friends we have, the work we do, and the mates we choose. Our interactions with our families, churches, peer groups, workplaces, and, of course, schools help shape our identities. If these forces were not enough, our consciousness is constructed by our involvement with changing technologies and the mass media and popular culture they help produce.

Embedded within the naïve notion of individualism is a historical amnesia, an atemporality. Duke's individuals, for example, have no connections with the past; they live in a freeze-frame of the present. The school in this conception is jerked out of history. What exists always has been, as school cannot be seen as an evolving institution that grows and falters through the years. We have no way of understanding the motivations of individuals or the purposes of school. We are incapable of self-analysis, for we have no grounding that empowers us to see where we originated. In the same way, we are incapable of critical analysis of school purpose, for we have no idea why schools do the things that they do. This is the condition under which much social studies teacher education takes place.

Peter McLaren (1991) extends this theme, arguing that, since teacher education has been mired in the Cartesian language of efficiency and the logic of management techniques and accountability schemes, it is not surprising that cultural questions have been ignored. Technically oriented teacher education programs don't study the power dimensions of tracking students into college bound or vocationally bound curricula. Higher status is accorded the college-bound track. This track reaches a knowledge more abstract and theoretical than the vocational track. A white student from an affluent home has less trouble with such material than a minority student from an economically disadvantaged home, because, in the affluent home, such knowledge is common in the linguistic and social dimensions of everyday life. When teachers fail to study such sociopolitical aspects of schooling, they tend to blame the victims of power inequalities for their failings. Without empathy, the vicious cycle of economic disadvantage and educational disenfranchisement continues uninterrupted.

Teacher education, both pre-service and in-service, is saturated with cognitive experiences that encourage conservative, individualistic, competitive, and decontextualized tendencies in the thinking of teachers. Prospective teachers encounter few experiences that challenge the status quo in schools. Given the way research is conducted in education, the knowledge base produced perpetuates that which is (Zeuli & Bachmann, 1986; Floden & Klinzing, 1990). As long as teacher educators believe that novice survival is a cardinal goal of professional education and that teachers learn to teach best by engaging in apprenticelike experiences, little substantive change will occur. Teacher education as apprenticeship induces neophytes to model the master teacher, rendering the study of teaching less essential than "correct" performance based on the master teacher's opinion and local standards within a particular school. The conformity encouraged results in a uniformity of thought, a mechanistic approach to the profession, and an inability to critically intervene in the world of school practice (Cruickshank, 1987; Britzman, 1991).

Students often enter the college of education with a set of conservative expectations and predispositions. They want to become teachers like the ones they've had or known, and they expect to teach students just like the ones who were their friends and associates in school. More often than students in other fields, they attend colleges close to their homes and desire to teach in their home states. Because of these and other factors, their acculturation into the profession marks little break with their pasts, their childhood values. Thus, teacher education students tend not to be seekers of alternative ways of seeing; they often are not especially interested in finding new lenses through which to conceptualize knowledge and pedagogy. Instead, they walk into classes searching for recipes for information delivery and classroom discipline. Questions of purpose, context, and power are alien, irrelevant. What does such information have to do with teaching?, they ask (Zeuli & Bachmann, 1986).

At least moderately successful in schools, prospective teachers are hard-pressed to forget the conventional educational practices that worked well for them. Thus, they feel that schools are all right as they are; with a few practice attempts out in the field and a few strategies to help with discipline, everything will be fine. The culture of passivity works at all levels: It certainly worked for the prospective teachers when they were elementary and secondary students; there is no reason to believe that listening well and following directions literally won't work now.

Questioning, interpretation, and intellectual flexibility rest at the core of what university faculty term essential cognitive acts. Rationalistic and technicist-oriented teacher educators tend not to appreciate these traditional academic values. Indeed, it is too often the case that teacher educators who work the closest to schools and to student and practicing teachers find themselves isolated from the more traditional culture of academia. Theirs is often a terrain of eight-to-five, punch-clock hours, little professional reading, ideological naivete, limited interpretative practice, and minimal analysis of the professional world. The logic of such working conditions emphasizes something quite unlike interpretive and critical thinking. There is an undertow in such an environment, an unseen tendency to surrender to the given, to view existing institutional arrangements as objective realities. Without the catalyst of interpretation, of an intellectually active analytical community, pronouncements tend to speak at a literal level; they speak "for themselves." Without an analytical view of the everyday and of institutional requirements and activities, thought is fragmented and conceptual synthesis is blocked. Indeed, our relationship to knowledge is severed. As a result, our role as participants in social and institutional life is unexamined and our power to anticipate the consequences of social actions is devoured (Zeuli and Bachmann, 1986; Greene, 1988; Britzman, 1991).

Jesse Goodman (1986) studied the effects of this modernist teacher education culture on student teachers. Even those students who entered practice teaching with beliefs in a teacher's responsibility to help determine curriculum, the inadvisability of emphasizing fragmented skills over the interpretation of social content, the value of curricular integration, the obligation to use learning activities to promote critical thinking, and the sanctity of creativity found themselves far more concerned with rationalistic school objectives by the end of their experience. Karen, one of the students Goodman observed, created an original, progressive unit on occupations at the beginning of her social studies student teaching. After a few week of immersion in the schools, she discarded the unit. Almost all of her lessons, Goodman tells us, came point-by-point from the teacher's guides. Karen became more and more concerned with using the textbooks effectively; indeed, this concern became far more important to her conception of good teaching than the ability to make curricular and instructional decisions. Her concerns with teacher power were virtually silenced, and she worked to win the approval of her student teaching supervisor, her practicing teachers, and the other personnel in the school.

Teachers don't need a cart of materials from methods professors; they need a schema, a sense of purpose that would help carry them through the acculturation to the anti-intellectual climate Karen found. As elementary teacher and author Susan Ohanian (1985) puts it: "Better that they [methods professors] show us a way to find our own ways than that they hand out detailed maps of the territory. A map is not of much use to people who don't know where they are headed" (pp. 697–98). The methods class must help us develop a way of "seeing"—a means of making sense of the multitude of simultaneous demands of a classroom. By helping prospective teachers in their consideration of where their teaching should be headed, methods professors bring sophistication to the study of education. If social studies teacher education students are not familiar with explorations of purpose, they are blind to the complex web of events taking place in any educational situation. William Heard Kilpatrick in 1926 argued that methods of teaching developed without a recognition of this complexity are doomed to failure.

Consider Kilpatrick's example of the relation of method to the complexity of student learning. A shy little girl enters kindergarten and begins to have trouble. She is unwilling to take part in activities with other children. One day a kindergarten aide gently coaxes her to try the sliding board. The little girl has to learn how to climb the stairs, how to prepare for the slide, and how to let go and slide down. The aide patiently takes her through each step. The next day, Kilpatrick continues, she comes to school a different person. She had a good time on the playground the day before, and she has decided that she likes school. The method employed to teach her to slide included instruction on all the technical aspects of sliding; but, it included much more. The kindergarten aide understood that some immeasurable attitudinal factors were at work: the child's disposition toward learning. The aide recognized the little girl's shyness and employed a subtle method. She gently coaxed the little girl to "try" sliding; detailed instructions were inappropriate. The effects of successfully involving the student in this one simple activity opened the door to her involvement in other, more academic, kindergarten activities.

Kilpatrick's example is, of course, quite simple, but it has important implications for other situations. For example, a junior in high school studies American history. In considering methods of teaching history we must also examine a variety of technical and attitudinal factors. What aspects of American history should we choose to teach our junior? What benefits are to be gained from such knowledge? How do juniors in high school often view the study of American history? At what level of abstraction is our student capable of thinking when he or she begins his study of American history? How do we instill a love for American history that will inspire our student to continue studying after he or she leaves our class? What methods of teaching American history will best facilitate the development of an analytical thinking ability transferable to other situations? Is there a way of conducting a history class so that our student's attitude toward learning in general is improved? What can we learn from the student's background which gives us insight into his or her attitude toward academic experiences? Can we connect school, the student's learning style, the social context from which the student comes, and various means of enticing the student to consider the study of history? No simplistic recipe of information delivery methods can provide this knowledge. Only a teacher who possesses such a knowledge and the thinking skill to apply it in constantly changing contexts can successfully accomplish all the demands of the always complex teaching act. To promote successful teaching, the methods class must go far beyond isolated technique.

CRITICAL TEACHER THINKING: AVOIDING TRIVIALIZATION

At a time when many social and educational analysts argue that work in general and teaching in particular are being made a more and more trivial process, it is important to reexamine the role of the social studies methods class. Recall our discussion of deskilling in Chapter 3: deskilling has involved taking jobs that demand skill and decision-making and dividing them into simplified actions. In this manner, less skilled, less costly, and more controllable workers and teachers can be employed. In this deskilled context, the last few decades have seen increased development of "teacher proof" and prepackaged materials. The logic of such materials rests on the assumption that many teachers are incapable of making professional decisions based on a general understanding of the goals of education. The use of such materials precludes the need for teachers to analyze the material that should be taught, understand the backgrounds and needs of individual students, or adapt certain subject matter and certain methods of information delivery to student needs. Such decisions are already made by the creators of the prepackaged materials. The job of teaching is reduced to merely executing plans that are made elsewhere.

Modern teachers are taught the trivialized, deskilled role in a number of contexts: the nonconceptual methods classes, in-service workshops, teacher journals (with their "100 ideas you can use on Monday"), methods textbooks, curriculum packets, and even the structure of the modern school. Let us expand our discussion of the ways in which school structure serves to "teach" teachers to think about their role and their methodological approach. Andrew Gitlin's (1983) ethnographic study of the effect of school structure on teachers' views of their role is a good place to start. Gitlin studied at Meadow School, the structure of which was marked by a curriculum directed by sets of predetermined objectives formulated by absentee professionals. Teacher fidelity to the predetermined objectives was measured by student performance on standardized post-tests.

Gitlin found that teachers rarely conceptualized their own curricula or their own methods. They generally followed the dictates of textbook writers, district curriculum guides, supervisors, or principals. The use of standardized post-tests pushed teachers to concentrate on getting students to master an objective rather than motivating them to think about the nature of the objective. For example, Gitlin watched a social studies teacher teach the following objective: "The student will discover that the period of industrialization was a time of rapid and great change in the production of goods."

To teach the objective, the teacher divided the children into assembly line workers to make a peanut butter and chocolate on graham cracker dessert. The point of the activity was that everyone would eat sooner if the dessert was made on the assembly line than if each person made a complete dessert. Students learned, therefore, that the Industrial Revolution ushered in an era of greater economic efficiency in the production of goods. The alienating and depersonalizing side effects of the industrialization process were not addressed, for they were not a part of the predetermined objective. The teacher, Gitlin reported, was even aware of the effect of industrialization and assembly line organization on worker self-direction and craftsmanship. She was aware that industrialists had found that they could make larger profits when deskilled workers performed repetitious and often boring tasks on the assembly line. Why was this important information not included in the lesson?, Gitlin asked. It was not in the predetermined list of objectives and would not be included on the post-test, the teacher replied.

The very considerations that moved the social studies lesson from a concrete exercise to a critical level of analysis were neglected. The teacher's job was trivialized. Her primary purpose was to facilitate good scores on the post-test, not to question the values, attitudes, or knowledge embedded in the concrete subject matter. A self-confident teacher, secure in his or her knowledge of educational purpose and subject matter, might have escaped the control of this structure. Gitlin's teachers, however, felt that such a structure dictated, to a great extent, the types of methods which could be utilized. Their methods had to emphasize the acquisition of measurable, concrete facts. Methods that facilitated student consideration of the assumptions underlying the factual materials were discouraged by the inevitable questions posed by the post-test.

As Gitlin observed teacher's meetings, he noticed that questions of execution and scheduling dominated the agendas. For example, teachers often discussed the amount of time a certain math or language arts objective would consume; they infrequently asked questions about what concepts students would consume; they infrequently asked questions about what they should be teaching in the first place or the implications of the objectives handed down to them. Reflection on questions of purpose was preempted by immediate concerns with meeting the dictates of the school structure, dictates that revolved around time expenditure, time coordination with other teachers, classroom management, and post-test anxieties. Teacher conceptualization of methods and content was obviously limited by the school structure. This format often reduced teacher work to prespecified, noncreative, trivialized routines. The challenge of the workweek had become for many teachers a race to get through the required objectives. Describing her attempt to complete an objective, one teacher commented: "I just want to get this done. I don't have time to be creative or imaginative."

This statement is informative on a number of levels. It reflects the important understanding that the limitations on teacher creativity imposed by school structure do not mean that teachers are incapable of creativity—far from it. To be effective in schools structured in this way, teacher abilities not usually considered creative were granted priority. Creative methods of approaching, delivering, questioning, or producing information were not deemed essential aspects of teacher repertoire. Proficiency in bureaucratic tasks, such as administering and checking post-tests, recording scores, grouping and regrouping students into ability groups, and time management were the essential talents. The lessons on method taught by the school structure, Gitlin concluded, tended to limit teacher reflection on how and what they taught. The constant demands of a teaching workplace, characterized by predetermined objectives and standardized tests, constrained teacher attempts to analyze the social and education assumptions of the school. At the same time, the demands of such a workplace negated the perceived value of thinking about alternate conceptions of what school could be.

TEACHING AS A SCHOLARLY ACTIVITY

After all the technically rational studies of what works are completed and all the practical methods are disseminated, teaching will still primarily be a scholarly activity. What does this mean? It implies that teachers must be capable of creating an environment in which scholarship can thrive and analytical thinking can develop. To accomplish such difficult tasks, teachers must be capable of analysis and synthesis themselves. The methods class must do its part to contribute to such abilities. Social studies methods professors must be aware of the ways in which the structure of school often subverts such abilities. Teachers must be prepared for the assault on their psyches that they will face in schools marked by pre-specified objectives, top-down standards, and strict accountability based on standardized post-tests.

Analysis and synthesis are the martial arts or self-defense for the twenty-first century teacher. Given the threat against teacher conceptualization and teacher control presented by the structure of many modern schools, educators need black belts. Teachers so equipped will be able to take data, concepts, methods of knowledge production, and theories and adjust them to the demands of diverse learning situations. Such teachers by necessity must be committed to independent critical democratic thinking rather than to an unanalyzed allegiance to rationalistic prespecific practices. Methods classes that promote such professionalism emphasize the type of contextual study that aids teachers in their quest to formulate questions of purpose. When they are able to formulate and contemplate such questions, teachers are ready to assume a larger role in redefining the nature and spirit of what an educator does. Empowered by such abilities, they are now ready to help change the conditions under which they work. These intellectually capable, self-directed, empowered social studies teachers will create a workplace in which scholarly work is nurtured and teacher control of the conceptualization of their own teaching is jealously guarded. Incompetent and authoritarian administrators will not survive very long as leaders of such a competent and self-confident teaching force.

Social studies teachers armed with theoretical and historical understandings will ask good questions of education. They will be seekers of patterns, revealers of hidden agendas and ideologies, and agents of educational progress. Such educators will demand modes of teacher evaluation that go beyond assessment of classroom cleanliness and order. First, the new evaluation will demand evaluators who themselves possess the aforementioned analytical skills; secondly, it will respect and appreciate the potential diversity of individual teacher goals, while it facilitates the attempts of teachers to work out the relationship between curricular conception and execution; and thirdly, it will patiently observe and aid the efforts of educators to glean meaning from the plethora of elements that continually shape and reshape a learning environment (Mathison, 2000).

Teachers who are good question-askers will hold subject matter knowledge up to creative critical inquiry. Teachers in higher education, while often possessing superior command of a body of information, sometimes fail their students when they fail to question the significance of certain knowledge in the overall education of an individual. The study of education promoted in the critical and conceptual methods class will concern itself with questions about the meaning of knowledge of a discipline, its connection with the lived world, its role in education, its proper place in a course of study, and its contextual relationship to the lives of the students (Cadenhead, 1985).

When methods professors view teaching as a critical scholarly activity, they automatically begin to think of such questions. Methods classes emerging from this viewpoint may choose to examine the great teachers of the past, focusing on the relationship between purpose and methods. As students note the diversity of methods and purposes utilized by successful teachers throughout history, they begin to recognize the repressive attempt to foist on teachers rationalized, predetermined, standardized methods applicable in all circumstances as an unfortunate expression of a rationalized bureaucracy. Such standardization serves the ideology of deskilling as it attempts to control teachers by specifying instructional behaviors and rendering them measurable. Thus, accountability is facilitated.

Teachers who are liberated by their ability to analyze and synthesize are free to choose methods that are based on their own knowledge production, consistent with their own beliefs, compatible with their own temperaments, and contextually sensitive to their students' needs. They are not obliged to follow a manual written by someone else; they are capable of determining their own guidelines. There is no finite quality of good methods; there are as many methods as there are imaginative teachers to think of creative ways of approaching, producing, and delivering information. The contextually grounded, conceptual methods class alerts social studies teachers to their limitless options. It frees them to consid-

er possibilities congruent with informed notions about engaged classrooms. The critical conceptual methods class provides teachers the meta
perspective which enables them to talk about the language, discursive
location, and ideological assumptions of a body of knowledge. In this
way, it takes students to a social and cognitive place where content classes in the liberal arts and science don't spend enough time.

If social studies teachers are to be scholars, the methods course must
become just as, if not more, important as historical, sociological, anthropological, geographical, cultural studies, political sciences, and economics content courses. Conceptual, critical theoretically grounded methods
courses build upon, massage, and analyze the content they have acquired
in such liberal arts courses. They use their all-important epistemological
understandings derived from the conceptual, critical methods course to
rethink the knowledge acquired in the content courses, how it was presented, and the ways they learned it. Was it presented unproblematically as truth? Were alternate interpretations provided? Were the values
implicit in the information exposed? What were the epistemological
assumptions of the professor? What were your (the student's) epistemological assumptions now that you understand what epistemology is? With
these understandings, social studies teachers become scholars who move
to a new level of consciousness. They see pedagogical and ideological features of schooling that were previously invisible. They experience critical enlightenment and the critical consciousness that accompanies it.

AN EPISTEMOLOGY OF COMPLEXITY: WHERE THE SOCIAL STUDIES RUBBER HITS THE PEDAGOGICAL ROAD

To escape from the TV-dinner pedagogies and the ideological repression
of dangerous social knowledge, while at the same time pushing for new
understandings and life-changing modes of teaching, it is important to
understand an epistemology of complexity. In this context, we can construct our own critical democratic social studies and imprint our creative
stamp on our professional practice. In that spirit, the following is a
delineation of a transformative epistemology that recognizes the complexity of the lived world and the teaching act. To be a scholarly,
researcher/knowledge worker who teaches social studies, this epistemological understanding is basic.

1. KNOWLEDGE IS SOCIALLY CONSTRUCTED. What we designate as knowledge is complex and always problematic. Social knowledge, knowledge about humans, and knowledge produced about social studies education are all shaped by a variety of forces. They are always constructed. The angle from which an entity is seen, the values of the researcher that shape the questions he or she asks about it, and what the researcher considers important all are factors in the construction of knowledge about the phenomenon. Any social studies knowledge presumes an epistemological stance. Most of the time, knowledge producers don't even know their own epistemological stance. Such a lack of consciousness exerts a dramatic effect on the nature of not only how knowledge is produced but on how the social, political, and educational spheres operate. Nonconceptual social studies educators do not understand the epistemological assumptions they are making. As democratic social studies educators, it is our charge to understand our own and other peoples' epistemological stance, to understand how the knowledge we come into contact with has been constructed. Such an understanding changes the way we see the world around us.

Thus, if knowledge is socially constructed, then democratic social studies educators are interested in the nature and effects of that construction. If knowledge about the sociopolitical world does not just exist "out there" waiting to be discovered but is more of a construction of human minds, then democratic social studies educators want to understand that process. This constructivist epistemological view holds profound implications for knowledge production and teaching in that democratic social studies teachers seek no final perspective on a topic; they know different constructions of political events will continue to be produced as times and, thus, perspectives change. Thus, constructivist social studies teachers are very suspicious of those who would offer the "final truth" or the "last word" on the Mexican War or the Civil Rights Movement.

Social scientists over the last 30 years have found themselves in the middle of an epistemological crisis. The crisis has produced some difficult questions for social analysts: What is the proper method of producing social, psychological, and educational knowledge? What constitutes knowledge in these domains? There is great dissatisfaction among social scientists and educational researchers with the positivistic definitions of knowledge, though the discomfort is not universal. This discomfort comes from the constructivist epistemological understanding that findings in the social and behavior sciences depend on the research methods used. The uniqueness of the information obtained from different approaches to research has led to the existence of separate bodies of social science knowledge. When the same event/phenomenon is studied by a variety of methods, the information produced has little covariation. This means that researchers using different methods share so little common ground that they have no way to relate their diverse findings.

Understanding that knowledge is a social construction, critical democratic social studies teachers come to realize that their job is much more complex than once perceived. Whose knowledge do we teach? Positivistic knowledge? Critical theoretical knowledge? Neither? Both? Why, or on what basis, do we choose our curriculum? These are not simple questions, but if social studies educators are to rise above a deskilled status, they must deal with them. In the domain of educational psychology, for example, consider how this dynamic plays out. When a specific intelligence test is examined by a critical, theoretically grounded sociologist and a psychometrician (a psychologist who statistically measures different aspects of cognitive functions), divergent constructions of the test's use and meaning emerge. To the critical sociologist, the test reflects an unexamined set of socioeconomic and cultural assumptions about the nature of intelligence. To the psychometrician, the test may suffer from internal inconsistency, that is, its rank ordering of individuals relative to their intelligence differs significantly from other intelligence tests. Thus, from the psychometrician's perspective it is a flawed instrument. The point, of course, is that, depending upon the paradigm (model used for making sense of a body of knowledge), our views of this test may vary widely.

The assertion that knowledge is a social construction, that information is produced by specific and identifiable forces, takes us back to our discussion of modernism. To understand the power of the epistemological change, we must return briefly to Descartes' splitting apart of mind and matter/body. This Cartesian dualism divided human experience into two different realms: 1) an internal world of sensation; and 2) on objective world composed of natural phenomena. Cartesian epistemology supported the belief that information, and even laws of physical and social systems, could be discovered objectively. Like their physical counterparts, social systems operated apart from human perception. It didn't matter who observed the social world; if they rigorously followed the scientific method and maintained their objectivity, they would discover the same data. A constructivist-grounded epistemology of complexity rejects this dualism and draws upon alternative epistemologies both from inside the Western tradition and outside in indigenous and other non–Western knowledge-producing traditions. It challenges the Cartesian epistemologies of realism and rationalism (Lavine, 1984; Lowe, 1982; Mahoney & Lyddon, 1988; Kincheloe & Steinberg, 1997). A brief explanation is necessary:

Realism presumes a singular, stable, external reality that can be perceived by one's senses; rationalism argues that thought is superior to sense and is most important in shaping experience. Our notion of constructivism contends that reality, contrary to the arguments made by proponents of realism, is not external and unchanging. In contrast to rationalism, constructivism maintains that human thought cannot be meaningfully separated from human feeling and action. Knowledge, constructivists assert, is constrained by the structure and function of the mind and can thus be known only indirectly. The knower and the known are Siamese twins, connected at the point of perception. Thus, knowledge is not simply "out there" to be discovered; it is shaped by the human mind in a complex interaction with lived reality.

Constructivism draws upon a Western anti-Cartesian tradition emerging from the New Science of Giambattista Vico in the early 1700s and extending to the phenomenology, critical theory, and women's epistemology of the twentieth century. Of course, as we will discuss in more detail, there are also numerous indigenous and non-Western sources as well. Vico insisted, to the consternation of the Cartesians, that a different conceptual apparatus was necessary for the analysis of social and cultural phenomena from that used to study the structure of the physical world. The tradition that Vico established insisted that human beings were more than objects. When conceived as such, the uniqueness of men and women is lost; they are reduced to things, to "its." When people are seen as objects, serious ethical questions arise. For example: Is manipulation acceptable? Is self-determinism a basic human right? Is the purpose of teaching and knowledge production the improvement of the human condition? Should democracy be considered in the conceptualization of the act of producing knowledge?

The point is clear: The objectivism, the separation of the knower and the known implicit in the Cartesian tradition, denies the spatiotemporal location of the knower in the world and thus results in the estrangement of human beings from the rhythms of life, the natural world (White, 1978). Alvin Gouldner extends the anti-Cartesian critique, arguing that the social sciences promote a form of inquiry suitable for an alienated age and an alienated people. The dominant expressions of the social sciences serve to accommodate researchers to sociocultural alienation rather than working to overcome it (Reinharz, 1979). Descartes argued that knowledge should be empirical, mathematical, and certain, and the orientation toward research that emerged worked to exploit the forces of nature in a way that mutated the landscape of the Earth. As a result of this objectivist epistemology and the positivism that emerged from it, we now inhabit a human-made, artificial environment. Emerging from the tradition was a behavioral science that set out to manipulate people and an educational system that utilized the behavioral sciences to mold students and their consciousness in a way that would foster efficiency and economic productivity, often at the expense of creativity, social justice, and knowledge necessary to perpetuate a democracy.

The "postmodern," counter-Cartesian epistemology of complexity understands the complications of producing knowledge. Central among these understandings is that the politics, values, research methods, and goals of social scientists profoundly shape what has been passed on to students as "truth" in social studies classes. Our complex epistemology lays bare the assumptions of Cartesian logic by illustrating the ways that the structure of traditional social science constructs imaginary worlds. Like a novel, science is "written;" both the novel and science operate according to the arbitrary rules of a language game. Our charge is to figure out the rules and effects of the Cartesian game. Such understandings constitute a giant first step in reshaping the world in a more just and humane way. Such a process marks a key role of a democratic social studies education.

Drawing upon feminist analyses of Cartesian science, our epistemology of complexity seeks the "formula" of the novel. Feminist scholars (Harding, 1991; Keller, 1985) maintain that science is a human act subject to all-too-human biases, contextual influences, and objectives. These forces shape science's values, ways of making meaning, production and interpretation of data, reasoning skills, and attributions of importance. Exploring the way these processes take place, critical social studies educators come to understand the logic behind the knowledge they are provided in the official curriculum. A key feature of my own democratic social studies teaching in high school embraced this search for the logic behind the construction of social studies knowledge. Teaching about the U.S. war with Mexico, I engaged students in an examination of several U.S. high school textbooks, college and graduate level U.S. texts, and Mexican secondary school textbook accounts of the war.

Much to the students' initial shock, the factors they were studying as the causes of the war were very different between the homogenized U.S. high school history texts and professional historical literature. The causes of the war were black and white in the U.S. history texts: Mexico was to blame, and the United States had little choice in entering the war if it were to achieve its divine "Manifest Destiny." The professional U.S. historical literature portrayed the causes of the conflict as more complex and difficult to discern. The Mexican texts provided a rather straightforward view of the war's cause: U.S. imperialism. Before 1846, the books reported, the area that became the states of California, Nevada, Arizona, New Mexico, Utah, Colorado, and parts of Kansas and Oklahoma was part of Mexico. After the war, this sizeable chunk of land constituted a huge part of the United States. Which book told the truth? Which one(s) were socially constructed? How do we make sense of such divergent depictions of the same event? Via such questions, we begin the study of the logic behind the knowledge. We just might, "get behind the facts."

This epistemological analysis of the construction of knowledge will provide social studies teachers multidimensional benefits. By studying the process by which knowledge is produced, students learn about the nature of learning. It is in this way that an individual student accomplishes that all-important goal of emancipatory education: learning to teach himself or herself. Because it is unconcerned with the attempt of men and women to control their own destiny, the Cartesian social studies curriculum is indifferent to learning that attempts to move beyond the acquisition of secondhand, authorized, ready-made facts. Operating with an eye on the ideological aspects of positivism, democratic social studies educators study the ways Cartesian knowledge and the pedagogy that promotes it induce us to accept the commonsense viewpoint that the social world is exactly as it is portrayed. Such a perspective can be paralyzing.

An epistemology of complexity can heal such cognitive paralysis faster than Pastor Benny Hinn. Be gone, evil paralysis! The critical epistemological consciousness, recognizing that all knowledge is socially constructed, asks: Whose knowledge are we teaching? Where did it come from? How was it produced? Whose interests does it serve? How did it get in the curriculum? Why are we teaching it? How does it serve the needs of students? How comfortable are we with it? Are we getting beyond the facts yet? Tom Puk (1994) picks up on this assertion, using knowledge produced and taught to U.S. students about Christopher Columbus. The typical American child is taught that:

> Christopher Columbus was the first person to discover (land on) North America and the United States in 1492 (the Vikings don't really count). He was a Spanish explorer (it was assumed that, in the United States, he would be thought of as being an Italian). He must have been a very brave fellow because he sailed into the unknown, fearing that he might fall off the edge of the world. He was attempting to find a new route to the Orient (with something to do with finding spices). How we know all this is not really known (it just is). He sailed straight across the Atlantic Ocean, from Spain to North America. He was a brave, amazing hero, although there are some rumors that he killed people.
>
> According to what we currently know about Columbus, this story line is essentially myth. In fact, we knew that much of it was myth long before the latest round of primary research. For example, there has long been the uncomfortable knowledge of existence of the Vikings. The most embarrassing annoyance must surely have been when we taught that Columbus met other human beings on the lands that he first "discovered" (p. 229).

So, according to Puk, U.S. social studies students, in relation to Columbus, are taught mythologies at best and misrepresentations at worst. Might it be important to ask the epistemological question: How was the knowledge that is presented about Columbus constructed? Puk argues that the quest for accuracy has little to do with the reason the Columbus fraud appears in U.S. social studies textbooks. Fear of reprisal from traditionalists who believe that there is some divine sanction to teaching the Columbus myth or that admitting to its inaccuracy would lead to a reappraisal of the entire curriculum may be more important justifications. A reappraisal of the entire social studies curriculum and the nature of the knowledge it presents as sacred is exactly what is being advocated in *Getting Beyond the Facts*. As the logic behind the construction of social studies knowledge is exposed, the house of cards will crumble. Maybe then, we can renegotiate our social, political, and historical knowledges, admit what we don't know, and proceed with a great deal more humility.

2. CONSCIOUSNESS IS A SOCIAL CONSTRUCTION. This constructivist theme runs throughout our epistemology of complexity. As with

knowledge, human consciousness is not something that exists independently of the world. Our consciousness, identity, self-concept,
view of our relationship to the world and other people is shaped by
the culture in which we live, our historical era, our family, our peer
group, and the information with which we come into contact. In
part, we are what we know. If, as Tom Puk argues, social studies students are taught a false history, a view of the past that never existed, then our understanding of knowledge as a social construction
takes on even more importance. Our study of epistemology/knowl-
edge production takes on (in the language of philosophy) ontological dimensions. As referenced previously, ontology is the branch of
philosophy that studies the nature of being, what it means to be
human. If we are what we know, then our very being is shaped by
these epistemological issues. In my opinion, that makes them more
than worthy of study.

Although we appear to one another as single, bounded identities,
we humans are socially superabsorbent—like humanoid Husky paper
towels. This simply means that our consciousness is shaped by that with
which we come into contact. Again, we are more complex social beings
than the Cartesians imagined. In hyperreality, we are all part TV game-
show host, evangelist, interviewee in a breakfast cereal commercial, cop
or criminal, and local news anchor. All personalities are latent and,
given the right stimuli, are ready to come alive. Thus, the boundaries of
individualism begin to fade like the chalk lines of a late-inning batter's
box. As they do, we become more aware of a critical constructivism's
(power-conscious) notion of the social construction of the individual.
Indeed, we even begin to recognize the limitations of middle-class
notions of individualism. In the name of individualism, we are taught a
"me first" perspective on self-gratification that renders us vulnerable to
appeals such as "I believe in equality: Everyone gets a tax cut—rich or
poor!" This emphasis on self-gratification trivializes critical conceptions
of citizenship, friendships, and sexual relationships, as each becomes
something designed to get what we want. Of course, we use testing not
only as a sound way of assessing the value of education but as a means
of motivating our individualistic students. As we gain a meta-awareness
of the construction of our consciousness, it becomes possible to critically reconstruct our understanding of the nature of individualism and
interdependence.

Always concerned with power, this epistemology of complexity studies the exaggerated role it plays in the social construction of consciousness. Democratic social studies teachers analyze their own and help students analyze their consciousness construction, especially around the ways race, class, gender, and religious dimensions of power contribute to the process. Novices in this context would explore the historical purposes of schooling and how these purposes were manifested in their own school lives and their own consciousness construction. In other words, a critical epistemology of complexity would transform colleges of education into serious academic institutions dedicated to an intense sociopsychological analysis of the effects of schooling. The ways that women and men construct their consciousnesses and the role that education plays in that process would become a guiding concern of teacher education in general and social studies education in particular, a concern that would necessitate interdisciplinary connections and research alliances across the university.

Democratic social studies teachers use this epistemological understanding of consciousness construction to shape the purposes of their teaching and self-explorations. In this context, such teachers seek methods to heighten individual awareness. Edmund Husserl, the great phenomenologist (phenomenology is concerned with the study of consciousness, as it attempts to grasp the ways individuals make meaning among themselves and other people), delineated research methods designed to facilitate understanding of the structure of consciousness and its relation to the world. One aspect of this method, bracketing, involves consciously setting aside everyday, accepted assumptions about one's immediate perceptions (Chamberlin, 1974; Schwandt, 1994). Once this bracketing of assumptions takes place, the individual examines and makes explicit all the meanings that were hidden in initial perceptions. In this way, individual awareness is heightened as previously hidden assumptions are revealed. The individual thus finds himself or herself more in touch with the values, political forces, fears, and associations that unconsciously direct his or her actions. Continued analysis of such factors may uncover their origins, thus contributing to greater self-understanding and self-knowledge. The foundations of the phenomenological method must rest on a self-knowledge that, once gained, allows teachers and students to turn their focus outward to more textured understandings of the interior experiences of others. Thus, we become more sensitive to the ways consciousness is socially constructed.

With these phenomenological insights, democratic social studies teachers become genealogists of consciousness who trace its formation in a variety of contexts and for a variety of purposes. Every time I walk into a classroom, I am concerned with both inducing students to bracket who they are and deploying the course in a way that helps them discern how they became that way. By recognizing the complex and contradictory forces that shape our consciousness, democratic social studies teachers begin to get a clearer understanding of how social knowledge is produced. They quickly learn that there is no all-knowing, God-like, transcendental view of reality that exists somewhere outside this reality. Indeed, they come to recognize that there are no value-free, privileged knowers who ask ideologically unfettered questions about the social world. Drawing upon the early work of Alvin Gouldner, critical democratic teachers come to recognize that research methodology and teaching are not simply logics but are moralities in the sense that they repress or liberate particular moral questions about social and educational reality. Educators, thus, are moral agents, rejecting or accepting the moral obligations of moral imperatives (McLaren, 1995, 2000; Kincheloe & McLaren, 2000; Goodlad, 1988).

Our self-critical genealogy, and the critical practice that grows out of it, constitutes an emancipatory right of passage as we leave behind our epistemological "adolescence." Exercising our new maturity, we come to formulate more penetrating questions about our professional practice, see new levels of activity and meaning in our classrooms, decipher connections between sociocultural meanings and the everyday life of school, and reconceptualize what we already "know." As we grow to understand the race, class, and gender locations of the students and others that we study, we come to appreciate our own location and the social relationships and perceptions such locations produce (Reinharz, 1982). Our social studies teaching takes on a new sensitivity and rigor, as we develop a clarified purpose of why we would want to teach history, anthropology, sociology, cultural studies, political science, economics, and geography. How do they help us understand who we have become? Do we really want to be this way? How can we become something different and better?

Without this social and ideological self-criticism, we cannot find the path to the *Lebenswelt*—the life world, the lived world of human consciousness. As philosopher Hans-Georg Gadamer (1975) argued, the critique of both the prevalent notions of objectivity and the way these ideas have shaped us allows us to get behind the objectivity of inquiry so that we might discover the life world. Standing at the intersection of his or her own consciousness and that which is being observed, the explorer discovers a crack in time and space through which he or she might crawl. From the other side of this temporal and spatial fissure, the world can be seen afresh: The trivial becomes the profound, comfortable assumptions are turned inside-out. This genealogical self-criticism has become an epic reconstruction of consciousness; indeed, we have stumbled on the process of not only how researchers make new discoveries but how fields of inquiry are transformed. Major advances in how we see social and educational phenomena do not emerge from a linear accumulation or extension within the matrix of previous discoveries. Major reconceptualizations come out of a meta-analysis of the ideological assumptions on which the framework underlying the accumulation of extant knowledge is grounded. Critical knowledge is produced not as much by asking questions within the framework as it is by asking questions about the framework (Kincheloe, Steinberg, & Tippins, 1999; Kincheloe, Steinberg, & Hinchey, 1999; Reinharz, 1979). Einstein did it in physics; together, we can do it in social studies.

Thus, insight into the ways our consciousness is socially constructed helps us change the field of social studies and change our lives in a way that is more ethical, more humane, more democratic, more free, and more happy. Through our knowledge of consciousness construction, we identify the sociopsychological demons that torture us and move us in pathological ways. Via the pathway of this understanding, a critical democratic social studies empowers, extends agency, and builds growth-inducing humane environments. By providing techniques that allow us all to see from new perspectives the nature of the school experience and its effects, a critical democratic social studies induces students, administrators, and other teachers to heighten consciousness of themselves as players on the educational stage, to take themselves less for granted, and to view themselves as subjects of study.

As epistemologically aware social studies teachers watch themselves be educators, they ask questions such as: Who do I call on in class? Who do I criticize, and from whom do I withhold criticism? Where in the school do I hang out? Where do I stand when I'm teaching? How do I arrange my room? Do I respond differently to the misbehavior of different students? Such a perspective grants teachers a dialectic of distance, that is, a closeness to students, marked by an awareness of who they are, their concerns, their interests, their experiences, their socioeconomic background, their diverse forms of intelligence. This perspective also establishes a metaphorical distance that allows them to step back and watch from afar how their backgrounds affect their daily lives at school, their self-definitions, the perceptions of them held by other teachers, and their educational success with students. Very simply, they become better social studies teachers.

3. POWER PLAYS AN EXAGGERATED ROLE IN SHAPING THE PRODUCTION OF "TRUTH," OF CONSTRUCTING OUR CONSCIOUSNESS. An epistemology of complexity understands that there is simply no such thing as neutral or unpoliticized knowledge. In its social construction, knowledge is shaped by the dynamics of power. Who's producing it and for what purposes? In the construction of our consciousness, power plays an exaggerated role in the process since one must hold power to produce certified public knowledge. Epistemologically aware social studies educators reject the reductionistic notion of politically neutral research into social phenomena as a form of ideological mystification, that is, an attempt to hide the political interests of educational practice and the research about it. If researchers fail to keep the normative, political, or value dimension of educational research in mind, the research they produce and the ends to which it is applied will simply serve to reproduce hegemonic social relations. Thus, from a critical democratic perspective, an awareness of the value orientation of research is essential, because it brings to awareness the fundamental embodiments of power which move social and educational events (Soltis, 1984; Kincheloe & Steinberg, 1997).

Beloved emancipatory educator Myles Horton put this power-related concept so simply in his conversation with Paulo Freire in 1990:

When I first started thinking about the relationship of learning and social change, it had nothing to do with Highlander. It was years earlier when I was debating with myself this whole idea of neutrality. Academicians, politicians, all the people that are supposed to be guiding this country say you've got to be neutral. As soon as I started looking at that word *neutral* and what it meant, it became very obvious to me there can be no such thing as neutrality. It's a code word for the existing system. It has nothing to do with anything but agreeing to what is and will always be—that's what neutrality is. *Neutrality is just following the crowd.* Neutrality is just being what the system asks us to be. Neutrality, in other words, was an immoral act. I was thinking in religious terms then. It was to me a refusal to oppose injustice or to take sides that are unpopular. It's an excuse, in other words. So I discarded the word neutrality before I even started thinking much about educational ideas. Of course, when I got more into thinking about educational ideas and about changed society, it became more and more obvious that you've got to take sides. You need to know why you take sides; you should be able to justify it (Horton & Freire, 1990, p. 171).

Thomas Popkewitz (1981) maintains that social and educational research expresses the researcher's interests in at least two important ways:

a. The research we undertake reflects our view of sociopolitical values. Our research allows us to reconcile what we see as social contradiction and to ponder the consequences of the actions of institutions. For example, we may see a class-stratified society beset by problems resulting from the existence of a so-called permanent underclass. We want to know how the arrangement of educational institutions affects this situation. Our research questions and the manner in which we approach our study have been shaped by our value orientations.

b. Since social research (especially quantitative social research) holds such a high status in the society, many individuals promote the belief that educational problems can only be solved through the application of rigorous science. Thus, solutions that emerge from community participation and democratic negotiation are dismissed; society has come to rely on the cult of the expert, those social scientists with precise, dispassionate answers to technical problems.

When researchers fail to note the existence of this omnipresent value dimension, Kenneth Howe (1985) contends that unpleasant outcomes typically result:

a. The research will be useless as information that informs practical action. Value judgments are inseparable from educational descriptions because of the relationship between educational research and educational practice. If researchers do not allow values to serve as a link between research and practice, educational inquiry will be irrelevant to what teachers and administrators actually do. In other words, the relationship between what we know and how we act upon the knowledge is problematic. Values not only inform what we claim to know but the actions that we take as a result of the knowledge.

b. Value-free research will be insufficient. If research in the field is not grounded upon explicitly-stated values that are open to evaluation little benefit will ever be derived from such research. Thus, energy and resources will have been wasted.

c. Value-free research holds the potential to produce harmful results. When research purports to be value-free, but covertly promotes specific values, various groups and individuals are rendered quite vulnerable. Students who are culturally different may be labeled emotionally disturbed, young girls and boys who attempt to transcend gender restrictions may be seen as maladjusted, or thoughtful young people with intelligent questions about social convention may be labeled as troublemakers. Power's ability to dominate hides in the shadows of knowledge producers' claim to neutrality and objectivity.

Obviously, values in social knowledge production affect human beings in very concrete ways. If the values of research are typically hidden, then the justifications for the educational politics which are based on them are also concealed. When such restrictions are out of sight, teachers have only a restricted view of why they do the things that they do. An analysis of the historical forces that have structured values is an integral part of a democratic social studies education. As we know, research is never a neutral means to a particular end. Research and its methodology grow out of the values of a particular world view. This particular world view, this paradigm, determines what constitutes legitimate research or an acceptable way of thinking. Even though positivistic, instrumentally rational research models have been challenged in some academic settings, they still dominate the mind-set of many elementary and secondary schools. Emerging from business and military sources, contemporary manifestations of positivistic research inject the values of business management and the military into the life of the school. Here is where the importance of phenomenological, semiotic, and ethnographic forms of research become so important to the democratic social studies teacher. They provide the tools with which we reveal the forces that make schools what they are, that tacitly construct the goals of social education (Orteza, 1988; Cherryholmes, 1988).

Why do social and educational researchers use particular words, metaphors, and models when they design their inquiry, interpret it, and suggest policies based on it? Their research language reflects the effects of the influence of power in the larger society. Power, as Michel Foucault has argued, has served to censor, exclude, block, and repress like a great superego; but, he continues, it also serves to produce knowledge, creating effects at the level of desire. As a censor in educational research, power serves to limit what constitutes a legitimate question, excluding "dangerous" investigations, such as explorations of how class factors affect student performances in school. As a producer in social and educational research, power serves to reward particular ways of seeing and particular activities. For example, educational researchers who desire success in the field learn and follow particular research norms which allow them the rewards of funded grants and promotions based on scholarly productivity. The way different research orientations draw boundaries between what is acceptable and what is not constitutes the ideological dimension of the act of inquiry (Cherryholmes, 1988). Here, power is at work, promoting particular views of educational excellence and educational failure, often around race and class demarcations.

As critical social studies teachers, we make a mistake when we assume that this power is always consciously exercised by a cabal of conspirators seeking to control the educational world. Much of the time, the ideological construction of consciousness emanating from sources of power does not take place at the level of conscious intention. For example, positivistic educational researchers, most of the time, do not seek to design research that results in the perpetuation of business and military values in school practices. School administrators do not typically seek to use educational research that represses ethical considerations and questions of justice in their efforts to run their schools. And teachers, most of the time, certainly do not consciously attempt to suppress their students' ability to think at a more critical level, nor do they try to punish the underprivileged or reward the privileged. But all of these unfortunate things happen, and, most of the time, we have no clue why. We don't catch on because we don't understand the subtle semiotic dimensions of power reproduction, i.e., how codes, symbols, and signs subtlty construct our world views. As social studies teachers who are researchers, we begin to see how educational research produced by such subtle forces legit-imizes particular values and delegitimizes others.

For example, in terms of concrete research practices, who is legiti-mate to interview, to use as a reliable source, and who is not? As a high school social studies teacher, I often watched other social studies teach-ers bring experts to their economics classes to speak and to answer stu-dent questions. In my high school these experts were usually successful businessmen who delivered a remarkably standardized ideological pack-age for student consumption. The idea of inviting individuals from other social classes or other ideological traditions (e.g., labor leaders, social workers, welfare rights leaders, etc.) was never considered. Dominant values and ideology were thus reproduced, not at a level of conscious intent on the part of the teachers, but at a tacit, unconscious stratum. On this same stratum, the records of any historical era favor those who direct public events or produce the records. Everyday people, the common voices of working people, are excluded from the picture. Democratic social studies teachers, aware of these hegemonic dimensions of power in inquiry, take special pains to collect testimonies of individuals outside of power and make sure they expose their students to them.

Expert researchers from academic settings like to believe that the university, because it is called "academic," is removed from these histor-ical realities, value dimensions, and ideological forces that shape the form their research takes. Our research, no matter who we are, is never as independent of outside influences as we would like to think; we are all caught at a particular point in the web of reality. Our epistemological goal, of course, is to understand what our particular vantage point is and how it limits our vision. This process involves our awareness of our own historicity, or place in history. We become conscious of our own ideolog-ical inheritance and its relationship to our belief and value structures, our interests, our questions about our professional lives. In his studies of the eugenicists and their influence on the way educators came to view intel-ligence and school performance, Steven Selden (1984) traces how social visions shaped eugenicist research design. Ideological conceptions of what constituted civilization, human progress, and a good society could not be separated from the formulation of eugenicist research. What is ironic in this case is that many of the instruments devised by eugenicist researchers to measure learning, intelligence, and ability are still employed in twenty-first century education. Thus, at an unseen level, the value assumptions of the eugenicist movement are embedded in contemporary educational practices (Cherryholmes, 1988; Kincheloe, Steinberg, & Gresson, 1996).

Mainstream researchers have ridiculed such claims, arguing that no one in modern educational research is an eugenicist. Indeed, they are correct in their assertion that eugenics is out of fashion and that educational researchers from almost any ideological perspective would rigorously reject association with the tradition. This is true even though one of the biggest selling books in history on the politics of race, *The Bell Curve* (1994), promoted overtly eugenicist, racist positions allegedly "proving" the inferiority of African Americans and Latinos. Knowledge production, however, derives its meaning and its importance from the purposes for which it was designed. Much of the time, the purposes are not known by those educators who consume the research. Unfortunately, educators and political leaders, too often, only notice that research serves particular ideological intentions when those purposes confront some aspect of the status quo (Bogdan & Biklen, 1982).

When an educational researcher, for example, contends that business sponsorship of excellence programs in particular schools serves to produce unquestioning attitudes toward the positive role of business in the local community and a one-dimensional perspective on the virtues of a Chamber of Commerce view of unregulated free enterprise economics, the status quo is challenged. It is at this point that cries of bias and politicized research make their way into the popular media as well as teacher, parent, and community awareness. Power has its ways; research emerging from a critical epistemology of complexity that challenges dominant ideology will typically be viewed as politicized and biased. Research that does not will often be deemed neutral and value-free. Speaking openly about its own political and ethical values, this book will be labeled by some as a dangerous politicization of the social studies. Meanwhile, other social studies texts that purport to provide us simply with the facts, that don't discuss knowledge production and the political forces that shape it, that grant us the proper methods of teaching students unproblematized social data, that hide their political affiliations will be considered unpolitical, objective, safe texts. Beware of social studies educators bearing gifts of power neutrality.

Thus, democratic social studies teachers, informed by a critical epistemology of complexity, seek a new angle, a unique insight into different ways of knowing, different forms of social knowledge, different approaches to knowledge production, and new ways of discerning the role of power in knowledge and consciousness construction. Research and the knowledge it produces is never neutral but constructed in specific ways that privilege particular logics and voices while silencing others. Why do science and math curricula in the United States, for example, receive more attention and prestige in public schools than social studies? Social studies teachers researching the way power helps shape individual and social consciousness uncover links between the need of large corporations to enhance worker productivity and the goals of contemporary educational reform movements. They discover relationships between the interests of business and the exclusion of the study of labor history in the social studies curriculum. They expose the connections between the patriarchal Eurocentrism of educational leadership and definitions of classics that exclude the contributions of women, minorities, and non-Westerners to the literature, art, and music canon.

Power regulates discourses; discursive practices are defined as a set of tacit rules that regulate what can and cannot be said, who can speak with the blessing of authority and who must listen, whose socioeducational constructions are scientific and valid and whose are unlearned and unimportant. In the everyday world of social studies teaching, legitimized discourses insidiously tell teachers what books may be read by students, what instructional methods may be utilized, and what belief systems, definitions of citizenship, and views of success may be taught. Schools may identify, often unconsciously, conceptions of what it means to be educated with upper-middle class white culture; expressions of working-class or non-white culture may be viewed as uneducated and inferior. In this context, teachers are expected to sever student identification with their minority group or working-class backgrounds, as a result, alienating such students through the disconfirmation of their culture.

Thus, the culture of schooling privileges particular practices and certain methods of discerning truth. Michel Foucault argues that truth is not relative (i.e., all world views embraced by different researchers, cultures, and individuals are of equal worth), but is relational (constructions considered true are contingent upon the power relations and historical context in which they are formulated and acted upon). If democratic social studies teachers accept Foucault's epistemological pronouncements, then we must grant the study of power a central role in emancipatory social studies. If truth is, as Foucault contends, relational and not absolute, then an important feature of our power work will involve discerning what criteria we employ to make judgments about social information. Such a task will demand a lifetime of study. I challenge you to join me.

Indeed, I challenge you to help democratic social studies teachers engage in this epistemological stakeout and help various individuals in differing situations seek the role of power in the knowledge they consume and the shaping of their consciousness. Epistemologically informed and socially committed social studies teachers help workers in their communities become agents of democracy in a power-saturated political economic landscape. Many times, the workers can help teachers and their students in their power detection, showing them the ways that capital exercises control over information flow and how, specifically, this affects the well-being of the workers. Informed workers show teachers and students how fewer and fewer corporations control more and more of the production of information. They discover that the postmodern corporation frequently regards the advertising of products to be secondary to the promotion of a positive corporate image.

Controlling information in this way enhances the corporation's power, since it engages the public in relating positively to the goals and the "mission" of the corporation. In this way, corporations can better shape government policy, control public images of labor-management relations, and portray workers in a way that enhances the self-interest of management. As a result, corporate taxes are minimized, wages are lowered, mergers are deregulated, corporate leaders are lionized, and managerial motives are unquestioned (Harvey, 1989; Kincheloe, 1999). Critical democratic social studies teachers must join with workers to address these power-shaped social and ethical distortions.

Democratic social studies teachers teach historical lessons on this power-knowledge nexus. Until the Vietnam War, many journalists (with significant exceptions) conceived of objectivity as "official-source journalism." Tom Wicker writes that journalists who did not rely on governmental and corporate official sources were considered subjective, if not subversive. But their front line experience in the Southeast Asian jungles changed the minds of many in the profession as they began to uncover the lack of accuracy in the information provided by official governmental sources. As reporters spent time with Vietnamese people, low-ranking U.S. officials in the hinterland, and soldiers and nurses— subjugated knowledges—they began to uncover a very different picture of how the war was going. These reporters surrendered their official-source objectivity, and, in the manner of democratic social studies researchers, began seeing for themselves and analyzing for themselves, often at the risk of physical harm and governmental wrath.

From the perspective of those who fought the war and cared for its victims, the claims of the Pentagon spokespeople, the generals, and the ambassadors began to appear fatuous and hollow. The reporters had taken a dangerous and subversive step: They had abandoned their so-called official-source objectivity for a phenomenological firsthand engagement with the lived world of the war. It was at this very point that they were accused of bias; the dominant view of proper reporter behavior was able to persuade a large portion of the American public of their "misguided, pro-Communist" motives (Bogdan & Biklen, 1982). This is just one of countless historical and contemporary examples of brave men and women getting beyond the facts and exposing power's complicity with knowledge regardless of danger to their safety and reputation.

These types of examples can be found in a variety of domains, locales, and forms. Philosopher of science Sandra Harding offers an example of these phenomenological concerns in the context of biological research. Using her understanding of socially constituted, gender-related influences on the *Lebenswelt* of biological researchers, Harding seeks to demystify the male power to produce knowledge in biology. In her analysis of attempts to explain human evolution in terms of the strides made by men in hunting societies, Harding uncovers an interesting gender bias. Assuming that sex-role distinctions (hierarchical distinctions at that) exist across all cultures, biological researchers have traditionally argued that man-the-hunter developed tools as aids to hunting. This exclusive masculine use of tools contributed to bipedalism and upright posture. This led to more effective hunting techniques that were characterized by a division of labor among the hunters. This hunting behavior was viewed as the evolutionary origin of male bonding in modern society, and, as such, justifies the reason why males should want to bar women from their economic activities, the pursuit of science included. The traditional hypothesis portrays men as the agents who precipitated the evolutionary break from prehuman cultures and took the giant evolutionary leap into human culture.

The biological account of the activities of women in contemporary societies presents them as basically the same as feminine activities in prehuman groups. Feminist scholars aware of the unexamined male-centered *Lebenswelt* of traditional biological scholarship, have, for the purposes of demystification, posed an alternative "woman-the-gatherer" hypothesis of human evolution. Where men had invented primarily stone tools, woman-the-gatherer invented tools made of sticks and reeds. Since women took care of the food gathering in the early societies, they also developed tools to defend against predators who interfered with their activities. Thus, it could be argued that woman-the-gatherer produced the tools that allowed the social organization that propelled humans into a new evolutionary epoch.

The point of the gynecentric (women-centered) theory of the origins of human cultural evolution is not to prove its superiority over the patriarchal interpretation. Harding specifically points out that it is equally impossible to prove one as it is to prove the other, and that is exactly the point. If one cannot be proved over the other, then what is the basis of the androcentric (male centered) theory? The origins of the interpretation come not from the data but from the gender assumptions of the researchers who formulated it. It was socially constructed, emerging from unexamined commonsense assumptions of male superiority, of patriarchal power. The theory was epistemologically arbitrary, based on a restrictive understanding of human possibilities. In biology, undoubtedly, but in all sciences, the value of intrapersonal and interpersonal knowledge has traditionally been seen as irrelevant. Harding alerts us to the value of such knowledge forms in a science as empirically based as biology. We see the power of androcentrism tacitly informing the research, since it dictates the selection of what might be considered a scientific problem, the important concepts and theories of the discipline, acceptable research methods, and interpretations of the results of research (Harding, 1986).

Harding's work alerts social analysts to the necessity of transcending surface appearances, of using the tools of phenomenology, ethnography, historiography, and semiotics to uncover the ideological constructions, the tacit assumptions, that drive social and educational research. In the postmodern context we learn that little is as it appears to be. When critical social studies teachers search for deep structures there to be uncovered in any classroom, they discover a world of personal meaning that is socially constructed by a variety of forces and often has little to do with the intended meaning of the official curriculum. With this understanding, the teacher studies how power shapes the learner's consciousness, its uniqueness, and the possible ways it may become more aware of the ways it has been constructed by power. This realm of personal experience is possibly the most unexplored aspect of school life. Testing and traditional assessment have no means of assessing it; it is not measurable in any positivistic sense. Yet, this is the part of the social studies curriculum that really counts, that involves the exaggerated role that power plays in shaping our consciousness. From a critical epistemological perspective, this strikes at the very reason we would study social studies in the first place.

Understanding why the world is as it is, why we are as we are, and what we're going to do when we learn these lessons is the basis of a critical democratic social studies. Of course, in this third aspect of an epistemology of complexity, we are concerned with the huge role of power in this process. Our larger critical concern with power involves the ways it shapes unjust action, and undermines democracy. Critical social studies educators understand that many aspects of the knowledge production and teaching process undermine democratic political action. Mainstream social science research that produces the information typically taught in social studies holds what might be considered bizarre perspectives toward the relationship between the researcher and researched.

Dominant hegemonic power-driven research orientations preclude researchers from pointing out forms of domination to the researcher; such orientations obstruct attempts to encourage emancipatory social change for the betterment of the individuals, groups, and communities being studied. An understanding of the hierarchical relationships between researcher and researched alerts social studies teachers to the dynamics of the emancipatory relationships they hope to establish with the students, other teachers, administrators, and community members with whom they work. Drawing upon our understanding of subjugated knowledge, we examine the hierarchical power relations between knowledge producers and minority groups, e.g., Blacks, Hispanics, and Native Americans. Because they intuitively understand the researchers' hierarchical view of them (listen to Sioux tribal member Floyd Westerman's insightful song, "Here Come the Anthros," as an example of the perspective of the researched), the subjugated objects of research view inquirers with distrust and often refuse to let them into their lives.

As researchers fail to understand many of the unique and subtle characteristics of the informant's world, their research distorts the lived conditions and the potentials of the researched. Such misrepresentations limit the possibility of the inquiry to serve as a basis for improving the life chances of the people being studied. The researchers just report what they see, and what they see may be severely limited by the ideological power construction of their own psyche (McLaren, 1995; Gordon, Miller, & Rollock, 1990). These power dynamics of research and knowledge production have been ignored by the field of social studies throughout its history. The importance of the epistemological emphasis here involves the fact that it brings these power issues to the discipline's front burner. Social studies cannot go back to the nonconceptual domain after its epistemological consciousness has been raised.

4. EMPHASIS ON CONSCIOUSNESS EVEN THOUGH IT IS HARD TO MEASURE EMPIRICALLY—WILLIAM PINAR'S CURRERE. Point 4 in our delineation of an epistemology of complexity is an extension of point 2 and its concern with the social construction of consciousness. Point 4 begins with this assumption and extends it by arguing that, even though consciousness does not lend itself to positivistic quantitative measurement, it still is the most important domain in the educational process. The behaviorist psychologist B. F. Skinner was so disturbed by the positivistic immeasurability of consciousness that he simply proclaimed that it didn't exist. Skinner was the perfect example of a modernist positivist and his pronouncement about consciousness is quite revealing for democratic social studies teachers: Even though it is the domain that may best express our humanness, if it doesn't lend itself to positivist method, then it is nonexistent. Skinner's pronouncement once again illustrates the way the world is socially constructed by our epistemological assumptions since the existence of consciousness was not as important in Skinner's formulation as the framework he used to understand reality.

Consciousness is obviously an essential part of what it means to be human, many analysts including the phenemonolgists, have argued, and should be studied if we are ever to gain significant insight into the affairs of human beings. However, the study of consciousness, phenomenologists warn, is limited by two important factors: 1) consciousness is not an object that is similar to the other objects of nature; and 2) there are aspects of consciousness that cannot be studied via traditional quantitative methods of science. Ever fascinated with the content of elusive consciousness, therefore, phenomenologists cannot be concerned with the empirical question of what is or is not real. They simply begin with the nature of consciousness—whatever that nature might be—as significant data to be studied. At the very least, the study of human consciousness is different than the study of nature in that humans, unlike rocks, acids, and atoms, are meaning making entities. This meaning making or thinking process will shape human's behavior in ways that differentiate people from rocks. If you kick a rock, for example, you know pretty well how it will react. Kicking a human, however, will elicit a wide variety of actions, depending on the human kicked. Such a human response does not lend itself to precise measurement and predictability.

Phenomenology attempts to render problematic all presuppositions about the nature of its own activity, the object being investigated, and the method appropriate to this kind of inquiry (Husserl, 1970). The attempt to rid oneself of as many presuppositions as possible grants phenomenology the possibility of unmasking hidden assumptions about the nature of reality. Phenomenologists also attempt to view consciousness as intentional, meaning that it is directed toward a specific object. Another way of expressing this thought is that consciousness is consciousness of something. Thus, phenomenologists think that it is absurd to divide reality (or the research process) into subjects and objects. The two cannot be separated, and the attempt to do so distorts reality (Steward & Mickunas, 1974; Schwandt, 1994).

Thus, an important concept about knowledge production in the social sciences that holds profound implications for the scholarly insights of social studies educators emerges in this context. As these educators attempt to evaluate and produce social knowledge, they begin to differentiate between research that does and does not understand the special status of human consciousness and the epistemological insights it necessitates. Democratic social studies teachers are suspicious of data that is produced by experts who don't grasp the difference between human beings and sedimentary rocks. Phenomenology may provide one of the best methodological pathways for social studies educators to grasp the specifics of this epistemological problem. It is concerned with the effort to grasp the meaning individuals ascribe to their lived worlds. Phenomenological understanding involves putting oneself in place of another person and attempting to recreate his or her feelings in oneself. Using this empathetic function, phenomenology provides a much more complex, deeper, and useful form of social knowledge than the Cartesian attempt to record the frequency of particular behaviors.

It is easy to see the impact of phenomenology on modes of research such as ethnography. When researchers ask not about the absolute meaning of a work of art but instead ask of its meaning for a certain individual or a group, they move research in new directions. The qualitative knowledge which emerges when researchers ask about and attempt to interpret the meanings that particular persons give to particular phenomena allows us new understandings and unique perspectives on social events and the human beings who participate in them. The human realm of intersubjective meaning becomes accessible in a way never imagined by Cartesian modernist researchers, when scholars interrogate the conventions, forms, and codes of everyday social life (Smith, 1983; Donmoyer, 1985; Soltis, 1984; Denzin & Lincoln, 2000; Kincheloe & McLaren, 2000).

Phenomenologically produced understanding of the way individuals construe their world and their place in it is one way in which intersubjective knowledge leads us to new dimensions of seeing social experience. In educational inquiry, such ways of seeing allow social studies educators to understand how teachers and students give meaning to their lived worlds in light of social and cultural forms they reflect and help produce. Indeed, such forms of inquiry facilitate our understanding of the often hidden and always ambiguous process by which education initiates us into our culture (Carspecken, 1996, 1999).

Phenomenology is a qualitative alternative to the epistemology of positivism. It presents, in a sense, a starting point for a critical democratic social studies teacher in the attempt to move beyond the mind-set that too often runs the schools, perpetuates teacher deskilling, and makes schools bad workplaces. Using our concepts of critical-theoretical enlightenment and emancipation and their concern with understanding and acting justly in the sociopolitical world, we embrace a critical phenomenology that helps us abandon the role of teacher as an implementor of administrative policy. No longer do we see research as a part of a process of explaining, controlling, and predicting. Phenomenology teaches us that we cannot understand an educational act without understanding the framework, the context within which teachers, students, and administrators make sense of their thoughts, feelings, and actions. Our critical phenomenology takes us one step beyond traditional conceptions of phenomenology by adding our concern with power to the mix. We must question the power relations, the ideological forces that shape that framework, that context, which helps construct our thoughts, feelings, and actions (Fowler, 1984; Wilson, 1977; Kincheloe & McLaren, 2000). We are comfortable on this difficult domain because ours is an epistemology that understands and seeks to deal with the complexity of the social world.

Phenomenology teaches us to abandon positivistic deductive devices, such as prior hypothesis formation that restricts researchers by directing their attention to often irrelevant variables. As with qualitative forms of research in general, the focus of our study in phenomenology emerges as the inquiry progresses. We focus on the perceptions of individuals, seeking the insiders' perspective. Of course, at the critical level, we search for the various ways this perspective is constructed by larger social forces. To the critical phenomenologist, the most influential reality of the many realities with which humans must deal is human perception. This reality is more important than any so-called objective reality because people act on what they perceive: Perceptions have consequences, they move events, they shape lives. Consider how these ideas affect social studies teaching and knowledge work. While the positivist seeks objective, factual, verifiable portrayals of reality, phenomenologists will seek to understand the participants' comprehension of what is happening and how such perceptions affect their lives. Because they hold such different goals, research data derived via the two approaches will present quite different perspective on the world and the school (Fetterman, 1988). They will construct profoundly different social studies curricula. Which one will you teach? I don't think you can stay neutral here.

Certainly one of the most important thinkers of the late twentieth and early twenty-first century about these issues is educator William Pinar. His work in this epistemological domain is essential for democratic social studies teachers. In his attempt to develop a practical method of analyzing the educational experience of the individual, Pinar takes this phenomenological orientation and fuses it with psychoanalysis and aesthetics. He calls his analytical form, *currere* (the Latin root of the world "curriculum," meaning the investigation of the nature of the individual experience of the public). We are returned once again to the inner world, the *Lebenswelt*, and to its relationship with the educational experience. A traditional criticism of much of the theoretical work in education is that it is not connected with the everyday experiences of teachers and students. Pinar's use of the concept of *currere* helps bring about the synthesis of theorizing and *Lebenswelt* with all the benefits that are to be accrued form such a fusion (Pinar, 1975, 1994, 1999).

Pinar claims that, in *currere*-based research, meaning is typically derived from the analysis of the relationship between signs and experience. Taking his cue from Maxine Greene (1975), Pinar contends that the quest for an understanding of experience impels researchers to tap their own subjectivity so that common sense may be transcended; i.e., we must go beyond what we take for granted. As knowledge workers in social studies, we must ask questions such as: What is involved in moving beyond the common sense world? How does one initiate the process? What possible benefits are to be derived? Are there examples of other individuals who have accomplished such a complex move and what did they gain? How do such attempts affect what we know in education? It is through such questions that we approach the *Lebenswelt* or, in Pinar's words, "that realm of the *Lebenswelt* associated with *currere*" (Pinar, 1975, p. 395).

As we engage in this phenomenological bracketing of experience in our own lives, Pinar argues that we are better prepared as researchers to apprehend the contents of consciousness as they appear to us in educational contexts. The liberation which results involves a freedom from modes of perception that reflect cultural conditioning and result in inauthentic and counterdemocratic behavior. We must loosen our identification with the contents of consciousness so that we gain some critical distance from them—a metaperspective. From our new vantage point, we may be able to see those psychic realms which are formed by conditioning and unconscious adherence to repressive social convention. Critical theorists would identify the process as part of the attempt to demystify the ideological construction of consciousness.

Once we have embarked on our quest to understand *currere*, Pinar tells us, we will uncover a great diversity of formats and sources. The educational *Lebenswelt* comes in a variety of packages; one package may contain historical information, another the insights of free association, another the contemplations of specific literary passages, and still another may hold ostensibly insignificant slices of school life. Both cognitive and intuitive insights (or a creative synthesis of the two) will inform our perception of *currere*.

At first, Pinar concludes, the information derived from our attempt to examine *currere* may be idiosyncratic. Eventually, however, our examinations will uncover aspects of a collective or transpersonal realm of educational experience. In other words, once we transcend the unique details of an individual's biography, we may unlock the doors to a secret room where fundamental structures of human experience have been hidden from view. Such structures may, as phenomenologists have anticipated (Merleau-

Ponty, 1962), appear very different when viewed at the stratum of individual personality but may be very similar when analyzed at the level of their roots. The understanding of these basic structures and their relationship to the sociopolitical world, and thus their impact on the world of social education, may be one of the most important outcomes of phenomenological research applied to the educational *Lebenswelt* (Pinar, 1975, 1994; Pinar, Reynolds, Slattery, & Taubman, 1995).

In our search as critical social studies educators for *currere* and the relationship between the basic structures of human experience and individual biography, we run head-on into the complex dialectic of particularity and generalization. When *currere* is extended by insights from semiotics and an epistemology of complexity and an awareness of the dialectic of particularity and generalization is moved to the front of the teacher's consciousness, the possibility for interesting and dangerous insight emerges. In our theorizing on place, Pinar and I address this interplay of particularity and generalization. Our sense of place, our grounded particularity, loses nothing when exposed (by way of *currere's* connection of private sensation to the public space) to the anticipatory accommodation notion of generalization derived from critical research.

Anticipatory accommodation is a very simple concept. It emerges in the rejection of the positivist notion of external validity—the extent to which a researcher can generalize her or his findings to other situations. The ability to make pristine generalizations from one research study to another accepts a simplified one-dimensional, cause-effect Cartesian universe. In a positivistic context, all that is needed to ensure transferability is to understand with a high level of internal validity the extent to which a researcher's observations and measurement are true descriptions of a particular reality, e.g., something about a particular classroom, and to know that the make-up of this classroom is representative of another classroom to which the generalization is being applied. The positivist would argue that the generalization derived from the first classroom is valid in all classrooms within that same population. Time or context factors are irrelevant in the positivistic context. Many qualitative researchers have argued that this positivistic concept of external validity is far too simplistic and assert that, if generalizations are to be made, if we are to be able to apply findings in context A to context B, we must make sure that the contexts being compared are empirically similar. This is a very difficult task.

If we accept a Piagetian notion of cognitive constructivism, we begin to see that, in everyday situations, humans don't make generalizations in this positivistic way. Piaget's notion of accommodation seems appropriate in this context since it asserts that humans reshape cognitive structures to accommodate unique aspects of what is being perceived in new contexts. In other words, through our knowledge of a variety of comparable contexts, we begin to understand their similarities and differences, and we learn from our comparisons of different contexts. Prediction, the goal of positivistic research, is not the desired outcome; thus, the notion of anticipatory accommodation: We learn from experience to anticipate a range of possibilities in particular circumstances. The cultivation of such an ability becomes a central goal of a democratic social studies. In many ways, anticipatory accommodation is a key component of wisdom. It is a form of wisdom that recognizes concurrently both similarity and difference in social and educational situations and thus allows us to anticipate what might happen and what we might do based on our foresight (Kincheloe & Pinar, 1991). In the difference between positivistic external validity and this notion of anticipatory accommodation rests the conceptual basis of our epistemology of complexity. Again, the world (the social cosmos in particular) emerges as far more complex than Cartesians thought.

Joel Kovel's (1981) concept of totality may extend our understanding of these issues. Totality implies a notion that is broader than either the particularity of private experience or the generalization of socioeconomic pattern; yet, it encompasses them both. Human beings are entwined in countless ways in this totality, which, in the particularistic domain, involves place and individual consciousness and, in the generalized realm, includes psychological, social, political, and economic patterns: e.g., in psychology, patterns of learning styles and in socioeconomics, patterns of school performance along the lines of class, race, and gender. Critical democratic social studies teachers must attend to both the particularistic and the general, especially the various levels of interaction between them. This is the totality, this is how we get to the *Lebenswelt*. The totality implies a radical reconceptualization of both the research act and social studies teaching. It not only directs our attention to the ways that socioeconomic and ideological forces construct consciousness but also to how individual children, real-life boys and girls, respond to such construction.

The totality connotes an understanding of individual consciousness in relation to history in all its complex multidimensionality. Critical knowledge workers cannot view themselves outside of history; they need to understand the place in the web from which they see reality. History viewed from the perspective of Kovel's totality becomes a working concept inseparable from the act of critical knowledge production and research. History becomes, thus, not a simple linear story of social, economic, and political forces; neither is it a series of particularistic anecdotes. The critical democratic social studies teacher sees history as an interplay between both the particularistic and the general that informs our understanding of our own consciousness, the forces which shape our professional lives, and the factors which help construct the world of our students.

Our historical understanding sets up our move to a new form of critical cognition; such a move allows us entry to the private world of experience from which we were previously excluded. An ossified Marxism, for example, that disregarded the particularistic was unable to account for the conservatism of many poor Americans—the working-class support of militarism and trickle-down neoclassical economics. It is by now a cliché to argue that control of the means of production is not a sufficient condition for emancipation. This recognition rests on Kovel's conception of totality which takes into account the ideological construction of individual consciousness (Kincheloe & Pinar, 1991). Critical democratic social studies teachers who understand the implications of an epistemology of complexity can make dramatic use of totality's synthesis of consciousness and history.

In this phenomenological domain, with its concern with new ways of exploring (not measuring) consciousness, we come to understand the ways this concern has shaped critical theoretically informed qualitative research and knowledge production. Democratic social studies educators must understand and be able to use these modes of research. This phenomenological focus on consciousness has shaped the evolution of ethnography and its application to education knowledge work over the past few decades. Ethnography is often described as the most basic form of social research. While ethnographers disagree over the relative importance of each purpose, ethnography attempts to gain knowledge about a particular culture, to identify patterns of social interaction, and to develop holistic interpretations of societies and social institutions. Thus, ethnography in social studies education attempts to understand the nature of schools and other educational agencies in these ways, seeking to appreciate the social processes that move educational events.

Phenomenology, ethnography, and historiography form a foundation for the paradigmatic challenge to positivism. Critical ethnography attempts to make explicit the assumptions one takes for granted as a culture member. The culture could be as broad as Japanese culture or as narrow as upper-middle-class student culture of George Washington High School. The critical ethnographer of education seeks to describe the concrete experiences of everyday school/educational life and the social patterns, the deep structures, that construct it. One of the most basic tools of the critical knowledge worker involves the research orientation derived from the phenomenological-ethnographic tradition (Hammersley & Atkinson, 1983; Denzin & Lincoln, 2000; Carspecken, 1996, 1999).

Another basic tool of critical research is semiotics. Semiotics involves the study of signs—it derives from a Greek word meaning sign—and codes. Semiotic researchers decode the systems of symbols and signs that enable human beings to derive meaning from their surroundings. Television wouldn't make sense to a Martian, for example, even if the alien could speak the language TV employed. Too many signs and codes exist which could only be deciphered by an acquaintance with the lived world that TV represents. This is why individuals from one culture, even though they speak fluently the language of another culture, might completely fail to catch the humor of a situation; it is contextualized in the culture in which they are aliens.

Each language, each system of codes and signs, is peculiar to a particular historically grounded culture. Semiotics views everything in a culture as a form of communication arranged in ways similar to that of verbal language. Critical knowledge workers who employ semiotics attempt to study culture as a communication phenomenon. They study it as a whole, always exploring interrelationships, never looking only at bits and pieces of it. They search for these relationships between phenomena in the context of an examination of the structures of institutions and individual consciousness. In the process, they uncover previously unnoticed manifestations of how power is reproduced and how consciousness is constructed (Scholes, 1982; Hodge & Kress, 1988).

In unexpected places, semioticians uncover new insights into social and psychological processes, e.g., the forms of what people call courtesy, the packaging of fast food, the facial expressions of an employee while talking to his or her boss, the points at which movie goers laugh during a film, etc. The school is a diamond mine for semiological study, for it abounds with codes and signs, and in conventions that call for unique insight. The way teachers, students, and administrators dress, pupils' language when speaking to teachers as compared to conversations with classmates, graffiti in a middle school restroom, systems of rewards and punishments for students, the use of bells in school, memos sent to parents, the nature of the local community's conversation about school athletics, are only a few of the many school topics which semioticians study.

Social studies teachers, employing semiotics in their repertoire of research strategies, might pay especially close attention to the ostensibly insignificant, offhand comments of their students, for it is here in what is typically dismissed as noise that semiological significance is revealed. An adolescent's observation that "You [the teacher] always pick on me," may be far more revealin, when pursued, than an expert's questionnaire. A pupil's excited attempt to interject a description of a DMX rap into a class discussion of *Sister Carrie* may provide unique and multidimensional insight when analyzed semiotically. James Anthony Whitson provides excellent examples of techniques of semiotic analysis and how such techniques can be used to open new vistas on the meaning of schooling that can be adapted by classroom social studies teachers (Gibson, 1984; Whitson, 1986).

To the semiotician, a text is not simply printed material. It is far more broadly defined, involving any aspect of culture that contains encoded meaning. For example, the text of a homecoming queen pageant holds multiple levels of meaning that can be read to reveal cultural insights and gender constructions. In the same way, a child's lunch is a map to a child's home culture: a Mexican student in South Texas who packs a single tortilla in a paper bag; the "lucky" suburban student whose single parent picks up lunch at McDonalds' on the way to school. A basic characteristic of semiotics involves its assumption that the interpretation of a text is not tied to the author's conscious understanding of its meaning. It thus follows that the socioeducational importance of a school practice may have little to do with what those who devised and implemented it had in mind. Certain disciplinary practices may have been formulated in the minds of school leaders simply as mechanisms to keep order.

The assumptions about the values, interests, and motivations of children, the purposes of schools, the meaning of democracy, the role of gender, definitions of good behavior, etc. embedded in such policies never entered into the consciousness of the school administrators when they conceived their discipline policy. The meaning of such practices is never static to the semiotician; meanings continue to reveal themselves as long as semioticians devise new questions of them. Thus, semiotics is a subversive form of research that teaches us to read the lived world in a new way. It is a form of reading that desocializes us from the official interpretations of the dominant codes; it frees us from the authorial interpretations of social texts that exploit those unequipped to question such impositions.

What does the flag mean? What does school spirit mean? What does maturity mean? What does popularity in school mean? What does good citizenship mean? Semiotic researchers uncover their dominant meanings, as well as a variety of subjugated, uncertified, oppositional meanings, and all of these dynamics provide us deep insight into the nature and construction of consciousness. As a result, semioticians cannot help but involve themselves in the study of ideology, and how it expresses itself and shapes consciousness in a variety of ways in a number of different places (Whitson, 1986; Scholes, 1982). Though we can never measure consciousness in the way positivists require for knowledge to be validated—we can never say that a student has a consciousness of 42—we can, through the use of ethnography and semiotics, paint a compelling and useful impressionistic picture of it.

5. CONCERN WITH LOGIC AND EMOTION/FEELING IN THE PROCESS OF KNOWING—THE IMPORTANCE OF EMPATHY. With a little reflection, we realize that in our everyday life we often speak of different epistemologies, different ways of knowing, without even thinking about it. We all have some idea of a Cartesian epistemology when we say that science proves that nicotine causes cancer in lab rats. But most of us make counter-Cartesian epistemological knowledge claims as well. Consider for instance: "I knew when I met him that he couldn't be trusted"—intuitive knowing; "My heart told me I loved her"—emotional knowing; "My "gay-dar" went off the screen when she walked in the room"—empathetic knowing; "I know there is more to life than meets the eye. I plan to enjoy the afterlife immensely"—spiritual knowing; "Don't tell me there's no God, I know Jesus is my personal savior"—divine knowing; "If I have to explain rap music to you, you'll never know anything about it"—cultural knowing. An epistemology of complexity recognizes that there are many ways of knowing, some more appropriate in some situations than others. For

example, I did not use a positivistic way of knowing to discern whether or not to marry my wife, Shirley. I relied much more on an emotional form of knowledge, a feeling. If I ever have to have my appendix removed, I hope my surgeon uses a different epistemological perspective as she decides where to make her incision. You get the idea. The epistemological idea I want to make for social studies educators in point 5 is that both logical and emotional ways of knowing are important in a democratic social studies. I will lay out how educators can use both epistemological orientations, sometimes together, sometimes separately, for emancipatory effect.

Feminist educator Madeleine Grumet (1988) extends our understanding of the counter-Cartesian attempt to transcend sole reliance of logic (logocentrism) by connecting with an epistemology of the body, of feeling. Social science, she argues, whether guided by regressive or emancipatory impulses, has been emeshed in a male-dominated snare of logical abstraction. Grumet has sought new methods of inquiry that are capable of drawing the body and feeling into the public conversation about education. Making use of qualitative methodologies such as history, theater, autobiography, and phenomenology, she confronts androcentric abstraction with the uncertainty, specificity, and contradiction of the private, the corporeal, the feminine. From the perspective of the guardians of the Cartesian tradition, such epistemological confrontations constitute overt subversion. After exposure to such concepts, inquiry can no longer be viewed as a cold, rational process. As feeling, empathy, the body, are injected into the research process, as the distinction between knower and known is blurred, as truth is viewed as a process of construction in which knowers play an active role, passion is injected into inquiry. Democratic social studies teachers see themselves as passionate scholars who connect themselves emotionally to that which they are seeking to know and understand.

Several decades ago Michael Polanyi wrote about personal knowledge, that is, a way of knowing which involves the passionate participation of the knower in the act of knowing. Guided by such notions, critical social studies educators embrace a passionate scholarship, a reconceptualized science, that is grounded upon and motivated by our values and solidarities (Belenky, Clinchy, Goldberger, & Tarule, 1986). Passionate knowers use the self as an instrument of understanding, searching, as Madeline Grumet has, for new methods to sophisticate the way the self is used in research. Søren Kierkegaard anticipated this notion of feminist passion, arguing in the first half of the nineteenth century that there is an intimate connection between commitment and knowing. Subjectivity, he maintained, is not simply arbitrary; instead, it reflects the most profound connection between an individual thinker and the world.

As inquirers grow passionate about what they know, they develop a deeper relationship with themselves. Such a relationship produces a self-knowledge that initiates a synergistic cycle, a cycle which grants them more insight into the issue being investigated. Soon, Kierkegaard argued, a form of personal knowledge is developed which orients the mind to see social life as more than a set of fixed laws. Social life is better characterized as a process of being, a dialectic where the knower's personal participation in events and the emotional insight gained from such participation moves us to a new dimension of knowing. Not only did Kierkegaard anticipate feminist theory's concept of passionate knowing and Polanyi's personal knowledge, but he also foreshadowed a post-Piagetian, post-Cartesian, postformal mode of thinking and producing knowledge that grounds our notion of a critical democratic social studies (Reinharz, 1979; Kincheloe, Steinberg, & Villaverde, 1999).

Another precursor of the feminist notion of passionate scholarship that shapes our social studies (and which should serve to humble Eurocentric academicians) concerns the ways that indigenous peoples have defined knowing. Note the similarities of Afrocentric and American Indian ways of knowing with the counter-Cartesian perspectives of Kierkegaard, Polanyi, and contemporary feminists. To such peoples, reality has never been dichotomized into spiritual and material segments. Self-knowledge lays the foundation for all knowledge in the African and Native American epistemologies. Great importance has traditionally been place on interpersonal relationships (solidarity), and a connected logic has moved these traditions to appreciate the continuum of spirit and matter, individual and world.

Indeed, indigenous ways of knowing and the European Cartesian tradition come into direct conflict over the epistemological issues of mind and body, individuals and nature, self and other, spirit and matter, and knower and known—a conflict which has generated serious historical consequences. It is only in the last 30 years that some Eurocentric people have come to recognize the epistemological sophistication of indigenous ways of seeing that discern a unity in all things and a connected spiritual energy embedded in both human and natural elements. Thus, that deemed primitive by traditional Western scholars becomes, from the perspective of democratic social studies teachers, a valuable source of insight into our attempt to extend an emancipatory education (Myers, 1987; Nyang & Vandi, 1980; Semali & Kincheloe, 1999).

The Italian philosopher Antonio Gramsci well understood some of these epistemological concepts, when he wrote from Mussolini's prisons in the late 1920s and 1930s. The intellectuals' error, he wrote, consists of believing that one can know without "feeling and being impassioned" (Gramsci, 1988). The role of intellectuals and researchers from Gramsci's perspective revolved around their attempt to connect logic and emotion in order for them to "feel" the elementary passions of the people. Such an emotional connection would allow the inquirer to facilitate the struggle of men and women to locate their lived worlds in history. Finding themselves in history, they would be empowered by a consciousness constructed by a critically distanced view of the ways that the structural forces of history shape lives. One cannot make history without this passion, without this connection of feeling and knowing, since, without it, the relationship between the people and intellectuals is reduced to a hierarchical formality. The logic of bureaucracy prevails, as intellectuals move to the higher rungs of the organizational ladder, assuming the privileges of a superior caste, a modern Egyptian priesthood (Gramsci, 1988). The essence of democratic knowledge work rests on an appreciation of Gramsci's exposure of the power relations between intellectuals and non-intellectuals.

The ability to create a new form of thinking that brings together logic and emotion and the human capacity for empathy is dependent on our understanding of the forces that shape the self. This is a theme that emerges time and again in our quest for a democratic emancipatory social studies. Knowledge of self allows researchers to understand how social forces and research conventions shape their definitions of knowledge, of inquiry, of effective educational practice. Knowledge of the self allows them consciousness to choose between epistemologies that depersonalize the process of knowing in hopes of gaining certainty, pure objective knowledge, and research orientations that assert that, since the mind of the observer is always involved, it should be utilized as a valuable tool. Humans possess a tacit knowledge which can be drawn upon to make sense of social and educational situations. Such tacit, intuitive knowledge guides researchers as they conduct interviews, observations, document analyses, etc. A primary purpose of the critical form of social knowledge work is to connect social studies teachers to the nature and formation of such tacit knowing and, in turn, to help them learn how to employ it for maximum benefit. Let us examine some of the dimensions of this tacit knowledge that makes humans the most valuable of all research instruments.

To begin with, humans are sensitive to subtle, hard-to-categorize dimensions of social life. Because of such sensitivity, the human inquirer can interact with a situation in such a way that the unspoken, the hidden, can be made explicit. The empirical research instruments that are capable of assessing particular factors are inappropriate for assessing other factors. Such is not the case with human instruments: They are almost unlimited in their adaptability. Researchers, as agents freed from reliance on particular instruments of inquiry, are capable of simultaneously collecting information about a variety of social factors at a variety of levels.

Humans, unlike research instruments, can perceive holistically. In the maelstrom of confusion that constitutes the socioeducational world, only humans can see connections between the disparate parts; only humans can grasp and perceive dominant themes in the ostensibly unrelated remnants of the socioeducational fabric. Human inquirers can extend knowing to a higher level through their capacity to grasp the realm of the felt, the emotional, the unconscious. Those unexamined usages, those unintended meanings, which reveal insights that open windows into the significance of experience, are the type of understandings that only humans are capable of grasping. These are the insights that allow us to comprehend the actual educational and ideological effects of schools and other social institutions. Here resides the central concept behind point 5 in our epistemology of complexity: Logic can be enhanced by interaction with the unique and often unexpressed emotional dimensions of human beings.

Unlike empirical instruments of research, humans can synthesize information, generate interpretations, and revise and sophisticate those interpretations at the site where the inquiry takes place. In the process the human, as research instrument, can explore the unusual, the idiosyncratic situation. The traditional empirical research instrument, on the other hand, may have no use for the unusual situation because it does not fit the categories delineated. Such uniqueness may serve as the path to a new level of understanding of the effect of a curriculum on a student or a community. While such dimensions of research are quite valuable and very sophisticated, we can look at them merely as extensions of everyday human activities: listening, watching, speaking, reading, etc. The cult of the expert will undoubtedly be uncomfortable with such research populism, but our understanding of social and educational life will be enhanced in the application of such a perspective (Lincoln & Guba, 1985; Denzin & Lincoln, 2000). Social studies teachers can revolutionize professional practice by viewing themselves as potentially the most sophisticated knowledge producing instruments available. In a very practical context, social studies teachers do not need experts to tell them what methods work in class; they can use their intuitive and empathetic capacities to discern what the students are learning and what they don't understand.

Empowered by an understanding of the power of their intuition, democratic social studies teachers refuse to allow a formal positivistic science to devalue what they perceive in their everyday practice. By validating what can be learned from life, feminist scholars have opened a whole new area of inquiry and insight. They have uncovered the existence of silences and absences where traditional scholars had seen only "what was there." Women scholars were able to uncover such absences by applying their own lived experience to the research process, thus connecting knower and known (Belenky, Clinchy, Goldberger, & Tarule, 1986). Traditional positivist researchers had weeded out the self, denied their intuitions and inner voices, in the process, producing restricted and object-like interpretations of socioeducational events. Using the traditional definitions, these object-like interpretations were certain and scientific; feminist self-grounded inquirers were inferior, merely impressionistic, and journalistic (Reinharz, 1979; Clough, 1998; Hicks, 1999).

Feminist theorists realized that the objective science of the Western tradition was released from any social or ethical responsibility. Objectivity in this sense became a signifier for ideological passivity and an acceptance of a privileged socioeconomic position. Thus, scientific objectivity came to demand separation of thought and feeling, the devaluation of any perspective maintained with emotional conviction. Feeling is designated as an inferior form of human consciousness; those who rely on thought or logic operating within this framework can justify their repression of those associated with emotion or feeling. Feminist theorists have pointed out that the thought-feeling hierarchy is one of the structures historically used by men to oppress women. In intimate heterosexual relationships, if a man is able to present his position in an argument as the rational viewpoint and the woman's position as an emotional perspective, then he has won the argument—his is the voice worth hearing.

The power dynamics of this relationship are projected onto a larger scale in the domain of knowledge production: The research experts occupy a male role, while the researched, and even the consumers of the research, occupy a female role. Thus, on a variety of levels, research is not a value-free, nonideological activity. Traditional science reproduces particular power relations which lead to the production of specific forms of knowledge. In this context, certain questions are asked, while others are deemed irrelevant. Presuppositions, try as positivistic science researchers might, cannot be eliminated. They can be brought to consciousness, confronted, and transformed over time, but they cannot be discarded (Fee, 1982; Reinharz, 1979).

Thus, the methodologies of scientific research emerge from these dominant presuppositions. Revered as sacred, traditional methodologies are rarely questioned even when they separate research technique from research purpose. To initiate inquiry with a question of method rather than with a question of purpose, feminist researchers alert us, is irrational. It is irrational in the sense that it bifurcates the way we obtain knowledge and make judgments. Flannery O'Connor argues that "judgment is implicit in seeing;" that is, constructing judgements is not an isolated process. When it is undertaken as such, it becomes so diluted that the insights derived are bland and trivial (Westkott, 1982). In this context, an epistemology of complexity attempts to heal the self-inflicted wounds of positivism. By removing judgment, emotion, and intuition from the knowledge production process, positivists shoot themselves in the foot before running the race. With these understandings, democratic social studies teachers can derive insights central to understanding and changing the social world that had previously been declared off limits.

Thus, a critical democratic perspective toward knowledge production helps social studies teachers connect knower and known, purpose and technique, by utilizing the human as a research instrument. From this perspective, inquiry begins with researchers drawing upon their own experience. Since the social researcher is a human being studying other human beings, he or she is privy to the inner world of experience. Utilizing his or her own empathetic understandings, the observer can watch social and educational phenomena from within, i.e., they can know directly, they can watch and experience. The gap between experience and scientific description begins to close. On a variety of levels the private is made public. Not only do we get closer to the private experience of our students, other teachers, and administrators, and the effect of these experiences on the public domain, but we also gain access to the private experience of the researcher and the effect of that experience on the public descriptions he or she presents of the social phenomena observed. In our situation as democratic social studies teachers, of course, we are the researchers, and it is our private experience and its relation to our public descriptions (and our public actions as teachers) that is being analyzed. Thus, not only do we learn about the educational world that surrounds us, but we gain new insights into the private world within us— the world of our constructed consciousness (Reinharz, 1979, 1982, 1992, Hicks, 1999). Such insight has profound consequences concerning how we teach our social studies students.

Continuing to take our cue from feminist scholarship in building our epistemology of complexity, democratic social studies teachers work to overcome positivism and the isolated egocentrism that accompanies it. In advocating their notions of intuitive and emotive ways of knowing, feminist knowledge workers call for a connected epistemology. Positivistic egocentrism (as opposed to connectedness) reduces our awareness of anything outside our own immediate experience. In this self-centeredness, we tend to reduce everything to an individual perspective. This ultimately causes us to miss meanings of significance. Many would argue that this self-absorption leads the way to an introspective self-knowledge that will move us to higher levels of experience, new dimensions of cognition. While self-knowledge is extremely important, egocentrism tends to reduce our ability to critique the construction of our own consciousness; we cannot get outside ourselves to recognize the social forces that have shaped us. Unless social studies teachers learn to confront egocentrism, the possibility of formulating critical perspectives in regard to ourselves and the world around us is limited. While we must make sure that social studies students have confidence in their own perceptions and interpretations, we must concurrently work to help them overcome the tendency to see the world only in terms of self. In a way, we must help them cope with a lifetime struggle between the tendency for self-confidence and the tendency for humility. We do not seek resolution, just a healthy interaction between the impulses (Greene, 1988, 1995; Pinar, 1994).

Overcoming egocentrism is an important first step in our epistemological quest for a connected consciousness. Feminist theory has emphasized the value of such a consciousness, since it has argued the importance of the feminine tendency for connectedness, that is, to experience the self essentially in relationship with others (Belenky, Clinchy, Goldberger and Tarule, 1986). Feminist theory distinguishes connectedness from separateness, which often eventuates in a moral stance grounded on impersonal methods for establishing justice. Separateness is often associated with an epistemology that is based on impersonal methods for establishing truth. Separateness has granted meaning to many of Western society's sacred political beliefs, such as freedom from interference or deregulation, self-dependence rather than an interrelationship with the community, and freedom as the right to do as we please (Greene, 1988, 1995).

As Fritjof Capra (1996) writes in his book, *The Web of Life*, this notion of interconnectedness is not only important in the social world but in the physical cosmos as well. In the development of life, for example, an interconnected synergy (the production of a combined effect greater than the sum of their separate effects) occurred when separate organisms actually blended together to produce a new higher-order (evolved) living entity. Such a synergistic, interconnected process challenges traditional notions of an individualistic evaluation of the species. Capra is interested in the epistemological implications of this process:

> Life is much less a competitive struggle for survival than a triumph of cooperation and creativity. Indeed, since the creation of the first nucleated cells, evolution has proceeded through ever more intricate arrangements of cooperation and evaluation (p. 243).

Interconnectedness, and the epistemology it supports, is a basic feature of the physical world, even of life itself. Such concepts are central to the very nature of our being as humans (ontology).

In this ontological context, we gain new insights into the nature of knowing in general and social knowing in particular. Connected knowing values intimacy and understanding instead of distance and proof. Separate knowing pursues autonomy, the highest state in the developmental taxonomies of Jean Piaget and Lawrence Kohlberg. Even some notions of critical theoretical emancipation privilege autonomous self-direction based on an understanding of how the influences of one's past shape and mold. A feminist reconceptualization of emancipation grounded on connected knowing uses this understanding of one's past not only to free oneself from its repressive characteristics but to facilitate connection with other people around visions of community.

The autonomy of Kohlberg and other liberals rests on the assumption that, once individuals reach a high cognitive development, their thinking is directed by principles of justice and egalitarianism. Simple rationality, then, is what is needed in the effort to create a just community (Lesko, 1988; Greene, 1988). Henry Giroux (1988) argues that this modernist rationalistic perspective on justice is not defined by results but through an obsession with logical process. Unconnected to real histories and lived experiences, modernist justice is conceived for a society of strangers who all have a relationship with the law but not each other (Siegel, 1986). The problem, of course, with this rationalistic, autonomous justice is what it excludes. As Max Horkheimer wrote decades ago, such rationalism fails to address the nature of happiness and the good life. Women have often pointed out the importance of attachment in the human life cycle, conceiving their role as teachers as purveyors of support and connectedness. Instead of presenting political procedures for justice, the supportive social studies teacher attempts to touch students, to grapple with them as world makers struggling to find their voice in the choir (Greene, 1988).

Logic and rationality retain their importance, but the ultimate end of cognitive development in an epistemology of complexity goes beyond simply grasping abstract principles. Cognitive development entails understanding everyday life from as many vantage points as possible. Indeed, a key to critical democratic thinking involves the ability to gain new angles of seeing, to contextualize in unique ways. Kohlberg, in his detached modernism, glorified Clint Eastwood, the self-contained H.P.D. (*High Plains Drifter*) who asked "nothing from nobody." The man with no name had no need to establish connections with a core of friends, to seek new perspectives on the conditions that he faced. Feminist cognition, on the other hand, operates within a network of relationships connected by an ethic of caring. In this way, feminism helps establish an epistemological basis for our critical democratic social studies. Leaving behind the myth of autonomy, moral and cognitive decisions are seen not as the constructs of individual minds but as the product of communion among people (Gergen, 1991).

Chapter 9

Social Studies Teachers as Knowledge Workers: Formulating the Epistemology of Complexity

Chapter 9 continues our effort to formulate an epistemology of complexity while, at the same time, thinking about its implications for social studies teaching. These epistemological concepts construct the basis of our concept of social studies as a form of knowledge work. To bring about the changes in the field that are necessary to making social studies a valuable feature of democratic practice, social studies teachers must become scholars who are knowledge workers—they research, they interpret, they expose embedded values and political interests, and teach students to produce their own knowledge. Epistemological understanding is central to this democratic objective.

6. CAN'T SEPARATE KNOWER FROM KNOWN. THUS, THE QUESTIONS THE KNOWER ASKS SHAPE WHAT CAN BE KNOWN. Throughout this discussion of an epistemology of complexity and what it means for critical democratic social studies teachers, I have often alluded to the inseparability of the knower and the known. Point 6 is a brief extension of this basic epistemological understanding and its highlighting of the profound importance of question formulation in shaping the knowledge we produce. Simply put, there is no knowledge without a knower. As a living being, a perceiving instrument, the perspective

of the knowledge producer must be granted the same seriousness of attention as is typically accorded the research design, the research methods in traditional forms of inquiry (Lowe, 1982; Gordon, Miller & Rollock, 1990).

Like knowledge, the knower also belongs to a particular, ever changing historical world. The human being as a part of history is a reflexive subject, i.e., an entity who is conscious of the constant interaction between humans and their world. Such a critically conscious knowledge worker recognizes that all knowledge is a fusion of subject and object. In other words, the knower personally participates in all acts of understanding. Moreover, the world in general, and the social and educational work in particular, is not an objective structure, but a constructed, dynamic interaction of men and women organized and shaped by their race, class, gender, and countless other features. Thus, it is impossible from the perspective of an epistemology of complexity to conceive knowledge without thinking of the knower (Reinharz, 1979; Lowe, 1982).

But the notion of knower-known inseparability has not been the dominant position in social and educational knowledge production. Social studies teachers need to understand that the Myth of Archimedes, the belief in an objective body of knowledge unconnected to the mind of the knower, has helped formulate how social studies educators have approached the curriculum presented to them. Such an assumption tacitly constructs not only what counts as valid knowledge but, via the shaping of research, it formulates what we "know" about society and education. The myth assumes that the human perceiver occupies no space in the known world; operating outside of history, the knower knows the social and educational world and its students, teachers, citizens, and leaders objectively.

This separation of the knower and the known is a cardinal tenet of the Cartesian-Newtonian paradigm. The impact of this way of seeing on the theory and practice of Western science has been profound. René Descartes' analytical method of reasoning, often termed reductionism, has formed the foundation of modern scientific research. Cartesian reductionism asserts that all aspects of complex phenomena can be best appreciated by reducing them to their constituent parts and then piecing these elements together according to causal laws (Mahoney & Lyddon, 1988). This is the opposite of an epistemology of complexity.

The social studies educational implications of this epistemological understanding are compelling. In particular, such an epistemological awareness highlights the importance of the questions a social studies educator might ask. What knowledge is produced in social studies and other domains depends on the questions asked about the topics at hand. Democratic social studies educators engage themselves and their students in the process of revealing the questions and the values that generate them that stand in the shadows of all data. This ability is necessary to the formulation of a critical democratic social studies because it helps unlock the secrets to why a curriculum contains this information and not other knowledges.

Such an epistemological analysis forces us to move beyond positivism's concern with simply answering unanalyzed questions or solving prearranged, structured problems. This question-formulating, problem-posing stage, Einstein argued, is more important than the answer to the question or the solution to the problem. Critical democratic social studies teachers are question analysts and problem posers. When epistemologically naïve teachers set up a problem, they select and name those things they will notice. Thus, questioning is a form of world making: how we select the problems and construct our worlds is based on the values we employ. Without an epistemological consciousness, teachers and administrators learn how to construct schools but not how to determine what types of schools to construct. In other words, teachers, school leaders, and teacher educators need to realize that school and classroom problems are not generic or innate. They are constructed and uncovered by insightful educators who possess the ability to ask questions never before asked, questions that lead to innovations that promote student insight, sophisticated thinking, and social justice (Schon, 1987; Ponzio, 1985).

If the genius of, say, an Einstein revolved around his ability to see problems in the physical universe that no one else had ever seen, then the genius of a social studies teacher revolves around his or her ability to see social and educational problems that no one else has ever seen (Kincheloe, Steinberg & Tippins, 1999). The application of such skills moves social studies education to a level unimagined by teachers trapped within the Cartesian tradition. Not only is such an educational orientation grounded on a democratic conception of teacher empowerment, but it serves to expose previously hidden forces that shape the consequences of the educational process. It is a testimony to what can happen, what can be revealed, when social studies teachers transcend the limitations of positivistic definitions of research and explore the relationships between the knower and the known.

With these understandings in mind, the very source of the knowledge found in social studies texts and curriculum guides involves the asking of value-laden questions. Julia Ellis (1998) writes that, in her classroom, she assigns interpretive exercises where students attempt to make sense of the texts they have encountered in class. In this context, she asks students to identify the questions that drive their interpretations and the origins of such inquiries. In this way, students can understand that questions produce knowledge, values produce questions, and that one's location in the web of reality produces the values we hold. Such recognitions provide social studies students and teachers a far more sophisticated view of why individuals (themselves included) believe what they do, why the social world operates the way it does, and what they might do to bring about democratic and egalitarian sociopolitical change.

Starting with questions such as "Why does this exist?" or, more specifically, "Why does homelessness exist?" or, "What can be done to improve the situation?" social studies teachers engage students in a reflective awareness of their own questioning processes. Being exposed to that which is different from our common experiences—different cultural understandings and epistemologies, for example—may be central to our attempt to raise new questions, to become the Einsteins of social studies. Paulo Freire helps us in this context since he not only teaches us how to expose the questions hidden in all knowledge forms but to formulate critical democratic questions concerning information with which we are confronted. When we are aware of our values and how they help shape our questions, we are much better equipped to make sense of an incoherent body of data. We become, in this context, critical interpreters of the social world who understand the roots of our own and other peoples' explanations of human affairs (Freire and Faundez, 1989).

7. OUR VIEW OF THE WORLD IS GROUNDED ON THE PERSPECTIVES OF THOSE WHO HAVE SUFFERED AS THE RESULT OF EXISTING ARRANGEMENTS. Often those who produce knowledge about the social world come from the dominant culture. Academics infrequently base their views of reality on the viewpoints of marginalized and excluded individuals. Because of this tendency, scholars who validate the views of the marginalized have in essence encountered difference. And, as we

have contended, our consciousness is raised when we take difference seriously. Valuing the productive power of difference, democratic social studies teachers take a cue from liberation theologians in Latin America and begin their analyses of social and educational institutions by listening to those who have suffered most as a result of their existence.

With these understandings in mind, a social studies based on an epistemology of complexity seeks a dialogue between Eastern cultures and Western cultures, as well as a conversation between the relatively wealthy northern cultures and the impoverished southern cultures (Bohm & Peat, 1987; Welch, 1991). In such a context, forms of knowing, such as the understandings of blue-collar workers that have traditionally been excluded by the modernist West, move social studies educators to new vantage points and unexplored planetary perspectives. Understanding derived from the perspective of the excluded or the "culturally different" allows for an appreciation of the nature of justice, the invisibility of the process of oppression, and the difference that highlights our own social construction as individuals. In this spirit, workers and educators who appreciate the insights of an epistemology of complexity begin to look at their work from the perspectives of their Asian, African, Latino and indigenous colleagues around the world. Such cognitive crossfertilization often reveals the tacit assumptions that impede innovations. For example, homebuilders who study Native American, Japanese or African ways of building houses may gain creative insight into their craft. After studying the way Zuni pueblos addressed problems of living space, they might be empowered to tackle space problems creatively in ways conventional builders hadn't considered.

In the context of cognitive development, Jean Piaget argued that conceptual change takes place when learners engage in the process of accommodation. As previously mentioned, Piaget described accommodation as the restructuring of one's cognitive maps to take care of an unanticipated event, that is, to deal with difference. In order to accommodate, an individual must actively change his or her existing intellectual structures to understand the dissonance produced by the novel demand. Accommodation is a reflective, integrative behavior that forces the realization that our present cognitive structure is insufficient to deal with the changing pressures of the environment (Kaufman, 1978; Fosnot, 1988). In a sense, accommodation becomes a subversive agent of change,

leading an individual to adjust whenever and wherever it might be necessary. When Piagetian accommodation is connected with Frankfurt
School critical theory's concept of negation in a context that appreciates
the critical notion of difference, interesting things begin to happen.
Common to both critical theory and accommodation, negation involves
the continuous criticism and reconstruction of what one thinks one
knows. For example, critical theorist Max Horkheimer argued that,
through negation, we develop a critical consciousness that allows us to
get beyond old ossified world views and incorporate our new understandings into a new reflective attitude (Held, 1980).

As critical democratic social studies teachers recognize the potential
of critical accommodation, they structure learning situations where individuals come to understand previously unrecognized aspects of the environment and expose the cognitive limitations that precluded insight in
the past. Horkheimer maintained that, through the awareness gained by
way of critical negation (the philosophical analogue to the cognitive act
of accommodation), an individual develops and becomes open to radical
change. In this context, critical accommodation can be described as a
reshaping of consciousness consonant with a critical understanding of
democracy and social justice. Thus, critical social studies educators see
the diversity of classroom experiences as an opportunity for cognitive
growth. An example from a democratic social studies classroom might
help to ground this concept. A teacher exploring the meaning of intelligence would develop (assimilate in Piagetian theory) an understanding
of the concept based on his or her personal experience and the coverage
of cognition in his or her teacher education. The teacher would accommodate the concept as he or she began to examine students who were
labeled unintelligent but displayed sophisticated abilities in the manual
arts or in the practical understandings of the trades and crafts.

At this point, the teacher might take note of this contradiction and
begin to integrate this recognition of exception (accommodation) into a
reconceptualization of the prevailing definition of intelligence in the culture of school. The old definition of intelligence would have been negated through exposure to diverse expressions of intelligence, and new ways
of seeing it would have been accommodated. In this way, an epistemology of complexity might alert teachers to the mainstream dismissal of the
talents of students from the margins—non-white and economically disadvantaged young people. Picking up on these concerns, teachers would
critically accommodate nontraditional expressions of intelligence that

would free them from the privileged, racially and class-biased definitions used to exclude cognitive styles that transcended the official codes. In this and many other situations, accommodation becomes the emancipatory feature of the thinking process. Critical democratic social studies educators recognize this and use it in the struggle for democratic economic, social, and educational change (Hultgren, 1987; Lather, 1991).

Derived from dangerous memories of history that have been suppressed and information that has been disqualified by social studies gatekeepers, subjugated knowledge plays a central role in an epistemology of complexity. Through the conscious cultivation of these low-ranking knowledges, alternative democratic and emancipatory visions of society, politics, education, and cognition are possible. In a critical democratic social studies curriculum, subjugated knowledge is not passed along as a new canon but becomes a living body of knowledge open to different interpretations. Viewed in its relationship to the traditional curriculum, subjugated knowledge is employed as a constellation of concepts that challenges the invisible social and cultural assumptions embedded in all aspects of schooling and knowledge production. The subjugated knowledges of African Americans, Native Americans, working-class people, women, and many other groups have contested the dominant culture's view of reality.

Confronted with subjugated knowledge, individuals from white mainstream culture begin to appreciate the fact that there are multiple perspectives on all issues. Indeed, they begin to realize that textbooks discard data about unpopular viewpoints and information produced by marginalized groups. Social studies curricula that include subjugated perspectives teach a lesson on the complexities of knowledge production and how this process shapes our view of ourselves and the world around us. The curriculum cannot stay the same if we take the knowledges of working-class men and women seriously, if we get beyond the rosy, romanticized picture of immigration to the U.S. and document the traumatic stories of the immigrants, if we seek out women's perspectives on the evolution of Western culture, or if we study the culture enslaved Africans brought to the New World.

The white dominant cultural power blocs that dominate North America in the first decade of the twenty-first century seem oblivious to the need to listen to marginalized people and take their knowledge seriously. Western power wielders are not good at listening to information that does not seem to contribute to hegemony, or their ability to win the consent of the subjugated to their governance. Knowledge that emerges from and serves the purposes of the subjugated is often erased by making it appear dangerous and pathological to other citizens. Drawing on work within the discipline of cultural studies that seeks to reverse conditions of oppression, subjugated knowledge seeks new ways of validating the importance and relevance of divergent voices. Such voices are excluded not merely from schoolrooms and social studies curriculum guides but from other sites of knowledge production, such as popular culture. Having become a major pedagogical force in Western societies over the past few decades, the popular culture "curriculum" is monitored for emancipatory expressions of subjugated knowledge. Though not always successful, power wielders attempt to neutralize the subjugated knowledges that find their way into TV, movies, popular music, the Internet, and other popular cultural sites (Dion-Buffalo & Mohawk, 1993; Fiske, 1993; Mullins, 1994; Nieto, 1996; McLaren & Morris, 1997).

Since the approval of subjugated knowledges is not contingent on the blessings of power wielders in the dominant culture, purveyors of subjugated knowledge can confront individuals from the white, upper-middle class cultural center with the oppressed's view of them. Some of the pictures are quite disconcerting for mainstream individuals who have never given much thought to the way they are seen from the social margins. Individuals from dominant social formations have never developed their imagination about how they look to marginalized others. As a result, women often make sense of men's image of women better than men understand women's view of men, individuals with African heritages understand the motivations of whites better than the reverse, and low-status workers figure out how they are seen by their managers more clearly than the managers understand how they appear to workers. Obviously, such insights provide us with a very different view of the socio-political world and the processes that shape it. Social studies teachers who employ subjugated viewpoints become transformative agents who alert the community to its hidden features, its submerged memories, and, in the process, help individuals to name their oppression or possibly understand their complicity in oppression. Such a naming process helps students, teachers, workers, and other community members to reflect on their construction of their lived worlds in such a way that they develop the ability to take control of their own lives—emancipation.

Thus, critical social studies teachers devoted to the value of subjugated knowledges uncover those dangerous memories that are involved in reconstructing the process through which the consciousness of various groups and individuals has come to be constructed. Such an awareness frees teachers, students, and other individuals to claim an identity apart from the one forced upon them. Indeed, identity is constructed when submerged memories are aroused. In other words, confrontation with dangerous memory changes our perceptions of the forces that shape us, which in turn moves us to redefine our world views, our way of seeing. The oppressive forces that shape us have formed the identities of both the powerful and the exploited. Without an analysis of this process, we will never understand why students succeed or fail in school. We will be forever blind to the tacit ideological forces that construct student perceptions of school and the impact such perceptions have on their school experiences. Such blindness restricts our view of our own and other people's perception of their place in history, in the web of reality. When history is erased and decontextualized, teachers, students, workers, and other citizens are rendered vulnerable to the myths employed to perpetuate social domination.

Teaching that is committed to subjugated knowledge has "friends in low places." In a critical social studies, the view from above of the traditional Eurocentric upper-middle-class male curriculum makes way for the inclusion of views from below. Emerging from an understanding of and respect for the perspective of the oppressed, such an epistemological position uses the voices of the subjugated to formulate a reconstruction of the dominant stories of traditional social studies. It is a radical reconstruction in the sense that it attempts to empower those who are presently powerless and to validate oppressed ways of thinking that open new cognitive doors to everyone. As critical social studies educators expose the way dominant power invalidates the cognitive styles of marginalized groups, we begin to examine testing procedures and their political effects. Eurocentric, positivistic psychometricians devise tests to evaluate student performance, forgetting in the process that evaluation is based on unquestioned definitions of intelligence and performance. When well-intentioned social studies teachers attempt to develop curricula based on a recognition of the existence of marginalized experiences, they miss the lessons provided by an understanding of subjugated thinking. Mainstream, multicultural social studies involves the inclusion of information on Africans, Latinos, Native Americans and women in a curriculum that has traditionally examined the contributions of famous white men. The power dynamics and cognitive orientation of the curriculum are not changed by such additions; they simply add a few new facts to be committed to memory. Such add-ons can be viewed as a tokenism that perpetuates the power relations of the status quo that, in turn, paves the way for a kinder, gentler oppression.

The advantage of subjugated perspectives, the view from below, involves what has been termed the "double consciousness" of the oppressed. If they are to survive, subjugated groups develop an understanding of those who attempt to dominate them; at the same time, they are cognizant of the everyday mechanisms of oppression and their effects. W. E.B. DuBois called this double consciousness of the oppressed a form of second sight, an ability to see oneself through the perception of others. A critical social studies curriculum of second sight is grounded on the understanding that a critically educated person knows more than just the validated knowledge of the dominant culture. For example, to understand science from a critical perspective would involve analysis of its specific historical origins (the seventeenth and eighteenth centuries) and its cultural location (Western Europe). A critical multicultural science curriculum would appreciate that, like other ways of understanding and studying reality, Western science is a social construction of a particular culture at a particular time. Such a cognizance would not induce us to dismiss and discard the accomplishments of Western science. That would be silly. But it would induce us to study other ways of knowing, such as the scientific theories of Native Americans and other cultural groups.

Science, as the term is typically used, is, Vandana Shiva (1993) writes, a Euro-centered ideology with parochial origins in male-centeredness and particular socioeconomic classes. Such culturally specific roots of science have been hidden behind a claim of a transcultural, transhistorical universality. Only when we study subjugated histories and cultures, such as those of women and non-Western societies, are we able to expose the socially constructed nature of Western science and the logic implicit within it that accepts ecological destruction and the exploitation of nature. Science is not the only area where an epistemology of complexity searches for alternative subjugated knowledges, for such information exists around each axis of domination. In the domain of gender, for example, critical analysts value ways of knowing that have traditionally been viewed as feminine. Such knowledges expose the hidden gender assumptions of male-centered social studies, since they provide alternative ways of looking at the sociocultural world. Ways of understanding and functioning in the world employed by disabled people, such as the use of sign language, are forms of subjugated knowledge that can be taught in a critical multicultural curriculum. Also important in this context is gay and lesbian subjugated knowledge that provides significant insight into the construction of sexual preference, sexual desire, and the cultural dynamics of gender role production. Both homosexually oriented and heterosexually oriented individuals can gain insight into the production of their identities from a confrontation with such subjugated knowledges.

Because of their race, class, and gender positions, many social studies educators are insulated from the benefits of the double consciousness of the marginalized and are estranged from a visceral appreciation of suffering. Until I was placed in a lower-track set of courses as a high school student—I was not viewed as a good student—I never understood what it felt like to be viewed as "slow." Such an experience alerted me to the pain of my fellow slow students and provided me with a second sight or a double consciousness of students in such a position. Such second sight has, in my opinion, served as one of the most important insights I have brought to my career as an educator. Such awareness is a subjugated knowledge, a way of seeing, that has been ignored in too many educational situations.

Contemporary social organization, and its sanctioning of the suffering of various individuals and groups such as low-track students, is often viewed as acceptable in the dominant curriculum. Educational leaders, who often come from dominant groups, don't typically challenge the ways of seeing that justify the prevailing social and educational system. What lived experiences would create a cognitive dissonance within the minds of such leaders that would make them uncomfortable with the status quo? The oppressed, while often induced by the mechanisms of power to accept injustice and to deny their own oppression, often use their pain as a motivation to find out what is not right and to discover alternate ways of constructing social and educational reality. The following points illustrate the benefits of a reconceptualization of social studies education in the light of an appreciation of subjugated knowledge (Ferguson, 1984; Fiske, 1993; West, 1993; Sleeter & Grant, 1994).

a. *Subjugated knowledges help us to rethink the social studies curriculum, the academic disciplines in general, and our purposes as educators and cultural workers.* An understanding of subjugated knowledge alerts us to the fact that there are different ways of seeing the world. With this understanding in mind, it becomes apparent that school and university curricula privilege particular views of the world. This can be illustrated by examining the discipline of mainstream educational psychology. If a foundational concept of the discipline involves the definition of intelligence as that which IQ measures, then what unstated cultural assumptions and values are embedded in such a definition? Throughout the history of Western developmental psychology, intelligence has been defined in a very exclusive manner. Interestingly, those excluded from the community designated as intelligent tend to cluster around categories based on race (the non-white), class (the poor) and gender (the feminine). The Western modernist tendency for logocentrism permeates definitions of intelligence.

According to mainstream Cartesian educational psychology and cognitive science, the way of knowing ascribed to "rational man" constitutes the highest level of human thought. This rationality or logic is best exemplified in symbolic logic, mathematics, and scientific reasoning. With the birth of modernity (the Age of Reason) and its scientific method in the seventeenth and eighteenth centuries, logocentrism was accompanied by a misogyny that associated feminine thinking with madness, witchcraft, and Satanism. As a result, scientific knowledge became the only game in town. In this context, individuals came to be represented in a dramatic new form—as abstracted entities standing outside the forces of history and culture. This abstract individualism eclipsed the Western understanding of how men and women are shaped by larger social forces that affect individuals from different social locations in different ways. Western society was caught in a web of patriarchy, a mode of perception that limited thinking to concepts that stayed within white, androcentric boundaries, far away from the "No Trespassing" signs of the feminine domain.

As social studies teachers begin to uncover these hidden values embedded in both the prevailing definitions of intelligence and our scientific instruments that measure it, they embark on a journey into the excitement of an epistemology of complexity. As they begin to search for forms of intelligence that fall outside traditional notions of abstract reasoning, they come to appreciate the multiple forms of intelligence that different individuals possess, especially those individuals who fall outside the racial, ethnic, or economic mainstream. It is not uncommon for us to walk through the halls of an urban high school, peeking in advanced placement (AP) or honors courses dominated by white faces. Further down the hall, the general education classes are filled with non-white, minority students and poor whites. Sensitive to the multiplicity of ways intelligence can be expressed, critical democratic social studies teachers begin to examine those students who have been labeled by mainstream educational science as unintelligent, slow learners who are at risk.

Upon further examination, teachers often uncover abilities in these students that are unconventional, but nevertheless, sophisticated. Students who are raised in cultures that value active engagement with reality over abstract rationality are the first victims of the scientific definitions of intelligence. Forms of intelligence that emphasize doing over abstraction regularly reveal themselves if teachers are sensitive to the social, cultural, and psychological dynamics discussed here. For example, a student's ability to draw, to build, and to fix are all sophisticated forms of cognition that are not measured by a standardized test. Critical social studies teachers can recognize, praise, cultivate, and connect these abilities to other forms of knowing. This process is an extremely important aspect of a democratic social studies. Once the values hidden in mainstream definitions are exposed, the possibilities opened for the education of the previously excluded are limitless. Valuing subjugated knowledge creates a new world for students condemned by the narrowness of traditional disciplinary ways of assessing them.

b. *Subjugated knowledges contribute to the analysis of the ways knowledge is produced and legitimated.* In Cartesian social studies, we are taught to believe that the social knowledge we consider official and valid has been produced in a neutral, noble, and altruistic manner. Such a view dismisses the cultural and power-related dimensions of knowledge production. Knowledge of any form will always confront other knowledge forms. When this happens, a power struggle ensues (evolution versus creationism, Western history or world history, the new or the old maths, anthropological studies of non-Western cultures versus a traditional patriotic curriculum). The decisions made in these struggles over knowledge exert dramatic, but often unseen, consequences in schools, economic institutions, popular culture, and the political sphere. For example, the role of the social studies teacher as a neutral transmitter of prearranged facts is not understood as a politicized role accompanying knowledge production. If schools are to become places that promote teacher and student empowerment, then the notion of what constitutes politicization will have to be reconceptualized. Battle with texts as a form of research, Paulo Freire and Ira Shor (1987) exhort teachers. Resist the demand of the official curriculum for deference to texts, they argue, in line with their larger critically grounded political vision. Can it be argued that capitulation to textual authority constitutes a political neutrality?

One of the great paradoxes of contemporary social studies education involves the use of a language of empowerment in school talk coupled with pervasive ignorance of the way power operates to subvert the empowerment of teachers and students, racially and economically marginalized students in particular. Such a contradiction undermines the effort of teachers and students to gain new insights into the way power shapes consciousness (Giroux & McLaren, 1988). Does it matter that we come from rich or poor homes, white or non-white families? These questions are not viewed as questions of power or knowledge production. Indeed, they are often not recognized at all. In a postmodern era of information saturation, with its TV, movies, databases, Internet, CD-ROM, and headsets, such issues become even more important. In a mutating, globally expanding technocapitalism that seeks to colonize everything from outer space to inner consciousness, questions of power and information become more important than ever before.

In the twenty-first century, postmodern power's control over information continues to expand. In book publishing, for example, 2 % of the publishers control 75% of books published in the United States. Corporations continue to gain power. Advertising expenditures have increased dramatically since the 1960s. Corporate images have become more and more important, not simply for marketing purposes but also for capital raising, mergers, gaining the competitive edge in the production of knowledge, the effort to influence government policy, and the advancement of particular cultural values. Indeed, through the power of their money, postmodern corporations have transformed the role of the university from guardian of knowledge to knowledge producer for business and industrial needs (Harvey, 1989; McLaren, 2000).

In this epistemological context, social studies teachers, students, and other cultural workers appreciate the need to analyze what they know, how they come to know it, why they believe or reject it, and how they evaluate the credibility of the evidence. Starting at this point, they begin to understand the social construction of knowledge and truth. In school, for example, they recognize that the taken-for-granted knowledges that are taught do not find justification as such universal truth. Instead, democratic social studies teachers appreciate the fact that the purveyors of such information have won a long series of historical and political struggles over whose knowledge and ways of producing knowledge is the best. Thus, critical social studies educators are able to uncover the socially created hierarchies that travel incognito as truth. Though everyone knows their nature, these hierarchies mask their "shady" backgrounds of political conflict. As truth, they are employed as rationales for cultural dominance and unequal power relations (McLaren, 1991, 2000).

c. *In the larger critical theoretical effort to construct more inclusive and just sociopolitical and educational spheres, subjugated knowledge must be justified in social studies education.* Multicultural and subjugated knowledges should be included in the social studies curriculum because it is more fair to include a variety of cultural expressions. We have emphasized issues of knowledge production and the construction of academic disciplines because these are the terrains on which the struggle for social justice can be won. Unless some form of cultural separatism prevails, we will have to work in existing academic structures. As critical analysts, we must raise questions about the weaknesses of these structures and how, in the name of justice and academic excellence, they must be reconceptualized. Thus, subjugated knowledge transcends status as a mere add-on that operates as inferior information, included merely to silence protestors from marginalized racial and ethnic groups.

If one of the basic features of a democratic social studies education involves making use of student experiences in curriculum development, then a democratic and critical approach to teaching that gains credibility in the academy must involve connecting student experience with the themes of the classroom. If the democratic aspect of this type of social education revolves around the provision of a meaningful education to those traditionally excluded from such an experience, then subjugated students and their marginalized cultural knowledge take on a new importance. In no way does mere reference to such knowledge constitute a critical democratic education. The move to the critical involves making use of such ways of knowing in a manner that challenges the hegemony of a monolithic form of social studies knowledge. Thus, in this context, student experience must be analyzed and subtly connected to larger sociopolitical and educational issues. Such a process is never easy, since it requires great skill and intellect on the part of the teacher. Critical epistemologically conscious teachers who are able to negotiate such an informed and nuanced process will render social studies meaningful in the lives of those who traditionally have discerned little connection between schooling and their lived realities. The success encountered by such teachers will help to legitimate the process in schools and communities (Darder, 1991; Ayers, 1992; Pruyn 1994).

d. *Subjugated knowledge helps to produce new levels of social insight by making use of indigenous knowledge.* Indigenous knowledge is a specified form of subjugated knowledge that is local, life-experience-based and non-Western-science-produced. Such knowledge is transmitted over time by individuals from a particular geographical or cultural locality. Indigenous ways of knowing help people to cope with their sociological and agricultural environments and are passed down from generation to generation. A critical democratic social studies that values subjugated knowledge realizes that indigenous knowledge is important not only for the culture that produced it but for people from different cultures. Only in the last couple of decades are European peoples beginning to appreciate the value of indigenous knowledge about health, politics, medicine, agriculture, philosophy, ecology, and education. Traditionally, these were the very types of knowledge that European education tried to discredit and eradicate. A critical education works hard to save such knowledges, which are, unfortunately, rapidly disappearing from the face of the earth.

A critical democratic social studies education sees a variety of purposes for the inclusion of indigenous knowledges in the curriculum. Since indigenous knowledges do not correspond to Western notions of discrete bodies or packages of data; they must be approached with an understanding of their ambiguity and contextual embeddedness. Thus, any effort to understand or use such knowledges cannot be separated from the world views and epistemologies embraced by their producers. The confrontation with such non-Western ways of seeing moves the power of difference to a new level of utility, because it exposes the hidden world views and epistemologies of Westerners unaccustomed to viewing culture—their own and other cultural forms—at this level. In this context, the critical encounter with indigenous knowledge raises epistemological questions relating to the production and consumption of knowledge, the subtle connections between culture and what is defined as successful learning, the contestation of all forms of knowledge production, and the definition of education itself. An awareness of the intersection between subjugated ways of knowing and indigenous knowledge opens a conversation between the "north" and the "south," that is, between so-called developed and underdeveloped societies. Critical social studies teachers seek to use their awareness of this valuable intersection to produce new forms of global consciousness and intercultural solidarity.

e. *If recognition and validation of subjugated and indigenous knowledges induce us to rethink knowledge production, then social studies educators must become adept researchers.* Contrary to the pronouncements of many mainstream educators, critical democratic social studies teachers believe that it is possible to create an education where students from all backgrounds can become researchers. By no means will this be easy; but it can be done. In critical democratic educational contexts, teachers, labor leaders, cultural workers, critical psychologists, and many other pedagogical agents can teach individuals to conduct secondary research (investigation of what other scholars have produced) by mastering the use of libraries, electronic databases, the Internet, and other compilations of data. Critical democratic social studies educators also maintain that individuals from all walks of life can learn to produce primary research (data collection taken directly from observations of the lived world). Indeed, critical teachers contend that elementary, secondary, and higher education, as well as informal pedagogies that take place outside of an institutional context, will be forever transformed when students learn skills of inquiry that allow them to collect, interpret, and apply subjugated forms of knowledge.

Contrary to the accusations of conservative educators that critical forms of multicultural education are destroying the standards of education, the forms of social studies promoted here call for higher academic expectations. Students are too rarely challenged. The schools and social studies teaching I envision situate research skills and knowledge production abilities at the core of elementary, secondary, and higher education curriculums. Thus, teachers become scholars who contextualize, interpret, and create knowledge, all the while modeling such behavior for their students. In this demanding context, social studies classrooms take on the appearance of "think tanks"—institutions where important knowledge is produced that has value outside of the classroom. In modernist Eurocentric education, teachers were instructed to say "Give me the truth, and I will pass it along to students in the most efficient manner possible."

In the new epistemology of complexity, social studies teachers are encouraged to support themselves, to assert their freedom from all-knowing experts. Such critical teachers often say "Please support me as I explore the world of history, sociology, or anthropology." In this context, teachers are intimately familiar with the Western canon but refuse to accept without question its status as universal, as the only body of cultural knowledge worth knowing. Thus, as scholars of Western knowledge, non-Western knowledge, and subjugated and indigenous knowledges, such social studies teachers are not content to operate in socioeducational frameworks often taken for granted. As critical analysts, they seek to rethink and recontextualize questions that have been traditionally asked about schooling and knowledge production in general. While they respect earlier insight and are reverential in respect to the genius of past eras, such educators display their veneration by continuing to question the work of their intellectual ancestors.

8. THERE ARE MULTIPLE REALITIES—REALITIES CONSTRUCTED BY OUR LOCATION IN THE WEB OF REALITY. An epistemology of complexity teaches us that the reality we construct depends on our location (or placement) in the web of reality. Cartesian reductionism privileges a single, scientifically validated vantage point from which we can perceive "the one true reality." With different locations in the web of reality come different perspectives on the world around us (Lincoln & Guba, 1985; Denzin & Lincoln, 2000; Briggs& Peat, 1989; Slaughter, 1989). Critical democratic social studies educators under-

stand that reality, schools, and texts of all types hold more within them to be discovered than first impressions sometimes reveal. In this sense, different frames of reference produce multiple interpretations and multiple realities. Contrary to the problem solving of positivism, an epistemology of complexity sees the mundane as multiplex and continuously unfolding (Greene, 1988, 1995; Haggerson, 2000).

An epistemology of complexity constructs a distancing from reality that allows an observer diverse frames of reference. The distancing may range from the extremely distant astronauts looking at the Earth from the Moon, to the extremely close, like Georgia O'Keeffe viewing a flower. At the same time, this complex epistemological perspective values the emotional intimacy of feminist connectedness that allows empathetic passion to draw knower and known together. In the multiplex vision of reality, linearity often gives way to simultaneity, as texts become a kaleidoscope of images filled with signs and signifiers to be examined. William Carlos Williams illustrated such complex qualities in the early twentieth century when he depicted multiple, simultaneous images and frames of reference in a verbal manner. Williams attempted to poetically interpret Marcel Duchamp's *Nude Descending a Staircase*, with its simultaneism serving as a model for what might be labeled "cognitive cubism." Democratic social studies teachers use such ideas to extend the holographic nature of their own and their students' memory, as they create situations where students come to view reality from as many frames of reference as is possible. The single angle of the traditional photograph is replaced by the multiple angles of the holographic photograph (Dobrin, 1987; Mandell, 1987; Talbot, 1986, 1991).

Armed with their cognitive cubism, democratic social studies teachers come to understand that the models of teaching they have been taught, the definitions of inquiry with which they have been supplied, the angle from which they have been instructed to view intelligence, and the modes of learning that shape what they perceive to be sophisticated thinking, all represent a particular vantage point in the web of reality. Like reality itself, schools and classrooms are complex matrices of interactions, codes, and signifiers in which both students and teachers are interlaced. Just as epistemological complexity asserts that there is no single, privileged way to see the world, there is no one way of seeing the classroom, intelligence, the purpose of social studies education, or teacher or pupil success. Once teachers escape the entrapment of the Cartesian-Newtonian way of seeing, they come to value, and thus pursue, new frames of reference in regard to their students, classrooms, and workplaces.

In this context of complexity, with its multiple frames of reference, the Cartesian-Newtonian quest for a final certainty about the knowledge we produce and consume seems silly. If we have learned anything in recent years, it is that our ideas about the world change and they will continue to change in the coming years. The chance of arriving at some juncture in human history, where further research will become unnecessary, as many social scientists and psychologists predicted rather recently, is slim. There are no social, psychological, or educational laws and thus no certainty. And, we should get used to it. There is unlikely to be any single research strategy or theoretical view that will allow us to grasp the whole of reality.

Given such prospects, an epistemology of complexity tells us that social knowledge workers should welcome a proliferation of research paradigms and take advantage of the new angles they provide for viewing the world. This epistemological pluralism or eclecticism will take our understanding of the social world to previously unexplored dimensions. Those who accept pluralism will recognize that divergent theoretical systems and research paradigms designate different phenomena as data and that what we consider reality cannot be separated from the methodological procedures employed to produce those conclusions (Eisner, 1984). The path to such eclecticism, however, is beset with obstacles. Indeed, philosophers of social science speak of a crisis in social inquiry. It is a crisis with roots in two attempts: 1) the fight to free social science from the positivistic quest for certainty; and 2) the struggle by those freed from the first quest to figure out what to do with their freedom, i.e., to cope with the choices presented by accepting multiple frames of reference.

Evidence of the crisis is manifested by an inability to agree upon standard criteria for judging the progress of a field of study. With so many frames of reference available, social scientists find it increasingly difficult to make evaluations across the wide range of activities undertaken in the name of their disciplines. Maybe even more disconcerting is the inability of knowledge producers in social sciences to understand the assumptions, aims, and languages of one another. Yet, what is the alternative? The attempt to bond our studies in a common language with shared assumptions takes us back to a positivistic quest for a universally under-stood language of research, an Esperanto of inquiry.

Shared aims in social knowledge production, advocates of an episte-mology of complexity maintain, stifle our creativity and interpretive pos-sibility. Much of the great physical and social scientific research seemed irrelevant to the patriarchs of the disciplines when it was first encoun-tered. In the most healthy scientific situation, there is generally little consensus about what the next step should involve, which method should be utilized to pursue the next step, or how exactly success should be measured. The price of our abandonment of the quest for certainty is untidy diversity, but the world itself (especially the social and education-al world) is not all that neat (Smith, 1983; Eisner, 1984).

Barbara Frankel (1986) states it well, arguing that those who are dis-turbed by this untidiness are simply lamenting the "confusion and noise" foisted upon social science by the complexity of humanness. Like the librarian who dreams of the tidiness of a library without patrons, neopos-itivists fantasize a spick-and-span social science where all researchers uti-lize identical, unbiased, infallible measuring instruments. Research would be so much easier, they dream, if researchers and the researched didn't have to interact through the imprecise medium of verbal language, disagree over standards of success, and find themselves separated by divergent value structures (Schweder & Fiske, 1986). We will never real-ly "know" anything, they warn, if we don't quickly deny the idea of mul-tiple realities. Social studies teachers who understand the multiple realities of an epistemology of complexity and use such knowledge in their classes will have to learn to deflect the attacks of the positivist gate-keepers of the social sciences and their educational cronies.

Throughout my career as a social studies teacher and writer, I've been confronted by teachers who asked in this context: Why all this talk about epistemology and multiple frames of reference, when I just want to do seven steps to teaching social studies? Why do we have to learn the counter-Cartesian epistemological response to positivism and its need for certainty? The reason such epistemological understandings are important is that positivism and the unquestionable "facts" it produces about the social and educational world shape both our personal and professional consciousness. The social knowledge we are taught as truth, the models of teaching we are presented in teacher education, the definitions of knowledge production that support our own inquiry, the angles from which we view intelligence, the modes of learning that shape the way we think, all emerge from the certainty of modernism. Like reality itself, schools and classrooms are complex webs of interactions, codes, and signifiers in which both teachers and students are interlaced. Just as a complex epistemology asserts that there is no single, privileged way to see the world, there is no one way of seeing the classrooms, seeing intelligence, seeing teacher or pupil success.

Once teachers escape the entrapment of the positivistic way of seeing, they come to value, and thus pursue, new frames of reference in regard to their students, their classrooms, their workplaces. They begin to look at their lessons from the perspective of their students—their black students, their Hispanic students, their white students, their poor students, their middle and upper middle class students, their traditionally successful students, their unsuccessful students. They examine their teaching from the vantage points of their colleagues or an outside lay observer from the community. Thus, they step out of their teacher bodies, looking down on themselves and their students as outsiders. As they hover above themselves, they examine positivistic technicist teacher education with its emphasis on bulletin board construction, behavioral objective writing, discussion skill development, and classroom management. They begin to see that such professional training reflects the certainty of modernity, as it assumes that professional actions are reducible to a set of skills applicable to all situations (Nixon, 1981; Carspecken, 1996, 1999).

One of the most practical ways for social studies teachers to gain access to and employ multiple frames of reference involves learning semiotic research skills. Through semiotics, social studies educators can better understand schooling and its terrain of contestation, of competing power interests where rival groups struggle over the meaning of differing representations. Few forms of inquiry are better equipped to reveal the hidden divisions within the social fabric, the mystified and often unconscious struggle between the dominant and the dominated. To sustain their privilege, the dominant must control representation and access to divergent frames of reference; they must encode the world in forms that support their own interests, their own power. But such an attempt is not as easy as some analysts (e.g., traditional Marxists) have tried to portray it. V. N. Voloshinov (1973) writing in the first three decades of the twentieth century argued that we misconstruct reality when we assume that power groups simply impose their meanings on the symbols and codes of a culture. Voloshinov maintained that symbols and language systems were always "multi-accentual," meaning that, lodged within cultural codes, were diverse, oppositional interpretations. Therefore, while dominant groups certainly attempt to impose their meanings on, say, the signification of school symbols, they are not necessarily successful (Whitson, 1986; Hodge & Kress, 1988).

The study of this struggle to define cultural and educational codes and signs is one of the most important aspects of semiotic research. When the dominated are seen as merely the blind victims of the dominator's encoding of the world, a one-dimensional, deterministic view of the social world has been constructed, a hegemonic, singular frame of reference has been privileged over all others. Hegemonized groups are not always ignorant of the attempts of the dominant to define social symbols. They resist: not all groups bought into the Bush administration's attempt to encode the American flag as a symbol of obedience to the dominant culture. Many Americans resisted, offering a counterhegemonic reading of the flag as a symbol of self-determination and freedom. Not all people accepted Ronald Reagan's attempt in the 1980s to appropriate the working class semiotic of Bruce Springstein as a symbol for a restrictive, obedient form of patriotism. Many people resisted, offering a very different interpretation of the meaning of Springstein's personal and musical imagery. Not everyone was positioned as Bill Clinton wanted them to be when he attacked Sista Soulja's call after the Los Angeles riots of the early 1990s for African Americans who insisted on rioting to loot white areas instead of their own neighborhoods. They realized that Clinton was using Sista Soulja to encode a message to white Americans: I'm a Democrat who will not pander to the African American community. Most African Americans recognized Clinton's semiotic maneuver; many white Americans applauded his actions as a warning to "dangerous black radicals"—different positions in the racial web of reality, different frames of reference.

In these examples, we can see the political features of this epistemological dynamic: power wielders work to make sure that one particular reading of reality that supports the interests of power takes precedence over other possible interpretations. Despite the protestations of reactionary forces promoting a homogenous culture that sees difference as a threat, particular groups within Western society have come to value the multiple perceptions of reality that emerge from encounters with difference. One aspect of this post-Cartesian valuing of difference involves a growing appreciation for local cultures with their diverse forms of meaning making. In *Curriculum as Social Psychoanalysis:*

Essays on the Significance of Place, William Pinar and I (1991) promote this notion of difference within a regional context, focusing on education in the southern place.

In considering the nature of the southern curriculum, we explore the concept of cultural renewal, a process where one's cultural history is confronted with the notion of difference. Avoiding any tendency toward nostalgic romanticization, perceptions of the past are interrogated by the present, by the social perceptions of other places. Thus, the curriculum becomes a form of critical psychoanalysis, as it analyzes the origins of present pathologies revolving around race, class, and gender oppressions. Put another way, social studies teachers help students understand where they are standing in the web of reality and how this placement helps shape the frames of reference they use to see themselves and the world. Southern students come to realize the specific nature of their consciousness construction, gaining the political and cognitive insights that come from such a realization. Such insights involve the understanding that they don't just happen to hold particular perspectives toward race, class, gender, religious, and political issues; particular historical forces have shaped those ways of seeing (frames of reference).

In the arts, a similar type of localism or "place" impulse can be found. Many advocates of the performing arts have, in the last few decades, gained an appreciation of ethnic and racial traditions as they incite new possibilities of aesthetic and dramatic expression. In politics the move toward localism transcends traditional liberal-conservative boundaries. Localities are increasingly separating themselves from state and national subservience as they utilize technology to make connections to those who share their social and political concerns. All of these localizing impulses undermine the "bigger is better" standardization tendencies of modernism. As place becomes more valued, the modernist dream of one great truth retreats and the subversive counter-Cartesian concept of difference becomes more influential (Gergen, 1991).

The growing pluralism of our student constituencies, with their multiple frames of viewing, has forced Americans to reconsider, whether they want to or not, the nature of a multiracial, multiethnic society. At the same time that some people read the twenty-first-century demographics of diversity as testimony to the need to value difference, others, such as all-American racist David Duke, see it as a clarion call to fortify the armaments and protect the "traditional Western heritage"—the white male frame of reference—at all costs. Americans have not yet recognized the significance of the early battles between Allan Bloom and the multiculturalists, William Bennett and the feminists. These were not simply struggles over the curriculum at Stanford or that presented by the New York regents. These skirmishes were the first outbreaks of a larger struggle to define who we are, to determine how we see the world and even how we learn to think. In the first decade of the twenty-first century, we are all still in a fight between a modernist traditionalism of consensus and a complex epistemological ethic of difference.

A basic principle of pedagogy maintains that good teaching takes the lives of all students seriously. Critical social studies educators affirm this principle, maintaining that it requires that they account for the race, class, and gender diversity of student populations. In this context, educators research and recover student experiences, analyzing the process of their construction and the ways they shape identity. Critical social studies insists that teachers learn to engage such experiences in a manner that respects them. In this situation, respect does not imply some form of facile validation but a mode of pedagogical intervention that induces students to look beyond their own experiences, wherever they might stand in the web of reality. Just because a student is African American or Native American doesn't mean that a teacher should romanticize his or her experiences. Most student experiences and frames of reference are contradictory, ambiguous, and complex, and it is the role of the critical teacher to help students, other teachers, and community members to understand them in relation to the forces of domination and hegemonic power. As they show students the ways their experiences shape the realities they construct, democratic social studies teachers also point out the ways that racist, sexist, and class-biased curriculum materials may shape their self-image and social consciousness (Banfield, 1991; Nieto, 1996).

The epistemology of complexity's concept of multiple realities and the power of difference constructs no fixed, transcultural view of self or world. In a pluralistic epistemology, especially living in the postmodern condition, individuals in everyday life experience multiple frames of reference, multiple forms of intelligence, diverse spiritualities, and a variety of ethical systems. Making use of multicultural and previously discussed indigenous knowledges and epistemologies, democratic social studies teachers search through premodernist societies in their quest for unique and practical ways to avoid the nihilism of modernism and reestablish human solidarity. The cognitive disease of modernism may best be cured by a postmodern broth of seven taro leaves, a recipe that borrows the democratic and egalitarian impulses of modernism, the communitarian and ecological respect of premodernism, and the self-awareness and the ethic of difference of post-Cartesianism. The recipe leads to a complex epistemological consciousness of the way all individuals, ourselves included, are presented by their cultural experience with particular frames of reference (Gergen, 1991). It is the job of the critical democratic social studies teacher to bring these frames of reference and the realities they create to consciousness and then to provide students with other cultural and ideological ways of seeing.

In the everyday life of the social studies, classroom teachers who understand this epistemology of complexity appreciate that there is no single historical past, no one story. History is constructed by multiple stories, told by people from diverse locations in the web of reality, each of whom holds different values and asks different questions of the past. Going back to our discussion of how one might teach about Christopher Columbus, a critical democratic social studies teacher might ask students to read not only their U.S. history textbook's account of Columbus, but passages about him from a Spanish historian's perspective or that of a Native American researcher. A classroom discussion of what was learned from these multiple frames of reference could be quite valuable for everyone concerned. A social studies based on an epistemology of complexity demands that we question what is presented to us as facts and learn to see the multiple social, historical, political, and economic realities constructed by diverse peoples (Puk, 1994). "Getting beyond the facts" is an overtly epistemological concept that induces us to avoid the passive acceptance of what is pitched to us as truth.

9. THUS, WE COME TO UNDERSTAND WHERE WE ARE LOCATED IN THE WEB OF REALITY—BECOMING HUMBLE KNOWLEDGE WORKERS. From the previous point, we can appreciate that individuals cannot separate what they perceive from where they stand in the web of reality. By understanding an epistemology of complexity, social studies educators can become more aware of where they stand in the web and how it shapes their views of world and self. These epistemological concepts lay the foundation for the concept of positionality. Positionality involves the notion that, since our understanding of the world and ourselves is socially constructed, we must devote special attention to the differing ways individuals from diverse social backgrounds construct knowledge and make meaning.

Thus, depending on our location in the web with its diverse axes of power, we will designate what constitutes the most important information in the social studies curriculum very differently. For example, when I read E. D. Hirsch's construction of what essential knowledge citizens should know, I never cease to be amazed at how his location as a white, upper-middle-class American male shaped his choice of knowledge; it is predominantly made up of data about white, upper/upper-middle-class males from a Western heritage. I want Hirsch (and myself) to understand the ways his location in the web of reality shapes his perspectives about it.

An epistemology of complexity teaches us about the social world's complicated web-like configuration of interacting forces. Knowledge producers, like all of us, are entangled in, not disengaged from, the web. As previously asserted, knower and known are inseparable—both are a part of the web of reality. No one in this web-like configuration of the universe can achieve a God-like perspective; no one can totally escape the web and look back at it from afar. We all must confess our subjectivity; we must recognize our limited vantage point. To recognize how our particular view of the web shapes our conception of educational reality, we need to understand our historicity, our position in time and space. Positivist epistemology, and the knowledge production it supports, tends to ignore the way our historicity shapes our consciousness. As a result, our concept of the social world is stripped of its complexity and reduced to a static, one-dimensional frame. Thus, the positivistic knowledge producer feels confident that he or she can make precise predictions, settle controversial questions, and ignore the complex, interactive process in which all social activity is grounded. From this positivistic perspective, linear mathematics controls the variables, eliminates extraneous variables, and paints a Norman Rockwell portrait of social studies education (Doll, 1989; Slaughter, 1989).

Because democratic social studies teachers understand their limited view of the world from their locations in the web of reality, they embrace a new humility in their knowledge work. They claim new perspectives, not truth, when producing information about the social world. For example, democratic social studies teachers avoid particular forms of patriarchal, positivistic knowledge production that promote a particular view of the social world as simply right or wrong. Drawing upon feminist research methods, critical democratic teachers understand that our location in the web of reality undermines the possibility of an absolute pronouncement about historical, social, or political "truth."

Thus, critical democratic social studies teachers always pause before announcing an interpretation. In a patriarchal culture, such a pause may not be viewed as a bow to complexity as much as it is perceived as a sign of weakness, an inability to "shoot from the hip" like John Wayne as researcher. Thus, feminist analysts tend to avoid the either-or thinking that can serve as an obstacle to the complex epistemological ability to conceptualize multiple frames of reference, to imagine a variety of solutions to perplexing situations. Positivistic either-or thinking promotes less investigation of the "whys" in a sociopolitical situation; an epistemology of complexity, always digging deeper, places great value on the asking of "why" questions. "Why" questions lead to ambiguity, uncertainty, and, hopefully, humility in a dominant epistemological climate of certainty (Greene, 1988, 1995; Anderson, 1987).

As we confront the postmodern condition, with its globalization, exploding imagery, and cultural interchange, our epistemology of complexity, with its self-reflection based on an awareness of where we are situated in the web of reality, becomes extremely valuable. No longer are we comfortable with macho proclamations of our ability to totally comprehend reality. We begin to speak in terms of constructions of reality. With our awareness of the various information filters that are employed by the media and other power groups, we begin to understand the process by which things get constructed. Such knowledge leads to an epistemological humility, a realization, in the words of Julia Kristeva, "that at the deepest levels of my wants and desires (I) am unsure, centerless, and divided" (Kristeva, 1987, 7–8). This humility is not a passing uncertainty but a critical resistance to all representations and interpretations that claim transhistorical certainty.

As democratic social studies teachers reject positivism's universal reason as the supreme form of knowing the sociopolitical world, they seek alternate forms of thinking and epistemological approaches that are historically and socially contingent, that are grounded on an awareness of what can be seen from particular locations in the web of reality. The view one gets of Manhattan standing in the canyons of Wall Street is very different from what one sees of the same island while making a low approach into JFK Airport. Both views are partial—just like all other perspectives on the city. There is no one correct point in the web from which we can see everything large and small about Manhattan.

Epistemologically aware social studies teacher educators can no longer direct students to some sacred body of professional knowledge that rises above all other bodies of data in importance. From their particular locale in the web of reality, social studies practitioners gain a unique and valuable perspective on the discipline. The partial, historically and socially specific knowledge of the practitioner must be respected for its insight, not its certainty. Understanding different individuals' location in the web of reality, social studies teacher educators can no longer maintain an uncrossable chasm between their so-called professional knowledge of the discipline and teachers' so-called practical knowledge. These two groups of social studies educators hold differing perspectives on the field; both base their view of it from different points in the web of reality (Aronowitz, 1994; Ferguson, 1980; Hicks, 1999; Feinberg, 1989).

One way of conceptualizing the type of social thinking promoted by an epistemology of complexity is to think of it as an infinite game. It is a game that makes fun of certainty and the fundamentalist excesses that accompany it. Whether the excesses be religious, political, pedagogical, or cognitive, they all denote a positivist epistemological arrogance that impedes self-reflection and interpersonal communication. Democratic epistemologically aware social studies teachers are fallibists who are unafraid to laugh at their own fallibility. No one wins the game, but all players benefit from the way it exposes the pseudocertainties that plague Cartesian modernism. Inclusionary and nonhierarchical, the game allows us to challenge the traditional rules that penalize the outsiders, the players from the margins (Gergen 1991). Like much play it makes sure everyone has a part.

Thus, critical democratic social studies teachers work hard to locate themselves in the web of reality and, in turn, expand their capacity for self-understanding. Such an understanding produces a metaconsciousness that is powerful enough to open the long-locked door of the primal as it moves individuals to transcend the boundaries of instinct. An epistemology of complexity promotes a self-reflection that asks why we are the way we are, that is, the origin of selfhood. As individuals explore personal meanings, the origins of their actions, they gain an awareness of possibilities in their lives. Metaconscious individuals refuse to accept or reject validity claims of any body of information without considering its discursive nature, that is, where the information comes from in the web of reality, what can be officially transmitted and what cannot, and who translates it and who listens. Without such reflection, individuals travel through life imprisoned by the prejudices derived from everyday existence or by what is often labeled common sense. The habitual beliefs of an individual's historical age become tyrants to a mind unable to reflect on its genesis. We often emerge from 16 to 20 years of schooling without having been asked to think about our own thinking. In this situation, we are unprepared to meet the demands of citizenship in hyperreality.

In the context of Howard Gardner's (1983) notion of multiple intelligence, we use the complex epistemological concern with our location in the web of reality to develop new forms of interpersonal intelligence. Social studies teachers as intrapersonal analysts generate strategies to promote web-of-reality understandings, self-reflection among themselves, their students, and the public at large. Once individuals begin to gain insight on how where they come from shapes their identities and worldviews, they are capable of taking emancipatory leaps. One fundamentalist Southern Baptist student I taught in Louisiana asked to meet with me because she was getting, in her words, "absolutely nothing from the class." We sat in my office and talked for a few minutes, and I encouraged her to speak about her background.

As she spoke, it became increasingly apparent that the only worldview she had ever been exposed to was a fundamentalist Christian perspective. Having been raised in this Southern religious context myself, I spoke to her about the ways she viewed the world and how it often conflicted with some of the ideas I brought up in class. As I detailed her social, political, religious, and even epistemological perspectives, she began to sob. "I'm sorry," I said. "I didn't mean to upset you. What did I say that hurt you?" "It's not your fault," she told me, "I just hate to be so predictable." We both laughed and ended the conversation on a pleasant note. The rest of the semester, this student worked hard to understand the relationships between her location in the web of reality and her view of the world, her identity, and her role as a social studies teacher. She learned the powerful lesson an epistemology of complexity can teach about the social construction of consciousness.

Other students have not reacted the same way to such an understanding. In addition to angry responses concerning the effort "to destroy my values or religious beliefs," some students have told me: "I understand now that our location in the web of reality influences what we see and the knowledge we produce." So, if all information is produced from a particular locale and can't claim the status of positive truth, why read social research? Why bother? Many teachers and students are disturbed by the contingent nature of social studies knowledge; their first impulse is to turn off the entire process. I understand how one who has been educated in a culture of positivism that teaches that knowledge is universally applicable could feel this way. Critical democratic social studies teachers must be empathetic with the anxieties of student students.

As I empathize, I attempt to make the point that even though social and educational knowledge production is contingent and possesses particular assumptions and value dimensions, it can be helpful. Epistemologically aware, critical research can be viewed as a democratic science of becoming. Certainty and prediction can be replaced with our notion of anticipation—the imaginative construction of the possible. Prediction is predicated on a positivistic body of empirical data and cause-effect relationships; anticipation takes empirical data into account but then moves into another dimension of the imagination. The quest for control of social and educational phenomena is abandoned as is the search for a precise reflection of educational reality. Epistemologically reflective knowledge is always tentative. It is a temporary perspective on a particular segment of the social and educational world, concerned with the humble process of anticipation with all of its attendant qualifications (Lincoln & Guba, 1985; Denzin & Lincoln, 2000; Noblit, 1985, 1999; Reinharz, 1979, 1992). Making use of these awarenesses, we move from positivistic data gathering to critical and complex forms of wisdom.

10. UNDERSTANDING WHERE WE ARE LOCATED IN THE WEB OF REALITY, WE ARE BETTER EQUIPPED TO PRODUCE OUR OWN KNOWLEDGE. As democratic social studies teachers learn their location in the web of reality, understand the ways it affects them and other producers of knowledge, and appreciate the contingency of social information, they begin to grasp the need to become producers of their own knowledge. In positivist teacher education programs, social studies teachers don't produce knowledge. James Garrison (1988) finds such a situation strange and remarkable. No wonder teachers are disempowered, Garrison argues; they are not even viewed as professionals. The knowledge they convey to students is on loan from the experts; it is not the property of the teachers. Social studies teachers as researchers audaciously claim the right to participate in the production of knowledge, while at the same time retaining their humility concerning the tentative, provisional nature of the knowledge.

The production of new knowledge gleaned from the lived world of the students and the members of the community surrounding the school is very much a part of a critical democratic effort to reconstruct culture and reconceive the role of education around a democratic system of meaning. As long as officially certified experts retain the power to determine what counts as social knowledge, little reform is possible. If we hold the power to produce our own knowledge, then we are empowered to reconstruct our own consciousness. The tyranny of expert-produced interpretations of traditions can be subverted, and our futures can be reinvented along the lines of a critical epistemology of complexity.

This issue of knowledge control moves us into a direct confrontation with teacher power. We cannot maintain a view of students as democratic participants and teachers as disempowered technicians. Over sixty years ago, John Dewey argued that teachers must assume the power to assert their perspectives on matters of educational importance with the assurance that this judgment will affect what happens in schools. Present nonconceptual technicist models of teacher education do not accept this argument, often teaching novices not to seek empowerment, not to think in an independent manner. Indeed, the hidden curriculum of technicist teacher education promotes a passive view of social studies teachers; they are seen as rule followers who are rendered more "supervisable" with their standardized lesson plan formats and their adaptation to technical evaluation plans. Such a reality teaches a hidden curriculum of disempowerment to social studies students. Critical democratic social studies teachers, for their students' sake, must rebel against such totalitarianism, encourage their students to be uncomfortable with authoritarian pronouncements of truth in social studies texts, and help them become researchers of multiple perspectives on the data provided. Both social studies teachers and their students must become knowledge producers (Puk, 1994).

This ethic of teacher and student as researchers is central to the notion of social studies promoted here. Our epistemology of complexity pushes this ethic even farther, asserting that if we are serious about our work as political agents of democracy, we must help all citizens become researchers: the future of democracy depends on it. Dewey argued that in a truly democratic society, where all parties have a voice in the formulation of policy, parents and community members must be participants in the public conversation about education. These citizens need the empowerment an understanding of critical research can provide. One of the most democratic roles a public educator might play involves sharing critical research skills with the public, especially the disempowered public. This is a radical action on a number of levels. First, it negates the cult of the expert. It helps destroy the myth that men and women should seek guidance from those blessed with society's credentials to direct them. In this way, it celebrates human self-direction. Second, it expands the role of the teacher. The teacher moves from classroom technician to active political agent as he or she views education as a vehicle to build an egalitarian community. And, third, it positions the school as an agent of democracy that is dedicated to an ethic of inclusion and negotiation. Operating as a democratic agent, the school seeks to uncover those forces that thwart participation as its teachers carefully map the web of reality that support such powers.

Critical research, of course, involves the production of new knowledge. Paulo Freire and Ira Shor (1987) write of a critical theory of knowing, arguing that there are two moments of knowing: 1) the production of new knowledge; and 2) when one knows the existing knowledge. What typically happens is that we separate these two moments. Critical research insists that they be brought together. Knowledge in technicist classrooms is produced far from the teacher and the students. Knowing is thus reduced to taking existing knowledge and transferring it. The teacher is not an inquirer who researches existing knowledge; he or she is merely a specialist in knowledge transference.

Teachers in this situation lose the indispensable qualities that are mandated by knowledge production: critical reflection, a desire to act, discomfort, uncertainty, restless inquiry, etc. When such qualities disappear from teachers, schools become places where knowledge that supports dominant interests is stored and delivered. Knowledge is produced by official researchers, scholars, textbook writers, and sanctioned curriculum committees; it is not created and re-created by teachers and their students in the daily life of the school. Teaching and researching, the official story goes, are separate entities. Critical teaching is not viewed as a form of inquiry. The symbiotic ties between teaching and research are not seen.

There are countless examples of the way critical democratic social studies teachers act on their research abilities. They develop curricula for their schools, they research problems and share their findings with other teachers during in-service education meetings, they devise methods grounded on their research to bring dignity and intelligence to self-evaluation procedures. Stephen Kemmis et al. (1982) describe the critical research of a group of junior high school teachers on ways of improving remedial reading in their school. They began by exploring various strategies that had been used by remedial reading teachers around the world and by examining a variety of problems associated with remedial reading. Different teachers examined different reading strategies and used the information to improve the remedial reading teaching. Based on their work, they implemented programs that involved more teachers in the attempt to help children with reading problems, altered the school day to devote more time to the development of reading, and formed teams of classroom teachers and specialist remedial teachers to tie remediation into the "regular" classroom.

Teachers involved in this project gained sophisticated understandings of remedial reading based on their own research, not the research and pronouncements of "experts." They learned how some techniques for teaching remedial reading worked to separate reading skills from the learning situations that necessitated them. Some of the methods utilized often served to perpetuate the status of students labeled remedial rather than allowing them to break away from the stigma. Other strategies resulted in student deskilling by removing remedial students from the learning context of the classroom, with the result that their poor classroom performance was maintained. Several techniques created situations where teachers found it hard to work together to develop reading skills in various curricular contexts. Teachers were becoming conceptualizers, not mere executors of someone else's plans (Carr and Kemmis, 1986). Examples of social studies teachers as researchers are numerous and can be found in a variety of recent publications (Kemmis, et al. 1982).

Another reason for democratic social studies teachers to be researchers involves the failure of positivist knowledge in the social and educational domains. Positivist research has failed because it has focused on the trivial and produced information that has little practical value. Positivist social, psychological, and educational information tells social studies teachers little about how the world works, how consciousness is constructed in the web of reality, or how schools operate. Positivistic verification of data is conducted in a non-naturalistic, decontextualized, artificial venue and attends only to particular, measurable, and isolated variables. Such variables are sometimes so isolated, so insignificant in light of the multitude of other variables not explored, that the results of the inquiry are irrelevant. The validity claims of such research are, to say the least, questionable.

Positivistic laboratory researchers present verified knowledge about how a particular technique produces success in teaching; understanding their process of verification, we may hold justifiable skepticism that such a technique will prove successful in a real school, in the everyday classroom that teachers inhabit. Remove this concept for a moment from the educational world and think of it in a zoological context. Ethnologists have written of similar insights into research on animals. Research conducted in animal labs or zoos produces data on wildlife that has little to do with how they behave in natural settings. Zoos, labs, and questionnaires in a sense become unique settings in their own right with their own dynamics and peculiar forces which help mold behavior (Orteza, 1988; Wilson, 1977). Democratic social studies teachers have only one choice in such an epistemological situation: they must learn to produce their own knowledge as they map the web of social and educational reality in which they and their students are entangled.

Educators who buy into the positivistic view of the world lay out a set of absolute standards that lay a foundation for an objective measurement of progress. Chester Finn (1982) is one of the better known champions of contemporary positivism and its cult of the expert. Let those who know, he maintains, determine the definitions of quality and the goals of schooling. In Finn's culture of the expert, teachers are expected to take prepackaged knowledge of the various subjects and "dish it out" to passive students. If successful, students will become "culturally literate" and "vocationally competent." They will also be ideologically naïve and easy to fit into the hierarchical workplace (Aronowitz & Giroux, 1985). Such a positivistic perspective induces social studies teachers and students to cave into the climate of deceit and redefine citizenship as consumption. If such a view prevails *public* education will "evolve" into a private function run by corporations who will be even better at adjusting teachers and students to the new corporate order. Knowledge production in this context will be controlled by a small elite. Epistemology, I wager, will not be a part of the corporate social studies curriculum.

The social studies will become more important in these privatized schools, as corporate leaders will want to make sure that teachers and students are "ideologically conditioned." Finn's educational vision grants us insight into the epistemological dimensions of this new educational order. Finn and his soulmates explicitly denounce the critical intent of knowledge production and acquisition. This critical intent involves an understanding of our location in the web of reality, the politics of knowledge production, and an understanding of how power works to construct our consciousness. The critical intent of knowledge production involves not only the ability to do research but to understand the relationship between the formal knowledge of mainstream social studies and the nature of everyday life. Of course, the ability to make connections and discern relationships is central to the critical process. The positivist evaluation techniques advocated by Finn and his cohorts are not capable of measuring the social studies student's or the teacher's ability to make these connections.

The evaluative knowledge produced by positivist researchers typically consists of fragmentary data that grants little insight into what is actually happening in the classroom. It completely dismisses the importance of understanding the web of reality in which teaching takes place. When critical, epistemologically conscious knowledge work is taking place, such positivistic evaluative procedures are particularly ineffective. Because positivism cannot conceive of such sophisticated cognition, it cannot develop instruments that would rate its existence. Positivistic evaluation demands a standardized, fact-based curriculum that focuses on short-term memory of unproblematized data. A social studies curriculum that engages in the analysis, interpretation, and production of knowledge has too many variables that cannot be controlled. Thus, it cannot be measured and compared to other curricula in an efficient and "validated" manner. Positivist education, therefore, has to change/fragment the curriculum to meet the demands of validation/evaluation procedures. Questions of what knowledge is of most worth, what type of curriculum best contributes to the needs of democracy, are irrelevant. The evaluation *tail* wags the curriculum *dog*. By definition the critical intent of knowledge work cannot be included in the social studies curriculum: it is much too imprecise, too subject to individual variation.

Always ahead of his time, John Dewey (1916) was uncomfortable with what many would call positivist or formal knowledge, a form of knowledge best described as neutral, objective, and detached from the knower and the social web of reality. External forms of information, Dewey wrote in 1916, might best be conceptualized as data suited for storage in a warehouse. Operating under this positivistic view of knowledge, academic study becomes a process where one draws on what is in storage. Such a perspective misses an important point, Dewey argued. The function of knowledge from his perspective was to connect, to find the relationship between different experiences. At this point, Dewey distinguished between knowledge and habit. His distinction is valuable because it helps us conceptualize knowledge in the social studies curriculum and prepares us to think about the nature and purpose of our own knowledge production. Dewey's description of habit sharpens our understanding of the type of information that is often taught in social studies when knowledge is controlled by positivist epistemological models. It also helps democratic knowledge producers in social studies appreciate the types of knowledge production they want to avoid.

When a learner has formed a habit, he or she has gained the ability to use an experience so that effective action can be taken when he or she faces a similar situation in the future. This is valuable, Dewey argued, for everyone will face similar situations in the process of living. A child who learns to solve long-division problems will certainly be faced with such problems again and again. But habit is not enough; it makes no allowance for change of conditions, for novelty. An individual who has learned a habit is not prepared for change and thus is vulnerable to confusion when faced with a previously unencountered problem. The habituated skill of the mechanic will desert him, Dewey wrote, "when something unexpected occurs in the running of the machine." The man on the other hand, who understands the machine is the man "who knows what he is about." This mechanic understands the conditions which allow a certain habit to work and is capable of initiating action that will adapt the habit to new conditions. The type of social studies teaching and knowledge production that engender such types of thought are far distanced from the positivistic schools that view all knowledge as empirically measurable.

In this context, we begin to get a more specific perspective on the nature of a critical form of knowledge production in the social studies. We are not attempting to create objective knowledge for storage in a warehouse, but a useful form of knowledge that can be applied to teaching and social problems, and one that is connected to the lived world and the complex web of reality. If social studies educators don't possess an understanding of the purpose of knowledge production and its relationship to their teaching, then studying research methods and epistemology is irrelevant. In point 11 I will explore this dynamic in more detail, focusing on a critical form of knowledge production that produces practical knowledge for social and democratic action.

11. PRODUCING PRACTICAL KNOWLEDGE FOR SOCIAL ACTION. Knowledge based on connections, John Dewey (1916) argued, is concerned not only with the immediacy of the knowledge itself but the vantage point it creates from which to consider a new experience. To Dewey the content of knowledge is what has happened, i.e., what is considered finished and settled. But the reference of knowledge, he argued, is the future. Knowledge, in the Deweyan sense, provides the means of understanding what is happening in the present and what is to be done about it. In a typical pragmatist context Dewey was concerned with the consequences of ideas—in the lexicon of point 11, the practical value, of knowing something. It is this pragmatic aspect of Dewey's theory of knowledge that informs the critical intent of education itself. As Aronowitz and Giroux (1985) put it: "the ability to connect contemporary experience to the received information that others have gained through their generalized experience" (p. 9).

Positivist social studies educators have never understood the notion of practical knowledge, of knowledge based on connections. This lack of understanding has profoundly shaped the history of social studies education and the type of knowledge that has been included in its curriculum across the decades. The notion of epistemological complexity is lost in this positivistic context, since social studies curriculum developers failed to comprehend the inexact and ever changing nature of practical knowledge. Technicist educators, Dewey maintained, regard knowledge as an entity complete in itself. Dewey's Hegelian background, with its emphasis on the dialectic, helped move his view of knowledge beyond the "knowledge in isolation" format. The dialectical notion of process grounded his view of the nature of knowledge. Knowledge from this perspective could never be viewed outside the context of its origins and its relationship to other information. We only have to call to mind, Dewey wrote, what passes in our schools as acquisition of knowledge to understand how it lacks any meaningful connection with the experience of students. A person, he concluded, is reasonable in the degree to which he or she sees an event, not as something isolated, "but in its connection with the common experience of mankind" (Dewey, 1916, pp. 342–43). Of courses, positivists do not possess the evaluative ability to measure such a practical, connected form of knowledge. Thus, they assume that it doesn't exist.

As we know, positivists seek to produce a form of knowledge—sometimes referred to as a formal knowledge—that is a timeless body of truth. Such formal knowledge is removed from connection with the world, from consideration of its consequences. Privileged in the schools, formal knowledge is viewed as separate from issues of commitment, emotion, or ethical action. Indeed, such formal knowledge often privileges social adaptation rather than social action. The objectivity inscribed in formal knowledge often becomes a signifier for political passivity and an elevation to an elite sociopolitical and economic location. Thus, in its "esteemed position," formalism refuses to analyze the relationship between knowledge production and social studies practice. Teachers obtain formal knowledge and then are expected to directly apply it in their classes.

Such application of formal knowledge involves pronouncements such as, "The research tells us to teach social issues in this way . . . ." The problem here involves formalism's failure to study the complex relationship between professional knowledge about education and educational practice. Formalism fails to discern the phenomenological complexity of social studies teaching, that is, the complicated ways that knowledge, consciousness, everyday life, and professional practice intersect. Without this critical recognition, knowledge production in colleges of education is somewhat irrelevant to social studies teachers. Formal knowledge production too often fails to question the relationship between professional knowledge and indeterminant zones of practice characterized by complexity, conflict, ambiguity, and uniqueness. Such a practical zone exists outside the boundaries of positivism and the formal knowledge it produces. Epistemological formalism can't cope with everyday life's and the social studies classroom's ill-formed problems.

The pedagogical aspect of the social studies teacher education curriculum is too often grounded on this formalist perspective. Such an orientation demands that social studies educators teach their professional education students the basic science and validated knowledge it produces. Upon completion of this phase, it requires that students be placed in a practicum where they can use this formal data to inform their practice. An epistemology of complexity questions such a process. The practical knowledge it seeks to produce is based on a meta-understanding of the epistemological assumptions on which any research rests.

With this type of understanding, critical democratic social studies teachers can develop new epistemologies of practice that employ multiple frames of reference. Such different views allow us to observe professional practice from the perspectives of different stakeholders in the educational process. We begin to understand that knowledge about practice is not universal but is contingent on the particular context in which it is applied. Viewing from the perspective and needs of marginalized groups, we may see that practices that might work with students from privileged backgrounds may serve to further oppress students facing the forces of class bias and racism. Social studies teachers with this epistemological understanding begin to understand, in a very practical way, that there is not one answer to any question, one accurate representation of an event, or one right way to teach macroeconomics.

Critical democratic social studies educators, guided by their epistemology of complexity, seek to produce a dialogical form of knowledge. Such knowledge is many times expressed as a series of questions and tentative answers rather than an arrogant factual knowledge. In this complex context, social studies educators produce knowledge that is less linear and procedural (the four steps to teaching the way a bill becomes law) and more circular and recursive (how do we help a group of low-achieving students perceive social studies research abilities as important in helping them achieve personal goals?). In this way, social studies knowledge producers are emancipated from formalistic, decontextualized, and universal rules for conducting research and teaching their students.

Such positivistic rules often allow social studies knowledge producers to see only what is there. That which is readily apparent often involves the least significant aspects of a social or political situation. As they are emancipated from the formalistic, knowledge producers decenter their perception in ways that allow them to see previously occluded relationships among entities, not just discrete features. Informed by these insights, researchers produce a practical knowledge characterized by three features: an integrative dimension, an applicative dimension, and a hermeneutic (interpretive) dimension.

The integrative dimension constructs meaning for isolated facts, in the process, placing data into a larger perspective, connecting it to understandings emerging from a variety of disciplines, and questioning its moral and political inscriptions. The applicative dimension questions how knowledge can be applied to important problems. The hermeneutic dimension searches for the variety of ways knowledge can be interpreted and the various horizons (contexts) within which it can be viewed. In all of these dimensions, emphasis is placed on the process of knowing rather than the production of a final, positive knowledge.

The practical knowledge championed here cannot even be produced by positivist researchers: positivist formal knowledge and practical knowledge are incommensurable, an epistemological mismatch. Complex practical knowledge must be produced by a process informed by and contingent on context. It is an embodied form of knowledge that cannot be separated from specific contexts. Like indigenous knowledge, practical knowledge is less informed by abstract rules of research procedures than by an intimate understanding of a specific situation. In line with the various features of an epistemology of complexity, practical knowledge is produced by a form of research that uses the human self as an instrument of inquiry and emotional/logical insight. Critical democratic social studies teachers feel they have contributed to the production of practical knowledge when they are able to describe the living context in which the knowledge is based. Human interactions and experiences that take place in these breathing contexts are not events to be simply described but complex circumstances to be interpreted. In this way, practical knowledge is produced—knowledge that can be used in social, educational, and psychological situations.

In their awareness of these living contexts, critical democratic social studies educators expose the values and contradictions in values that shape the contexts themselves and their own questions about them. Thus, the level of awareness of social complexity is raised. The practical benefits of such a heightened awareness of complexity help us escape the simplistic, reductionistic data of more traditional paradigms. Awareness of such omnipresent values helps us explain the meaning of the context and the uses to which such meaning can be applied. In this context, the critical knowledge producer comes to understand that these values are not absolute qualities but are perpetually subject to questioning, interpretation, clarification, and transformation. Appreciating the complex relationship connecting knowledge, values, and context, critical analysts can cope with random occurrences via their self-reflective, self-evaluating, and self-adjusting orientation. Thus, they are attuned to and undaunted by the messy aspects of everyday life.

The move from explanatory knowledge to practical knowledge demands a profound sociocognitive and epistemological leap. Such a move constitutes a criterion for a reconceptualized notion of rigor. Such a criterion falls outside the boundaries of formal research, with its prearranged, operational definition of rigor as fidelity to an objectivist methodological procedure. It is important to delineate this new notion of rigor in an era marked by a language of educational excellence and high standards. Our reconceptualized notion of rigor, and the epistemology of complexity that grounds it, can help social studies teachers reshape the public conversation about high quality, rigorous education. This new notion of rigor is also important as critical democratic social studies teachers produce practical knowledge for inclusion in the social studies curriculum.

How do we exercise critical citizenship in diverse communities? How do we reconceptualize our social values in light of the epistemological concept of difference? Where do we begin the process of helping the public rethink its notion of intelligence as more than high scores on standardized tests? How do we help students and other teachers understand the ways poverty and racism inscribe themselves on the consciousness of the oppressed? All of these questions form the basis for the production of practical forms of knowledge that set up the possibility for emancipatory action. With such questions in mind and an understanding of an epistemology of synthesis, integration, and application, we can begin to produce knowledge and engage consciousness in a way that leads to progressive social change. As epistemological horizons are expanded, human possibility is enhanced. We can all become something we have never been before.

 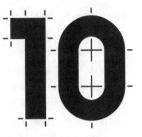

Chapter 10

What's Complex about Our Notion of Complexity? Extending the Epistemology of Complexity

Democratic social studies teachers in the twenty-first century understand that knowledge production and consumption are not simple matters. As they gain an epistemological consciousness, they appreciate the multitude of factors that contribute to what is validated as official social studies knowledge and how this information shapes students in particular ways. They also come to understand the myriad of political and ideological influences social studies knowledge exerts. In Chapter 10 we will dig deeper into the nature of the complexity of knowledge production while examining its relationship to the role of the social studies teacher in an era where such insights are suppressed by the educational establishment.

12. APPRECIATING THE NATURE OF COMPLEXITY—OVERCOMING REDUCTIONISM. The simplicity of mainstream knowledge production does not work. The web of reality is composed of too many variables (or as scientist Ilya Prigogene puts it, "extraneous perturbations") to be taken into account and controlled. One extraneous variable, for example, in an educational experiment can produce an expanding, exponential effect. Inconsequential entities can have a profound effect in a complex nonlinear universe. The shape of the physical and social world depends on the smallest part. The part, in a sense,

is the whole, for via the action of any particular part, the whole in the form of transformative change may be seen. To exclude such considerations is to miss the nature of the interactions that constitute reality. The development of a counter-Cartesian reconceptualization of social studies and social studies knowledge production does not mean that we simplistically reject all empirical science. Obviously, there are questions in education that involve counting, figuring percentages, averages, etc. It does mean, however, that we conceive of such empirical questions as one part of the web, i.e., the interactive configuration.

A counter-Cartesian reconceptualization of social studies means recognizing, as Dewey did, as feminist epistemology does, that the knower and the known are intimately connected, that a science that separates fact from value, purpose, belief, and complexity is a pseudoscience divorced from the *Lebenswelt*, the lived world of human consciousness. Such a reconceptualization reminds us, as social studies knowledge producers that we can display our findings and argue for their value, but always with a hesitation, a stutter, a tentativeness—never as the simple truth (Besag, 1986b; Doll, 1989; Briggs & Peat, 1989).

The complexity of reality may be illustrated by medical and mechanical examples. When the human body breaks down, doctors may identify a certain factor, but the "cause" of the illness is always multiple. Living entities are always composed of a multitude of feedback loops, a cardinal concept in chaos theory. A home furnace is one of the most familiar forms of a simple feedback loop. We all know, that when the room cools down below the temperature set on the thermostat, it responds by switching on the furnace. As the furnace heats up the room to a point above the second temperature set on the thermostat, the furnace automatically shuts off. The ear-splitting screeches produced when a microphone is placed close to a speaker, feedback, is another example of a feedback loop. Output from the amplifier is detected by the microphone and looped back into the amplifier. The chaotic sounds which result are the consequence of a feedback loop where the output of one stage turns into the input of another. Because human beings are composed of so many feedback loops, e.g., the transformation of food into energy, the increase in heart-rate in the presence of danger, etc., the attempt to study them takes on far more complexity than traditional conceptions of cause-effect linearity could imagine (Lincoln & Guba, 1985; Briggs & Peat, 1989; Capra, 1996; O'Sullivan, 1999).

In order to study such complex systems, social studies educators have to move from hierarchic to heterarchic conceptions of order. Positivism saw an inherent order in the physical and social world, e.g., the divine right of kings to govern or Carl Brigham's (the founder of the Educational Testing Service) hierarchy of the intelligence of ethnic groups. Counter-Cartesian researchers maintain that, if orders exist, they exist side by side: if one order dominates, it is merely temporary and is subject to a variety of rapidly shifting forces. Because of this heterarchic conception of order, any simplistic notion of determinism is destroyed. In a hierarchic universe, positivists have maintained that, if a knowledge producer knows the location and velocity of all the bits and pieces of the world, the future can be predicted and controlled. But change is complex, and qualitative researchers informed by a postmodern understanding have to accept the notion that change occurs dramatically and unpredictably (Lincoln & Guba, 1985; Denzin & Lincoln, 2000; Briggs & Peat, 1989).

Operating in a closed system where variables are controlled, positivists have often promoted an orderly and predictable view of change. When the variables were controlled and protected from outside contamination, equations could be formulated and exact predictions about the social and educational world could be devised. But even ostensibly very minor variables could have dramatic effects, sometimes not exhibiting themselves for long periods of time. When they did manifest themselves, their effect seemed to the positivistic researcher as an aberration, probably a mistake in the construction of an equation. Not only does the critical analyst in the counter-Cartesian context lose the possibility of certainty, but he or she is faced with a need to find methods of exploring these complex multiple constructions of reality.

In this context, marked by complexity, think of the social studies classroom. A wide variety of kids with different backgrounds, special needs, different home experiences, diverse strengths and weaknesses and changing moods and dispositions inhabit those desks in our rooms. As we survey our classrooms, we come to realize that there is more to teaching social studies than meets the modernist eye, more than is included in technicist teacher education programs. The purpose of an epistemologically complex social studies teacher education is not to learn the right answers, the hand-me-down knowledge of the research experts; on the contrary, critical democratic teacher education consists of making the most of the unanticipated complications of the classroom. Technicist methods courses and student teaching do not address the innate and complex uncertainty of teaching; they attempt to deny it. Thus, complex teacher educators refuse to promise the provision of a generic form of social studies teaching applicable to all students in all contexts. Neither do they promise to reduce the uncertainty of the profession by the application of quick technical fixes. The counter-Cartesian turn implies an admission that teacher educators also agonize over the confusing uncertainties of everyday practice. To do otherwise would be to revert to the dishonesty of modernism's veil of simplicity and certainty (Clark, 1987).

An epistemology of complexity adopts a progressive view of knowledge that, even as social information is being gathered by researchers, it is being analyzed and interpreted. A more positivistic view of knowledge assumes that only after one knows the facts is he or she ready to analyze. Such a view misses the important point that what we designate as the facts is an act of interpretation; in the case of positivistic research, it is an unconscious act of interpretation. Privileged knowledge producers often assume that knowledge is a static or inert entity; writers of elementary and high school social studies textbooks often take this viewpoint. Knowledge production, operating with an understanding of an epistemology of complexity, proceeds tentatively, ever mindful of ambiguity and uncertainty. When we know for certain, little need exists to pursue alternative ways of knowing. "Deviant ways of seeing" are dismissed as irrelevant; they are not viewed as an important source of new insight and socioeducational innovation (Romanish, 1986; Schon, 1987).

This view of social studies knowledge production and teaching within an epistemology of complexity revolutionizes the way we conceptualize social studies education. The negative consequences of the quest for certainty are avoided, when teacher researchers and teacher educators begin to imagine and construct new ways of thinking about social studies teaching and teacher education. If the act of teaching were known and constant, social studies teachers could act on empirical generalizations, and teacher educators would know exactly what teachers needed to know to perform successfully. But teaching is not constant and predictable: it always takes place in a microcosm of uncertainty. Thus, what we call valuable practitioner knowledge is elusive. How to teach teachers what to do in conditions of uncertainty is even more elusive.

The positivism of professional schools of education in the early twentieth century used Cartesian science to eliminate the uncertainty of professional practice and replace it with empirical knowledge about the
teaching act. The cult of the expert in the educational sphere precluded
an admission of uncertainty. The uniqueness of particular teaching situations was ignored by educational researchers/experts whose clients
demanded official knowledge, knowledge that specified the scientifically
sanctioned "right way" to proceed (Schon, 1987). In a culture that relies
on the expert for guidance, uncertainty doesn't play well. Indeed, denial
of the useless complications of complexity, with the attendant certainty
that can be asserted, signifies strength and positive, affirmative leadership
in a macho patriarchal culture. The higher our levels of epistemological
understanding, the weaker our perspectives often appear to a culture that
has been conditioned to buy into a quest for certainty. This cruel irony
tends to impede the attempt to teach complex, sophisticated, critical
thinking and to retard the movement to put social studies teachers into
positions of control over their workplaces. Social studies teachers with an
epistemological consciousness of complexity must resist asking experts to
tell them what to do when they experience difficulty. This does not mean
they can't ask experienced educators for advice; they must also adeptly
resist frustrated students' calls to "Just tell us what you want us to memorize, and we'll do it." Teaching with an understanding of epistemological complexity is a subtle task that takes practice and patience.

One of the major problems of U.S. schooling involves its inability to
understand this epistemology of complexity, its inability to deal with
ambiguity, or to perceive ambiguity as a valuable characteristic. Without
such an understanding, educational leaders have continually sought
naïve and simplistic answers to the complex social and cognitive questions that confront education, a reflection of the epistemological predisposition of modernism to seek certainty in its inquiries about human and
educational affairs. Critical complex social studies education attempts to
overcome our socially engrained discomfort with the enigmatic, our
desire to have something we can all subscribe to together, our need for a
shared certainty.

Cartesian certainty cannot withstand the pressure of deconstructive
epistemological analysis. In this context, French philosopher Jacques
Derrida ridicules the certainty with which modernist science constructs
valid arguments. Such arguments begin with primitive and undefined
terms and premises, he maintains, and to ignore this situation is to seek

a fictional security. Meaning, like an eroding hillside, slowly dissolves until language and texts take on a configuration quite different from the original state. A reader in 2018 may derive a very different meaning of this paragraph from the one I intend. Different social experiences, different circumstances, may alter the codes that give this paragraph meaning in the first decade of the twenty-first century. Meaning derived from research data or frames of reference that serve as the starting place for educational inquiry cannot help but reflect the ideology and social norms that surround them. Unexamined frames of reference lead to claims of scientific certainty that perpetuate privilege for the privileged and oppression for the oppressed (Cherryholmes, 1988).

These ideas have important implications for social studies teaching when they are used to analyze contemporary teacher education and to help teachers formulate questions about their own thinking and the thinking of their students. Unlike the tendency of Cartesianism, thinking cannot be conceived as mere problem solving; problems, as the proponents of complexity would tell us, do not unambiguously present themselves. If a problem is identified as a result of particular ideologies and social frames, then the Cartesian predisposition to look at it as a puzzle to be solved misses some cardinal aspects of the process of thinking about a problem (Altrichter & Posch, 1989). Formal thinking does not allow teachers and students to explore the origins of the problems, the assumptions that move us to define some situations as problems and others as not problems, or the source of authority that guides us in our formulation of criteria for judging which problems merit our thinking and teaching time. This is where our epistemological consciousness helps us understand the complexity of our role as social studies teachers. Employing such a perspective, we begin to uncover the hidden ways ideology shapes the questions that underlie our classrooms. Thus, we see far more clearly the shaky foundation on which the quest for certainty rests.

The Cartesian faith in the constancy of meaning shapes our lives as social studies teachers. The meanings that students and teachers attribute to terms such as reading, teaching, or learning influence the forms our evaluations of teachers, students, and schools take. For example, think about a teacher as researcher seeking to determine whether a critical complex method of teaching geography produces more learning than a drill-and-recite method. The researcher begins the inquiry by identifying what learning is and what behaviors should be examined to determine whether it has or has not taken place. There is nothing objective about such a process; absolute, certain knowledge does not emerge from such a study. The knowledge that does emerge is inherently conditional, dependent on an acceptance of a variety of assumptions about the goals of geography education, the definition of a good student, the nature of learning, and so on. From a critical and democratic perspective, these teaching issues are not technical questions; they are questions of meaning. As our political and epistemological perspectives fashion our evaluation strategies, the designation of who is a competent or incompetent geography teacher or student is contingent on the system of meaning we employ. Without this notion of epistemological conditionality, of context, we find that teachers and students are easily hegemonized, co-opted into covert systems of meaning that undermine their emancipatory trek, their efforts to come to terms with ambiguity.

When teachers possess a cognitive style that has accepted ambiguity and prefers complexity, they seem better suited to encourage such higher-order forms of thinking on the part of their students. This high-complexity teacher tends to challenge social studies student thinking, because he or she expects more factual and conceptual support for student argumentation, greater analytical divergence, and more self-analysis in light of the concepts under study. The high-complexity teacher is better able to establish more pervasive and authentic interaction between students and students, and students and teachers. Such interaction heightens self-awareness, as students (and the teacher) are attuned to the power of their own words and those of others, and to the nature of the contexts and codes and the ways they construct the meaning of communication (Peters & Amburgey, 1982).

These higher-complexity social studies teachers tend to operate on a sophisticated level, as they encourage the active interpretation and negotiation necessary to the critical process of cultural reconstruction. As they gain the power to reconstruct their own consciousness, they are able to help their students reinterpret their traditions and reinvent their futures together in solidarity with other self-directed human agents. Teachers who are comfortable with ambiguity and prefer complexity operate at an ideological level that seems to be more tolerant, flexible, and adaptive and employs a wider repertoire of teaching models. They are better equipped to enter a postconventional world where certainty is sacrificed in order to overcome bureaucratic definitions of the deskilled role teachers often play in school. This counter-Cartesian view of teacher consciousness helps us move beyond the negative consequences of the quest for certainty, since social studies teacher educators and teachers themselves begin to imagine emancipatory educational futures. If the act of teaching followed the modernist pattern and was constant and predictable, teachers could act on empirical generalizations, and teacher educators would know exactly what teachers needed to know to perform successfully. But teaching is not constant and predictable; it always takes place in the microcosm of uncertainty (Schon, 1987).

Such arguments may strike you as terrifically strange and unsettling, given your lifelong exposure to an uncritical Cartesian epistemology. In this mind-set, complexity is irrelevant because we all know that the purpose of science is to produce universal laws/truths and the purpose of education is to pass those truths along to students. What's the problem here? This is the way it has always been or seems to have been. Positivists have harbored grand ambitions: to provide, for example, the truth about the nature of entities such as intelligence or culture. Psychologist Donald Fiske, arguing the Cartesian position, contends that psychologists and social scientists must ignore all of this concern with complexity and focus on the discovery of the regularities in the behavior of social objects. Strongly disagreeing with an epistemology of complexity, Fiske argues that social laws exist and can be discovered. The regularities to which he refers are the building blocks of social laws. In other words, Fiske contends that our search for the laws of society must start small with microscopic methods of investigation. The objects of social inquiry, he says, must be small objects and short temporal periods. Fiske is confident that years and years of such microscopic research will eventuate in an accurate portrayal of social reality (Frankel, 1986).

Fiske rejects a counter-Cartesian conception of disorder. It is this positivistic discomfort with uncertainty that motivates the construction of logocentric designs: build more jails and get the deviants into them; re-establish old-fashioned discipline and solve school management problems; allow administrators to determine what textbooks teachers should use and adopt them; inquire into what strategies improve test scores and require teachers to use them; give principals and deans more responsibility to fire people; pass a law or a constitutional amendment that requires citizens to respect the flag; do research that is simple, orderly, and elegant and produces verifiable data; devise questionnaires that soothe our quest for certainty by subtly requiring respondents to answer questions in ways that prove that the world is stable and predictable; as a research analyst, assume that the word and the deed are consistent. All of these designs are based on the assumption of common frames of reference. They are all based on reductionistic notion of the simplicity of the lived world. The fact that they are arrived upon in a way that reflects the tacit dominant ideology of a time and place is not considered in the quest for certain knowledge of the world of education. Thus, in its assurance, its refusal to examine the assumptions that guide it, the Cartesian quest for certainty often obscures more than it uncovers (Gordon, Miller & Rollock, 1990).

Practicing social studies teachers have always suspected as much. They have always intuitively felt that something was wrong with this type of simplified, but scientifically validated, research about teaching. The community of experts was not so insightful. The positivistic mainstream assumed that laboratory research findings were the source of solutions that could be applied in every classroom setting (Doyle, 1977; Ponzio, 1985). Positivistic researchers failed to understand that every classroom possessed a complex culture of its own, a culture that defines the rules of discourse in classroom situations. Meanings are negotiated around who should talk, and what are the consequences of particular behaviors. Thus, the meanings of specific social studies classroom events depend on a researcher's knowledge of what happened previously, how classroom meanings, codes, and conventions were negotiated. For a positivistic researcher to walk into a class without an understanding of the previously negotiated meanings and expect to make sense of the situation is unrealistic; it is even more unrealistic for him or her to expect that generalizations applicable to other classrooms can be made from this incomplete and often misleading snapshot of a classroom.

To understand the complexity of the classroom, alternative research methods must be employed. This realization has sparked the mushrooming acceptance of qualitative, naturalistic research. Contrary to positivism's attempt to make quick and clean observations devoid of context, this research orientation places a high priority on detailed, long-term observation of behavior in natural settings. Qualitative, naturalistic researchers realize that the space between teaching and learning outcomes is shaped by a cornucopia of variables. Because of this complexity, the attempt to explain divergence in student performance by reference to a few generalizable aspects of teacher action is reductionistic and misleading (Doyle, 1977). Who is better suited to make long-term, detailed, multidimensional observation of classroom behavior than a teacher?

Ignoring the intuition of the social studies teachers who occupied the bottom rungs of the professional education status ladder, the positivist experts donned their blinders and pushed forward. Their modernist certainty created a host of rigid dichotomies that have affected the educational research act and social studies practice: objective reality and subjective experience, tact and imagination, truth and opinion, neutrality and partisanship, logic and emotion, secular and sacred, and public and private. The cause-effect linearity of modernist positivism, with its emphasis on decontextualized problem solving, sets the agenda for what has been considered important about teaching social studies. From the perspective of Ilya Prigogine, the 1977 Nobel Prize winner in chemistry and proponent of postmodernist chaos theory, such linearity not only determines what we consider important about the world but distorts our view of the world in the process.

Prigogine argues that unstable dissapative structures—structures that, depending on their contexts, reveal fascinating new layers of complexity—are far more common than structures that are stable (Prigogine & Stengers, 1984). The recognition of these unstable dissipative structures is a major step in the human attempt to make sense of the physical and social world. We need to move beyond both modernity's simplistic linearity and its yearning for certainty and adopt more sophisticated tools of analysis. Picking up on this epistemological understanding, social studies teachers could no longer teach isolated simple facts about the social, political, economic, and cultural cosmos. They would have to study data as part of larger contexts and processes. Indeed, the very meaning of the information depends on its relationship to the contexts and processes.

Critical democratic social studies teachers who understand and act on their understandings of an epistemology of complexity must not fall victim to a "new and improved" form of certainty. Our counter-Cartesian humility must become an everyday feature of our scholarly and professional lives. All knowledge, all aspects of the social studies curriculum, are inherently complex and problematic and demand questioning by everyone involved. While I personally embrace many revisionist historical interpretations of American diplomatic and sociopolitical history, I must always present my beliefs as interpretations—not final truths. Social, historical, political, and economic knowledge is so complex in its contextuality and its status as part of an ever-evolving process that it is never "finalized." There will always be new interpretations to consider.

Critical democratic social studies teachers deal with a realm so complex that they must accustom themselves to the mistakes they will make in their attempt to make sense of it all. We will never have enough data to be assured that we "have it right." In this complex context, our goal for social studies teachers is not that they parlay the truth to their students, but that they turn out students who are aware of the complexity of the process and their own and other individuals' fallibility in their quest to understand the social landscape. What an amazing scholarly insight this could be.

13. ALL KNOWLEDGE IS IN PROCESS, A PART OF A LARGER PROCESS. An epistemology of complexity is inseparable from an epistemology and pedagogy of process. Positivism, and the social studies education it supports, sees the fundamental nature of reality as "separate things." Reality and consciousness itself in a process-oriented epistemology are seen as fundamentally a collection of processes, always interacting with other things and processes, and thus always changing. Process, thus, is the fundamental state of the physical and social worlds. Processes are more fundamental to reality, therefore, than separate entities—a notion that flies in the face of Cartesianism and the social studies it supports (Mashalidis, 1997). Knowledge in this epistemological context has a past and a future; we always see it in a particular stage of its development. When knowledge is removed from its process(s), it is no longer capable of being known: it has become known, resulting in its life-force being stripped away (Postman, 1995; Krievis, 1998). When social studies teachers witness such a move in the top-down, technical content standards they are provided, they witness an epistemological murder.

Aware of a complex epistemology of process, critical democratic social studies teachers understand that the knowledge of today changes tomorrow. It is not stable, immobile, or static. Albert Einstein clearly understood this dynamic and used it to change the way we understood the world around us. Using his understanding of nineteenth century German philosopher George W. E. Hegel's concept of process, Einstein walked through a conceptual window unimaginable to most individuals trapped in a Cartesian house. Writing in the nineteenth century, Hegel was conceptually uncomfortable with Isaac Newton's absolutist explanation of gravity and the way things work. Most important for our educational, social, and cognitive concerns, Hegel was unimpressed with the manner in which Newton reached his conclusions. From Hegel's perspective, every entity's existence could only be understood in relation to other things. In his philosophical view, the concept of relationship took on an importance not valued by Newton and his scientific descendants.

Relationship was so significant to Hegel that he described the interaction between entities as a living process. In such a process, all things in the world were affected and shaped by all other things, just as in Einstein's relativity theory, mass worked on space and space worked on mass ("Einstein on spacetime," 1998). Operating without the benefit of this lesson, social studies educators fall into the irrationality of the fragmentation of conventional reason. We see the importance of the world in things in themselves, in isolation from their contexts, removed from the larger processes that provide their meaning. Informed by Einstein's lesson, social studies education and the thinking it teaches, become more than the accumulation of fragments of data. In the call for educational standards over the last few years, we have seen the effects of this failure to learn Einstein (and Hegel's) lesson: we judge educational quality by the quantity of data accumulated (Woods & Grant, 1998; Madison, 1988).

An epistemology of process was so important to Einstein that he could not have developed the General Theory of Relativity without it. A quick look at the relationship between process and the genesis of the theory is instructive to social studies teachers. Einstein often used the notion of a rubber sheet stretched over a backing dish to explain the complex notion of space. When a bowling ball or a BB is placed on it, the sheet is bent or warped around the object. This distortion exemplifies what massive objects, such as the sun or the moon, do to the fabric of space. This is one of the basic concepts of Einstein's General Theory of Relativity. The rubber sheet is flat when no objects are placed upon it; Einstein referred to this as the absence of gravity. When the bowling ball depresses the sheet, the curvature around the depression represents a gravitational field. A BB rolled along the sheet will fall into the trough just as an asteroid will fall to Earth if it gets too close to its gravitational field. The more massive the object, the greater the bending of space. The bowling ball will distort the sheet more than the BB.

So, according to Einstein, mass causes a depression in space. If a comet, for example, moves too close to a star, it is drawn into its gravitational well and seized. Thus, entities in space follow the shape of the universe when they fall to Earth. They are not pulled by some gravitational force! While the rubber sheet is merely a metaphor and reduces the complexity of Einstein's relativity, it does help us appreciate the structural unity of space, matter, and motion, the process of space. (A tricky part is that we have to add time to that unity as well.) Gravity, therefore, is simply a part of the structure of the universe, and, amazingly, Einstein figured that out. Objects fall into the valley in space-time produced by the bowling ball/sun. In this context, the orbits of the sun's planets can be better conceptualized; Mercury and Venus as well as Neptune and Pluto "roll" around the indention in space caused by the sun's gravity trough.

The General Theory of Relativity even asserted that, if a massive object in space is disturbed, it will cause ripples in space like ripples from a rock splashing in a pond. In space, these "gravity waves" are illustrated again by the rubber sheet, as we imagine dropping a ball bearing on it. BBs and bowling balls placed on other portions of the sheet will be affected by the dropping of the ball bearing. Einstein asked us to use our rubber sheet to imagine a massive object that revolves. In this situation, the "gravity well" it produces in space is not just a depression in the rubber sheet but a spinning indentation that twists space. Such twisting induces other objects around it to move in particular ways. While the General Theory of Relativity is, undoubtedly, very complex and mysterious, the point I am making about it is quite easy to understand. This point holds revolutionary significance for social studies teachers.

As Einstein sought to understand the force of gravity, he discovered that there is no such thing as "nothingness" in the structure of the universe. Space like everything else is *something*; it is an intrinsic part of the fabric of the cosmos. Space is neither empty nor separable from matter. The relationship between space and matter is central to making the universe what it is. In light of Einstein's assertion, the old Newtonian notion of gravity was destroyed; but most importantly to our point, the Newtonian universe and the Cartesian-Newtonian way of looking at the universe (epistemology) was overturned. When Newton developed his Universal Theory of Gravitation in the 1600s, he focused on gravity as a thing in itself. If gravity, as he believed, was simply a force, why would one look at it in any other way? Thus, he, and especially those who came after him, followed the emerging scientific method and removed gravity from its larger process so it could be efficiently analyzed. And this was exactly their mistake ("Astronomical Instruments," 1999; "Gravitational Radiation," 1998; "Still right . . . .," 1998; Evans, 1997; Woods & Grant, 1998; Peoria Astronomical Society, 1998).

Einstein, operating in the first decades of the twentieth century, was able to escape the Newtonian mistake that had misled physicists for a quarter of a millennium by one conceptual move. Instead of searching for gravity as a thing, he saw it as a relationship, a part of a grander process. Einstein saw gravity in relation to other aspects of the universe. Indeed, he understood that the relationship between matter and space—illustrated by the rubber sheet, bowling balls, and BBs—is exactly what makes the world what it is. What we experience as gravity is not a force made up of tiny gravitrons but a reflection of the structure of the universe moving us along a path existing in curved, multidimensional space. Space, he figured, is not the package in which the universe is stored; it is a key aspect of the process of creation. For those who understood the basic idea of Einstein's theory, the physical world could never be viewed the same way again (Levenson, 1997; Woods & Grant, 1998).

The focus on process, connecting space, time, and matter, that eventuated in Einstein's revolutionary theories can also change our social consciousness, cognition, and education. As we pursue modes of thinking that account for changes and interactions in the physical, social, and psychological domains, we begin to gain dramatically different and more complex perspectives on that which surrounds us. In this concept of interactive processes, the etymology of Shirley Steinberg's and my concept of postformalism or postformal thinking is revealed. (We will describe postformalism in detail later in the book.) At this point, however, it is important to explain Einstein's role in leading us to new ways of making meaning, to new appreciations of the process of both being and becoming (Kovel, 1998).

Using Einstein's example of thinking in physics and Hegel's dialectical insights, we are led to critical and post-Cartesian-Newtonian forms of analysis. In this context, we begin to appreciate the hidden processes that place the physical, social, psychological, and educational worlds in a sea of constant change. Newtonian and Cartesian ways of seeing often provide a metaphorical photograph of an entity. This photograph is an isolated moment in time, a still life that may miss the significance of the larger dynamic of which it is but a part. When we see it as postformalists, we see facts as part of a larger process, we begin to understand how things move beyond what they are but still retain their identity. For example, while gravity no doubt exists, it moves far beyond its existence as an entity involved merely with the attraction of one object to another when conceived as a part of an inclusive whole—the structure of the universe. Imagine the difference between a science lesson taught to middle school students about gravity that takes this processual feature into account and one that doesn't.

The process-based thinking delineated here is a form of holistic analysis that insists on the inseparability of mind and body, politics and economics, consciousness and cultural context, facts and values, the biological and the social, and gravity and matter. What education in its disciplinary organization, or in its fragmentation of information, treats as separate, an epistemology of complexity considers parts of larger processes. There is nothing wrong, process analysts maintain, with separating entities for the purpose of labeling and analysis as long as this step is followed by the act of putting them back together. Step one: gravity is defined as the attraction of one object for another; step two: this attraction is viewed as a result of the interrelationship among space, mass, time, and motion. Thus, this mode of analysis can be described as examining an entity from differing vantage points: 1) gravity as experienced by an earthling throwing a baseball into the air and watching it return to Earth; and 2) gravity from the perspective of one who views (or like Einstein is capable of imagining) the universe as a whole and frames it in such a perspective. Understanding both modes and their relationship is important in the critical effort to make sense of gravity (Bookchin, 1995; Kovel, 1998; Levins, 1998).

Thus, informed by these ways of seeing, an epistemology of process and complexity assumes that little in the universe is as it appears to be. Critical democratic social studies teachers argue that considering an entity only as a thing in itself can be viciously misleading. The reason for this examination of Einstein's educational life and thought in a social studies context involves his phenomenal ability to avoid this Cartesian-Newtonian quicksand and to model a rigorous form of process-oriented cognition that can lead us out of the cognitive and educational confusion in which we are presently ensnared. The implications of such a critique of Cartesian-Newtonian logic (conventional reason) are sobering and are not offered frivolously. Based on Einstein's mode of thinking and numerous analyses of the limitations of mainstream Western epistemology, critical democratic social studies teachers come to understand that there are important flaws in accepted forms of logic, research, and knowledge production.

Do not misread this assertion. I am not arguing that we throw out the Cartesian-Newtonian baby with the bathwater, that is, that mainstream science is of no benefit. Of course, it is. Its contributions are significant and well documented. An epistemology of complexity maintains that we can do better, go further, and address the limitations inherent in the Cartesian-Newtonian system, in particular, the limitations Einstein had to overcome to develop his frame-shattering theories. In many ways an epistemology of complexity demands a new rigor in social studies cognition and education. Such an epistemological approach helps social studies teachers develop ways of transcending conceptually impoverished definitions of high educational standards grounded on recall of fragmented bits of knowledge, long on memorization and recitation, short on an understanding of larger processes, interpretation, applicability/transferability, and connectedness. When students and teachers move into the processual realm, they gain the ability not only to explain the dynamics that move events but, like Einstein, develop the capacity to transform them in progressive ways (Kovel, 1998; Woods & Grant, 1998; Lawler, 1995).

With these Einsteinian insights into an epistemology of process, we begin to notice the processural nature of other aspects of the lived world. Consciousness, for example, can be understood as a process-oriented dynamic. Consciousness and knowledge acquisition in this context are not separate entities, things in themselves, but parts of a mutually constructive process. As with the process connecting the knower and the known, consciousness cannot be understood separate from the world. With this understanding, we can reconceptualize social studies education not only as an epistemological dynamic but as an ontological force as it shapes who we are as human beings (Mashaldis, 1997). In such a processural context, social studies cannot be separated from other disciplines but must be viewed as part of a larger multidisciplinary context. I hope you have already discovered that this is exactly what I am attempting to do in this chapter. Social studies is analyzed in light of the larger process shaped by its interconnections with physics, philosophy, psychology, the social sciences, and education.

Critical democratic social studies teachers who attempt to act on their understanding of this epistemology of process, of course, have to continually battle the forces of positivism within the schools. Instead of exploring and constructing new, emancipatory social, cultural, and political processes, social studies teachers and students in the grips of Cartesianism are fed a diet of isolated, unproblematized data. Such a pedagogy works not to promote analytical thinking and stimulate the social imagination but rather to adjust one uncritically to the status quo.

Contrary to such Cartesian social studies teaching, a complex epistemology of process alerts teachers and students to the realization that social meanings are never closed but remain forever open in light of the appreciation of another process in which they can be understood. Positive knowledge doesn't age well; it often turns to vinegar. New facts come to light; fresh interpretations uncover new processes that render traditional accounts passé. Albert Einstein, as a student, is viewed as a failure; as a scientist, a genius. Yesterday's certainties are tomorrow's superstitions. Deliver me from the dreary universe where everything can be known (Slaughter, 1989; Rineharz, 1979; Lincoln & Guba, 1985; Denzin & Lincoln, 2000).

14. THE IMPORTANCE OF INTERPRETATION—CRITICAL HERMENEUTICS. Ever since positivists applied physical science methods to social science research, there has been a struggle to address those aspects of the human condition that need not just counting but understanding. The information that social analysts collect may include observed behavior, documents, and artifacts, but these source materials cannot be separated from the meanings granted them by past, present, and future human agents. The hermeneutic dimension of research attempts to appreciate this question of meaning by focusing on the interpretive aspects of the act of knowledge production. In the Cartesian academic universe, this hermeneutic dimension is often dismissed. Understanding that all knowledge is an interpretation, a critical social studies, based on an epistemology of complexity, places great emphasis on the hermeneutic dimension.

An epistemology of complexity appreciates that, in critical knowledge production, no matter how much Cartesian experts may argue that the facts speak for themselves, interpretation is always at work. Sometimes it is a conscious process (as in critical theoretical knowledge production); many times it is unconscious (as in positivistic research). Nevertheless, it is always there (Grondin, 1994; Gross & Keith, 1997; Rosen, 1987; Vattimo, 1994). The hermeneutic act of interpretation involves, in its most elemental articulation, making sense of what has been observed in a way that communicates understanding. Not only is all knowledge production merely an act of interpretation, but, hermeneutics contends, perception itself is an act of interpretation. Thus, the quest for understanding is a fundamental feature of human existence, since encounter with the unfamiliar always demands the attempt to make meaning, to make sense. The same, however, is also the case with the familiar. Indeed, as in the study of commonly known texts, we come to find that sometimes the familiar may be seen as the most strange. Thus, it should not be surprising that even the so-called objective writings about the social domain are interpretations, not value-free descriptions (Denzin, 1994; Gallagher, 1992; Jardine, 1998; Smith, 1999).

Learning from the hermeneutic tradition and an epistemology of complexity, critical social studies educators have begun to reexamine textual claims to authority. No pristine interpretation exists. Indeed no methodology, social or educational theory, or discursive form can claim a privileged position that enables the production of authoritative knowledge. Knowledge producers must always speak/write about the world in terms of something else in the world, "in relation to . . . ." As creatures of the world, we are oriented to it in a way that prevents us from grounding our theories and perspectives outside of it. Thus, whether we like it or not, we are all destined, as interpreters, to analyze from within its boundaries and blinders. Within these limitations, however, the interpretations emerging from the hermeneutic process can still move us to new levels of understanding, appreciations that allow us to "live our way" into an experience described to us.

Despite the impediments of context, hermeneutically informed social studies teachers can transcend the inadequacies of thin descriptions of decontextualized facts and produce thick descriptions of social texts characterized by the contexts of their production, the intentions of their producers, and the meanings mobilized in the processes of their construction. The production of such layered descriptions/interpretations follows no step-by-step blueprint or mechanical formula. As with any art form, hermeneutic analysis can be learned only in the Deweyan sense—by doing it. Researchers in this context practice the art by grappling with the text to be understood, telling its story in relation to its contextual dynamics and other texts, first to themselves and then to a public audience (Carson and Sumara, 1997; Denzin, 1994; Gallagher, 1992; Jardine, 1998; Madison, 1988; Ellis, 1998).

These concerns with the nature of hermeneutic interpretation come under the category of philosophical hermeneutics. Working this domain, hermeneutic scholars attempt to think through and clarify the conditions under which interpretation and understanding take place. The critical hermeneutics that grounds critical knowledge production moves more in the direction of normative hermeneutics in that it raises questions about the purposes and procedures of interpretation. In its critical theory-driven context, the purpose of hermeneutic analysis is to develop a form of cultural criticism, revealing power dynamics within social and cultural texts. Social studies teachers familiar with critical hermeneutics build bridges between reader and text, text and producer, historical context and present, and one particular social circumstance and another. Accomplishing such interpretive tasks is difficult, and researchers situated in normative hermeneutics push ethnographers, historians, semioticians, literary critics, and content analysts to trace the bridge-building processes employed by successful interpretations of knowledge production and culture (Gallagher, 1992; Kellner, 1995; Kogler, 1996; Rapko, 1998).

Grounded by the hermeneutic bridge building, educators in a hermeneutic circle (a process of analysis in which interpreters seek the historical and social dynamics that shape textual interpretation) engage in the back-and-forth of studying parts in relation to the whole and the whole in relation to parts. No final interpretation is sought in this context, since the activity of the circle proceeds with no need for closure (Gallagher, 1992; Peters & Lankshear, 1994; Pinar et al., 1995). This movement of whole to parts is combined with an analytic flow between abstract and concrete. Such dynamics often tie interpretation to the interplay of larger social forces (the general) to the everyday lives of individuals (the particular). A critical hermeneutics brings the concrete, the parts, the particular, into focus, but in a manner that grounds them contextually in a larger understanding of the social forces, the whole, the abstract (the general). Focus on the parts is the dynamic that brings the particular into focus, sharpening our understanding of the individual in light of the social and psychological forces that shape him or her. The parts, and the unique places they occupy, ground hermeneutic ways of seeing by providing the contextualization of the particular, a perspective often erased in traditional inquiry's search for abstract generalizations (Gallagher, 1992; Kellner, 1995; Miller & Hodge, 1998; Peters & Lankshear, 1994).

The give-and-take of the hermeneutic circle provokes analysts to review existing conceptual matrices in light of new understandings. Here the analysts reconsider and reconceptualize preconceptions so as to provide a new way of exploring a particular text. Making use of an author's insights hermeneutically does not mean replicating his or her response to his or her original question. In the hermeneutic process, the author's answer is valuable only if it catalyzes the production of a new question for our consideration in the effort to make sense of a particular textual phenomenon (Gallagher, 1992). In this context, participants in the hermeneutical circle must be wary of techniques of textual defamiliarization that have become clichéd. For example, feminist criticisms of Barbie's figure and its construction of the image of ideal woman became such conventions in popular cultural analysis that other readings of Barbie were suppressed (Steinberg, 1997). Critical hermeneutic analysts in this and many other cases have to introduce new forms of analysis to the hermeneutic circle—to defamiliarize conventional defamliarizations—in order to achieve deeper levels of understanding (Berger, 1995).

Within the hermeneutic circle, we may develop new metaphors to shape our analysis in ways that break us out of familiar modes. For example, thinking of movies as mass-mediated dreams may help critical researchers of postmodern popular culture to reconceptualize the interpretive act as a psychoanalytic form of dream study. In this way, critical scholars could examine psychoanalytic work in the analysis of dream symbolization for insights into their cultural studies of the popular culture and the meanings it helps individuals make through its visual images and narratives. As researchers apply these new metaphors in the hermeneutic circle, they must be aware of the implicit metaphors researchers continuously bring to the interpretive process (Berger, 1995; Clough, 1998). Such metaphors are shaped by the sociohistorical era, the culture, and the linguistic context in which the interpreter operates. Such awarenesses are important features that must be introduced into the give-and-take of the critical hermeneutic circle. As John Dewey (1916) observed decades ago, individuals adopt the values and perspectives of their social groups in a manner that such factors come to shape their views of the world. Indeed, the values and perspectives of the group help determine what is deemed important and what is not, what is granted attention and what is ignored. Hermeneutic analysts are aware of such interpretational dynamics and make sure they are included in the search for understanding (Madison, 1988; Mullin, 1999).

Critical democratic social studies teachers with a hermeneutic insight take heart as they pursue their inquiry and teaching. They are aware that the consciousness, and the interpretive frames, they bring to their tasks are historically situated, ever changing, ever evolving in relationship to the cultural and ideological climate (Hinchey, 1998; Kincheloe, Steinberg, & Hinchey, 1999). Thus, there is nothing simple about the social construction of interpretive lenses: consciousness con-struction is contradictory and the result of the collision of a variety of ideologically oppositional forces. Critical qualitative researchers who understand the relationship between identity formation and interpretive lenses are better equipped to understand the origins of their own asser-tions, especially the way power operates to shape them. Linguistic, dis-cursive, and many other factors, typically hidden from awareness, insidiously shape the meanings knowledge producers garner from their work (Goodson, 1997). It was this dynamic that Antonio Gramsci had in mind when he argued that a critical philosophy should be viewed as a form of self-criticism. The starting point, he concluded, for any higher understanding of self involves consciousness of oneself as a product of power-driven sociohistorical forces. A critical perspective, he once wrote, involves the ability of its adherents to criticize the ideological frames that they use to make sense of the world (Coben, 1998).

Analyzing Dewey's and Gramsci's notions of self-production in light of the aims of critical hermeneutics vis-à-vis critical democratic social studies education, we begin to gain insight into how the ambiguous and closeted interpretive process operates. This moves us in a critical direc-tion, as we understand that the "facts" do not simply demand particular interpretations. Social studies teachers who fail to take these points into account operate at the mercy of unexamined assumptions. Because all interpretation is historically and culturally situated, it is the lot of criti-cal knowledge workers to study the ways both interpreters (often the ana-lysts themselves) and the objects of interpretation are constructed by their time and place. In this context, the importance of social theory emerges. Operating in this manner, researchers inject critical social the-ory into the hermeneutical circle to facilitate an understanding of the hidden structures and tacit cultural dynamics that insidiously inscribe social meanings and values (Cary, 1996; Gallagher, 1992; Kellner, 1995). This social and historical situating of interpreter and text is an extreme-ly complex enterprise that demands a nuanced analysis of the impact of hegemonic and ideological forces that connect the microdynamics of everyday life with the macrodynamics of structures such as White supremacy, patriarchy, and class elitism. The central hermeneutic of much critical knowledge work involves the interactions among research, subject(s), and these situating sociohistorical structures.

When these aspects of the interpretation process are taken into account, analysts begin to understand Hans-Georg Gadamer's (1989) contention that social frames of reference influence researchers' questions, which, in turn, shape the nature of interpretation itself. In light of this situating process, the modernist notion that a social text has one valid interpretation evaporates into thin air. Researchers, whether they admit it or not, always have points of view, disciplinary orientations, social or political groups with which they identify (Kincheloe, 1991; Lugg, 1996). Thus the point, critical hermeneuts argue, is not that knowledge producers and teachers should shed all worldly affiliations but that they should identify those affiliations and understand their impacts on the ways a researcher approaches social and educational phenomenon. Gadamer labels these world affiliations of researchers their "horizons" and deems the hermeneutic act of interpretation the "fusion of horizons." When critical researchers participate in the fusion of horizons, they enter into the tradition of the text. Here they study the conditions of its production and the circle of previous interpretations. In this manner, they begin to uncover the ways the text has attempted to represent truth (Berger, 1995; Ellis, 1998; Jardine, 1998; Miller & Hodge, 1998; Slattery, 1995).

The hermeneutic tradition puts the politics of interpretation at center stage in social studies education and the knowledge production that takes place within the field. Like ordinary human beings, critical knowledge workers make history and live their lives within structures of meaning they have not necessarily chosen for themselves. Understanding this, critical hermeneuts realize that a central aspect of their sociocultural analysis involves dissecting the ways people connect their everyday experiences to the cultural representations of such experiences. Such work involves the unraveling of the ideological codings embedded in these cultural representations. This unraveling is complicated by the taken-for-grantedness of the meanings promoted in these representations and the typically undetected ways these meanings are circulated into everyday life (Denzin, 1992; Kogler, 1996). The better the analyst, the better he or she can expose these meanings in the domain of "what goes without saying," that activity previously deemed noise unworthy of comment. Such critical interpretations often involve dangerous knowledges previously excluded from the social studies curriculum.

In the postmodern and hyperreal first decade of the twenty-first century, electronic modes of communication become extremely important to the production of meanings and representations that culturally situate human beings in general and textual interpretations in particular

(Goldman & Papson, 1994; Hall, 1997). In many ways, it can be argued that the postmodern condition produces a second-hand culture, filtered and performed in the marketplace and constantly communicated via popular mass media. Critical analysts understand that the pedagogical effects of such a mediated culture can range from the political/ideological to the cognitive/epistemological. For example, the situating effects of print media tend to promote a form of linearity that encourages certain forms of rationality, continuity, and uniformity; on the other hand, electronic media promote a nonlinear immediacy that may encourage more emotional responses that lead individuals in very different directions (du Gay, Hall, Janes, MacKay & Negus, 1997). Thus, the situating influence and pedagogical impact of electronic media of the postmodern condition must be assessed by those who study cultural and political processes and the social research processes itself (Bell & Valentine, 1997; Berger, 1995; Bertman, 1998; Denzin, 1992; Kellner, 1995).

A critical hermeneutics in an epistemology of complexity is, of course, suspicious of any model of interpretation in social studies that claims to reveal the final truth, the essence of a social, economic, cultural, or political text or experience (Goodson and Mangan, 1996). Critical hermeneutics is more comfortable with interpretive approaches that assume that the meaning of human experience can never be fully disclosed—neither to the researcher nor even to the human who experienced it. Because language is always slippery, with its meanings ever in process, critical hermeneutics understands that interpretations will never be linguistically unproblematic, will never be direct representations. Critical hermeneutics seeks to understand how textual practices, such as scientific research and classical social and economic theory, work to maintain existing power relations and to support extant power structures (Denzin, 1992).

As critical social studies educators, we draw, of course, on the latter model of interpretation, with its treatment of the personal as political. Critical hermeneutics grounds a critical research that attempts to connect the everyday troubles individuals face to public issues of power, justice, and democracy. Typically, within the realm of social studies and cultural analysis in general, critical hermeneutics has deconstructed sociocultural texts that promote demeaning stereotypes of the disempowered (Denzin, 1992; Gross & Keith, 1997; Rapko, 1998). In this context, critical hermeneutics is also being deployed in relation to cultural texts that reinforce an ideology of privilege and entitlement for empowered members of the society (Allison, 1998; Fine, Weis, Powell, & Wong, 1997; Frankenberg, 1993; Kincheloe, Steinberg, Rodriguez, & Chennault, 1998; Rains, 1998; Rodriguez & Villaverde, 2000).

In its ability to render the personal political, critical hermeneutics provides a methodology for arousing a critical consciousness through the analysis of the generative themes of the present era. Such generative themes can often be used to examine the meaning-making power of the contemporary cultural realm (Peters & Lankshear, 1994). Within the social studies profession, there is still resistance to the idea that movies, television, and popular music are intricately involved in the most important political, economic, and cultural battles of the contemporary epoch. Critical hermeneutics recognizes this centrality of popular culture in the postmodern condition and seeks to uncover the ways it impedes and advances the struggle for a democratic society (Kellner, 1995). Appreciating the material effects of media culture, critical hermeneutics traces the ways cultural dynamics position audiences politically in ways that not only shape their political beliefs but formulate their identities (Steinberg & Kincheloe, 1997).

In this context, Paulo Freire's (1985) contribution to the development of a critical hermeneutics is especially valuable. Understanding that the generative themes of a culture are central features in a critical social analysis, Freire assumes that the interpretive process is both an ontological (pertaining to being) and an epistemological act. It is ontological on the level that our vocation as humans, the foundation of our being, is grounded on the hermeneutical task of interpreting the world so we can become more fully human. It is epistemological in the sense that critical hermeneutics offers us a method for investigating the complex conditions of our existence and the generative themes that shape it. In this context, we gain the prowess to both live with a purpose and operate with the ability to perform evaluative acts in naming the culture around us. This ability takes on an even greater importance in the contemporary electronic society, where the sociopolitical effects of the cultural domain have often been left unnamed, allowing our exploration of the shaping of our own humanness to go unexplored in this strange new social context. Critical hermeneutics addresses this vacuum (Kincheloe & Steinberg, 1997; McLaren, 1997; Peters & Lankshear, 1994).

Critical hermeneutics deployed in social studies names the world as a part of a larger effort to evaluate it and make it better. Knowing this, it is easy to understand why critical hermeneutics focuses on domination and its negation, emancipation. Domination limits self-direction and democratic community building, whereas emancipation enables them. Domination, legitimated as it is by ideology, is decoded by critical hermeneuts who help critical researchers discover the ways they and their subjects have been entangled in the ideological process. The exposé and critique of ideology is one of the main objectives of critical hermeneutics in its effort to make the world better. As long as our vision is obstructed by the various purveyors of ideology, our effort to live in democratic communities will be thwarted (Gallagher, 1992). Power wielders with race, class, and gender privilege have access to the resources that allow them to promote ideologies and representations in ways individuals without such privilege cannot (Bartolomé, 1998; Carlson & Apple, 1998; Denzin, 1992; Hinchey, 1998; Jipson & Paley, 1997; Leistyna & Sherblom, 1996; Peters & Lankshear, 1994; Pinar, 1998; Gresson, 1995).

15. LOCATING THE FRONTIER OF CLASSROOM KNOWLEDGE AT THE POINTS WHERE ONE'S PERSONAL EXPERIENCE INTERSECTS WITH SECONDARY INFORMATION. In an epistemology of complexity, social studies teachers are hermeneutical scholars who engage in rigorous thinking, extensive reading, ongoing dialogue, thorough analysis, and synthetic reflection. Too much of the current teaching and curriculum standards developed for social studies accept the Cartesian epistemological assumption that knowledge is an external body of information independent of human beings. The social studies teacher's role in this context is to insert this knowledge into the minds of students. Frequently, this "knowledge" is a body of isolated facts (factoids) to be committed to memory by uninterested social studies students. Evaluation procedures that emphasize the retention of isolated bits and pieces of data strengthen this view of knowledge.

Conceptual thinking vanishes as modernist social studies classes trivialize learning. Students are evaluated on the lowest level of human thinking: their ability to memorize. This "stupidification" process is directly related to the unstated, tacit Cartesian epistemology lurking in the hallways of the school. Thinking skills, involving the ability to ask unique questions, to see connections between concepts, or to apply conceptual understandings, lose importance. Emancipated and empowered social studies teachers, aware of this epistemology of complexity, focus on using these thinking skills to guide the interaction between them and their students and the social studies content they all want to engage. In this process, both students and teachers reinterpret their own lives, and in the process, uncover new insights and talents. Unless students and teachers can incorporate social studies information into their lives to produce new knowledge, the discipline will remain an ideological rite of passage into a politically unconscious adulthood.

If social studies teachers cannot engage their students in the development of an epistemological consciousness where they can produce knowledge, my effort to educate thoughtful, emancipated, knowable teachers is quite irrelevant. Why bother requiring a college degree if social studies teachers simply deliver factoids? Why struggle to interest social studies teacher education students in the task of knowledge production, the quest for an epistemological consciousness, the effort to expose the values hiding in particular kinds of information, or the formulation of questions about the effects of social context or power? The genius of great social thinkers lies much less in their ability to retain the information they encounter than in their ability to produce new knowledge. When social studies teachers gain an epistemological consciousness and the collision of student experience with the information of the humanities and social sciences produces new knowledge, traditional information is not simply discarded. Critical democratic social studies teachers, indeed, reexamine what constitutes traditional knowledge, the traditional canon, but, at the same time, recognize value in the knowledge others have produced.

The important epistemological point here is that we interrogate this social knowledge and consider it in light of new contexts and questions. As we develop point 15 the new contexts and questions on which we are focusing here involve our personal experiences and consciousness. How does this social information, we ask, help us rethink, reinterpret our prior experiences? How does it affect our political beliefs? our view of citizenship? How does it help (or hinder) us from becoming the people we want to become? What does it mean to us, given where we have lived our lives? These questions and others like them are important steps in the creation of emancipatory knowledge because they preclude the epistemologically reductionistic concrete-level "mastery" of secondary (secondhand) data and the disempowerment it leaves in its wake. There has to be more than this to social studies education. Brilliant social studies teachers are always working on new ways to help their students connect their lives to secondary data in ways that create new syntheses of knowledge, new ways of being.

Appreciating the epistemology of complexity, critical democratic social studies teachers understand that there is nothing simple about setting up this synthesis of secondary information and personal experience. Such social studies teachers have grown comfortable with the uncertain, tentative syntheses that they and their students develop. They are keenly aware of the presence of contradiction and treasure the effort to integrate ostensibly dissimilar phenomena into new, revealing combinations. Critical social studies teachers, conscious of these epistemological dynamics, escape the confines of Cartesianism and set foot into new pedagogical, ontological, and even cosmological (used here to mean the nature of the universe and the inseparability of the nature of life and human consciousness from this larger whole) realms.

Only an individual with a critical consciousness of epistemological complexity, who understands self in its critical cosmological (interconnected) context, is ready to jump into this new realm. Where the formal operational orientation of Cartesianism functions on the basis of isolation of parts, linear causality, and determinism, the epistemology of complexity assumes a holism based on a complex, nonlinear interconnection of events. In particular, in the context of point 14, this holism is based on the continuum of cosmos and self. Where does the cosmos and the self begin? The frontier that connects (not separates) world and self is a living part of both (O'Sullivan, 1999; Van Hesteran, 1986; Kramer, 1983).

As democratic social studies teachers grow accustomed to this self-world connectedness, they are reminded once again of the counter-Cartesian rejection of universal, correct ways of viewing the social and educational worlds. Such teachers will see not only multiple interpretations of social phenomena but will be able to identify the contexts from which they emanate and the ways they intersect with the life experiences of themselves and their students. They appreciate what systems of meaning various knowledge producers have employed to shape the data they disseminate and from whose perspective their stories are told. Critical democratic social studies educators, in this context, understand the deterministic epistemology of some analysts, such as traditional Marxists. Traditional Marxists argued in their own deterministic way that humans see only what their conceptual lenses allowed them to see, what their context of understanding permitted.

In the spirit of hope, possibility, and antideterminism, social studies teachers, with a complex epistemological consciousness, liberate themselves from such determinism by monitoring the intersection of information and consciousness, by gaining a new awareness of their own perceptual process, and by transcending what the context allows. In this way, critical democratic social studies educators emancipate themselves from Cartesianism and the structural forces that limit human ability to see the social world from outside our restricted place in the web of reality. In logic-centered modernism, this monitoring of self-perception was subverted in Cartesianism's discounting of the centrality of the terrain of private inner reality. In line with the modernist impulse, what purpose did the realm of consciousness serve in the process of industrialization, the quest for material progress, or the "manly" conquest of nature? As counter-Cartesianism rediscovers the sensuous and erotic dimensions of humanness, an epistemology of complexity incorporates such notions into new ways of exploring and perceiving the social, educational, and even intrapersonal domains (Gordon, Miller, and Rollock, 1990; Kramer, 1983; Slaughter, 1989).

Such new modes of thinking, knowledge-production, and teaching incorporate sensual- and self-knowledge in interesting and emancipatory ways. Social studies teachers, researchers, and teacher-researchers who do not understand the way information interacts with their own experiences and shapes their own consciousnesses tend to misconstrue the pronouncements, actions, and feelings of others. The complexity and multiple readings characteristic of a counter-Cartesian epistemology are remote to modernist formal teachers and knowledge producers, because they seek comfort in the prescribed methods, the objectivity, and, especially, the depersonalization of traditional positivistic social and educational science. Such positivistic teachers and knowledge producers are only nervous purveyors of the correct answers (Van Hesteran, 1986; Steinberg and Kincheloe, 1998).

In a sense, the Cartesian objectivist tradition provides a shelter in which the self can hide from the deeply personal issues that permeate all social and educational phenomena. Such personal issues, if it were not for the depersonalization of Cartesian knowledge production, would force an uncomfortable element of researcher self-disclosure. Epistemologically conscious social studies teachers, of course, move beyond this Cartesian veil of secrecy, exploring and revealing how their own perspectives and values came to be constructed and how the social information they encounter shapes their pedagogies and world views. They transcend Cartesian formalism's concern with problem solving by seeking the genesis of the problems they discern. In this way, they develop a form of intrapersonal intelligence, as they learn to contextually examine the origins and nature of their own thinking.

In his effort to explore post-Piagetian, post-Cartesian forms of cognition, Robert Kegan (1982) theorizes that an essential characteristic of such thinking involves the individual's attempt to disengage himself or herself from socio-interpersonal norms and ideological expectations. The epistemology of complexity's concern with questions of meaning, emancipation via ideological disembedding, and attention to the process of self-production rises above Piaget's formal operational level of cognition and a Cartesian form of inquiry, with its devotion to proper procedure. What I will explain later in the book and label postformalism is a form of thinking that grapples with purpose, devoting attention to issues of human dignity, freedom, authority, and social responsibility.

Many conceptions of such post-Cartesian forms of analysis and cognition contend that an appreciation of epistemological complexity, with its multiple frames of reference and concern with self-production, necessitates an ethical relativism that paralyzes social action. My conception of postformalism and its complex forms of perceiving and inquiring is tied to an epistemologically complex understanding of critical theory that is used to examine the frontier where personal experience intersects with secondary information. Social studies teachers who understand this dynamic are never content with what they have constructed, never convinced of any social, political, or educational system's appropriateness, and always concerned with the expansion of self-awareness and consciousness. In this mode, they engage in a running dialogue with self and a perpetual reconceptualization of the nature and purpose of their teaching. They stand ready in this context to rethink the ways the information they deal with intersects with their own and the experiences of their students.

16. CRITICAL ONTOLOGY—SEARCHING FOR NEW FORMS OF HUMAN BEING. One of the most important ways that a critical education moves us to new levels of consciousness and being involves gaining awareness of ourselves as social and historical beings. Individuals who gain such an awareness understand how and why their political opinions, religious beliefs, gender role, or racial perspectives have been shaped by

dominant perspectives. Our epistemology of complexity plays such an important role in this attempt to gain new understandings and insights as to who we could become. As it exposes the particular ways knowledge is produced and the impact it exerts on the shaping of self, we all begin to understand that our present state of being (our ontological self) is, in part, a social and historical construction. Just as they have been shaped by social action, they can be rethought and reshaped by social action. Point 16, our last feature of an epistemology of complexity, blurs the lines of knowledge production and being (ontology), as we focus on how we move from the gaining of epistemological consciousness to new ways of being human. In this context critical democratic social studies teachers move into a realm where they pursue what might be labeled a "critical ontology."

A critical epistemology of complexity promotes self-reflection that results in attitudinal change. The basis of this change rests on insights into the scars and traumas of the past. Social studies teachers, thus, help their students begin the process of understanding themselves by bringing to consciousness the process by which their identities were formed. Action that is to be taken by students to address social pathologies, such as racism, sexism, or class bias, that shape individual consciousness can begin to be negotiated once self-reflection has taken place. Prudent ontological action that involves asking questions of ethics, morality, politics, emotion, and gut feeling does not take the form of rules and precise regulations. Our understanding of critical theory vis-à-vis an epistemology of complexity provides a framework of principles around which action can be discussed rather than a set of procedures. Social studies teachers who engage in the quest for new, expanded, more just and interconnected ways of being human—a critical ontology—are never certain of the exact path of action they will take in such a pursuit. An awareness of contextual factors will always complicate the effort.

A part of the emancipatory action we might take involves questioning accepted definitions of particular social entities such as intelligence, school success, a good society, popularity, or competence. As active interpreters with a social/ontological imagination, we can redefine such notions in more just and conceptually expanded ways. In such a context, we can involve ourselves and others in a process of social reconstruction, educational reconceptualization, and self-improvement. According to an epistemology of complexity, we hold the power to reconstruct our consciousness. If this is the case, then, in a critical ontological context, we possess the ability to reshape ourselves, a process that, given our location in the social web of reality, concurrently demands that we reinterpret our traditions and reinvent our futures together, in solidarity with other self-directed human agents.

The thinking of social studies teachers and students is intimately connected to these ontological features. As epistemologically conscious teachers and students "get beyond the facts," they come to understand both the complexity and the limitations of history. Social studies teachers not only ask, How do we know, but Why does it matter to us in this particular place and time? How does this historical knowledge shape me? What does it demand of me now that I know it? Such questions are central to the reconceptualization of the civic self and to the future of democracy in a world where power quashes democratic impulses (Pang, Gay & Stanley, 1995). Given such hostile socio-political circumstances, critical democratic social studies educators seek catalysts for ontological evolution. How do we use our epistemological consciousness to push the boundaries of humanness?

A key step involves freeing ourselves from the machine metaphors of Cartesianism. An epistemology of complexity recognizes the reductionism of viewing the universe as a well-oiled machine and the human mind as a computer. Such ways of seeing subvert an appreciation of the amazing life force that inhabits both the universe and human beings. This machine cosmology has positioned human beings as living in a dead world, a lifeless universe. Ontologically, this Cartesianism has separated individuals from their lifeless surroundings, undermining any organic interconnection of the person to the cosmos. The life-giving complexity of the inseparability of human and world has been lost and the social study of people abstracted—removed from context. Such a removal has exerted disastrous ontological, psychological, and social effects. Human beings, in a sense, lost their belongingness to the world and people around them (O'Sullivan, 1999).

Again, Ladi Semali's and my (1999) concept of the importance of indigenous knowledge in postmodern times emerges. With the birth of modernism and the scientific revolution, many pre-modern, indigenous epistemologies, cosmologies, and ontologies were lost, ridiculed by European modernists as primitive. While there is great diversity among premodern world views, there do seem to be some discernible patterns that distinguish them from modernist perspectives. In addition to developing meaning systems that were connected to cosmological perspectives on the nature of creation, most premodern viewpoints saw nature and the world at large as living systems. Western, often Christian, observers condescendingly labeled such perspectives as pantheism or nature worship and positioned them as an enemy of the notion of monotheism. As such, they needed to be stamped out and replaced with a belief in the one true God. Not understanding the subtlety and nuance of such indigenous views of the world, Europeans subverted the sense of belonging that accompanied these enchanted views of nature. European Christomodernism transformed the individual from a connected participant in the drama nature to a detached, objective, depersonalized observer.

The modernist individual emerged from the process alienated and disenchanted. As Edmund O'Sullivan (1999) puts it, Cartesianism tore apart "the relationship between the microcosmos and the macrocosmos" (p. 82). Such a fragmentation resulted in the loss of cosmological significance and the beginning of a snowballing pattern of ontological imbalance. A critical ontology involves the process of reconnecting human beings on a variety of levels and in numerous ways to a living social and physical web of reality, to a living cosmos. Social studies teachers in this context help students connect to the civic web of the political domain, the biotic web of the natural world, the social web of human life, and the epistemological web of knowledge production. In this manner, we all move to the realm of critical ontology where new ways of being and new ways of being connected reshape all people.

Philip Wexler (2000) picks up on these ontological issues, arguing that an intuitive disenchantment with Cartesian fragmentation and its severing of the self-environment relationship is fueling a diffuse social revaluation. He employs the term "revitalization" for this mass, decentered movement taking place throughout Western societies. It constitutes an attempt, he contends, to resacralize our culture and ourselves. Such an effort exposes the impact of Eurocentrism and Cartesianism on what human beings have become, as, at the same time, it produces an ontological "change from within." Understanding the problems with Cartesianism's lack of self-awareness or concern with consciousness and interconnectedness, Wexler's resacralization picks up on wisdom traditions, both premodern and postmodern, to construct an ontology of complexity. In this context, the Cartesian bifurcation of the mind and body is repaired, and new relationships and comfort with the body, mind, and spirit are pursued. In the transcendence of modernist notions of bodily ego-greed, a new understanding of the body's role in meaning making is obtained.

Resacralization positions the body in relation to cognition and the process of life itself. The body is a corporeal reflection of the evolutionary concept of *autopoiesis*, self-organizing or self-making of life. Autopoiesis involves the production of a pattern of life organization. Cognition in this ontological context involves the process of the self-production. Thus, life itself is a cognitive activity that involves establishing patterns of living, patterns that become the life force through self-organization. If life is self-organized, then there are profound cognitive, epistemological, and ontological implications. By recognizing new patterns and developing new processes, humans exercise much more input into their own evolution than previously imagined.

Evolution (and in the context of our discussion, cognitive evolution) is not as random as previously thought. Life is self-produced in forms of escalating diversity and complexity. The interaction of different living forms can catalyze the self-production feature of living systems. In both its corporeal and cognitive expressions the autopoietic life process reaches out for difference, for novelty, to embrace its next ontological level (Wexler, 2000; Capra, 1996). Social studies teachers who understand an epistemology of complexity can use these ontological notions to rethink their lives and their teaching. With these understandings, we can self-organize and reorganize the field to new levels of complexity where new patterns and processes allow us to rethink the nature of our being and the possibility of our being. Social studies in this complex context takes on an unprecedented importance, while it pursues ways of knowing and being that shape the evolution of the human species.

Chapter 11

Social Studies in the Web of Recent Educational Reform: Schooling for Social Regulation

Since the early 1970s, there has been a consistent right-wing pressure on educational reform in general and social studies education in particular. Reacting to the perceived social, political, and educational changes of the 1960s, right-wing strategists located an opportunity to call for a return to traditional values, neoclassical economic policy, traditional power relations, a Cartesian, fragmented, fact-based school curriculum, and a Eurocentric, Americentric view of the patriotic indoctrination role of social education. In this context the right wing in the United States promoted a new dominant cultural story that played well to White audiences frustrated with the changes taking place in the world: the recovery of White supremacy perceived to be lost in the Civil Rights Movement.

Aaron Gresson (1995, 2000) argues that this new right-wing White story inverts a traditional Black narrative. Because of the media portrayal of the economic success of Black and other minority groups—a portrait less accurate than represented—the right-wing story contends that non-Whites in the last three decades of the twentieth and the first decade of the twenty-first century have greater power and opportunity than Whites. This preposterous position posits that this new African American, Latino, and Native American privilege has been gained at the expense of more deserving White Americans, especially White males.

The story is promoted in a variety of spheres, including education, and in a number of ways, but always with the same effect: the production of White anger directed at non-Whites and women. Such anger works, of course, to divide poor and working-class people of all races and genders, to support the interests of privileged power wielders, and to shape the social studies curriculum.

Such a dominant sociopolitical and educational story induces many Whites to see themselves as people under threat. Sociologists have long maintained that individuals and groups who perceive themselves under threat often react with an attempt to reassess their power and regain their former social position: the phenomenon of status anxiety. This reassertion, of course, takes many forms and many degrees. Manifestations may include modest efforts to reassert one's self-worth by way of private expression of racial disdain ("I hate the way Deion Sanders struts around the end zone like a rooster every time he scores a touchdown") or racial superiority ("Many of the people who work in my office don't make a very good impression with their loud 'street talk' and everything").

Other examples of White reassertion in the United States may work more at the level of group recovery, with the passage of "English only" legislation in heavily Latino areas, such as Florida, California, and Arizona, or battles over "multicultural curricula" as evidenced throughout the nation (Frankenberg, 1993). More extreme expressions involve the recent dramatic growth of White supremacist organizations and the terrorist activity associated with some of them: for example, the April 1995 bombing of the Oklahoma City federal building and the shootings at the Jewish Day Care Center in Los Angeles in 1999. The vast majority of Americans are dismayed by this level of angry White reassertions, yet the perception of Whites as the real victims of U.S. racism becomes more and more deeply embedded into the White collective consciousness. In the domain of social studies, this White reassertion impulse can be seen in the debates over history and social studies standards in the 1990s and early twenty-first century. When confronted with standards that attempted to depict African American, Latino, Native American, and women's issues, many political and educational leaders charged that the effort constituted a new form of reverse racism. How could Harriet Tubman be mentioned as often in the history curriculum as many of our nation's founders? opponents asked. In this recovery context we will examine the forces shaping social studies education via the impulse of recent educational reform.

GETTING CONTROL:
REGULATING WORKERS AS A LARGER GOAL OF EDUCATION

After the social upheavals of the 1960s and the economic problems of the 1970s, conservative educational reformers in the 1980s moved on a variety of fronts to gain control of American education. In the early and mid-1980s, a panoply of reports emerged criticizing American schools for a variety of reasons. The report, of course, that received the most attention was the National Commission of Excellence in Education (NCEE) report in 1983. Based on a set of assumptions that viewed education as an arm of business in America, the NCEE argued that one of the most important roles of schools was to further technological development in American society. If the main role of schools was to further technological development, where did that leave social studies? If social studies was, as Project SPAN tells us, already viewed with indifference before the reform movements of the 1980s, the field of study found itself in an even less favorable position after the reports and the reform. The types of questions a critical democratic social studies education asked were deemed irrelevant, as reformers pushed the schools and society into a new corporate-dominated future.

In a period when Americans needed to be asking questions of social consequence—of course, these questions need to be asked in all eras—education reformers have placed less emphasis on social education. As they have rushed headfirst into high tech industry, computerization, productivity improvements, and technical solutions for human problems, conservative reformers failed to ask some of the basic social and cultural questions. What are the human consequences of postindustrialism? How do high tech jobs affect human beings? Do technical solutions to human problems take into account the complexity of human emotions and feelings? As political economic leaders devoted resources to the improvement of economic productivity, did they have a sense of our vision of a good society? In other words, were they guided by economic expediency or by visions of justice, social happiness, human freedom, and aesthetic appreciation, and our concept of critical ontology?

These were some of the important questions of the 1980s that were not asked then and, unfortunately, are not asked now. While economic prosperity was and is, of course, desirable, it is not the only goal of human beings. Economic prosperity itself may not be desirable if it doesn't include everyone and destroys the ecological balance of the planet in the process of its achievement. We all lose if economic prosperity is achieved at the expense of the emotional quality of our lives. This section examines the role of technological innovation in the American workplace and the ways it has come to affect American education in general and social studies education in particular. In the following pages, we will analyze how technology has served to change the face of the American workplace, change the role of schools, and how, when unexamined it has come to limit the freedom of men and women.

How exactly does technology come to limit human freedom? When most of us think about technology, we often concentrate on laborsaving aspects that grant us greater control over our time. In this context, technological innovation does not constrain human activity but allows greater choice over how we live our lives. The automobile and the interstate highway, for example, grant us more expendable time than our ancestors could ever have envisioned. There is another side to technological innovation, however. Other than laborsaving devices, technology has rarely served to make for a humane workplace in modernist America. In fact technological innovations, such as the assembly line and accompanying efficiency procedures, have often served to limit worker options. New technologies of worker control, often called scientific management, may have extended the tendency of industrial supervisors to view workers as objects to be manipulated. Too infrequently have techniques of scientific management served to encourage a view of workers as human beings with emotions to be considered and individual talents to be cultivated.

Industrial managers have often sought specific worker personality types to meet the needs of the technicalized workplace. According to many industrial analysts, workers who possess the following personality traits are more valuable to the enterprise than employees who do not: 1) an acceptance of a subordinate role in the hierarchy; 2) submission to the rigid discipline required by the bureaucracy of the workplace; 3) comfort with the lack of concern for human emotions and the subtle dynamics of human interaction that is characteristic of the technicalized, bureaucratized workplace; 4) an acceptance of motivation based not on the value of the work itself but on the external reward structures of monetary incentives.

The role of education often revolves around the production of these personality traits in students. Men and women are students before they are workers. The workers who give up the control of the planning and direction of activities that comprise their jobs first surrender their autonomy to teachers. A teacher sometimes simulates the role of the boss, granting rewards and assessing penalties. As far as discipline is concerned, the corporatized school attempts to prepare the future worker for the requirements of the dehumanized, bureaucratic workplace. Some of us have experienced that workplace directly through our own work histories. Others have experienced it vicariously through the stories of our friends or by reading about the line workers in Studs Terkel's *Working* or Ben Hamper's *Rivithead*. It is a structured world, marked by highly standardized routines and degrading requirements of conformity, of time schedules, regulations, and stifling technocratic procedures. Schools prepare our psyches for such a place with their oppressive and petty rules which govern student behavior.

The schools often condition students to remove their affect and emotions from their schoolwork, a characteristic highly valued in the workplace. The more dehumanized a bureaucracy becomes, the more "success" it attains. When love, hatred, irrationality, and other emotional elements are removed from the official business, then rules and regulations can work more predictably. Thus, as educational studies have indicated, Cartesian educators tend to value student personality traits related to the cognitive mode of expression. Students with highly developed affective personality traits are often not rewarded for their compassion and empathetic insight. Also, students, like workers, frequently are not intrinsically interested in their work. In both cases, the organization has to rely on external rewards, such as grades, pay incentives, class ranks or titles, to motivate the individual.

What are the implications here? Simply put, this view of schooling turns our conventional notions upside down. To see one of the roles of school as the production of personality types that better suit the needs of those who run the technical workplace challenges the assumption on which many modern discussions of education rest. We often look at schooling as a force that frees us from ignorance, helps us envision alternatives, gives us choice in direction of our lives, and opens the doors of opportunity. Viewed in the context of "personality adjustments," schools serve not as a force for freedom but as a vehicle of constraint. Instead of granting us power to shape our lives, education often "regulates" us so that we better serve the needs of capital. This is not the way many Americans interpret the role of schools in a democratic society.

If schools serve this sometimes regulative role, why don't more Americans understand that this is the case? Why do we rarely hear this view expressed in the public discussion of education? The answers to such questions are very complex and ambiguous, and this is not the forum for a full discussion of them. Suffice it to say that many Americans intuitively understand that something is wrong with their education; they have just not articulated precisely what it is. Many Americans, especially those who have worked in low-status jobs, know that school was similar to work. And in neither school nor the workplace do these Americans feel that their talents were appreciated or that they had much input into what went on. It is important that these voiceless workers, these victims of technocracy, understand that school does not have to be an institution that limits choice. It is important that the concerns of these Americans be considered in the national conversation about educational policy. The concepts of technocracy and technicalization are valuable in the attempt to understand the role of schooling, for they provide us with a means of articulating our vague feelings that contemporary society and education are somehow hostile to individuality.

EXPLORING THE RELATIONSHIP BETWEEN THE REGULATION OF THE WORKPLACE AND THE PURPOSES OF SOCIAL EDUCATION

What is the nature of the process by which technocracy quashes the individuality of the worker? Because of its complexity and subtlety, it is often unrecognized. The process merits examination in some detail. Employers, to exist, must extract labor from their workers. In this society, the employer must make an effort to avoid the appearance of treating labor harshly. The ideal situation, employers have reasoned, would involve a labor force which voluntarily cooperated with management to increase profit margins and boost productivity. Through the use of scientific management, employers have found several ways to avoid harsh treatment of labor and to contribute to the creation of a cooperative workplace. The procedure that has worked best, however, has been to design technologies that simplify and specify the activities of workers. If the technology is sufficiently sophisticated, workers will not have to think for themselves because, as in the fast food industry, they merely follow a predesigned routine. The employer doesn't have to worry as much about supervision, when workers relinquish their control of the process of production. Observers of this situation perceive that it is the technology, not the employer, that forces the employee to follow orders.

One of the most important outcomes of this technicalization of the workplace is the creation of a hidden, but well-delineated, hierarchy. The hierarchy accentuates the division of labor and de-emphasizes thinking and decision making by the workers. Such a workplace conditions workers to take orders. Since workers do not control decision making about the execution of their jobs, the hierarchical structure necessitates the hiring of many foremen and supervisors, quality control specialists, administrators to coordinate production, efficiency engineers, and researchers and consultants to provide the information necessary for the few at the top to make intelligent decisions. Unfortunately, this description of the technicalization of the workplace and the solidification of the workplace hierarchy sounds hauntingly familiar to the organization of our school systems. We will examine the similarities between the workplace and the schools later in greater detail.

The hierarchy in the workplace attempts to keep those workers at the lowest rung of the ladder ignorant of the way the production process works as a whole. Management tries to insure that low-level workers see only a minute part of the process and that they see it in isolation from the larger logic of the total operation. Such a placement attempts to persuade workers to accept the fact that decisions regarding their work will be made by higher-ups. Many workers realize that they could perform the jobs at a higher level of the hierarchy just as well as, if not better than, the people who now hold them. They are discouraged by the higher formal education requirements necessary for such high level jobs. Seeing limited access to higher education, many low-level workers give up their aspirations to higher positions. Thus, in some cases, workers come to accept the view that their "ignorance" justifies management's relegation of them to nonthinking jobs.

Workers in this situation come to separate their spirit, their affect, from their work. Work is not a time of fulfillment of creative impulses, nor is it a time of unification of themselves with other workers. As a result, the worker sees gratification in other spheres of his life. Some analysts have argued that workers turn toward consumption of goods as an activity for happiness and fulfillment. A new boat, car, motorcycle, camper, or swimming pool substitute for meaningful work activity. As a rock song of the 1970s put it, employees start "working for the weekend." Older workers work toward retirement.

As workers find that the possibility of promotion to higher level jobs is minimal and learn to devote their energies to concerns outside of work, management devises new ways to minimize their indifference to their work. One such way is the use of mini-hierarchies of job ladders for low-level employees. Such ladders give workers hope of at least some advancement and encourage stable work behavior. The ethic of not rocking the boat or not making waves comes to dominate the workplace. Workers who offer too many creative suggestions or appear to be too enthusiastic about doing a good job are not viewed as ideal employees but potential troublemakers. Left unrestrained, these workers may disrupt the orderly flow of daily events and initiate discontent among fellow workers. Employers come to want employees with a moderate level of interest in their work: enough interest to do what they have to do but not enough to want to devise ways to do it better. Thus, technocracy, in a bizarre way, celebrates mediocrity. Another result of the hierarchical structure produced by the technocratic workplace is the disruption of common interests between the workers. As low-status employees gain seniority and conform to the ethic of the workplace, they move up the rungs of the mini-ladder. As a result, they acquire an interest in the preservation of the system and lose concern for the welfare of their workmates on the lower rungs. Worker camaraderie is further damaged by the fact that management arranges a situation where the lower-level workers rarely come into contact with persons near the top hierarchy. The agent who supervises them is another worker: a foreman, an efficiency supervisor, or a quality control administrator. Their frustrations and resentments are directed toward one another. This serves to hide the exploitative role of both the technology and the individuals at the top of the hierarchy who use it to control worker behavior (Behn et al., 1976; Wirth, 1983).

Though the process is complex and leaky, schools tend to prepare students for the place in hierarchy that "best fits" their social class origins. Thus, the poorer kids are trained to adopt the personality traits necessary for low-status jobs. The more affluent children are socialized for managerial and professional roles. Most of the time, such differential training takes place within individual schools, rationalized by so-called ability grouping and level testing. Any observer can notice the difference between the management of a "low group" and an "advanced group." The low group is subjected to a high degree of external discipline. There are copious rules, accompanied by rigid disciplinary procedures. In these situations, students learn to take orders and respect authority. Low-level students have few choices as they are prepared for their low status role in the workplace. Advanced students are subjected to fewer rules and less consistent enforcement of rules which exist. For such students, conflicts are often settled through negotiation and discussion rather than through the arbitrary action of authority. Such experiences serve to prepare the more affluent students for decision-making managerial or professional positions. They reflect the relative freedom such students will find in their adult roles in the workplace as bosses (Behn et al., 1976).

As technology changes in postmodern society, the type of education provided slowly changes. Schools in America typically are designed to meet the needs of corporations. It logically follows, therefore, that, when technology mandates new types of industry, schools slowly adjust their curricula to produce new types of workers. The claim that the high-tech economy of the twenty-first century will need masses of highly educated scientific workers is problematic. Indeed, the high-tech economy has become an important part of American life in the first decade of the twenty-first century, but it will soon require fewer and fewer highly skilled workers. The fastest growing employment categories are in the service sector: e.g. secretaries, office workers, etc. With the decline of jobs in hard industries, such as steel and automobiles, the nature of the American workplace has dramatically changed. It probably was not necessary that an automobile assembly line worker, educated in 1955, be able to read and write to perform his job. To perform competently, the new service worker, in addition to the desirable personality traits of the workplace, must possess basic literacy skills. Thus, it is not surprising that 1983 was the year when the National Commission on Excellence in Education (NCEE) called for a dramatic reform of education to rescue "a nation at risk."

THE NATIONAL COMMISSION ON EXCELLENCE SETS THE STAGE FOR 20 YEARS OF EDUCATIONAL REFORM

What is the relationship between the reform movement initiated by the NCEE and the technocracy with which we are concerned? The NCEE assumed that the role of school was fundamentally an economic one. When all is said and done, "excellence" and technical standards reformers agree, schools serve economic ends, and curricula can be justified only to the degree those ends are accomplished. In the 1980s economic context, technological improvement was viewed as paramount. Thus, education was viewed primarily as a means of furthering technological improvement and providing manpower to serve the new technology. American business in the 1980s found itself in a technological crisis. Let us briefly examine the genesis of this technological crisis and its effect on education. Such an examination may help illustrate the role education, and social studies education in particular, plays in a technocracy.

The 1970s were years marked by declining productivity, reduced capital investment by American industry, and high unemployment, especially among young, entry-level workers. High unemployment did not result from a decrease in the demand for labor during the period. High unemployment resulted from the baby boomers coming of age and entering the workforce. Because of this circumstance, governmental educational policy focused on youth unemployment. Career education and vocational education were pushed by all levels of government.

American business responded to the labor surplus by becoming more labor-intensive and by reducing expenditures on new machinery. Many companies decided to add second and third shifts in lieu of replacing equipment that had grown old and obsolete. As a result, productivity declined: American workers were producing less than their Japanese and Western European counterparts. Between 1960 and 1977, American productivity remained virtually the same, while Japanese productivity increased by 255%. In the 1980s, the situation changed dramatically as the baby boom ran its course, and fewer and fewer youth entered the job market. In the 1970s, 2.5 million workers were entering the labor force annually; by the late 1980s, that number had decreased to around 1.5 million new workers per year. Simply stated, there were fewer young people in the 1980s than there were in the 1970s—in the 14 to 24 age group. about twenty percent less.

What is important to our discussion of technocracy involves the response of American business. There were two main business responses in the educational sphere: 1) Business sought to improve the basic education of youths who would have been marginally employable in the 1970s; and 2) Business sought to improve the technological training (math and science) of those who would work in high prestige industrial jobs (engineers, scientists, and technicians). An examination of the first response: As the baby boom subsided, fewer qualified employees were available for entry-level jobs. Knowing that too great a decrease in labor would drive up wages, business responded in its own best interest and sought to maximize the number of potential laborers. Thus, U.S. business concerned itself with improving the academic competence of the marginally employable student of the 1970s. It called for a renewed concern for "the basics" and strict accountability to insure that such basic teaching and learning took place.

The second business response in the 1970s also merits further analysis. Because of the reluctance of manufacturers in the 1970s to improve equipment, American business had to face the consequences of a technological crisis. One result, of course, was reduced productivity. When productivity declined, American industry found itself less able to compete equally with foreign competition. Thus, like the challenge presented by Sputnik in the late 1950s, American business began calling on the schools to supply them with technically competent professionals (Spring, 1984). Business leaders were especially concerned with increasing math and science requirements for high school graduation. Reading the NCEE report of 1983, one is reminded of a call to arms against a more technologically competent enemy:

> Our nation is at risk. Our once unchallenged preeminence in commerce, industry, science, and technological innovation is being overtaken by competitors throughout the world. . . . If an unfriendly foreign power had attempted to impose on America the mediocre educational performance that exists today, we might well have viewed it as an act of war. . . . The risk is not only that the Japanese make automobiles more efficiently than Americans and have government subsidies for development and export. It is not just that the South Koreans recently built the world's most efficient steel mill, or that American machine tools, once the pride of the world, are being displaced by German products. It is also that these developments signify a redistribution of trained capability throughout the globe. Knowledge, learning, information and skilled intelligence are the new raw materials of international commerce and are today spreading throughout the world as vigorously as miracle drugs, synthetic fertilizers, and blue jeans did earlier (1983).

The NCEE report reflected the concerns of the business community and its desire to solve its technological problems. Many of the members of the NCEE were directly associated with the Shell Oil Company, Bell Labs, the California Farm Bureau, and the Foundation for Teaching Economics. The economic concerns of these organizations were translated into the educational concerns of *A Nation at Risk*. When the NCEE report is compared with other studies of American education in the 1980s (such as John Goodlad's or Ernest Boyer's), the economically motivated technological focus of the NCEE becomes apparent. The strategy that business took involved marshaling public support of the business-directed educational goals of expanding the numbers of potential employees, a move that exerted downward pressure on wages. American business wanted to flood the job market with: 1) high school graduates with the "proper" personality traits and minimum literacy skills for entry-level jobs; and 2) college trained, highly qualified, scientists and engineers.

Many educators were (and still are) uncomfortable with the business-oriented call for reform and its assumptions about the role of education. These detractors have consistently maintained that: 1) Schools do not exist to meet the demands of business and industry; 2) The short-term demands of business and industry do not necessarily result in benefits for the economy in general or the individual in particular; 3) The technological and labor problems of business and industry were not caused by the failure of public schools. Indeed, it was not school leaders who chose not to invest in new plants and equipment in the 1970s, and, when productivity began to rise in the 1990s, no one credited the work of schools as the cause. 4) It is difficult to predict manpower needs for business and industry, and there is little agreement that an educational curriculum specifically designed to address those needs even accomplishes its goals (Kincheloe, 1995, 1999). Many agree that a general education, steeped in the sciences as well as the humanities, may, in the long run, best serve not only the nation's economic but even its social and spiritual needs (Winegar, 1984).

Thus, the business-oriented education reforms of the 1980s served as a celebration of technocracy. If technocracy implies that the demands of the prevailing technology come to outweigh our democratic concerns about the welfare of people, then, American education is in part a servant of the technocracy. The social studies curriculum, if the business-oriented reforms continue to prevail, will not be dictated by the desire to learn those skills and that knowledge that are of most worth; students will be presented material that best prepares them to adjust to the technology of the workplace. In the process, humane concerns in educational planning disappear; democratic participation is ignored as a goal for social studies in particular and schooling in general; and the celebration of the individual as a free agent who plots his or her own destiny is viewed as an inefficient impediment to economic growth. What matters is determined by the technological and economic demands of the moment. Humans surrender to the needs of the machine in the name of international competition.

This perspective and its implications for social studies education is well illustrated by former Secretary of Education William Bennett's (1987) book of the era, *First Lessons*. In his discussion of the state of modern elementary education, Bennett offered an educational vision that reminded one of John Dewey. Progressive, child-centered, concerned with critical thinking, surprisingly, Bennett took one through an inquiry-based vision of what elementary schools in America could be. Reflecting a pedagogical progressivism, Bennett argued that science should be taught in a hands-on manner. Students should learn science by doing it. Math, he continued, should be related to the lives of the children. Lo and behold, Bennett even argued that teachers should avoid emphasizing tests to the point that critical thinking was sacrificed—sounds like *Getting Beyond the Facts*. Bennett promoted a Deweyan vision of schooling until he reached the subject of the social studies. Immediately, the progressive pronouncements ceased, and a new attitude emerged.

In this new context, the Secretary was horrified by what he called the social studies obsession with issues that come from sociology, psychology, anthropology, and law. These fields of study, in particular their emphasis on matters of race and culture, he wrote, have little relevance for social studies. What we need, he asserted, is not sociology, psychology, and anthropology, and law, but history, geography, and civics. From Bennett's comments about what should be included in the social studies, we gain a valuable insight into right-wing perspectives in the curriculum. Obviously, there is nothing wrong with history, geography, and civics as subjects in the social studies curriculum: They should be taught with rigor and enthusiasm. But Bennett had some very peculiar ideas about the nature and purposes of such subjects. History should involve teaching students the great facts of American history (i.e., a sanitized, white-washed view of America's virtuous past); geography should emphasize place names and map skills; and civics should focus on the necessity of obedience and respect for authority. Bennett viewed the goal of social studies as a repressive form of social regulation.

Social studies from the right-wing perspective should concern itself, therefore, with the rote-based transmission of a body of socially beneficent, order-producing truths: 1) The United States represents the flowering of Western culture; 2) America's great values involve its Anglo-Saxon heritage and free enterprise economics; and 3) Life is good in these United States and any criticism of the society borders on misanthropic behavior. Bennett's pronouncements of the 1980s told us that courses in cultural history, perspectives that advocate pluralism, or lessons that encourage social introspection are somehow anti-American. The test of a good elementary social studies program, the Secretary contended, involves its willingness to engage uncritically in the rituals of national life: saluting the flag and singing the national anthem, for example.

There is a bizarre double standard at work here. Where science and math are areas where freedom of inquiry is cherished, critical thinking is a prized goal, and questioning is a virtue, social studies is an area where freedom of inquiry is denied, critical thinking is dangerous, and questioning borders on disloyalty. In essence, students are to be smart in science and stupid in social studies. But, given the technocratic workplace promoted by corporate leaders and the role of school as the producer of an efficient and politically passive workforce, are we surprised? Social studies teachers and critical democratic citizens, who are aware of the foundations of democracy and the dangers of economic power, must understand these efforts to recast social studies as a form of social regulation.

RIGHT-WING EDUCATIONAL REFORMS OF THE LATE-TWENTIETH CENTURY: SOCIAL REGULATION AND THE PROTECTION OF THE TRADITIONAL SOCIAL NARRATIVES

Human beings use stories to give meaning to their lives. On a personal level, we become heroes or heroines who make meaning and act on particular understandings of why we are here, what is of great importance, and what is insignificant. In our stories about what constitutes a good society, justice, an ethical act, or an authentic way of being human, the substory of education takes place. As we analyze the educational debates of the 1970s and 1980s, we can discern that the conflicts we trace are intimately connected to differing personal, social, and educational stories. Since the 1960s, many of the traditional stories of European superiority, Cartesianism, the benefits of technological innovation, the supremacy of a competitive ethic, patriarchal social structures, and nature as an enemy to be conquered have been questioned by a variety of groups and individuals around the world. The post-Civil Rights Movement, Gay Rights Movement, Indigenous Peoples Movement, and Women's Rights Movement social, political, and educational world since around 1970 may best be understood as a period where conservative groups attempted to reconstitute, repackage, and promote the traditional stories (Postman, 1989).

As they watched the old stories maligned by the faithless, conservative political and educational leaders rode to power in the late 1970s on their depiction of a good vs. evil struggle. The modernist story of progress, characterized by a faith in traditional science, time as money, a cult of reason, an idealized notion of freedom framed within a decontextualized vague humanism formed a tentative alliance with fundamentalist Christianity and its Puritan vision of America as a Christian city (theocracy) on a hill (Giroux, 1991). Education, especially social education, became a primary battleground for the conservative forces, as a "battle for the mind" took shape around issues such as school prayer, textbook content, government support for private Christian schools, the evaluation of teachers, phonics, the curriculum, and school management. The conservative story has certainly established itself as the dominant narrative, but it is not without opposition, and internal tensions have plagued the right-wing coalition from the 1970s to the first decade of the twenty-first century.

As critical democratic social studies teachers come to understand and situate themselves and their teaching in recent educational history, they appreciate the need to delineate for their students and readers the foundations on which they construct their interpretations. My hermeneutic (interpretive) stance is grounded on our counter-Cartesian epistemology of complexity, a Deweyan progressivism, and critical theory. In this analytical context, I question the benefits of an exclusive focus on Western reason and its social, political, and educational effects. My position questions the Enlightenment and traditional Marxist stories, with their obligatory "heroes" and the supposition of their privilege to historically situate, define, and judge other stories without applying such analyses to themselves. This critical counter-Cartesian critique contends that the Grand Narratives of Western Civilization, with their stories of progress, expansionism, and the success of science, have presented us with unexamined notions of knowledge, truth, objectivity, and reason. Such definitions can be exposed as forms of social power, a victory of a particular narrative's way of representing the world that benefits some while harming others.

If definitions of knowledge, truth, objectivity, and reason are indeed contingent on power and its construction of the Eurocentric grand narrative, are we not in danger of lapsing into a relativism, a nihilism that chokes our ability to act ethically, to act as self-direct human agents? As conservatives have confronted the critique of our progressive, critical, and counter-Cartesian position, they have answered this question affirmatively, arguing that such a viewpoint degenerates into a call for anarchy and a destruction of all that is sacred. I disagree, of course, and maintain that our position, grounded in a critical democratic system of meaning, can help social studies educators formulate new, socially just, ways of seeing themselves, the sociopolitical world, and the purpose of the social studies, new ways that are more honest and cognitively stimulating than the right-wing, less reflective, and more certain social stories.

Our critical democratic system of meaning makes no pretense about neutrality. I want my students and readers to know up front my identification with the subjugated stories, the narratives of the excluded and the dominated. Thus, my view of recent educational history and the role of social education/social studies in this drama is grounded in the effort to expose the ways the dominant recovery stories and the educational policies that emerge from them serve to perpetuate the hopelessness of the oppressed. At the same time, as emphasized throughout this book, I attempt to understand how my own, my students', and my readers' perspectives have been shaped by exposure to the right-wing stories. What do we know about sociopolitical concerns? How do we come to know it? These are questions that a critical democratic system of meaning never lets us forget.

THE CRITICAL DEMOCRATIC SYSTEM OF MEANING VIS-À-VIS THE RIGHT-WING STORY

Our critical democratic system of meaning is clarified and extended by a fusion of an epistemology of complexity, critical theory, counter-Cartesianism, feminist theory, and subjugated and indigenous knowledges. Salvaging the most progressive elements of the modernist story, articulations of social justice, solidarity, and equality, our critical democratic system of meaning asserts an educational politics and a social studies that challenges right-wing regulatory stories while creating an emancipatory narrative for social studies. It includes four basic features: 1) a recognition of the power of racial, gender, ethnic, religious, and economic difference to shape consciousness and the objectives of social studies; 2) an exposé of the way power covertly works to structure inequality; 3) the promotion of an optimistic narrative that recognizes the complexity of the relationship between humanity's attempt to achieve self-direction and the social structures and narratives that impede the effort; and 4) the conceptualization of a new and more self-conscious way of approaching parenting, work, schooling, play, citizenship, and happiness. Hope exists in the formulation of the critical democratic stories. The struggle between these different stories and visions is essential knowledge in the educational of social studies teachers (hooks, 1989; Giroux, 1991; Hinchey, 1998; McLaren, 2000).

I mention these critical democratic insights in this context in order to emphasize the need for understanding the educational struggles of the last few decades. Only via an understanding of the right-wing stories and their quest for regulation can we appreciate the forces that exclude the critical democratic system of meaning from inclusion in twenty-first century social studies. During the late 1970s and early 1980s, the New Right captured the social and educational imagination with its narrative portrayal of an American decline initiated by the liberalism of the 1960s. The right wing made the traditional Puritan dream fashionable again, and education was viewed as an avenue to individual fortune. The conservatives told a story of a permissive liberal ethic that precipitated a breakdown of authority, patriotism, and discipline.

Framing the story as "the crisis of schooling," the New Right, since the late 1970s, has forced democratic progressives of any stripe into the position of having to defend failed or unpopular policies of the 1960s. Even though some of these policies were never given a chance to achieve their promise, and despite the fact that many of the progressives forced to defend such programs have little or no historical connection with 60s reforms, the Right has won hearts and minds with such a tack. While it is accurate to argue that the educational reformers of the 1960s often produced a theoretically immature vision of school reform, based on a romantic celebration of student culture and an insensitivity to the economic concerns of minority and working-class parents, it is not fair to argue that they produced a crisis in education (Giroux and McLaren, 1989). The inaccuracy of the story revolves around the fact that most American schools were unaffected by such reforms (Cuban, 1984). Even more ridiculous was the attribution of economic decline to the progressive reformers. Nevertheless, it worked, and during the 1980s and 1990s voices of critical democracy and egalitarianism were heard less and less in the public conversation about the purposes of social education.

Even though conservatives by the 1980s gained the power to tell the educational and social studies stories in the public venue, they did not represent a cohesive and monolithic ideological force. The right-wing alliance forged in the late 1970s was an unholy pact among corporate leaders, conservative scholars, and fundamentalist Protestants newly awakened to their own political power. Ronald Reagan was perfectly suited to tie the coalition together. Part right-wing ideologue, part defender of the corporate world, and part purveyor of fundamentalist Christian pieties, Reagan appealed to all fringes of the conservative alliance with a naivete that, on TV, played as an Ozzie Nelson honesty. Taking his cue from clippings collected from *Reader's Digest* and *Guideposts*, Reagan told a story of an America guided by Providence to greatness. The role of social education in the Gipper's story was to make sure that all understood America's favored standing in the eyes of God.

But even the popularity of Ronald Reagan could not quell the tensions in the alliance. Corporate and business advocates, pushing for a back-to-basics education designed to regulate workers and enhance their productivity, vied with both fundamentalists, supporting a prayer-based, Christian-oriented curriculum and academic guardians of tradition, advocating an old-time, humanities-based retelling of the Western tradition. Though common ground for the three conservative positions was found, emphases have changed during the last couple of decades. After 1984, the fundamentalists exerted less power at the national level, although they found (and continue to find) pockets of great success in particular state and local situations. Schooling, as cultural uniformity based on a narrow reading of the Western tradition, fused with business-oriented schooling as job training. Consequently, by the late 1980s, the Right maintained that not only had the public schools put the American economy at risk, but they were subverting Western civilization as well (Aronowitz, 1989).

Despite the waxing and waning of the influence of particular perspectives within the right-wing phalanges, common ground in conservative education has revolved around the role of the teacher. Our notion of teacher as scholar and researcher does not fit in this context, since right-wing groups tend to see the teacher as a technician who passes along the information and belief structures of the standardized testmakers and the state curriculum guides. Under the banner of teaching as the transmission of the best of our cultural heritage (read White), teachers are deskilled and deprofessionalized.

Through these lenses, teachers do not need to help students interpret, question, relate, or apply the information they transmit. What need is there for scholars in the teaching profession? Indeed, the tendency to be scholarly may get in the way, impeding the orderly transmission of the "facts." Here the accountability-based, standardized orientation of the conservative excellence movement dovetails with the concerns of the advocates of Western tradition. The politically "inoffensive" story of the West can be transmitted and then scientifically assessed to make sure that teachers are performing their jobs properly (Ryan, 1989; Giroux & McLaren, 1989).

Indeed, teachers must "get the story right." Attacked by so many and in such an "unfair" way, the American Pageant began to disappear from the schools, the right-wing story proclaimed. American virtue was doubt-ed, charges of racism, sexism, class bias and imperialism entered the con-versation (Reitz, 1988). Schools set out to reclaim the legacy of American greatness and to quell the doubts. Turning to the authority of tradition, the right-wing leaders re-told the story of Manifest Destiny, only in early 1990s garb. Basking in the "great victory" in the Persian Gulf, George Bush the Eldar heralded the story to the world, proclaim-ing that America had quieted her detractors. "Who can doubt us now?" he rhetorically asked.

THE COLLAPSE OF AMERICAN LIBERALISM: DEVELOPING A SOUND PROGRESSIVE ALTERNATIVE TO CONSERVATIVE SOCIAL EDUCATION

Where was the opposition to the right-wing co-option of education? Liberalism in the 1980s and 1990s offered little help. For example, the liberal presidential candidates of the 1980s, Walter Mondale and Michael Dukakis, denied their own liberalism, devoting much campaign time in an effort to run from the liberal label. Liberal opposition to Reagan, Bush, and Bennett's educational initiatives was minimal, as lib-eral politicians and educational leaders, understanding prevailing opin-ion, cowardly echoed right-wing concerns. When the Democrats won the White House in 1992, Bill Clinton basically carried forward the con-servative educational reforms established by his predecessors. To his cred-it, Clinton did not support the right-wing effort to "privatize" public education (i.e., destroy it) or to cut its funding to absurd levels, but most of his educational policy was an echo of Reagan and Bush.

Liberal academics sometimes addressed questions of educational opportunity for marginalized students but typically reframed them with-in ideological contexts of worker productivity, GNP, and economic competitiveness. The public perceived the bankruptcy of liberalism: It had lost its ability to tell convincing cultural stories. Though he viewed it from the conservative perspective of the guardians of the Western tradition, Allan Bloom in 1987 in his *The Closing of the American Mind* sensed liberalism's forfeiture of moral leadership. Unable to take a moral stand, late twentieth century liberalism lapsed into an ethical relativism that reflected positivism's separation of fact from value. Indeed, liberalism became the standard bearer for a disintegrating Cartesianism and, as a result, was unable to articulate a compelling reason to challenge the right wing. About the only policy it could advocate was increased public expenditures for education.

Liberalism's inability to critique the educational perspectives of the conservatives involved its failure to develop a sense of its location in history. Such an ability would have allowed liberalism to understand the sociocultural and political economic forces that gave birth to and shaped the forms that domination and cognitive deskilling would take. Without such contextual grounding, late-twentieth century liberalism became impotent, unable to formulate educational alternatives that find their strength in an awareness of the process by which justice and democracy are repressed by schools. Without such an awareness, liberalism became an "unindited co-conspirator" in the preservation of race, class, and gender inequality and a poverty of socioeducational vision.

At their worst, contemporary liberals reject conservative educational policies without a clear understanding of just what it is they seek to substitute in their stead. Liberals speak of victimization but lack the theoretical frames to connect the process to larger political struggles. Pluralism does not substitute for a deep recognition of the forces of difference, i.e., the deep social structures that isolate individuals and groups and pit them against one another. While democratic social studies teachers study liberal notions of tolerance, multiculturalism and acceptance, these tacit forces that pull us apart perform their insidious work. Liberalism can be an ally of the forces of critical democracy when liberals begin to gain a self-awareness of their own limitations, emerging from their failure to recognize the deep structures that work to pit human actors against one another. The liberal desire for us all to connect to one another, does not have to fail, and it does not have to be dismissed as just another naïve effort of do-gooders. A post-liberal movement for human interconnection that is grounded in an understanding of difference and refuses to forge the connection in the confines of a dominant culture's ideological and discursive practices can extend human solidarity and the struggle for freedom, justice, and happiness.

In a liberal vein, Marilyn Ferguson (1980) has written that we have learned that Western culture does not have all the answers. Beginning with this recognition, liberals examined their consciousness construction, seeking a "higher consciousness." Make no mistake, critical democratic social studies educators agree with Ferguson and work hard to develop such a consciousness. For all this concern with self-understanding/knowledge, however, liberalism has often remained quite naïve to the socio-ideological construction of consciousness, the production of self. Here rests liberalism's opportunity to crawl through the crack in the wall that limits perception. Outside the confines, liberals will find a new place where there is a recognition of their location in the web of reality, their historical moment, an emancipatory epistemological consciousness.

Such a new perspective will allow liberals to understand the naivete which results from an unawareness of how the lived world precludes escape from the Enlightenment narrative and their own complicity in the unexamined use of patriarchal and Eurocentric ways of framing educational experiences. Referring to a critical democratic system of meaning, liberals may gain a historical, theoretical grounding which empowers them to move beyond their present position and effectively confront the repressiveness of conservative education. Indeed, the power of the Right to dictate educational policy reflects a failure among democratic progressives to initiate a public conversation about education.

DEMOCRATIC SOCIAL STUDIES AND THE RIGHT-WING NOTION OF TRADITION

Drawing on our epistemology of complexity, our critical emancipatory system of meaning, our view from below, critical democratic social studies educators can cultivate a public educational conversation that takes seriously the notions of citizenship and social justice. Such a conversation can lead to an empowerment that is predicated on the identification of oppressive school and social practices that place unnecessary limitations on human actions, emotions, and cognition. Such educational oppression impedes citizens and students from egalitarian participation in social and educational institutions alongside those who possess the status of "competence" (Simon, 1989). Emerging from this public conversation about justice and schooling will be a recognition of the effects of the right-wing educational policies on the human mind and spirit.

Democratic social studies educators will encourage students to draw upon their own cultural heritages or subjugated knowledges in order to develop academic abilities that empower them to deconstruct existing school knowledge. Extending their analysis, students will question the uses of their empowerment. Thus, they will be forced to confront the task of developing progressive social visions, new stories of what could be. Such new stories allow social studies teachers to engage students in the analysis of how experience is named and rewarded in schools and how such naming affects different students in different ways. Such analysis leads to a higher level of thinking that moves teachers beyond the unexamined cultural transmission model of their task and students beyond the nervous test-taking role with which they have grown so familiar.

Thus, as an act of educating students for the moral and ideological imperatives of an authentic democratic society, critical social studies transcends the repressive right-wing notion of Tradition. The questioning of the educational canon becomes an act of democracy, a manifestation of higher order thinking; knowledge is engaged in tandem with ethics and cognition. Contrary to the pronouncements of right-wing analysts, critical engagement with the wisdom of the past is not a mark of closed minds and distorted personalities. Where would we be if many of our intellectual ancestors had failed to question tradition, racism, sexism, class bias, and religious intolerance? A social education that is uninterested in justice and an engagement with everyday life is not compatible with a democratic society. It is, in its own way nihilistic, devoid of hope, in the sense that it assumes that all the great ideas have been thought, that the jury is in on the great questions of humanity, that community is lost and cannot be regained, that history has ended (Nussbaum, 1987).

This progressive attempt to subject the social studies curriculum, and subsequently the Western tradition, to a reexamination in light of democratic and complex epistemological precepts is not a legitimate act in the eyes of the Right. While proclaiming their own ideological innocence, advocates of unquestioned Tradition have not been hesitant to hurl charges of educational politicization at their democratic progressive adversaries. Listening to the conservative story, one gets the impression that schools are about ready to wave the scholarly white flag and surrender educational institutions to a group of bizarre radicals. Portraying themselves as besieged underdogs, conservatives write of school leaders running from the advancing enemy, leaving their intellectual principles and moral grounding behind (Weisberg, 1987, Kimball, 1990).

Evoking memories of Richard Hofstadter's description of "the paranoid style of American politics," right-wing proponents write of a grand leftist educational conspiracy. Interest groups pressure schools to revamp their curricula, conservative Roger Kimball (1990) writes, in a way that only 10 or 20 years ago would have been disregarded because of its flagrant political bias. Questions such as "Where are women in the curriculum?" or "Where are Blacks in the curriculum?" represent a blatant politicization of the social studies curriculum, but a conservative curriculum that continues to exclude them is framed as politically objective. Are there not political assumptions underlying both positions? Is education not an inherently political act, since it inevitably confronts questions of power and power distribution?

The conservatives have trouble understanding that reading, whether it be of the traditional canon or of student and teacher lives, is a sociopolitical act; our interpretations cannot be separated from where we are standing when we read, i.e., our location in the web of reality. The simplistic right-wing notion of objectivity will continue to impede a serious analysis of the way postmodern schools and the educational reform movements of the last 25 years exclude the socially marginalized. In this context, social studies teachers are often asked to parrot prearranged and isolated fact-bits without attending to their underlying assumptions. Right-wing reform leaders cannot encourage teachers to reflect on the political presuppositions of their lessons (e.g., who is excluded, who is included) because they themselves are blind to the presuppositions of their school reforms in general. This blindness results from their denial of the very existence of political presuppositions. Critical democratic educators must help social studies teachers develop strategies to analyze how knowledge and policy are produced. At this level of deconstruction, teachers will begin to comprehend the "logic" behind the facts, their context and significance, and the difference competing assumptions about knowledge and policy make on the way teachers teach and students live their lives.

This is the point where our critical democratic, post-Cartesian critique and its accompanying vision informs social studies efforts to transcend the right-wing curriculum of regulation. The paradigm shift, the reconceptualization of our way of seeing the educational world, allows us the insight to understand our role in a historical moment where cultural and educational boundaries are disappearing. This disappearance of boundaries involves a panoply of conflicting social changes including, but not limited to, the influence of mass media through its power of representation (i.e., the way our view of the world is constructed) on the restructuring of our self-identity, and our political orientation, our relationship to social and educational institutions.

The Right reacts to the breakdown by retreating into a nostalgic hiding place, a social amnesia that blinds us to the forces which shape our consciousness. Drawing upon the breakdown of these boundaries, we begin, as educators, to formulate new questions of knowledge, pedagogy, and cognition. We transcend the questions dictated by the narrative of the Right: How do we raise test scores? How do we produce workers who are better suited to work in degrading, deskilled jobs? How do we better control teachers so they teach the standardized materials their superiors deem appropriate? Making use of the postmodern sense of possibility, of freedom from the old stories and questions, we begin to reconceptualize the purposes of social studies.

THE COUNTER-CARTESIAN RECONCEPTUALIZATION OF SOCIAL STUDIES: MOVING TOWARD THE POSTMODERN DOMAIN

A critical counter-Cartesian reconceptualization of social studies questions the foundational metaphors and assumptions of the right-wing socioeducational story. Take, for example, the assumption concerning what constitutes successful social studies student and teacher performance, i.e., the nature of what type of thinking is deemed desirable on the part of students and teachers. Our critical democratic counter-Cartesian way of seeing seeks to expand the limits on human thinking imposed by evaluation procedures. When we apply our critical system of meaning and our deconstruction of the dominant stories, we begin to anticipate new ways of seeing and knowing. These are levels of cognition that move beyond the type of thinking demanded by standardized measurements of aptitude/ability/intelligence and even beyond Jean Piaget's notion of formal thinking. Men and women do not reach a final cognitive equilibrium beyond which no new levels of thinking can emerge. Indeed, there have to be modes of cognition that transcend the formal operational ability to formulate abstract conclusions, understand cause-effect relationships, and employ the traditional scientific method to explain reality.

Piagetian formalism implies a comfort with a Cartesian-Newtonian mechanistic view of the world that is unable to escape the confines of a cause-effect, hypothetico-deductive system of reasoning. Trapped within the language of certainty and prediction, formal operational thinking organizes verified facts into a theory. Those pesky facts that do not fit into the theory are discarded. The theory that emerges is the one best suited to eliminate contradictions in knowledge. Thus, formal thinking proceeds on the assumption that the resolution of contradiction is a central objective of cognition. Understanding an epistemology of complexity, we quickly discern a Cartesian reductionism at work in formalism. Critical social studies teachers move quickly to "call out" such reductionism and the subtle modes of social regulation it supports. Contemporary high-standards schools of excellence in the conservative mode and the omnipotent standardized test makers, assuming that formal operational thought represents the zenith of human potential, focus their labor on its cultivation and measurement. Indeed, this assessment may be too generous, for, many times schools of this type fail to transcend low-level concrete forms of thinking. Students who move beyond formality are often not rewarded and sometimes even punished for excessive independence.

Postformal thinkers are not uncomfortable with the ambiguous, contingent, and complex nature of knowledge. They are tolerant of contradiction and value the attempt to integrate divergent phenomena into new, revealing syntheses. In other words, they are pioneers of the mind, attempting to expand the cognitive envelope, to escape the limitations of Cartesian-Newtonian modernity and venture into a new exciting cognitive and ontological realm. Postformalism can be viewed as a form of cognition that suits the complexities of a postmodern world. Where formalism functions on the basis of the Cartesian paradigm's assumptions of linear causality and reductionism, postformalism assumes reciprocity and holism (the ambiguous, nonlinear interconnection of phenomena). No simple, privileged vantage point exists for postformal thinkers, no perspective that grants them the "truth." Drawing upon women's ways of knowing, subjugated knowledges, and the insights of indigenous peoples, postformal thinkers rediscover the synergism between logic and emotion and the benefits of disengagement from the socially acceptable, the expected.

Such speculations about the reconceptualization of cognition necessitate a critical confrontation with the old regulatory story of education as simple cultural transmission. We cannot escape a self-dialogue (and, hopefully, a larger cultural conversation as well) concerning educational purpose. Postformalism opens a dialogue with the past that holds dramatic implications for that which is not yet. Thinking about the purposes of education in ancient Greece, stoic philosopher Musonius Rufus offered a protocritical perspective, maintaining that a philosophical education is practical in its attempt to improve the student's own life and the life of the surrounding community. In this sense, it is action-oriented, eschewing the assumption that students are passive recipients of timeless truths. From Musonius Rufus' ancient perspective, education works to invigorate the student's ability to think and act ethically in specific situations. Thus, it follows that, like the prescriptions of a wise doctor, social studies education must be tailored to the particular strengths and weaknesses of each student as well as to the contextual setting (the place) in which he or she emerges (Nussbaum, 1987; Kincheloe & Pinar, 1991; Pinar, 1991; Weil, 1998).

INTERPRETING TRADITION: SOCIAL STUDIES AND ACTS OF POSTFORMAL TRANSFORMATION

Such thoughts are not unlike those of Nietzsche who also advocated the abandonment of education as unexamined cultural transmission in favor of developing the capacity for interpretation. To Nietzsche, interpretation involved acquiring the ability to see, think, speak, and write. When viewed as inseparable processes, Nietzsche theorized that this interpretative facility allowed learners to sneak through the morass of conventional perception and view individual cases from a variety of angles (Greene, 1987, 1995). Such notions not only conceptually anticipate this admittedly unoriginal notion of postformal thinking but also challenge the right wing's reading of just what constitutes Tradition. Tradition, even Western Tradition, is a cacophony of conflicting voices, of which the Right has chosen only a few to build its standardized, Eurocentric, androcentric curriculum.

Thus, the postformal challenge refuses to allow Allan Bloom to dictate the official story of how our students came to be so shallow, William Bennett to define educational excellence, E. D. Hirsch to proclaim what constitutes cultural literacy, or Madeleine Hunter to determine the correct strategies by which the official knowledge is to be transmitted to social studies students. Postformal social studies educators don't allow such right-wing stories to turn their discipline into an antidemocratic pedagogy of regulation. They work diligently to transform social studies education into a pedagogy of complexity and emancipation. Such democratic work is an intense struggle in a postmodern era when informal, out-of-school education positions individuals in a conservative framework.

Reading right-wing educational literature, one is often struck by the omnipresent assumption that only the conservative guardians of Tradition care about the past, about the teaching of history. A central tenet of a critical democratic social studies that values a postformal cognitive orientation is the notion of etymology, an awareness of the genesis of knowledge, of self-production, of institutional form. Indeed, it is possible to draw upon the past while avoiding a Bloomian worship of Tradition. One of the outcomes of a critical democratic reconceptualization of social studies education involves a reworking of Tradition in light of current concerns. Such a reworking initiates a more general consideration of how postformalism confronts texts and how this relates to educational purpose. Education as simple cultural transmission fails to confront the complexity of the contemporary significance of what have been deemed the classic texts.

Stanley Aronowitz (1989) argues that classic texts in a democratic educational context are appropriated, not revered, and, in this appropriation, transformed. Postformal social studies teachers recognize this, and, in their understanding, unveil contemporary meanings without ignoring the text's historical significance (Weisberg, 1987). Thus, in a semiotic mode, postformal history teachers ask new questions of the cultural heritage, in the process, revealing themselves and the forces that have shaped our institutions. Such teachers may study the traditional Western canon (and certainly the nontraditional Western canon and non-Western canons) as a form of social knowledge. But it is more than just that; it is us. It holds, buried within it, revelations about the tacit dimensions of our consciousness construction, our ontological configurations.

The knowledge revealed by such study is ever-surprising and unpredictable. Because postformal educators refuse to simply revere the traditions, the analysis that results creates a question about our frame of reference: How and from where do we see historical knowledge? When conservatives fail to question their frame of reference, a tyrannical certainty emerges that perpetuates privilege for the privileged and oppression for the oppressed. This allows, for example, what the school defines as the classics to include mainly male Europeans, while denying contributions, and, in many instances, excluding Third-World, non-White, or female innovators. To avoid such outcomes, Tradition must be subjected to a democratic analysis which explores tacit assumptions, underlying sources of authority used to ground judgments, and unexamined ideological assumptions that shape the questions we ask about the canon. Thus, what the Right has defined as a crippling relativism emerges as a liberating sense of the inconstancy of meaning, an uncertainty that allows us to see what before was hidden from view.

Our critical uncertainty and understanding of complexity here avoids nihilism and relativism via its grounding in our democratic system of meaning. Contrary to the pronouncements of Bloom and Bennett, the Western heritage does not represent the unfolding of the absolute spirit (Aronowitz, 1989). As John Dewey (1916) argued decades ago (though it was often misunderstood by the public), education should avoid the cultural transmission model of preserving "the standard," of perpetuating the myth of the West as the benchmark of civilization. In this context, the notion of Human Nature is identified with our heritage and, Dewey maintained, education is reduced to a cowardly quest for certainty. Humans, thus, relinquished their gift of self-creation and constant redefinition; instead, education as cultural transmission assumed that men and women were already finished, completed projects, unchangeable entities. The possibility of the enlargement of our moral imaginations offered by the uncertainty that came out of an engagement with other cultures with their different frames of reference was lost. The benefits of the interaction with difference were squandered.

What do we mean by the expansion of our moral imagination? Our notion of postformal thinking is intimately connected to such an expansion of consciousness because it forces us to confront the concept of mind. In contrast to modern right-wing assumptions, Dewey conceived it as the variety of ways that we consciously engage the events that confront us. Thus, mind is a verb. This means that it is never self-contained, separate from the world, but contingent, ever interacting with situations and other minds. Mind is never complete, for it never stops assimilating, restructuring itself as a result of its contact with new stimulation (Greene, 1987, 1995). Thus, our moral imagination emphasizes relationships and meaning, not mastery or simple isolated "being." For example, we sometimes humiliate geography students who may have grown up around, played, and fished in a river when we demand that they define the word, "river", employing the dictionary definition "water flowing within a channel." What about their experience with rivers, the effects of rivers on their lives and the lives of other people who live around them, the floods, the politics of water rights, irrigation, recreation, pollution, etc.? These questions of meaning, not the dictionary definition, make the study of rivers important.

These questions of significance, which are always questions of relationships, form the basis of postformal thinking, of the expansion of our moral imaginations. Neither E. D. Hirsch's "List," Allan Bloom's "Great Tradition," Mortimer Adler's *Paideia Proposal*, nor Lynne Cheney's history standards deal with Dewey's concept of mind. The crisis of postmodern education revolves no more around our failure to teach Tradition or to prepare our students for the workplace than the solution to the crisis revolves around improving standardized test scores and teaching rote-memorized facts about our civilization. Postformal thinking and the expansion of our moral imagination demand a social studies grounded on a reconceptualized function of reason and a search for meaning in the relationship between self and world (Silliman, 1990). This does not allow for an order-obsessed curriculum of regulation that mandates what social studies students should think and the ways they must act. Stated another way, a democratic social studies education should help students develop wisdom, i.e., the cognitive ability and the contextual grounding to make intelligent choices and commitments in the way they shape their personal and civic lives.

Part of this life-shaping process involves the role of students as members of a larger political community (Feinberg, 1989). In this context, the expansion of the moral imagination involves the development of a scholarly grounded and practical civic courage. Caught in a media-dominated world of manipulative consumerist images, of irresponsible corporate power, of covert and morally indefensible governmental activities, of limited access to diverse information sources, social studies students, unacquainted with the postformal exposé of the tacit dimension, will have limited ability to make informed civic choices (Greene, 1987; Kincheloe, 1995). The educational vision sold to the public by conservative theorists does not address such concerns. Civic courage, the ability to see beyond overt forms of regulation and the covert control of imagery, the grappling with the meaning of democracy and the responsibilities it demands, are not a part of the conservative educational story. There are alternatives. There are more thoughtful answers to the questions we ask about education than the ones provided over the last 30 years. There are other stories to be told by a critical democratic social studies that can be used to democratize schools, workplaces, and the society at large.

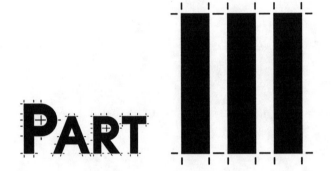

PART III

Research and the Social Studies

Chapter

Social Studies Teachers as Researchers: Action Research as a Teaching Method

My call for social studies teachers as researchers picks up where calls for inquiry in social studies left off a few decades ago. To go beyond the calls for inquiry in social studies, Chapter 12 argues that teachers as well as students must become researchers who are epistemologically aware and who understand critical social theory and notions of complexity. Thus, contemporary critical social studies teachers have a well-defined sense of emancipatory purpose and an inclination to understand the context in which their teaching takes place. If teachers are to become scholars who model scholarship for their social studies students—a necessary task in reforming twenty-first century social studies education—they must be adept researchers. These research abilities constitute a key task in our notion of critical knowledge work.

THE POVERTY OF RESEARCH IN TEACHER EDUCATION— THE HISTORY OF ACTION RESEARCH

Teacher education's historical encounters with the domain of research have produced very few benefits. Assuming this failure, Chapter 12 analyzes the action research movement in a critical democratic context, attempting in the process to theorize new ways of conceiving of social studies teachers as researchers engaged in reflective and complex practice. The research component of teacher education programs traditionally involved a watered-down statistics course in the master's curricula and nothing at all in pre-service programs. Action research concepts, such as the promotion of greater teacher self-understanding of his or her practices, conceptual change, the formation of student consciousness, and an appreciation of the social forces that shape the school are ignored in the traditional teacher research classes. Such classes, with their circumscribed notions of research, miss the specificity of the teaching act, the uniqueness of the teaching workplace, the ambiguity of practitioner ways of knowing. If we are serious about the production of critical, reflective social studies teachers, then democratic action research cannot be separated from any component of teacher education. The critical form of this democratic action research in a social studies context demands analysis.

I will begin that questioning with an examination of the roots of the contemporary action research movement in education. As early as the 1940s, Kurt Lewin called for action research in social psychology. Taking their cue from Lewin, leaders in spheres as disparate as industry and American Indian affairs advocated action research. During the post-World War II era, Stephen Corey, at Teacher's College, led the action research movement in education. Corey argued that action research could help reform curriculum practice when teachers applied the results of their own inquiry. There was considerable enthusiasm for the movement in the postwar period, but, by the late 1950s, action research had become the target of serious criticism and started to decline. Analysts have posited that the decline was precipitated by the bifurcation of science and practice that resulted from the growth of the cult of the expert. As policy makers came to rely more and more on expert educational research and developmental laboratories, the development of curriculum and pedagogical practices was dictated from top-down positivistic dictates. Thus, the production of research was separated from the ambiguous and complex world of the social studies practitioner.

When action research was rediscovered in the United Kingdom in the 1970s, the motivation for its resuscitation involved a reaction to the growing acceptance of the positivistic view of knowledge, with its emphasis on prespecified, measurable learning outcomes and its degradation of the role of teacher as a self-directed professional. Democratic educators were beginning to question the usefulness of positivism's abstract generalizations in the concrete and ambiguous situations in which they operated on a daily basis (McKernan, 1988; Elliott, 1989a). Still, however, teacher education continued to assume that the research dimension of professional studies involved the training of teachers in the use of quantitative methods. Research was defined as a positivistic form of data gathering and generalization production. So ingrained and unchallenged were such definitions of research that, when action research advocates involved teachers in on-site teacher inquiry projects, the teachers reported that they did not consider themselves to have taken part in "real" research. Even those who felt that they had taken part in research maintained that it was a very low-quality activity. Their college of education-generated definition of research as a controlled experimental design, replete with systematic statistical analysis, seemed to undermine their ability to reconceptualize what form research might take or how it might be connected to their lives as practitioners (Van Hesteren, 1986; Ross, 1984).

Fighting the image of research in the conventional wisdom, advocates of action research began to evoke new interest in the late 1970s. Aligning themselves with the attempt to redefine teacher professionalism, action researchers gained unprecedented respectability in the 1980s. In the midst of its success, action research found itself being molded and defined by many of the same people who had promoted the traditional forms of research in colleges of education. More critical teacher educators began to express concerns over the foundations of what often passed for teacher action research. Fearing a technocratic co-option of such inquiry, Patti Lather argued in the 1980s that much of the action research conducted in schools was not critically grounded. Lather was correct then and now, as, unfortunately, much of the teacher research in the first decade of the twenty-first century remains ahistorical and apolitical. As such, it lends itself to subversion by educational leaders who are tempted to employ a technical form of action research as a means of engineering practitioners' "improvements" (Lather, 1986).

For example, many school projects have viewed teachers as researchers as implementers of theoretical strategies devised by researcher experts or administrators. In such situations, teacher research involves testing how well particular strategies work through the analysis of particular techniques in their own classrooms. Promoted as teacher-friendly, these projects, in the name of creating democratic workplaces, actually promote a very restricted view of the role of teachers. Teachers are supporting actors incapable of playing leading roles, that is, in developing critical perspectives at the level of ideas (Connelly & Ben-Peretz, 1980). Teachers in this context are still seen as mere executors. Advocates of teacher research who support this implementation orientation are quite naïve when it comes to the realm of ideology. They do not realize that the act of administrators selecting problems for teachers to research is an ideological act, an act that trivializes the role of teacher. When administrators select problems for teacher researchers to explore, they negate the critical dimension of action research.

When the critical dimension of teacher research is negated, the teacher-as-researcher movement can become quite a trivial enterprise. Uncritical educational action research seeks direct applications of information gleaned from specific situations; a cookbook style of technical thinking is encouraged, characterized by recipe-following teachers. Such thinking does not allow for complex reconceptualizations of knowledge and, as a result, fails to understand the ambiguities and the ideological structures of the classroom. Teachers, in this context, retreat to cause-effect analysis, failing to grasp the interactive intricacy (complexity) of a classroom. The point that educational problems are better understood when considered in a relational way that transcends simple linearity is missed. Thus, teacher research becomes a reifying institutional function, as teachers, like their administrators and supervisors, fail to reveal the ways that the educational bureaucracy, and the assumptions that support it, constrain one's ability to devise new and more emancipatory understandings of how schools work (Orteza y Miranda, 1988).

Teacher research is co-opted; its democratic edge is blunted. It becomes a popular grassroots movement that can be supported by the power hierarchy; it does not threaten, nor is it threatened. Asking trivial questions, the movement presents no radical challenges or offers no transformative vision of educational purpose, since it acts in ignorance of deep structures of schooling, such as the positivistic view of educational knowledge. Teachers are assumed to be couriers, that is, information deliverers, and are accorded a corresponding lack of status in the workplace (Ruddick, 1989; Ponzio, 1985). Uncritical educational action research fails to recognize that inquiry must always subject its findings to assessment and some form of critical analysis, and critical analysis is always dangerous in its unpredictability and transformative character.

A CRITICAL FORM OF ACTION RESEARCH

What exactly is the difference between a co-opted form of teacher research and critical form of teacher research? In both *Teachers as Researchers: Qualitative Inquiry as a Path to Empowerment* (1991) and *Toward a Critical Politics of Teacher Thinking: Mapping the Postmodern* (1993), I attempted to delineate the requirements of critical action research: 1) It rejects Cartesian-Newtonian notions of rationality, objectivity and truth. Critical action research assumes that methods and issues of research are always political in character; 2) Critical action researchers are aware of their own value commitments, the value commitments of others, and the values promoted by the dominant culture. In other words, one of the main concerns of critical action research involves the exposure of the relationship between personal values and practice. 3) Critical action researchers are aware of the social construction of professional unconsciousness; 4) Critical action researchers attempt to uncover those aspects of the dominant social order that undermine our effort to pursue emancipatory goals; and 5) Critical action research is always conceived in relation to practice—it exists to improve practice. Indeed, it becomes a central and highly sophisticated aspect of a critical social studies teaching methodology.

With these criteria in mind, critical action research is the consummate democratic act, because it allows social studies teachers to help determine the conditions of their own work. Critical action research facilitates the attempt of teachers to organize themselves into communities of researchers dedicated to emancipatory experience for themselves and their students. When teachers unite with students and community members in the attempt to ask serious questions about what is taught, how it is taught, and what should constitute the goals of a school, not only is critical self-reflection promoted, but group decision making becomes a reality (Carr & Kemmis, 1986; Aronowitz & Giroux, 1985; Steinberg & Kincheloe, 1998; Carson and Sumara, 1997).

Action research, as defined here, becomes the (logical) educational extension of a critical social theory. Since critical theory is grounded on a recognition of the existence of oppression, it stands to reason that the forces of this oppression have to be identified. Action research serves as a perfect vehicle for such a search. Without this critical recognition of domination and oppression, action researchers will simply consider the school site as value-neutral and their role as disinterested, dispassionate observers. Change in this context is irrelevant, and, according to Cartesian-Newtonian perspectives on research, this is the way it should be. Researchers are to maintain an uncommitted view toward the actions they encounter. In a world of oppression, critical theorists argue, ethical behavior demands that such dispassion must be confronted (Giroux & McLaren, 1991; Codd, 1984; Hinchey, 1998).

Whenever we dispense with values, political considerations, or historical context, our attempt to understand the situation we are researching is weakened. Our appreciation of an educational situation is contingent on the context within which we encountered it and the theoretical frames we brought with us to the observation. Cartesian-Newtonian modernism has told us that our research must serve no specific cause, but critical counter-Cartesianism has caused us to realize that every historical period produces rules that dictate what nonpartisanship entails. In other words, different rules privilege different causes. Thus, what we "see" as researchers is shaped by particular world views, values, political perspectives, conceptions of race, class, and gender relations, definitions of intelligence, etc. Research, thus, can never be nonpartisan, for we must choose the rules that guide us as researchers; critical theory's exposé of the hidden ideological assumptions within educational research marked the end of our innocence (Aronowitz, 1983; Elliott, 1989b).

To be critical is to assume that humans are active agents whose reflective self-analysis, whose knowledge of the world, leads to action. Action research is the logical extension of critical theory in that it provides the apparatus for the human species to look at itself. Critical action research that is aware of critical perspectives on the production of identity and the context of hyperreality can contribute to the sociocognitive emancipation of men and women. Such a sociocognitive emancipation is the first step in a cognitive revolution—our effort, as social studies teachers, to see the world, ourselves, and our students from new angles. Based on a democratic dialogue, an awareness of historical moment, and a passionate commitment to the voice of the oppressed, the counter-Cartesian insurrection redefines research, in the process, producing a knowledge between the cracks, information previously swept under the rug.

In schools, the first-hand, up-close perspectives of social studies teachers previously relegated to a lesser significance are valued by action research as kinetic knowledge, that is, knowledge with the potential to

wreak havoc. This information, gained through action research's emphasis on observation and reflection, promotes democratic change grounded
on the understanding of participants. In the modernist discourse of science, such an emphasis constitutes a radical change of approach (Codd,
1984; Young, 1990). Action that reflective individuals take to correct the
social and individual pathologies uncovered by critical social studies
teachers and students can be negotiated after the action research process
is completed. The critical core of critical action research involves its participatory and communally discursive structure and the cycle of action
and reflection it initiates. Such a cycle does not produce a set of rules and
precise regulations for the action it promotes. Critical postmodern action
research provides a provisional framework of principles around which
action can be discussed rather than a set of procedures (Young, 1990,
Popkewitz, 1981).

A central part of this action reminds us of our epistemology of complexity: the redefinition of knowledge. There are many dimensions to
this redefining process, but one of the most important involves democratizing access to knowledge in schools and society. If knowledge is a form
of cultural capital, then lack of access to it spells major problems for
those on the margins of the culture of knowledge. Foucault has convinced us that knowledge is power; and though it is a hard pill for advocates of teacher empowerment to swallow, part of the reason that the
teaching corps is delegated to the margins is that too many of them are
ill-educated in colleges and teacher education programs. As previously
argued, social studies teachers with weak academic, theoretical, and pedagogical backgrounds must defer to the judgments of educational leaders,
the certified experts. The culture of technicist teacher education has tacitly instructed social studies teachers across the generations to underval-
ue the domain of social theory while avoiding questions of the
ideological, psychological, and pedagogical assumptions underlying their
practice. The power that comes from such understandings is a prerequisite for the critical attempt to redefine knowledge. Teachers must understand the social and political factors that contribute to knowledge
production. Indeed, the gaining of such an awareness should be a central
concern of critical action research (May & Zimpher, 1986; Porter, 1988;
Maeroff, 1988; Tripp, 1988; Kincheloe & McLaren, 2000).

Critical knowledge production begins when action researchers illuminate the taken for granted. Dewey focused our attention on such a
process when he argued that social studies teachers should operate on the

basis of a reflective action that disembodies moral, ethical, social, and political issues from mundane thinking and practice. As action researchers maintain such a perspective on their everyday experience, they are able to explore the tacit forces that have encoded their own lives and their students' lives. In a sense, critical action researchers relearn the way they have come to view the world around them. Indeed, they awaken from the modernist dream with its unexamined landscape of knowledge and unimaginative consciousness construction. Once awake, critical social studies teachers as researchers begin to see schools as human creations, with meanings and possibilities lurking beneath the surface appearances. Their task becomes the interpretation of schools and the students who attend them, not just the chronicling of surface characteristics devoid of context (Hultgren, 1987; May & Zimpher, 1986; Lesko, 1989; Carspecken, 1999). A brief example is in order.

SOCIAL STUDIES TEACHERS AS RESEARCHERS OF STUDENTS

An important example of social studies teachers performing critical action research involves the researching of their own students. A critical complex social studies pedagogy is simply not possible without understanding the ways the social and cultural context produces the students they face every day. Critical social studies teachers as researchers study their students' writing, their everyday actions in classrooms, their interactions with them, and the stories they tell both inside and outside of class. Do students see themselves as knowledge receivers or knowledge producers? Do they sense that they have a voice in their own education or that they operate merely at the mercy of the educational system? Inquiring social studies teachers want to know, so they can adjust their teaching appropriately (Pruyn, 1994).

Thus, as social studies teachers research their students, they learn more and more about how to teach them, how to connect the social studies curriculum to their lives. Teacher researchers come to understand that the way students relate to the social studies is often shaped by factors about which they themselves are not fully conscious. Social conditioning at an unconscious level moves them to react to lessons in a variety of interesting ways. Thus, teacher researchers analyze conflicting and contradictory student behaviors in relation to the social context that produces them. As a result of their research, they are often able to bring these sociopsychological dynamics to student consciousness. The fact that social studies students get much of their information and attitudes about the field of study from the larger culture, media, family, and peers is rarely acknowledged in the microdynamics of the teaching process. Social studies teachers as researchers explore such student learning experiences and refer to them every day (Darder, 1991; Davis & Fernlund, 1995).

In my career as a high school and university social studies teacher, I am sad to report that action research in the social studies is rare, teacher research on students is rarer still, and inquiry into the social and cultural context and the ways it shapes student consciousnesses and their views of social studies, almost nonexistent. Rarely discussed is the change in childhood and adolescence after World War II and the way young people began to create their own unique culture, their own private spaces, to avoid adult surveillance. Rarely studied is the way this cultural change dramatically altered the nature of youth and their relation to adults and schooling. Youth, by the 1950s, increasingly became a time when young people attempted to construct their own values and mattering maps. One of the few social institutions that understood this cultural dynamic was business. In the social space these changes created, businesspeople attempted to colonize youth by creating lifestyles that demanded particular types of products.

When Shirley Steinberg and I researched and edited *Kinderculture: The Corporate Construction of Childhood* in 1997, it was this process that we were researching. We were doing what I am writing about here. Our argument, as social studies teachers as researchers of the cultural forces that shape students, was that teaching was often irrelevant in students' lives because teachers did not understand the forces that shaped children. Our effort was to study some of the ways these changes had been shaped by corporate power wielders. The first paragraph of that book illustrates this attempt.

The theme of this book is very simple: New times have ushered in a new era of childhood. Evidence of this dramatic cultural change surrounds each of us, but many individuals have not yet noticed it. Unfortunately, many of the people who make their living studying or caring for children have not recognized this historical watershed. Furthermore, few observers have appreciated the fact that the information explosion so characteristic of our contemporary era has played a central role in undermining traditional notions of childhood. Those who have shaped, directed, and used the information technology of the late twentieth century have played an exaggerated role in the reformulation of childhood. Childhood is a social and historical artifact, not simply a biological entity. Many argue that childhood is a *natural* phase of growing up, of becoming an

adult. The cardinal concept here involves the *format* of this human phase that
has been produced by social, cultural, political, and economic forces operating
upon it (Steinberg & Kincheloe, 1997, p. 1).

By researching children and the products that were advertised directly to them, we began to discern larger social trends about childhood that
had specific educational consequences. We found that the cultural distance between children and adults was diminishing by noting processes
we called the "childification of adults and the adultification of children."
Many contemporary adults refuse to surrender their youth, while many
youth insist on being viewed as adults. Such processes can be discerned,
especially, around issues of sex and violence. As the nature of childhood
and adulthood change, our research seemed to indicate that difficulty was
emerging around their interrelationship. As a result, the incidence of
child neglect and abuse increased, adolescent depression reached epidemic levels, the rate of youth suicide increased, and child poverty
became more and more common.

As young people were increasingly facing such problems, the
American public was less and less willing to support the social needs of
children. They voted down taxes for education and child welfare; they
refused to support child care programs; they were generally uninterested
in the effects of advertising on children; they were unwilling to protect
the constitutional rights of young people; they supported legislation to
treat juvenile offenders as adults; and they produced cultural texts illustrating a thinly concealed contempt for contemporary young people.
Numerous movies have portrayed young people as killers who have to be
stopped at any cost. It is amazing how many popular films represent youth
as pure evil. In *Kinderculture*, we researched the evolution of this adult
anger toward children and its effects.

These features of the contemporary cultural landscape of youth and
its social construction are important examples of the type of information
social studies teachers need to be producing, analyzing, interpreting, and
connecting to their professional practice. We can trace these contemporary themes of childhood and adolescence in a variety of cultural expressions, from concerns with violence to the conversation about family
values (Grossberg, 1992). At the same time that conservatives attempt
to contain youth by a return to patriarchal family values, we see the
ambiguous portrayal of the smart-ass child. The postmodern child is
worldly, often presented on TV and in the movies as a wise-cracking
know-it-all. Such a child is easy to hate and is particularly threatening to

adults. Child abuse in this context is made to appear almost justifiable. Indeed, the only way to counter such deplorable trends is to bring back a right-wing masculinist form of child raising that uses any means necessary to stop this youth crisis from destroying our nation.

Social studies teachers as researchers work with their students to support them and explore with them these contemporary cultural influences. Not only does this contribute to an understanding of self-production and a sense of mutual respect between teachers and students, but it also helps connect social studies to the lived world outside of school. It is a powerful way to help students understand the manner in which seemingly unconnected and abstract social and cultural forces shape their lives and make them feel the anxieties and tensions that sometimes plague them. As students involved in such research become rigorous scholars, they also learn to make sense of the invisible forces that work on them constantly. Everyone benefits from such a critical research-based curriculum.

THE ACTION IN ACTION RESEARCH: CHANGING PRACTICE

Research in a critical democratic social studies has so many uses and benefits. Obviously, a major theme of *Getting Beyond the Facts* involves using research as a means of reforming social studies practice in a way that improves scholarly ability and one's capacity to operate as a democratic citizen. The focus of social studies action research is unlimited. What, for example, do particular forms of teacher evaluation tell us about the purposes and values of our schools? teacher researchers ask. Looking below the surface of standardized-test-driven, behavioral assessment models of teacher evaluation, action researchers begin to uncover patterns of technicalization that erase teacher input into the determination of their own professional lives. Empowered with such knowledge, teachers gain the language to argue a case for their involvement in school policy. When principals and supervisors, for example, argue that teacher evaluation instruments necessitate particular forms of assessment, teachers will be able to point out that embedded within such instruments is an entire set of political, epistemological, cognitive, and pedagogical assumptions. Thus, teachers will enter into a sophisticated, theoretically grounded negotiation with administrators about the terms of their evaluations, the terms of their professional lives.

In such a context, critical theory-based action research attempts not simply to understand or describe the world of practice but to change it.

Proponents of such inquiry hope social studies teacher education students will learn to use action research in a way that will empower them to shape schools in accordance with well-analyzed moral, ethical, and political principles. Teachers who enter schools with such an ability are ready to make a cognitive leap; indeed, the stage has been set for movement to the realm of a post-Cartesian practitioner thinking. As critical action researchers endowed with a vision of what could be and a mechanism for uncovering what is, these social studies teachers are able to see the sociopolitical contradictions of schools in a concrete and obvious manner. Such recognitions force such teachers to think about their own thinking, as they begin to understand how these sociopolitical distortions have tacitly worked to shape their world views, their self-images, and their understanding of the purposes of social studies.

Social studies teachers as researchers cannot help but turn to biographical and autobiographical analysis in their inquiry. Aware of past descriptions of higher-order thinking, such teachers in this situation become researchers not only of students but also of themselves, researchers of the formation of their own cognitive structures. Such inquiry produces a meta-awareness of an omnipresent feature of the role of critical teachers: They are always in the process of being changed and changing, of being analyzed and analyzing, of being constructed and constructing, of learning and teaching, of disembedding and connecting. The purpose of critical action research, thus, is not to produce data and better theories about education; it is to produce understanding of the purposes of a democratic social studies supported by reflection and grounded in sociohistorical context (Carr & Kemmis, 1986; May & Zimpher, 1986; Carson and Sumara, 1997).

The understanding of purpose and the self-reflective qualities of social studies teacher research are forever intertwined with the process of sharing this practitioner research with others. One practitioner sharing his or her research with another is the best way to know how to foster a healthy questioning and a meaningful dialogue between practitioners. Successful dialogues will produce "felt responses" and further introspection, further revelations of ideological domination. Such interactions will move social studies teachers to expose the sociopolitical values in their research and teaching, uncover the ideological assumptions which have directed their practices, and reveal the impact of their own race, class, gender, and religious affiliations on their everyday lives (Reinharz, 1982; Kincheloe & Steinberg, 1997). This self-reflective quality of the teacher as researcher brings to center stage an extremely important dimension that uncritical teacher research misses. As the critical action researcher begins to reflect on his or her own consciousness, the realization begins to emerge that it has been shaped by a panoply of ideological forces—forces that often blind the teacher to an understanding of a multitude of important dimensions of classroom life.

DECONSTRUCTING HARRY, OR, AT LEAST, THE CONCEPT OF EMANCIPATION IN ACTION RESEARCH

If this is true of practitioners themselves, then the same ideological forces must work to shape the everyday understanding, the self-perceptions, of research subjects, i.e., people in general. The very essence of critical teacher research involves the return to the realization that subjects participating in social practices understand what is happening in their own lives, their own microcosms. Of course, the ways we teach or conduct research are products of these influences (Cherryholmes, 1988). If we are to ever operate as emancipated self-directed adults, we must confront the power of these forces. Indeed, in this confrontation we are obliged to deconstruct the power relations and the assumptions embedded in the term "emancipation," as we implied in our previous discussion of critical theory. When deconstructionism confronts emancipation, some interesting things begin to happen. Deconstruction can be defined in many ways: a method of reading, as an interpretive strategy, and as a philosophical strategy. For our purposes, it involves all three of these definitions, since it views the world as texts to be decoded, to be explored for unintended meanings.

Jacques Derrida has employed deconstruction to question the integrity of texts, meaning that he refuses to accept the authority of traditional, established interpretations of the world. This becomes valuable in a variety of situations, inasmuch as deconstruction focuses on elements that others find insignificant. The purpose is not to reveal what the text really means or what the author intended but to expose an unintended current or an unnoticed contradiction within it (Culler, 1981, 1982). Social studies action researchers should carefully watch the deconstructionist encounter. First, emancipation (as discussed in Chapter 6) can no longer claim to be the "blessed redeemer" of educational and sociopolitical life once exposed to the provisionality of deconstructionism. Second, after a deconstructionist encounter, emancipation's patriarchal foundations are revealed. Third, informed by these concerns, advocates of the concept of emancipation never again allow emancipation to escape questioning, to assume the position of a grand narrative. Fourth, humbled by deconstruction, emancipation is promoted as one way that an educational or a political situation could be improved, not as *the* way.

Despite this deconstructionist humility the problem remains: The goals of critical action research violate the "neutrality," the nonpolitical claim of the dominant school culture's view of inquiry. Attempts of critical teacher researchers to examine and expose the forces that shape our consciousness and the assumptions of our research are viewed as efforts to politicize the research process. Again, deconstructionism forces us to question more deeply social and discursive assumptions. Rejecting a binary opposition between subjectivity and objectivity, we begin to uncover a modernist cult of objectivism. Devotees of the cult attempt to make invisible their own social beliefs and practices (the political domain) while concurrently pointing to the subjectivities and "bizarre" customs of the individuals they are studying (Roman & Apple, 1990). They don't seem to realize that reality is tattooed by power, that the world's imprint on knowledge cannot be removed (McLaren, 1992a).

What mainstream empirical researchers can't seem to understand is that meaning is a contested entity. What an event, an action, or a text means may depend on what question is asked about it or what is hidden from an observer. When operating from this perspective, analysts of research divert their attention from questions concerning the bias of the data to questions concerning the interests served by the bias—questions of whose meanings prevail. Such questions forsake the positivist search for a privileged reference point from which the truth of educational practice may be discerned. Thus, what mainstream researchers once termed human predispositions, researchers informed by critical theory and deconstructionism refer to as discursive imprints on subjectivity, i.e., the consciousness construction that results from immersion in particular language games (McLaren, 1992b; Lather, 1992).

Based on their negotiations with those they have researched, critical action researchers assess information on the basis of its ability to move its consumers and producers in an emancipatory and humanistic direction, i.e., to help them achieve empowerment and self-direction through an understanding of the ideological forces that shape humans. For example, if action researchers are unaware of the unequal power relations in the school in which they are conducting their inquiry, how can they possibly grasp the importance and meaning of what they might perceive? When studying the school performances of a selected group of students, action researchers would be handicapped if they failed to account for the interaction between socioeconomic class and a student's language usage.

A student's usage of language, of course, seriously affects how well he or she does on a standardized test. Embodied in particular discursive fields, students from specific backgrounds, as well as the action researchers who analyze them, will tend to perceive in the context of these fields (McLaren, 1992a). If action research in social studies education is to be transformative, such understandings are central and must be shared with those being researched. As students from cultures shaped by repressive forces of race, class and gender begin to understand the power discourses that have molded them, appreciate the causes of powerlessness, and use such insights to form the basis of collective and individual actions to change repressive conditions, they are empowering themselves in the critical sense of the term (Shapiro, 1989; Lather, 1991).

UNCRITICAL ACTION RESEARCH: THE SAME OLD SAME OLD IN A NEW PACKAGE

Such considerations, however, are conceptual light years away from the forms of action research approved for use in the school. Arguing from a different set of assumptions, noncritical advocates of action research maintain that the everyday knowledge of teachers is the most important form of educational knowledge we possess. While the everyday knowledge of social studies teachers is more insightful than positivistic knowledge, it is not enough. It is not all that social studies teachers need to know. Action research in education, critically defined, is not content to confine teachers as researchers to the task of collating what they and their colleagues already know. Even though the packaging of noncritical action research appears new and fresh, its flavor is the same. The theoretical assumptions are tailored to the cult of objectivity that blinds participants to the complexity of forces that move events in educational settings.

The critical social studies teacher researcher asks questions of deep structure of his or her school or classroom setting. In other words, he or she is concerned with the emancipatory potential of social knowledge. Thus, critical teacher research will always aim to aid individuals in the attempt to take control of their lives, assuming that such autonomy is a moral right of human beings. This moral principle extends into the process of action research since it demands that individuals who are studied have the right to participate in decisions that portend to produce knowledge about them. The dignity of those being researched is respected when power is shared in both the application and the production of knowledge about them. Such power sharing allows the researchers to gain new insights into the deep social structures that shape their own consciousnesses, thus enhancing the possibility of self-determination.

Bringing everyday practical knowledge to the forefront of our consciousness may be the first step in such a process but it is not the last. It must be supplemented by an awareness of the ideological construction of our consciousness and the educational and political results of such construction. Given such a purpose for critical action research, Patti Lather (1991) has proposed the notion of catalytic validity. Catalytic validity points to the degree to which research moves those it studies to understand the world and the way it is shaped in order for them to transform it. Noncritical action researchers who operate within an empiricist discursive community will find catalytic validity to be a strange concept. Action research that possesses catalytic validity will display not only the reality-altering impact of the inquiry process, but it will also direct this impact so that those under study will gain self-understanding and self-direction (Altrichter & Posch, 1989; Van den Berg & Nicholson, 1989; Lather, 1991, Reason & Rowan, 1981).

Teacher research that ignores the emancipatory interest ends up only ankle-deep in the school ocean, missing a kaleidoscope of undersea activity. Social studies action research needs to move beyond exclusive concern with the individual and institutional levels of inquiry toward an understanding of the social and cultural structures that help shape the educational lives of individuals and help determine the consequences of schooling. When all three levels of inquiry are pursued by social studies teacher researchers, a view of education far more sophisticated than the one produced by an uncritical attention to teacher practical knowledge emerges. It is more sophisticated in that it is multidimensional, genuinely practical, reflective, politically savvy, and emancipatory. This uncritical action research orientation is quite dangerous because, in the name of innovation and democratic pedagogy, it fosters severely limited views of social studies teaching and the educational process in general. It covertly upholds the status quo since it is unable to analyze the dominant forces that constrict teacher insight and school policy. As it ignores wider social and political frameworks, it unwittingly reproduces dominant ideology and denies social studies teachers the privilege of questioning the authority of past disciplinary practices (Ruddick, 1989; Hinchey, 1998).

As uncritical action research denies teachers the right to self-direction, it also shuts its eyes to the values that appear throughout any effort to do research. It pretends that what counts as an educational improvement is obvious to all. If such a view is accepted, research becomes simply a value-free, neutral technique used to measure how well we have reached consensual goals. What we call "improvement" is always problematic, always embedded with tacit epistemologies, politics, views of human psychology, and ideologies (Wallace, 1987). When researchers and educational leaders assert, or even imply, that there is consensus on social studies goals, alarm bells should ring in the ideology detection center staffed by critical teacher researchers.

Many of the pronouncements of advocates of uncritical action research illustrate an unacquaintance with our social embeddedness and epistemology of complexity when they assume that everyday language is politically neutral and value-free. John Elliott, for example, has argued that everyday teacher concepts, expressed in everyday teacher language, should substitute for outsider perspectives. While Elliott makes a valuable point when he argues that teachers should protect themselves from the domination of the expert, he comes across as xenophobic when he maintains a "conceptual isolationism" for teachers. Concepts from social theory, when presented with sensitivity for the unique role of the practitioner, are necessary in the development of deeper understandings of the everyday life of the classroom and alternative perspectives on the goals and purposes of teaching. When it is not viewed as verified truth and not presented as a justification for top-down imposed goals for teachers, social theory can, of course, be very valuable. Elliott himself suffers from the effects of this conceptual isolationism since he fails to comprehend the social construction of consciousness. Teacher language and concepts seem to him somehow miraculously free of ideological interference. Elliott needs to take his analysis to another level.

VILIFYING THOSE DAMNED CRITICAL THEORISTS AND THEIR "POLITICIZED RESEARCH"

Focusing his attention on critical educational action research, Elliott calls it a dangerous conception of the teacher-as-researcher movement. Action researchers, he tell us, influenced by critical theory, have perpetuated the false notion that the self-understandings teachers hold of their everyday activities make up ideologically distorted misrepresentations of the world. The purpose of critical theory, according to Elliott, is to provide teachers with modes of analysis that explain how this ideology distorts teachers' views of themselves and their teaching and works to justify hegemony. Since he rejects the possibility that a teacher's perspective on the world could be ideologically shaped, Elliott sees the intent of critical action research as mere politicization. The most important effect of critical action research, Elliott contends, is that it requires a dialogue between the critical theorist and the teacher. The critical theorist, thus, becomes merely the latest in a long line of experts who impose their opinions on teachers.

Elliott seems to forget that most people, teachers included, may identify with or embrace ways of seeing that do not serve their best interests. Thus, when teacher perceptions of the world of school are left unquestioned, the effects of power are left invisible. No matter what the way of seeing in question, critical deconstructive analysis points out the partiality of any perspective. As deconstruction alerts us to how our economic, gender and racial positions shape our comprehension of various social and political phenomena, we begin to understand that the questions generated in our action research reflect where we are standing in the web of reality—a key understanding of our epistemological consciousness. In light of such understandings, Elliott's tendency to unprovisionally celebrate the perspectives of teachers conducting action research is misguided. Whether the perspective be that of the critical academic, the educational leader, the student, or the social studies teacher as researcher, the historical and cultural placement of the subject must be exposed and analyzed. Without question, the voice of teachers must be respected, but respect does not imply a disinclination to question their location—in the web of reality (Lather, 1991; McLaren, 1992b; Kincheloe & McLaren, 2000).

Elliott neglects another important point in his critique of critical action research: As opposed to other "outsiders," critical advocates of action research are not a part of a bureaucratic power structure which mandates teacher behavior. Whenever critical theorists would, in the mode of positivism, force their perspectives top-down on social studies teachers, I would join Elliott in his condemnation of them. At present, this is not happening. No room for outside opinion exists in Elliott's view of teaching and action research; in a critical action research context, he laments, "teachers' self-understandings cannot alone serve as the basis for their emancipation from ideological control" (Elliott, 1989b, pp. 50–53). Elliott's view of hegemony is quite unusual, for, while it excludes the identification of many of the forces that reproduce power in our consciousness, e.g., media, traditional teacher education, gender relations, etc., it includes all "outsiders" who analyze educational situations.

Elliott's perspectives have influenced other supporters of action research who also condemn critical teacher research for its desire to end open-minded inquiry. Jim McKernan (1988) writes in the spirit of Elliott that action research cannot be "held hostage" to the political ideology of the critical theorists. While he supports the effort to link critique and action in education, McKernan contends that this educational action should involve education and not politics; it should be an action that concentrates on issues of curriculum and instruction not on political matters like social justice. In the name of educational improvement and political neutrality, positivism pops up like a jack-in-the-box. McKernan's view is plausible only if we accept the positivist separation of facts and values and see the role of schools as politically neutral. My reading of educational history tells a very different story: a tale of schools many times used for political purposes, schools undermined by unequal power distribution.

Such uncritical perspectives are not simply the province of traditional quantitative researchers or researchers who accept the tenets of positivism. The perspective is alive and well in, of course, the action research movement and also within qualitative educational studies in general. The ability to make judgments is not viewed as a goal of qualitative research, many researchers argue. Of course, there is an element of truth in the pronouncement that we don't do qualitative research in order to judge how well a teacher is doing, but this is not the final word of judgment in a qualitative research context. We can refrain from making personal judgments while developing a set of criteria that allows us to judge the value of particular educational goals and outcomes. This is why it is so important for us to develop a provisional critical system of meaning. We need to ask and answer questions such as: are these goals and outcomes just? Are they respectful of human dignity? Whose interests do they serve? What are the epistemological assumptions embedded in these goals and outcomes? On what set of political beliefs are they grounded? This is judgment and, indeed, it is political. But to refrain from some form of judgment even in the name of neutrality is also political: Critical awareness smokes us out of our pseudoneutral "high ground." We cannot avoid making political choices as social studies teachers. To teach, to develop social studies curricula, is to make a political choice.

It seems obvious that any teacher's perspective, unaided by different vantage points, will guarantee that he or she will remain unconscious of these tacit assumptions that direct one's practice. Most people would be unaware, say, that they hold sexist or racist viewpoints that affect their teaching or do not correspond to their avowed principles. I do not doubt that those I refer to as the uncritical proponents of action research are genuinely concerned with granting teachers more insight into their professional practice, but such advocates fail to ask whether, in the contemporary workplace, teachers are free to initiate changes they consider necessary. Uncritical advocates of teacher research are uncomfortable with the so-called elitism of critical action researchers, such as Wilfred Carr, Stephen Kemmis, and myself, in our focus on the theoretical and organizational structures that constrain the everyday practice of teachers.

Can teachers make changes derived from their research and reflection? Carr and Kemmis ask. Often times the answer is no, given the self-perpetuating organization of schools and the ideological blindness and/or orientation of many school leaders. Uncritical action researchers, it seems, meet teachers only halfway: They throw one-half the length of the rope needed to pull them out of the water to safety. They speak the language of empowerment, and they concern themselves with the reflective power of teacher research, but they refuse to confront the structural conditions of schools and the larger society that preclude the translation of teacher reflection into emancipatory educational action (Wallace, 1987; Kincheloe, 1991, 1993; Steinberg & Kincheloe, 1997).

Uncritical advocates of teacher research are more and more using a critical vocabulary to describe their activities. Words such as "emancipation", "hegemony", and "domination" are heard and read quite often in the literature of action research. "Emancipation", for example, is not employed in the same way by Elliott as it is by Lather, Hinchey, McLaren, Carr, Kemmis, and myself. To Elliott (and many others) emancipation is a very specific situation: teachers freeing themselves from perspectives which emanate from outside the classroom. Lather, Hinchey, McLaren, Carr, and Kemmis use the term to evoke the image of teachers freeing themselves from the hegemonizing influences of larger sociocultural forces. Elliott's concept of emancipation does not allow for a critical reconceptualization or decentering of dominant views of the purpose of teaching. Employing a language of critique in relation to particular teacher expectations, critical forms of questioning become, from Elliott's perspective, an unwelcomed political imposition from outside the school.

Is it not possible to respect teachers and the sanctity of teacher knowledge and, at the same time, question particular interpretations and actions teachers derive from their reflection (Elliott, 1989a)? Maybe an analogy outside an educational context would help. There is little doubt that a lawyer with thirty years of courtroom experience possesses a unique form of knowledge that could only be attained by this particular experience. This does not mean that we have no right to argue or disagree with his or her purposes for trying or not trying a case or for accepting one case and turning down another. Indeed, an outsider with a different set of experiences may provide valuable insight into particular aspects of the lawyer's work. Critical action researchers in social studies education cannot allow their language to be co-opted and stripped of its emancipatory meaning by analysts who don't understand the reality of power relations, the socially constructed nature of knowledge, and the suffering which comes out of the existence of domination in the social and educational world, in short, by those who don't possess a consciousness of an epistemology of complexity.

Lest I be misunderstood, I will close Chapter 11 with a few reminders. In my attempt to preserve a role for advocates of critical action research in the conversation about social studies teacher research, I am not attempting, as Elliott and McKernan would suggest, to argue that teachers should not become authorities on the discourse of schooling. Critical democratic social studies educators demand respect of teachers and teacher knowledge and seek to expose the insidious ways that outside experts can come to dominate teachers. This is not, however, the position of Elliott and McKernan, inasmuch as they fail to discuss the discursive and power restrictions on understandings derived from teacher-conducted action research. Neither are they (or am I) attempting to pose as outside experts ready to come in and "correct" the "false consciousness" or distorted perceptions of practicing social studies teachers.

As critic Teresa Ebert (1988) maintains, we are interested in uncovering the ways that all of us, teachers included, are shaped by the ways lives are connected to dominant relations of power. Critical analysts, teachers, students, or other interested parties do not possess a consciousness that situates us beyond history and political practices. None of us, as Peter McLaren (1992a) contends, stands outside the policy structures of

Chapter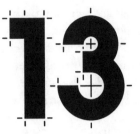

Exploring Water:
Students as Researchers in the
Social Studies Methods Course

Social studies teachers, who are scholars and knowledge workers, who possess an epistemological consciousness, and who engage students in a complex social studies that matters, understand the importance of both teachers as researchers and students as researchers. Using Chapter 12's understandings of a critical teacher research, Chapter 13 explores how such insights can be applied to producing student research as part of a social studies methods class. Social studies teachers must not only help their students make sense of the social, political, economic, and cultural world, but they should also help students make sense of themselves as participants in the world. Nothing prepares students for these roles better than learning to become rigorous researchers—inquirers who can read the world in such a way that they not only can understand it but can change it. The research act rests at the center of the complex, rigorous social studies curriculum.

Students as researchers in the critical democratic social studies classroom possess a vision of "what could be" and a set of skills to uncover "what actually is." Such students are empowered to delineate the social, political, and pedagogical contradictions of schooling, and in the process, ascertain the ways these contradictions have shaped their own and other students' consciousness. As our social studies students as researchers progressively deepen their appreciation of the contradictory dynamics, they concurrently gain a power literacy, that is, the ability to recognize the ways power operates to create oppressive conditions for some groups and privilege for others. Thus, students as researchers gain new ways of knowing and producing knowledge that challenge the commonsense views of sociopolitical reality with which most individuals have grown so comfortable.

Social Studies Teachers and Students as Collaborators In Research: Exploring the Obstacles To Democracy

No reason exists to preclude most elementary, secondary, and university social studies students from becoming critical student researchers. A democratic and informal, but intellectually disciplined, classroom can become a venue in which teachers and students create and re-create knowledge. Myles Horton, the founder of Tennessee's Highlander Center, argued that students and teachers need to learn how to find answers to the problems that confront them. In his simple, but not simplistic, manner, Horton delineated the central theme of critical social studies student research: Students and teachers should be collaborators in inquiry into the obstacles that block the achievement of their goals and dreams. Social studies teachers who facilitate the delicate task of engaging students as researchers must possess a well-informed and sophisticated sense of how to involve students in an analysis and clarification of their goals and dreams. Horton argued that teachers needed to share their theories of where they were going with students, so students could decide how to respond to the purposes of the classroom. If students didn't agree with the direction the teacher and other members of the class were moving, then alternative paths could be devised. The important concepts at work in such a context involve both the social studies teacher's effort to help students formulate a purpose for their research and education in general and the student's right to reject such a formulation (Long, 1995; Horton & Freire, 1990).

Recently, I talked with a group of teachers studying practitioner research and its various applications. As I listened to them, it became increasingly apparent that, while they understood a variety of action research techniques, they really had little sense of what larger purpose such research might serve. They were motivated to conduct teacher research but had no vision of what it could accomplish. The same is true of most new educational reforms; those who implement them often have no sense of the new ways of thinking they demand. Make no mistake about my purpose for social studies students as researchers. As I engage students in such work, I want them to develop a higher level of understanding, a critical literacy. Such a literacy would allow them the ability to understand the social construction of the world around them and their relation to it. Student researchers in this critical democratic vision learn to act in informed, socially just, and communitarian ways. I would not measure my success in terms of student ability to raise standardized test scores or gain admission into prestigious colleges. The critical democratic vision involves student inquirers as courageous citizens, not merely "good students."

Kathleen Berry (1998) writes of extending children's initial wonder about the world via student research. As student researchers analyze mainstream representations, they "reclaim wonder" in a manner involving the illumination of the taken-for-granted. John Dewey focused our attention on such a process when he argued that individuals should operate on the basis of a reflective action that disembeds moral, ethical, and political issues from mundane thinking. As student researchers in social studies pursue such a reflective relationship to their everyday experiences, they gain the ability to explore the hidden forces that have shaped their lives. Just as Berry thinks of students reclaiming wonder, students as researchers relearn the ways they have come to view the world around them. Indeed, such students gain the ability to awaken themselves from a mainstream dream with its unexamined landscape of social knowledge and consciousness construction. In their newly awakened state, critical student researchers begin to see schools as human creations with meanings and possibilities lurking beneath surface appearances. Their ability to grasp these understandings moves them to a new level of consciousness, a cognitive domain where knowledge intersects with moral imperatives resulting in previously unimagined activities.

Social studies students as researchers operating at a new cognitive domain go beyond so much: words on the page, dominant forms of ideology (constructs that maintain the status quo and its unequal power relations by producing particular meanings and interpretations of reality), and conventional purposes of education. This ability to go beyond is made possible by Paulo Freire's concept of "problem posing." Such a position maintains that the social studies curriculum should in part be shaped by problems that face teachers and students in their efforts to live just and ethical lives. Thus, in this context, students as researchers become

one feature in a problem-posed social studies curriculum that seeks to foster critical reflection on the forces that shape the world. Such a critical
reflection engenders a healthy and creative skepticism on the part of students. It moves them to be suspicious of neutrality claims in economics
textbooks; it induces them to look askance at, say, Phillips Petroleum's
legitimation commercials that position the oil company as the organization that has done more than any other to save our environment.

PRODUCING EXPERT STUDENT RESEARCHERS: PROMOTING DEEP LEVELS OF SOCIOPOLITICAL UNDERSTANDING

The social studies student research referenced in this critical context
involves both primary and secondary forms of inquiry. Primary research
involves conducting research directly in particular contexts, whether
they be ethnographic studies of events in their natural settings, semiotic
studies of symbols, signs, and codes that inscribe meaning in everyday
life, phenomenological studies of human consciousness and the meanings individuals give to certain phenomena, or historical studies of the
unfiltered writings and other cultural productions of the past. Secondary
research involves studying the ethnographies, semiotic analyses, phenomenological studies, and histories produced by other researchers. The
contention here is that students should be able to perform both types of
research as early as possible. As far as secondary forms of research are
concerned, social studies students should develop in-depth library skills
as soon as possible. In addition they should gain awareness of sources of
information offered by the community, both its institutions and particular members. A central aspect of secondary research involves the critical
ability to evaluate the assumptions of researchers and to identify the vantage points from which they are observing a phenomenon.

An important aspect of this ability to locate and critique secondary
research involves the skill to name what has been excluded. Students as
researchers exploring secondary materials will find that school texts consistently leave out issues of social conflict, injustice, and institutional
bias. In such secondary materials students will often discover what Henry
Giroux (1997) calls a "reified view of knowledge," meaning a form of
knowledge that is beyond question, that erases the fact that it was produced by humans operating in a particular context with a specific set of
values. Understanding these dynamics, student researchers gain an
awareness of the subjective nature of all knowledge and of the need to

interpret and deconstruct it in order to appreciate the tacit presuppositions about human beings and the world inscribed within it. In a time when traditional educators criticize progressives for a lack of intellectual rigor, we find such accusations odd in light of the type of scholastic abilities we want both teachers and students to possess. Democratic social studies teachers are often connected by their opponents to low standards; the more authoritarian the pedagogy, the more conservative critics bestow the blessings of rigor.

In the eyes of the advocates of traditional education, critical efforts to democratize social studies teaching and empower students are characterized as less-than-rigorous therapeutic sessions designed to help students get in touch with their feelings and to feel good about themselves. (Bob Dole made this charge in his presidential campaign in 1996.) While I have no problem with students who are happy and feel good about themselves, my purpose here is to produce emotionally and physically healthy social studies students who possess numerous methods of gaining, interpreting, producing, and applying social knowledge. There is nothing rigorous about pedagogies that require all students to concurrently "master" decontextualized bits of information—a lockstep absurdity. In this context, knowledge, despite all of its complexity, is reduced to a discreet entity that holds no past or no future.

Such data outside its context holds no significance. Students as researchers help explore and develop that context, as they search for the genesis of knowledge and analyze the reasons many have thought it was sufficiently important to place specific information in the official social studies curriculum. Without such contextual understandings, the memory-work pedagogies of traditionalists fail to achieve their most basic objective: the memorization of the validated knowledge of "our cultural heritage." Once the standards test is over, most students no longer have any use for such information and quickly forget it. Students as researchers in this critical context not only delve deeper into topics and move to a deeper level of understanding, but they even remember data better than students in traditional social studies programs. Their contextualized understandings help them mentally file social information in a manner that allows it to be easily recalled (Abercrombie, 1994; Capra, Steindl-Rast & Matus, 1991; Fiske, 1994; Ayers, 1992; Fried, 1995). Thus, they beat the traditional social studies educators at their own game.

AN EXAMPLE:
STUDENTS RESEARCHING SHREVEPORT'S WATER PROBLEM

One successful implementation of a primary, research-based critical social studies methods class involved student exploration of the water problems of Shreveport, Louisiana. The class convened one fall term immediately after a summer marked by a rash of water problems in this northwest Louisiana city. A mayoral election was being held during the period, and citizen dissatisfaction had pushed water to the front of both candidates' agendas. As the social studies education class considered what problem to explore, water could not be ignored. The class consisted of 10 students. None of them had ever engaged in a research project of any magnitude, but who all planned to teach elementary social studies. As the project began, they were unsure of themselves and frightened by the prospect of the research.

Indeed, the research background of most students was weak. Many confided that they had never before had to undertake a research project of any magnitude. This reevaluation illustrated a broader problem among elementary and even many secondary social studies teachers: the inability to conduct research. It is no wonder that inquiry methodology has often not worked in the public schools—too many teachers do not have the research skills necessary to make it work. Students in an inquiry project are lost if they do not have a teacher who can give directions on where to go for further information on a topic. Before social studies classes can escape the rote memorization, and textbook-oriented strategies that have paralyzed young minds for so long, sophisticated teacher research skills are a necessity.

At the beginning of the project, the students were hesitant to jump into the research. Being so inexperienced with primary research, they didn't know quite where to begin. This realization of research deficiency, when combined with the fact that they would soon be in the schools teaching social studies, seemed to awaken them to the need for better preparation of social studies teachers. Understanding their own backgrounds in light of the goals of social studies personalized the insufficient preparation in social science methodology that most elementary teachers possess. Some of the students had no understanding of what exactly sociology and anthropology, for example, were designed to study. Political science, some thought, was an alien discipline that had something to do with politics and politicians. This lack of understanding had little to do with the failure of colleges of education alone. Such realities indicate problems in all branches of the educational establishment. Once alerted to these considerations, the students' outlook toward the project become quite positive, and their commitment to an improvement in the quality of social studies teaching was unqualified.

The students had rarely thought of the relationship between social studies skills and everyday life, nor had they considered the application of social studies skills to real problems in their community or nation. The project enabled them to see social studies as a living entity, something that served to explain real events and that could be applied to real problems. Coming into the class, these students were no more nor less informed about social studies than students in other social studies classes taught over the years. For all the talent that exists among social studies/social science teachers in public schools, colleges of education, and colleges of liberal arts, student awareness of the potentialities of social studies is very low. The problems are apparent. College level social studies methods teachers must initiate a campaign of awareness. Social studies methods teachers must induce teachers to think in terms of the applicability of social studies concerns and insights. They must illustrate the need for those concerns and insights in contemporary society.

The city of Shreveport had been having trouble with the taste of its water for years. The city government and the water department had been deluged with complaints for a long time, and a sometimes bitter debate over the solutions to the problem had affected city planners in administration and after administration. Numerous studies had been commissioned, but, because of competing political interests, progress toward any solution had reached an impasse. The summer before the class met in the fall had been a particularly bad time for the water department, and complaints had risen to a near-record level. So, when the class began its research, city water was a hot political potato, fresh on everyone's mind.

The water problem found its origin in the fact that the source of Shreveport's water, Cross Lake, was an aging body of water plagued by all the problems that accompany lake maturity. As a lake ages, organic matter collects on its bottom, and, in periods of low water, the algae growth, which coincides with the build-up of organic matter, causes aesthetic problems of taste and color. Add to this the development of homesites within the Cross Lake watershed, accompanied by homeowners' use of phosphate fertilizers that eventually ran off into the lake, and the problem was magnified. Not only did the phosphates "fertilize" the yards but

they stimulated organic growth in the lake as well. The summer is a particularly bad time for an aging lake because of increased nutrient con-
centrations, warm water temperatures, and long periods of unobstructed
sunlight, all of which promote algae growth.

Some water officials argued that the Environmental Protection
Agency's decision to discontinue the use of chlorine in water purification
contributed to the city's water problem. The EPA ruling forced water
departments to substitute the weaker chemical, chloramean, for chlorine.
The addition of chlorine to water was found to produce chloroform, one
of the trihalomethanes that have proved to be a human carcinogen. The
uses of the less potent chloramean did not limit algae growth as effectively as did chlorine, and, as a result, the taste and odor problems were
accentuated. [The debate over the use of chlorine continues in
Shreveport and around the country. Public concern over Shreveport
water has also continued since the class project, as new city administrations continue to fund studies of the problem.]

The term opened at a running pace, as an attempt was made to provide the students a background in the goals and major issues of elementary
social studies. The students examined different perspectives on the goals of
elementary social studies, and, during the third week of the term, completed a comparative content analysis of a couple of elementary textbook
series in light of specific elementary social studies goals. Before students
could tackle a project with its emphasis on skill development and its variety of objectives, they needed to gain an understanding of traditional social
studies goals. Also, students were informed about more traditional ways of
teaching elementary social studies methods courses in order to provide a
context in which they could better understand the logic behind the primary research project as a means of teaching social studies methods.

A key point in the course involved the choosing of the topic and the
formulation of a plan for dividing the study into components. As students chose one of the subtopics, they conducted preliminary research for
the purpose of producing a tentative outline for the inspection of the
teacher. This division of the project components was important on a
number of levels. In the first place, it was a necessary step in the completion of a successful project. Unless the topic was viewed from a number of perspectives, there would be no way that any holistic sense of the
problem could be gained. If the various perspectives did not complement
one another while avoiding redundancy, project success was highly
unlikely. Secondly, the division of the topic was based on the disciplinary

breakdown of the social sciences (political science, sociology, history, anthropology, etc.), and it was through the different perspectives provided by the various social sciences that students could learn the problem solving value of the social studies. In other words, this division of responsibility had to be performed effectively if the students were to understand the value of the method. Thirdly, the teacher had to be aware of the process of dividing the project into manageable parts, for this would probably be the only time that the prospective teachers would see such a method of division before they attempted to implement it in their own classrooms. Thus, each step had to be fully explained so that the students understood the logic behind the procedure.

The project forced the students to confront the question: How does a group go about studying a city's water problems from the perspective of the social sciences? Using the divisions of the social sciences to get started, the problem was examined from historical, economic, and political vantage points, as well as from a comparative perspective borrowed from anthropology. In addition to these basic divisions, one student served as a synthesizer, attempting to present an overview of the role water plays in our lives while introducing the readers of the final report and the audience at the public forum to the scope of the study and the contributions of the specific student participants. Other reports involved a special look at all the problems associated with Shreveport water, a study of environmental aspects of the water problem, and two papers on practical alternatives to the present system. The table of contents of the students' final report read as follows:

   I.   An Introduction to Water
  II.   History of Shreveport Water, 1839–1917
 III.   History of Shreveport Water, 1917–the Present
  IV.   An Overview of Shreveport Water Problems
   V.   Political Aspects of Shreveport Water
  VI.   Shreveport's Water Source: A Comparative Study
 VII.   Shreveport's Water: Economic Considerations
VIII.   Shreveport Water: Environmental Considerations
  IX.   Alternatives to Shreveport's Existing Water Supply: Part 1
   X.   Alternatives to Shreveport's Existing Water Supply: Part 2

After the topics were agreed upon and each student chose his or her part, the research began in earnest. The students quickly found that the director of the water department and his staff were especially helpful. Not only did the water department officials welcome a parade of students to their offices, but they came to the university and worked with students who felt uncomfortable with the technical aspects of the topic because of weak or nonexistent backgrounds in chemistry. All told, water department personnel donated hours of their time to the edification of the social studies students, consistently maintaining the attitude that such services were merely a part of their job. Also invaluable was the help of specific members of the university community. One chemistry professor, who was also a leader in the region's environmental awareness movement, spoke to the class on numerous occasions and granted interviews to students who had further questions. The students were impressed by the fact that there were so many people in the community, including water department staff members, university professors, and local political leaders, who were willing to help them. It was a realization that would not be lost when they acquired teaching positions in the public schools.

The students' first meeting with the water department staff was interesting on a number of levels. Not only did the students realize how interesting and controversial the topic was, but they came to understand how technical some aspects of it could be. They realized that a better understanding of chemistry was a necessity and set out to sophisticate their understanding of the discipline. This was one of their more impressive accomplishments, i.e., their success in acquainting themselves with the basic physical scientific knowledge so as to make sense of the water controversy. Once such understandings were gained students, could talk comfortably about trihalomethanes and their production in the chlorination process.

As the project proceeded, the students kept diaries in which they examined the nature of their research, their frustrations and successes, and how the process could be related to the teaching of elementary social studies. Some students displayed a sophisticated insight into the connection between the project in a college setting and its use in an elementary context. Some students needed the point explained that there was not a direct transfer between a college social studies project and an elementary project. The idea of primary source orientation, a flexible problem-centered curriculum, an emphasis on skills improvement and not simply factual acquisition, the need for teacher research abilities, the view of social studies as a pragmatic tool for investigation, and the liberation of students and teachers from a textbook-oriented program were all concepts that students were encouraged to address in their diaries, along with personal feelings, observations, and suggestions to the teacher for future improvement of the class.

After a couple of months of research, the students presented oral reports to the class on their findings. They were questioned by the professor about inconsistencies, and their attention was directed to further research where it was needed. The oral reports were very valuable because students had an opportunity to question one another, not in a competitive way but in an attempt to reconcile contradictory findings and induce one another to ask new questions of their material. The project was designed to culminate in a public forum with the students presenting information and facilitating a public discussion of the issues. Newspaper and TV reporters were invited, along with individuals who had played some role in the students' search for information. The forum added an element of excitement and offered an overt reminder of the connection between the project and the world outside of the classroom.

The students turned in their research papers to the professor two weeks before the forum. At this point, mechanical errors were corrected, a few sentences were added or deleted, and students were asked to check any questionable assertions. The papers were returned with corrections, and the students rewrote their final drafts. These were resubmitted, copied, collated, and bound into a volume to be distributed at the forum. Many students found this part of the process to be valuable, in that they had to present a "perfect" copy for public distribution. They had never been involved in this final step where a professor had edited parts of their final drafts.

The forum was well attended. Members of the university community, the visual and print media, environmental groups, the water department, as well as students and politicians, were present. Students presented a brief overview of their research, and a set of agreed-upon recommendations were issued after the individual presentations. The floor was then opened for discussion, and the students and the audience exchanged questions and considered the major issues involved. Local TV and radio stations ran features on the event on their news programs. Local newspapers reported on the forum, and one newspaper followed up with a front-page feature on the project and the unique method it presented for educating social studies teachers. The project was certainly a success in introducing students to alternative methods of teaching elementary social studies, improving their primary source research skills, connecting the social studies classroom with actual social problems, improving student writing, speaking, and organizing skills, alerting students to resources in the community and ways of incorporating them into education, and providing students with an opportunity to work with a group in a research-based problem solving activity.

The project was also a success in informing the community of the sophisticated capabilities of prospective elementary teachers, the creative potential of teacher education, the value of social studies in the public schools, and the possibilities provided by education that transcends mere rote memorization. In other words, the students were not just learning to teach social studies but were actually serving as ambassadors for education in a larger community that often looked at them, and others like them, with condescension. This multidimensional role was one that they would not lose after their association with the class had ended. Teachers must wear many hats as educators, with classroom teaching a primary, but not solitary, concern. If social studies education is to improve, critical social studies teachers must display the possibilities of the subject to the communities in which they teach. The water project provided teachers with good practice for such a goal.

Chapter 14

Thanksgiving in the Elementary Social Studies Classroom: Students as Researchers Yet Again*

I (Joe) am constantly attempting to devise new "scams" for engaging students in research projects that are meaningful to them and to which they can invest their concerns and emotions. A particularly successful example in which I was able, with the help of gifted colleagues, to engage a group of elementary social studies education students involved a study of Thanksgiving. The class consisted of a group of wonderful, committed, talented, and comedic students who devoted considerable time and effort to the goals of the class. This chapter is dedicated to that personable group of social studies education undergraduate students.

MAKIN' FRIENDS AND INFLUENCIN' PEOPLE: A THANKSGIVING STORY

I have been personally obsessed with the teaching of Thanksgiving in elementary social studies since an incident that occurred early in my career as a teacher educator. While engaging in student teaching supervision in a small southern university, I visited one of my students in a local elementary school. It was the Wednesday before Thanksgiving Day, and I had arranged to observe her teach a lesson. Upon arriving in her

---

* This chapter was co-authored by Leila Villaverde.

classroom, I was surprised to find her cooperating teacher giving a lecture to the fifth graders about the origins of the Thanksgiving holiday. I tiptoed to the back of the room and sat down beside my student teacher.

She told me that she would not be teaching that day because the cooperating teacher had requested time to give the lecture. I arranged to see her at the same period on the following Monday and listened with her to the remainder of the cooperating teacher's lesson. I was fascinated by the similarity of the teacher's depiction of the loving Pilgrims' inducing the "wild" Indians to share a bounteous turkey dinner with them to celebrate their friendship and a good harvest with the accounts I had heard as a child from my elementary teachers in the mountains of rural Tennessee. The teacher spoke of how the Pilgrims introduced the "godless" Indians to Jesus and brought the gift of salvation to their lives. After the glorious Thanksgiving dinner, she told the class, the Pilgrims and the Indians lived happily together ever after.

At this point I turned to my student teacher and whispered in mock seriousness: "I think there's something missing in that account that I just can't put my finger on: Oh yeah, the little part about the Pilgrim's genocide of the Indians." I thought I had established a sufficiently personal relationship with the student teacher that she would understand my ideological reference point and the purpose of my sardonic comment. But, unfortunately, I was wrong. I would come to find out that I had not exercised good judgment.

On Monday morning, I nonchalantly walked into the elementary school ready to observe my student. I was met at the door by an obviously upset and visibly angry assistant principal who asked me if I was Kincheloe. "Yes," I replied and extended my hand for a handshake. Ignoring my gesture, the assistant principal told me to follow her to the principal's office. Walking silently four steps behind her, I knew that there was a problem. But what it could be, I could not imagine.

When I entered the office, the principal sternly told me to sit down at the conference table dominating the room. Already seated were my student teacher and her cooperating teacher who was red-faced and weeping. Without a moment of hesitation, the principal told me that I would no longer be welcome in the elementary school and that he had called my dean at the university to report my "deplorable behavior." As a principal, he admonished me, he would not allow some young professor to come into his school spreading lies about sacred American institutions. In all his years as an educator, he said, he had never heard nonsense comparable to what I had told the student teacher. He would make sure that he told other principals in the area about me so I wouldn't be allowed to "spread my poison" in other schools. ~

He dismissed me from the meeting, telling me to report to my dean's office immediately on my return to the university. As I drove to the university, I thought about the notion of competing ideas in a democratic marketplace and how such a concept was alien in many U.S. schools. I thought about whether or not my comment to the student teacher was inappropriate. Was I taking advantage of a teaching moment, or was I exercising poor judgment? I honestly wasn't sure. My meeting with my dean offered no surprises, as he reprimanded me for my behavior. He had worked hard to establish good relationships with the local schools, he said, and was infuriated by my disrespect for him, the school-university relationship, the cooperating teacher, my student teacher, and the "truth".

While we can debate the appropriateness and timing of my comment in the context of the student teaching observation, this story raises other questions about social studies teaching and the role of the school as a democratic space. I don't believe that my concern with the genocidal aspect of the Pilgrims' actions would have ever been welcomed in the elementary school in question or that any teacher, speaker, or community member who raised questions about the veracity of the teacher's Thanksgiving story would have been allowed to speak again. What does this tell us about the teaching of social studies? What does it say to those social studies teachers who possess an understanding of emancipatory goals and an epistemological consciousness? Throughout the class described in this chapter, I raised these questions with my students. They found the story and the questions both fascinating and disturbing. They struggled to figure out what I should have done in the circumstance. Let us now turn our attention to Leila Villaverde's and my description of the social studies methods class.

THE ENIGMA OF THANKSGIVING

Thanksgiving is one of many enigmatic celebrations in the North American pantheon of holidays. A large part myth and historical erasure, Thanksgiving celebrations and school lessons paint a picture of American Indian-English settler relations that is quite misleading. Such a depiction is important because Thanksgiving serves the central cultural role of providing a national origin myth. From the traditional morality play of the settler-Indian interaction, students gain an ideological understanding of America as specially blessed by God, America forged by civilizing both the savages and the wilderness in which they resided, America as the representation of order in the sea of indigenous chaos, in short, an ethnocentric vision of nation and self. The complexity and importance of the holiday are revealed when such ideological understandings intersect with the portraits of the Plymouth settlement provided by historians of seventeenth-century Massachusetts.

In these chronicles, we find a group of settlers giving thanks to God for the smallpox plague spread by pre-Plymouth European explorers that devastated the Native populations of the region. The Pilgrims are often seen as graverobbers who relied on Indian generosity and food stores to survive the early years of the settlement. The English settlers are also viewed as violent neighbors who, within a half century after the Plymouth landing, had killed a large percentage of the Indians living in their proximity. As to Thanksgiving as a holiday, we find that, even though Abraham Lincoln proclaimed Thanksgiving a national holiday in 1863, the association of Pilgrims, Indians, and a grand feast with the holiday didn't emerge until the end of the nineteenth century, almost three centuries later. Indeed, school curriculum with the morality play between settler-Native replete with Squanto and the planting of corn is, for the most part, a twentieth-century phenomenon.

When such historical images are contrasted with mainstream elementary education's curriculum of turkey bulletin boards, handouts with Pilgrims in their starched black and white suits extending outstretched hands to the near-naked Indians, descriptions of the divinely inspired piety of the Christian settlers and the moral foundations of America's settlement, elementary social studies teachers find themselves faced with some profoundly troubling decisions concerning how they should teach Thanksgiving. As social studies methods teachers, we wanted our elementary teacher education students to appreciate the moral and pedagogical dilemmas caused by the collision of the mainstream school's expectations for the teaching of Thanksgiving with their sophisticated historiographical understandings of the foibles of the traditional story. In this problematic context, we asked the students to conduct research on seventeenth-century Indian-settler relations as well as on curricula taught in mainstream schools. Grounded in both their research and speculation, students devised Thanksgiving units for various elementary grade levels that indicated their awareness of the complexities involved in such curriculum making.

RESEARCH IN THE CRITICAL METHODS CLASS:
QUESTIONS OF PURPOSE AND CONTENT

Research is crucial for the success of any pedagogical model, particularly when the focus is on the critical empowerment of students. When students are engaged in taking an active role in the learning process, they are empowered to shape their experiences, what they search for, interpret, understand, and apply. Not only do methods students as researchers become critically aware of what is included and excluded in and out of traditional curricula but they are forced to continually expand their fund of knowledge as one question leads to the next in any line of research. The excerpts in this chapter are taken out of the interdisciplinary Thanksgiving units designed by our students. The class was taught by Joe Kincheloe, Shirley Steinberg, and Leila Villaverde and revolved around questions raised by a critical democratic approach to social studies education.

We introduced the class by focusing on issues of what social studies education is and what it could be. Social studies in elementary schools have been abused, misused, misunderstood, hated, and ignored. When researchers examine the teaching of social studies in elementary education, they find few bright spots. Good teachers do great things in some schools, but too few elementary teachers have a sense of purpose in relation to social studies education. Too many are victims of a lack of interest in social studies. In this class, we attempted to acquaint the students with the problems of social studies, and what elementary teachers can do to overcome them in their professional lives. To begin this process, we wanted our students to search their consciousnesses and their own educational history to understand what they already knew about social studies. Then we asked questions: What are the social studies? What are methods? How can teaching and methods be critically and significantly taught? What do you expect from a social studies "methods" class? We worked together in the class as teachers/students/researchers to explore, in the spirit of the Frankfurt School, what social studies can be.

As we discussed cognition, social studies, and elementary education, we demonstrated different methods within the classroom. We covered integrated education in regard to using other content areas within social studies to enhance and broaden our curriculum. As a class, we explored new ideas on higher orders of teacher thinking (postformalism) and how we might share these abilities with our students. We tied these new forms of thinking into social studies methods that are connected to the fine arts (art, drama, and music). In addition to learning to think in new and exciting ways, we learned some very specific and practical teaching methods that could be applied directly to the students' future elementary social studies classes. As methods teachers, we engaged students in the analysis of social studies in terms of the larger society, and in terms of race, class, gender, power, sexuality, religion, economics, etc. Constantly acting as researchers, we asked questions about traditional methods (our own student histories) and what we would keep or improve upon.

In their units, students were asked to draw upon their research, use and/or expand on the approaches we discussed in class, and make reference to their understanding of the purposes of social studies as they created an interdisciplinary two-week Thanksgiving curriculum. They were given the flexibility to create any type of situation for their classrooms. Thus, some students included famous speakers or planned for a variety of extravagant field trips. What follows are excerpts from the units created by three excellent students: Elizabeth McNeil, Melissa Shine, and Kristin L. Persichini. Although there were many excellent units, we found these particularly interesting, given their use of a research-grounded interdisciplinary, critical democratic, epistemologically and socially conscious approach towards teaching about Thanksgiving in elementary school. All three units relied primarily on giving the students every opportunity to be researchers, taking advantage of every resource possible, including an emphasis on the Internet. This chapter provides a conceptual and practical framework for a methods course that empowers teacher education students as researchers creating the experience necessary for successful and confident application of these concepts in their own classrooms.

Elizabeth McNeil's Thanksgiving Unit

McNeil begins her unit with a quote from Michael Dorris's "Why I am Not Thankful for Thanksgiving":

> Considering that virtually none of the standard fare surrounding Thanksgiving contains an ounce of authenticity, historical accuracy, or cross-cultural perception, why is it so apparently ingrained? Is it necessary to the American psyche to perpetually exploit and debase its victims in order to justify its history?

She then states:

> Until recently, I had this notion in my head that I wanted to create a Thanksgiving unit that would include none of the stereotypical aspects of the holiday. I did not even want to mention the word Pilgrim in the unit. I considered it a challenge to go beyond the norms of what we believe Thanksgiving to be, and to introduce new definitions for the word "Thanksgiving."
>
> I began with the subject of dance. Dance has always been a way to express a myriad of feelings, from anger and hate, to love, and finally, to thanksgiving. I wanted to concentrate on how various cultures use dance to give thanks; in this way, I would be reinventing the word "Thanksgiving" for the imaginary class for whom I was designing this unit.
>
> Then, after reading the endless amount of information available on Thanksgiving, I decided that I would be doing a disservice to my imaginary class if I did not try to problematize the subject with them. I still wanted to integrate dance into the unit, but I wanted it to be a part of what the holiday called Thanksgiving was and is in the United States.

There is a consciousness evident in this passage that demonstrates a concerted effort to challenge and analyze the standard in order to mediate between the traditional curriculum and one that would empower the students and better prepare them for society. Her unit is designed for 10 days of work, integrating basic curriculum subjects with various subjects within the arts and technology.

McNeil designates Day One: "Tradition, deconstructing the Thanksgiving holiday and discussing the word tradition." She asks the students to create a Thanksgiving page in their class webpage, addressing the multifaceted topics in their units with only the requirement of starting the webpage with the word "tradition". She states:

> I will open the unit with the class by brainstorming with the kids what the word tradition means to them. I will ask them if their families or friends have any special traditions that they would like to share with the group. After discussing traditions within the family, we will talk about the above definition, which I will have posted on the board. We will spend quite some time discussing what each definition means, and whether people are active or passive in the definition. I will ask them if they notice any faults in the definition, and why. Following the discussion, the class will compose together a new definition of the word tradition, which would address all the problems, such as the gender biases, in the antiquated Webster's version . . . .
>
> After lunch, the kids will go to art class which will be taught by our guest lecturer, Annie Liebowitz. After a discussion of the specifics of her photography, the artist will talk about different methods of capturing light and shadow in photographs. A science lesson will ensue, as the kids ask the artist how film

works. The kids will turn again to the Internet to find information on film . . . .
Ms. Liebowitz gives the students the assignment to create a photographic essay
on traditions they see every day. The essay is to be completed using the newly
created definitions of the word tradition . . . . They also have been assigned to
go to the library and find information on photography and science behind film
developing.

The first day began with one word, tradition. From that one word, our
amazing class branched out to learn creative writing, computer, science, and art
skills. We explored different cultures through our traditional lunches and
gained appreciation for the art of photography.

She stresses research of the unknown and familiar, provides experientials,
and caters to the differences within her classroom. She also respects the
natural flow of research and learning in revolving the day's lessons
around where the research leads.

Every day, McNeil begins the day with a discussion of the student's
photographic essays, monitoring their progress and answering any questions. Day Two: "Thanks, but no thanks!" addressed stereotypical
Thanksgiving feasts, events, and books that represent Thanksgiving erro-
neously. She shows films depicting the feasts:

Especially offensive is the "Brady Bunch" portrayal of the first feast, using a
Brady-made movie to capture the event. The kids will watch that footage and
then discuss what they have seen. I will ask them what they know about the
holiday, and if they think that the event happened as it was portrayed on television.

She places a quote from James W. Loewen's *Lies My Teacher Told Me*
on the overhead projector which the students discuss. Instead of imposing a topic on the students, discussions are facilitated so that the students
are part of the deconstruction and construction of knowledge.

We will talk about the implications of placing stereotypical images in books
and in media and representing them as the norm. We will then go to the library
to locate books that perpetuate the stereotypes of Pilgrims in black and Indians
wearing war paint and carrying tomahawks. . . . I will pose to the class the question: "What is the truth about Thanksgiving?" Has this tradition been handed
down to us inactive receptors of knowledge as *Webster's* definition indicates?
We will again turn to the Internet for help. The Center for World Indigenous
Studies has an excellent website. . . .

The students were assigned to research specific aspects that the webpage
included so that at the end of the day they would come together to pres-

ent what they found. They also had the option of presenting their information in a variety of ways—a multimedia production, book, song, etc.—as long as it would help in the creation of the unit home page. Overall, McNeil encouraged the students to use a variety of resources, to question, compare, contrast, and discuss.

Day Three: "Irreconcilable differences?" highlights an excerpt from a 1970 speech on the 350th anniversary of the Pilgrim's arrival. As always the day began by discussing the photographic essays. But the focus of the day was on the diseases that indigenous people often contracted from European settlers.

> First, we will examine the disease from the perspective of a traditional sixth grade history book. We will then compare the depiction of the diseases to those indicated in *Lies My Teacher Told Me.* . . . The kids will be asked to write a reflective journal assuming the role of the person who spoke at that 1970 ceremony. They will be encouraged to write about their life as a Wampanoag or about the day that they were to give the speech. Was that person nervous? Did that person have the help of another to write that speech? What circumstances brought that person there to give that speech?. . . The kids will be free to find a quiet place to compose their pieces.

Creating a space to imagine another's consciousness is crucial to demystifying biases and racist behaviors. Exploring other experiences through research and intellectual as well as emotional knowledge is also very important to fostering a well-rounded student.

> The kids who have finished their stories early will begin a large mathematics assignment which will encompass the rest of the unit. Because the class agreed that books and the media are influential in how people see the Native American people of this country, they will begin a "detective mission." They will become introduced to statistics by analyzing the books in their library. They will have to look up all the books dealing with Native American issues and devise a way to interpret that information on their website. They may do graphs, charts, etc., but it must be clear what the ratio of stereotypical books is compared to more appropriate books. . . . This statistical analysis will be completed over the course of the next two weeks.

Day Four: "Detectives aren't just for television;" "Statistics aren't just for college kids" deconstructs the meaning of "detective" and the implications of what the students find in the library.

If the kids are being detectives by hunting down stereotypical books, then does that make the library an accomplice to the crime? Furthermore, does that make the authors punishable by law? The children will discuss courses of action to take in the school in order to relay the message to the other students that some of the books in their school are problematic.

The students spend the rest of the day in the library researching and exploring other books that stereotype people. A highlight of this day involves the emphasis on action-oriented research utilizing the knowledge students have learned to raise others' awareness in regards to how and why knowledge is constructed.

Days Five and Six: "Letters with a mission" provides the final steps for the students to apply what they have learned through their detective assignments.

Many of the children will start to have concerns about the quality of books in their library. The kids will begin letter-writing campaigns to the libraries in their school district and to the people responsible for purchasing the books. Included in the letters will be the students' research findings on the materials promoting negative stereotypes in the school libraries. Also included in the letter will be a list of recommended books by and for Native Americans . . . The letters will be . . . mailed to the appropriate locations by day six. The children will also call their local news media to explain what they have been doing to increase awareness of stereotypical books in schools.

McNeil provides a good example here of how to use math within the classroom so that the numbers do not become sterile, but useful, a means to a socially productive end. Continuing to work on the photographic essays, the students experiment with different settings, as they photograph traditions outside of their families.

Day Seven: "Return to day three" goes back to working on the reflective journal the students began on day three. The day continues as follows:

Today we will be talking about the Native American commitment to nature and how we can work to encourage ecologically sound practices. . . . The kids will talk about their own ecological practices and those of their families. . . . We will make a book about the possible dangers imposed upon us if we do not begin to recycle. . . . We will discuss the work we have done throughout the past few days which has led us to the place where we are at the moment.

The children will spend the rest of the afternoon working on their webpage. They must maintain it by adding any new material to it or answering questions posed by outside sources. While working on their pages, some of the children may start receiving responses to the letters they wrote regarding the book debate. The kids will probably receive a lot of "thank yous," but not a lot of action. Perhaps another sixth grade class somewhere in the country could respond to our page by asking questions about our findings. This will instill in my students a sense of accomplishment for all their hard work. It is possible that news will travel and people will start questioning Disney's Pocahontas book and movie.

Day Eight: "Shall we dance?" looks at dance for its international and cultural significance. McNeil plays traditional Wampanoag music and asks the students for their reactions. She then induces them to dance to the music, perhaps even closing their eyes if they feel comfortable in order to feel the music.

> From there, I will brainstorm with the kids some other times people dance to give thanks. In Europe, at Oktoberfest, for example, . . . We will spend a good part of the morning studying different dances intended to give thanks. . . . The children will spend the rest of the morning writing short narratives about a child their age who lived during the time of an ancient harvest celebration. They can write about Asian, Native American, European, and African cultures, among many others, as long as they have some historical background included in the narratives. The kids will rehearse these narratives as if they were soliloquies and be ready to present them on day 10 of the unit.

The students research their characters and read more books that will help them in their soliloquies. During the dance lessons, the students examine the kinesthetic effects of dancing.

Day Nine: "Photographic essay day with Annie Liebowitz" culminates the students' experience as photographers. During the morning, they develop the film and in the afternoon they display their essays for their families, explaining what they meant to them. Traditional food representing the students' culture is a part of the afternoon events. Realistically, the students would need extra days for the film to dry, a contact sheet to be printed, and the specific shots to be selected, printed, and dried. Also, they would need some time to organize the sequence of the essay and decide whether or not to include text.

Day Ten: "The final day":

> On the last day of our Thanksgiving unit, the kids will reflect on the cognitive restructuring that they had to go through in order to reinterpret the holiday in a new light. They will rehearse their soliloquies in the morning and then perform them in the afternoon for their families.

McNeil's unit comes to a close with a variety of experiences, resources, and demystifying practices designed for elementary students. Using her abilities as a researcher, McNeil is empowered to lay out a set of compelling activities for her students. Aware of the importance of research as a pedagogical act, she is able to tie research, interpretation, and knowledge production to the Thanksgiving activities.

Melissa Shine's Thanksgiving Unit

Shine's unit begins with a description of the school and classroom for which it is designed. Her classroom is a third grade full of ethnic and religious diversity and includes students from stable and abusive families, as well as some children with varied physical and developmental disorders. In her school, Melissa has made it a priority to include aides to work alongside the teacher. She states, "This allows the teacher to present challenging lessons to all of the students and still ensure that all of the students are learning and benefiting." Her unit is divided into eight parts that deal with the historical construction of the time period from which Thanksgiving was supposedly born.

Part 1: "Planning the voyage" (Day 1, part of 2) introduces the students to the story of the Pilgrims and strangers who boarded the Mayflower to come to the New World. For the next two weeks, the students would be acting the parts of both the newcomers and the Wampanoag Indians.

> The first activity that we will do will be making journals to record our events in the following days. The students will be encouraged to write and draw how they feel, what everything looks like, and the events that are happening around them. The students can write these journals from a newcomer or a Wampanoag Indian's point of view. They can also choose to be a man, woman or child and write from that perspective as well. The students will write in the journals every day, and the first day's activity will be to write about why they are traveling on the Mayflower.

From this activity, the students plan and map the boat trip, study the wind currents, and calculate the mileage and supplies needed. The students will also rewrite the Mayflower Compact and design the Mayflower to be an appropriate vessel. Shine uses *If You Sailed on the Mayflower* to read aloud to the children throughout the unit.

Part 2: "The New World" (second part of Day 2, Day 3) paves the arrival of the newcomers from setting up their village to building their homes. Math skills are used to lay out the village so that all the families have an equal share. The students are divided into three groups that read *The First Thanksgiving Feast, Samuel Eaton's Day*, and *The Pilgrims of Plymoth*. The students will then present the information to their classmates, comparing and contrasting the stories in order to design their own village from all they have read and heard.

Part 3: "Pilgrim Life" (Day 4) discusses the vestments and customs of the newcomers, considering the temperature in order to later design appropriate clothing.

> The teacher and students will then discuss the roles of the men, women, and children in each group. The journal entry for today will have the students explain what their role as a man, woman or child is in the village and how they compare to the roles that each of these groups hold in today's society.

The class also discusses nutrition and caring for the crops the newcomers cultivated on the plantation. The students experiment with planting seeds and monitoring the effects of water, sunlight, and fertilizer on the plants' growth. Shine carefully weaves a variety of subjects into the day's lesson to maximize the students' learning and create a more holistic approach to teaching.

Part 4: "Indian Life" (Days 5 and 6) concentrates on the dress, customs, and culture of the Wampanoag Indians so that the students can design clothing.

> The students will be asked to draw a picture of what these Indians looked like. Since there is the stereotypical view that most Indians had headdresses and Mohawks, many students will draw pictures emphasizing these looks. The teacher will show the students how the Wampanoag Indians actually dressed so that the students can become aware of the fact that what they are sometimes told or think is not the truth in all cases.

The students are also asked to observe and discuss the phases of the moon and draw what the moon looks like in their journal every night. This is designed to initiate the student in reading and discussing the significance of nature for the Native American culture.

> The students will . . . read and discuss *Lightning Inside You*, . . . "How Glooskap made human beings' which is found in *How Glooskap Outwits the Ice Giants*. The

students would then record in their journal a story in which they think of a way the Great Spirits and nature can collaborate and teach a lesson.

The students also learn some Algonkian language as well as the history behind the meeting between Squanto and Captain Miles Standish. The students will prepare a reenactment of this meeting.

> The journal entry for this section will have the students record how they, as Wampanoag Indians, would feel about the newcomers, and how the newcomers would feel about the Wampanoag Indians. . . . The students will also learn about the autumnal Thanksgiving feasts that the Indians had each year and will realize that they celebrated these feasts long before their Thanksgiving with the newcomers. They will find out that this Thanksgiving feast was actually the Wampanoag's fifth of the year.

At this point, the students invite each other to the Thanksgiving festivities. Throughout this lesson, the students have had the opportunity to expand their frames of reference by adopting another's position or consciousness as a simulation of Thanksgiving and its history.

Part 5: "Preparing for the Feast" (Day 7), the students plan for the event as newcomers, deciding how much food needs to be prepared, what ingredients are needed, and how much time is needed to cook.

> The students will spend half of the day in the library researching books and the Internet to find authentic Thanksgiving recipes to serve at their feast, such as corn soup, succotash, white fish, red meat, fowl, berries, beans, squash, pumpkins and sweet potatoes. . . . They will also be able to use their research to find games that the children of this time period played, and they can also invent games that could have been played using the available resources of the land back then.

As the students prepare everything, Shine asks another class to join it in hopes of reproducing the story as closely as possible by having more guests come than expected and then solving the dilemma presented by the need to stretch and divide the food.

Part 6: "The First Tthanksgiving" (Day 8). At the outset, the students must tend to the insufficient food.

> "Squanto," one of the children in the other class, will instruct some of his tribe members to go hunt and get more food for the feast. These students will leave and return with the food they have prepared.

Before eating, "Squanto" will say the Thanksgiving Prayer from the Iroquois People. Both classes will eat their meals and will participate in activities that happened during the first Thanksgiving. The students from the other class will have previously learned how to make corn husk dolls. They will then partner off with someone from my class and will teach them the story of the corn husk dolls and . . . teach them how to make one. By having the other class tell the story out loud, the students will be able to see how the Indians usually passed on their stories orally and not in written language. Each partner group will discuss what the moral of the story was and then ask another group to tell their version of the story. Most likely, the stories will be somewhat different and the students will be able to see how oral stories can become distorted if they are continually passed down. The teacher will then explain that, to prevent this from happening, the Indians often had storytellers who were really good at telling their own stories but also at telling the traditional stories accurately.

The students will read both versions of *The First Thanksgiving* . . . and the teacher will finish *If You Sailed on the Mayflower* . . . then *The Thanksgiving Story* . . . and ask the students how it was different from what they had learned in the past few days. . . . At the end of the day (the students will be informed that the First Thanksgiving actually lasted three days), "Captain Standish" and "Squanto" will decide to write a peace treaty between the Wampanoag Indians and the newcomers. Both classes will collaborate and write in the treaty what they feel are important issues.

The students are empowered in the continuous application of what they research and learn. History is not left untouched or regarded as sacrosanct; it is understood, deconstructed, and revamped from a socially conscious agenda.

Part 7: "The Thanksgiving celebrations since then" (Day 9) compares and contrasts how Thanksgiving celebrations have changed throughout the decades.

They will discuss the foods and customs that their families celebrate, as well as the information that they learned this year and how it differed from years in the past. The students will read the "Thanksgiving Day" chapter of Celebration, which describes how Thanksgiving became a national holiday and how it has been celebrated through the years.

In this same part of the unit, students monitor the progress of their plants and write a letter to a person in the school for whom they are thankful.

As the final discussion, the teacher will read "Lin's first Thanksgiving" aloud. The story explains how a young girl from Vietnam interprets Thanksgiving by comparing it to her leaving Vietnam because of the new political power. The students and teacher will discuss Lin's story and the story of other immigrants and why they choose to move to America.

The class will end the day by discussing the fact that some people do not celebrate Thanksgiving simply because they have no family or money to do so. As a prearranged class trip, the students will then spend the rest of the afternoon working in a soup kitchen for the homeless. Their homework for the night will require them to reflect in their journals about the people that they met there and how they felt about it.

The students' learning is expanded cross-culturally through the above lesson and internalized in the reflective writing captured in the journal. Providing these kinds of experiences for elementary students fosters an experiential research opportunity that allows for the paradigms of inquiry to be transformed by what is being studied or experienced. In this way, it transcends the mechanical delivery of "proper methods" from methods professor to teacher education student.

Part 8: "Indian life now and human rights" (Day 10):

Today's class will wrap up the Thanksgiving unit, but will also provide a lead-in to a discrimination and human rights unit. . . . The students are shown a copy of the treaty signed by the newcomers and the Wampanoag Indians, as well as the one the students wrote in class. . . . The Pilgrims did not think that the Wampanoag Indians were equals because they found their religion and beliefs to be inferior. Even though they had endured religious persecution, they continued the cycle by inflicting oppression on others. The teacher will then talk about King Philip's War and how the two groups ended up killing each other with the death toll much higher on the Indian side.

Shine's students read and respond to the 1970 speech from the Thanksgiving ceremonials held annually at Plymouth Rock. They also analyze how different groups are treated unfairly and study actions that can be taken to oppose such injustice.

Today will also include a discussion of what Indian life is like now. We will talk about how Indians were forced onto reservations and the attitudes and stereotypes that people have about Indians. The students will reflect in their journals about how they feel about these issues and how they would feel if someone treated them like this.

Shine's unit provides a good flow and progression of information and experiences as she finishes the unit with relevant race relations in contemporary society. Ending with yet another goal, another pursuit, is the backbone of my research-oriented pedagogical model that empowers students to make learning a lifelong endeavor in and outside of the institution of school. Like McNeil, her consciousness of the role of research in pedagogy empowers her students to think and act in exciting ways.

Kristin L. Persichini's Thanksgiving Unit

Persichini's unit is structured completely differently, partitioned by themes flexibly overlapping during the two-week period. Her unit is designed for a middle-class fourth grade with children from diverse backgrounds. She provides a rationale for her unit:

> Our world is constantly changing, and therefore, I believe that our teaching strategies should also be changing in order to accommodate our learners.
>
> I have reached this conclusion only through many nights of struggling with right and wrong, traditional and non-traditional, accepted and perhaps a bit controversial teaching styles. However, after reflecting on my own learning experiences, I have finally realized why nothing in the area of history ever made sense or even interested me in all my years of school. Unfortunately, a movement of "information feeding" educators have created numerous generations of people who do not know anything about our country's history. The problems occur due to the obvious gap between the information being "taught" and the lives of those learning it. The material needs to be meaningful, and in order for this to happen the children have to be involved in the research of these facts. Simply, teachers should present crucial issues and children should actively research the issue as problematic situations which directly or indirectly affect their lives.
>
> Knowing this, I have constructed a unit on Thanksgiving entitled, "You're invited" . . . invited to a unified world composed of many differences. In this unit, I have asked the children, using the history of Thanksgiving as their focus problem, to investigate differences which are included in our world. . . .
>
> The children will begin each day of this two-week unit by expressing their feelings in a journal which will allow them to consistently reflect on their progress in beliefs. . . . They will be allowed to work on these activities as they wish throughout the unit as long as they complete them all by Thursday of the second week. At this time, the children will come together and discuss each activity as a group. These discussions will allow the students to discover new ideas from one another. These collaboration days can include anything from poetry readings, commercial reviews, and drama skits to food samples, sports activities, and song rounds. . . . The end of Friday will be dedicated to a "Thanksgiving feast" which recognizes a wide variety of cultural celebrations that occur throughout the year. In actuality, we will be giving thanks to our own individual family traditions and creating our own ideas of a Thanksgiving celebration.

The above situates her unit and her particular agenda for her students and demonstrates an acceptance of difference and an encouragement of students who are finding their own voice throughout the research and learning process. She has also made it a point to include the parents as much as possible for their cooperation and input. The students will look at mainstream Thanksgiving stories and then at other stories that have been marginalized by the western paradigm. Through a variety of experiences, the students will look critically at the knowledge that is usually presented to them as unquestionable. Persichini's activities are described under different subject areas; only a few will be highlighted.

Language Arts: The students will write about what they already know about Thanksgiving, including family traditions, historical knowledge, and personal concerns.

> After completing a written description of what Thanksgiving is to you, interact with a partner on the Internet and in the library to research another point of view pertaining to the history of Thanksgiving as we know it.

The students will also read *The True Story of the Three Little Pigs* by Jon Scieska, discuss it and compare the different versions of the same story in light of their research.

Science: Through the use of science, the students become active participants in their learning process, learning to utilize a variety of resources available to them.

> Locate a local farmer and interview him or her about agriculture within your community. Survey what crops are grown and then analyze their usefulness to your community as opposed to other areas. You may want to consider the effects of weather on the various crops.

Social Studies: This section expands the student's imagination and cross-cultural awareness.

> Pose an "I Wonder" question that you can research using any and all resources accessible to you. Please feel free to work with others that wonder the same thing you do. For example, if you wondered what type of activities the Amish participated in for fun, you may contract a person from this culture, surf the Internet, or read informational literature pertaining to Amish culture. Prepare an oral presentation of this newly gained knowledge for the gathering at the end of the unit.

Mathematics: The first assignment deals with entering the results from tomato experiments they were previously working on into Microsoft Excel in their computers. Two other assignments follow:

Get a partner and go to the media room. While there, watch 15 minutes of television. During this time, one of you keep track of how many times reference was made to male stereotypes, such as associating males with roughness or the stereotypical assumptions. The partner needs to keep track of references of female stereotypes such as a mother in the kitchen. After recording the results, discuss why these stereotypes are continually portrayed and where we are most likely to encounter them. Then, use your discussion to decide why such stereotypes as face painting and savage behavior are associated with Indians.

Design the ideal playground in your neighborhood. Be sure to specify the calculated area, or length times width, which this will take from your neighborhood. How do you think the people living in the house where the playground was just built felt when they lost their home so that children had a place to play? Now, look at a map of the land which the Indians once occupied. Mark what portion was originally taken from them. Be sure to specify the calculated area of this land using the proper scale from the map. How do you think the Indians felt when the Pilgrims showed up only to take their already cultivated land, as one story claims?

Health: Here the students will look at the stereotypical Thanksgiving dinner menu and analyze the nutritional value of the foods. They will also investigate the causes for the deaths in the "Trail of Tears" while identifying the unhealthy conditions which led to the deaths. Then Persichini poses:

Your best friend just admitted to you that he/she has been starving him/herself because of the extra weight put on over the summer. Does this "difference" seem like a problem? Explain. Should we treat those starving themselves differently because of their eating habits?

Physical Education: The students are instructed to:

Surf the Internet to find a site that discusses various dances common to the Indian culture. Watch the video footage and attempt to learn the dance in a sequence of short, simple steps. Collaborate ideas with others to come to a consensus of what role dance played in the Indian culture.

Again, we see the students exposed to the Internet so that they can have a plethora of information at their fingertips.

Music: The arts in general are given much attention in Persichini's unit as basic subjects offering a variety of experiences.

> Work in groups to establish an overall opinion of the benefits which result from a diversified community. Take these ideas and incorporate them into a song of any style that tells your story. Experiment with homemade musical instruments to enhance the performance.

Also, above improvisation is encouraged which is pivotal for fostering creativity.

> Discuss with others why music is or is not important in your life. Look at another culture's view of music and observe how music affects their lives. How do the differences between music in cultures affect our society? You may want to look at some issues including group interaction, home environment with or without music, and the communication skills of various groups.

Art: Through visual representation and imagery, Persichini focuses her lessons on identifying, deconstructing, and displacing dubious representations assigned to various groups.

> Often, Indians are stereotyped to wear head dresses and face paint. However, they are people just like you and me. They dress in clothing and do not make it a habit to paint their skin on a daily basis. Identify another stereotype found within a culture of interest to you. With the intent to put an end to such stereotypes, create a portrait of a member from this culture which illustrates the invalidity of the ideas currently held.
> Videotape a commercial which tells me how differences affect your lives and what the society looks like which makes you feel that "You are invited." Please be open with your ideas and share the rationale to your beliefs. After this is completed, attempt to create a commercial that depicts the way the Indians felt when differences entered their society. Why were the reactions conflicting between your ideas and the Indian's ideas?

Drama: The lessons and activities planned for this section recognize the need for fourth graders to kinesthetically express themselves as well as emphasizing other ways of knowing.

> Create a skit which portrays the story of Thanksgiving that you created in this two-week period. Feel free to be creative with language, costumes, personalities, and roles. "Different" interpretations of his holiday are welcome. Make it a goal to give us an inside view of your Thanksgiving celebration.

Play charades with a group of peers that depict the typical stereotypes involving gender, culture, race, attitude, and socioeconomic status. After using stereotypes, take interesting facts that you have learned within this unit that disprove these assumptions and attempt to act them out.

Finally, during the last day of the unit, we will all contribute our own traditional family gatherings to an "Around the world" dinner feast. By doing this, we will be able to rewrite our own stories of the Thanksgiving feast. Hopefully, this culminating activity will provide a sense of being "invited" for all of the members of this learning experience.

It is Persichini's belief that students would experience a substantial amount of success given the flexibility and freedom permeating the unit. She states, "Overall, I hope that this learning experience will open up the children's minds to many views of stories and also encourage them to problematize traditional stories which have previously been taken for granted. Persichini also offers the following websites for further research:

http://www.night.net/thanksgiving/lesson-plan.html "Teaching About Thanksgiving"

http://media3.com/plymouth/thanksgiving.html "The Truth About the Pilgrims and Thanksgiving"

http://www.census.gov/ftp/pub/edu/diversity/llele.html "Creating Our Nation's Diversity"

http://www.census.gov/ftp/pub/edu/diversity/divtext.html "Our Diverse Nation"

gopher://ericir.syr.edu:70/0R0-14688-/Lesson/Subject/LanguageArts /ceclang.37 "Spiro Mounds"

gopher://ericir.syr.edu:70/0R0-1765-/Lesson/NewLesson/SocialStudies /diversity "Diversity of Cultures in America"

gopher://ericir.syr.edu:70/0R0-5087-/Lesson/Subject/SocialStudies /cecsst.82 "Native American Interdisciplinary Educational Unit"

http://www.eduplace.com/ss/act/wonder.html "What's the Wonder?"

http://www.eduplace.com/ss/act/celtime.html "A Celebration Timeline"

http://raven.ccukans.edu/kansite/ww_one/comment/Cmrts/Cmrt3.html "Portraying the Indian"

http://www.minnetonka.k12mn.us/support/science/lesson45/thanks.html "Thanksgiving Unit"

http://www.eduplace.com/ss/act/fabric.html "The Fabrics of Our Lives"

http://pc65.frontier.osrhe.edu/students/plumleyo/cloth.html "Women's Southern Cloth"

http://pc65.frontier.osrhe.edu/students/plumleyo/straight.html "Men's Southern Straight Dance"
http://one-web.org/oneida/lacrosse.html "Lacrosse: An Iroquois Tradition"
http://www.si.edu/organiza/museums/amerind/edu/eduschol.html "School Programs"
http://www.si.edu/organiza/museums/amerind/exhibit/index.html "Exhibitions"

CONCLUSION: THE POWER OF STUDENT RESEARCH

In order to summarize the three units we have delineated in this chapter, we will list the strengths and highlights that all three units share that make them such powerful pedagogical documents. The list contains the components to successful student researcher frameworks that are applicable to any subject or grade level. The list is as follows:

1. Research expertise.
2. Deconstruct/question/compare/contrast.
3. Utilization of multiple resources.
4. Experientials/multiple, varied experiences
5. Expanding knowledge (traditional)/focusing on other ways of knowing.
6. Exploring other's consciousness.
7. Interdisciplinary focus.
8. Consciousness of students' needs.
9. Studying bias, stereotypes, culture, and tradition.
10. Emphasizing cross-cultural definitions.
11. Journaling—a respect for the need of private self-expression resulting in heightened learning, reflection, analytic skills, and empowerment.
12. Inviting speakers, family members, and other classes.
13. Focusing on multifaceted, kinesthetic, emotional, intellectual, and artistic expression and development.
14. Encouraging respect for and demystification of difference.

McNeil's, Shine's, and Pesichini's Thanksgiving units model the use of research in elementary education. These three young women were teacher education student researchers conceptualizing, writing about, and creating conditions for their students to become researchers. These teacher education students experienced and practiced the research and pedagogical skills they will apply in their classrooms. They and many of their fellow classmates, whom we are unable to mention here, prove that teachers who are intepreters and knowledge producers are better equipped to become inspirational teachers. Particularly impressive in their curricular plans is their savvy about the controversial nature of Thanksgiving as a scholarly topic and the politicized nature of schooling. In all three units, the students were able to use research as a means of defusing the volatility of their lessons. None of them can be accused of indoctrination or politicization, since they allow their students as researchers to find differing perspectives on the ideological meaning of Thanksgiving as part of their inquiry process.

One of the central tenets of any critical democratic social studies—whether it be in graduate school, college, secondary, or in this case, elementary education—involves the ability to conduct research. Critical teachers provide students with the skills and space to do it, interpret it, use it, and continuously change it within different contexts. As much as student abilities allow, critical social studies teachers acquaint students with secondary research skills in libraries, book and magazine outlets, and the Internet. In the same way, they acquaint students with primary research methods, including historical, ethnographic, semiotic, textual, and other processes of producing original knowledge. We argue that such methods can be taught to all students, even young elementary students. The ability to perform research provides students with a cognitive skill immeasurably important in all phases of life. It grants them a historicity and a contextual appreciation of learning that no other skill can furnish. As a result students (and their teachers) experience the empowerment that many pedagogies only reference in the abstract. They are empowered by what they can do and what they know. Doors are opened to new ways of seeing that expand the cognitive envelope and move human beings to new levels of consciousness.

Many thanks to Penn State education students Elizabeth McNeil, Melissa Shine, and Kristin L. Persichini.

Chapter

Teachers Researching Localities in Social Studies Education: An Example— The History of Education in Shreveport, Louisiana*

The ability of teachers to conduct research is central to the democratic social studies advocated in this book. In addition to the numerous advantages already delineated concerning the value of teacher (and student) research, this chapter provides yet another benefit. Whenever I have moved to a new teaching location, I have modified my research agenda to include an exploration of the social, cultural, economic, political, geographical, educational and historical dynamics of the new place. Not only does such work ground me in the forces shaping the locality in which I am living, but it also helps me understand the schools in which I'm working and the students I'm teaching.

While teaching in Louisiana, I discovered that few of my colleagues in the college of education knew much about the area's educational history. When it came to African American education, few individuals in the university had any knowledge at all. Understanding these dynamics, I buried myself in numerous historical archives. I was attempting to use my historical research abilities to construct a story of education in Shreveport and Caddo Parish that could help my students understand

---

* In this chapter references are arranged in the endnote format. In historical research where archived documents and other primary sources are used, this form of source documentation is less intrusive to the textual flow that the parenthetical motif used elsewhere in this book.

how education and larger sociopolitical forces had interacted to shape contemporary institutions in the area. When I completed my work, I found, much to my delight, that I could integrate the knowledge I had gained in a variety of ways and for many different purposes in every class I taught. Students who read the material gained an enhanced sense of place (Kincheloe & Pinar, 1991) and were able to connect the insights gleaned to their own social education and pedagogy. Such observations convinced me that my hard work was well worth the time investment.

I present the following history of education in Shreveport and Caddo Parish as a model for the types of "place research" that social studies teachers can conduct anywhere. Histories of local places can inspire and move students in profound and surprising ways.

THE NINETEENTH CENTURY ORIGINS OF EDUCATION IN SHREVEPORT AND CADDO PARISH—THE PRIVATE ACADEMIES

The history of education in the South has often been marked by neglect and provincialism. The results of neglect are obvious, and much work remains to be undertaken on the nature and meaning of the Southern educational experience. The results of the provincialism are less obvious to many observers. Many of the works on Southern history of education have actually been chronological accounts of White people's schooling, Blacks being rarely mentioned except as obstacles to White progress.[1] Flawed by racist assumptions and an obsession with "firsts" (the first school, the first graduates, the first superintendent, etc.), these provincial works portray only a partial and often inaccurate view of the Southern educational experience. State and local educational histories have suffered the most from this provincialism, and the educational histories of Louisiana and Caddo Parish are no exceptions.

Founded in the late 1830s, Shreveport quickly became the commercial center of Caddo Parish. From its founding until the Civil War, the port city was often viewed as a hangout for mean-spirited steamboat men, toughs, and drifters.[2] Dance halls, saloons, and gambling dens were reported to outnumber more reputable business establishments, and in the very early days of the city righteous observers were shocked by the absence of churches.[3] In this environment, survival was the main concern of the pioneers, and, as a result, education, in the formal sense of the term, was viewed as a low priority.

Within only a few years after incorporation, various factors began to change the social and cultural structure of the town. By the beginning of the Civil War in 1861, Shreveport was more "cultured" and more metropolitan than most early residents and observers would have believed. Nevertheless, the "rough and tumble" aspect of the city remained, causing subsequent historians to refer to the "dual personality" of early Shreveport. This municipal schizophrenia must be taken into account when attempting to understand the educational expression of the young city.

The schizophrenia involved the diverse people who migrated to Shreveport in those early years and the different and sometimes clashing needs they expected the town to address. Indeed, the concerns of the steamboat men, gamblers, drifters and prostitutes who called frontier Shreveport home in the 1830s, 1840s, and 1850s were very different from the family-oriented "men on the make."

These respectable types along with their wives and families struggled with the "baser elements," as they were called, for social and political supremacy. The establishment of order and stability became priorities for the upwardly mobile citizens of Shreveport, as they struggled to set up their businesses, professional practices, trades, churches, and farms.[4] As they began to win the battle for social and political dominance, they caught glimpses of the new world in which their children would live. In this new world of respectability, formal education would play an important role. In addition to providing skills of literacy, it would provide the veneer of culture that would visibly separate the respectable types from their social inferiors. Thus, the town's dual personality moved the townspeople to establish formal institutions of learning to supplement the informal (non-school) education provided by apprenticeships, on-the-job training, the church, and the home.

The academies established by the early Shreveporters were basically privately funded and privately supported. Contrary to traditional historical assumptions, however, there were antebellum Southern supporters of public education. Indeed, in some Southern cities, public school systems flourished before the Civil War. Shreveport was one of these cities. To begin with, the town's youth and frontier demeanor worked against a public system of schools. Furthermore, Shreveport's population (in 1850, the population was only 1,728) was not sufficient to produce a large urban underclass which threatened the upwardly mobile townspeople. In cities like Mobile and Savannah, public school supporters promoted schooling as a way to improve the bad manners and to elevate the morals of such "undesirables," many of whom were immigrants.[5] While the population of antebellum Shreveport included immigrants from many places, there were not enough of them to cause alarm.

Nevertheless, the academies in Shreveport did derive minor benefits from the efforts of Louisiana reformers to promote publicly supported education. Agitation for state aid to education in Louisiana had existed intermittently since territorial days. Throughout the antebellum era, funds were sporadically appropriated for education. Sometimes coming from the sale of public lands, sometimes from lotteries, the funds were granted to privately managed academies. Caddo Academy was one such recipient. Formed in 1838, the academy received a building appropriation of $1,500 from the state. In typical fashion, the state grants had ended by 1842, when education money was retrenched.

In 1845, a new state constitution was adopted which mandated the formation of free public schools. Based on this constitutional requirement, the Louisiana legislature passed the first free school act in 1847, and a special session of the legislature in December of 1848 authorized the appropriation of $550,000 for the support of free schools. Because of its rural character, Shreveport benefited very little from such educational activity. Private academies receiving minimal state grants would remain the order of the day until the Civil War.[6]

Determining what went on in the academies and who attended them is sometimes obscured by the school experiences of contemporary observers. The nineteenth-century use of the terms, "colleges" and "academies", is different from the meanings ascribed to them by moderns. It was hard, for example, to distinguish the academy from the college in the nineteenth century. There was a tendency for the college to admit a slightly older student and to present a little more advanced curriculum. But this can in no way be assumed. Academies admitted students as young as nine and colleges graduated students as young as fifteen. There are examples of students over the age of 30 being admitted to both institutions. As far as the average age is concerned, we have no clear picture of the typical student. It is important to note that, since academies were seen as an alternative to college rather than a preparation for college, academy students could come in a variety of ages and could enter at a variety of levels.[7]

A. H. Leonard was 11 years old when he entered George Wyche Rives' Classical Academy in Shreveport in 1850. Judging from the experience of Leonard and other students, the academies in Shreveport were generally populated by youngsters in their early to mid-teens. Like other pupils, Leonard came to school when his parents could spare him and the money. The financial burden of academy attendance was not the result of tuition. Indeed, tuition at Rives' Classical Academy was only one dollar per month. The monetary costs of an academy education in the 1850s involved the removal of the youth from the marketplace and the resulting loss of income. These lost earnings, rather than the expense of tuition, limited academy education to middle and upper-middle income people.[8]

Leonard entered Rives' Academy as an ambitious, highly motivated student but quickly was faced with the realities of academic life in the 1850s. The academies were rough places, and a young scholar had to contend with establishing his place in the pecking order to avoid constant trouble. As an old man, Leonard described the ridicule and laughter he faced during his first few days at the school. "My school mates," he wrote, "soon saw that I was . . . a thing for laughter, scorn, and jeers . . . and they 'socked it' to me."

Soon the verbal abuse turned to physical abuse. At first, Leonard withheld retaliation, having been taught that "fighting was a deadly sin." But when an older and larger boy argued with Leonard, and "finding words inadequate to express his emotions," slapped Leonard's face, Leonard expressed his rage physically. "I knew nothing about fighting," he wrote, "but I could and did hit, scratch, and kick with some effect." Though he lost the fight, Leonard established himself as a fighter and a boy willing to defend his interests at school. Thereafter, he disregarded his early training, fought just as the other boys did, and, much to his satisfaction, was admitted to "the fraternity of bad boys."[9] Thus, the "hidden curriculum" in the early Shreveport academies did not reward young scholars but pushed them to forsake scholarship for peer acceptance—a situation common to schools in any era.

The formal curriculum of the Shreveport academies, of course, had a very different intent. Academies found their origins in the eighteenth century and were conceived on the premise that there was a need for an institution which offered practical and modern courses. Such an institution would offer a distinct alternative to college education which emphasized the classical. But this new type of practical academy was not to be.

In the first place, teachers and parents wanted a classical curriculum in the academies. Classical education, with its emphasis on Latin and

Greek, was the essence of an elite education, and that was exactly what the parents of most academy students wanted for their children. Secondly, few teachers were equipped to teach practical or modern subjects. Texts in subjects like botany and trigonometry appeared late in the academy period and emphasized that which could be memorized rather than that which could be put to use. It can be concluded that in those infrequent occasions when practical subjects were offered, they were not very practical. And finally, most academies stressed a classical curriculum because it was inexpensive. Modern and practical courses required surveying equipment and laboratories. Because of the classical orientation of the colleges, almost any man with some college experience could teach Greek and Latin. Also, the classical academy could get by with one faculty member, since an educated man was expected to know all the classical subjects.[10] Their need for faculty and materials minimized by the classical curriculum, the underfunded academies could survive even in frontier areas such as Shreveport in the 1850s.

When A. H. Leonard entered Rives' Classical Academy in 1850 he faced memorization and recitation exercises in Latin, math, grammar, history, and geography. When he quit school a couple of years later, he could "spell and define words very well and write legibly." According to Leonard, he had mastered Andrew and Stoddard's Latin grammar, read Virgil, Caesar, and part of Sallust, and had made his way through Emerson's *Arithmetic* to cube roots.[11]

Although there were curricular differences (especially between male and female programs), the course of study Leonard undertook was similar in other Shreveport and Caddo Parish academies. In the North Louisiana Collegiate institute, located two miles outside of Shreveport, students studied the typical classical curriculum with its emphasis on ancient language, grammar, mathematics, and history. Directed by the Rev. S. P. Helme, who founded the school in the early 1850s, the academy "strictly limited" the number of pupils admitted and charged extra for the teaching of French, Italian, and Spanish.

The Providence Academy located two miles west of Spring Ridge in Caddo Parish operated as a boarding school before the Civil War. Headed by Charles E. Crawford, who was only an honorary graduate of the Baptist College of Mississippi, the academy charged its students a boarding fee of ten dollars a month. In typical fashion, students had to pay an extra charge for each course taken. For orthography (spelling) and reading, students were charged $2.50; for primary arithmetic, $3.00; for Latin, Greek and mathematics, $4.00.[12]

A. H. Leonard's story is typical of the students of the academy, and his experiences highlight the experiences of many of his contemporaries. His family background was typical of those upwardly mobile families who formed the core of support for the academies. Leonard's father was a steamboat captain from Mobile, Alabama, who, at the urging of his wife, gave up his career for a life which allowed him more time at home. Hard working and desiring respectability, the elder Leonard took a job in 1850 as the manager of the Palmetto Hotel in Shreveport. As a man who wanted success for himself and his children in the evolving young town, the senior Leonard sensed a need for the academy.

The Leonard family's view of education and schooling is very interesting on many levels. In the first place, the family valued learning for its own sake. Like many other academy students, A. H. Leonard had received an intensive home education before entering Rives' Classical Academy in 1850. "My sister Cecilia," Leonard wrote, "taught me to read, write, and spell." After learning the rudiments of reading, Leonard sophisticated his skills and "developed a passion for books which has never been satisfied." During his life, he read, in his words, thousands of books. As one studies Leonard's memoirs, his self-education becomes obvious since his knowledge, writing skill, and recognition of subtlety far surpass the academic abilities of a person with less than three years of formal schooling.

By the time he entered the academy, Leonard was an emerging scholar. His formal academic experience could not compete with the quality of his home schooling and subsequent self-education. Indeed, his most important concern in the academy was self-preservation. Thus, in his own mind, Leonard separated schooling from the concept of education. Discussing Sir Francis Bacon, Leonard praises the Englishman's revolt against the formalistic and impractical scholastic education of the European universities. He laments Bacon's lack of success, concluding that "it is still true that educators do not educate."[13]

In the eyes of Leonard and his family, therefore, learning was intrinsically important, but the school was not the best place to pursue it. The curriculum of the academy was staid and impractical, but nevertheless important. The academy achieved its importance not academically but socially. However superficial the classical training in the Shreveport academies may have been, it provided students with access to classical knowledge. And classical knowledge served as a badge of culture and refinement.

The ability to make classical allusions became a necessary skill for public speakers, for a knowledge of the classics proved the speaker's credibility. This classical veneer became a means of access to the professions and the leadership roles that nineteenth-century American society considered the province of the educated. Thus, the training of the academies was important in a very practical way that had little to do with the pursuit of knowledge: The academies provided a ticket to social status.

While the Leonard family needed that ticket, more aristocratic families did not. They had already arrived at their destination. The academies were often condescendingly viewed as annoyances by the elite in Caddo Parish society. Aristocratic planters in the area viewed education as a matter of family responsibility. Accordingly, they hired private tutors for their children and on occasion sent them to school back East.[14]

Such aristocratic behavior illustrates an important aspect of the antebellum academies in Shreveport and Caddo Parish. The academies did not cater to the aristocrats but were vehicles for social and economic mobility in the ambitious middle-income members of northwest Louisiana society. The academies held no pretensions in the creation of a Louisiana aristocracy. The academies prepared the professional classes to assume their positions in late nineteenth century Shreveport society. Businessmen, doctors, educators, lawyers, ministers, and politicians received their culture in the academies.[15] Most of these men assumed their positions by work, not by birth. The academy was a necessary step in their mobility.

Nineteenth Century Women's Education: The Obligations of Womanhood

Women in antebellum Shreveport also needed the veneer of culture that formal education could provide, but their veneer, of course, was different. In the antebellum period, women's role was well-defined and quite rigid. In the minds of both men and women, the ideal female role involved an identifiable list of chores: to fill the world with children; to educate those children; to instill religion, virtue, and chivalric principles in those around her; to encourage other women to be commendable and feminine; to assist her husband in his plans for the social advancement of their family; to mend his bad temper by her perseverance and gentleness;

and to make the home a happy refuge for him.[16] Antebellum academy education for women can only be understood in the context of this list of feminine obligations.

Many of the academies which were open exclusively for women were teaching a curriculum similar to the male curriculum by the 1850s. The main differences between these academies and the male academies was the addition of special domestic courses for the females. Other female academies made a concerted attempt to provide a very different course of study from their male counterparts. These academies sought to provide improvement in the household arts, such as sewing, embroidery, piano, etiquette, and other social graces.[17]

Whether the academy was pursuing a classical or a domestic curriculum, the purpose was to make women better homemakers, mothers, or wives, and, maybe, even better, elementary teachers. Ever fearful that education would strip women of their femininity, the educators were quick to point out that education would add to, not subtract from, the feminine character.[18] Education will not change women, they argued. Indeed, feminine learning will make for a better society, it was agreed, because educated women will be better home managers and will serve their families more effectively.

During the push for social respectability by the upwardly mobile Shreveporters of the 1850s, female academies sprouted up around town. A Professor Bernard opened both a male and a female academy in 1856, while, at approximately the same time, the Cottage Grove Female Seminary was founded with Miss Louisa M. Ricksas, principal. Just before the war, more female academies opened, and women continued to attend the academies during the hostilities.[19]

The Cottage Grove Female Seminary is a good example of an academy which emphasized the household arts. The school told parents that "Domestic Science" was a "leading feature" of Cottage Grove. The academy emphasized "system, neatness, and regularity" and promised to help women fit into their divinely sanctioned role as a "helpmate for man" who makes a happy home and sheds "a halo of joy and peace on each family circle."[20]

The Daughters of the Cross opened a female academy in 1860 which not only emphasized the domestic arts but academic subjects as well. Spelling, reading, writing, arithmetic, geography, etymology, rhetoric, astronomy, and philosophy were all included in this parochial curriculum.[21] The Catholic schools founded in the years following the war continued this curricular tradition. In 1868, St. Vincent's Academy provided Domestic Arts as well as English, French, Latin, mathematics, science, history, and astronomy. Other area schools for women, including Mansfield Female College, offered a classical academic curriculum which emphasized courses in the Bible, spelling, reading, writing, grammar, arithmetic, algebra, history, mythology, Latin, and botany. Again, the point is illustrated that the designations, "college" and "academy", denoted little difference.[22]

These academic experiences for women reflected broader changes in the social role of women in American life. The Shreveport female academies were designed to uphold a social order where women held a domestic role. The academy founders and teachers did not realize that they were contributing to a larger social revolution that would lead to an altered perception of women's place in the world.

The changes in women's role, of course, would not occur immediately, nor would they come about as a direct result of their academic education within the academies. Like their male counterparts, women in the academies were subjected to rote-based methodologies where memorization and recitation for competitive daily grades were the order of the school day. Such methods did not encourage women to engage in independent critical thought or to ask questions about their subservient social conditions. Rote memorization and recitation had a stifling effect on male academy students as well; but, with men, such academic experiences probably had some type of instrumental value. In preparing the sons of the ambitious for professional roles, the unthinking repetitive training of the academies provided discipline and practice in the work habits required for monetary success.

What benefit did this academic training provide women? On a broader social level, the academic experiences of the academy possibly hastened the time when women would be viewed as the intellectual equals of males. If women could handle the more rigorous academic subjects, they were probably not as intellectually inferior as many people thought. On a more personal level, the lessons of the academy were less significant. The academic training was probably more of an escape from the lived world than a preparation for it. While the women studied Latin and history, they were expected to remain aloof from the political issues of their day; to do otherwise would be too unfeminine.

One of the few outlets in antebellum Shreveport for a woman who wanted to use her academic training involved elementary education.

Before the public school movement in Shreveport, elementary education was a private affair for those who could afford it or for those who could provide it themselves. With the emergence of the female academies in the 1850s, more and more of the women teachers possessed an academic background. After a stint at the academy, many young women used their training to teach their own children or younger brothers and sisters at home. Some opened small schools in their homes where neighbor children could come for a hour or so of reading and writing a day. With the rise of the Caddo Parish public schools in the 1880s, some of these female academy graduates would step into public school positions.[23]

RACIAL GHOSTS: EDUCATION'S STRANGE FRUIT IN THE CIVIL WAR AND RECONSTRUCTION

Though many of the Caddo Parish academies continued to operate during the Civil War, the upheaval of the period would change the nature of education in Shreveport permanently. While the war affected most aspects of Shreveport life, the residents of the town attempted to carry on life as usual. This was easier for Shreveporters to accomplish than for many of their fellow Southerners because the ravages and horror of the war did not touch Shreveport as it did other parts of the South. Shreveporters who did not serve in the military often did not understand firsthand the reality of the Civil War.[24]

Confederate political authority remained intact and was supported by Shreveporters throughout the war. Pro-Confederacy Democrats retained control of the city and parish governments from succession to surrender, and Shreveport government officials refused to cooperate with the federally controlled "puppet regimes" in New Orleans. Even after the war ended in the west, Shreveport had to wait two weeks for federal troops to occupy the city. Mayor Jonathan L. Gooch and his city governmental officials did not resign when the troops entered the city and even remained in power after the troops established control. In other words, Shreveport continued to be controlled by men from the same well-to-do families who had governed before the war.

With the support of political leaders in Shreveport, state officials attempted to "win the peace" by putting Louisiana society back together in its prewar arrangement. In November of 1865, the legislature passed Black Codes, which limited the freedom of the emancipated slaves and severely infringed on their political liberties. After the failure of the

Louisiana legislature to grant Blacks the right to vote and the killing of Blacks in the infamous New Orleans riot in July of 1866, the actions of the Louisianans were perceived to be defiant and belligerent. In the minds of many Northerners, a response was demanded. That response would take on the form of the passage of the First Reconstruction Act of March, 1867 which placed Louisiana under military rule.[25]

Shreveport, however, was again unlike the rest of the state. Even after Gen. Phillip Sheridan imposed an appointed government on the rest of Louisiana, Shreveport retained White Democratic government. While Shreveport's Democratic leaders were forced to compromise their "conservative" principles as they cooperated with the military occupation, they retained their offices until 1871. In that year, the Louisiana Legislature passed legislation which did away with Shreveport's Board of Trustees and established Republican rule in the city. It was at this point that the political and racial hatreds of Shreveporters were raised to their highest level. These hatreds would affect Shreveport politics, social relationships, and education for decades.[26]

Though the framers of the Louisiana Constitution of 1864 provided the legal structure for public schooling, the dominant Whites in the early years of Louisiana Reconstruction had strong reservations about publicly supported education. *The Shreveport Times* explicitly stated the conservative position on the social role of government arguing that "we are . . . opposed to governmental charity in any shape. The province of government is not the dispensation of charity."[27] Education at the public expense was considered charity.

Governor James Madison Wells, in his 1865 message to the legislature, advocated the abolition of public education outside of New Orleans. Public education in north Louisiana had little support from either the state government or the north Louisianans themselves. Most Louisiana citizens, Shreveporters included, were especially uninterested in education during the period surrounding the end of the war. Their thoughts were directed toward rebuilding their lives and their war-shattered economies.[28]

Not only did education, and especially public education, at the end of the war suffer from popular indifference, but there was often active opposition to it. During Andrew Johnson's presidential Reconstruction in 1865 and 1866, opposition was so great that few public schools existed outside of New Orleans and Baton Rouge.[29] The opposition came from several sources. The aristocratic planters had traditionally resisted appropriating money for public education or, as they called it, pauper education. They never balked, however, at appropriating money for private instruction at their own plantations.[30]

On the other hand, poor people were often opposed to public education, as they needed all the labor their children could provide during the planting, growing, and harvest seasons. Teachers noticed that, sometimes, when the children of poor illiterate parents gained merely the barest rudiments of reading and writing, they were immediately removed from school and declared to possess sufficient education.[31] Important opposition also came from religious sources. The Catholic clergy were opposed to all public education, and, in Louisiana, such resistance carried significant political weight. Even the Presbyterians argued against public education on the grounds that public institutions were "Godless," filled with disorderly and corrupt ruffians, and that Presbyterians had an obligation to educate their own.[32]

The most important opposition emerged as a result of radical Reconstruction in Louisiana. After March of 1867, the process of readmission to the Union underwent great changes as the first of Reconstruction Act was passed, imposing military rule on the South. Shreveporters were depressed by the change of policy. A bulletin published in Shreveport immediately after the passage of the first Reconstruction Act summed up the feelings of many White Shreveporters when it described the city as enveloped in "rain, snow, sleet, frost, and gloom."[33]

Schooling was looked upon as one of the key elements of Radical Reconstruction. It would "Americanize" the Southerner just as it was supposed to do with the poor and the immigrants in the North. Schooling would discipline the Southern "delinquents" in the same way it disciplined the rowdy poor of the North. Not only would Northern reformist education bring the Southerners "back in line," but it would also solve the vexing race question. Education, the Radicals naively assumed, would bestow culture and learning on Black people, and, as a result, Whites would quickly accept the Freedmen as social equals. The stains of racial hatred and prejudice were far harder to remove than the Radicals suspected. Thus, the schools were doomed to failure as they embarked on a mission which they were unequipped to accomplish. Indeed, the attempt would evoke resentment that would last for generations.[34]

The coming of Radical government in Louisiana brought the adoption of the Constitution of 1868 which required at least one public school in each parish. Much to the consternation of the White people of Caddo Parish and the rest of the state, these schools were open to both Blacks and Whites. A system of school administration based on an urban northern model was established for the state. Under the new setup each police jury ward was designated as a separate school district, and the parishes were charged with levying a school tax to supplement the funds provided by state taxes. Such an administrative system was more elaborate than the small number of schools required.

Thus, the schools were saddled with a bureaucracy requiring paperwork and reports unnecessary in small towns and rural areas. School personnel in Shreveport during the Reconstruction period were constantly asking for more forms to facilitate the filing of reports to the state superintendent. Caddo school officials regularly complained to state officials about the mandated weekly and monthly reports, arguing that, without clerical help, it was impossible to complete the reports on time. Reports were late or never filed, and excuses for late filing were creative. The Caddo Parish Police Jury was charged with identifying educable children in the Parish between the ages of 6 and 16. They also were required to estimate the amount of money that would be needed to educate the children. The exercise was futile; the funds would never come.[35] Educational bureaucracy had to come to Caddo Parish.[36]

Radical school superintendent Thomas W. Conway attempted to enforce compulsory school attendance for children between the ages of 8 and 14 in 1868. He was unsuccessful because of the general indifference of the citizens to education and, most importantly, the requirement that the schools be open to children of both races. In Caddo and other parishes, local officials were required to levy taxes to support the schools. In reality, however, police juries did not levy taxes for schools. In the rare cases when they did, tax collectors refused to collect them.[37]

White parents in Shreveport and Caddo Parish simply would not send their children to racially mixed schools. Moreover, the citizens adopted a general policy of noncooperation with public schools associated with the Radical governments. Indicative of this policy was the refusal of the prominent citizens of Caddo Parish to serve in school board positions.

Unwilling to cooperate with Blacks and Republicans, the Whites left school board positions vacant or occupied by recently freed slaves who had yet to acquire literacy skills. "We must have someone there on the board besides Mr. Powell that can read and write," wrote District Education Superintendent James McCleery to Thomas W. Conway in the summer of 1870. Samuel J. Powell, president of the Bayou Sara school board in Caddo Parish, had previously told McCleery that the election of a secretary and treasurer of the board was postponed because no one on the board could read and write well enough to do these jobs.[38]

In order to engender any public interest in education, the Caddo schoolmen had to give the public the impression that they were working to thwart the Radical goals for public education. Powell told McCleery that he had generated some interest in education in Caddo by offering the possibility of racially segregated schools. Powell asked McCleery to forsake the Radical goal of racially integrated schools.

> . . . with an assurance from you to me and from me to them that there will be no attempt to mix the school, I have induced some of our best men . . . to accept the school [school board] appointments. I am laboring under disadvantages, as you must know, having no one on the Board besides myself who could spell *education* without prompting, and as a necessary consequence entirely and utterly unfit for the positions assigned them.[39]

Thus, like many of their White brothers and sisters around the South, Shreveporters often claimed that they would abandon the public schools before they would go to school with Blacks.[40] With racial attitudes so polarized, the Radical attempt to establish integrated schools evoked some of the most vile rhetoric Shreveport had ever heard. The carpetbaggers and scalawags were hated, and the schools of the period were associated with their efforts to bring about racial equality. The carpetbaggers were best represented by the Freedmen's Bureau and the Bureau was best represented by its schools. The Whites considered the Bureau schools a threat because they provided agitators an opportunity to excite the freedmen with promises of equality.[41]

Some of the Whites in Caddo Parish responded to the threat violently. The White League was formed in Caddo Parish during the period and was championed by *The Shreveport Times*. Dedicated to White supremacy and unafraid to use violence to achieve it, the White League attempted to free which Louisianans from "the polluting embraces of such a hybrid pack of lecherous pimps as Kellogg [Reconstruction governor of Louisiana] . . ., Durrell [Reconstruction federal circuit judge] . . . and their followers who were conceived in sin, brought forth in pollution, nursed by filthy horbies . . . ."[42]

Some Whites in Caddo used terrorist tactics to overthrow the Reconstruction regime. Threats against freedmen, lynchings, intimidation of Black voters, and violence against White Republicans were in evidence in the parish throughout the era. Justifying their actions on the grounds of racial superiority and on the claim that they were being robbed blind by the Radicals, violent members of Shreveport society fought carpetbaggers and their education until the restoration of White-controlled government in 1877.[43]

In the meantime, the White Shreveporters who could afford it continued sending their children to the private academies. An editorial in *The Daily Southwestern*, published in Shreveport, recommended that private education continue in light of the prevailing social circumstances.

> We cannot trust solely to the advantages of a common school system in a population so sparse as ours, nor can we wait on the logic of events to settle the question of mixed schools. We must hope that the already established schools [the academies] of this section may continue to merit a liberal home patronage.[44]

The academies during the Reconstruction Era would be more important than private institutions would ever be again. The White resistance to Reconstruction gave rise to new academies which carried on the same academic traditions as the antebellum academies. In both the antebellum and postbellum academies in Caddo Parish, little permanence and stability existed. Academies came and went capriciously, their survival usually resting on whether or not the founder chose to remain in the area.

In 1870 several academies existed: the Caddo Academy, Shreveport Female Institute, Dodd's Institute for Females, German School, Catholic Female School of the Daughters of the Cross, and St. Vincent's. Female.[45] Established soon thereafter was the Thatcher Military Institute. The most prestigious academy in the postbellum period, Capt. George E. Thatcher's military institute catered to Shreveport's well-to-do.

> The school was patronized by the influential people of the city, and the alumni of this school are today prominent in the professional, business and social life of the city, parish, state and nation. . . . The teachers of this school . . . all played prominent parts in the school and the social life of the city.[46]

Combined with Thatcher's military training, French, Latin, Greek, history, mathematics, and sciences reflected the classical curricula of the antebellum academies.[47] Catholic education was an important component of Shreveport's formal education for White people during Reconstruction. In addition to the Catholic Female School founded in

1860 by the Daughters of the Cross, St. Vincent's Academy was founded by the Daughters of the Cross in 1868. St. Vincent's prospered in the late 1860s and early 1870s, as boarding school and day school enrollments increased. Like other schools in the town in 1873, St. Vincent's was closed because of the disastrous yellow fever epidemic. Unlike some other institutions, however, St. Vincent's survived and resumed classes in the spring of 1874. Combining Catholic religious instruction with classical studies and domestic sciences, St. Vincent's provided women with a four-year course of study. Courses included religion, English, French, Latin, mathematics, science, history, astronomy, philosophy, plain needlework, embroidery, piano, voice, art, etiquette, and the "social graces."[48]

Thus, Shreveporters with sufficient financial resources continued to rely on private education from the academies during the days they described as "the times that try men's souls." The souls of Black Shreveporters had been tried for a long time, however, when they faced the daily regimen of slave life. The Reconstruction period offered Blacks new hope fro freedom and an improvement in the quality of their lives. From the perspective of Reconstruction leaders in Louisiana and Caddo Parish and of the Blacks themselves, education was the main avenue to the promised land of freedom and equality. The promised land painted by the Reconstruction leaders was a mere mirage for Black people, however, as the commitments of the Radicals were temporary and the tolerance of the Whites was limited.

THE TASTE OF DEGRADATION: AFRICAN AMERICAN EDUCATION AND THE RESTORATION OF WHITE SUPREMACY

Outside of an isolated few private schools for free Blacks in antebellum New Orleans, Natchitoches, and Baton Rouge, formal educational experiences for Blacks in Louisiana did not exist in the antebellum period. The Black Codes of the state limited Black education and decreed heavy fines and punishment on people who would teach slaves.[49] The more common educational experience for Blacks in Louisiana, was the "school of slavery."

Often termed the "hidden passage to education," slavery surprisingly presented a few vocational and even academic educational experiences. Many masters trusted aspects of the economic administration of the plantation to their slaves. In order to perform such tasks, slaves had to read and write. Thus, a hidden passage to education was created and nurtured by masters who were often quite proud of the educational accomplishments of talented slaves. Of course, most slaves did not benefit directly from this opportunity, but the point is that such experiences constituted the first academic educational experiences for many Black people in America.[50]

Blacks in Louisiana and Caddo Parish had to take advantage of educational opportunities whenever and however they were presented. Not only were Blacks often denied formal educational opportunities in the parish in the nineteenth century, but when opportunities were offered, they were rarely equal, marked by a hidden agenda, and bitterly resented by some segments of the White community.

Historical accounts of Black history and Black educational history reflect this bitterness. Often, the Black educational experience was completely ignored in these studies. When the *Shreveport Journal*, for example, examined the history of education in Shreveport for its 1935 centennial edition, Black education was not mentioned except in citing contemporary school enrollment figures.[51] More commonly, attempts were made to justify the benevolence of the White community regarding the education of Blacks. "Shreveport and Caddo Parish met their share of the responsibility in providing for the education of the Negro" in the nineteenth century, chroniclers proclaimed. Arguing that the Black population only paid a small portion of the taxes, Shreveport and Caddo Parish historians pointed out the benevolence of the White population in providing "equal educational advantages."[52]

Other historians presented a more hostile attitude toward Black education. Viewed in the context of the Reconstruction Era, Black education was a part of the vindictive Radical attempt to wipe out White supremacy and "put the heel of the Negro on the White man's neck." In these accounts, Blacks become the scapegoats for the area's economic problems in the later nineteenth century. At the end of slavery, the story goes, the scattered Blacks became unruly and potentially dangerous. The plantations deteriorated from lack of labor, and the northern carpetbaggers used the freed Blacks to humiliate and degrade White citizens by elevating the freedmen to positions of political power. During this Reconstruction period, Black politicians, the early historians wrote, legislated against Whites and stole them blind. These accounts were quite bitter and were accepted as fact for decades after the period ended.[53] To these historians of previous generations, the attitudes of Black people toward their own education was deemed unimportant or irrelevant.

As slaves gained their freedom in Louisiana, they displayed an almost pathetic belief in the power of education to provide a better life. Black publicly supported education in Louisiana followed the army. A s early as 1862, Black schools were formed by Union officers, and, by 1864, a formal structure of education for former slaves was set up in New Orleans and the parishes along the Mississippi.[54] While Blacks in Confederate Shreveport did not benefit from these Union schools, they were ready to take advantage of educational opportunity when it finally availed itself. Education was a form of magic, and grandmothers and grandfathers sat in makeshift schools alongside their grandchildren, reading and reciting passages from the Bible and more secular material. After emancipation, reports came in from all over the South, especially Louisiana, concerning the acute desire of former slaves to learn. In addition to schools established for them, Blacks established private schools on their own and staffed them with their own people.[55]

The first Black schools in Caddo Parish were established by Blacks themselves in small churches throughout the parish. Even the so-called Black public schools of the last three decades of the nineteenth century were conducted, for the most part, in small churches. Indeed, after the Civil War, more than half of the Black schools in existence were supported entirely by Black people themselves.[56]

Helping Blacks establish educational institutions was the Freedmen's Bureau, formed in March of 1865. The objective of the Bureau was to help ease the transition of four million former slaves to freedom. In South Louisiana, efforts to deal with freedmen had been alternately administered by the War Department and the Treasury Department since 1862. One aspect of these efforts was the attempt to provide for the education of former slaves. Once the Freedmen's Bureau was established in Louisiana, education would become its major focus. Education, it was believed, could provide the skills necessary to ease Blacks into the economic life of the state.[57]

In July of 1865, the Freedmen's Bureau took control of Black education in Louisiana. Caddo Parish was unaffected, since most of the schools for Blacks were located in New Orleans and Baton Rouge. The Bureau undoubtedly played an important role in Black education in Louisiana, but every Black school received aid from the agency. Some Black schools received aid from Northern benevolent agencies; others were supported by local societies and churches; and a large number were completely self-sufficient.[58]

In those schools in which the Freemen's Bureau held complete control, teachers from Northern benevolent societies were often recruited. Somewhat out of touch with Southern realities and operating with a specific ideological agenda, these schools took on an interesting and often ludicrous atmosphere. Bound by their culture and political vision, the teachers offered a curriculum design fro students who would live in an urban, industrialized society such as Boston. Opportunities for industrial jobs for freedmen did not exist in the 1860s and 1870s, even discounting racially biased hiring practices. It must have been quite a spectacle to watch newly freed slaves react to a curriculum based on Greek, Latin, and dialectics. Possibly the most surprising aspect of the entire process was the faith the freedmen placed in such a curriculum.[59]

In Shreveport, the Freedmen's Bureau worked to establish schools for Blacks with some success. In the summer of 1865, Thomas W. Conway, head of the Bureau in Louisiana and future Radical superintendent of education, made Shreveport one of three regional offices for the Bureau in the state.[60] Work soon began to help promote and support Black education in the area.

While the Bureau did promote Black education in Caddo, the going was tough. By the late fall of 1866, only one school for Blacks had been in operation in the entire district which consisted of not only Caddo but Bossier and DeSoto Parishes as well. Local Bureau officials blamed the lack of education activity on White outlaws who periodically terrorized Black teachers and students and then escaped into Arkansas and Texas. The local planters were to blame also, the officials continued, for they refused to help protect the teachers and students from the violence.[61]

Even with the Bureau's bid in Caddo Parish, the Bureau schools were mainly supported by the freedmen themselves. The schools were generally held in Black churches, and teachers were paid in large part by student tuition. That the schools were able to remain open during the period was a phenomenon, given the heavy reliance upon Black financial support. Blacks in Caddo were poor to begin with in the 1860s, and when that poverty was coupled with a bad cotton crop and wages to Blacks paid not in money but by a share of the crop, conditions only deteriorated.[62]

Most of the support for Black education in Caddo Parish provided by the Freedmen's Bureau involved the appropriation of small grants of

$100 to $250 to small Black churches to help pay the cost of holding classes. Endorsing a request for $250 for educational aid from the First Baptist Church for Colored People of Shreveport, District Education Superintendent Jones McCleery wrote:

> These people are subject to humiliating actions. They have in a sense almost had to go back into bondage in order to educate their children and worship God. I hope the Commissioner can see his way clear to approve their request for the amount asked.[63]

Another form of Bureau support was the direct grant to the plantation owner who wanted to set up a school for his Black laborers. Planters in Caddo Parish, like planters all around the South, were very uncomfortable with the education provided by the Freedmen's Bureau and Northern philanthropy. Many of them agreed that the "Negro problems" could best be taken care of through education; education, that is, "Southern style."

By way of education, the planters argued, the Blacks would be made "safer" and more moral. Indeed, fear of Blacks and "colored retribution" was an omnipresent concern during the Reconstruction period. The safer, more moral Black would become more dependable and thus a better worker.

It is in this context of fear that the appeal of those conservative Southerners for Black education can be best understood. The goals of the conservatives were the same: the safe control of a newly freed Black population. The means to accomplish the goal sometimes differed. Could the goal best be accomplished, they asked, by denying the freedmen all educational opportunities or by carefully controlling the educational opportunities provided? That debate would determine the nature of Black education in Caddo Parish for decades after the Reconstruction era.

With these concerns in mind, the Caddo planters applied for Bureau grants to set up schools on their plantations. Worried about the adverse effect of planter education, Superintendent McCleery approved these applications with the condition that the school property be deeded in advance to some Northern philanthropic society.[64]

Many historians consider the work to provide education for Black people the most significant accomplishment of the Reconstruction Era. While the Freedmen's Bureau aid was important to Black education in Louisiana and Caddo Parish, it was never sufficient to establish a system of schools even when combined with aid from missionary and philanthropic societies. Congress was unwilling to levy the taxes necessary to support a system of Black education; thus, the burden of support, both moral and financial, often came from the former slaves themselves. The faith that Black people placed in the power of education to solve their problems is one of the more moving aspects of American educational history.[65]

As bad as the public system of education formed by the Radical Reconstructionists proved to be, it was still better than the system established by the Redeemers in Louisiana's post-Reconstruction period. These aristocratic, former Confederates (often called the Bourbons) would have been happy to have terminated all public education, especially Black education. But they did not. Because of the strong foundation laid by the Radicals, the Bourbon Redeemers did not dare attempt the disestablishment of the legal structure of the state's school system. This is not to imply, however, that they tried to make it work.[66]

In April 1877, as part of the political deal that allowed Rutherford B. Hayes to assume the presidency, White Democratic rule was restored in Louisiana. Stephen B. Packard, a Republican, and Francis T. Nicholls, a Democrat, both claimed the Louisiana governorship. In order to assume the presidency, Hayes had agreed to end Reconstruction and allow the establishment of "home rule" (i.e. White rule) to the South. The presidential commission which arrived in New Orleans on April 5, 1877, had one task: to establish the Democrat, Nicholls, as the legitimate governor of Louisiana. This they did, and, as a result, White government was again in full control of Louisiana.[67]

Not only were the Redeemers in political control of the state, but they had little to fear from the archenemies, the Northern reformers. The Northern humanitarians had pinned grandiose but naïve hopes on the power of education to free freedmen from the effects of slavery in only two, three, or four years. In the South after the Civil War such an expectation was ludicrous, given the prevailing social and economic conditions. When their hopes for speedy educational and social change for Blacks were not realized, the Northern educators began to take a new look at some of the Southerners' racial prejudices. They began to blame the Blacks for not learning fast enough and for not improving their social conditions. Thus, they abandoned the Blacks to the Redeemer governments. With the retreat of the reformers, Black education was without serious and widespread support. By the summer of 1877, the Bourbon Redeemers controlled all of the state's institutions, education included.[68]

Upon the establishment of the Redeemer government, the legislature adopted a General School Act which required the formation of a State Board of Education, parish school boards of five to nine members serving at the appointment of the State Board of Education, district school boards appointed by the parish boards, school funds distributed on the basis of the educables in each district, a $100 per year salary for parish superintendents, and a state property tax of two mills for the support of education. The act was 11 pages long, and 7 pages dealt with an intricate system of finance. The length of the document is ironic, considering the fact that the state government would exhibit so little concern for public education for the rest of the nineteenth century.[69]

When 1877 and 1888 legislature slashed state expenditures by over $2.7 million, educational services suffered, and Black education suffered in particular. Wealthy planters and businessmen received tax breaks, but such legislation was irrelevant because they rarely paid taxes anyway. The refusal of the wealthy to pay taxes, the Shreveport city attorney explained in 1881, was a behavior "they got in the habit of" during Reconstruction.[70]

In Caddo Parish public and educational affairs were beginning to return to their "proper order." By 1877, separate school systems were in the process of being established. On June 7 the first Caddo Parish School Board was organized under the Redeemers with William Seay as president. The board reported that 28 schools existed in the parish with an enrollment of 976 pupils and property valued at $1,288.52. Six schools were located in Shreveport—three White and three Black. The school board possessed so little money during the late 1870s and 1880 that no school buildings could be constructed and most schools were mere makeshifts. Even by 1889, when the parish owned merely 55 schools, the total value of school property was only $12,000. In rural portions of the parish, schools were conducted in churches and in any available empty buildings, while, in the town, classes were held mainly in vacant houses. At this same time, some of the state school money was being diverted to the White private schools.[71]

Schoolteachers could not expect much compensation for their labors in this climate of social and economic retrenchments. In 1877, rules established for the payment of teachers stipulated that when "the number of scholars is under twenty the teacher shall receive $2.00 per head a month." If there were over twenty students, the board agreed to pay teachers forty dollars per month.

With the salary for the parish superintendent set at only $100 per year, Louisianans could not expect to hire professional schoolmen to administer their systems. Thus, men of means were asked to "oversee" the schools as a gesture of civic service. The first superintendent of Caddo Parish was John J. Horan, and he was succeeded by T. F. Bell who served as parish superintendent until 1891. Bell was the archetypal Redeemer. Having served as a Confederate soldier, Bell was described as one of the courageous men who fought the Black attempt to wipe out White supremacy. He helped rout the carpetbaggers and taught the Black people a lesson that they did not soon forget. Typical of the leadership of Shreveport society in the post-Reconstruction era, Bell was not sensitive to the educational needs of Blacks in the period. Times were hard, however, and, while Blacks received a disproportionately small portion of state funds, no one received enough support to pursue a high quality education.[72]

The few friends of education hoped that, when the Redeemer legislature met for the Constitutional Convention of 1879, some provision for education would be granted. Given the promise of the Redeemers to slash state expenditures, no one was surprised by the meager attention afforded schooling in the state. The new Constitution mandated a $1 poll tax for school purposes; no other definite tax for schooling was guaranteed. Article 224 stipulated only that the General Assembly provide for "establishment, maintenance and support of public schools." The same article stated that a free system of public schools will be established "for the education of all children of the state between the ages of six and eighteen years." Still fearing the few Radicals left in Congress, the legislators avoided an explicit segregationist statement in the Constitution. They left the formation of the segregated schools in the hands of the local school boards.[73]

Leading the fight to reduce the support of public education all across the South were Redeemers—well-to-do former Confederates. They were most often conservative Democrats with economic ties to the railroads and the emerging industrial powers. Though they controlled the power strings in post-Reconstruction society, the Bourbon Redeemers were not socially or economically representative of the large percentage of struggling small farmers in the South during the era. As unconcerned as they were with the educational opportunities of poor Whites and Blacks, they were more concerned with protecting the freedmen's right to at least some education than were the poor Whites.[74] Bourbons in Caddo Parish,

however, were less inclined to support Black education than their aristocratic brothers across the South. In Shreveport, "Negrophobia" was so
strong that the local Bourbons opposed almost any act designed to
improve Black opportunity.

In addition to the hostile attitude of the state's Redeemers, Louisiana
education faced many obstacles in the last decades of the century, including dire poverty, a lack of leadership in the field of education, and the
omnipresent fear of a return to racially integrated schools. Working in
this context, the Redeemers reduced the state government to a point
where public education almost disappeared in portions of the state. Even
in the late 1890s, the Bourbon legislature would refuse to increase the
tiny state appropriations to education. Writing about the bill to increase
education funding, *Shreveport Times* founder Major Henry J. Hearsey laid
down the Bourbon attitude: "The education of a bad citizen will increase
his power for evil and make him a worse citizen."[75]

In a state marred by race hatred in the post-Reconstruction period,
few localities in the state had a more consistent record on the race issue
than Caddo Parish. "White supremacy, first, last and all the time, has
always been the motto of the White people . . . of Caddo," the
Shreveport *Evening Judge* proudly proclaimed, "and they prove their faith
by their works." The citizens of Caddo were so unembarrassed by their
reputation for terrorism against Blacks and Republicans that they named
one of their baseball teams in the late 1870s and early 1880s, the
Shreveport Bulldozers. "Bulldozing" was a word commonly used during
the era to refer to the terrorist tactics employed by Whites to keep Blacks
in line.[76]

Not only was Shreveport a bastion of White supremacy, but it was
also a state leader in the battle for fiscal conservatism. The push to reduce
all forms of state expenditures always found support in Caddo Parish.
Although barred by state law from issuing special taxes for education,
localities could appropriate a portion of their budgets for the support of
public education. Even with state aid so inadequate during the 1880s and
1890s, the Shreveport City Council often refused to give the school
board the monies they had appropriated for education. In 1891 the
school board actually brought suit against the city council for the unpaid
funds appropriated to the schools between 1878 and 1890. Such fiscal
parsimony in the words of one old Caddo Parish resident created a situation where "the most outstanding thing about [Shreveport schools in
the 1880s] was we didn't have a system."[77]

The Shreveport City Council was not the only governmental entity to withhold appropriated funds from the schools: Caddo Parish officials also refused to relinquish school monies. The parish sheriff would not release funds derived from poll taxes, fines, and forfeitures that were earmarked for education. Thus, in 1892, the school board once again empowered attorneys to bring suit, this time against the sheriff for the disputed money.[78]

At the same time that public education in Shreveport was struggling to stay alive, the United States Congress was debating the Blair Bill. This proposed legislation to aid education would have granted four million federal dollars to Louisiana schools. No state needed such aid any more than Louisiana. The state legislature had passed petitions for its support, and both of Louisiana's US senators pressed for the bill's passage. However, editorial comment in Shreveport was adamantly opposed to the bill. *The Shreveport Times* called federal assistance to education a humiliation that moved the nation "in the direction of centralization." Federal aid was not the real issue; support of education, whatever the source, was. Ironically, the same people who spoke so vehemently against the Blair Bill had for years called on the federal government to provide Louisiana with money to build and fortify levees.[79]

In the eyes of modern historians, distanced by time from the racial hatreds of the period, Bourbon misrule followed Radical misrule. Fear of Black government was so widespread after Reconstruction that Louisiana Whites were ready to accept any form of despotism that was forced on them—as long as it was White.[80] Sharing the prejudices of the Bourbons, subsequent historians often rationalized the governmental abuses of the Redeemers and their educational actions. The traditional historiographical view of the period blamed the people's refusal to fund education adequately on their outrage over the excesses of Radical Reconstruction. They had watched the Radicals squander educational appropriations for years and were not ready to allow such abuse again. The Radicals robbed the people in the name of public education the historians asserted, and tried to force the races to go to school together.[81]

Justifying their highhanded and often cruel techniques, the Louisiana Bourbons claimed that their government, with its social stagnation, was the only alternative to turbulence. Of course, the turbulence to which they referred had a racial implication. So secure were the Shreveport Bourbons with the justness of their cause and the necessity of their methods that they used the newspaper to call for political misdeeds against those who would oppose them.

> It is the religious duty of Democrats to rob Populists and Republicans of their votes whenever and wherever the opportunity presents itself and any failure to do so will be a violation of true Louisiana Democratic teaching. The Populists and Republicans are our legitimate political prey. Rob them! You bet! What are we here for?[82]

The Bourbons were rarely forced to justify their educational neglect during the 1880s and 1890s, but when they did, they relied on two main points. The first was the sometimes tacit understanding that no education was preferable to racially integrated education. The second point involved the economic realities of the time. Not only do we live in a poor state, the Bourbon leaders argued, but we need to use our resources to encourage manufacturing, railroads, and capital investment. In the name of low taxes and economic growth, the Louisianans allowed their educational institutions to fall to a lower condition than any other state. Indeed, illiteracy increased in Louisiana between 1880 and 1890. Such conditions elicited an uncharacteristic reaction in the West Baton Rouge Sugar Planters in 1881: "How much are we better off now than when under Radical rule? None but the officeholders see it; the masses do not."[83]

Much of the corruption and zeal of the Bourbon government was aimed at Louisiana Blacks as retribution for their actions during Reconstruction and as a warning for the future. Black education was particularly singled out for Bourbon vindictiveness. By 1890, only 37 percent of Louisiana Black children (ages nine to nineteen) could read. Mississippi Black children at this time ranked 20 percent higher in literacy. Local officials had the prerogative to divide state schools between Blacks and Whites in whatever manner they preferred. In some parishes Black education was not funded at all. Bourbon neglect of Black schooling in the latter part of the century was well-illustrated by the census of 1890 which indicated that, counting public, parochial, and private schools, there were only 828 teachers for over 200,000 Blacks of school age.[84]

The Shreveport *Weekly Caucasian* reflected a Bourbon view of education popular in Caddo Parish. Ignorant Negroes present us with a bad problem, it argued, but "education is the most dangerous remedy for the evil yet proposed." Education's danger, the paper innocently asserted, is based on the fact that it leads Blacks toward social equality.[85] The

Bourbon position favoring Black education was illustrated by a
Louisianian in the summer of 1880, commenting on a Black school he
had observed. As long as the schools taught Blacks to be respectful of
Whites, he maintained, he could support Black education. After meeting
Black children on their way home from school, he stated that "it is real-
ly amusing . . . to see them all pull off their hats and bow."[86]

Our knowledge of the reactions of Black people to all of this Bourbon
mistreatment is limited by the fact that few Blacks at the time could
leave written evidence of their reactions. Black people in Shreveport
sometimes spoke louder through their actions than their words. With the
establishment of the "redeemed government" in the late 1870s, many
Black Shreveporters tried to organize mass exoduses. First attempting a
migration to Liberia and later to Kansas, the Freedmen understood what
lay in store for them under White rule in Shreveport. Unable to organized the journeys, Shreveport Blacks had to brace themselves for
Bourbon abuse.[87]

And the abuse did come. From the modern perspective, the most
surprising aspect of Bourbon racism in Shreveport is not that it existed,
but that the leaders of the city were so unembarrassed in expressing it.
The Shreveport *Evening Judge* described a lynching of a Black man as
"beautiful." All Black brutes should be dealt with in this way, the paper
opined. "Before the war [the Black] kept their places like the other
beasts of the field."

In 1889 the *Daily Caucasian* conceived what came to be known as the
"Shreveport Plan" to deal with Blacks. Based on the belief that Blacks
were not fully human, the plan contended that Blacks should not hold
easy jobs, e.g., bootblacks, waiters, porters, cooks, clerks, and teachers.
The spirit of the plan was captured by the statement that Whites should
be forbidden "to employ a colored man . . . in any other manner than at
the hardest and most degrading tasks." Of course, the Shreveport Plan was
never completely practiced, for Blacks continued to hold jobs as waiters,
porters, and cooks, and a number of Black teachers continued to teach.[88]

THE ORIGINS OF PUBLIC EDUCATION: THE PAUPER STIGMA
AND OMNIPRESENT RACIAL FEARS IN THE NEW SOUTH

With racial feelings this intense, it is not surprising that many
Shreveporters looked condescendingly on the school system that Black
children attended. Public schools, Shreveporters of the 1870s, 1880s, and

1890s often claimed, were for the Black and the poor. Public support of education was looked upon as an imposition, and those who could afford it sent their children to private school. Little was said about those who could not afford private education. Before publicly supported education could prosper, the pauper stigma would have to be removed.

Before the pauper stigma could be removed, however, school facilities would have to be improved. Thus, a vicious circle was established. The public would not support the schools because they were for the Black and poor; and, without such support, the school facilities were so horrendous that "respectable" people would have nothing to do with them. The only children who attended them, therefore, were the so-called paupers.[89]

The public education facilities were indeed primitive during the era. Held in abandoned buildings or churches, both the rural and city schools consisted mainly of one-room frame buildings. Walls were poorly stripped rough boards that allowed in the rain and the cold. In winter, teachers would hang children's coats on the walls to keep out the freezing wind. The schools were heated by small stoves maintained by the larger boys who carried out the ashes and brought in the wood or coal. There were no individual desks but, instead, several long benches with desks as long as the benches. On each bench 15 to 20 children could sit. Since the schools were held in vacant buildings, teachers and students were constantly prepared to move when the property was sold or rented. The concept of spending public funds for well-equipped and comfortable schools was not within the imagination of most people living in Shreveport during the era.[90]

Gradually, however, the educational imagination of some Shreveporters was awakened. By the 1890s, the memories of Reconstruction had begun to fade, as the residents realized that White supremacy reigned again. Slowly the White population came to understand that nothing or nobody was prepared to upset the racial relationships that White Shreveporters had worked so hard to reestablish in the years following Reconstruction. The Radicals were a distant memory and the new generation of White leaders knew them only as the scary phantoms of an old nightmare. Once the Radicals, with their goals of racial equality were seen as mere memories, school reform could proceed.

Coupled with these fading memories was the emergence of a so-called New South ideology. While industrialization and scientific agriculture rested at the heart of the movement, there did exist an educational impulse. When all of these factors were combined with an emerging Southern Progressivism concerned with reform of Bourbon governmental corruption and the creation of a participant democracy, the origins of the public school crusade in the South are revealed.[91]

Like Progressives throughout the country, Shreveport Progressives were concerned with honest government and uplifting the poorer elements of society to make them more orderly and more capable of working as participants in the industrial and political life of the community. This participation would give the people a stake, or at least the perception of a stake, in the society. As a result, the Progressives argued, these people would concern themselves with the good of the community. It was the role of the public schools to teach them how to participate.

By no means should the movement for public schooling in Louisiana and throughout the South be confused with a liberalization of attitudes toward Blacks and Black education. Indeed, the efforts to establish a viable system of public education in the South in the 1890s and early twentieth century often was pursued at the expense of equal educational opportunities for Blacks. In most areas, Caddo Parish included, reformers unembarrassedly published statistics indicating the separate but unequal educational treatment of Black students. Even those reformers who were genuinely concerned with Black educational opportunity knew that the attempt to include Blacks in the educational crusade would destroy any support they had mustered for improved education.[92]

By the late 1880s, Shreveport was beginning to advertise itself as a center of the New South. Like business leaders in other Louisiana cities, Shreveport businessmen saw industrialization as part profit-making and part moral crusade. Importantly, the New South movement was sometimes seen as a nonviolent continuation of the Civil War. If we could not compete with the Yankees on the battlefield, the Southerners concluded, we can surely compete with them in the factory. At the same time that industrialization was seen in competitive terms, education was beginning to be viewed from the same perspective. The inferiority of Southern schooling was becoming a matter of Southern shame.[93]

Moved by all of these factors, a few Shreveporters began to push for public support of education in the 1890s. Aided by an increasing educational interest throughout the state, some Shreveporters pushed for an extension of public education into the high school years. In 1888, the State Legislature granted parish school boards the authority to establish high schools. Four years later, the school board took advantage of the provision and established the first high school in the area in 1892. The beginnings were humble. The school board rented two rooms in a YMCA building to house the high school and its forty "poorly prepared students."[94]

Since neither the parish nor the city were authorized to tax specifically for school purposes, Shreveporters interested in educational expansion had to devise a way to raise money for a separate high school building. In 1895 Superintendent of Caddo Parish Schools, H. H Hargrove, proposed a voluntary tax for a high school building. Acting on Hargrove's proposal, a citizen's committee appealed to property owners and raised about $60,000 for the school. Public educational concern was thus awakened, and Central High School opened in October of 1899.[95]

Along with the concern for New South Industrialization, Southern and civic pride, the fading memory of Reconstruction resulting from the security of White supremacy, and the Progressive desire for social order and political participation, the public schools were beginning to draw support from the small farmers of the Populist movement. The interest of the Populists often clashed directly with the Bourbons, and the issue of schooling was no exception. The Populists resented the Bourbon neglect of the public schools, for, as poor farmers, they often could not afford to send their children to the private academies.

The Populists gained strength in the early 1890s and began to assert themselves on the Louisiana political scene. Uniting with Republicans and even Blacks, the party offered credible representation fro the less affluent members of Louisiana society. It was a hopeful era for Louisiana Blacks, as they shared platforms at conventions and were even nominated for political offices. But the era was short-lived. By 1896 the Bourbons had crushed any hope of Populist success, and the movement broke into factions, never to gain significant support again. The losers were the Blacks, for, with the demise of Populism, they once again had no one to represent their cause.

During their heyday, the Populists offered some interesting critiques of Bourbon education policy. The Bourbons, Populists argued, had deliberately sabotaged public education in Louisiana. Bourbons had undermined the schools, not so much to save state money, they contended, but for the purpose of reducing the people's knowledge to the lowest common denominator and, as a result, keeping Blacks and rural Whites docile.

Many of the farmers of Caddo Parish agreed with such sentiments, though Caddo, with its Bourbon control, was never a center of Populist activity. Nevertheless, one of the popular parish newspapers of the period was the independent Shreveport *Progress*, which sometimes leaned toward the Populist Party. Still, Shreveport's conservatism was apparent, for, where most North Louisiana parishes had at least one explicitly Populist newspaper, Shreveport had none. The Shreveport Bourbons would have the last laugh when, by 1900, the Populists had deserted the Blacks. By the early twentieth century, state school monies were being divided in the "best interests of the school district," which simply meant more money for White education. The support for education from the Populist-oriented poorer segments of late-nineteenth-century Louisiana was important, but it was quickly crushed by the powerful Bourbons. The demise of poor White and Black input into the public school crusade in the 1890s would leave the leadership of the movement to the more well-to-do members of Louisiana society.[96]

Worried by the lack of Bourbon support, the public school supporters in Shreveport contrived a public relations move to gain the backing of the well-to-do. Understanding that Bourbons supported the private schools, the public school people asked the women teachers of the private schools to teach in the public schools. Also, the "ladies of the more cultured homes" were asked to hold classes in the public schools. The ploy was very successful, and popular private school teachers and other well-bred ladies helped dissolve some of the patrician condescension toward the publicly supported "pauper schools." Thus, by the turn of the century, the more prosperous members of Shreveport society were beginning to pay attention to public schooling. With their backing, the "cultured ladies" brought not only their prestige to the schools but their values as well.[97]

Combined with the credibility granted by the ladies, the Constitution of 1898 allowed increased support and funding of the public schools. As a result of the new Constitution, parishes could levy taxes specifically designed to fund school building and maintenance. Such funds provided a vital boost to the financially needy Caddo school system. The benefits derived from the provisions of the new Constitution moved many historians to designate 1898 as the birth date of modern public education in Louisiana.[98]

PROFESSIONALIZATION, RATIONALIZATION, AND
BUREAUCRATIZATION: EDUCATION FOR REGULATION

Before public schools would be accepted by the prosperous citizens as places to send their children for an education, the widespread perception of teacher incompetence would have changed. The campaign to change such views of teachers continued through the better part of the twentieth century. The attempt to educate teachers and make teaching a profession is a central theme of the history of education in Caddo Parish.

In the early public schools of Caddo, the attempt to hire competent teachers was relatively unimportant. In the 1870s and 1880s school officials were sometimes content with merely filling unoccupied positions. The greatest evil in Louisiana public education, many early observers argued, was the incompetence of the teachers. By the 1890s, the situation had improved only slightly.[99]

Often, the teachers who taught in the small one-room schools of the late nineteenth century were teenagers rarely possessing a high school education. They were paid between $25 and $50 a month, and most of the more able quickly left for another profession. Intelligent young men who taught did so only long enough to earn money to prepare them for another vocation such as law. Young women rarely stayed in the profession after marriage, for many Louisianans believed that the schoolroom was no place for a married woman. It was assumed that long-term employment as a teacher was not a vocation for the highest caliber of young people. For an 18-year-old on his way to the legal profession, teaching was socially acceptable; for the 35-year-old who saw it as a career, it was not.[100]

Before the bureaucratization of the schools in the early twentieth century, teacher certification was often a capricious affair. While there were attempts in Louisiana and in Caddo parish to improve the standards of those hired, officials were thwarted by a dearth of qualified choices. School boards in the latter nineteenth century were granted unlimited power to bestow licenses to teach. Criteria for granting licenses usually revolved around the political contracts and loyalties of the candidate and the need of the school system. If an applicant wanted a position in a system with a shortage of teachers, he or she usually got the job.[101]

The prospective teacher was given an examination and awarded either a first- (the highest), second-, or third-degree certificate. The holder of a first-degree certificate was authorized to teach grammar and high school subjects. Teachers with second-degree certificates taught in the lower elementary grades, and those with third-degree certificates taught in the lowest grade levels.[102] Oftentimes the third-degree certificate was given primarily to Black teachers, as performance on the test had little to do with degree granted. Shreveport native Hattie Lake described the examination she was given by the superintendent of the East Baton Rouge Parish schools in 1877:

> For the next few days I reviewed as best I could. When the time came we went tot he superintendent and presented the application. I told him I had not expected an examination and was not prepared.
>
> He was a lawyer, and knew people as well as his business. He began talking to me and before I knew it had drawn me into an examination. I missed the first question he asked me, but his manner was reassuring, and I soon recovered self-possession. After questioning me for some time a lady who was with us and a mutual friend said to him, "I think you have questioned her enough." He replied, "Just wait. I want to give her as high a certificate as I can."
>
> He finally said to me, "I must congratulate you on your examination" and gave me a First Grade Certificate.[103]

After several years of administering oral exams, Caddo school officials in 1885 mandated content tests in arithmetic, grammar, geography, and history. The highest possible score was 40; not only did no one reach that standard, but even the most respected and successful teachers scored below 15. Teachers thought that the tests were extremely hard and could only be passed with extensive content knowledge. Because of limited choices, parish officials were forced to hire teachers who were "woefully lacking in the fundamentals of elementary knowledge."[104]

Recognizing the serious problems with teacher quality, the state attempted, throughout the late nineteenth century, to improve the situation. Until taxpayers were willing to delegate more funds to teacher salaries and until condescending social attitudes toward the profession changed, little could be done to improve conditions. The focus of the state's efforts to improve teaching involved the standardization of teacher evaluation criteria. Like many subsequent attempts to improve educational quality, uniformity and bureaucratization were relied upon as reform measures.[105]

By 1900, the public school crusade in Louisiana was well under way. The efforts of the previous two decades to improve teacher quality were intensified as the public school movement picked up steam around the turn of the century. If the public was to support public schools, it had to be convinced that teachers were worth supporting. Caddo Superintendent J. C. Moncure and the board of education passed a resolution on October 6, 1900, requiring each teacher and assistant teacher in the parish to present information specifying: 1) the grade of teacher certificate they held; 2) the name of the school from which they had graduated (if any) and the number of years of teaching experience; 3) the professional subjects they had studied for the purpose of improving the quality of their teaching since they entered the teaching field; and 4) the educational periodicals they read regularly. The superintendent was to examine the responses to the information and to endorse or not endorse the teacher's qualifications as a Caddo Parish teacher.[106]

C. E. Byrd, who would serve as superintendent of Caddo Parish schools from 1908–1926, was a guiding force behind these early attempts to improve teacher quality. As city principal (i.e., supervisor of all schools within the city limits of Shreveport), Byrd argued incessantly for stricter teacher standards. Working for more rigorous and longer teacher preparation, Byrd demanded that teachers also strive for professional self-improvement. Byrd was instrumental in the founding of early teacher organizations in Caddo Parish—organizations designed with teacher self-improvement as their cardinal objective. Illustrative of his catalytic role in teacher improvement, Byrd arranged for teacher paychecks to be issued at the meetings of the Caddo Parish Teachers Association.[107]

The growing professionalization of teaching was sometimes resented by the teachers themselves but was welcomed by the leaders of education. Many of the teachers at the beginning of the twentieth century, especially in Louisiana, had no training in pedagogy and were unaware of the innovations in the field. Educational leaders, however, had attended seminars and courses offered around the country by educational specialists. C. E. Byrd, for example, had attended college in Virginia, seminars on education at the New York Chautauqua, and educational forums at the Southern Education Association meetings to name just a few.[108]

The teachers were accustomed to teaching in ways they had traditionally been taught and were uncomfortable with the emerging "scientific methodologies." The leaders were excited by the status that such innovations bestowed on the profession. The scientific pedagogy of the early century provided a special language that separated and thus protected educators from the lay public. If laymen could not understand what the educators were talking about, they would be hard pressed to criticize the teachers. Thus, professionalization meant that, like lawyers and physicians, educators could now establish their role as experts in an industrializing society that was increasingly dependent on experts.

As technology became more sophisticated in the early twentieth century, it slowly began to make its mark in all areas of the country. Telephones and automobiles began to pop up in Shreveport by the first decade of the new century, heralding the passing of an old age and the dawn of "modern times." Social and educational theorists in turn-of-the-century America advocated a new education for a new era. The schools were called upon not only to teach academic skills but to teach social skills as well—skills which would prepare youth to fit into the new society of the twentieth century.[109] The role of the teacher was beginning to change and Caddo Parish had educational leaders working to make sure that all Caddo teachers were aware of their changing responsibilities.

With the development of high school education in Shreveport in the 1890s and its growth in the first decade of the twentieth century, the new role of the Caddo teacher became quite apparent. Curricula were designed to help "fit the student to the changing society." In order to administer such an undertaking, a whole new class of educators developed who were not classroom teachers. The role of supervisor had emerged. By the end of the first decade of the twentieth century, the developing discipline of educational psychology had provided a quantitative means of measuring student and teacher performance. This quasi-scientific "objective" means of determining competence rested on the development of a battery of tests designed to evaluate measurable outcomes of teaching.

By 1909, Louisiana had made provisions for supervision of the state's teachers. That year the State Board of Education set aside two periods of a high school principal's day for teacher supervision. A state high school inspector had been appointed as early as 1907, and, by 1914, new elementary and high school supervisors had been hired to oversee and improve teaching in the schools. With teaching objectives quantified and measurable, principls and supervisors evaluated teacher performance, suggesting specific methods for improvement if work was deemed inferior.

By 1893, C. E. Byrd exercised strict control of Shreveport teachers. The Caddo Parish School Board granted Byrd the power to dictate how teachers should teach and manage the discipline of their classes. He prepared all examination questions for student promotions and was in charge of grading them. Byrd observed the teachers in their classrooms to determine if they met the standards of the parish and called teachers into his office for consultation if he was not satisfied with their performance. Because of Byrd's dynamic supervisory role, Shreveport teaching was more standardized and teacher choices were often more limited than in other Louisiana parishes in the late 1890s and the early decades of the twentieth century.[110]

By the 1920s, the supervisory bureaucracy had expanded further on the state level. The Louisiana State Department of Education initiated a statewide program of supervision designed to improve teaching methods in both city and rural schools. Supervisors taught demonstration lessons which they expected teachers to imitate. Teachers were checked to see if they met the objectives adopted by the parish school boards, and, if found wanting, the teachers were required to attend in-service workshops conducted by supervisors. In their attempt to improve Louisiana teachers, the supervisors judged the educators on the basis of their fidelity to preestablished teaching techniques and the efficiency with which they carried out their educational tasks, e.g. the amount of material covered, the time required to begin class, the time required to move from one task to another, etc. Thus, the definition of good teaching was standardized. When the supervisors performed their tasks diligently, which they often did not, teacher individuality and creativity was discouraged.[111]

Administrators and educational leaders sought other methods of improving what they perceived to be the low quality of teaching in both the state and in Caddo Parish. One way to encourage the professionalization of the teaching force was the establishment of teacher organizations. The first teacher organization in Louisiana was the Louisiana State Education Association. Founded in 1883, the organization was open to White teachers, school officials, and interested laymen. This organization was succeeded nine years later by the Louisiana State Public School Teachers Association, which was open only to White school personnel. Public school teachers, however, did not dominate the organization, since school administrators and leaders of higher education directed the group.[112]

When C. E. Byrd came to Caddo Parish in 1892, Matttie Williams, a teacher and principal in the local schools, had helped to organize the Caddo teachers into the Caddo Teachers Association. The organization was designed for two central purposes: to improve the professional quality of teachers and to elicit support for public education in Caddo Parish. Byrd was elected president of the organization in his first year in Shreveport upon the recommendation of Caddo Parish Superintendent

H. H. Hargrove. Under Byrd's strict direction, the organization served less as a teacher organization and more as a training unit for educators. Under the auspices of the organization, Byrd saw that proscribed readings for teachers were completed and that teachers were present at the monthly meetings.[113]

The monthly meetings were training sessions, and teachers were confronted with lessons on teaching methods. Caddo teachers heard lectures on sand modeling, elocution, psychology in connection with child life, and many other educational topics. During the 1890s, the organization brought in nationally known platform speakers to raise money to buy books for libraries and teaching aids for classrooms. By the first decade of the twentieth century, Byrd felt that the organization should devote even more time to professional improvement. He opened the March 1906 meeting with remarks about the need for periodic gatherings of teachers "to perfect and establish a closer relationship of all grades.[114]

Byrd, not the teachers, was in charge of the teacher organization, and his goals for it were clear. Those goals did not include the use of the Caddo Teachers Association as a vehicle for teacher grievances. Evidence exists that teachers were quite dissatisfied with salaries in the early decades of the century. Indeed, schools experienced shortages of male teachers, since men were forced to quit teaching in order to go into higher paying vocations.[115]

The professionalization of the teaching force was impeded by the lack of well-educated candidates and by limited access to higher education. Before 1940, when all teachers were required to hold a college degree for certification, state and parish officials devised numerous ways to provide pedagogical training for their faculties. Alarmed by the fact that less than 5 percent of his educators held college degrees, Byrd pushed his teachers into Chautauqua courses, teacher institutes, parish institutes, and summer normal schools.[116]

For 15 years, Caddo teachers attended the Louisiana Chautauqua, held in a wooded enclave north of Ruston. Beginning in 1892, the Chautauqua teacher sessions were conducted for a month each summer. All the subjects in the curriculum were taught by nationally known educators. Byrd not only encouraged Caddo teachers to attend but took an active role in the administration of the Chautauqua program. For several years, Byrd even managed the institute and planned its programs. By 1907, the Chautauqua was discontinued when other state-sponsored means of teacher training dominated teacher time.[117]

Another agency employed to educate teachers was the teacher institute. Similar in purpose to the Chautauqua, the teacher institutes usually lasted for a week during the summer. Often financed by the Peabody Fund, the institutes held meetings in the day for teachers and at night for parents. The teacher programs usually stressed methodology, while the parental meetings emphasized the benefits to be derived from tax-supported schools.[118] The directions given to the leaders of the teacher institutes by the state superintendent and his staff, however, indicate a more manipulative role for the institutes. Instructors were exhorted to arouse the people's interest in tax-supported schools and to cause the public to "feel that they must have that kind of school." As for the school teachers, the superintendent urged instructors to inspire:

> . . . the teachers to greater efforts and higher ideals; cause the teachers to fall in love with the profession of teaching, so deeply in love with it that the question of salary be made secondary to the question of the greatest good for the children.[119]

Professor Byrd continued to urge Caddo teachers to attend summer school even after Chautauqua and the teacher institutes were discontinued. After 1907, Byrd insisted that teachers take classes on a college campus one out of every three summers. At Byrd's insistence some Caddo teachers spent their summers at Harvard, Columbia, the University of Tennessee, or other colleges known for their teacher training. The state superintendent's desire that teachers value the good of the children over the question of salary was fulfilled with these dedicated Caddo teachers. For their summer pilgrimages, the teachers received a monthly salary increase of two dollars.[120]

The normal school movement, beginning in the latter nineteenth and early twentieth century, changed the nature of Louisiana teacher education because it centralized and standardized the process. Early normal schooling in Louisiana was weak in comparison to modern standards, since most students merely studied a high school curriculum. Attendance was irregular, and years would pass before even a semblance of college-level work was offered. In the 1910s and 1920s, standards at the Louisiana State Normal at Natchitoches were gradually raised. With the urging of the state department of education, more and more Shreveport teachers received their degrees at Natchitoches and at the educational department at Louisiana State University in Baton Rouge. In Caddo Parish in 1908, there were 94 White teachers; only 18 of them had obtained normal degrees. By 1926, there were 458 White teachers in the parish, with 284 having earned normal degrees. With a standardized set of experiences, the normal school graduates were excused from taking a teacher examination.[121]

When analyzing the professionalization of teachers in Caddo Parish, it is extremely difficult to examine Black and White teachers simultaneously because of the vast differences in their experiences. Bourbonism actually increased its power in Caddo Parish during the early part of the twentieth century,[122] and, as a result, Blacks continued to suffer both politically and educationally. While Black education in general suffered, the education of Black teachers languished. Even at mid-twentieth century some observers would be alarmed by the lack of educational opportunity for Black Caddo Parish teachers.

In the late nineteenth century, no provisions for Black teacher education in Louisiana had been made other than the minimal work undertaken at Southern University, then located in New Orleans. The standards of the work at Southern were quite low since much of the university's work was high school and even primary level. In the first two decades of Southern's existence, the normal department only turned out 167 teachers. Shortages of trained Black teachers existed in New Orleans; the situation in northern Louisiana was critical.[123]

As Black teachers struggled to teach with little if any education, they were confronted with schools without furniture, crowded classes, and school terms of three to five months. State Superintendent of Education T. H. Harris argued in 1913 that the state should provide eighth grade level training for Black teachers. Such training, he claimed, would produce Black teachers who "would know ten thousand times more than the Negro teachers who are now teaching in the Negro public schools of this state." Even in the eyes of the White leaders of education in Louisiana in the first and second decades of the twentieth century, something had to be done about Black teacher education.[124]

Because of racial discrimination and the resulting lack of opportunity, improvements in Black teacher education were delayed. As a result, the summer schools and institutes for teachers used as strategies to educate White teachers were also employed for Black teacher improvement. While White teachers by the 1920s had gained opportunities to attend colleges and normal schools, such was not the case with Black teachers. The piecemeal education of the summer schools and the institutes continued for Black teachers until almost mid-century.

In response to the depressing lack of Black teacher education in the early part of the twentieth century, State Superintendent of Education James Aswell established summer normal schools for Black educators. In 1905, Shreveport hosted a month-long summer normal school for Blacks in which prominent Black educators conducted sessions. By 1911, the state was offering parish training schools for Black teachers. The training schools undertook the dual role of training Black teachers and, at the same time, offering vocational training for Black communities. The parish institutes continued to train teachers until the late 1930s, when most of the agencies dropped their teacher education function and became vocational high schools. The summer schools continued for decades, with Shreveport often serving as a host city. Like teacher education for Whites, Black normal schools and colleges slowly usurped the function of the summer schools and the institutes. With the Blacks, however, this would not take place until the late 1930s.[125]

Also, like their White counterparts, Black educational leaders in Louisiana and Caddo Parish felt that the cause of Black teacher professionalization could be advanced by the development of teacher organizations. Thus, in 1901, a group of Black educators met in Alexandria and formed the Louisiana Colored Teachers' Association (LCTA). Understanding the hostility many Whites held against organizations of Blacks, especially educated Blacks, the LCTA leaders trod gingerly in their agitation for educational change. Leaders established the *Louisiana Colored Teachers' Journal* with the goals of unifying, improving, and stimulating teacher preparation. The organization also helped build small libraries for Black youth and helped conduct research on the inequality of Black educational facilities in the state.[126]

Despite the efforts of the LCTA, racial discrimination in Caddo Parish and Louisiana in general thwarted the attempt to educate Black teachers. Paralyzed by inadequate very low teacher pay, parsimonious state funding, and the prevalent poverty of Black people in general, educational leaders concerned with Black teacher improvement found themselves perpetually frustrated. Some educational leaders in Caddo did not favor teacher education of any type for Blacks: The less education they had, the easier they were to control. Sentiment favoring higher education for Black teachers began to gain ground by the late 1920s and 1930s. such support resulted in the founding of the Louisiana Negro Normal and Industrial School, later to be known as Grambling College.

Black teachers in Caddo Parish slowly began to take advantage of the teacher education program offered at Grambling.

In 1931, the state board of education passed regulations placing certification of Black teachers on the same level with White teachers. Too few Blacks, however, were graduating from teacher education programs to place a large percentage of certified teachers in Black schools. As a result, graduates of the institutes continued to receive certificates as late as 1947.[127]

Another factor which affected the professionalization of teaching in Caddo Parish was the increasing public dissatisfaction with unprepared teachers in the second decade of the twentieth century. Throughout the state, political and business leaders called for more qualified, and in the context of industrialization, more efficient teachers. As the high school movement developed in the early decades of the century, citizens lamented the fact that teachers were not prepared to offer much more than upper-elementary grade work. By 1912 and 1913, the state department of education issued resolutions requiring higher standards for high school teachers. At the same time, the state board of education took control of the teacher certification process, creating a state examining committee to examine teachers.

The results of the first few state examinations were alarming. Only 52 percent of the White applicants and only 14 percent of the Black applicants achieved certification in the first examination in August of 1912. The second examination was administered in January and February of 1913, and, this time, 47 percent of the White and 41 percent of the Black applicants passed. The chairman of the state examining committee, John R. Conniff, admitted that, in order to certify more Black teachers, "a more elementary set of questions was given to the Negro applicants than to the White third-grade applicants." In compliance with the new state clarification requirements, Superintendent Byrd was asked not to hire any teacher without a valid state teaching license.[128]

As the result of Byrd's relentless efforts, White teacher educational credentials, at least, continued to improve in the last half of the 1910s and in the 1920s. By 1922, all but five teachers in the White high schools of Shreveport were college graduates. Statistics for the elementary teachers were not nearly as impressive. This improvement in credentials was effected despite the phenomenal population growth in Caddo Parish accompanying the oil boom of the 1920s. Between 1919 and 1924, the teaching staff at Central High School, Shreveport's White high school, increased from 16 to 56, while the student population jumped from 372 to 1,793. still, Byrd managed to keep most positions staffed with certified personnel. The public was impressed with Byrd's efforts.[129]

Continuing the push to gain public credibility, the state department of education mandated that all future certification of White high school teachers would rest on the completion of a baccalaureate degree, a requirement extended to elementary teachers in 1940. Byrd responded to the new state regulations in characteristic style. The Caddo superintendent mandated that all Caddo teachers not holding a certificate with academic work commensurate with the new state certification requirements would be required to attend school every summer until the new standards were met.[130]

Not until the mid-1930s in Caddo Parish did teachers begin to assert themselves as an organized profession, and then only minimally. Across the state, teachers had been granted tenure legislation and state-supported retirement by 1936 and sick leave by 1940. Still, Louisiana teachers and Caddo teachers were very dissatisfied with the low pay. The average yearly salary for a White teacher in Louisiana in 1935 was $994.81, while the average Black teacher received $411.59 per year. Because of such low pay, a chapter of the American Federation of Teachers was organized in Caddo in January of 1935. Such organization disturbed the residents of Shreveport, and the public and the teachers fought over the issue of teacher pay throughout the late 1930s and the war years. By 1950, teacher salaries had improved to an annual average of $2,817.99, an increase attributable more to better economic times than to effective teacher organization. Still, by mid-century, the struggle for teacher professionalization faced a long fight.[131]

PROGRESSIVISM WITH A SOUTHERN ACCENT: EFFICIENTLY ADJUSTING STUDENTS TO THE NEEDS OF BUSINESS

Around the turn of the century, educators began to look at the role schools played in society from a different perspective. Awed by the social changes wrought by industrialization and technology, some educators argued that schools should not just teach information but should help students adjust and fit the emerging new society. In other words, schools would not only embrace academic goals, but they would address social goals as well.

This new social role for education would mean that schools would determine the slot students would occupy in society and then educate them for it. With the disruption of traditional family and social life that industrialization and technology threatened to bring about, schools offered the hope of social order and the elimination of conflict. If industrialization was pulling Americans away from the familial roots, then schools could take over many of the traditional socializing functions of the home. If the new technical and industrial order was destroying the agricultural and craft orientation of the American labor force, then schools could train students for new types of jobs in the new society.

Thus, the old classical curriculum of the academies and the early high schools was giving way to more practical studies. This curriculum was designed to make the student capable of participating in a dynamic democratic society and to help the youth find his or her "proper" role in it. Ultimately, however, the concern of these new educators was social rather than individualistic. These new educators were Progressives, closely aligning themselves with the Progressive political reform movement of the period. Contrary to some traditional views, not all Progressives were "liberal," and many of these new Progressive educators envisioned very conservative political outcomes for their version of school reform.

Like conservative Progressives, egalitarian Progressives planned to use education as a means of reducing social conflict within the society. The egalitarians, however, envisioned a more just society where rich and poor both had access to a democratic school system which provided the skills necessary to economic opportunity. Such educators saw the monopolistic entrepreneurs and the special interests as the bad guys—villains who sapped the country's resources for personal economic gain. When these forces were regulated and the schools had helped provide social and economic justice for the poor, all classes of men and women could come together in a peaceful community where resources were equitably distributed.

The conservative Progressives did not accept the "idealistic" egalitarian social vision. Social conflict would be ended, they argued, only when scientifically trained experts and managers wrestled control away from the monopolistic entrepreneurs and enacted their vision of a harmonious society. The only way that harmony could be achieved in a complex industrializing society was through imposition; individuals had little choice concerning their role. The educational managers would determine the student's aptitude and accordingly assign him or her a special social position. Thus, the school took on a significant function in the formation of the new society. The school was to adjust students to life and to prevailing social conditions, oftentimes without sufficient attempt to study or question those conditions.[132]

Enamored by the principles of scientific management, the conservative Progressives wanted the schools run as scientifically and efficiently as the industrial society they envisioned. The leaders of the Caddo Parish schools shared the goals of the conservative Progressives. In their attempt to build an efficient educational system designed to meet the needs of an ever-changing and developing area, the Caddo educational leaders designed a scientifically managed educational program. By 1911, the bureaucracy was in place, and rules and regulations governing the behavior of pupils, teachers, parents, van drivers, and janitors were submitted to the school board. In order to insure efficiency, principals were required to make a monthly written report to the school board on each teacher; the city school supervisor and the rural school supervisor were required to submit a monthly written report on the schools; and soon, a committee was formed to present a written report on the administration of Caddo Schools and the methods employed by Caddo teachers. Efficiency ruled: Educational paperwork had come to Caddo Parish.[133]

If the leaders of Caddo education were successfully to fulfill their role of efficiently matching the child to the social role best suited for him or her, students would have to be classified. An editorial in the Shreveport Times in 1924 reflected the perspective of the educational leadership in Caddo concerning the classification of students. We believe in "fitting the children according to their natural endowments for useful careers," the Times editorialist argued. It is unwise, he continued, to make pupils follow a core curriculum, "a fixed path, willy-nilly . . . achieving little."

> Some children are retarded naturally, these children should not be forced to feel their inaptitude for certain subjects, for Divine Providence has created us with a view to making us all fit into the great clock-work of the universe. There are important functions for every man, woman, and child to perform in this life.[134]

Forward-looking educators, the editorialist concluded, should see to it that today's children "fit according to their peculiar abilities . . . the manifold tasks of the morrow." In the early days of Shreveport High School, Byrd attempted to classify all students the week before school began. As enrollments grew and guidance became more ostensibly scientific, more efficient and comprehensive means of classifying students would be developed.[135]

Standardized testing emerged as a key to assessing the abilities and aptitudes of students. Through observation and testing, counselors could objectively decide who best fit into specific curricula and who should be trained for specific vocations. Testing became so pervasive in Louisiana education in the 1920s that elementary students were given standardized tests by the state every six weeks. It was inevitable that such testing led to formalization and standardization of the curriculum. Nevertheless, it was assumed by educational leaders that evaluation must be precise if students were to be accurately advised concerning their vocational aptitude.[136]

It was during the first decades of the twentieth century that the social goals of school and the goals of business merged. Reports indicated that students who did not stay in school did not make good workers. With the classical curriculum and the absence of practical studies, reports also suggested that even children who stayed in school were not being supplied with so-called, industrial intelligence. In other words, the classical curriculum was not providing business with good employees. If schools were not providing business and industry with able workers, then a locality's competitive economic condition was undermined. There was but one solution: The schools would have to change.[137]

Various civic groups pressured the Caddo schools to become more sensitive to the business and industrial needs of the Shreveport area. Frances Shuttleworth, the Education Chairman of the Louisiana Federation of Women's Clubs, asked Superintendent Byrd to improve the vocational and educational guidance in Shreveport schools. Coupled with the call for vocational guidance was the suggestion that the school system devote more study to local economic, social, and industrial conditions and adjust school vocational education policies to contribute to their improvement. School dropouts should be brought back into vocational educational programs, Shuttleworth continued. This the schools were only happy to do, for, if the school was to perform the role of supplying industry with efficient labor, then dropouts were embarrassments.[138]

Thus, the Caddo schools undertook the goal of training students to become efficient workers for the labor force. As early as 1901, Byrd applied for, and was granted, a manual labor school for boys that was constructed adjacent to Shreveport High School. The students at the manual training school learned to work with tools, usually carpentry and woodworking related implements.

By 1907, Caddo schools were expanding vocational course offerings designed to provide training for specific jobs. By the 1920s, domestic sciences, shorthand, bookkeeping and typewriting were all regular electives in the high school curriculum. Manual training was offered in both the senior high and the junior high in Shreveport. Vocational and manual education were always popular with teachers and administrators because they gave educators a means of dealing with those whom they perceive to be the less bright students. Often coming from the homes of the economically less well-to-do, the vocational and manual students were perceived to be much safer when removed from the academic classroom.[139]

The education of the efficient worker was but one of many goals undertaken by the schools of the new century. All across the country, educators were calling for more subjects in the school curriculum, subjects that would educate not merely the mind but would socialize the child and make him or her a better citizen of the new society. By 1909, the State Department of Education had issued a curriculum guide for Louisiana elementary schools which called for new courses. Nature study was required in grades one through six; agriculture in grade seven; art in one through seven; gardening in the first to the fifth grades; civics in grade seven; physiology and hygiene in the fifth, sixth, and seventh grades; and vocal music in the first through the seventh grades.[140]

The role that school played in Shreveport society expanded dramatically in the early twentieth century. By 1908 Caddo schools took on the responsibility of improving the health of their students. Health education became a top priority, and monthly health inspections of all schools and all pupils were conducted. At the same time, local doctors presented lectures on the proper care of eyes and teeth, improving sanitation, and disease prevention. By 1909, school officials had arranged for the board of health to set up a plan for vaccinating all school children against prevalent diseases. In 1911, the schools successfully focused their efforts on the eradication of the hookworm which afflicted about 50 percent of the rural population.

By 1915, the first school cafeteria in the parish was established at Shreveport High School. It was justified on the basis that one of the most important roles of the school was the improvement of student health. No longer, proponents proclaimed, would students have to buy the unhealthy, dust-covered sandwiches sold by the vendors who lined up next to the school entrance.[141]

Another aspect of the health education movement in Caddo Parish was the call for sex education in 1911. The Louisiana Federation of Women's Clubs, which had been so supportive of vocational education to meet the business needs of Shreveport, now insisted that sex hygiene be taught in the schools. Education Chairman Frances Shuttleworth sent a letter to State Superintendent T. H. Harris requesting his support for the measure. The movement for sex education was stymied when Harris told the group that any attempt to teach the subject in Louisiana schools was "unthinkable."[142]

Another role the schools assumed during the era was agricultural education. In 1908, the state legislature required that agriculture be taught in all Louisiana elementary schools and, by 1910, it was mandated in all secondary schools. Agricultural problems, such as the boll weevil plague in the first decade of the century, had heightened Louisianan's awareness of the need for scientific farming. Agricultural education was designed not only to improve knowledge of farm procedures, but it was designed to change unfavorable attitudes toward the farming life. Louisiana, in the second decade of the twentieth century, was beginning an era of organization and industrialization. Some of the new urbanites no longer viewed the farmer as the noble yeoman but as a hick and a rube. Agricultural education, in the words of Superintendent Harris, was designed to 'break down the false attitude which exists in the mind of so many people toward country life and country pursuits."[143]

The teaching of home economics or domestic science also became an important school priority during the period. Shreveport High School was one of the first schools in the state to teach regular courses in home economics. Justified on the basis that an important role of the school was to improve the quality of a student's family life, home economics took on greater importance in female education as the years passed. Louisiana educators touted its virtues, claiming that "no other single phase of the high school curriculum has been more effective in producing good results than home economics."[144]

As early as 1895, girls at Shreveport High School had formed a basketball team that competed with other clubs (school and non-school) in the area. Athletics quickly became an important aspect of school life after the turn of the century, with football and baseball teams formed by the second decade of the century. Physical education, as a responsibility of the school, gained acceptance during the first decades of the century. By 1913, supervised play, which included athletics, acrobatic stunts, and games, occupied an important part of the curriculum. Equipment was purchased by the city, and funds were raised to purchase a two-acre playground for each school. In the 1924 school year, the school board hired a physical education director to oversee the supervised plan to help plan the inclusion of a daily physical education period.[145]

Military training gained entry into the curriculum at the time of World War I. Byrd took a census of the boys enrolled in Shreveport High School between the ages of 14 and 18 and submitted the information in his application to the War Department for an instructor and equipment for the establishment of a Junior ROTC program. After studying the value of military training, Byrd and the school board agreed that the program would contribute physical and mental training and bring about better discipline in the school.[146]

Thus, the curriculum continued to expand. Caddo schools requested more and more social responsibilities, and, in the process, the public came to expect more and more from them. By the 1930s, art and music were accepted components of the curriculum, dramatics were promoted for their social and academic value, and the vocational curriculum had expanded to include auto repair and metalwork. "The schools were attempting to do all things for everybody."[147]

In an era which placed so much emphasis on industrialization and urbanization, and at a time when the school devoted much of its efforts to helping students adjust to a new industrialized, urban society, one might think that rural education was neglected. Such was not the case; school leaders extended the concept of school as preparation for life into a rural environment. Indeed, turn of the century conservative Progressive educators saw the rural farm problem as an educational problem. Inadequate education, the educators contended, had contributed to the bad state of affairs in rural Louisiana and rural Caddo Parish. Conversely, they reasoned, innovative, practical education could be used to improve rural life.[148]

The first years of the twentieth century had been rough years for farmers, especially cotton growers. Many farmers lost their land, and others watched profits drop dramatically as bad weather and boll weevils plagued their crops. Schools in the rural areas did not serve a large percentage of farm children. In Caddo Parish, most of the early twentieth progress in education was taking place within Shreveport, yet two out of every three children of school age in the parish lived in the country. As parish superintendent, Byrd made one of his top priorities the improvement of rural schools and the development of a specially developed rural curriculum.[149]

Besides the lack of financial support, rural schools were plagued with bad transportation conditions in country areas. Caddo Parish began the Good Roads Movement early in the century as a part of the larger attempt to improve rural schools through consolidation. If the curriculum were to be expanded and standardized so that every group of pupils could be prepared for a particular role in society, schools would have to be consolidated. Indeed, the basis of the conservative Progressive educational agenda of social efficiency rested on school consolidation. Before Superintendent Byrd could initiate his progressive plans for the education of rural youth, the Caddo rural schools would have to be consolidated. Byrd eventually won the battle, but not without some resistance from rural Caddo Parish communities who maintained that consolidation had destroyed their control over the education of their children.[150]

By 1910, the state department of education was beginning to treat rural education seriously. That year, a state supervisor of rural education was appointed and a course guide for rural schools in the state was published. In conjunction with the law that agriculture had to be taught in all elementary schools, Louisiana educational leaders were trying to insure that a bureaucracy was established which would encourage rural schools to improve rural life. In 1913, the state department specified the courses that would be offered by the rural schools. Included in the new curriculum were classes in agriculture, domestic economy, shop work, general science, rural sociology, rural economics, agricultural botany, agricultural zoology, agricultural physics, agricultural chemistry, algebra, and plane geometry. The department also specified the methods that should be used to teach these classes.[151]

The educational leaders of Caddo Parish warmly embraced the new ideas for rural education and embarked on a plan to implement the curriculum and its goals. Byrd and the school board agreed that rural schools could elevate rural people along economic, social, and moral lines. They believed that, through the public schools, a new type of farmer could be trained. He would be an efficient farmer who applied urban principles of scientific management to his agri-business.[152] Caddo progressives cheered when rural agricultural leader V. L. Roy addressed a Shreveport audience in May, 1913. Rural schools, he argued, had the power to bring about unprecedented changes in rural life. Up until this point, he continued, rural education had been disgraceful. It had been housed in shanties and had presented itself as merely city education administered in the country.

> The rural child may learn how Europe is drained but he learns nothing about the drainage of his father's farm. He may know who Ponce de Leon was, but know nothing about humas, potash, and phosphoric acid. He can bound Montana, but does not know where Franklin Parish is. . . . He identifies the pictures of Socrates and Caesar . . . but cannot recognize the breed of a Polled Angus cow.[153]

Roy closed his argument with the contention that the most important mission of the rural school "lies outside the school house." In the final analysis, he said, the rural school must be judged by its ability to improve the life of rural people. "Its influence must extend . . . to the life of the community . . . the rural school of the future must stand for country life betterment."[154]

Caddo educators worked to make Roy's vision a reality in the parish. Caddo Parish School Board President W. E. Glassell called for a new kind of country school which taught the practical skills of rural vocations. Byrd supported the formation of corn clubs for boys and girls and hog clubs for all boys between 9 and 18 years of age to supplement the rural curriculum. Even neglected Black schools received some attention in the push to educate the model rural citizen. Negro farm leagues were formed in the rural Black schools to teach farming techniques to raise money for Black education. Funds raised from the sale of the crops grown by the leagues were used to build Black schools and to pay for the extension of school to eight months. In Caddo Parish the progressive expansion of the curriculum took many forms."[155]

In the training of citizens to occupy specific roles in society, curriculum expansion was not enough; a new methodology also had to be implemented. The child-centered movement within the larger Progressive education movement would provide this new methodology. While child-centered teaching methods had accompanied the expansion of the curriculum in other areas of the nation by the 1920s, such was not the case in Louisiana and Caddo Parish. Louisiana education in the 1920s was still quite formalistic, with subject matter outcomes and objective testing the order of the day.

The leaders of teacher education programs at Louisiana Polytechnic Institute and Southwestern Louisiana Institute began to introduce child-centered methodologies to their teacher education students in the 1920s. The more relaxed and informal methods were championed as a reaction to the high-tension teaching, the standardized testing, and the resulting curriculum standardization being promoted by the state department of education during the period. The teacher educators argued that such formalistic methods of teaching caused educators to neglect the more subjective, hard-to-quantify aspects of education. The emphasis on testing, they contended, caused teachers to overvalue test scores "to the neglect of highly desirable processes of thinking and working." By the middle of the 1930s, the advocates of child-centered methodology had won many converts around the state and in the educational leadership of Caddo Parish.[156] As the advocates defined it, child-centered methodology consisted of five basic points:

1. Pupils work cooperatively as a social unit.
2. Pupils participate in planning what is to be done, how it is to be done, and in the evaluation of the results of their efforts.
3. Concern for the overall growth and development of the child is central.
4. Every pupil is given an opportunity to experience the feeling of success.
5. As pupils and teachers work cooperatively, interests and needs of the pupils in a dynamic society take precedence over textbooks or formal courses of study.[157]

The influence of the child-centered Progressives in Caddo Parish was more apparent in the rhetoric of the parish school leadership than in classroom teaching. While some teachers did employ Progressive methods, most found that the techniques required too much prior planning and content knowledge to be performed successfully. Like teachers who came before them and after them, the Caddo teachers of the 1930s were, for the most part, content to teach as they had been taught. Thus, the supervision of the schools changed more than the teaching.[158]

The change in educational rhetoric was real, however. Caddo Parish Superintendent E. Weldon Jones argued in 1935 that the old style mental drill was unnecessary. More learning can e gained, he argued, "in the same amount of time devoted to something interesting, practical and adapted to the present day." With these considerations in mind, the superintendent pointed with pride to the automobile repair training, the restoration of old furniture, the art training, and the interior decorating found in Caddo schools. In the 1920s such subjects would have been considered supplementary, but by the 1930s they constituted a central role of the schools.[159]

The new science of teaching in the child-centered 1930s was the ultimate educational expression of the new industrialized and urbanized society of the modern era. In the new world, Mary Willis Shuey wrote in the 1935 *Shreveport Times* Centennial Edition, "future happiness depends on the way we learn to work with a group and play with a group." It is the schoolroom and school playground, she continued, where this adjustment to group participation is best learned. Shuey unintentionally captured the spirit of the era in education when she contended that, in the modern education of the 1930s, the talk was of social adjustment. Teaching theories had changed radically, she wrote.

> In the old days the three "Rs" of Reading, 'Riting, and 'Rithmetic were the chief things taught. Today the schools play to develop the child fully. The three Hs they say now, and surely to round head, hand, and heart is a better system than that of the past.[160]

THE CONTINUING OBSESSION WITH RACE IN THE TWENTIETH CENTURY

Often neglected in the midst of twentieth-century educational change, be it building improvement or new methodologies, was the large percentage of Black students in the parish. Educational goals and priorities may have changed, but the racial feelings which had dictated so much of Caddo Parish's social, political, and educational history remained the same. Educational leaders, even those who genuinely were concerned with Black educational progress, were handcuffed by the intensity of racism in the parish.

As the role of education expanded to match the goals of school to the needs of business and the industrializing society, some educators in the early part of the century began to call attention to Black education in the parish. Blacks in Shreveport, one educator proclaimed, "are ideal and thus growing up in ignorance and will be a curse to the city, parish, and state."[161] From the perspective of many citizens of Caddo Parish, Blacks deserved no educational support for two reasons: 1) They paid so few taxes; and 2) They were Black. In the eyes of the conservative Progressives, Blacks were viewed as another special group to be provided with a special form of education to fit them to their proper social role. To the new breed of educators "blackness" was a defect which would be repaired with scientific application of educational principles.[162]

The panacea for Black education involved enrolling Black youth in industrial education programs. By 1909, the Caddo Parish School Board had expressed its support for the establishment of a Black industrial school in the Allendale community. Five years later, the board discussed the establishment of another industrial training school, but Superintendent Byrd could not persuade the board to fund it. Byrd head-ed a committee which examined the possible formation of the school. The committee reported that, if some outside financial help could be secured, the school could become a valuable asset to the community. Funds were secured in 1915, and plans were submitted to the school board, outlining the organization of an industrial school which would operate six months a year. Six months was a significant improvement over the usual three-to-five-month terms for the Black schools in Caddo Parish during the period.[163]

As Roscoe White, the assistant superintendent of Negro schools in Caddo Parish in the 1930s and later superintendent of Caddo Schools, put it, "The Negro schools were better than nothing but they were not much better." White's assessment rings true when one examines Black schools in Shreveport, even in the midst of the crusade for better educa-tion in the early twentieth century. Though 62 percent of Caddo's 58,200 residents in 1910 were Black, the value of Black school property consti-tuted only 6.5 percent of the total Caddo school property value. In other words, in a parish predominately Black, 93.5 percent of the school monies were delegated to White schools. In 1911 almost 2,000 Black children in the city of Shreveport could not attend school due to the lack of classroom space for them.[164]

Since the parish school board would not spend more than a token of the taxpayers' money for Black education, Blacks in the twentieth cen-tury had to provide for themselves much as they had done in the nine-teenth century. In the first decades of the new century, most Black schools were still conducted in Black churches. In 1913, for example, of the 85 Black schools (most of which were one room shacks) in the parish, the school board owned only 26.[165]

Conditions were deplorable. Superintendent Byrd found in 1915 that at the Stoner Hill School for Blacks there were three teachers with 250 pupils in poorly ventilated rooms with insufficient equipment. Most Black schools were overcrowded with 60 to 80 students in a room. Roscoe White reported that overcrowding persisted into the 1930s and 1940s, with Black students having to work at desks made from apple crates. Textbooks used in the schools were the discards from White schools. Black teachers had to use whatever books they could get, and students in the same class worked from a variety of sometimes unrelated texts.[166]

The racial prejudices of the parish were so strong that they often overcame the conservative Progressives' desire to use the schools to fit Blacks into a specific, albeit inferior, role in the society. Vocational and industrial education for Blacks would continue but never at a level of funding which would satisfy proponents. As World War II ended, the child-centered Progressivism would fall out of favor with Caddo educators, and conventional educational wisdom would return with a renewed call for basic education. The dominant theme in Caddo education would still revolve around the issue of race, since the fear of desegregation would dominate the educational picture. Concern with racial politics and racial integration would become so obsessive that attention to educational purpose would sometimes be relegated to the back burner.

NOTES

1. See Harvey Neufeldt and Clinton Allison, "Education and the Rise of the New South: An Historiographical Essay," in Ronald K. Goodenow and Arthur O. White, *Education and the Rise of the New South* (Boston, 1981), 250–293. This essay is the best existing source for exploring historiographical trends in Southern educational history.

2. A. H. Leonard, "Reminiscences," unpublished manuscripts, L.S.U.-Shreveport Archives. [hereafter referred to as LSUSA], 28.

3. Perry Anderson Snyder, "Shreveport, Louisiana, During the Civil War and Reconstruction," (Ph.D. diss., Florida State University, 1979), 25–26.

4. Leonard, "Reminiscences," 28–34.

5. Robert L. Church, *Education in the United States* (New York, 1976), 123.

6. Edwin W. Fay, *The History of Education in Louisiana* (Washington, D.C., 1898), 38, 54, 60, 62–63, 66, 69–70; Lilla McLure and J. Ed Howe, *History of Shreveport and Shreveport Builders* (Shreveport, 1937), 161; Rachel B. Rodgers, "The History of Public Education in Bossier Parish, from 1843 to 1956," (M.A. Thesis, Louisiana State University, 1956), 12–13, 17–18;

Hilda A. Kohler, "A History of Public Education in Louisiana During Reconstruction," (M.A. thesis, Louisiana State University, 1938), 30–31. Secondary sources on this topic are sketchy and dated. Much work needs to be undertaken on antebellum education in Louisiana.

7.   Church, *Education in the United States*, 35.

8.   Leonard, "Reminiscences," 45; Mary Willis Shuey, "Public Schools of Shreveport Enroll 11,000 Students, Housed in nearly Score of Building," *Shreveport Times*, June 28, 1935, 13; Church, *Education in the United States*, 24.

9.   Leonard, "Reminiscences," 43–44.

10.   For a detailed discussion of the academies see Theodore R. Sizer, (ed.), *The Age of the Academies* (New York, 1964).

11.   Leonard, "Reminiscences," 45.

12.   Maude Hearn O'Pry, *Chronicles of Shreveport and Caddo Parish* (Shreveport, 1928), 195–197; James William Mobley, "The Academy Movement in Louisiana," *Louisiana Historical Quarterly*, XXX (July, 1947), 796–797.

13.   Leonard, "Reminiscences," 9, 42–43.

14.   Dora Currie, "Some Aspects of the Development of Public Schools in Caddo Parish During the Administration of Superintendent C. E. Byrd, 1908–1926," (M.A. Thesis, Louisiana State University, 1942), 4.

15.   See McLure and Howe, *History of Shreveport and Shreveport Builders* for biographical sketches of the professional leadership of Shreveport society in the late nineteenth century.

16.   Review of Harriet Martineau, *Society in America, American Quarterly Review*, XXII (September and December, 1837), 37.

17.   S. Alexander Rippa, *Education in a Free Society* (New York, 1971), 236–253.

18.   Carol Wells, "Kind and Gently Admonitions: The Education of a Louisiana Teacher," *Louisiana History*, XVII (Summer, 1976), 303.

19.   O'Pry, *Chronicles of Shreveport and Caddo Parish*, 195–196; Snyder, "Shreveport, Louisiana, During the Civil Way and Reconstruction," 83–84.

20.   O'Pry, *Chronicles of Shreveport and Caddo Parish*, 196.

21.   Ibid, 195.

22.   Sister Dorothea Olga McCants, D.C., "St. Vincent's Academy: The First Century, 1866–1971," *North Louisiana Historical Association Journal*, III (Winter, 1972), 75; Wells, "Kind and Gently Admonitions," 305.

23.   For an insightful personal glimpse at an academically educated woman of the era, see Wells, "Kind and Gentle Admonitions."

24.   Snyder, "Shreveport, Louisiana, During the Civil War and Reconstruction," 83–84, 141.

25. Joe Gray Taylor, *Louisiana Reconstructed, 1863-1877* (Baton Rouge, 1974), 108–113; Snyder, "Shreveport, Louisiana, During the Civil War and Reconstruction," 134–175.

26. Snyder, "Shreveport, Louisiana, During the Civil War and Reconstruction," 175–200.

27. *Shreveport Times*, February 11, 1873.

28. Taylor, *Louisiana Reconstructed*, 459–461; Kohler, "A History of Public Education in Louisiana During Reconstruction," 71.

29. Taylor, *Louisiana Reconstructed*, 461.

30. Roger W. Shugg, *Origins of Class Struggle in Louisiana* (Baton Rouge, Louisiana, 1939), 74–75.

31. Taylor, *Louisiana Reconstructed*, 464–465.

32. Ibid, 468.

33. Ibid, 134.

34. Church, *Education in the United States*, 34.

35. Entry for August 19, 1867, Caddo Police Jury Minute Books, LSUSA.

36. James McCleery to M.C. Cole, June 21, 1870, and Charles W. Keeting to M. C. Cole, December 4, 1873, both in Caddo Folder, Louisiana State Board of Education Collection, Louisiana State Archives.

37. Taylor, *Louisiana Reconstructed*, 462.

38. James McCleery to Thomas W. Conway, July 2, 1870 and Samuel J. Powell to James McCleery, June 25, 1870, Caddo Folder.

39. Powell to McCleery, June 25, 1870, Caddo Folder.

40. Patsy K. Barer, "Clifton Ellis Byrd, Educator" (Ph.D. diss., Louisiana State University, 1968), 23.

41. Kohler, "A History of Public Education in Louisiana During Reconstruction," 40.

42. Snyder, "Shreveport, Louisiana, During the Civil War and Reconstruction," 202.

43. Taylor, *Louisiana Reconstructed*, 92, 93, 158, 299.

44. Editorial in *The Daily Southwestern* (Shreveport) as quoted in Currie, "Some Aspects of the Development of Public Schools in Caddo Parish," 5–6.

45. O'Pry, *Chronicles of Shreveport and Caddo Parish*, 181.

46. Frank Grosjean, "Splendid Educational Facilities Always Afforded Youth of Shreveport," *Shreveport Journal*, June 27, 1935, 10.

47. Mobley, "The Academy Movement in Louisiana," 799.

48. McCants, "St. Vincent's Academy," 75.

49. Betty Porter, "The History of Negro Education in Louisiana," *Louisiana Historical Quarterly*, XXV (July, 1942), 730–735.

50. Henry Allen Bullock, *A History of Negro Education in the South* (New York, 1967), 1–12.

51. Grosjean, "Splendid Educational Facilities Always Afforded Youth of Shreveport," 10.

52. Currie, "Some Aspects of the Development of Public Schools in Caddo Parrish," 7, 34.

53. Taylor, *Louisiana Reconstructed*, 12; McLure and Howe, *History of Shreveport and Shreveport Builders*, 161, 245, 286; John C. Engelman, "The Freedman's Bureau in Louisiana," (M.A. thesis, Louisiana State University, 1937), 34.

54. Porter, "The History of Negro Education in Louisiana," 738; Taylor, *Louisiana Reconstructed*, 455; Engelman, "The Freedman's Bureau in Louisiana," 77.

55. James D. Anderson, "Ex-Slaves and the Rise of Universal Educational in the New South, 1869–1880," in Goodenow and White, Education and the New South, 3–6; Taylor, *Louisiana Reconstructed*, 455–456; Kohler, "A History of Public Education in Louisiana During Reconstruction," 41–42.

56. R. P. Player, "Negro Development Greatly Aided By Churches," *Shreveport Journal*, June 27, 1935, 16; Kohler, "A History of Public Education in Louisiana During Reconstruction," 44.

57. Church, *Education in the United States*, 128; Howard A. White, *The Freedmen's Bureau in Louisiana* (Baton Rouge, 1970), 7–9; Willie Malvin Caskey, *Secession and Restoration of Louisiana* (Baton Rouge, 1938), 142; Taylor, *Louisiana Reconstructed*, 456.

58. Taylor, *Louisiana Reconstructed*, 456; Englesman, "The Freedmen's Bureau in Louisiana," 82.

59. Church, *Education in the United States*, 133.

60. White, *The Freedmen's Bureau in Louisiana*, 20.

61. Entry for November 30, 1866, Records of the Bureau of Refugees, Freedmen and Abandoned Lands. LSUSA.

62. Entry for November 30, 1866 and Thomas Monroe to Frank R. Chase (Superintendent of Education for the Louisiana Freedmen's Bureau), June 30, 1867, in ibid.

63. Endorsement Memorandum from James McCleery, January 3, 1870, in ibid.

64. Henry J. Perkinson, *The Imperfect Panacea: American Faith in Education, 1865–1965* (New York, 1968), 19; Church, *Education in the United States*, 136; Entry for August 26, 1869, Endorsement Memorandum form James McCleery, September 4, 1869, entry for October 29, 1869, Records of the Bureau of Refugees, Freedmen and Abandoned Lands; Snyder, "Shreveport, Louisiana, During the Civil War and Reconstruction," 117; White, *The Freedmen's Bureau in Louisiana*, 183, 185; O'Pry, *Chronicles of Shreveport and Caddo Parish*, 154–155.

65. Taylor, *Louisiana Reconstructed*, 456–457; White, *The Freedmen's Bureau in Louisiana*, 188–190.

66.   Currie, "Some Aspects of the Development of Public Schools in Caddo Parrish," 6; Taylor, *Louisiana Reconstructed*, 467, 495–497, 507.

67.   Taylor, *Louisiana Reconstructed*, 498–499.

68.   Church, *Education in the United States*, 137–138.

69.   C. W. Hilton, Donald E. Shipp, and J. Berton Gremillion, *The Development of Public Education in Louisiana* (Baton Rouge, 1965), 12; Wells, "Kind and Gentle Admonitions," 312.

70.   William Ivy Hair, *Bourbonism and Agrarian Protest* (Baton Rouge, 1969) 60.

71.   McLure and Howe, *History of Shreveport and Shreveport Builders*, 162–163; Viola Carruth, *Caddo: 1000* (Shreveport, 1970), 108; Currie, "Some Aspects of the Development of Public Schools in Caddo Parish," 9, 13; Barber, "Clifton Ellis Byrd, Educator," 29.

72.   Currie, "Some Aspects of the Development of Public Schools in Caddo Parish," 8–10; McLure and Howe, *History of Shreveport and Shreveport Builders*, 245.

73.   Edwin Lewis Stephens, "Education in Louisiana in the Closing Decades of the Nineteenth Century," *Louisiana Historical Review*, XVI (January, 1933), 47; Hilton, Shipp, and Gremillion, *The Development of Public Education in Louisianana*, 12; Currie, "Some Aspects of the Development of Public Schools in Caddo Parish," 6–7.

74.   Church, *Education in the United States*, 142–143.

75.   Hilton, Shipp, and Gremillion, *The Development of Public Education in Louisianana*, 12; Taylor, *Louisiana Reconstructed*, 508; Hair, *Bourbonism and Agrarian Protest*, 268.

76.   Shreveport *Evening Judge*, February 24, 1896; *New Orleans Daily Picayune*, May 29, 1879.

77.   McLure and Howe, *History of Shreveport and Shreveport Builders*, 163; Currie, "Some Aspects of the Development of Public Schools in Caddo Parish," 18–20; Barber, "Clifton Ellis Byrd, Educator," 34.

78.   Currie, "Some Aspects of the Development of Public Schools in Caddo Parish," 20.

79.   Hair, *Bourbonism and Agrarian Protest*, 124.

80.   Ibid, 107.

81.   For traditional views on the Redeemers' educational policies see Stephens, "Education in Louisiana in the Closing Decades of the Nineteenth Century," and Fay, *History of Education in Louisiana*.

82.   Shreveport *Evening Judge*, December 15, 1985.

83.   Hair, *Bourbonism and Agrarian Protest*, 119, 122, 113.

84.   Porter, "The History of Negro Education in Louisiana," 805; Hair, *Bourbonism and Agrarian Protest*, 113, 121, 125.

85.   Shreveport *Weekly Caucasian*, February 6, 1890.

86.   Hair, *Bourbonism and Agrarian Protest*, 127.

87. John G. Van Deusen, "The Exodus of 1879," *Journal of Negro History*, XXI (1936), 119; Hair, *Bourbonism and Agrarian Protest*, 84.

88. Hair, *Bourbonism and Agrarian Protest*, 190–191.

89. Shuey, "Public Schools of Shreveport Enroll 11,000 Students," 13; Currie, "Some Aspects of the Development of Public Schools in Caddo Parish," 12.

90. Shuey, "Public Schools of Shreveport Enroll 11,000 Students," 13; Currie, "Some Aspects of the Development of Public Schools in Caddo Parish," 13–14.

91. Neufeldt and Allison, "Education and the Rise of the New South," 259–260; Church, *Education in the United States*, 147.

92. Church, *Education in the United States*, 148.

93. Hair, *Bourbonism and Agrarian Protest*, 56, 190.

94. Grosjean, "Splendid Educational Facilities Always Afforded Youth of Shreveport," 10; Barber, "Clifton Ellis Byrd, Educator," 34–35; Shuey, "Public Schools of Shreveport Enroll 11,000 Students," 14.

95. J. David Cox, "An Evaluation of the Pupil-Activity Program of C. E. Byrd High School," (M.A. thesis, Louisiana State University, 1942), 15–16; Shuey, "Public Schools of Shreveport Enroll 11,000 Students," 14.

96. Taylor, *Louisiana Reconstructed*, 508; Hair, *Bourbonism and Agrarian Protest*, 234–281; Church, *Education in the United States*, 150–152.

97. Wells, "Kind and Gently Admonitions," 313; Grosjean, "Splendid Educational Facilities Always Afforded Youth of Shreveport," 10; Shuey, "Public Schools of Shreveport Enroll 11,000 Students," 13–14; Currie, "Some Aspects of the Development of Public Schools in Caddo Parish," 12; Barber, "Clifton Ellis Byrd, Educator," 33.

98. Hilton, Shipp, and Gremillion, *The Development of Public Education in Louisiana*, 15; O'Pry, *Chronicles of Shreveport and Caddo Parish*, 154; Carruth, *Caddo: 1000*, 108. Grosjean, "Splendid Facilities Always Afforded Youth of Shreveport," 10; Shuey, "Public Schools of Shreveport Enroll 11,000 Students," 13; Stevens, "Education in Louisiana in the Closing Decades of the Nineteenth Century," 49.

99. Rodney Cline, *Education in Louisiana—History and Development* (Baton Rouge, 1974), 91; M.S. Robertson, *Public Education in Louisiana After 1898* (Baton Rouge, 1952), 13; Currie, "Some Aspects of the Development of Public Schools in Caddo Parish," 15–16.

100. Robertson, *Public Education in Louisiana*, 13; Cline, *Education in Louisiana*, 91, 95.

101. Robertson, *Public Education in Louisiana*, 125; Cline, *Education in Louisiana*, 90.

102. Cline, *Education in Louisiana*, 91; Wells, "Kind and Gentle Admonitions," 317.

103. Wells, "Kind and Gentle Admonitions," 317–318.

104. Currie, "Some Aspects of the Development of Public Schools in Caddo Parish," 16; Barber, "Clifton Ellis Byrd, Educator," 46; Robertson, *Public Education in Louisiana*, 130.

105. Robertson, *Public Education in Louisiana*, 12–13.

106. Currie, "Some Aspects of the Development of Public Schools in Caddo Parish," 16; Barber, "Clifton Ellis Byrd, Educator," 46.

107. Barber, "Clifton Ellis Byrd, Educator," 82–83, 49–40.

108. Ibid, 15, 35.

109. Church, *Education in the United States*, 290–291, 303.

110. Robertson, *Public Education in Louisiana*, 57–74; Barber, "Clifton Ellis Byrd, Educator," 39–40.

111. Spencer J. Maxey, "Progressivism and Rural Education in the Deep South, 1900–1950," in Goodenow and White, *Education in Louisiana*, 57–74.

112. Steven, "Education in Louisiana in the Closing Decades of the Nineteenth Century," 48; Cline, *Education in Louisiana*, 26, 96; Robertson, *Public Education in Louisiana*, 211.

113. Currie, "Some Aspects of the Development of Public Schools in Caddo Parish," 42; Barber, "Clifton Ellis Byrd, Educator," 47.

114. Barber, "Clifton Ellis Byrd, Educator," 47–49.

115. Currie, "Some Aspects of the Development of Public Schools in Caddo Parish," 46; Robertson, *Public Education in Louisiana*, 13.

116. Cline, *Education in Louisiana*, 92; Currie, "Some Aspects of the Development of Public Schools in Caddo Parish," 17; Shuey, "Public Schools of Shreveport Enroll 11,000 Students" 13.

117. Rodney Cline, *Builders of Louisiana Education* (Baton Rouge, 1963), 89–90; Currie, "Some Aspects of the Development of Public Schools in Caddo Parish," 17; Barber, "Clifton Ellis Byrd, Educator," 41, 137–141; Stevens, "Education in Louisiana in the Closing Decades of the Nineteenth Century," 48; Cline, *Education in Louisiana*, 30–31.

118. Barber, "Clifton Ellis Byrd, Educator," 41, 43; Cline, *Education in Louisiana*, 31–32; Robertson, *Public Education in Louisiana*, 28, 35–36.

119. Robertson, *Public Education in Louisiana*, 35–36.

120. Barber, "Clifton Ellis Byrd, Educator," 44–45.

121. Church, *Education in the United States*, 302; Cline, *Education in Louisiana*, 25, 28–29, 51; Currie, "Some Aspects of the Development of Public Schools in Caddo Parish," 57–58; Robertson, *Public Education in Louisiana*, 132.

122. Perry H. Howard, *Political Tendencies in Louisiana* (2nd ed.; Baton Rouge, 1971), 203.

123. Porter, "The History of Negro Education in Louisiana," 770–806; Robertson, *Public Education in Louisiana*, 128.

124. Robertson, *Public Education in Louisiana*, 131–132.

125. Porter, "The History of Negro Education in Louisiana," 806–810.
126. Ernest J. Middleton, *History of the Louisiana Education Association* (Washington, D.C., 1984), 53–60; Cline, *Education in Louisiana*, 96.
127. Robertson, *Public Education in Louisiana*, 132–136; Interview with Roscoe White conducted by B. E. Tabarlet, June 28, 1977; Oral History Collection, LSUSA.
128. Currie, "Some Aspects of the Development of Public Schools in Caddo Parish," 43; Robertson, *Public Education in Louisiana*, 57, 71–72, 128–129; Barber, "Clifton Ellis Byrd, Educator," 45; Cline, *Education in Louisiana*, 91.
129. Barber, "Clifton Ellis Byrd, Educator," 88; Currie, "Some Aspects of the Development of Public Schools in Caddo Parish," 44.
130. Cline, *Education in Louisiana*, 92; Currie, "Some Aspects of the Development of Public Schools in Caddo Parish," 45.
131. Interview with Roscoe White; Cline, *Education in Louisiana*, 97–99; Robertson, *Public Education in Louisiana*, 157.
132. Church, *Education in the United States*, 192, 204, 256, 297, 302, 314.
133. Currie, "Some Aspects of the Development of Public Schools in Caddo Parish," 40; Barber, "Clifton Ellis Byrd, Educator," 38.
134. *Shreveport Times*, October 13, 1924.
135. *Shreveport Times*, October 13, 1924; Barber, "Clifton Ellis Byrd, Educator," 39.
136. Robertson, *Public Education in Louisiana*, 95–97; Cline, *Education in Louisiana*, 62–63.
137. Church, *Education in the United States*, 304–05.
138. Barber, "Clifton Ellis Byrd, Educator," 86.
139. Barber, "Clifton Ellis Byrd, Educator," 63, 76; Currie, "Some Aspects of the Development of Public Schools in Caddo Parish," 48; Church, *Education in the United States*, 217–221, 224, 306.
140. Robertson, *Public Education in Louisiana*, 90.
141. Barber, "Clifton Ellis Byrd, Educator," 76, 89–90, 107, 123–124.
142. Ibid, 76, 86.
143. Robertson, *Public Education in Louisiana*, 75, 91–92.
144. Ibid, 76–78, 91.
145. Barber, Clifton Ellis Byrd, Educator," 84–85, 105; Currie, "Some Aspects of the Development of Public Schools in Caddo Parish," 50.
146. Currie, "Some Aspects of the Development of Public Schools in Caddo Parish," 50; Barber, "Clifton Ellis Byrd, Educator," 83.
147. Shuey, "Public Schools of Shreveport Enroll 11,000 Students," 14.
148. Maxey, "Progressivism and Rural Education in the Deep South," 48.
149. Robertson, *Public Education in Louisiana*, 90–91; Barber, "Clifton Ellis Byrd, Educator," 116–117.

150. Maxey, "Progressive and Rural Education in the Deep South," 52–53; Barber, "Clifton Ellis Byrd, Educator," 116–117; Currie, "Some Aspects of the Development of Public Schools in Caddo Parish," 36–39.
151. Robertson, *Public Education in Louisiana*, 92–93.
152. Barber, "Clifton Ellis Byrd, Educator," 119; Maxey, "Progressive and Rural Education in the Deep South, 48, 52–53.
153. The *Shreveport Times*, May 8, 1913, 6.
154. Ibid.
155. Barber, "Clifton Ellis Byrd, Educator," 119, 123; Robertson, *Public Education in Louisiana*, 91.
156. Cline, *Education in Louisiana*, 63–64; Robertson, *Public Education in Louisiana*, 97–98.
157. Cline, *Education in Louisiana*, 65.
158. For a flavor of the teaching of the era, see interview with Roscoe White.
159. Shuey, "Public Schools of Shreveport Enroll 11,000 Students," 14.
160. Ibid, 13.
161. The *Shreveport Times*, January 2, 1911, 2.
162. Barber, "Clifton Ellis Byrd, Educator," 111; Church, *Education in the United States*, 204.
163. Currie, "Some Aspects of the Development of Public Schools in Caddo Parish," 51–52.
164. Interview with Roscoe White; Currie, "Some Aspects of the Development of Public Schools in Caddo Parish," 54; Barber, "Clifton Ellis Byrd, Educator," 111.
165. Currie, "Some Aspects of the Development of Public Schools in Caddo Parish," 34.
166. Barber, "Clifton Ellis Byrd, Educator," 112; Interview with Roscoe White.

Chapter

Socially Studying Science and Scientific Research: Integrating Social Studies and Science Education

Always scrambling to make social studies germane to students, teachers, and educational leaders, I constantly look for ways to integrate the discipline in other areas of the curriculum. In Chapter 16, I lay out a picture of what might happen when social studies and science educators pool their resources and begin to examine knowledge production in relation to the cultural and epistemological issues previously delineated. Critical democratic social studies teachers with an epistemological consciousness can profoundly affect the perspective of their science teacher colleagues as they help them view science as the product of a particular historical place with a specific set of cultural assumptions.

CONTEMPORARY SOCIAL AND CULTURAL STUDIES OF SCIENCE

The first decade of the twenty-first century in Western societies is a time of critical analyses of the scientific establishment by scholars engaged in cultural studies of science, sociologists of scientific knowledge, multiculturalists who uncover the gender and race-inscriptions on the scientific method, and philosophers exposing science's claims to objectivity. The purposes of such studies do not involve some effort to critique the true value of Western scientific knowledge, that is, the correspondence of a scientific pronouncement to a reality existing in isolation to the knower. Rather, such critiques of science point out that Western science has created a self-validating frame of reference that provides authority to particular Western androcentric, culturally specific ways of seeing the world. Typically, this way of seeing is viewed as superior to all others. As a result, too little self-criticism exists on the part of the Western scientific establishment.

Contemporary social and cultural studies of science apply the same forms of analysis to both physical and social sciences, asking in both domains how knowledge is produced and how do implicit worldviews shape the knowledge construction process. Such questions, unfortunately, tend not to come from within the scientific establishment but from outsiders such as students of the social domain. From the voices and the knowledges of non-Westerners and indigenous peoples, Westerners may be induced to take a new look at modernism's decontextualized rationality and the harm it can cause in people's lives around the planet. Indigenous knowledge (Semali & Kincheloe, 1999) provides a provocative vantage point from which to view Eurocentric discourses, a starting place for a new conversation about the world and human beings' role in it (Ross, 1996; Aronowitz, 1996; Kloppenberg, 1991; Harding, 1996).

The goal of such a learning process is to produce a transformative science, an approach to knowledge production that synthesizes ways of knowing expressed by the signifiers of hand, brain, and heart. It may be possible to examine the relationship between Western Cartesian science and global, multicultural, and indigenous ways of knowing in a manner that highlights their differences and complementarities. The purpose here is not only to deconstruct Western methods of knowledge production or to engage Western scientific researchers in a process of self-reflection. While deconstruction and self-reflection are important, I am more concerned with initiating an conversation resulting in a critique of Western science that leads to a reconceptualization of the Western scientific project around issues of multiple ways of seeing, justice, power, and community. The notion of a multiculturally informed transformative science is not one that simply admits more peoples—"red and yellow, black and white" into the country club of science but is an approach that challenges the epistemological foundations of the ethnoknowledge known simply as science.

A transformative scientist understands that any science is a social construction, produced in a particular culture in a specific historical era.

Via a study of indigenous knowledge, Western scientists come to understand their work in unprecedented clarity. As they gain a critical distance from their scholarship, they also gain new insights into the culturally inscribed Eurocentrism of the academy in general. Such informed scientists could begin to point out the similarities that connect indigenous perspectives with certain schools of feminism, agroecology, ecological theory, critical theory, and affirmative forms of postmodern critiques. While, obviously, these perspectives are different and come from diverse contexts, there are points around issues of knowledge production where they all intersect. Important and strategic alliances among physical scientists and cultural scholars, social studies teachers, and science educators can be constructed around these intersections. Operating in solidarity, individuals from these different backgrounds can ask new questions about what it means "to know," and about the role of love, empathy, and civic courage in the epistemological process.

A transformative science of education, for example, takes these epistemological and cultural dynamics into account as it reconceptualizes the way students are traditionally assessed. Rejecting the tendency of modernist educators to judge students on an arbitrary, allegedly neutral standard unconnected to them, the transformative educator develops personalized means of evaluating an individual's performance. The arbitrary norms of science are never disinterested; they are always culturally specific. In these questioning practices, transformative analysts are rejecting the universalizing tendency of modernist science, interrogating the power dynamics and cultural assumptions inscribed upon so-called universal propositions. In this manner, they are valuing locality and the insights the process of "de-universilization" can provide. When agricultural scientists, for example, begin to question the universal truth of scientific agriculture, they become far more receptive to the genius of the local knowledge accumulated by farmers around the world. Examples of such local ways of knowing are numerous and fascinating in their wisdom (Shankar, 1996; Kloppenberg, 1991; Apffel-Marglin, 1995; Airhihenbuwa, 1995).

Science educators can learn from critical social studies teachers about the social power science exerts and how it is used to discredit and oppress diverse individuals and groups. A key to comprehending the power of Western science involves its ability to depict its findings as universal knowledge. Modernist science produces universal histories, defines civilization, and determines reality. Such capabilities legitimate particular ways of seeing and, concurrently, delegitimate others. Such an ability is imperialistic, since it operates to characterize multicultural knowledges as inadequate and inferior. Too often in the mainstream philosophical study of epistemology, these power-related features of knowledge production are ignored. Epistemology, such Cartesian scholars contend, is a philosophical issue—nothing more. They fail to appreciate the ways modernist scientific universalism excludes "White science" as a cultural knowledge, a local way of seeing. Ethnoscience, like ethnicity itself, falls within the category of otherness. Indeed, whiteness itself took shape around the European Enlightenment's notion of scientific rationality, with its privileged construction of a transcendental, universal, White, male subject who operated at the recesses of power. But, even in this central position, he gave the impression of escaping the confines of time and space (Ashcroft, Griffiths, & Tiffin, 1995).

In this context, whiteness was naturalized as a universal entity that operated as more than a mere ethnic positionality emerging from a particular time, the late seventeenth and eighteenth centuries, and a particular space, Western Europe. Reason in this historical configuration is whitened and human nature itself is grounded upon this Cartesian reasoning capacity. Lost in the defining process in the socially constructed nature of scientific reason itself, not to mention its emergence as a signifier of whiteness. Thus, in its rationalistic womb, whiteness began to establish itself as a norm that represented an authoritative, delimited, and hierarchical mode of thought. In the emerging colonial contexts in which Whites would increasingly find themselves in the decades and centuries following the Enlightenment, the encounter with non-whiteness would be framed in rationalistic terms: whiteness representing orderliness, rationality, and self-control and non-whiteness, chaos, irrationality, violence, and the breakdown of self-regulation.

Rationality emerged as the conceptual base around which civilization and savagery could be delineated (Alcoff, 1995; Keating, 1995). This rationalistic, modernist whiteness is shaped and confirmed by its close association with science. As a scientific construct, whiteness privileges mind over body, intellectual over experiential ways of knowing, and mental abstractions over passion, bodily sensations, and tactile understanding. In the study of global and indigenous knowledge, such epistemological tendencies take on dramatic importance. In educators' efforts to understand the forces that drive the curriculum and the purposes of Western education, modernist whiteness is a central player. The insight it provides into the social construction of schooling, intelligence, and the disciplines of psychology and educational psychology in general opens a gateway into White consciousness and its reactions to the world around it.

These Western rationalistic dynamics of whiteness as a colonial impulse were well articulated by Sir Francis Bacon in his ruminations on the scientific method. Bacon conceptualized science as an entity that would "bind" nature and reduce her to a slave. As a slave, she could perform useful services for Europeans. This dominant-submissive relationship between scientist and nature is reproduced in the colonial relations between European and non-European and, in the power relations between universal and local knowledge. Such political dynamics have been rarely addressed in the literature of Western scientific scholarship, or in the literature of social studies, for that matter. Of course, great anger is elicited when non-Western or Western analysts point out the assumptions of Western superiority, racial hierarchy, and colonial relationships inscribed in Cartesian epistemologies. Since such assumptions are seen as natural or even God-given, critics who expose their social construction and ethnocentrism are viewed as enemies of the Western "regime of truth" or of the culture itself. Western society in general, and its educational institutions in particular, need to rethink this dynamic.

Thus, as a student of social studies and knowledge production, I engage in a critique of Western epistemological tyranny and the oppressive educational practices that follow it. Western epistemological tyranny decrees that the reality constructed by Cartesian-Newtonian ways of seeing is the only reality worth discussing in academic settings. Knowledge in this context becomes centralized, and the power to produce knowledge is concentrated in the hands of a limited power bloc. In this process, one begins to understand that science is the most powerful cultural production of Western society. The knowledge Western science produced became the benchmark by which the productions of non-Western civilizations were measured. In this context, Europeans, by the late-seventeenth century, became increasingly condescending toward the "primitive" knowledges of other cultures. Such perceived primitivism justified the civilizing efforts of the White man's burden and the pedagogical dynamics embedded in the concept (Harding, 1996; Hess, 1995; Dei, 1994; Jegede, 1994). Science teachers have rarely studied these social and cultural concepts.

DEMOCRATIC SOCIAL STUDIES EXPOSÉ
OF THE POWER OF SCIENCE:
CONSTRUCTING CRITICAL RESEARCH IN SCIENCE TEACHING

Since critical theory is grounded on the recognition of the ways power oppresses, it stands to reason that the forces of oppression have to be identified (Semali & Kincheloe, 1999; Codd, 1984). In the context of critical research in science education, one of the first places critical inquirers might look for oppression is, of course, modernist science itself. Critical observers have maintained that prediction and control of external phenomena are presupposed in the language of science as well as in mathematics and statistics. The external phenomena in question involve the control of nature to serve human ends (Aronowitz, 1988). Modernist science is committed to expansionism or growth. These are terms frequently confused with progress. Expansionism of this type demands that individuals be programmed for the progress-oriented agenda even when it conflicts with their best interests or the best interests of the community. Modernist science is committed to the production of profit. Too often, ideas, commodities, and people themselves are evaluated in light of their relation to profits. When individuals engage in actions that are contrary to the interests of profit making, science tends to reshape their behavior by labeling it deviant or pathological. Finally, modernist science is committed to the preservation of bureaucratic structures. Science serves as the force that processes people in relation to the smoothly functioning needs of bureaucracies. It is the bureaucratic need, not the human need, that takes precedent when a conflict arises. Obviously, these are key issues in both social studies and science education. Important interdisciplinary and collaborative work can take place around them.

Science is a force of domination, not because of its intrinsic truthfulness but because of the social authority (power) that it brings with it. "Scientists contend" . . . "science has proven" . . . "the test results tell us" . . . signify a power difficult to counter (Jenks, 1993). Critical social studies educators are quick to warn their science teaching colleagues not to perceive this "science-as-power" concept too simplistically. The way science exerts its power is quite subtle and rarely takes place without eliciting resistance. Men and women are not cultural dupes who are manipulated by some cabal of grand conspirators in unspecified high places. If people were merely cultural dupes, how could we teach them anything? We could possibly use some vulgar manipulative behavioral conditioning, but any respectful, reflective progressive pedagogy would not work with such dupes. At the same time, however, if men and women were not duped on occasion by power interests, there would be no need to promote their self-awareness and sense of agency. The development of such a consciousness would empower them to regain control of their lives from those who would use them to serve interests other than their own (Grossberg, 1994). *Thus, the power of science to shape and control demands to be analyzed by informed researchers who refuse to allow grand ideological pronouncements to substitute for specific inquiry.*

Consider, for example, the ways that an unexamined scientism subverts twenty-first century democracy. With the increase of environmental hazards resulting from scientific "progress," citizens sometimes seek to legitimate a "totalitarianism of hazard prevention" (Beck, 1992, p. 80). Here a pattern is created where in the attempt to prevent something bad (environmental side effects), something worse (suspension of democratic principles) is produced. In this context, the population is divided along a new set of axes, i.e., expert versus nonexpert, or those who possess the magic language and methodology of modernist scientific research versus those who don't. The mass of nonexperts, the experts maintain, must be provided with technical details that will condition them to respect the magic of the scientific elite. The cultivation of such respect is tantamount to a pacification program designed to quell public protest, criticism, or resistance, that is, to disempower and depoliticize. This is both an issue of social studies and science education. It can't be fragmented into separate domains.

Such an example of antidemocratic scientism highlights the empowerment impulse in critical democratic research. Inquiry that aspires to critical status is connected to the larger effort to confront various kinds of antidemocratic impulses, especially those embedded in the discourse of science. Such research thus becomes a transformative effort, unembarrassed by the label "political" and unafraid to consummate a relationship with an emancipatory consciousness. Emancipatory consciousness, as we know, involves the attempt to free oneself from the tacit controls of racial, class-based, and gendered discourses and lived practices. Often, these forms of control are justified in scientistic forms of rationality, e.g., Herrnstein and Murray's psychometrically validated discourse of racism. Max Horkheimer (1972) put it succinctly when he argued that critical research has never been satisfied with merely increasing the knowledge base. Therefore, a critical rendition of a socially informed science education research attempts to do more than understand the dynamics of science and pedagogy and the interesting ways they intersect. *Critical science education research attempts to change science and pedagogy by moving them into the emancipatory domain.* Critical democratic social studies teachers employ their work to empower science educators to construct their practice along well-analyzed moral, ethical, and political principles.

Science teachers who enter classrooms with such understandings and research abilities are prepared to make a cognitive leap; indeed, the stage has been set to move to a new domain of practitioner thinking (see my discussion of postformalism in Kincheloe, 1993, 1995; Kincheloe & Steinberg, 1993). As critical researchers endowed with a vision of what could be and a mechanism for uncovering what is, these teachers are able to see the sociopolitical contradictions of Cartesian science teaching and research in a concrete and obvious manner. Such recognitions encourage reflection, and thinking about one's own thinking, since they induce teachers to understand how these sociopolitical distortions have tacitly worked to shape their world views and self-perceptions. With a deeper understanding of such processes, practitioners recognize the insidious ways power operates to create oppressive conditions for some groups and privilege for others. Thus, critical research opens new ways of knowing that transcend formal analysis (Quantz, 1992; McLaren, 1989; May & Zimpher, 1986; Hultgren, 1987; Lesko, 1988; Carr & Kemmis, 1986; Porter, 1988; Tripp, 1988; Kincheloe, Steinberg, & Hinchey, 1999).

Excitement over the life of the mind and the effort to extend these new ways of knowing and researching constitute the lifeblood of a critical science education. Such grounded enthusiasm can generate interest among students, prevent burnout of teachers, and engage parents and community members in the world of science education. Critical research, with its power to latch on to and amplify excitement about thinking, is the type of educational activity that, unfortunately, right-wing activists have been attempting to quash over the last 25 years. Those who seek to narrow human possibility, to subvert the effort to redefine science for the twenty-first century, to undermine the quest for a science compatible with social justice, and to impede the progress of a cognitive revolution need to be held ethnically accountable.

THE IRRATIONALITY OF SCIENTIFIC RATIONALITY

Over the last two centuries, social analysts have repeatedly noticed a persistent irrationality embedded in modernist thinking that tends to devalue human beings and their needs. Nowhere is this impulse easier to identify than in the ways production decisions are made. Because modernist scientists and economists fail to account for natural and social realities, industrial policy often undermines the local and concrete concerns of democratic citizens. Raising the GNP becomes, in the spirit of raising standardized test scores, the purpose of economic activity. The GNP fails to distinguish among different kinds of production. The construction of more Burger Kings and Pizza Huts or shopping centers is just as important as steel or oil production. In this type of science-based economy, the value of economic activity and products is determined by considerations that have nothing to do with social needs. The short-term visions that dominate the economic sphere destroy concerns such as human creativity. Indeed, workers, for example, are reduced to mere pawns if profit parameters are modified (Chesneaux, 1992; Falk & Lyson, 1988; Aronowitz, 1992; Aronowitz & DiFazio, 1994).

The same neglect of social needs and irrational perspectives toward production has produced an industrial machine that laughs derisively at those who raise questions of ecological concern. George Bush, in the last days of the 1992 presidential campaign, called Al Gore, "Ozone Man" because of his book on the environment. Rush Limbaugh elicits a very positive response from listeners and viewers when he attacks the environmentalists as kooks and screwballs. When we examine the health hazards of modernist workplaces in the past and present, we realize the irresponsibility of American corporate leadership. Organized labor has finally begun to address the dangers posed to workers by the various chemicals and substances produced or used in production. The near epidemics of cancer and other industry-related diseases are forcing industrial leaders to reassess their policies of shameful neglect. One out of every four citizens in the United States now gets cancer, while one out of every five Americans dies of it (Kellner, 1989). Though corporate America has begun to earmark more money for public relations concerning environmental issues, the cleanup industry has only just begun.

A revolution of scientific thinking must occur before environmental protection becomes a common theme of management training, and social studies can help science teachers understand this dynamic.

Accounting methods, for example, must begin to view the environment as something inseparable from issues of economic production (Block, 1990). Improvements in the environment and increases in the quality of air and water would be treated as material contributions to the larger social and economic good. Growth for its own sake would no longer serve as an axiom of economic life. Suggestions that growth be considered in light of social needs or environmental concerns would no longer elicit cries of heresy in the corridors of American corporations (Aronowitz, 1992). The disorderly growth of California's high-tech Mecca, Silicon Valley, would become a symbol for the failure of modernist science in terms of its ecological and human damage. Toxic waste overruns the area; chemical leaks and accidents are hidden from public view; housing costs are ridiculous; traffic is horrendous; and desperate executives take amphetamines to get going and tranquilizers to calm down. The techno-logical consciousness that produced Silicon Valley would be reassessed vis-à-vis the demands of democracy. It would not become the prototype of the American future or the future of scientific progress.

Thus, democratic social studies educators maintain, contrary to the prevailing wisdom, that technological development does not necessarily improve our quality of life. The irrationality of the modernist marriage of science and economics, with its emphasis on short-term profits, has cre-ated an atmosphere where technological development has been viewed as a way to reduce labor costs. Technological development has allowed machines to take the place of skilled labor. Those involved in the pro-duction process, therefore, could be reduced to a few highly paid man-agers and R & D (research and development) experts and a division of low-wage skilled or semi-skilled workers attending to machines. Where there is evidence of a need for higher skilled workers in some high-tech industries, most advanced technological operations can be operated by low-skill, low-paid workers. The computer, for example, shows no sign of eliminating, or even reducing, the monotony and stress of service and information workers. Indeed, some studies indicate that word processing typists experience twice as much fatigue and lack of challenge as tradi-tional clerical workers. The irrationality of the workplace continues, and little effort is made to address the human consequences of work (De Young, 1989; Pollin and Cockburn, 1991). Modernist science continues its dehumanization of contemporary life. The modernist dream of a rational society fueled by disinterested scientific research has not worked out according to plan. This should be an important aspect of the socially informed science curriculum.

MAKING USE OF THE CULTURAL STUDIES CRITIQUE OF SCIENCE

One of the most important sites of theoretical production in the history of critical postmodern research has been the Centre for Contemporary Cultural Studies (CCCS) at the University of Birmingham. Attempting to connect critical theory with the particularity of everyday experience, students of cultural studies (which will be described in more detail in Chapter 26) argued that all experience is vulnerable to ideological inscription. At the same time, these researchers maintained that theorizing outside of everyday experience has resulted in formal and deterministic theory. Over the last 20 years, cultural studies' popularity has exploded in universities throughout the world, especially in the United States. In the last several years, this success has elicited a backlash against cultural studies that claims the goal of cultural studies is the destruction of Western science. Many academics have bought into this distortion. Given its new prominence, cultural studies demands specific definition. As an interdisciplinary, transdisciplinary, and sometimes counterdisciplinary field, cultural studies functions within the dynamics of competing definitions of culture. Unlike traditional humanistic studies, cultural studies refuses the equation of culture with high culture. Instead, cultural studies asserts that myriad expressions of cultural production should be analyzed in relation to other cultural dynamics and social and historical structures.

Such a position commits cultural studies to a potpourri of artistic, religious, political, economic, and communicative activities. In this context, it is important to note that, while cultural studies is associated with the study of popular culture, it is not primarily about popular culture. Cultural studies interests are much broader and generally tend to involve the production and nature of the rules of inclusivity and exclusivity that guide academic evaluation, and, in particular, the way these rules shape and are shaped by relations of power. Such insights are especially important for researchers in science education, since they allow insights into scientific assumptions typically outside the purview of the field.

Like any critical field of research, cultural studies is concerned with its application to the world outside the academy. Proponents maintain that the project of cultural studies is to address the most urgent social questions of the day in the most rigorous intellectual manner available. Thus, the everyday concerns of cultural studies are contextually bound. Indeed, the work of this interdisciplinary discipline is constantly being articulated and rearticulated around new social, cultural, and political conditions. Its engagement with the ever evolving historical context subverts any tendency on the part of cultural studies scholars to become complacent about the field's contributions both inside and outside the academy. So important is this notion of context that some scholars label the work of cultural studies as radical contextualism. To conceive cultural studies as radical contextualism, or a theory of context making, speaks directly to the field's contribution to the reconceptualization of analysis. In this context, cultural studies becomes extremely valuable to social studies educators working in collaboration with science teachers.

The decontextualization that cultural studies addresses is derived in part from the disciplinary structure of the social and physical sciences. So fragmented is research and scholarship among the disciplines that communication between scholars is undermined. Awareness of the risks produced by modernist science slips between disciplinary cracks, disappearing through the sieve of overspecialization. Scholarship has become so isolated that scholars work in private, focusing on narrow areas, rarely analyzing the way this isolated work fits into a larger whole. Producing knowledge that is so specialized, scholars often have little concern with the meaning of the knowledge produced, its application, or its possible effect. Cultural studies attempts to overcome this fragmentation by highlighting culture as a living process that shapes the way we live, view ourselves, and understand the world around us. By adopting cultural studies' overtly multidisciplinary approach, social studies and science teachers can study larger social issues, such as race, class, gender, sexuality, ethnicity, immigration, and pedagogy from unique perspectives and theoretical positions. As students of cultural studies question the dominant ways of seeing that evolve around the "normal science" of disciplines, they free themselves from the self-validating redundancies that limit insight and chain them to familiar explanations (Nelson, Treichler, & Grossberg, 1992; During, 1994; Grossberg, 1994; Beck, 1992; Aronowitz, 1993). The pulse of critical democratic social studies is beating in cultural studies.

HOW THEY GONNA KEEP'EM DOWN ON THE MODERNIST FARM, AFTER THEY'VE SEEN QUANTUM THEORY?

Science teaching has never been the same after its confrontation with a critical democratic, epistemologically conscious social studies. Physics could never be the same after the discovery of the subatomic world of the quantum in the early twentieth century. Depending on what questions are formulated about this realm of reality, a different picture of the quantum emerged. Two years after Werner Heisenberg issued his philosophical interpretation of quantum mechanics in 1927, John Dewey published in *The Quest for Certainty* an explanation of the way human action participates in the scientific formation of an object. It is not simply, Dewey postulated, that scientific understanding of the mysterious realm of subatomic particles can no longer fulfill the requirements of Newtonian research (Aronowitz, 1988). A much more dramatic implication has emerged from the study of the quantum, Dewey concluded: The object of the inquiry is altered by the inquiry itself. Simply put, the knower shapes, at least in part, the known. Science, therefore, becomes a social construction, and society becomes a scientific construction. The implications for scientific research and science teaching are powerful.

The New Paradigm Takes Shape

Such heretical thoughts created a philosophical/paradigmatic crisis that has lasted for almost seven decades—a crisis with staying power. Knowledge producers from all scientific and humanistic domains have had to examine the assumptions about knowledge with which they had grown so comfortable. Here physics begins to inform sociology and vice-versa, as researchers begin to notice the blurring of the boundaries between science and culture (Aronowitz, 1993). It is not far from this recognition to the deconstruction of science's tacit role in the prevailing social order. In this context, the deconstructive role of cultural studies can be appreciated, not only as a part of, but as a sophistication of, the effort to trace the social, cultural, and political footprints of science as a discourse. French social analyst Michel Foucault's project can be well-understood in this milieu. Foucault attempted to lay out the relationship among prevailing definitions of science, definitions of the normal and pathological, and the ways social behavior is policed. Like exhausted boxers hanging on to one another in the 15th round, postquantum science and society cannot be separated.

Sciences informed by a critical democratic social studies cannot ignore the limitations of Cartesian-Newtonian research. Biologists from the new paradigm contend that classical biology can only recognize one set of causes as operating in a living organism: external relations, or, those mechanistic factors that dictate its behavior. Rene Descartes conceived the laws of biology as merely the laws of matter in motion. Animal behavior, human physiology, even life itself, were viewed as undeviating mechanistic processes (Birch, 1992). The modern scientific certainties of rigid conceptions of space and time, impenetrable matter, and infallible laws of motion are in ruin. The chaotic world of an epistemologically informed science taunts the old boundaries with new theories of physical holism, dynamic interrelationship, and integrated life forms (Zohar & Marshall, 1994). Biologists in the twenty-first century can write, almost without embarrassment, about levels of organizations of electrons, molecules, and cells that behave not like the smaller units that constitute them but like a larger organizational whole.

Here the organizational whole becomes not only greater than the sum of its parts, and the parts themselves are transformed in the process of the whole's transfiguration from one evolutionary level to another. A dramatic principle has emerged in this context that transcends the construct of mechanistic modernist biology. In addition to interpreting higher levels of biological organization in terms of the lower, researchers make sense of the lower levels in terms of the higher. Biologists, informed by an epistemology of complexity, pursue the unsettling implications of this self-organizational dynamic, arguing that, when such activity occurs, it invades the space traditionally designed by scholars as "mind." Molecular geneticists have been sometimes forced to conclude that cell activity is more mind-like than machine-like in its constitution by internal relations. Buoyed by such understanding, some post-Cartesian scientists have contended that human experience is the high-level prototype of physical and biological building blocks, e.g., cells, atoms, and electrons (Birch, 1992). Thus, the ecological dynamics of a relational science, a way of seeing reasonably comparable to the radical contextualism of cultural studies and a critical social studies, emerges.

One of the ironies of the rise of Einsteinian/post-Newtonian physics and its influence on science in general involves the movement of the staid fields of philosophy of science and sociology of science to a prominent state. Once merely a handmaiden of the "important" work of science, philosophy of science involved little more than developing precise language to clarify the meaning of scientific research. With the rise of quantum research, philosophers of science have increasingly concerned themselves with important observational questions concerning what is seen in an experimental situation. Scientifically produced "facts," philosophers of science are quick to tell us, are no longer easily designated in a postmodern culture and a quantum universe. Questions of complex epistemologies, of knowledge production and validation, are central dilemmas of the new times. Research, for example, in molecular genetics that identifies a gene as having particular qualities can no longer be so easily verified once researchers uncover a manifestation of self-organization among genetic material. Research in subatomic physics that is unable to plot the trajectories of electrons like bullets shot from a gun raises complex validation questions that thwart any simple resolution. Classic objectivity no longer exists in such uncertain circumstances (Aronowitz, 1988, 1993; Birch, 1992; Courteney, 1988).

New epistemological models began to develop around these discoveries. Niels Bohr and his Copenhagen Interpretation specified the nature of knowledge in the quantum epistemology. Connecting observer and observed, Bohr and his colleagues refused to talk about atoms or electrons when they were not being observed. Thus, quantum epistemology delved into the irrational in nature. We must accept the irrational, the Copenhagen physicists argued, for, when we try to ignore it and build rational pictures or models of the quantum world, the classical ideas of Newtonian physics slip in to distort it (Peat, 1990; Talbot, 1986.) Picking up on the work of Bohr, physicist David Bohm developed a series of theories that pushed physics to a new dimension, while, at the same time, expanding our social and epistemological imaginations (Bohm & Peat, 1987; Briggs & Peat, 1984). While many have contributed to the avant-garde physics of the late twentieth and early twenty-first centuries, Bohm's work helps focus analysis on the interrelationship among quantum physics, critical democratic social studies, scientific research, and the concerns of science education.

*Dangerous Intersection: Quantum Physics and Critical Democratic
Social Studies—Contextualizing Research In Science Education*

The following nine points conceptually contextualize critical post-
Cartesian-Newtonian science education by delineating the social and
pedagogical lessons of quantum physics:

1. The universe is an undivided whole. Nature cannot be analyzed as if
   it were a conglomeration of parts.

David Bohm argued that, while employing the language of holism,
science has in practice studied the physical world as if the fragments
explored under microscopes and accelerated in particle chambers were
actual reality. Drawing on the ideas that would form the basis of his
notion of the implicate order (the order of reality that is yet to be unfolded), Bohm called for a reconceptualized scientific research agenda that
sought the enfolded connections among events. Bohm theorized the
existence of what he called an explicate and implicate order of reality.
The explicate order involves simple patterns and invariants in time, that
is, characteristics of the world that repeat themselves in similar ways and
that have recognizable locations in space, e.g., the level of reality we
inhabit that is marked by overt characteristics such as particular leaf
shapes on oak trees (Combs & Holland, 1990). Explicate orders are often
what is identified by the categorization and generalization function of
classical science.

The implicate order is a much deeper structure of reality. It is the
level at which ostensible separateness vanishes and all things seem to
become a part of a larger unified process. Implicate orders are marked by
the simultaneous presence of a sequence of many levels of enfoldment
with similar dissimilarities existing among them. The totality of these
levels of enfoldment cannot be made explicit as a whole. They can be
exposed only in the emergence of a series of enfoldments. In contrast to
the explicate order (already unfolded), where similar differences are all
present together and can be described in Cartesian-Newtonian terms,
the implicate order has to be studied as a hidden process, sometimes
impenetrable to empirical methods of scientific research (Bohm & Peat,
1987; Briggs & Peat, 1984).

In the implicate context, therefore, researchers study the flux and
flow, the stages of events—not simply the event itself. Critical post-

Cartesian-Newtonianism, like Bohm's physics, has decried the fragmentation of Cartesian-Newtonian epistemology and the research strategies that accompany it. Human and social experience, not to mention aspects of the physical world as well, has been reduced to discrete and arbitrary bytes that are separated from the combination of forces that provided the context in which distinctiveness emerged (Britzman, 1991). Cartesian-Newtonian love, for example, involves a raised heartbeat, a specific percentage increase in hormonal secretion, and a behavioral expectation of positive reciprocation. Science curriculum designers operating in this context remove science education from the social and physical realities that grant significance to the material to be learned. Operating on similar epistemological assumptions, quantum physicists and critical democratic social studies educators and researchers see human beings, society, and the physical world as interconnected aspects of a broader framework, an implicate order, which reveals itself when the evolutionary possibility of humanity is entertained (Oliver & Gershman, 1989). Operating with such understandings, science educators can identify a disciplinary discourse as an implicate order. Enfolded in the exclusions and inclusions of, say, the discourse of psychometric research is a set of enfolded patterns designating who will be deemed intelligent and who won't. An understanding of implicate orders, previously missed in the conversations of "normal science," opens researchers to exciting new insights.

2. Transcending dominant, certified ways of seeing: scientific and critical democratic social studies researchers as cognitive cartographers.

Bohm has maintained that to take wholeness seriously is to give up all that is familiar and comfortable about our understanding of the physical world. In other words, Bohm is asking us to step through the postquantum looking glass to the other side of the mirror. For example, Bohm and others have recognized that quantum systems are related in a manner which insults the traditional explanations of Cartesian-Newtonian physics. Subatomic level processes are connected in ways that have nothing to do with commonsense conceptions of fields, pushes, pulls, waves, particles, direct or indirect correlations. Dominant ways of seeing have nothing to do with such disconcerting quantum processes. For example, correlations between particles in different locations are often instantaneous, not requiring intercommunication. Labeled nonlocality, such interactions (or noninteractions) are irrational from a

Cartesian-Newtonian perspective. The time has come for a deconstruction and redefinition of the term, "rational" (Bohm & Peat, 1984; Peat, 1990). The process of redefinition may bring us to a level of understanding of physical reality which opens doors only imagined by science fiction writers.

Drawing upon the critical democratic insights of Frederick Jameson, Stanley Aronowitz and Henry Giroux (1991), I take the idea of transcending familiar ways of seeing into the realms of social and educational research. The counter-Cartesian critique alerts us to the dominant ways in which social reality is "mapped" and thus gives us the power to formulate new cognitive maps which take into account the unique conditions created by new electronic and informational technologies. In many ways, the socioeducational space created and occupied by television, mass advertising, computer technology, music videos, video games and the like is as uncomfortable and as unfamiliar as the microspace described by quantum physics. The counter-Cartesian creation of new constellations of forms, that is, the rewriting of our lives and the ways we represent ourselves, is similar to the attempt of avant-garde physics to rewrite our understanding of physical reality. Critical democratic social studies teachers illustrate these connections to their colleagues.

Various scholars (Kitchener, 1988; Doll, 1993) have argued that we should characterize the eighteenth century in terms of "clockwork order," the nineteenth century as an era of organic growth, and the twentieth century as a time of turbulence. Is the twenty-first century a time of breakthrough to a new level of turbulent social and scientific reality? If turbulence is the watchword of an era, not only are new forms of mathematical and scientific research strategies necessary but so are new forms of pedagogy as well. Along with new epistemologies and cosmologies, social studies educators, scientific researchers, and science educators will have to come to terms with chaos theory in a variety of disciplinary settings. Such a cognitive process, William Doll (1993) argues, demands that we embark on a new attempt to formulate "a description of nature." Such a process requires science educators to involve themselves in a redefinition of self and personal value. This transformative effort will help them deal cognitively, emotionally, and spiritually with what Doll calls "a major turning point in our relations with the world" (Doll, 1993, p. 97).

3. Theory construction as means to insight, not as begetter of absolute
    knowledge and truth—the development of a science grounded on an
    epistemology of complexity.

Bohm is quite concerned with producing insights into the physical
world. An insight, he argues, is not a rigid truth but an act of perception,
a new angle on the "wholeness." We have to say good-bye, for example,
to the type of permanence Newton experienced when looking at the
night sky with its predictable stars and star paths. The turbulence of the
twentieth century focused our star-gazing on a new set of celestial bodies:
quasars, pulsars, black holes, galaxies rent apart, etc. (Doll, 1993). The
insights to be gained from such astronomical observations challenge
everything our scientific ancestors held dear. But all insights need not be
this cataclysmic. Just because it cannot claim epistemological certainty,
a poet's insightful ability to connect individuals to an empathetic flash on
the "taste of sorrow" does not relinquish its value. Knowledge of sorrow
is transitory. Each time we experience it, we find ourselves in new circumstances. The taste in the new context is slightly different, and we
slowly understand the feeling in subtly different ways.

Advantages can be gained from giving up the traditional epistemological quest for final knowledge. In a complex epistemological world of
science, emphasis is placed on the delicate, ever shifting nature of relationships between physical objects, and the undivided nature of reality,
and not on the individual pieces of our existence. Seen from a Cartesian-
Newtonian perspective, the heart is undoubtedly not the brain, but on
another more subtle plain, there is no way to separate the function of the
two organs. Indeed, to separate them is to lose insight into the genesis of
heart function and disease (Briggs & Peat, 1984).

Jean-Francois Lyotard (1984) maintains that the postmodern world is
an environment in flux, a social cosmos where the epistemological certainties of the past have been destroyed by technical and scientific innovation. Thus, individuals must steer their own courses, develop their own
insights without the guidance of validated benchmarks, unquestionable
philosophical assumptions, or universal definitions of reason. Knowledge is
constantly changing in the postmodern world, as the pace of social change,
in general, accelerates to a dangerous speed. Cartesian-Newtonian modernism attempted to control the changes by stepping outside of history,
developing permanent fixtures of truth, and using them to produce discursive closure, in an end to history and an end to conversation (Hutcheon,

1988). A science based on an epistemology of complexities operates from within history, knowing that present circumstances will change (probably tomorrow), and that history cannot be escaped. Critical science educators, like their social studies counterparts, understand that no curriculum is final, no canon sacrosanct, no research strategy ubiquitous in its application. There is always tomorrow in the post-Cartesian world (Pinar, 1994; Kellner, 1991; Grumet, 1988, 1992; Garrison, 1988; Fehr, 1993; Slattery, 1995; Cherryholmes, 1988; Carr & Kemmis, 1986; Capra, 1982; Bakhtin, 1981; Ashley, 1991; Wertsch, 1991).

4. Stretching beyond mechanistic ways of seeing—the coming collapse of the Cartesian-Newtonian world.

Many researchers and science teachers continue to practice their craft as if the mechanistic world view had never been questioned. They do not see that the *agent provocateur*, quantum physics, has already performed its subversive task with aplomb, sowing the seeds of ruination for Cartesian-Newtonian mechanistic fragmentation. Showing that the concept of separate atomic particles cannot be maintained, previously validated fragments of reality lost their definition as discrete entities existing in time and space. As the result of quantum analysis, physicists' pictures of individual subatomic particles blurred into postimpressionistic portraits of ill-defined clouds (Briggs & Peat, 1984).

The Cartesian-Newtonian master narratives and mechanistic ways of seeing are also crumbling in the social sciences, humanities, and education. In Western philosophy, poststructuralist, critical, and feminist perspectives have raised challenges to tradition via questions of ethics and justice. Critical theory is, in a sense, the quantum physics of social theory since it reframes the Cartesian-Newtonian picture of fragmented social and educational reality. Foucault, Derrida, Lyotard, Habermas, and Baudrillard have successfully challenged the empiricist assumptions (the metanarratives) of science and other cultural systems. As they challenged the epistemological authority of consensus, they exposed the illusion of consensus. They tapped in to the subjugated ways of seeing of the marginalized, the dispossessed.

The counter-Cartesian-Newtonian scientific research tradition can be traced back to the time of Descartes and Newton themselves. Outsiders such as Giambattista Vico in the early 1700s and Søren Kierkegaard in the first half of the nineteenth century argued that mechanistic ways of knowing reduced humans to mere objects to be manipulated, not subjects with the power to gain consciousness and control their own lives (Lowe, 1982; Mahoney & Lyddon, 1988; White, 1978; Reinharz, 1979, 1982). The subjugated knowledge in this dissent tradition rejected the Cartesian-Newtonian definition of a substance as something that exists independently of anything else. There is a difference between an organism, a natural entity, a human being, and a machine. When nature is measured mechanistically (like a machine), it dies. Indeed, the sacred and spiritual nature of life is rendered mundane. The amazing capacity of living things to organize themselves is ignored when scientists climb over one another to measure the rate of their "growth." In science education, the phenomenal ability of a child to organize a picture of her role in the natural world is lost in the mad rush to count her correct responses (Birch, 1992; Doll, 1993).

5.   Siamese twins connected at the point of perception—the inseparability of the knower and known.

After quantum theory, the assumption that the observer and that which he or she observes constitute discrete parts of the universe cannot be supported (Briggs & Peat, 1984). Of course, the questions we ask about quantum reality shape the picture of the subatomic cosmos we paint. As previously argued, our location in the web of reality, our vantage point, influences our questions. Thus, to remove the knower from the object of study is to distort the process of knowing. Post-Cartesian science and social studies are grounded on this constructivist conception of knower-known inseparability. It transforms the "givens" of modernism into the "constructions" of postmodernism. Thus, while reality may exist, it is molded by the discourses, concepts, and categories of human interpretation. Many have taken such an assertion to mean that the world is meaningless. Why should social scientists and educators even attempt to perform their tasks? Counter-Cartesians respond that constructivism does not imply meaninglessness, just that any meaning which remains to be found is created by us ourselves (Hutcheon, 1988). Such an understanding holds dramatic implications for the ways we inquire and teach. It grants us a critical distance which allows us to uncover that which was hidden by the assumptions of certainty: the ironies, the ambiguities, the complexities, the intentions that shape what we have become.

When science educators and researchers refuse to separate the observer and the observed and focus on the nature of the knower, interesting insights begin to emerge. Humans are sensitive to subtle, hard-to-categorize dimensions of social life. Because of such sensitivity, the human inquirer can interact with a situation in such a way that the unspoken, the hidden, can be made explicit. The empirical research instruments that are capable of assessing particular factors are inappropriate for assessing other factors. Such is not the case with human instruments; they are almost unlimited in their adaptability. Physical and social science researchers, as agents freed from reliance on particular instruments of inquiry, are capable of simultaneously collecting information about a variety of factors at a variety of levels. Humans, unlike impersonal research instruments, can perceive holistically. In the maelstrom of confusion that constitutes the socioeducational world, only humans can see connections between the disparate parts; only humans can grasp and perceive dominant themes in the ostensibly unrelated remnants of the socio-educational fabric. Human inquirers can extend knowing to a higher level through their capacity to grasp the realm of the felt, the emotional, the unconscious. Unexamined usages and unintended meanings reveal insights that open windows into the significance of experience, which are the types of understandings that only humans are capable of grasping. These are the insights that allow us to comprehend the actual educational and ideological effects of schools and other institutions.

6. The inseparability of whole and part—abandoning the idea of a rigid body for the notion of "world tube."

To Bohm, structures of reality are parts of larger flowing movements, like a vortex in a stream. Albert Einstein initiated the concept with his idea that there are no Newtonian rigid bodies existing absolutely in space and time, only relative ones. In the place of rigid bodies, Einstein introduced the idea of world tube or the history of a region of space. Rejecting the notion of the particle as smallest unit of physical analysis, Einstein's world tube implied that matter was best conceived as a process, as an interaction of whole and part. Indeed, where does the river end and the vortex begin? Of course, there is no way to tell because physical reality is an infinitely complex, rationally unanalyzable continuous process (Bohm & Peat, 1987; Briggs & Peat, 1984).

In the same way that avant-garde physics subverts the notion of the unified or rigid particle as the smallest coherent unit of analysis in the physical universe, counter-Cartesianism subverts (decenters) modernism's notion of the free, coherent, transcendent, unified individual (or subject). The idea of a free, coherent individual is grounded on an acceptance of a rational, self-determining consciousness, free from any type of consciousness construction. Critical democratic social studies educators contend that human subjects gain their "subjectivity," their meaning in the world, through their social relations. Thus, the human subject is shaped by multiple and contradictory forces. The self is no longer a simple warehouse for consciousness. It is a site of the ambiguous pushing and pulling of a multitude of influences. As with a vortex, it is hard to determine where human consciousness ends and social and discursive acts begin.

Modernist biologists, operating in the mechanistic paradigm, held that an organism grows in complexity from a single fertilized egg to a multidimensional living entity in the same way a tinker toy bridge is built—separate piece by separate piece. Now, however, we understand that, if you sever the limb bud of an embryonic frog, jumble the cells, and randomly throw them back together, a normal frog leg still develops. Whole and part are inseparable, because the frog embryo exhibits qualities not found in machines. The fragments of the embryo gain their identity as a result of their spatial relationships at strategic phases in the growth of the embryo. Developmental biologists, employing Cartesian-Newtonian research strategies, were occupied for 60 years on a futile search for a discrete organizer, a single molecule or a single group of molecules, that served to organize the various portions of an embryo (Birch, 1992). The bloodhounds were called home, the hunt was canceled, and the futility of the search was acknowledged. Embryonic development, like countless other biological, physical, and social realities, can't be reduced to the causation of a single chemical, sub-atomic particle, or "great man."

7. The instability of language—scientific language is the progeny of the Cartesian-Newtonian world.

We must talk, David Bohm argues, but we must remember that our words are never about absolute things. At our best, we express insights. At our worst, we communicate illusions. Quantum theory, for example, undercuts our complacency about the meaning of words such as "path." It is not that the electron's path is uncertain. It is the linguistic use of path in this context that doesn't work. Echoing Wittgenstein, Niels Bohr often reminded his colleagues that reality is just a word in the particular word game of science. Drawing upon Bohm's theory of enfolded order, we can see that all science is grounded in a language designed only to describe the explicate order. Thus, language is a prisoner of the Cartesian-Newtonian wardens. What we can conceptualize is significantly limited by the failure of language to keep up new dimensions of reality (Briggs & Peat, 1984; Peat, 1990).

A central tenet of a critical democratic pedagogy involves its description of the instability of language. Frames of reference seem to be a matter of systems of description, discursive rules, rather than of that being described. Language, thus, does not possess a fixed and absolute correspondence to reality. The individual's construction of meaning, as a result, with this counter-Cartesian understanding, is freed from the confines of traditional usage. Viewed critically, we are empowered to see that the meanings considered most legitimate are significantly determined by power groups who exert influence over the economic and social workings of a culture (Hutcheon, 1988; Aronowitz & Giroux, 1991). Indeed, one of the tragedies of any absolutist or essentializing school of thought is that, having accepted the need to free language and thinking from its Cartesian-Newtonian constraints, some wish to immediately place a new set of constructive meanings upon society. A complex democratic social studies understands the absurdity of such a goal.

8. The wholeness of the universe cannot be captured by one grand theory—there is always another vantage point from which to question reality.

Each time in the history of science that we arrived at a point where a particular paradigm failed to provide consciousness expanding, meaningful answers, we have reached an epistemological watershed. In effect, what happens during this period of dissonance is that we discover a deeper wholeness to the cosmos than we had ever before anticipated. The holistic nature of reality extends far deeper than our maps, theories, or equations ever portrayed it. Philosopher Martin Heidegger once provided an insightful example in attempting to illustrate the difficulty of one description capturing the wholeness of reality. Comparing truth to a drinking glass, Heidegger explained that, as one rotates the glass to see one particular aspect, another aspect is concealed. The glass, he concluded, can never be positioned in a manner that allows one to see the whole glass. From a previously unconsidered angle, we may see another dimension of the wholeness (Briggs & Peat, 1984).

"Let us declare war on totality; let us be witnesses to the unpresentable," Lyotard (1984) wrote in an attempt to reflect the counter-Cartesian notion that wholeness cannot be captured by one grand theory. Within the socioeducational domain, critical democratic social studies educators reject attempts to delineate an essential transhistorical human nature, a fixed theory of intelligence or ossified stages of cognitive development, or the correct human goals that must be pursued. Typically, such totalities wrap themselves in the banner of objectivity and scientific disinterest, thus freeing themselves from a distasteful debate. The counter-Cartesian attack on totality is offered in the attempt to deflate an authoritarian epistemological machismo, replacing it with a complex diversity of perspectives and voices. The stories of the subjugated emerging from particular historical struggles offer new perspectives on the wholeness of society—perspectives that allow us to see Heidegger's glass from new angles (Aronowitz, 1988).

9. The inability of old orthodoxies to name the changes that are shaping our lives in the twenty-first century.

Newtonian physics assumes that we live in a world where the scale of size and energy is taken for granted. The quantum world in Newtonian terms is an irrational land of mystery, a fun house of mirrors, where objects instantly transform themselves from particles into waves, entities "walk" through two doors at once, and "distant relatives" use the telephone whenever communication is needed. The Mad Hatter, the Door Mouse, and psychometricians reign supreme. Physicists have been baffled by the action of subatomic particles and their ability to maintain a "nonlocal" connection that has nothing to do with space or time. Newtonian concepts have little relevance for such a terrain (Peat, 1990).

The postmodern condition, marked by a media-propelled landscape of consumerism, is a cosmos markedly different than the world into which the modern physical and social scientific disciplines were born. In the postmodern world, political and consumer discourses merge into a grammar of manipulative images. Counter-Cartesian critique assumes that such unprecedented conditions cannot be understood within the framework of modernism (Hutcheon, 1988). One of the few chances we have to escape the tortuous possibility of falling deeper into the pit of mindless consumerism and objectivism is to understand the critical democratic analysis of power relations within texts, codes, and cultural signs, indeed, within curricula and school definitions of success. Like Cartesian-Newtonian scientists, the attempts of traditional liberals and conservatives to explain the power relations of the postmodern world are inadequate. Indeed, an epistemology of complexity, and the knowledge production it supports, gives us a chance to go beyond, to explain what has traditionally eluded us, to explain the construction of the conscious operation of power, and to understand the ways that our schools unwittingly promote particular views of reality and self.

The types of paradigmatic conflicts detailed here often produce incommensurate perspectives about the world. Fields of study don't change in evolutionary and progressive steps but cataclysmically and contentiously with fervent debate and hostility. The counter-Cartesian pronouncement that Western technoscientific rationality has failed will not set well with many science educators and researchers. The modernist scientific establishment has too often failed to react to possible side-effects of its work (Aronowitz, 1988; Beck, 1992). Expert scientists have assured us that no causal link between tobacco and cancer can be established, that Agent Orange did not produce adverse health effects among U.S. soldiers in Vietnam, that Gulf War Syndrome is a creation of Gulf War veterans, that nuclear testing in the 1950s was safe, etc. Indeed, it has been the science establishment that has allowed the nonverifiable, value-laden goal of increased economic productivity to take precedence over human/environmental hazards. It is ironic that scientists, invoking their Cartesian objectivity and disinterestedness, have become the bestowers of legitimation on polluting industrialists who compromise the planet's air, water, food, plants, animals, and people in the quest for higher profit margins.

By the dawning of the twenty-first century, scientific miscalculation of nuclear risks in the 1950s and 1960s looks as naive as the eighteenth century medical practice of bleeding a sick patient or the nineteenth century "science" of phrenology. Few among us would not recognize the humor of the "Do not panic" male voice-over of the nuclear war sci-fi movies of the 1950s and 1960s or the "Prevent panic" reference of the following scientific expert-produced "Official Instruction Sheet" from

1959. A postmodern consciousness can read such a document only in a comedic context similar to the way Joel, Mike, and the robots on *Mystery Science Theater 3000* read a health education film (also produced by scientific experts) from the same era.

> A strong, blinding flash of light is the first sign of the detonation of an atomic bomb. Its thermal effects can produce burns. Therefore: *immediately cover sensitive body parts like eyes, face, neck and hands!*
>
> Immediately jump into a hole, a pit or a ditch! In an automobile, immediately duck beneath the dashboard, stop the car, fall to the floor of the new vehicle and protect your face and hands by curling up! If possible look for protection behind a heavy table, desk, workbench, bed or other furniture!
>
> You have a better chance of surviving in a cellar than in upper floors. *Not every cellar has to cave in!* If chemical or biological weapons are used, immediately put on your protective mask! If you don't have a protective mask, don't breathe deeply and protect your breathing passages by holding a moist handkerchief over your mouth and nose.
>
> Clean up and decontaminate yourself from radiation or poisons as circumstances warrant. *Prevent panic, avoid unthinking haste, but act!* (Beck, 1992, p. 60)

As the characters on *South Park* have learned: *Duck and cover.*

METHODS IN THE MADNESS: SHAPING POST-CARTESIAN KNOWLEDGE PRODUCTION IN SCIENCE EDUCATION

The attempt to construct a universal critical democratic research method is as futile as a physicists' quest for the ether. Critical post-Cartesian research in science education can make no guarantee about what particular questions will be important in varying contexts. Thus, no one methodology can be privileged over others, but, at the same time, none can be eliminated without due examination. Ethnography, textual analysis, semiotics, deconstruction, ethnography, critical hermeneutics, interviews, phonemic analysis, psychoanalysis, rhizomatics, content analysis, survey research, and phenomenology only begin a list of methods a critical postmodern researcher might bring to the table (Nelson, Treichler, & Grossberg, 1992). Such an eclectic view of research has been labeled *bricolage* by several scholars (Denzin & Lincoln, 1994; Weinstein & Weinstein, 1991; Becker, 1989). Bricolage involves taking research strategies from a variety of disciplines and traditions as they are needed in the unfolding context of the research situation. Such a position is

pragmatic and strategic, demanding a self-consciousness and an awareness of context from the researcher.

The Bricolage of Critical Research

The critical researcher is able to negotiate a panoply of data-gathering
techniques and a plethora of interpretive theoretical constructs (e.g.,
feminism, Marxism, cultural studies, critical constructivism, critical theory, post/counter-Cartesianism). Most critical methods can be deployed
at some point in one context or another to achieve critical democratic
goals. Such efforts hinge on the researcher's theoretical understanding of
the critical tradition and her ability to apply this understanding to the
social and interpersonal aspects of her life, e.g., understanding the relationships between one's way of seeing and the race, class, and gender
location of her personal history. Appreciating research as a political act,
the critical bricoleur abandons the quest for objectivity, focusing instead
on the clarification of the values he or she brings to the inquiry (Denzin
& Lincoln, 1994).

A few examples of critical postmodern methods in education are in
order. Semiotics is the study of codes and signs that help humans derive
meaning from their surroundings. Science education researchers can use
semiotic methods to gain insights into deep structures moving classroom
events. Indeed, classrooms are diamond mines for semiotic study, for they
abound in codes and signs, in conventions that call for unique insight.
The way teachers, students, and administrators dress; pupils' language
when speaking to teachers as compared to conversations with classmates;
graffiti in a middle-school restroom; systems of rules of behavior; the use
of bells in schools; memos sent to parents; language used by students to
describe science and scientists; and the nature of the local community's
conversation about school athletics are only a few of the many school
topics a semiotician could study. Critical researchers of the profound in
the mundane begin to move beyond traditional questions of teaching
into the uncharted territory of inquiries involving the question, Who are
we becoming as a result of this science education experience (Whitson,
1991; Britzman, 1991)?

The brilliance of semiotics is that it makes the given an object of
thought, of critical focus. Semiotics refuses the shallowness of lived experience, as it searches for ways of seeing that describe the invisible, the
empty spaces of the picture. Viewed from this perspective of the critical,

a gifted program in science or social studies involves far more than a set of enrichment activities for the smarter children. Levels of obscured assumptions begin to jump out of such programs when the light of grounded critique is shown upon them—assumptions unseen by even those making them. Thus, research moves from the glorification of the novel to the analysis of the assumed. In this context language transcends its role as conduit for information. Semiotic analysts view the relationship between speaker and listener or writer and reader to be based on constant interpretation in the context of the semiotic matrices brought to the act of communication by all participants. Thus, we are faced with the realization that communication becomes not a matter of extracting meaning from communiqués but of constituting meaning based on the cultural context, values, and social identities of those involved (Greene, 1988; Britzman, 1991; Bowers & Flinders, 1990; Manning & Cullum-Swan, 1994).

When researchers turn such interpretive strategies upon their own practice, they engage in semiotics of introspection. As researchers analyze their actions with attention to ritual, metaphor, and questioning strategies, they begin to uncover hidden dimensions of their belief structures, their familiar cognitive strategies, their assumptions about students, and their attitudes toward the "proper" deportment of a teacher (Courteney, 1988). No longer can knowledge producers hide in the shelter of the Cartesian-Newtonian objectivism that shields the self from the deeply personal issues that saturate all educational acts. Semiotic researchers cannot view themselves as transhistorical beings. They need to understand their place in the web from which they see reality. Contextualized in this way, the schemata, the values, the belief structures, that defy recognition as they fade in the familiarity of our consciousness are highlighted when they are dyed by the ink of semiotics. Historical contextualization of self in this situation utilizes the insight of difference when we finally begin to see ourselves placed against a social backdrop of values and ways of perceiving that are unfamiliar (Scholes, 1982; Hodge & Kress, 1988; Kellner, 1991).

Critical ethnography is another example of a critical research methodology that can be adapted to the bricolage. Ethnography, the study of events as they evolve in their natural setting, is often described as the most basic form of social research. While ethnographers disagree over the relative importance of each purpose, ethnography attempts to gain knowledge about a particular culture, to identify patterns of social interaction, and to develop holistic interpretations of societies and social institutions. Thus, ethnography in education, seeking to appreciate the social processes that move educational events, attempts to understand the nature of schools and other educational agencies in these ways. Ethnography attempts to make explicit the assumptions one takes for granted as a culture member. The culture could be as broad as Japanese culture or as narrow as the upper-middle-class student culture of George Washington High School. The critical ethnographer of education seeks to describe the concrete experiences of everyday school/educational life and the social patterns, the deep structures, that construct it. One of the most basic tools of the critical researcher involves the research orientation derived from the ethnographic tradition (Hammersley & Atkinson, 1983; Smith, 1989; Clough, 1998).

Counter-Cartesian forms of ethnography have focused on the discontinuities, contradictions, and inconsistencies of cultural expression and human action. As opposed to modernist forms of ethnography, counter-Cartesian methods refuse the attempt to reconcile the differences once and for all. The poststructuralist critique of classical ethnography highlights the tendency of the tradition to privilege a dominant narrative and a unitary, privileged vantage point. In the effort to conflate knower and known, the poststructuralist ethnographer proposes a dialogue between researcher and researched that attempts to smash traditional hierarchical relations between them (Atkinson & Hammersely, 1994). In the process, the modernist notion of ethnography as an instrument of enlightenment and civilization of the "native" objects of study dies an overdue death. Counter-Cartesian ethnographies are texts to be argued over, texts whose meanings are never natural but are constructed by circumstance. Such characteristics are obviously colored by poststructuralist ethnography's rendezvous with contemporary literary criticism and its Derridian influences (Aronowitz, 1993).

Some of the poststructuralist ethnographies of the last few years have taken a ludic turn, ignoring critical concerns while pursuing a high-vogue deconstructionist posture. Such practitioners avoid any epistemology that promotes critical action for socioeconomic change (West, 1991). Critical ethnographers have slammed such ludic practice, joining with feminist, African American, and postcolonial researchers to reemphasize questions of power's impact on identity, history, and social relations. The critical ethnography associated with feminism, antiracism, and postcolonialism has exposed the status quo apologetics of both traditional and ludic postmodern ethnography. In the tradition established by critical ethnography, advocates argue, practitioners must continue to document the rituals of resistance that have separated class cultures and subcultures from dominant society (Aronowitz, 1993; Nelson, Treichler, & Grossberg, 1992; Willis, 1977; Marcus & Fischer, 1986; Griffin, 1985; Clifford, 1992; Taussig, 1987).

The Feminist Dynamic of Critical Postmodern Research

Feminist research in the 1990s and the first decade of the twenty-first century has defined the center of critical counter-Cartesian scientific research. Feminist researchers have laid the groundwork for the new critical post-Cartesian paradigm by constructing a revisionist history of science that debunks many of the glorification myths of modernist science as religion (Aronowitz, 1988; Kincheloe, 1991; Clough, 1998; Hicks, 1999). Aware of the tacit subjectivity of modernist science and the political power it has wielded under the flag of disinterestedness, feminist researchers refuse to pay homage to its authority. The androcentric principle of a neutral, hierarchical, and estranged interaction between researcher and researched is subverted by feminist scientists (Fee, 1982; Mies, 1982; Olesen, 1994; Hekman, 1990; Flax, 1990; Ferguson, 1993; Collins, 1990; Butler, 1990).

It is important to point out that no monolithic body of feminist theory exists. Three forms of feminist analysis have dominated the feminist critique. 1) Liberal feminism has focused on gender stereotyping and bias. While such analyses have provided valuable insights, liberal feminism in general has failed to engage issues of power. As a result, the position has been hard pressed to make sense of social reality with its subtle interactions of power, ideology, and culture, an interaction that needs to be analyzed in the larger effort to understand both the oppression of women and male privilege (Weiler, 1988). 2) Radical feminism has maintained that the subjugation of women is the most important form of oppression in that it is grounded on specific biological differences between men and women. In radical feminism, concerns with race and class are more rejected than ignored, since radical feminists maintain the irrelevance of such categories in the study of women's oppression; 3) The form of feminist theory privileged in this chapter is, not surprisingly, critical post-Cartesian feminism. This articulation of feminism asserts that feminism is the quintessential counter-Cartesian discourse. As feminists focus on and affirm that which is absent and/or peripheral in modernist ways of seeing, they ground the critical democratic critique in lived reality, in the material world (Kipnis, 1988; Jagger, 1983). As critical counter-Cartesian feminists challenge modernist patriarchal exclusions, they analyze the connections between an unjust class structure and the oppression of women (Weiler, 1988; Rosenau, 1992). Often, they contend, male domination of women is concretized on the terrain of class, e.g., the feminization of poverty and the growth in the number of women who have become homeless over the last 25 years. A detailed analysis of critical counter-Cartesian feminism and its implications for research in social studies and science education is needed.

Ever grounding critical theory and research in everyday practice, feminist analysis extends our appreciation of the effort to connect emotion and reason, knower and known. Renate Duelli Klein describes a research project involving battered women. The researched (the battered women) were never considered objects of research but were viewed as subjects who were sisters, as mirrors of self. Researchers approached the project with the assumptions that the battered women were co-researchers. As such, the researchers and the researched compared their own experiences as women and negotiated the findings of the project in a way where the experience of each group was extended by interaction with the other (Klein, 1982). Such research strategies hold direct social, political, and epistemological implications for science educators. As researcher and researched interact, new insights into the interactions of teachers and students, teachers and teachers, teachers and administrators, and science education professors and teachers can be deconstructed on the cognitive, pedagogical, and affective levels, to name just a few.

Because of such benefits, feminist analysis has quickly moved to the center of the stage of late twentieth and early twenty-first century critical research. After its marriage to and transformation by feminist insight, a complex critical theory can never return to a paradigm of inquiry in which the concept of social class is simplistically privileged and exalted as the master concept in the Holy Trinity of race, class, and gender. A critical theory reconceptualized by poststructuralism and feminism promotes a politics of difference that refuses to pathologize or exoticize the Other. In this context, communities are more prone to revitalization. Periphalized groups in the thrall of a condescending Eurocentric gaze are able to edge closer to the borders of respect, and previously classified objects of research potentially acquire the characteristics of subjecthood.

Kathleen Weiler's *Women Teaching for Change: Gender, Class and Power* serves as a good example of critical research framed by feminist theory. Weiler shows not only how feminist theory can extend critical research, but how the concept of emancipation can be reconceptualized in light of a feminist epistemology (Aronowitz & Giroux, 1991; Lugones, 1987; Morrow, 1991; Weiler, 1988; Young, 1990). Emancipation run through the feminist filter loses its status as the final state one achieves by applying the "correct" theory. It becomes a contingent state, ever entwined with changing context and new insights and constantly grappling with unrecognized forms of oppression and regulation.

Such a rethinking of emancipation, as discussed earlier, with its concern with the specificity of context, focuses the attention of critical democratic researchers on the particularity of lived oppression. Realizing that concern with the particular and the local cannot be dismissed by abstract theories of macropolitics that privilege structural explanations of power, postfeminist critical inquirers understand the complex interaction between larger structural political dynamics and the particularity of individual experience [See my analysis of this dynamic as manifested via the power McDonald's exerts over children in Kincheloe (2001) and Steinberg & Kincheloe (1997)]. Feminists, such as Britzman (1991), Fine (1988), Benhabib and Cornell (1987), Flax (1990), Pagano (1990), Hutcheon (1989), Kipnis (1988), and Morris (1988), and analysts of gender and race, such as hooks (1989), Fox-Genovese (1988), and Jordan (1985), have taught critical theorists that, whereas larger social forces clearly exert a profound impact on society at large, their impact on individuals and localities is ambiguous and idiosyncratic. In this same context, William Pinar's and my theory of place in *Curriculum as Social Psychoanalysis: Essays on the Significance of Place* (1991) expands the notion of particularity and its relationship to wider, discursive regimes in the context of critical social theory and the politics of curriculum theory.

Madeleine Grumet (1988) extends our understanding of the feminist attempt to transcend logocentrism by connecting the language of the body, of feeling, with inquiry. Social science, she argues, whether guided by right-wing or left-wing impulses, has been enmeshed in a male-dominated snare of abstraction. Grumet has sought new methods of inquiry that were capable of drawing the body and feeling into the public conversation about education. Making use of qualitative methodologies such as history, theater, autobiography, and phenomenology, she confronts androcentric abstraction with the uncertainty, specificity, and contradiction of the private, the corporeal, the feminine. From the perspective of the guardians of the Cartesian tradition, such epistemological confrontations constitute overt subversion. After exposure to such theorizing, inquiry can no longer be viewed as a cold, rational process. As feeling, empathy, the body, are injected into the research process, as the distinction between knower and known is blurred, as truth is viewed as a process of construction in which knowers play an active role, passion is injected into inquiry. Critical researchers see themselves as passionate scholars who connect themselves emotionally to that which they are seeking to know and understand.

Here is the point where feminist theory blows the lid off of the Cartesian-Newtonian tradition. Modernist researchers often weeded out the self, denying their intuitions and inner voices, and, in the process, produced restricted and object-like interpretations of socioeducational events. Using the traditional definitions, these object-like interpretations were certain and scientific: Feminist self-grounded inquiries were inferior, merely impressionistic, and journalistic (Reinharz, 1979, 1982). Rejecting the authority of the certainty of science, feminist researchers charged that the so-called objectivity of modernist science was nothing more than a signifier for the denial of social and ethical responsibility, ideological passivity, and the acceptance of the privileged sociopolitical position of the scientific researcher. Thus, feminist theorists argued that modernist pseudo-objectivity demands the separation of thought and feeling, and the devaluation of any perspective maintained with emotional conviction. Feeling is designated as an inferior form of human consciousness. Those who rely on thought or logic operating within this framework can justify their repression of those associated with emotion or feeling. Feminist theorists have pointed out that the thought-feeling hierarchy is one of the structures historically used by men to oppress women. In intimate heterosexual relationships, if a man is able to present his position in an argument as the rational viewpoint and the woman's position as an emotional perspective, then he has won the argument: His is the voice worth hearing.

Drawing from feminist researchers, critical democratic social studies educators have learned that inquiry should be informed by our humanness, that we can use the human as a research instrument. From this perspective, inquiry begins with researchers drawing upon their own experience. Since the educational researcher is a human being studying other human beings, he or she is privy to the inner world of experience. Utilizing her own empathetic understandings, the observer can watch educational phenomena from within, i.e., she can know directly, she can watch and experience. In the process, the private is made public. Not only do we get closer to the private experience of students, teachers, and administrators and the effect of these experiences on the public domain, but we also gain access to the private experience of the researcher and the effect of that experience on the public descriptions he or she presents of the phenomena observed (Reinharz, 1979, 1982). Thus, not only do we learn about the educational world that surrounds us, but we gain new insights into the private world within us—the world of our constructed consciousness. (Remember William Pinar's insightful explanation of his notion of currere—the investigation of the individual experience of the public; Pinar, 1994).

No longer can critical counter-Cartesian researchers allow science to blind the knower intentionally, thus restricting what science can "see" in the world of education. By revealing what can be learned from the everyday, and the mundane, feminist scholars have opened a whole new area of inquiry and insight. They have uncovered the existence of silences and absences where traditional scholars had seen only "what was there." Such silences and absences typically revolve around the ostensibly value-neutral language of modernist science. To initiate inquiry, feminist researchers argue, with discussion focused only on method/technique instead of value assumptions is irrational. It is irrational in the sense that it tries to separate the way men and women obtain knowledge and make judgments. Flannery O'Connor has argued that "judgment is implicit in seeing;" that is, constructing judgments is not an isolated process. When it is isolated, the act of judgment is trivialized to the point where the insights derived from it are bland and trivial (Westkott, 1982). The work of Donna Haraway (1991), Evelyn Fox Keller (1984), and Sandra Harding (1986) has been especially important in exposing the silent values that drive modernist science. When this powerful feminist critique is deployed with the methodological bricolage of critical democratic research and the epistemological insights of quantum physics, science education is transformed forever more.

Respecting the Complexity of It All: Full Speed Ahead, Mr. Sulu

Critical democratic research respects the complexity of the world; it takes our epistemology of complexity very seriously. The nature of this complexity can be illustrated by the relationship between research and the domain of theory. The dense language of critical postmodern theory has too often discouraged the uninitiated in their effort to discern the relationship of such discourse to their everyday professional lives. Behind the language, there rest some very important insights for those interested in extending the conversation of science education. All scientific observation is theory saturated in that theory provides the language that frames what is observed. Theory in a modernist scientific mode is a way of understanding that operates without variation in every context. Since theory is a linguistic and a cultural artifact, its single interpretation of the object of its observation is inseparable from the historical dynamics that have shaped it (Rosenau, 1992). The task of critical research in social studies and science education is to address this complexity, methodically uncovering the invisible artifacts of culture and describing the nature of their influence. Scientific theory in this context is exposed for what it is: not an explanation of nature but an explanation of our relation to nature.

This is not to say that critical counter-Cartesian research has no use for theory. Indeed, theory is very important in the bricolage of critical democratic research. Theory involves the conceptual matrix analysts use to make sense of the world. Theory, whether it is held consciously or unconsciously, works as a filter through which researchers approach information, designate facts, identify problems, and devise solutions to their problems. Different theoretical frameworks, therefore, privilege different ways of seeing the world in general or the purposes of science education in particular (Aronowitz, 1993; Giroux, 1988). The theory behind a critical post-Cartesian way of seeing recognizes these theoretical dynamics, especially the potential tyranny that accompanies theoretical speculation. The problem that has undermined the traditional critical project of understanding and changing the inequality plaguing modernist societies has involved the production of a theory that was too totalizing (all encompassing) and rigid to grasp the complexity described here.

Critical post-Cartesian theory is committed to a theoretical stance that guarantees the individual or community the capacity to make meaning and to act independently. Any theory acceptable to critical democratic social studies and science educators, thus, must take into account local divergence. This is not to adopt a position that insists researchers allow phenomena to speak for themselves. Theory, critical post-Cartesians argue, is a resource that can be used to generate a dialogue with a phenomenon; it is always contingent, and it never whispers the answers to the researcher in advance (Rosenau, 1992; Dickens & Fontana, 1994; Grossberg, 1995; During, 1994). Theory is prone to motion sickness, in that it doesn't travel well from one context to another. Indeed, theory's usefulness is always mitigated by context.

Science educators of all stripes can learn from their encounter with the vicissitudes of the complexity of socially aware scientific research. Critical democratic research and the educational forms emerging from it assume that science educators must understand the conditions and effects of knowledge production, while, at the same time, engaging in knowledge production themselves. Maybe in the present regime this strikes us as a difficult, if not insurmountable, task. Given my experiences with science educators and science education students and the brilliance they bring to their tasks, I believe that such understandings are possible. As knowledge producers, science educators can weave understandings of knowledge validation, student experience, and the notion of consciousness construction with the latest research in, say, quantum physics or molecular biology. Students can be introduced to the ethnographic, semiotic, phenomenological, critical hermeneutical, deconstructive, and psychoanalytical dimensions of the bricolage, meanwhile coming to understand the social, political, and epistemological forces that shape science, education, and their lives in general. In this context, science educators gain the ability to step back from the world and look at it anew. Seeing from a sociocultural/epistemological perspective different from the one to which they have been conditioned, they uncover new vantage points to observe the constructing forces (Noffke & Brennan, 1991; Adler, 1991; Slaughter, 1989). As they produce knowledge, they remake their professional lives, and they rename their worlds. They benefit from their interaction with critical democratic social studies teachers, and the social studies gain new insights from them. The disciplinarity that keeps these two domains separate is counterproductive.

Part **IV**

Issues of Power in the Social Studies

Chapter

Addressing Patriarchy in a Critical Democratic Social Studies: The Recovery of a Dominant Masculinity

Little agreement exists on the meaning of patriarchy and how the term might be used in critical theories and a democratic social studies. Some scholars have called for the term to be abandoned, while others argue that, despite its analytical fuzziness, it can be used as an orienting concept in the study of male domination of women. When used in sociological literature, patriarchy falls within four general frames: 1) a system of government based on kinship; 2) a generalized form of masculine oppression; 3) a technology in the reproduction of capitalism; and 4) a system of gender and class relations.

From feminist theoretical perspectives, four views of patriarchy and patriarchal oppression have been employed:

1. LIBERAL FEMINIST VIEW OF PATRIARCHY: No one structure around which women's oppression is organized exists. Indeed, within liberal feminism, no search for grand social structures is undertaken. Instead, liberals look for small-scale problems of injustice, typically revolving around the refusal to provide equal rights for women in employment and education and the existence of sexist attitudes that help maintain the inequality of these rights for women. In focusing on rights and attitudes, liberal feminism fails to address the deep

social roots of gender inequality and the interconnections between these various dimensions;

2. RADICAL FEMINIST VIEW OF PATRIARCHY: Men as a social group oppress women as a social group. This gender opposition constitutes the most important structure of social oppression, deriving its power from the social structure of patriarchy and patriarchy alone. This is to argue that the patriarchal oppression of women is not a by-product of capitalism. In such radical feminist accounts, there exists a propensity for essentialism, meaning that social oppression is reduced to a biological dynamic. In this context, males are viewed as by nature predisposed to oppressive behavior toward women. In addition, this predisposition tends to become universal, dismissing differences between both women and men in terms of ethnicity, race, class, and religion. No matter what the social context, the patriarchal oppression of women remains relatively the same, and little possibility for change exists;

3. MARXIST FEMINIST VIEWS OF PATRIARCHY: Gender inequality is derived from capitalism, not from a structurally independent form of patriarchy. The way class relations are structured ultimately determines the nature of gender interaction. The focus on capitalism and economics in the Marxist version of patriarchy is deemed too narrow by many feminist critics, moving scholars to ignore the ways that gender subjugation operates differently than economic domination. The conversation about the relationship between capitalist oppression and patriarchal oppression continues to be central in the discourse of feminist theory (see Carol Johnson, 1996);

4. DUAL SYSTEMS FEMINIST VIEW OF PATRIARCHY: In this theoretical formulation, Marxist and radical feminist analyses of patriarchy are synthesized into a capitalist-patriarchal interrelated view. Sylvia Walby (1990) and others criticize dual-systems theory in that it doesn't go far enough in its electicism. These critics want to include in their analysis a wide variety of structures around which gender oppression takes place (Waters, 1989; Walby, 1990; Jonasdottir, 1994).

The purpose of this chapter involves helping social studies teachers develop a post-Cartesian theory of patriarchy that examines gender and gender oppression as socially structured ever evolving phenomena. Such a theory will focus on the various ways that masculinity is shaped by these complex power dynamics. The chapter will focus on developing an understanding of dominant constructions of masculinity, the crisis of this dominant patriarchal masculinity, the conservative recovery of this patriarchal masculinity, and progressive efforts to provide alternatives to this oppressive gender formation in the form of a critical democratic social studies analysis of patriarchy. Such a theory, I believe, transcends the limitations of each of the previous theories delineated, inasmuch as it draws upon recent advances in the domain of social theory and cultural studies.

Kate Millett's *Sexual Politics*, published in 1970, revived an almost dormant sociological conversation about patriarchy. Deployed as a counterhegemonic device, Millett's radical feminist view of patriarchy worked to identify the nature of gender inequality for the feminist movement's developing struggle against male domination. Almost three decades later, it is less difficult to understand the modernist assumptions that were driving this compelling, but conceptually underdeveloped, early work in feminist theories of patriarchy. With the benefits of hindsight and the insights of recent critical social theory, we can begin to formulate a critical counter-Cartesian view of patriarchy. Modernist methods of analysis induced feminists to theorize a universalistic, cross-cultural view of patriarchy that assumed a common subjugated experience for all women. Millett's "notes toward a theory of patriarchy," which set the terms of the discourse on patriarchy for years following its release, couldn't deal with the diversity of women's experiences, especially in relation to class, race, and ethnicity. The modernist tendency to essentialize women's identity around only the power axis of gender subverted analysis of women's subjectivity and experience outside a generally White, middle-class, heterosexual norm.

The theory of patriarchy delineated here draws upon a nontotalizing conception of male power that understands that patriarchal power does not emanate from a single nexus, nor does it work for the same outcomes, no matter what the historical place and historical time. This is why John Fiske's (1993) notion of a power bloc is always helpful, since it views power structures as ever changing and shifting alliances around specific issues in particular conditions. Thus, for example, particular men and groups of men may align with wealthy women around issues that support their mutual upper-class interests. On another issue, the power bloc might shift and realign itself in such a manner that these same men and women find themselves on opposing sides. In addition, the modernist tendency to view masculinity as a monolithic concept, devoid of masculine diversities around issues of class, ethnicity, race, or sexual preference, is no longer acceptable in a critical democratic social studies formulation. Early feminists used such a monolithic conception as a political device in their critique of patriarchy, since they were understandably afraid that male ambiguity and complexity would undermine the solidarity of the movement. Because of these and other concerns with a totalizing and essentialized view of patriarchy, the use of the term, "patriarchy" has often been avoided over the last fifteen years among students of gender. It is my contention that a critical democratic social studies education needs to reconceptualize and reclaim the critique of patriarchy in light of an epistemology of complexity and a study of the structural and ontological ways it works to construct masculinity and subordinate women (Waters, 1989; Butler, 1990; Walby, 1989; Gore, 1993; P. Smith, 1996).

CONSTRUCTING THE CRITICAL COMPLEX THEORY OF PATRIARCHY

The concept of patriarchy is important because it asserts that gender inequality is a pervasive feature of contemporary society. To invoke patriarchy is to problematize the social construction of gender and gender relations in a way that moves us to consider what constitutes a just and democratic academic curriculum, politics, and social consciousness. Any critical, complex, counter-Cartesian theory of patriarchy must draw upon a critical, poststructuralist, feminist theory for academic sustenance. Critical postmodern feminism posits that humans are social constructions, not entities who are determined by innate biological, universal characteristics. Such a position should not be taken to mean that biology plays no role in the production of humans or that we can merely change who and what we are simply by wishing it so. The theoretical position does imply that the potential of humans is far more open-ended than traditionally believed and that we should not blame our dispositions merely on biological or psychological determinism.

At the same time a critical complex theory of patriarchy relies on a critical poststructuralist feminism, it is very careful (especially when theorists happen to be men) to consider the political dynamics of using feminism as it does. Too often, men's engagement with feminism can be perceived to be, or actually is, an appropriation of such scholarship and political work for purposes not consonant with the feminist project. For example, patriarchal theorizing can serve to return the focus of scholarly attention to men in the process of helping to recover patriarchal authority. Given this possibility, any attempt to construct a complex theory of patriarchy must carefully examine the danger of appropriation. Fred Pfeil (1995) is acutely aware of this possibility and offers in *White Guys: Studies in Postmodern Domination and Difference* an excellent example of how male theorists might deal with it. Any emancipatory attempt to redefine masculinity without a humble nod to feminist theory and the help of women in general collapses into traditional patriarchy's male bonding rituals—activities that always involved the exclusion of women. The form of patriarchal theorizing and political practice delineated here always takes place in the presence of, and with the collaboration of, women (McLean, 1996a; Gore, 1993; Dowell, 1996).

In the spirit of this nod to feminist theory, a critical complex theory of patriarchy is informed by poststructuralist feminism's politics of difference that actually works to subvert traditional notions of gender difference in patriarchal societies. Such a traditional notion of difference divides individuals neatly into males and females and unequally distributes power to men. A critical complex patriarchal theory emulates poststructuralist feminism's effort to subvert this system, and end the exploitation of women and traditional patriarchy's disowned sons: gay men and non-White men. In this context, a critical complex theory of patriarchy employed in social studies begins to rethink notions of gender, subjectivity, and sexuality, in the process of setting the stage for a reinvention of masculinity. Operating in this manner, theorists have come to realize that the essentialization of male and female difference precludes the recognition that men who reject dominant notions of patriarchal masculinity and who struggle against race, class, and gender domination are ideologically closer to feminists than are other women who unquestionably accept traditional notions of gender difference.

Such understandings hold dramatic implications. Indeed, a critical post-Cartesian complex theory of patriarchy demands nothing less than a questioning of comfortable assumptions about everything from male/female difference to the gender inscriptions of social institutions and the power relations that sustain them. For example, our theory of patriarchy understands the ways that the Western intellectual tradition has developed in an androcentric soil. Such a realization doesn't mean that social studies teachers simply dismiss the entire Western canon, but it does induce us to examine and develop alternatives to the epistemological assumptions that ground the tradition. A key function of our theoretical work—the function that earns it the label, "critical"—involves an analysis of the ways that power shapes knowledge forms, the definition of truth, and the rules of academic and other cultural discourses. Western democratic societies, bathed as they are in a liberal ideology of equal opportunity, a just world, and egalitarian social relations, find this power dynamic hard to fathom. Understanding this social tendency, a critical complex theory of patriarchy works hard to demonstrate the ways that society is structured by collective power differences constructed along lines of race, class, gender, ethnicity, and sexual preference. If the construction of masculinity and the oppression of women are to be understood, such a process will take place only in the context provided by an analysis of structured power relations (Ebert, 1988; Clough, 1994; Gore, 1993; Hedley, 1994; McLean, 1996a; Walby, 1990; McLean, Carey, & White, 1996).

Gender, in our critical conceptualization, is a structural system of power and domination, and masculine identity is a socially constructed agent of this power. In this context, the social construction of patriarchy helps shape men's self-interest that, in turn, structures their dominant gender identities as contained within individuals. A critical complex patriarchal theory sees notions of masculinity implanted throughout powerful social institutions, including education, the welfare establishment, the police, the military, the legal system, the media, etc. Indeed, corporations, colleges, and sports organizations are shaped by patriarchal/masculinist values of social Darwinism and success for those who conform. The liberal notion of individualism champions the problematic belief that "personal problems," such as spousal abuse, violence, and misogynistic attitudes, can be solved by appeal to individuals. Our critical complex theory of patriarchy contends that such problems demand both personal and social solutions. Men's oppressive relationships with women cannot be understood until we expose the ways various social institutions attempt to socialize men and women and shape their gender identities in a manner saturated by patriarchy.

Any emancipatory transformation in the attitudes and behavior of men will take place only in a situation where these social institutions are challenged. Male employees who confront the implicit patriarchal values of the corporation may lose their jobs, male students who confront the tacit androcentric knowledge of the academy may fail, and male social studies teachers who call out the patriarchal structures of the discipline may be ridiculed. These are the stark prospects that face those who would challenge patriarchy. Critical social studies scholars of patriarchal power must gain insight into the ideologies and discourses that constitute ever changing articulations of patriarchy. By ideology, I do not mean a misrepresentation of what is "real" in society. I use the term in a more post-Cartesian sense to define a process involving the maintenance of unequal power relations by mobilizing meaning in a way that benefits the dominant group. Thus, a patriarchal ideology in this articulation involves a tacit process of meaning making and affect mobilization that induces women to accept a passive view of their femininity and men to embrace unproblematically their gender privilege. All of this takes place in ever changing ways in a variety of social venues in a manner that camouflages gender antagonisms and conflict. Patriarchal forms of discursive power work through what are often perceived as neutral conduits of language to produce a set of tacit rules that regulate, in the context of gender, what can and cannot be said, who speaks with the blessing of authority and who must listen, and whose social constructions are scientifically valid and whose are unlearned and unimportant. Discursive analysis disputes the traditional assumption that individuals possess stable properties such as an identity or a personality. In our critical complex theoretical frame, patriarchal language is viewed as a sociopolitical arena where gender identity is continuously renegotiated and remade.

Understanding the ways that patriarchal power works allows us to gain insight into methods of interrupting oppressive patriarchal practices. It prepares us to understand the pain that many heterosexual White men claim to experience in the early twenty-first century without ignoring men's privilege and dominant gender position. These theoretical assertions understand that patriarchy is ever mutating as it reacts to challenges from feminists, gay rights advocates, and other individuals and groups. In the same context, this critical complex theory of patriarchy views masculinity as possessing multiple and ambiguous meanings and different expressions in different contexts. Indeed, masculinity is not the same for all men, and, as a result, our patriarchal theory refuses to essentialize or universalize the concept. Operating without the crutch of a universalized masculinity, our critical complex view of patriarchy induces analysts to study the conflicting stories a culture tells itself about men and the ideological and discursive dynamics that help construct and frame these narratives. As we examine these stories, the question we seek to induce social studies students to ask is, What is masculinity (Hedley, 1994; McLean, 1996a)?

In many ways, asking such a question represents a potential radical act. Naturalized assumptions are opened to analysis and negotiation in an unprecedented manner and the historical existence of other masculinities confronts those who would repress awareness of their reality. In the men's movements that have emerged in the last decade or so the question, What is masculinity? has often been answered with a set of assumptions very different from those embraced by our critical patriarchal theory. Men's movement leaders have often sought a "true masculinity" (Bly, 1990). A more critical and emancipatory search might involve an analysis of the effects of men's narratives and beliefs about masculinity on both themselves and women. In this same spirit, does the adoption of an alternative nontraditional masculinity result in the forfeit of patriarchal privilege? Can a critical complex theory and social studies pedagogy of patriarchy help men who seek alternative masculinities to understand gender power dynamics in a way that induces them to resist falling into power fields that result in their oppression of women and gay males? In this situation, such men, I believe, must seek the help and support of women, gay men, and non-White men and the insights they can provide for dealing with asymmetrical power relations (Clatterbaugh, 1997).

In a social studies context, how does a critical complex theory of patriarchy help us teach boys to step way from dominant masculinity and the power that accompanies it? Social studies and educational institutions in general in this culture, unfortunately, have rarely considered such a question. In fact, they have traditionally taught boys to embrace a patriarchal masculinity. The patriarchal nature of mainstream education, taught by both male and female teachers as surrogates for absent patriarchs, reproduces unequal gender relations. Such an education teaches young men to join in the power struggle that surrounds dominant notions of masculinity and the sacrifice of humanness that accompanies it. Educational institutions that "make men out of boys" often brutalize young men, use homophobia to induce them to conform to an insensitive masculinity, de-emotionalize them, and train them to physically and emotionally abuse one another. Those who don't internalize the messages and gain significant validation for mastery of the masculinity curriculum must live in the shadow of self-doubt and male inadequacy for the rest of their lives.

The de-emotionalization process holds very negative consequences for boys and men—and for women also. Public display of emotion is not allowed in dominant constructions of masculinity, unless the emotion is anger. The dominant masculinity curriculum not only teaches boys not to show emotions but not to feel them either. Such a process induces boys to avoid intimacy and self-disclosure, since it attempts to humiliate those who engage in such activities. A key feature of masculine education, connected to this process of de-emotionalization, involves teaching young men to hate those who engage in open display of emotions. Such disdain, often marked by homosexual or effeminate-based name-calling, is part of a larger feature of the curriculum involving the tendency to teach boys to hate what they fear. A critical complex theory and pedagogy of patriarchy is empowered to name this often hidden curriculum and construct emancipatory alternatives to it. In this pedagogical context, such a theory explores ways that boys can be engaged in rituals of connection rather than the glorification of separation. In this way, the theoretical understanding of the rational/emotional split of Cartesian-Newtonian epistemology informs a pedagogy of transformation that values the narratives of diverse groups of people. Such a critical social studies curriculum moves beyond traditional forms of Western education because it refuses the universal vantage point of Western science that validates the official position and challenges a way of seeing that dismisses diverse narratives as trivial and irrelevant "noise" (P. Smith, 1996; G. Smith, 1996; McLean, Carey, & White, 1996; Pagano, 1990; Gore, 1993; McLean, 1996a).

THE CRITICAL COMPLEX THEORY OF PATRIARCHY: EPISTEMOLOGY, MALE POWER, AND REASON

A critical complex theory of patriarchy understands that the rise of Western science in the Enlightenment and the Age of Reason cannot be separated from the political dynamics of gender relations. When Western society moved away from the interdependent perspective on reality of the Middle Ages to the logocentric, mechanistic view of modernity, there came to exist an accompanying misogyny that associated feminist thinking with madness, witchcraft, and Satanism. Intuition and emotion were thought to be incompatible with androcentric logic and reason, and, as a result, scientific knowledge became the only game in town. The masculinization of thinking was a cardinal tenet of Western social evolution.

Individuals came to be represented in a dramatic new form—as abstracted entities and as individuals standing outside the forces of history and culture. Society was caught in the cognition of patriarchy, a matrix of perception that limited our imagination to concepts that stayed within the androcentric boundaries, far away from the "No Trespassing" signs of the feminine domain.

Standing outside of the forces of history and culture involved observing at a distance. Valid knowledge was produced exclusively by personally detached, objective observers. As delineated in previous chapters, knowers were separated from the known. Masculinist autonomy, abstraction, and distance deny the spatial and temporal location of the knower in the world and thus result in the estrangement of human beings from the rhythms of life, the natural world (Lowe, 1982; Mahoney & Lyddon, 1988; Anderson, 1987; Bowers & Flinders, 1990; White, 1978). Feminist theory has asserted that the autonomy and isolation of the logical, masculine individual have necessitated a mechanistic perspective on the universe. Such a perspective guards against the ascendance of more feminine forms of meaning and identity based on connecting, caring, empathy, inclusively, and responsibility. Devoid of such characteristics, masculinist modernism created a behavioral science designed to manipulate individuals and an educational system that utilized the behavioral sciences to mold students and their consciousness in a way that would foster efficiency and economic productivity, often at the expense of social justice and creativity.

Enlightenment science, as a traditional masculine way of knowing, has denigrated the importance of context, thus allowing for a decontextualized science that produces a dissociated and fragmented body of knowledge about the social, psychological, and educational world. Such a decontextualized science produces a quick and dirty analysis of human behavior and social interaction. The study of gender itself provides an excellent example of the problematic nature of such ways of seeing, since gender is viewed as a causative factor without taking into account the existence of other variables in a social situation. When positivistic research ignores the wider context and the multitude of other variables which attend it, the conclusions drawn from such studies typically suggest innate differences (often hierarchical) between the sexes. Studies, for instance, that look only at gender differences in math achievement might discover (accurately) that boys do better than girls on particular standardized math tests. By not examining the results contextually, and by not pursuing explanatory factors, positivistic researchers fail to consider the panoply of reasons for the different scores. Appealing to the accuracy of their statistics as authority, researchers fail to confront the quick and dirty simplicity of their research design. Thus, what is appears to be only what has to be; the public is provided with further "proof" that boys are naturally better than girls in math (Jayaratne, 1982). Scientific "proof" of the superiority of "rational man" has been mobilized. Gender differences have been essentialized.

Feminist scholar Schulamit Reinharz (1979, 1982, 1992) is always helpful in analyzing the failure of patriarchal positivism in social research. The use of questionnaires, she contends, which force a "yes," or "no opinion," is an example of the positivistic distortion of the lived world. Using such instruments, positivistic researchers substitute a controlled reality, a social situation with its own conventions and rules, for the ambiguity of the world of schools. They make a serious conceptual error when they correlate respondents' answers to questionnaires (responses peculiar to the controlled situation of being questioned about their attitudes) to their attitudes in another, completely different, social situation, the lived world of their workplace, or their educational situation. Reinharz appreciated the limitations of such questionnaires when she tried to answer the questions herself. She could not answer the questions seriously, for her feelings and thoughts were not capable of being translated into simple, codable responses. Like the lived world itself, her attitudes were complex and subtle, often ill-defined and were capable of being discovered and articulated only in dialogue with friends or during silent introspection (Reinharz, 1979).

Patriarchal positivistic science, then, can be very misleading for practitioner fields, such as education, communications, or social work, because it fails to produce insights germane to professional lives. Patriarchal positivistic educational research is limited in the sense that its language, the language of propositions, does not speak to the practitioner. Propositional language is concerned with the specification of the criteria by which statements about the world can be verified or refuted. The needs of the teacher transcend the language of propositions, for they often revolve around the particularity of certain entities: the creativity of one child, the "feel" of a child's anger or affection, the ambiance of a classroom full of students captivated by a lesson. This is the stuff of teacher knowledge, and this is precisely the type of situation that andro-centric positivistic prepositional language cannot address. It is irrelevant in such contexts, for it cannot capture the subtleties of interpersonal emotion—the subtleties, feminist educators maintain, that move us to the heart of the teaching act. Simply put, patriarchal positivistic measurements or frequency studies cannot convey a nuanced understanding or feeling for the individuals and social contexts under observation. In its quest for propositional generalization, positivistic research misses an essential point. For the practitioner, it is often the infrequent behaviors, the deviations from the general tendency, that are most important to pedagogy (Mies, 1982; Doyle, 1977; Eisner, 1984).

School is an excellent venue for the study of rational man and patriarchal forms of analysis and knowledge production—and their lived consequences. Few institutions reflect the patriarchal nature of modernist ways of seeing more than the school. Bastions of male supremacy and dominant cultural power, schools have been shaped by what patriarchy has viewed as acceptable behavior and appropriate ways of being. Sophisticated thinking, indeed humanness itself, has been equated with maleness. Because of male-centered nature of schooling, White male students from middle-class homes are imbued with a confidence that allows them to see failure as more a reflection of the teacher's inadequacies than their own. Because female cognitive development proceeds along a different path, women's interpersonal and connected qualities are sometimes viewed as inferior to the androcentric notion of intellectual autonomy. Women find it risky to go with their intuitions in school because such a cognitive style is so seldom recognized as valuable. Over the years, many women students begin to lose confidence, often coming to feel that their failure is a result of their own inadequacy (Maher & Rathbone, 1986).

Often when I talk about these gender dynamics with teachers in social studies and other fields, they are taken aback with my connection of gender to science, research, knowledge production, and professional practice. They have been convinced by androcentric scientific realism that objectivity is a precondition for scientific discovery, the production of relevant knowledge, and the reporting of that knowledge. A critical complex post-Cartesian theory of patriarchy understands that objectivity is not some transcultural, transhistorical way of knowing but merely one of the many human ways of making sense of the world. Objectivity in this theoretical perspective is a belief structure that grew up in a particular time (the eighteenth century) in a particular place (Western Europe) and that values androcentric cognitive strategies more than those tending to be embraced by many women and men subjugated on the basis of class, race, and ethnicity. This is to argue that positivistic objectivity tacitly hides political dynamics of race, class, ethnicity, and (central to our concern here) gender. The claim to objectivity has allowed scientists since the eighteenth century to make the separation between knower and known a decoy for using a dominant male mode of understanding and representing the world to increase their power to control it.

Objectivity as a patriarchal myth has allowed a dominant masculinist perspective to become a "God's eye" vantage point. As such a social construct, objectivity has provided a form of transhistorical validation for dominant masculine values of reason, system, and order. Such validation promotes dominant masculine identity and the rational consciousness that accompanies it as the preferred ways of being in the world. These cognitive styles/ways of knowing shape everything from definitions of intelligence to constructions of success. Obviously, a corollary of such validation is an invalidation of femininity and nondominant forms of masculinity. Indeed, it is such disdain that often fuels misogyny, racism, and homophobia. A critical complex theory of patriarchy understands the gendered, hegemonic nature of objectivity and seeks to expose such a power dynamic in numerous other ostensibly neutral social expressions. Engaged in such a process, social studies students studying patriarchy begin to imagine new forms of inquiry and social analysis. An area of particular concern for educators in this context involves the gender dynamics involved in the construction of what constitutes sophisticated cognitive activity. Understanding that diverse race, class, gender, and ethnic groups may hold different views of what constitutes intelligence or genius, many advocates of a critical democratic social studies have called for a reconceptualization of cognitive theory (Ward, 1996; Ramsay, 1996; Gore, 1993; Clough, 1994). This, of course, is the basis of postformalism.

PSYCHOLOGY IN PATRIARCHAL CONTEXT

Modernist psychology has been an excluding discipline that has sought to canonize the norms of Western White males from the upper-middle class. Intelligence, creativity, mental health, and normality in general have been defined by narrow guidelines that exclude diverse cultural manifestations of such concepts. One standard has worked so far, and it is the obligation of the guardians of the discipline to preserve that standard from the feminist and mluticulturalist barbarians at the gate. What is obvious to many is that the standards and guidelines delineated by the discipline are the ones best met by the guardians themselves. America is a Eurocentric country by necessity, gatekeepers such as E. D. Hirsch (1987) maintain. So blatantly do Hirsch and his compadres erase the role of non-Europeans in American life and scholarship, one wonders how such scholars convinced themselves that the culture is devoid of African, Asian and Native American influences. Toni Morrison (1993) refers to these absences as so "ornate" that they demand our attention. Even those who have understood the impact of history and culture in shaping psychological functions could not escape the broader gravitational pull of patriarchal Eurocentrism. Though Russian psychologist Lev Vygotsky opened an extremely important psychological conversation about the intersection and culture and mind, even he assumed the superiority of European male cultural tools and forms of mental functioning to those of other cultures (Wertsch, 1991).

Such Eurocentrism, when combined with the return of White supremacy and the growing disparity of wealth between Whites and non-Whites, points to an epistemological crisis of knowledge and human purpose. The way we produce knowledge in the modernist paradigm often focuses exclusively on the macrolevel, ignoring the social differences that reside at the microlevel, the domain of the particular. Positivist psychology has assumed that what is statistically most common is, accordingly, most significant. The postformal (see Kincheloe & Steinberg, 1993) psychology advocated here, in the context of a critical counter-Cartesian theory of patriarchy, seeks out the marginal, the subordinate, and the "deviant," while gleaning insights that demand the reconfiguration of the field, the reconceptualization of common assumptions. In this postformal context, the center-margin hierarchies so common to modernist psychology begin to break down. The new psychology forces disciplinary change in light of the exposure of the race, class, and gender-grounding of basic psychological concepts. In the process, it reveals the ways the field has served to disempower subordinate groups. At the core of the epistemological crisis of modernism is its inability to deal with diversity.

In social studies programs supported by modernist psychology, marginalized students are often lost and alienated. Unlike students from the dominant culture, they cannot draw upon their personal histories and cultural backgrounds to facilitate their negotiation of school requirements. From the modernist psychological perspective and the pedagogy that emanates from it, such personal and cultural experiences constitute the problem, the reason for these students' academic difficulties, their "cultural disadvantage." Consistently confusing intelligence with social advantage (whiteness, middle-classness, and often masculinity), modernist psychology buries knowledge both about individuals from marginalized cultures and the insights they have historically produced. From the perspective of postformal analysts, modernist psychology, like the whiteness and dominant masculinity that culturally grounds it, operates as a form of arrogant perception, an epistemological stance that approaches culturally different situations and individuals from a position of power. Thus, patriarchal White culture uses its science to disseminate images of the world and its people that allow Whites to maintain their power position. The arrogant perception of Eurocentric psychology provides middle/upper- middle-class White men with a sense of privilege that undermines their ability to make sense of the world and their relation to it. Such a position in the web of reality blinds such individuals to the need for constant self-analysis, for contemplation about one's role in the world. Such inquiries provide the raw materials for creative insight. It is obvious that, when individuals consider themselves privileged to the point they are exempted from such activity, they are held captive by the power of the status quo.

PATRIARCHY AND POWER

Any critical complex theory of patriarchy must focus on the privilege men derive from their male power as well as the oppression women experience in relation to it. In this context, the ways that power shapes gender subjectivity becomes a central concern, for this analysis focuses on both the discursive and ideological dynamics of patriarchal masculinity. In order to appreciate the ways power shapes gendered subjectivity and produces gender oppression, it is important to briefly provide a matrix for a theory of power. Power involves far more than a unidirectional hierarchy from oppressor to oppressed. First, the oppressed have power, albeit weaker, to resist, and sometimes overthrow, the oppressor; and second, those individuals, groups, and social structures often labeled the oppressors may exist in a far more complex set of relations with both one another and the oppressed than has traditionally been understood. Thus, power is exercised by both dominant and subordinate forces.

John Fiske (1993) as always provides a language that helps us conceptualize this power dynamic. The dominant, top-down forces are labeled "imperializing" powers and the subordinate, bottom-up forces are termed "localizing" powers. Imperializing powers, in the form of White supremacy, class elites, and patriarchy, attempt to extend their influence as far as possible over various societies, the tide of history, social organizations, and individual consciousnesses. Localizing powers, on the other hand, in the form of individuals or alignments of oppressed peoples, attempt to shape the immediate conditions of everyday lives. Such conditions may involve beliefs, social relationships, and identities/subjectivities and, typically, must be protected from the impact of imperializing powers. In this context, imperializing power, operating under the guise of a neutral social institution or as a cultural production such as a movie or a TV show, may control individuals' access to relevant information or influence their preferences in relation to gender identity formation. Within the dynamics of this understanding of power, individuals are never completely free agents, for they are always affected by social conditions they had no role in creating. Thus, human agency (the ability to shape one's own life) involves operating within the social field one is provided, a social field shaped by imperializing power's tendency to dominate, to some degree, legal, media, and educational institutions and social forms such as language and the family (Lewis, 1990; Walby, 1990; Wartenberg, 1992a; Cooper, 1994; Keat, 1994).

It is important to note that imperializing and localizing powers are not fixed, stable entities. Instead, they can be characterized as ever changing social allegiances marked by two consistent features: Imperializing powers operate with entitlement and privilege; Localizing powers operate with limited access to economic, social, and political resources. Thus, those who exercise localizing powers are marginalized but are still able to promote their own interests. Those who study power understand that imperializing powers do not have the ability to conquer the social domain to the point that identities are homogenized and resistance permanently quashed. The appreciation of Fiske's notion of imperializing and localizing powers opens a new dialogue about the two-way production and reception of power (imperializing to localizing and localizing to imperializing) that may be expressed in terms of macro/micro power theory. In this context, we can no longer assume the pedagogical impact of macro-organizations on micro-individual/oppressed group consciousness.

To understand both how power operates and the impact of hegemonic/ideological macropower, we must analyze power relations at the microlevel. For example, men themselves may understand that a macroforce called patriarchy works to dominate women in various contemporary societies, yet they may disclaim any participation in such power relations. Because of patriarchal macropower structures, unmarried women may be treated differently from men, finding access to social goods quite limited. For example, the way the workplace is structured limits women's job opportunities. When they do gain jobs, their pay is significantly less than men's, and they are vulnerable to on-the-job sexual harassment. Single women have a harder time obtaining bank loans and, as a result, find it more difficult to start or expand a business that might support them financially. Even though a husband might not participate in any conscious or unconscious gender bias toward his wife in their everyday marital relations, given such macroeconomic gender structures, the wife is more dependent on her husband economically than he is on her. The wife must consider her actions in light of what her life would be like without him and, as a result, understands she gains something from the marriage that a man doesn't need to contemplate. Thus, the micropower that husbands possess sometimes has little to do with their intentions; careful analysis, however, may reveal subtle ways that husbands deploy their power in order to gain advantages in everyday marital interactions. Different husbands will use the macropower of patriarchy in different ways. Thus, patriarchy, as a form of macropower, elicits very different effects when it is deployed at the microlevel of everyday life.

The critical theory of power proposed here sees the social world as structured by competing interests between macro imperializing powers and micro localizing powers. It is no longer sufficient to identify dominant powers without an analysis of how individuals make diverse meanings of the ways these powers influence their lives. When these powers set limits on the range of possibilities through which men and women construct their identities, how, for example, does this play out in the construction of masculinity and femininity? In the electronic reality of contemporary society, with its movies, TV, CD's, Internet and video games, how does dominant power's circulation of ideological signs and meanings shape these processes? When hegemonic structures reinforce meanings made in, say, school, with ideological representations purveyed on TV, dominant power alignments are shaping the way individuals see themselves and their relation to the world. When such alignments can mobilize pleasure around particular ideological representations, their power to shape subjectivity increases substantially. Again, John Fiske's notion of a power bloc is helpful in providing language and concepts to sophisticate our power theory.

Expanding our earlier reference to the concept, Fiske argues that macropowers come together and break apart around particular issues that arise in particular conditions. With an appreciation of the ever shifting and realigning nature of power blocs, analysts begin to understand that a particular individual can operate within the macropower alignment on one issue but operate in opposition to such an alignment on another issue. For example, African American men, subordinated by class and racial macropower, can work in concert with the patriarchal power bloc along the axis of gender. In this context, the patriarchal power bloc is not a centralized social formation but a decentralized array of individuals and structures that produces patriarchal hegemonic ideologies designed to win the consent of oppressed individuals to accept the patriarchal system that subjugates them. These individuals and structures operate by the rules of dominant masculinist discursive practices, construct and purvey the knowledge of male-centered academic disciplines that frame patriarchal ways of seeing and being as universal norms, and attempt to coercively control the bodies of those who threaten the patriarchal power bloc, such as women, gays, and others who reject dominant notions of masculinity. Thus, in this context, we recognize forms of macropower deployed by power blocs to protect their privilege: hegemonic ideological power, discursive power, disciplinary power, and coercive power. Different situations will demand the deployment of different forms of power. For example, if a husband's attempt to use hegemonic ideological power to win the consent of his wife to his domination of her ("I'm the head of the household, and I don't want my wife working") fails, he may resort to physically coercive power to control her (Cooper, 1994; Fiske, 1993; Tomlinson, 1991; Wartenberg, 1992b; Bizzell, 1991; Musolf, 1992; Giroux, 1994; Abercrombie, 1994; Ball, 1992).

The deployment of these various forms of power takes place in a variety of places and constitutes a form of education—or pedagogy. Pedagogy has been used for decades to refer to the art of teaching. In our critical pedagogical context, we expand the use of the term to think about its meaning outside of its identification with the technical aspects of classroom practice. In this context, we begin to understand that the domain of pedagogy involves ways that knowledge is produced, accepted, and rejected, as well as the processes by which identity is formed.

Pedagogy, in this sense, examines the variety of ways individuals receive dominant representations and encodings of the world and the variety of places in which such a process takes place. Seen in this way, pedagogy takes on a heightened importance in light of our macro-micro power theory. Indeed, pedagogy describes the process that occurs when macro-power intersects with the micropower dynamics of everyday life, an intersection marked by interaction with various forms of knowledge, identity formation, the development of values, and the process of forging one's place in the world. A critical complex theory of patriarchy sees this pedagogical process, marked by the intersection of the macro-micro domains, as a key operation in understanding the workings of patriarchy.

Since more traditional forms of sociology and social theory examined the macro dynamics of power, it is no surprise that the analysis of patriarchy has concentrated on this level. Thus, our analysis of patriarchal power, taking its cue from macro-micro power theory, examines both patriarchal social structures and the ways they intersect with the production of gendered subjectivity. In this context, we will ask the question of how social structures and the psyche connect. One important aspect of this connective process involves the ways consciousness is engaged by patriarchal power around expressions of affect and emotion. In popular culture and its pedagogy, for example, such affective and emotional considerations induce men and women to consent to stereotypical gender representations. Affective and emotional arousal, and the pleasure that accompanies it, moves even individuals intellectually conscious of patriarchal oppression to let down their guards against such insidious patriarchal power. This arousal of affect is central to developing an understanding of the way the macro is connected to the micro. Emotions and affective states are shaped by interactions in specific lived (micro) contexts, which in turn are framed by broader sociocultural (macro) contexts. Too often, psychological efforts to make sense of these emotional/affective dynamics exclude the effects of the broader sociocultural context.

The creation of subjectivity is one of the central concerns of the macro-micro power theory. The creation of gendered subjectivity is one of the main concerns of a critical theory of patriarchal power. What is at stake in this discussion is nothing less than the production and reproduction of people. Of course, the gender roles of the family, shaped as they are by patriarchal power, play a central role in this production process. But various social structures are also involved in the process, inasmuch as the state endorses the ideology of the privatized, patriarchal family that reinforces dominant notions of masculinity and femininity. Indeed, gendered subjectivity is created in a plethora of sites. A critical complex theory of patriarchy privileges no particular social space in this process. Patriarchal ideologies, justifying particular forms of dominant masculinity and femininity, emanate from a variety of social locations. Three specific patriarchal ideologies that contribute to the oppression of women include: 1) the ideology of domesticity; 2) the woman-as-caretaker ideology; and 3) the ideology of romance.

The ideology of domesticity involves the implantation of the belief among men and women that women are responsible for unpaid work at home; the women-as-caretaker ideology induces men and women to believe that "good" women will defend their husbands and protect their patriarchal power and privilege, whether men are present or not; and the ideology of romance teaches that women's status emanates from her male relationship. With working-class women, in particular, such ideologies situate home and family as the central concerns for women. When their identity is shaped around such ideologies, these women are set up for failure in a patriarchal society. They become, in a sense, patriarchy's women. Because of their identification with the domestic sphere, they become especially vulnerable to the whims and moods of their male partners. If a man leaves a domestically identified woman as the sole supporter and caretaker of the family, she has little experience to draw upon in her attempt to find wage labor outside the home. This is not an isolated scenario. Feminization of poverty over the last couple of decades, as women face the patriarchal reality that devalues their talents and abilities, has increased exponentially. Indeed, the domestic ideology dictates that women's work in the economic marketplace is worth about 60 percent of men's work and does not provide single mothers with sufficient resources to support their families by themselves (Valli, 1988; Weis, 1988).

Lois Weis (1988) contends that women are caught in a double bind: They define themselves around themes of home and family but are forced by economic realities to work outside the home. When declining Western economics forced married women into the workforce, little change took place in the social dynamics and work responsibilities within the home. Women found themselves bound by a double workday—full shifts in both the home and the workplace. Recent studies indicate that employed, married women perform three hours of housework for every one performed by their husbands. In addition to their jobs outside the home, married employed women engage in housework an average of five hours a day. If a married woman's domestic work were monetarily compensated, her family's income would be increased by more than sixty percent. Critical social studies educators understand the negative impact of these ideologies on women. In doing so, they appreciate the reality that has been created by patriarchy's refusal to provide special support for women in these circumstances. Therefore, critical social studies teachers prepare their female students to deal with the social dynamics surrounding these gender issues while engaging them in a larger struggle to help increase public awareness of the need to redistribute some of women's caretaker functions. Such redistribution can relieve women of their mind- and body- numbing double workday. Hopefully, the critical consciousness that surrounds such an understanding can be used to help the public employ these caring qualities traditionally relegated to women to humanize society, schools, and workplaces (Sidel, 1992; Wolff, 1977).

This so-called feminine ethic of caring holds great potential when applied to the reconceptualization of social studies, schools in general, and other social institutions. At the same time, as a patriarchal ideology, this caring/caretaker dynamic can be turned against women. It can be used to undermine women's best interests when it is employed without a cognizance of power relations between women and men. When working class women, operating out of an ethic of caring, place their own concerns and own needs last, they inadvertently reinforce patriarchal power relations between themselves and their husbands. Indeed, many working class women can justify their educational pursuits only in terms of their commitment to their husbands and families. "I'm doing this for them," they often tell their teachers. Such a nurturance ideology, such a way of making sense of women's role in the world, reached the level of social obsession in the years immediately following World War II. The ideologies of domesticity, caretaking, and romance expressed themselves in TV's June and Ward Cleaver, Alice and Ralph Kramden, and Lucy and Ricky Ricardo—visions of mother in the kitchen and father at work. The roots of contemporary feminism can be traced to the emotional toll this view of womanhood exacted on the "loving housewife" of the 1950s and early 1960s. Housewife depression, increasing divorce rates, and a general discomfort with the family life characterized this era of hyperdomesticity (Luttrell, 1993; Rubin, 1994).

Women caught in the patriarchal trap, who fail to understand the underside of the ideologies, are less able to protect themselves from the social forces that oppress them. Self-sacrifice and passivity, common features of patriarchal notions of femininity, should come with the Surgeon General's health warning in the twenty-first century. Young women who embrace such traditionalism, Michele Fine (1993) reports, are more likely to find themselves with unwanted pregnancies and child care than more assertive teenagers. In a study of girls in a public high school in New York City, Fine noticed a large number of the students who got pregnant were the quiet and passive ones, not those girls whose dress and manner signified sexuality and experience. Such an observation should not be interpreted to mean that teenage mothers are always a certain type of female. Obviously, the issue is far more complex than this. What it does mean is that the traditional practices of femininity often subvert the economic, social, and educational development of young women (Fine, 1993).

Some social studies students assume that these patriarchal ideologies are now behind us, a relic of an era past. Such is not the case, critical democratic teachers tell them, focusing their attention on a hidden gender curriculum, the "girl curriculum" that operates covertly in American schools. Researchers have found that schools offer more career choices for boys, White upper-middle-class boys in particular, and fewer for girls, lower-economic-class non-White girls in particular. Career education booklets often list four career options for boys for every one listed for girls. Thus, career counseling often directs female students to career choices that dramatically undermine their wage-earning possibilities and lead them toward a life of poverty (Johnson, 1991). Even in the newest job programs, these gender dynamics are still at work. Analysis of the fifteen federal school-to-work demonstration programs developed in the 1990s indicated that three of the programs enrolled no girls and four enrolled three girls or less. The types of programs attended by students conformed to the stereotypes of the patriarchal ideologies: Girls were guided into office, allied health, clerical programs; boys enrolled in electronics, metal working, and automotive programs.

Such ideologies help construct and sustain social structures of patriarchal power. Men are often able to impose their will against women because of the structural support they tacitly receive. So important are these structures in supporting patriarchy that Sylvia Walby (1989) defines patriarchy as a system of social structures. Such structures are surrounded by, and help support, patriarchal practices, in the process, shaping and being shaped by human experience—the interaction of the macro and the micro. John Fiske (1994) refers to the processes as the interface between structures and everyday lived practices, the crucial site of the hegemonic process. Of course, practices can be complicit with the interests of the patriarchal power bloc or they can be confrontational. In this context, it can be argued that structures constitute the locations where the imperializing power of patriarchy is mobilized, while practices are the social spaces where localizing powers might defend themselves against such domination. The conflicts between a man and woman in a marriage or the relationship between men and women in a university faculty simply cannot be understood outside of the imperializing power of patriarchy exerted through social structures. To analyze only the specific relationships and the practices involved with them is to focus only on the microlevel and to see everyone operating on an equal field of power and privilege. The mistake of ignoring macrostructures and their invisible role in everyday gender relations is made daily and works to perpetuate the power of patriarchy (Hedley, 1994; Walby, 1989; Holstein & Gubrium, 1994; Fiske, 1993; Wartenberg, 1992b).

In this context, the importance of Sylvia Walby's six structures of patriarchy can be appreciated. In no way does she mean to imply that the six structures are totally autonomous; each structure both reinforces and blocks all other structures. Walby's structures include: patriarchal household production relations, patriarchal relations within paid work, the patriarchal state, male violence, patriarchal sexuality/compulsory heterosexuality, and patriarchal cultural institutions.

1. PATRIARCHAL HOUSEHOLD PRODUCTION RELATIONS. Husbands expropriate the household labor of women. In such a context, women must learn to read their husbands and adjust themselves to the emotional distance of men. The ideological dynamics of this structure revolve around the domesticity, romance, and caretaker triad discussed earlier. In this context, a patriarchal pedagogy is purveyed that teaches women to give up aspirations of self-sufficiency and independence and settle into an emotional dependence on men. In such dependence, women become protectors of men, especially from feminist attempts to delineate the nature of male oppression of women.

2. PATRIARCHAL RELATIONS WITHIN PAID WORK. The most important aspect of this structure involves the exclusion of women from the workplace or their segregation within it. In this context, women's

work is devalued and inevitably undercompensated. Such a process cannot be fully understood, Walby alerts us, outside the context of marketplace and racist forces. In the workplace, women find themselves corralled into professionally subordinate roles that involve nurturing, comforting, and operating as sexual objects. The same ideological forces are at work here as in the household context, since women are enculturated to accept their subordinate place in the workplace hierarchy without resistance.

3. THE PATRIARCHAL STATE. Women are consistently excluded from equal access to governmental influence and power by this patriarchal structure. Not only do women not have a direct presence in the state, but, more importantly, they are unable to muster political forces to pressure the state about gender issues. Women are not equally represented in state institutions, such as courts, the judiciary, the police, or the legal system, and, as a result, sensitivity to issues that affect females is not as great as it should be.

4. MALE VIOLENCE. The violent behavior of men is not attributable merely to the psychological problems of a few men; rather, it assumes the characters of a social structure. Women's knowledge of men's common use of violence against women holds serious consequences, because they modify their conduct and mobility in fear of the possibility of harm. In the context that shapes male violence, men in patriarchal societies possess a sense of entitlement to hold power over women. This patriarchal ideology of male privilege enculturates men to embrace violence when their entitlement is challenged. Indeed, in this ideological context, men learn to challenge the authority of assertive and self-directed women. This male rage at female agency can be viewed quite clearly in relation to feminist assertiveness over the past few decades.

5. PATRIARCHAL SEXUALITY/COMPULSORY HETEROSEXUALITY. This structure produces an ideology that induces women to become heterosexual and seek marriage relationships. Within this context, sexuality has been traditionally constructed as an activity centered around male pleasure. Indeed, male sexual desire is inseparable from an effort to master/gain power over the object. Within this sexual domain, many argue that sexual liberation has placed women in a position

where they are expected to have heterosexual sex with men. Such male expectations can be configured as a new form of patriarchal power over women. Obviously, this issue is quite complex, for sexual liberation offers women many benefits, including freedom from the stigma associated with having illegitimate children and premarital sex. The point a critical complex theory of patriarchy raises in this context is the problematic nature of reductionistic proclamations that sexual liberation is an unequivocal benefit for women.

6. PATRIARCHAL CULTURAL INSTITUTIONS. Such institutions include religious, educational, and media organizations, and all play a very important role in shaping masculinity and femininity. In every cultural institution, patriarchal discourses have developed that are regulatory in their intent. Religious institutions have set a variety of technologies of control to police women's behavior and limit their power. Educational institutions have differentiated men and women, validating male power by conferring males with more valuable credentials than women. Also, educational institutions have, as we have discussed, tended to validate masculine cognitive styles more often than feminine ways of operating. Media institutions have produced representations of women from a dominant masculinist gaze that positions women as objects of male heterosexual desire (Walby, 1989, 1990; Dubino, 1993; Lewis, 1990; Pagano, 1990; Vande Berg, 1993; Ramsey, 1996; G. Smith, 1996; Hedley, 1994; Layton, 1994; Hauser, 1992).

THE PATRIARCHAL CONSTRUCTION OF SUBJECTIVITY: DESCRIBING DOMINANT MASCULINITY

When theorists and researchers analyze the various stories men and women tell about gender identity, they come to understand that there are competing notions of femininity and masculinity. Operating with this understanding, I will offer a description of what has constituted a dominant masculinity in contemporary Western societies—a dominant masculinity, that like whiteness, tends to erase its function as a norm and creates the illusion of universality. Indeed, being a "real man" means never having to talk about masculinity, patriarchy, or power. In a patriarchal culture, dominant masculinity avoids reflection and attends to practical matters at hand, leaving men oblivious to the ways their gendered subjectivity contributes to the oppression of women and non-dominant men. It is always surprising how such an unreflective masculinity shapes social studies education, and academic and university life in general, just as much as any other social domain. Such an observation concerns not only the androcentric curriculum, epistemological assumptions, and the research methods commonly employed, but also the types of men who gain administrative roles and the forms of masculinity that are deemed appropriate for leadership. Even in progressive schools and colleges, it is difficult to find men in leadership roles who fall outside the boundaries of dominant masculinity. We must be careful to describe this form of masculinity as a socially constructed gender form that is inscribed by power and continually reshapes itself in light of ever evolving circumstances.

Drawing up Cartesian-Newtonian rationality and a classically informed modernist notion of the bourgeois man, dominant masculinity is a careful combination of mind and body, consciousness and unconsciousness, and rational and irrational. The rational dynamic provides certainty in knowing, while the body's readiness for aggression and violence provides an ideal way of being (ontology). In combination, the masculine mind and body make the rules and enforce them. In the gender context, reason and violence are not opposites but symbiotic dynamics in the shaping of dominant masculinity. Nevertheless, in the domain of the mind, dominant rationality positions men as being above emotions. One can discern this devaluation of emotions in much of the Western philosophical canon, where men have been represented as transcending matter, while women have been viewed as connected to nature. The misogynistic dynamic at work in this context has involved dominant masculinity's devaluing of women's abilities and disdain for their "weak" emotionality. The theme also emerges in Western psychology in the description of the supreme manifestation of a human being as a self-actualized person. Such an individual is "individuated" in the sense that he or she is capable of existing separately from others. A community-actualized person in this therapeutic context is unmentioned in the discourse of modernist psychology; the concept has not even been conceived. In addition, we see the same gender forces at work in the disciplinary conversation about moral development, especially in Lawrence Kohlberg's theory of the stages of moral development. Despite Carol Gilligan's critique in her book, *In a Different Voice*, Kohlberg's androcentric theory maintains wide acceptance (McLean, 1996a; Mosse, 1996; Ramsey, 1996; G. Smith, 1996).

In this volatile mix of patriarchal, rationality/mind, and violence/body, dominant masculinity's desire for power cannot be separated from the fear of failure. To understand one's masculinity is to appreciate the fact that other men may choose to destroy you. Indeed, no matter how great the success of dominant men, most seem to be plagued by the possibility of failure. Many analysts have concluded that men positioned by dominant masculinity are motivated more by avoidance of failure than the possibility of success. Thus, male complicity with dominant masculinity creates men whose privilege is mitigated by a constant gnawing terror of humiliation, while it makes sure neither women nor men win in the gender relations it structures. Men seek a form of power that can never be possessed; women suffer from male oppression. The question many students of patriarchy have asked concerning men's need to use their gender power to impose their will on women begins to answer itself in this context. It is not sufficient for a man ensnared in dominant masculinity to just be; such a man must prove his unequivocal manliness. He does this by demonstrating his power over women and by proving what he is not: not woman, not queer, not emotional, not reflective. In the milieu of dominant masculinity, the greatest male failure possible involves the taboo against homosexuality. Any form of male disempowerment, of male shortcoming, of a man's rejection of competition can be inscribed with the signifier of queerness. In this way, homophobia serves as a powerful hegemonic tool in the prevention of opposition to patriarchal power (Clarke & Henson, 1996).

In the public sphere of men's lives, almost all of their institutional interactions involve dealing with hierarchies. Living and operating in such contexts involves constant emotional struggle with the fear of not rising in the hierarchy and the development of competitive competence to make sure failure is avoided. In this competitive context, men learn to conceal feelings about their emotional struggle from their workplace colleagues. After all, they are competitors who might use such disclosure as a sign of weakness that could be used against other men. One of the many reasons that women face glass ceilings and job discrimination in workplaces and academic institutions involves the tendency of many women to feel comfortable with a form of emotional intimacy perceived by dominant males as giving themselves up to the enemy. Such emotional disclosure is viewed as a sign of weakness that can be exploited in the patriarchal institution. How can we place such women in positions of power, men on the make ask, when they are likely to "spill their guts" to someone from a rival organization? Given their sociopolitical power positions, men's construction of masculinity affects a wide range of individuals, women and nonpatriarchal males in particular. Despite, ironically, the power of patriarchy, dominant men as a group often feel a sense of impotence. Especially in the economic uncertainty characteristic of post-Fordism (the form of economic production that follows Fordist mass-production focusing more on niche markets and targeted forms of production), the promise of upward mobility and a steady increase in personal power in the organization has evaporated. Men in the web of dominant masculinity find themselves more vulnerable than ever before. In this troubling context, the pathologies that develop around men's fear of failure intensify, producing what we will discuss later as the crisis of masculinity.

Our description of dominant masculinity must make sure to clarify the complexity of patriarchal emotionality. Men, like women, are intensely emotional beings that seek love, intimacy, and affinity with others, but in dominant masculinity these affective propensities must be repressed in the pursuit of power. Repression of a volatile psychic conflict between desire for connection with others and the dominant masculinity demand for individuation and separation has profound costs. Male violence is ignited in the interplay of the rancor between desire and its mandatory muzzling—phosphorous and water, bonding and autonomy. This kinetic ambivalence causes great consternation for many men, as well as for the people who love them. When the argument is made in dominant masculinity that men are out of touch with their emotions, this is not the same, of course, as arguing that men are not emotional. Within the context of dominant masculinity, public display of emotions other than anger is out of bounds. Operating in this discursive/ideological universe, education for masculinity teaches boys that emotional display and self-revelation will bring them little but abuse from other boys.

The pain that many contemporary men feel in a situation that may be described as a crisis of patriarchy is not the motivation for their oppression of women and nondominant males. The point is that dominant masculinity's tendency for oppression necessitates that men be guarded emotionally and rendered insensitive to their emotional state. The power dynamics and competitive demands of dominant masculinity necessitate particular male personality types. Theodor Adorno and his co-researchers labeled these types authoritarian personalities decades ago. When men are emotionally anesthetized, they can become dangerous weapons in the military, the corporation, or in their interpersonal interactions. Within a patriarchal society, men are sometimes socialized to view women and nondominant males as enemies who seek to control and emasculate them. Such an other-as-enemy, gender/sexuality xenophobia is often accompanied in patriarchal culture by the socialization of women to attend to men's emotional needs. Thus, the attempt to talk about the construction of dominant masculinity outside the power relations that accompany the production of gendered subjectivity is misleading (Hedley, 1994; Ramsay, 1996; McLean, 1996a).

Christopher McLean (1996a) is extremely insightful about questions of power and dominant masculinity. In relation to various men's movements that have developed over the last decades, questions concerning men's pain and suffering in dominant masculinity have arisen. After pointing out that many men endure great suffering because of poverty, racism, and homophobia, McLean addresses the pain of men who occupy the most privileged positions in patriarchy: White, upper-middle-class, heterosexual males. This question, it seems to me, is central to a study of dominant masculinity and power because it helps those who pursue gender justice determine how to deal with such men in their pedagogical interventions. Do dominant males have something to gain by surrendering their gender power and redefining their masculinity? I insist that White, upper-middle-class, heterosexual men as well as non-White, working-class, and poor men have much to gain by such an act. Just as importantly, women and nondominant males will profit immensely from such a large-scale action. This is not to argue that dominant males are oppressed by patriarchy—they are not. The quality of their lives, however, and their access to love and affection are severely limited by patriarchy's demands. In patriarchy's construction of dominant masculinity's workplace, men's lives are played out in a theater of war where many fall victim. Such casualties are taught to believe that they're personally incompetent, not that the system itself is grounded in a set of values incompatible with the concept of human dignity.

THE CRISIS IN PATRIARCHY'S DOMINANT MASCULINITY

In the critical post-Cartesian complex theory of patriarchy, it is understood that patriarchy is not a stable social form but one that is ever responding, changing, and adapting to new challenges. In this context, Sylvia Walby (1990) points out that patriarchy experienced dramatic alterations in the twentieth century, moving from a private to a public social structure. Walby's public patriarchy operates in public venues such as workplaces and the state. Private patriarchy's focus on the household is not abandoned in the shift from the private to the public, but it is no longer the focal point of patriarchal domination. Patriarchy in its public format replaces private domestic individualistic oppression of women with a more collective form. The exclusion of women from the public space is replaced by their subordination and segregation within it. While once patriarchs openly barred women from public spheres of life, the evolving patriarchy of the last few decades finds patriarchs denying that any discrimination against women exists in the workplace. Such a strategy constitutes a form of patriarchal counterattack against its enemy, feminism. In this ever changing and evolving conception of patriarchy, the oppression of women has moved from containment and exploitation within the home to a positioning of women as sexual objects for men's gratification. This change from domestic caretaker to low-paid worker and sexual prey of men is profound in its implications for how patriarchy and dominant masculinity operate.

In this evolving public patriarchal context, men tend to control the ever important cultural representation of gender roles in general and women in particular. In the post-Fordist, electronic hyperreality of twenty-first century Western societies, the power and impact of such representational ability is especially important. For example, the control of gender representation helps create a climate in the post-Fordist economy where, despite widespread feminist protest, women performing roles that reflect the caretaker ideology is seen as natural and unproblematic. Women's professional careers are assessed in terms of masculinist expectations, devoid of sensitivity and institutional strategies for dealing with childbirth, child care needs, and other issues related exclusively to women. In this context, it is important to understand that pronouncements of progress for women ("You've come a long way baby!") may often be a manifestation of changes in patriarchal form from private to public rather than a diminishing of patriarchal power and oppression. Like racism and other forms of oppression, patriarchal domination continues to reshape itself in new and previously unthought of ways. A critical complex theory of patriarchy understands that one of its primary missions is to track these changes and develop pragmatic responses to them.

Critical democratic social studies teachers can make profound use of these responses.

One of the most important of recent patriarchal mutations involves efforts on the part of some men to blur the lines between male and female identity by feminizing maleness. Obviously, this is a very complex and ambiguous dynamic that must be addressed carefully. On one level, a critical complex theory of patriarchy applauds the blurring of gender lines that enables a replacement of monolithic notions of gender identity with pluralistic conceptions of subjectivity. On another level, we must be cognizant of the possibility that such reconstructions of male identity may be used as a means of establishing a new form of patriarchy—a "vampire patriarchy"—that sucks the nurturing blood of femininity for strategic advantage. In this way, a feminized maleness works to contain feminism by hegemonically winning women's consent to a kinder and gentler patriarchy. While tyrannical male behavior depends on the supremacy of dominant masculinity, liberal patriarchal hegemony is grounded in a sensitized dominant masculinity. The emergence of sensitized male hegemony signals one response to the crisis of masculinity that began to take shape in the late 1960s and early 1970s. It was during this period that masculinity was being redefined, as White men observed a questioning of their age-old privilege. A critical complex theory of patriarchy is not fooled by the efforts of many so-called sensitive males to respond to the crisis by dehistoricizing, depoliticizing, and denying the power structures of patriarchy in an attempt to reshape male privilege (Waters, 1989; Vande Berg, 1993; Rattigan & McManus, 1992; Dowell, 1996).

Believing that it was under attack by feminists, multiculturalists, and gays and lesbians, dominant masculinity, caught in the post-Fordist economic decline beginning to manifest itself in the early 1970s, struck out in a seemingly helpless rage against the "feminazis," "queers," and "wimpy liberals." Men who viewed themselves as belonging to the lodge of dominant masculinity found themselves anxious about their gender identity in a way very few of them had previously experienced. The traditional gender certainties that had established relations of female dependency and male autonomy were breaking down. Men operating within the dominant masculinity paradigm were shaken by the emotional realization that established patriarchal axioms, such as the power of reason to establish male dominance and order, were open to question. If patriarchal power was fragile and dominant masculine identity not a manifestation of higher human consciousness, then subjectivity—male subjectivity in particular—was a fragile entity. Such realizations signaled a secular "mark of the beast" to men comfortable in their dominant masculine roles. Indeed, there was no doubt about it: Masculinity was in crisis.

The helpless rage of dominantly masculine men was (and still is) an interesting counterpose to the patriarchal ideal of self-directed men civilizing the world by categorizing it, ordering it, and controlling it. The raging bull of dominant masculinity under threat was a reaction to the social claustrophobia of the multidimensional challenges to its supremacy. Faced with pressures to reconstitute themselves, even in the once sacrosanct domestic situation, many men committed to a dominant masculinity began to bail out, to abandon their wives and familial commitments. Such an important dynamic has been typically ignored in the analysis of the changes in family life in the last third of the twentieth century. After the women's movement and economic necessity combined to move women into the public space, men could no longer hang on to the fantasy that women's desire was limited only to their husbands and children. Women's desire had also gone public. Women were now investing libidinal energy in careers, women's organizations, officemates, and other nondomestic interests. Such outwardly directed feminine desires served to accentuate the threat to dominantly masculine males and fan the flames of their rage.

The crisis of patriarchy cannot be separated from the transformation of the American family of the last 30 years. In this period the circumstances of family life and social life have come together, causing the boundaries between them to blur. The dominant ideologies, including patriarchy and its dominant masculinity, that have traditionally been deployed to reconcile social contradictions have failed to resolve the problems caused by changing family structures. The bourgeois patriarchal family has been characterized by a variety of people from diverse social locations as horrific, with its child abuse, spousal beatings, emotional traumas, etc. Representations of such horror exhibited themselves in support groups, TV talk shows, women's organizations, tell-all books, and movies. The portrayal of Jimmy Stewart's happy family in *It's a Wonderful Life* had mutated into the dysfunctionality of *Ordinary People* by the 1980s and *American Beauty* by the end of the century. In these cultural spheres, we can observe both the weakening of patriarchal authority and a conservative attempt to recover it (Layton, 1994; Ramsay, 1996; Sobchack, 1991).

The conservative effort to recover patriarchy involves the "rebirth" of men. In movies such as *ET*, *Starman*, and *The Terminator*, the loss of a husband or father—the dominant male fleeing from the domestic space—is replaced via a process of transformation of the adult male body. In science fiction, the childlike paternalism of ET, the benevolence of the humanized alien, Starman, and, in *The Terminator*, Reese, the loving rebel from the future, and the Terminator himself, the cyborg assassin, all lay claim to patriarchal authority, albeit in absentia. ET, as Elliot's surrogate, must phone home and leave; Starman fathers a human child, bestows him with the consciousness of an alien race, and leaves; and Reese dies with the promise of an eventual return from the future via a complicated time warp. Such paternal roles could be imagined only within a sociopolitical unconscious grappling with the familial/patriarchal role of men.

In this context, the role of children emerging from confused paternal figures in the crisis of patriarchy became increasingly problematic. Within the crisis of patriarchy, the nineteenth century bourgeois construction of childhood as a time of purity and innocence began to break down. No longer could the child be protected from the "corrupting" knowledge of the adult world. As the father leaves, the child must emerge as the little adult to hold the broken family together. At one level, such children become threats to patriarchy, in assuming the abandoned paternal or parental role; on a second level, they lose their status as children and childhood as it developed in nineteenth century when bourgeois society begins to collapse (Sobchack, 1991). Increasingly plugged into the electronics entertainment of hyperreality, children have grown less and less dependent on parental figures. Such independence both frustrates and angers fathers at the same time as it exposes their parental failure. Fatherly anger toward children is clearly visible in *The Other*, *The Exorcist*, *The Bad Seed*, *Firestarter*, and *It's Alive*, even though there is an attempt to hide it by portraying children as hideously evil. This child-based xenophobia positions children as foreigners whose presence marks the end of the family's configuration as a couple (Paul, 1994).

Even in supposedly family-friendly movies such as *Home Alone* 1 and 2, the adult males, Kevin's father and uncle, are overtly contemptuous of him and are unconcerned with his problems. All the viewer can discern is that the father and uncle are caught in a crisis of patriarchy, fighting for their manhood, expressing it, perhaps, in their resistance to the "breadwinner-loser" male character who forfeits his male energy in his domestication and subsequent acceptance of fidelity in marriage, dedication to job, and devotion to children (Lewis, 1992). Such a male figure was ridiculed by beatniks as square, by *Playboy* devotees as sexually timid, and by hippies as tediously straight. The search for a hip male identity, along with a healthy dose of irresponsibility, has undermined the family as a stable and loving environment. Indeed, to "do the right thing" in regard to one's family as a man is to lose status among one's fellow men. Thus, contrary to the right-wing construction, patriarchy and dominant masculinity may have had much more to do with undermining the family than feminism. An examination of adult male behavior in families indicates that many men are in crisis, desperately concerned with peer group status. For example, men, on average, pay pitifully inadequate child support to their former spouses, if they pay it at all. Only half of the women awarded child support ever receive what they are owed; another quarter receive partial payments; and the remaining quarter get nothing at all (Galston, 1991). The ambiguous role of the father and his relationship to his son in the crisis of patriarchy's wounded family is addressed in an overtly oedipal manner in a number of movies over the last two decades.

The Shining focuses attention on a father's hostility toward his son. Danny, the child protagonist in *The Shining*, develops the psychic power to see beyond the limits of time and space after his father (Jack Nicholson) in an alcoholic stupor breaks Danny's arm. Danny's power, his shining, is expressed through his imaginary friend, Tony, who lives in Danny's mouth. Tony exists to help Danny cope with his violent and abusive father.

Danny's presence and growth remind his father of his emasculation, his stultification by the family. The father's solution to his problem—the attempted ax murder of his wife and child—allows for no ambiguity; the movie jumps headfirst into the maelstrom of the conflict between virile masculinity and the demands of domesticity. The movie slaps viewers in the face with the crisis of masculinity through Jack Nicholson's Jack Torrence character.

As the screen image of the crazed ax-wielding Nicholson fades into a blurred image of *Jurassic Park* (1993), the continuity of the child-hating adult male remains intact. Even in this "child-friendly" Spielberg-produced dino-drama, the paleontologist (Sam Neill) holds such an extreme hatred of children that he won't ride in the same car with them. At one point in the film, in response to a prepubescent boy's sarcastic question about the power of dinosaurs, Neill evokes the image of the violent Nicholson, circling and threatening the child with the ominous claw of a velociraptor. The difference between *Jurassic Park* and *The Shining*, however, involves Neill's moment of epiphany. When the children are endangered by the dinosaurs, Neill sheds his hatred and, like a good father, risks mutilation and death to save their lives. As in the *Home Alone* movies, the issue of the father's hatred is buried in a happy ending: the safe children celebrating with the "reformed" Neill, and the happy, reunited McAlister family celebrating Christmas in a frenetic gift-opening ritual in *Home Alone 2*. The effort to recover dominant masculinity and patriarchal power through the Republican-directed and Clinton co-opted notion of family values was changing the cultural landscape in the 1990s. Family values must triumph; adult men must be depicted as ultimately devoted to their children; the feminists' portrayal of the "bad father" must not be reinforced.

The male response to the crisis of masculinity is extremely complex and diverse. From escaping the domestic scene, exploding with rage toward wife and children, to an effort to resituate themselves within the dominantly masculine role of family protector, men have struggled to negotiate the crisis. In light of the disappearance of the traditional bourgeois childhood, an inverse trend can be identified that expands our list of men's responses to the crisis. Along with the adultification of the child, we can observe the childification of the adult—the father in particular. In the same model of vampirism described earlier in the context of men in crisis sucking the feminine blood/social capital of nurturance, men suck the lovability of the child so as to regain the patriarchal power lost via the attacks on more machismo modes of domination. With the childlike father, we find that the patriarch has given up practical authority, much like the Dustin Hoffman character in *Kramer vs. Kramer*, and like the loving but deferential dads of the 1980s sit-coms, such as *Family Ties*. Such playful and happy dads ground the emergence of nonauthoritarian paternalism that transforms the angst-ridden family into a virtual playground.

Such a childlike father finds it difficult to operate with a wife/mother present to remind him of his bumbling, yet precious, ineptitude. The child, of course, assumes the role of the wise one who validates or repudiates dad's performance as parental unit. Importantly, in this context, the father is transformed into a poignant and sympathetic figure who is loved like a child for his lack of corrupting and *adult*erating knowledge about the ways of the world. It's as if the strains of the guilt of patriarchy are being washed away from men in this childlike male. Surely, this cute and inept character could not have participated in the napalming of children and the other war crimes of Vietnam, the spousal abuses documented by feminism, or the child abuse described by children in therapy. Jack Torrence was dead, and men needed some form of a social "amazing grace" to save them from the perception of wretchedness. This salvation was inseparable from the redemption of mainstream America and its dominant whiteness in the city-on-the hill rhetoric of Ronald Reagan and his conservative Christian supporters. If men and White people could be represented as innocents and, ultimately, victims persecuted by radical feminazis and militant Blacks, the formation of a new political order was possible. The dominant male had to be weakened and transformed into an insignificant figure before he could reclaim the mantle of patriarchal power (Sobchack, 1991).

RESOLVING THE CRISIS: THE RECOVERY OF PATRIARCHY

Aaron Gresson (1995) names the tendency in the American sociopolitical cosmos, emerging in the 1970s and continuing into the twenty-first century, as the recovery of White patriarchal supremacy. The power of White males, he maintains, was perceived to be weakened by the Civil Rights, Anti-war, Feminist, and Gay/Lesbian movements of the late 1960s and early 1970s. In order to understand subsequent American politics and social discourses, one must understand them as a part of this larger effort to regain lost power. With Gresson's context in mind, it is not hard to understand that every victory won for women and nondominant males has been followed by a patriarchal backlash. Such a backlash is often characterized by patriarchal forces consolidating their power so as to reassert their domination in a reconfigured way.

The patriarchal counterattack often refocuses attention on previously uncontested issues, changing the nature of the conversation about gender relations and power. For example, after the women's movement, most women gained the freedom to leave unhappy marriages, but surveys reveal that more and more single women with children live in poverty. Such a reality changes the focus of patriarchal domination, much in the private-to-public context described earlier by Sylvia Walby. Instead of attempting to control women's pursuit of work outside the home, patriarchal power exerted itself in lower pay for women doing the same work as men and unequal access to more desirable, higher-paying jobs. Patriarchal oppression is recovered, albeit around different issues and in different venues.

In this recovery and reformulation of patriarchy, men are represented as victims in a variety of contexts—from Vietnam to domestic battlegrounds where feminist wives leave them and take their children away. Much of the academic scholarship and the popular cultural representation of men's relationships with women fail to contextualize them in terms of the social conflicts about patriarchy or male domination that occurred in the 1960s and 1970s. Often, such portrayals only depict the male being "victimized," in the process, deleting the legacy of patriarchal oppression that led wives or lovers to particular actions. Such recovery texts fail to depict asymmetrical power relations between men and women, allowing men to shift the focus of concern from women back to men. Thus, in the academy, women's studies becomes gender studies, and men are returned to the center of attention. In this way recovery serves as a containment of feminism, a hegemonic act that gives the impression that men have changed feminism by becoming more sensitive and concerned with gender equality. In this scenario, women operating under the mantle of feminism will express conservative anti-feminist sentiments and employ the values of dominant masculinity in their actions.

Discussing this male appropriation of feminism as part of the recovery of patriarchy is not meant to imply that other more direct forms of patriarchy are not at work. The Christian Right is very clear in its efforts to promote patriarchy and dominant masculinity by condemning feminism, gay/lesbian activism, and any other threats to straight White male power. I have chosen to focus more on the liberal hegemonic recovery of patriarchy because such a form of domination operates at a more concealed level and, in the long run, may exert more influence than more overt forms of patriarchy. In this liberal hegemonic context, men's movements attempt to redefine masculinity in the victimized rhetoric of recovery. In these articulations of gender, men, because of their socially constructed emotional inhibition and the psychological deformations they construct, are represented as worse off than women. Men are worse off in the sense that they are not allowed to engage in emotionally fulfilling interpersonal relationships. Described as the most important human experiences, such relationships are essentialized as being easy for women to join in and difficult for men. The argument here is not that many men are harmed by these emotional inabilities; the point is that, in

the strategy of patriarchal recovery, no attention is given to power relations between men and women, diverse constructions of masculinity, and
the patriarchal power structures that permeate Western societies.
Psychology is consistently separated from the cultural context and privileged over sociology, as individual therapy is promoted as the path to
social reform. Because of the success of such liberal perspectives, the need
for a critical post-Cartesian theory/pedagogy of patriarchy is profound in
the first decade of the twenty-first century (Walby, 1990; Vande Berg,
1993; Layton, 1994; P. Smith, 1996; McLean, 1996a).

A CRITICAL DEMOCRATIC SOCIAL STUDIES PEDAGOGY OF PATRIARCHY

In conclusion, a few points about a social studies that addresses these
patriarchal issues is in order. In this context, the purpose will not be to
lay out a set of methods for teaching about patriarchy but to provide a
framework for making sense of the problems that social studies teachers
who embrace such a pedagogy will have to address. Such thoughts are
contextualized by the concerns of many feminist mothers about the differences between their progressive, socially concerned daughters and
their apathetic and sometimes hostile sons. Obviously, students of both
genders need experience with a critical analysis of patriarchy, but at the
beginning of the twenty-first century, boys may be especially needy. The
violence-saturated, often anti-intellectual, features of various racial, ethnic, and class-based boys' cultures position many male students in opposition to the life of the mind. Yet, at the same time that boys are
negatively positioned in relation to the goals of learning, they are also
situated in educational institutions that are patriarchal to their core.

Schools reproduce dominant masculinity despite the presence of
women in the process. Indeed, the patriarchal structures of school help
boys make meanings of their educational experiences that, in turn, shape
their lives. School, as an enclave of male power, validates dominant masculinity's cultural impulses among male teachers and their male students
and naturalizes their discomfort with women, gays, and other nondominant males. Despite their academic apathy and dominant masculine
resistance to the overemphasis of scholarly values, boys, operating within the confines of patriarchal power, know that teachers will spend more
time with and devote more energy to them. Male teachers, caught in the
crisis of patriarchy, have recently worked more diligently to maintain

male power under the perceived threat from feminist educators, homo-sexual rights advocates, and critical teachers. Advocates of nonconceptual social studies can be blind to these social forces that are constantly shaping the gender lives of students, teachers, and administrators. When one examines the ways the cultural curriculum of the commercial youth culture often supports the dominant masculinity of school, an understanding of the power of patriarchy as an educational force begins to emerge (McLean, 1996b; Bersani, 1995; Salisbury & Jackson, 1996).

In this context a critical democratic social studies that addresses patriarchy can be successful only if it understands the various ways patriarchy shapes the educational process and holds a complex awareness of the way patriarchy itself is constructed. Such an awareness has been missing from many educational strategies developed over the last decade or so. Not understanding the multidimensional nature of patriarchal power, anti-sexism education has viewed boys as passive victims of gender enculturation. Masculinity here is viewed as an essential concept that fits boys to particular gender norms, often in a deterministic manner. The emphasis in these articulations of boys' gender education revolves around the internalization of masculine stereotypes, a focus that underestimates the degree of personal agency males bring to the process of gender construction. Identity formation is complicated by constant struggles and resistances that must be mapped and addressed in any critical pedagogy of patriarchy. Without such appreciations, pedagogies of masculinity devolve into efforts to induce boys to choose between positive or negative articulations of maleness. Such dualistic expressions create categories of "acceptable" and "unacceptable" males that subvert our understandings of how all men are privileged by patriarchal power. In this dualistic pedagogy, more often than not, middle/upper-class males come to be seen as acceptable while lower-class men are viewed as unacceptable (Sedgwick, 1995; Champagne, 1996).

In many areas education about masculinity is being shaped by assumptions emanating from the men's movements we have discussed. Critical and feminist educators fear that education programs emerging in the context may reflect the backlash against feminism and become part of the recovery of patriarchy. In programs of this type, boys are segregated into all-male groups, and emphasis is placed on the absence of male role models. As fathers have played a lesser role in childrearing, masculine authority, such educators argue, has been lost. Social problems such as domestic and street violence, they conclude, are caused by an absence

of masculine authority. Often ignoring the specific nature of how masculine authority might be exercised, the position calls for a vague paternal
presence that implies the inadequacy of women in such matters. Thus, in
the name of a progressive gender education, misogyny is reinforced and
the recovery of patriarchal power is accomplished. The disconcerting
aspect of such a gender education involves its claim to progressivism
because it simultaneously equates the position of boys with that of girls.
In the process, the power differential between the genders is erased along
with questions of race, ethnicity, and class. Such erasure allows boys'
underrepresentation in homemaking classes to be equated with girls'
underrepresentation in the physical sciences and math. Examined within a critical context of power relations, it is not difficult to understand
the status difference between homemaking classes and science/math.
Girls suffer a significant loss from their underrpresentation; boys don't
(Salisbury & Jackson, 1996; McLean, 1996b; Clatterbaugh, 1997;
Popenoe, 1996; Connell, 1995; Dench, 1996).

Such power-insensitive pedagogies need a critical post-Cartesian theory of patriarchy to help them rethink the disturbing aspects of their practice. Informed by such a model, such educators would gain a deeper
understanding of gender identity as a dynamic terrain of struggle. Boys'
experiences in schools and in the culture at large are diverse and contradictory. Any pedagogy that fails to understand both this complexity and
the lack of any easy correspondence between patriarchal power and the
production of male identity is doomed to failure. A critical democratic
social studies recognizes the opportunity allowed by the nondeterministic
nature of identity formation, because it opens oppositional locales from
which dominant masculinity and patriarchal power can be challenged. At
the beginning of the twenty-first century, the male struggle for identity is
omnipresent and sometimes virulent. In schools, male behavior (misbehavior) should always be viewed within this context. Even the most mundane male activity—the ways boys walk, communicate with one another,
speak in class, interact with girls, react to humor, dress, etc.—is inscribed
by this struggle. At some level, most boys (and men) are more insecure
with their masculinity than they let their peers, parents, and teachers
know. A central task of a critical democratic social studies that addresses
gender is to access this masculine uncertainty in a way that induces boys
to think both logically and affectively about the nature of masculinity in
general and their own masculinity in particular (Pagano, 1990; Miller,
1993; Grumet, 1988; McLean, 1996b; Connell, 1995).

Building trust and the capacity for honest communication around this pervasive masculinist uncertainty, a critical analysis of patriarchy in social studies defines its ultimate purpose as the pursuit of gender justice. The ability to examine various situations and one's own actions in light of questions of gender power and justice is the pedagogical aspect of this critical pursuit of gender justice. The development of this ability to engage in a critical gender hermeneutics always takes place in a context where boys are actively engaged with girls and women. Central to a critical complex theory of patriarchy is the understanding that a central cause of social pathology in the lives of many men involves their alienation from women. Thus, a social studies education that embraces this study of patriarchy always takes place with an alliance between men and women and positions the feminist goal of the empowerment of women as one of its central objectives as well. Within such a social studies education, such empowerment does not involve mere female success in the existing patriarchal school system but a reconceptualization of school organization and purpose in light of a critical feminist critique and our complex theory of patriarchy (McLean, 1996b; Salisbury & Jackson, 1996; Yudice, 1995; Radford & Stanko, 1996).

Such theoretical insights fix the attention of social studies educators on the relationship between the social domain and the construction of subjectivity. Such understandings, when carefully shared with our male students, can help them appreciate the ways they consciously and unconsciously oppress females and males who fall outside nondominant masculinity. In an era when gay bashings and violence against women are everyday practices, the time has come to challenge the educational practices that deify dominant heterosexual masculinity and maintain the silence about patriarchy and everyday life. I am amazed by the way educational institutions, the media, and various social agencies can consistently ignore the pathological expressions of dominant masculinity that terrorize those who are viewed as weak and/or different (Kelly, 1996; Salisbury & Jackson, 1996). These dynamics have played a central role in almost all of the school shootings of the last few years. Until we are able to engage boys and men in the development of an interpersonal intelligence that allows them to connect with the experience of others, violence will continue to be a significant part of our daily lives. Until we induce boys to understand and take action in opposition to asymmetrical power relations surrounding categories of race, class, gender, and sexual preference, social pathology will continue to be the order of the day.

Chapter

Fingerprints at the Crime Scene: Power, Knowledge Production, and a Critical Democratic Social Studies

In Chapter 18 constructivism once again plays a central role in the social studies concepts under analysis. Implying that nothing represents a neutral perspective, constructivism shakes the epistemological foundations of modernist grand narratives. Indeed, no truly objective way of seeing exists. Nothing exists before consciousness shapes it into something we can perceive. Such an understanding, of course, is basic to an epistemology of complexity. In this context we understand that what appears to us as objective reality is merely what our minds construct, what we are accustomed to seeing (Leshan & Margenau, 1982; Bohm & Peat, 1987). The knowledge that the world yields has to be interpreted by men and women who are part of that world (Besag, 1986b). Whether we are attempting to understand football, education, or art, the constructivist epistemological principle tacitly remains. For example, most observers don't realize that the theory of perspective developed by fifteenth-century artists constituted a scientific convention. It was simply one way of portraying space and held no absolute validity. Thus, the structures and phenomena we observe in the social and physical worlds are constructions of our measuring and categorizing mind (Frye, 1987).

As such, these creations always take on a fictional dimension—a dimension dependent upon a variety of social, psychological, and discursive dynamics. One important thread running through these dynamics involves the role of power and its ability to shape our representations of the world along the lines of particular patterns. In this context, these fictions, though complex and idiosyncratic, become formulaic, reflective of dominant ideologies at work in the larger society.

Because social studies scholar teachers are often unable to discern the way in which power and its dominant ideologies position them in relation to the texts they produce, the development of analytical methods for exposing this dynamic becomes a central feature of critical constructivist knowledge production. Social studies educators must understand these fiction formulas in their professional work. An individual who gains such a critical insight would better understand how his or her political opinions, religious beliefs, gender role, racial self-concept, or educational perspectives had been influenced by the dominant culture. Understanding these power-driven fiction formulas helps social studies teachers in their critical struggle for self-reflection and an understanding of the role of power in the web of reality. In this critical constructivist context, democratic social studies teachers develop a dynamic and textured understanding of the way power works at both macro (deep structural) and micro (particularistic) levels to shape our understandings of the world and our role in it. Such theoretical work might begin its analysis of macropower with Gramscian notions of hegemony and its analysis of micropower with Foucauldian notions of discursive construction with its intrapersonal and interpersonal dimensions. The theoretical innovation that critical constructivism seeks involves the identification of contact points where these macro and micro manifestations of power connect. The search for these contact points takes place on the individual terrain of consciousness, necessitating, in a sense, a phenomenology of power—in a Foucauldian sense, an archeology of consciousness.

Such understandings open new possibilities for insights into knowledge production and teaching. A power-conscious critical constructivism allows social studies educators to step back from the world as they are accustomed to perceiving it. Such an ability highlights the way fiction formulas are shaped by linguistic codes, cultural signs, and, of course, embedded power. This power-conscious critical constructivism gives birth to what Bill Pinar and I have described as "social psychoanalysis," a method of analysis grounded on the integration of critical theory and French poststructuralism. As social psychoanalysts trace the fingerprints of power, they investigate the conditions under which knowledge is produced. In the electronic hyperreality of the present, attention may focus on forms of popular culture and media and their relation to identity production. A critical constructivist analysis of contemporary power structures quickly realizes that power is more powerful in hyperreality than ever before. The power of electronic media has no historical precedent. Never before has human understanding of the production of self (subjectivity) been so contingent on the manipulations of power. In this social context, power has invaded what John Fiske calls "the last terrain of control." By this, he is referring to the colonization of the internal domain of human beings: consciousness, social interaction, and the human body. The charge of critical constructivism and the critical social studies it supports, therefore, is the development of more insightful and specific analyses of power, its sociopolitical effects, and the fiction formulas it produces in our descriptions of the world, the world of education in particular. We are, of course, discussing what constitutes a rigorous social studies education.

Thus, the critical constructivist researcher seeks to untangle the complex knot of power in a manner that affords critical democratic social studies teachers insight into social practices and institutions. Such insight uncovers buried networks of power relations that constrain human possibility. Recognition of these networks empowers individuals who seek to resist and challenge social constraints. Every power relationship represents a site of potential struggle. The critical constructivist social studies educator peers into the micropolitics of everyday life, exposing points where intervention is possible. In the process of such analysis, researchers highlight distinctions between just and unjust educational arrangements, democratic and undemocratic deployments of power, and inclusive and exclusive definitions of success. Critical constructivist researchers inject dye into the capillaries of power, exposing the tissues that have been formed and malformed by power's presence (Wartenberg, 1992a; Ball, 1992; McCarthy, 1992). Compare this mode of social studies analysis with that proposed by top-down, technical standards. I'll see your educational standards, President Dubya Bush, and raise you.

WHAT IS POWER?

Though the nature and effects of power constitute a topic of contentious debate, rarely does anyone take time out to define the subject of the debate. In recent years a consensus seems to be emerging around the notion that power is a basic reality of human existence. Consensus, however, dissolves at this point with various scholars running like quail in diverse theoretical directions. Critical constructivists seem to agree that this fundamental constituent of human existence works to shape the oppressive and demeaning nature of the human condition. Scholars from both the Symbolic Interactionist and the Cultural Studies traditions accept the fundamental "constituent of reality" thesis, contending that power is embedded in the social frameworks of race, class, gender, occupations, and everyday interaction and communication. Poststructuralists such as Foucault agree, maintaining that power is present in all human relationships, be they the interactions of lovers, business partners, or researchers and the researched. Indeed, Foucault concluded, after reading Nietzsche, that, like the existence of capillaries in the circulatory system, power is inseparable from the social domain. As to the form of this pervasive social feature, Foucault never offered a definition more specific than that the exercise of power is a way in which particular actions modify others or guide their possible conduct. Since power is everywhere, therefore, it is not something that can easily be dispensed with or overthrown. Simplistic politics or pedagogies that propose to put an end to power relations do not understand its relation to the web of reality (Musolf, 1992; McCarthy, 1992; Cooper, 1994).

Thus, power relationships involve more than simply a one-way flow of power, an unidirectional hierarchy. Critical democratic social studies educators familiar with poststructuralist insights understand that omnipresent power can be deployed by servants as well as masters, that the subjugated are capable of avoiding the control of their oppressors, and indeed, in some situations, they can use their power to overthrow those who control them (Wartenberg, 1992a). As Amelie Rorty (1992) puts it, "we are all empowered . . . and we are all unempowered" (p. 5). We are empowered in the sense that we all possess capabilities, traits, and talents; we are unempowered in the sense that we all, at one time or another, experience failure in the attempt to satisfy our needs and desires. Foucault expressed this same concept with his notion of "disciplinary power." Such a form of power can both punish and transform individuals into subjects via the disciplines of the human sciences, such as, medicine, education, psychiatry, penology, criminology, and the various social sciences. The power of these disciplines has created a regulated culture through the use of "scientific expertise" at particular social sites—hospitals, schools, asylums, prisons, etc. Social psychoanalysts document the microworkings of disciplinary power in these venues. Such microworkings involve the variety of ways the wielders of disciplinary power engage the individual in the process of his or her own consciousness construction, a sociopsychological makeover that renders him or her more amendable to the requirements of the "normalizers," the "disciplinarians" (Ball, 1992).

SHADOW POWER: I SENSE IT EVERYWHERE BUT NEVER SEE IT

Real power is clandestine in its stance of plausible deniability. Critical social studies educators and knowledge producers maintain that most of us look at schools from the outside, never sensing the raw power covered by mundane artifacts such as bulletin boards and student art. When students emerge after the final bell, their social reconstitution has already begun. The new identity is replacing the old one in a process of cell-by-cell ideological metamorphosis. The success of the process is intricately connected to its ability to render itself invisible. Coercers hide their threat. Social researchers fall prey, identifying power as the province of the king, the state, or the legislature. Whatever the name of authority, power hides in the top-down configuration (Rorty, 1992; Airaksinen, 1992; Thiele, 1986; Fiske, 1994). Because power is everywhere, it can pass itself off as being nowhere. Thus, meanings are produced covertly—cloak-and-dagger hermeneutics. Liberal researchers produce narratives unable to penetrate the façade constructed by power. Thus, power is portrayed as a peripheral player in their version of everyday sociopolitical life.

Indeed, power is so well hidden that even those who deploy it are unaware of its existence. Despite the fact that many men are cognizant of the patriarchal domination of women, they often deny their complicity in such a power dynamic. In this particular case, they are unable to perceive the culturally situated, pervasive nature of patriarchal domination characterized by a social structure in which women have more trouble gaining access to goods, services, and opportunities than do men. In such a circumstance, wives must often depend upon their husbands to help them meet their material needs. Thus, wives need husbands in ways that husbands don't need wives, a need that creates power asymmetries in their relationships. Once these situated power dynamics are made visible, human beings, and those who study them, begin to appreciate the ways that power falls to individuals when they occupy particular social roles (Wartenberg, 1992b).

STANDING IN THE SHADOWS OF POWER:
DISCIPLINING SOCIAL STUDIES KNOWLEDGE PRODUCERS

As we begin to make sense of shadow power and to uncover the places in which it hides, we can begin to appreciate the subtle ways that power unconsciously shapes our consciousnesses, our teaching, and our knowledge production. Any analysis of social knowledge production should address the social and political construction of the consciousness of the researcher. Knowledge of self allows researchers to identify the ways power shapes research conventions, definitions of knowledge, and the purposes of inquiry. Knowledge of self, of positionality (one's location in the web of reality), creates a consciousness that empowers researchers to choose between research models that avoid power relations in the process of depersonalizing knowledge and models that use intuition and emotional empathy to gain access to the dynamics of power. Researchers attuned to the ways power shapes the form inquiry takes can no longer accept, unproblematically, the assumptions of mainstream social research (Yeakey, 1987). As they develop a sense of reflexive awareness, they focus on the ways they are molded by linguistic codes, cultural signs, and embedded ideology. At this point they begin to reconstruct their perception of the world, not just in a random way, but in a manner that deconstructs what appears natural, that reopens questions ostensibly answered. They ask new questions about how that which is came to be, whose interests do particular institutional arrangements serve, from where do their own frames of reference emanate, and what is the nature of their relationship with those they research. In such a context, researchers are engaging in a critical construction/deconstruction of the world and their relation to it (Lincoln & Guba, 1985; Denzin & Lincoln, 1994; Noblit, 1984; Slaughter, 1989; Fine, 1993).

Critical democratic social studies scholars concerned with power engage in a metaconversation with themselves about their relations with power. This metaconversation continues its demystification process as it turns its attention to the discursive construction of their research. Why do social studies knowledge producers use particular words, metaphors, and models when they design their inquiry, interpret it, and suggest teaching strategies based on it? Their research language reflects the effects of the influence of power in the larger society. Power, as Foucault has argued, has served to censor, exclude, block, and repress like a great superego. But, he continues, it also serves to produce knowledge, creating effects at the level of desire. As a censor in social research, power serves to limit what constitutes a legitimate question, excluding "dangerous" investigations, such as explorations of how class factors affect student performances. As a producer in social research, power serves to reward particular ways of seeing and particular activities. For example, social studies researchers who desire success in the mainstream field follow particular research norms that afford them the rewards of funded grants and promotions based on scholarly productivity. The way different research orientations draw boundaries between what is acceptable and what is not constitutes the ideological dimension of the act of inquiry (Cherryholmes, 1988). Here, power is at work, promoting particular views of social studies excellence and failure, rewarding particular forms of knowledge production and punishing others.

As critical social studies analysts, we make a mistake when we assume that this power is always consciously exercised by a cabal of conspirators seeking to control the world of social studies. Much of the time the ideological construction of consciousness emanating from sources of power does not take place at the level of conscious intention. For example, mainstream social studies professionals often do not seek to design research that results in the perpetuation of business and military values in social studies classrooms. Most school administrators do not seek to use educational research that represses ethical considerations and questions of justice in their efforts to run their schools. And most teachers certainly do not consciously attempt to suppress their students' ability to think at a more critical level, nor do they try to punish the underprivileged or reward the privileged. But all of these unfortunate things happen, and most of the time, we have no clue why. We don't catch on because we don't understand the subtle semiotic dimensions of power reproduction, i.e., how codes, symbols, and signs subtly construct our worldviews. As critical constructivist social studies scholars, we begin to see how educational research produced by such subtle forces legitimizes particular values and delegitimizes others.

For example, in terms of concrete research practices, Who is legitimate to interview, to use as a reliable source, and who is not? Remember my story of how, as a high school social studies teacher, I often watched social studies teachers bring experts to their economics classes to speak and to answer student questions. In my high school, these experts were usually successful businessmen who delivered a remarkably standardized ideological package for student consumption. The idea of inviting individuals from other social classes or other ideological traditions (e.g., labor leaders, social workers, welfare rights leaders, etc.) was never considered. Dominant values and ideology were thus reproduced, not at a level of conscious intent on the part of the teachers, but at a tacit, unconscious level. On this same level, the records of any historical era favor those who direct public events or produce the records; the masses, the common voices of working people, are excluded from the picture. Critical constructivist social studies researchers, aware of these hegemonic dimensions of power in inquiry, take special pains to collect testimonies of individuals outside of power. Thus, they attempt to avoid particular fiction formulas that insidiously shape research oblivious to the workings of dominant power (Reinharz, 1979, 1992).

Expert researchers from academic settings like to believe that the university, because it is called "academic," is removed from these historical realities, value dimensions, and ideological forces which shape the form their research takes. Our knowledge production, no matter who we are, is never as independent of outside influences as we would like to think. We are all caught at a particular point in the web of reality. A central goal of a critical democratic social studies, of course, is to understand what our particular vantage point is and how it limits our vision. This process involves our awareness of our own historicity, or place in history. History in this context becomes not a self-contained subject with a body of knowledge but a process of knowing, of making sense of, the social world around us. We become conscious of our own ideological inheritance and its relationship to our belief and value structures, our interests, and our questions about our lives as social studies educators.

In his studies of the eugenicists and their influence on the way educators came to view intelligence and school performance, Steven Selden (1984) traced how social visions shaped eugenicist research design. Ideological conceptions of what constituted civilization, human progress, and a good society could not be separated from the formulation of eugenicist research. What is ironic in this case is that many of the instruments devised by eugenicist researchers to measure learning, intelligence, and ability are still employed in modern education. Thus, at an unseen level, the value assumptions of the eugenicist movement are embedded in contemporary educational practices (Cherryholmes, 1988). Indeed, the power of, in this case, White supremacy works in mysterious ways to represent educational and other aspects of reality. Here rests what I would consider central concerns of any social studies curriculum—of course, they are not to be found in social studies curriculum or in content standards.

Vox Domesticus: Distinguishing Power and Domination

As something that cannot be eliminated from the social process, power is everywhere—a source of pleasure and pain, liberation and regulation. In the context of social studies, knowledge production, and teaching, particular aspects of power assume more importance than others. Domination emerges at this point as the particular form of power that solidifies unequal relationships. While subordinate forces also wield power, they cannot be conceptualized simply as countervailing dynamics of power or as forces of counterdomination. Domination emanates from these asymmetrical mechanics because it taps what has been defined as "extractive power," i.e., the ability acquired by power wielders to exploit and draw benefit from the exertions of others. When social researchers are unable to speak of patterns of domination—because they are unable to identify them in everyday life—they become naively complicit in the process of domination. Power wielders such as corporate leaders continue to covertly derive extractive power from, for example, recent graduates of vocational schools who are taught to see as natural top-down managerial regulation of their daily lives, the logic of capital as superior to the logic of justice, exclusive access to information about production as a privilege of management, etc. Thus, the new employees tend to submit to the corporate appropriation of their productive abilities. Hence, the voice of critical democratic social studies teachers is desperately needed even in vocational education—a place where it is presently excluded.

Critical in the process of domination is the capture of the dominated's capacities, that is, their "power to." Thus, the corporate domination of young workers involves the acquisition of their extractive power through the firm's "power to" represent the ways of the world to them. Corporate "power to" control the concepts around which the social, economic, and political world is constructed and portrayed is an ideological precondition of domination or power over workers. When the voice of the researcher is concurrently domesticated (*vox domesticus*) by the same corporate power to represent the ways of the world as natural and unworthy of comment, domination is extended by, as previously mentioned, its ability to hide. Thus, the power to dominate, to construct the fiction formulas of social researcher's descriptive narratives, revolves around this capacity to represent. Indeed the most powerful manifestation of power is capable of defining individuals' priorities, curiosities, incentives, and desires (Miller, 1990; Cooper, 1994; Patton, 1989; Rorty, 1992; McLaren, 1995). The raison d'être of critical social studies knowledge production involves the unveiling of these conditions and methods of textual production and the relationship between cultural representation and ideological domination. While power interests have always concealed the process by which they attempt to depict reality, the strategies by which dominant interests represent the world in the first decade of the twenty-first century are far more sophisticated than ever before (Brown, 1993). The need for researchers capable of decoding the power relations embedded in cultural texts, therefore, has never been more urgent.

FINGERPRINTS AT THE CRIME SCENE: POWER AND TEXTUAL REPRESENTATIONS IN POSTMODERNITY

Whose interests are served by a politics of representation? What ideological codes can be identified in particular representations? How are certain representations positioned in relation to questions of race, class, and gender? The development of critical constructivist forms of social knowledge production is not important merely in the continuing effort to sophisticate research but also in the traditional task of citizenship education, i.e., civics. When the power to represent reality clusters in the hands of a relative few, and representational techniques achieve an unprecedented level of sophistication, power and representation become central features in the life (or death) of a democracy. If people are to assume authority over their lives, not to mention self-government, the ability to deconstruct power-saturated representations becomes essential. Proponents of critical forms of education (Giroux, 1994; McLaren, et al., 1995; McLaren, 1995; Steinberg & Kincheloe, 1996, 1999; Kincheloe, 1995; Haymes, 1995; hooks, 1994; Britzman, 1991; Aronowitz, 1993) argue that all representations must be positioned historically and politically in contexts that expose their content, targeted audiences, structure, and power dynamics. Critical democratic social studies warn educators that representations aimed at the political domain are deployed not only in traditional political sites but also on the terrains of art, entertainment, religion, and various forms of popular culture. Critical analyses of representations closely attend to questions of ethics, solidarity, and public responsibility in relation to the ways they intersect with issues of profit, corporate legitimation, worker exploitation, and race, class, and gender oppression.

Analysis of the crime scene (the postmodern condition), the dusting for the fingerprints of power on the representations of reality now taken for granted, call for a new form of "criminology," i.e., new techniques of social analysis and knowledge production. A sea change has taken place in knowledge production, in what counts as knowledge, in the last 30 years. The power of mass media has demonstrated to critical social studies educators the need for analysis of how textual, aural, and visual representations are produced and distributed. Indeed, as the mass media have changed the ways that culture itself is constructed, identities, voice production, and self-images cannot be removed from the analysis of TV, film, CDs, computer networks, advertising imagery, etc. A major transformation in cultural epistemology necessitates analysis of such systemic changes and their implications. As an interdisciplinary, transdisciplinary, and sometimes counterdisciplinary field, cultural studies has emerged as a new means of addressing the new times. Thus, cultural studies pushes researchers beyond the limits of what we already know, investigating the interaction between power, domination, and the private terrain of affect, feeling, and pleasure.

In the name of cultural studies, Norm Denzin (1989, 1994) has examined and called for further examination of these dynamics as they manifest themselves in postmodern mass communications. Communications itself is power, he contends, and is intrinsically ideological. Ideologies of White supremacy, patriarchy, and the upper-middle and upper socioeconomic classes permeate American cultural representations. Images are produced that tacitly favor the powerful, as producers, all the while proclaim the neutrality of their productions. The research bricolage described in Chapter 16 offers a range of methodologies (ethnography, textual analysis, semiotics, deconstruction, ethnomethodology, critical hermeneutics, phonemic analysis, psychoanalysis, social psychoanalysis, rhizomatics, content analysis, interviews, survey research, and phenomenology—just to begin a list) that attempt to flush out the ways that power produces research narratives and representations of the social (Musolf, 1992; Nelson, Treichler, & Grossberg, 1992).

The Eclectic Art of Exposé:
Cultural Studies and Bricolage

Cultural studies scholars pursue power and its effects by any means necessary. The panoply of different methodologies that constitute cultural studies' interdisciplinary projects, the fields' eclectic view of research has been labeled "bricolage" by several scholars (Denzin & Lincoln, 1994; Weinstein & Weinstein, 1991; Becker, 1989). Bricolage involves taking research strategies from a variety of disciplines and traditions as they are needed in the unfolding context of the research situation. Such a position is pragmatic and strategic, demanding a self-consciousness and an awareness of context from the researcher. Some, or many, aspects of the bricolage can be deployed to get a better look at power. As one labors to expose the fiction formulas that covertly shape our own and other scholars' research narratives, the bricolage highlights our appreciation of the relationship between one's way of seeing and the social location of his or her personal history. Appreciating research as a power-driven act, the critical social studies researcher as "bricoleur" abandons the quest for objectivity, focusing instead on the clarification of his or her positionality and the social location of other researchers and the ways they shape the research narrative (Denzin & Lincoln, 1994).

Just a Little Bit of Respect: Bricolage and Complexity

Bricolage has emerged as a direct result of critical constructivism's respect for the complexity of the lived world; it is grounded in an epistemology of complexity. The nature of this complexity can be illustrated by the relationship between research and the domain of theory. The dense language of critical postmodern theory has too often discouraged uninitiated social studies teachers in their effort to discern the relation of such discourse to their everyday professional lives. Behind the language, there rest some very important insights for those interested in extending the conversation about researcher positionality. All observations are theory-saturated, in that theory provides the language that frames what is observed. Theory, in a modernist empiricist mode, is a way of understanding that operates without variation in every context. Since theory is a linguistic and a cultural artifact, its single interpretation of the object of its observation is inseparable from the historical dynamics that have shaped it (Rosenau, 1992). The task of critical constructivist research is to attack this complexity, methodically uncovering the invisible artifacts of culture and describing the nature of their influence. The domain of theory in this context is exposed for what it is: not an explanation of nature but an explanation of our relation to nature.

This is not to say that critical constructivist research has no use for theory. Indeed, theory is very important in the bricolage of critical complex social research. Theory involves the conceptual matrix analysts use to make sense of the world. Theory, whether it is held consciously or unconsciously, works as a filter through which social knowledge producers approach information, designate facts, identify problems, and devise solutions to their problems. Different theoretical frameworks, therefore, privilege different forms of textual representation (Aronowitz, 1993; Giroux, 1988). Traditional researchers in the Cartesian empirical paradigm, of course, have had no use for discussions of representation, the text, or the narrative voice of the inquirer. The facts they produce after all are, as Sergeant Joe Friday of *Dragnet* fame might put it, "just the facts." "What you talking about," such researchers might ask, "with all this discussion of theoretical pre-assumptions?"

The appearance of theory freedom renders traditional empiricist research the great deceiver. It wraps itself in the cloak of objectivity while unconsciously promoting specific values and a certified definition of a "proper" relationship to sociopolitical life. To engage in social studies research without understanding the epistemological and value assumptions behind it, critical constructivists argue, is to miss the complexity of the lived world and to guarantee the irrelevance of the research produced (Astman, 1984; McNay, 1988; Kincheloe, 1991). Theoretical understanding is a precondition to the critical constructivist analysis of the complex constellation of sociallyconstructed values that shape the social studies curriculum. No research tradition, in my opinion, can match the bricolage's capacity to expose the nature of this power-driven process of social construction. I hope that social studies knowledge producers will exploit its benefits in the coming decades.

UPPING THE ANTE: EXTENDING DOMINATION/HEGEMONY— HYPERREALITY AND THE MANAGEMENT OF MEANING

Extending our brief references to power at the "crime scene" of postmodernity, an extended discussion of mutating forms of domination in postmodernity's hyperreality is in order. Domination at the macrosocial level is best conceptualized by Antonio Gramsci's notion of hegemony. Power blocs have become less and less dependent on violence as a means of domination and more reliant upon the consent of citizens in their own domination, Gramsci wrote in Mussolini's prison decades ago. The organization of consent is a very complex affair, he argued, that takes place in everyday life. The power bloc wins popular consent by way of a social studies pedagogical process, a form of learning that engages people's conceptions of the world in such a way that transforms (not displaces) them with perspectives more compatible with the elite (Giroux, 1992). The existence and nature of hegemony is one of the most important and least understood features of sociopolitical life in the twenty-first-century U.S., even among social researchers. They, too, are hegemonized, since their ideological field is structured by limited exposure to competing definitions of the sociopolitical world. Indeed, no one is excluded from the hegemonic field. Its bounded mental/ideological horizon garners consent to an inequitable social matrix—a set of social relations that are legitimated by their depiction as natural and inevitable (McLaren, 1994a; Goldman, 1992).

The technologies of hegemony (the methods by which social consent is garnered) move social domination from condition yellow to condition red. Critical constructivists find themselves in a state of full alert in regard to the exacerbation of domination in the postmodern condition. This power-saturated hyperreality is marked by a blurring of the distinction between the real and the unreal. The success of social studies knowledge producers hinges on: 1) their ability to link the production of the images and signs of hyperreality to power blocs in the political economy; and, 2) once this linkage is exposed and described, their ability to delineate the highly complex and ambiguous effects of the reception of these images and signs on individuals located at various coordinates in the web of reality. No easy task, this effort, but to avoid it is to turn our backs on the democratic experiment and the possibility of producing a social studies that promotes social justice. This is why the effort to trace the effects of power in the ways researchers represent reality and formulate narrative voices is so important.

We must be very specific about the nature of domination in contemporary life. Power in hyperreality, in its obscured yet ubiquitous guise, is amplified by corporate control of the means of simulation and representation. Corporations are the most important social studies educators of our era. By determining what is important (worthy, for example, of time on TV) and what is not, corporate-owned media can set agendas, mold loyalties, depict conflicts, and undermine challenges to the existing power bloc without a modicum of public notice. The question of power/domination that we are grappling with in this chapter cannot be too important an issue, for it is not a topic addressed on the mediascape. CBS will not present a two-minute story on domination in hyperreality on tomorrow night's evening news; neither will a single local affiliate do so on any of their news programming in the foreseeable future. Electronic media will make programming decisions on the basis of issues of commodity exchange; that is, cultural codes will be conveyed to the viewing audience on the basis of their capacity to engage men and women in their duty to consume. The constituency of hyperreality serves the needs of the power bloc with honor and civic reverence. Their "patriotic" acts of consumption constitute the life-affirming producing energy of postmodern capitalism. In this regime of economic accumulation and social regulation, artistic production unites with industrial production to produce commodities that assume sign value as aesthetic signifiers of status and dominant cultural capital (Luke, 1991).

If "we are what we eat," then we also are what we know. The implications here are obvious if social, political, and economic information production and delivery are predominately controlled by an ever decreasing number of corporate power wielders. In such a context, the attempt of individuals, social studies researchers included, to gain access to nonprocessed information always requires motivation, effort, and some degree of both critical consciousness and investigative expertise. Media and related forms of information production in hyperreality constitute the central forces of hegemony in their role of meaning organizers and pattern revealers for people attempting to make sense of their own lives and the world. Related as they are to the techno-economic and social interests of corporate America, the forms of meaning that media organize and the types of sociopolitical patterns they reveal fall reasonably close to the tree of corporate ideology. The process is by no means heavy-handed and monolithic. Rather, it is subtle and contradictory, inasmuch as media and their corporate underwriters refrain from attempts to simply supplant the social, familial, interpersonal, and existential experience of the public. Instead, they suggest a way of constructing such lived phenomena in a sensible manner that reduces friction between the interests of the power bloc and the desires of the public (Tomlinson, 1991).

Technopower and the Politics of Information

Analysts of research and social theory make a serious mistake when they separate researchers from the macro- and micropolitics of hegemony, with its regulatory relationship to information and meaning. The pedagogical features (e.g., identity formation and knowledge production) for corporate-dominated media and the hyperreality it helps produce are profound. Such a repressive social studies pedagogy shapes our view of knowledge production, obscures our recognition of where we are located in the web of reality, and subverts our conception of the complexity of textual representations. These dynamics, ostensibly operating exclusively in the political domain, bleed over into the realm of education and the research that surrounds it. Critical constructivists, concerned with social justice, egalitarianism, democratic pedagogies, liberatory teaching, and the social impact of their work as social studies educators, must examine issues of social studies curricula and knowledge in light of power and the politics of information. The use of terms such as postindustrialism, post-Fordism, or high-tech economy has created a misleading picture of power relations in contemporary and future American society. To listen to former Speaker of the House Newt Gingrich speak of technological innovation in relation to his political vision is to hear a "techtopian vision of social harmony and capitalist paradise." Unfortunately, more grounded projections, based on present conditions, do not portend such a free-market Garden of Eden.

The development of new technologies over the last couple of decades has not created a new era of power sharing. As the wealthiest in America have become much wealthier and more entrenched, the working class and the poor have lost power and financial security. In this context the term "technopower" can be used to describe the expansion of corporate influence through the development of sophisticated new technologies. Via technopower, firms are better equipped to control and exploit their workers while silencing their critics. Critical constructivist social researchers, arguing that we all construct our worldviews, understand that some worldviews fit better with the dynamics of technopower than others, and that some worldviews will bring emotional corroboration and financial reward more effectively than others. Those researchers who attempt to expose such realities understand that their narrative voice, whatever form it might take, will find fewer avenues for expression than those who celebrate them.

The politics of corporatism, with its technopower have exacerbated capitalist hegemony over production, capital, credit, and commodity markets, including media and mass/popular culture producers. This unparalleled concentration of power reframes questions of social studies knowledge production into a carnival-fun-house-of-distorted-mirrors context that changes all the traditional rules of inquiry. The social studies pedagogy of technopower emanates from centralized control of data banks, radio and TV transmissions, transnational communications systems, and global networks. Controlled by corporate leaders, such a megasystem allows them to regulate macro-markets from Argentina to Zaire while reshaping individual consciousness in cities, villages, and rural areas in a way that weds men, women, and children to corporate values like competitive individualism, the superiority of an unregulated market economy, and the necessity of consumption. Such forms of knowledge control induce people to bond with worldviews of the powerbloc in their depiction, for instance, of blue-collar workers as incompetent. If a sizable portion of the public fails to contest this particular representation, the power relations of the status quo are concretized. In the politics of labor-management relations, for example, managers can more effectively rally particular segments of the public to support their denial of higher wages and more power on the shop floor to workers with the contention that, after all, they don't deserve such rewards. With public information about the concerns of social studies quickly mutating into a private commodity, with fewer and fewer corporations controlling the flow of information—two percent of publishers, for example, now control over 75% of the books published in the U.S.—public accessibility to information outside of the orbit of technopower contracts. In the process, technopower expands (Peace, 1990; Smart, 1992; Brosio, 1994; McLaren, et al., 1995).

FURTIVE FORMULAS: EXHUMING THE COLONEL AND HIS SECRET RECIPE

Our discussions of power/domination, consciousness construction, and representation have brought us to an important crossroads. Understanding that all research texts are haunted by an authorial voice, two questions emerge: What is the nature of that voice? and How does it reflect the consciousness construction of a social studies teacher-researcher? A language-of-research way of posing these questions might involve creating the concept of political validity—evaluating the manner in which a piece of research confronts questions of power and the ways such power shapes the content and presentation of the research. The history of ethnography, for example, connected as it is to the attempt to understand and control the countercolonialism movements beginning in the 1940s, is awash in the blood of domination. Questions of power in this context were repressed far too long. In some cases, the difference between CIA-sponsored ethnographic research and espionage was indistinguishable (Miller, 1993). To those subjects of research, whether finding themselves oppressed in Iran in the late 1940s or in America in the first decade of the twenty-first century, questions of political validity and the nature of representation and presentation of research data become quite significant. The fiction formulas employed for the purpose of narrating the stories of their lives help shape their relationship to the center and the margins of the social galaxy (Rosenau, 1992). Because all social researchers' representations of reality and their narrative presentations of it are fraudulent to the degree they are tendered as true pictures of the social cosmos, critical constructivists seek the patterns of the fraud, i.e., the fiction formulas.

The critical constructivist exposure of fiction formulas constitutes a direct challenge to modernist modes of social representation. When modernist discourses of social research are subjected to the archeological "exhumation" of the critical constructivists, they are often revealed as promiscuous exercises of power. Such discursive schemas constitute the microfeatures of consciousness construction, the taken-for-granted components of subjectivity that prompted Gramsci to envision the purpose of philosophy as self-criticism. A critical philosophy, he argued, cultivates the ability of its adherents to criticize the ideological frames they employ to make sense of the world (Keat, 1994; Reynolds, 1987; Mardle, 1984). The criticism of dominant ideological frames and the exposure of petrified fossils of power, embedded in the modes of representation and presentation of mainstream social research, in no way should be read as anarchist strategies for nihilism, for the destruction of human agency. To the contrary, the exposé of shadow power is the foreplay for the consummation of political action, of counterhegemonic, taboo-breaking forms of informational representation and presentation. It is a primary objective of a critical democratic social studies.

Modernist Fables and Dangerous Deceits

The modernist interpretivist fable asserts that there is a correct way to describe social, political, and economic reality. Post-Cartesian critiques of the fable condemn it as fraudulent in its certainty, and in its denial of ideological complicity in the dynamics of its construction (Fontana, 1994; Rosenau, 1992; Probyn, 1993). The unitary, modernist, Cartesian self, the narrative reflection of liberalism's abstract individual (the subject who transcends the weight of historical and cultural engagement) is removed from power's construction of consciousness. As a covert form of autobiography, the narrative formula of traditional data presentation positions the social reporter as a privileged producer of texts; the social studies researcher in this context fails to achieve power validity. He or she fails to gain a power literacy. At this juncture, the critical constructivist analyst specifies the discursive forms of the modernist narrative (the fiction formulas) and their power-connected seductions. Understanding power's pervasiveness as well as its construction of a researcher's ideological horizon, the critical constructivist social analyst itemizes the male-specific, class-dominated, White-oriented, unified-subject-assumed fiction formulas that produce the naïve narratives at the hub of academic research.

These same types of furtive (hidden) formulas (secret ideological recipes) can be uncovered in the attempt to mobilize public memory. Such historical fiction formulas operate on both school and cultural terrains, creating narratives that are conflict-free, seamless, objective, and official. Such fiction formulas arise not from the need to remember but from the need to forget. The formula calls for a bleaching of the blood-stains that help prop up established power. The power of such memory construction in education is revealed in the formulaic histories of the Educational Testing Service that exclude the eugenicist origins of, and influence on, what passes as a value-neutral, objective evaluation organization (Kincheloe, 1990; Owen & Doerr, 1999) Power's secret recipe survives. As a force of domination, it produces subjectivity, renders itself invisible, makes meaning, reflects and exacerbates asymmetrical social relationships, and insidiously wins consent.

THE WAY OF TRANSGRESSORS IS HARD:
ELUDING DOMINANT FICTION FORMULAS

The post-Cartesian redefinition of social knowledge production has gained momentum in the last three decades. The critical constructivist reformulation of social studies knowledge production does not reassure the epistemologically timid, and it pays no homage to the traditionalist's historical, social, and political certainties. Such democratic transgression not only calls sacred memories into question but diverts and dams up their narrative flow. Even the superiority of scientific narrative forms over literary stylistics is no longer assumed. Using the passageway created by cultural studies and bricolage, critical constructivism finds new vantage points from which to reassess the relationship among culture, knowledge production, researcher positionality, and power. Employing the bricolage, critical constructivists come to appreciate the unique demands that hyperreality's shifting cosmos of representations places on the methods and goals of their research (Goldman & Papson, 1994). An ever evolving, unfixed subject cannot speak with the same authority as the male voice-over of a National Geographic Special TV presentation on the "Bantu natives of the copper-rich Belgian Congo." Post-Cartesian decentering of authority/power demands a move to a dialogue between researcher and researched, a reassessment of the relations of domination hidden within the social studies knowledge production process.

The critical constructivist reformulation of social research speaks an uncertain language of dialogical representation. An ethnographic analysis of American high school students' perceptions of, say, the purposes of schooling held by their teachers and administrators may demand nontraditional research strategies. Such students' perceptions may be constructed by two differing, possibly conflicting, discourses. The primary discourse may be that of the official curriculum with its litany of noble social studies objectives: citizenship training, a "well-rounded" knowledge of the world, vocational preparation, literacy, cultivation of the ability to live together, etc. The secondary discourse may be that of the covert, oppositional culture of youth with its own interpretations of school purpose: control of the libidinal impulses of young people, babysitting, conformity, adjustment of poor kids to low-status jobs, psychological preparation of students for toleration of boring life situations, etc. Critical social studies teachers as researchers understand both dimensions of this dynamic. They understand complexity, appreciating that students can hold both perceptions simultaneously. The fingerprints at the social studies crime scene are always a little smudged and difficult to read. Power is elusive but omnipresent. A critical democratic social studies demands a power literacy.

 Chapter

Social Studies and the Intersection of the Critical and the Cognitive: The Future of Critical Education

Critical education has, over the last few decades, revolutionized the way we have come to think about education and teaching. It has undoubtedly sophisticated the democratic conversation about social studies and the goals of schooling in general and provided hope to what was a pessimistic progressive conversation. It has expanded the envelope of social studies education with its attention to race, class, and gender issues and has redefined inclusivity in its complex democratic form. By no means has critical education reached its ultimate expression or its final synthesis. Indeed, if it is to retain its critical dimension, it must seek out, listen carefully to, and act on the basis of the critiques of those who uncover its failures and shortcomings. It is only with this humility and fallibist (the belief that one is capable of making mistakes) predisposition that critical education will continue to play a subversive/productive role in a democratic social studies.

CRITICAL CONSTRUCTIVISM: COGNITION IN THE SOCIAL STUDIES

As we think about the future, I am convinced that the implications of the intersection of critical theory and an epistemology of complexity must be examined in all areas of schooling and in teacher education.

Much of my work over the last decade has been concerned with the implications of this intersection for the study of cognition. Critical ideas, as we all know, are often missing from the discourse of cognition and educational psychology in many colleges of education around the world. Importantly, social studies education, especially a critical variety, has operated without the benefit of a cognitive theory. The focus of this chapter involves some beginning thoughts about this one segment of the future of a critical democratic social studies: the study of cognition and the development of a critical constructivism and postformal psychology of education.

As previously asserted, constructivism, in the process of shaking the empistemological foundations of modernist grand narratives, maintains that nothing represents a "neutral" perspective. Indeed, no truly objective way of seeing exists. Nothing exists before consciousness shapes it into something we can perceive. What appears to us as objective reality, Piaget argued, is merely what our minds construct, what we are accustomed to seeing (Leshan & Margenau, 1982; Bohm & Peat, 1987). But where do these creations and the predispositions that shape them come from? It is with this question that the attempt to examine cognition from the perspective of critical epistemology of complexity begins. In addition to a variety of problems with Piaget's version of constructivism, including a dehistorization, a logocentrism, an essentializing tendency, and a positivistic impulse, two major questions arise in relation to this notion of predisposition: Are our psycho-social predispositions beyond our conscious control? And do we simply surrender our perceptions to the determinations of the environment, our context? Because individuals are often unable to see the way their environment shapes their perceptions (that is, constructs their consciousness), the development of cognitive methods for exposing this process must become a central goal of a critical democratic social studies. This is where a critical epistemology of complexity collides with constructivism. Hence, the genesis of our term, "critical constructivism."

THE DIALECTIC OF ASSIMILATION AND ACCOMODATION: CRITICAL NEGATION AS A COGNITIVE ACT

Using the tenets of a critical epistemology of complexity, let us explore what happens when our emancipatory source of authority intersects traditional Piagetian notions of cognition. To Piaget, intellectual adaptation is an equilibration between assimilation and accommodation. Assimilation involves the shaping of an event to fit into one's cognitive structure. No event, even if a student has never encountered it before, constitutes a new beginning. In other words, as assimilation fits an experience to the demands of one's logical structures, it is grafted onto previously developed schemes. Accommodation, on the other hand, refers to the restructuring of one's cognitive maps to take care of an event. In order to accommodate, an individual must actively change his or her existing intellectual structure to understand the dissonance produced by the novel demand. Piaget described accommodation as a reflective, integrative behavior that forces the realization that our present cognitive structure is insufficient to deal with the changing pressures of the environment (Kaufman, 1978; Fosnot, 1988).

Piaget argues that, at the beginning, assimilation and accommodation tend to move in different directions: assimilation, as the conservative protector of existing cognitive structure, subordinating the environment to the existing organism; accommodation, as the subversive agent of change, leading the organism to adjust to the imperatives of the environment. In the long run, however, Piaget contends that the ostensibly divergent tasks are inseparable in the larger process of equilibration—the dynamic process of self-monitored behavior that balances assimilation and accommodation's polar behaviors. Over the past 30 years, however, critics have asserted that, as Piaget described higher orders of thought, he privileged assimilation over accommodation. The effect of this assimilation-centeredness has been the progressive removal of the individual from her or his environment. The emphasis, thus, becomes not so much on what an individual can do in the world of objects, or what actions she or he can undertake, but how quickly the individual can learn to think outside of reality. The more an individual engages in disembedded thought, the higher level of cognition Piaget will ascribe to him or her. In a Cartesian-Newtonian framework, the higher order thinker is detached from personal experience. The Piagetian image of the active learner in charge of his or her own fate is subverted by the lack of exchange between the thinker and the world of objects. Because of this removal of women and men from experience, Piaget's theory abstracts individuals from the cosmos while reducing the possibility of emancipatory individual and social change.

To Piaget, knowing involves the transformation of contradictory experience into stable structures. When subjected to a post-Cartesian challenge to the stability of meaning, Piaget's confidence in the viability of structures is undermined. Meaning is far too ephemeral for an epistemologically complex study of cognition to claim the existence of a stable structure, a balance between assimilation and accommodation—in Piaget's word, "equilibration." The concept of negation, central to critical theory and to accommodation, involves the continuous criticism and reconstruction of what one thinks one knows. For example, critical theorist Max Horkheimer argued that, through negation, we develop a critical consciousness that allows us to transcend old codified worldviews and incorporate our new understandings into a new reflective attitude (Held, 1980). Let us delve deeper into these connections between critical theory and constructivism.

Critical equilibration denies the possibility of any stable balance between assimilation and accommodation. Aware of the tendency of Piagetian formalism to de-emphasize accommodation, critical equilibration recognizes the radical potential of constructivist accommodation. As accommodation changes consciousness in order to understand new aspects of the social environment, subjects gain awareness of their own limitations. Horkheimer maintained that, through the awareness gained by way of critical negation—the philosophical analogue to the cognitive act of accommodation—an individual develops and becomes open to change (Held, 1980). Thus, a key cognitive dimension of any critical democratic social studies will involve accommodation—indeed, a critical accommodation. Critical constructivist teachers understand the value of difference, with its power to initiate the process of critical accommodation, as a reshaping of consciousness consonant with the concerns of a critical system of meaning. Such social studies teachers see the diversity of classroom experiences as an opportunity for cognitive growth.

Critical constructivist social studies teachers, for example, exploring the meaning of intelligence and its relationship to their students, would assimilate an understanding of the concept based on their own experience. The teacher would accommodate the concept as he or she began to examine students who were labeled unintelligent but, upon a second look, exhibited characteristics which, in an unconventional way, seemed sophisticated. The teacher would then integrate this recognition of exception (accommodation) into a broader definition of intelligence (Kincheloe, Steinberg, & Villaverde, 1999). The old definition of intelligence would have been negated; through exposure to diverse expressions of intelligence, new ways of seeing it would have been accommodated.

The new ways of seeing would be critically accommodated in the sense that they would emancipate us from the privileged, racial, gender, and class-biased definitions of intelligence which were used to exclude cognitive styles that transcended the official codes. In this and many other cases, accommodation becomes the emancipatory aspect of the thinking process in question. Critical constructivists recognize this and use it in the struggle for democratic social and educational change.

Critical accommodation in the social studies classroom is the key to the creation of new student attitudes. Dialogical encounters between critical constructivist teachers and their students often involve the presentation of information that disrupts assimilated world views—for example, an encounter with a Mexican historian's interpretation of the Mexican War. It is at this point, a point where cognitive dissonance reaches its zenith, that students realize that something in their consciousness is out of order and adjustment is required. This moment of accommodation is not to be subverted by the unethical social studies teacher who takes advantage of it to indoctrinate, or to provide a facile resolution to the dissonance. Such resolutions are ethically tantamount to behaviorist manipulation or the indoctrination of religious or political zealots. The critical constructivist teacher prolongs the accommodation moment for days or weeks at a time, using it to stimulate searching, research-based student activities (Hultgren, 1987).

TEACHING A CRITICAL CONSTRUCTIVIST SOCIAL STUDIES

Critical constructivist social studies teaching proceeds in no prearranged, standardized manner, but it does seem to embody a few common characteristics. At some point, teachers and students are encouraged to examine the cognitive structures that impede transformative action, whether on the self or the social environment. For example, an individual may be stuck at a Piagetian formal level that emphasizes a procedural form of abstract logical thought, a form of thinking that removes the relationships among thinking, consciousness construction, and praxis (informed action) from consideration. Such forms of thinking tend to relegate teaching and learning to a cognitive realm, separate from commitment, emotion, and ethical action. As is so often the case in cognitive and educational psychology, individuals are removed from their social context. Such a removal runs contrary to an epistemology of complexity and a social study of anything.

At the same time, transformative action may be impeded not only by cognitive structures but by sociopolitical structures as well. This sociopolitical impediment may be found in economic and linguistic structures, in geographic places, religious dimensions, and many other ideological social domains. Critical constructivist social studies teachers strive to identify these impediments and their effects on how individuals come to see and act on the world (Codd, 1984). For example, no matter how "intelligent" a young woman might be, her identification with a religious sect that viewed women as the metaphorical body and men as the head would impede transformative action on her part. Such forms of sociopolitical oppression would be exposed by critical constructivist social studies. In both the cognitive and the sociopolitical situations, impediments serve to impede the disruption of critical accommodation. Critical democratic social studies teacher education would prepare teachers with the skills to map the assimilation and accommodation experiences of their students in relation to the cognitive and sociopolitical interactions that affect these experiences. Learning action research techniques discussed in previous chapters, such as semiotics, ethnography, phenomenology, and historiography, prospective teachers would be empowered to uncover the evidence to construct their sociocognitive maps.

This sociocognitive mapping of critical constructivist social studies teaching consistently involves the revelation of irony at one or more points in the accommodation process. Irony, Hayden White writes, alerts us to the inadequacy of the grand narrative in question to characterize, and to account for the elements that don't fit into the order of the narrative. Often in the context of critical accommodation, the grand narrative may be an individual's story about her or his self-production, the person's self-identity. Irony may be seen as a linguistic strategy that sanctions skepticism as an explanatory strategy, satire as a form of social critique, and agnosticism as an ethical approach (White, 1978). The critical epistemological perspective, infatuated with irony, is hard to separate from critical accommodation. Nothing is as closed, self-sufficient, autonomous, or consistent as it seems. All entities are riddled with contradictions. What we think of as real, profound, or stable is merely a reflection of conventions. Indeed, the world in general is an imagined series of places (Hutcheon, 1988; Shapiro, 1992). With this in mind, critical accommodation becomes a counter-Cartesian act because it draws upon such ironic recognitions to initiate the disruptive process. As Paulo Freire characterizes emancipation as risk, so, too, is critical accommodation. As social studies teachers and students ironically interrogate past sociopolitical understandings, they embark on an agnostic venture into the unknown. Exploring and rereading sedimented meanings, these "geologists" critically accommodate ironic perception into new, albeit tentative, perceptions of reality and self (Greene, 1988, 1995; Grimmett, Erickson, Mackinnon, & Riecken, 1990).

An important aspect of this accommodation of ironic perception into new understandings of reality and self involves the disembedding of personal knowledge from the specific experience in which it developed. Only after this disembedding takes place can accommodations be transferred into new contexts. This critical transference involves a form of anticipatory accommodation that moves beyond a traditional Piagetian notion of formal generalization. The formal thinker, according to Piaget, possesses the ability to construct pristine generalizations from systematic observations. Such a cognitive process accepts a one-dimensional, Cartesian-Newtonian, cause-effect universe. In the formalistic empirical context, for example, all that is needed to ensure transferability is to understand, with a high level of internal validity (the extent to which observations of a particular reality are true), something about a particular classroom and to know that the make-up of this classroom is representative of another classroom to which the generalization is being applied. Individuals operating in this tradition argue that the generalization derived from the first classroom is valid in all classrooms with the same population (external validity).

When we apply our understanding of critical constructivism and disembedding, we begin to see that in everyday situations people don't make generalizations in this formalistic, empirical manner. Our notion of critical accommodation tells us that we reshape cognitive structures to account for unique aspects of what is being perceived in new contexts. Through our knowledge of a variety of comparable contexts, we begin to understand similarities and differences; we learn from our comparisons of different contexts. The Cartesian-Newtonian concern with generalization and prediction is not the goal of our disembedding and critical transference, our critical accommodation. Instead, we begin to think in terms of anticipatory accommodation, that is, we anticipate what we might encounter in similar situations, what strategies might work in our attempt to bring about emancipatory outcomes (Barrett, 1985; Benson, 1989).

Thus, we end up at a political and cognitive place very different from the location of the depoliticized modernist cognition so typical of Cartesian colleges of education. We have begun to see the social construction of cognitive science and the ways it contributes to the construction of our consciousness, our definitions of intelligence, and our social studies teaching. Critical accommodation allows us to incorporate multiple definitions of cognitive sophistication, definitions that include feminist, Afrocentric, and subjugated reconceptualizations. In this way, critical constructivism reveals its democratic, inclusive, and, indeed, its critical epistemological impulse.

A social studies education grounded in a critical constructivism will contribute only marginally if it fails to penetrate the barriers erected by the various strands of teacher education. In addition to the confrontation with cognitive science, a critical constructivist social studies must engage the gatekeepers in special education (challenging the criteria by which assessments and placements are made), methodology/instruction (unveiling the rationalization of the teaching act and its effects on schools), educational research (revealing the decontextualized half-truths that often distort the literature of the field), and educational leadership (disclosing the embedded patriarchy and regulatory assumptions in the descriptions and definitions of "effective administration"). In these situations critical social studies educators bring much needed critical social analysis to educational institutions. We are at our best when we reveal the tacit structures that shape comfortable perceptions about the nature of teaching and learning. Ideally, we will produce even more of these forms of educational analyses in the future.

POSTFORMALISM AS A COGNITIVE GROUNDING FOR A CRITICAL SOCIAL STUDIES

Postformal thinking serves as an outline for the forms of critical, social, and educational analyses referenced here. Consider this basic outline of postformalism in a critical constructivist social studies context and the ways it can be applied to research and interpretation in the social, cultural, historical, political, and economic realm. Social studies teachers who are concerned with the social construction of knowledge, an epistemology of complexity, and knowledge work are always aware of how student experiences interact with the academic disciplines. If they are not concerned with these dynamics, if knowledge is viewed as simply an external body of information independent of human beings, then the role of the social studies teacher is simply to take this knowledge and insert it into the minds of students. Evaluation procedures that emphasize retention of isolated bits and pieces of data are intimately tied to this view of knowledge. Conceptual thinking is discouraged, since such a social studies trivializes complex learning. Students are evaluated on the lowest level of human thinking: the ability to memorize without contextualization. Thus, unless students are moved to incorporate social information into their own lives, social studies will remain merely an unengaging rite of passage into adulthood, an adjustment to the social status quo.

The point is clear. The way we define thinking exerts a profound impact on the nature of the social studies, the role that social studies teachers play in the world, and the shape that society will ultimately take. In the following characteristics of postformal thinking, each feature contains profound implications for the future of social studies. Indeed, postformal thinking can change both the tenor of schools and the future of teaching. Self-reflection would become a priority with teachers and students, as postformal social studies educators attend to the impact of school and society on the shaping of the self. In such a context, teaching and learning would be considered acts of meaning-making that subvert the technicist view of teaching as the mastering of a set of techniques.

Teacher education could no longer separate technique from purpose, reducing teaching to a deskilled act of rule following and concern with methodological format. A school guided by empowered postformal thinkers would no longer privilege White male experience as the standard by which all other experiences are measured. Such realizations would point out a guiding concern with social justice and the way unequal power relations in school and society destroy the promise of democratic life. Postformal social studies teachers would no longer passively accept the pronouncements of standardized test and curriculum makers without examining the social contexts in which their students live and the ways those contexts help shape student performance. Social studies lessons would be reconceptualized in light of a critical notion of student understanding. Postformal teachers would ask if their classroom experiences promote, as Howard Gardner (1991) puts it, the highest level of understanding that is possible.

Postformal thinking involves:

1. ETYMOLOGY (a study of origins, historicization)—the exploration of the forces that produce what the culture validates as knowledge. Individuals who think etymologically inquire into the sources of their intuitions and "gut feelings." Rarely do we come up with such feelings independently, for most thoughts and feelings are collective in origin (Bohm & Edwards, 1991; Senge, 1990). Consider, for example, language: It is entirely collective. We may think that our assumptions are self-generated, but, typically, we get them from the core of culturally approved assumptions. The concept of "thinking for oneself" must be reconsidered in light of these concerns. Indeed, without an awareness and understanding of etymology, women and men are incapable of understanding why they hold particular opinions or specific values. Without such appreciations, the ability for reflection and analysis is seriously undermined. It is not an exaggeration to maintain that the capacity for critical thought is grounded upon the postformal concern with etymology.

   a. *The origins of knowledge*—Postformalism induces us to ask what we know, how we come to know it, why we believe or reject it, and how we evaluate the credibility of the evidence. Where did the epistemological and cultural forms that undergird our knowledge originate and gain social certification?

   b. *Thinking about thinking*—the examination of the social construction of consciousness, of our own inner world of psychological experience.

   c. *Asking unique questions—Problem detection*—the transcendence of mere problem solving and the subsequent move to problem detection. Postformalists see problems where others see equilibrium and thus gain insight into aspects of the cosmos previously missed. With this understanding social studies educators can trace the etymology of what is, and is not, considered a problem in a cultural setting.

2. PATTERN—the understanding of the connecting patterns and relationships that shape the lived world. Having, in 1992, spent a harrowing night in a small bathroom with three of our children and three dogs seeking shelter from Hurricane Andrew, I am aware of the power of the cyclonic weather pattern that creates unfathomable power.

High- and low-pressure centers developing in differing locations, are part of the hurricane system and interact with prevailing wind patterns to direct the path of the storm. Each component of the pattern influences the others in a way that is typically hidden from view. One can only comprehend the system of a hurricane by thinking of it as a totality, not as independent, discrete parts. Knowledge of various types is also constructed by invisible patterns characterized by interlocking activities. From our vantage point in the middle of these patterns, they are extremely difficult to identify. Modernist science and education have typically focused on separate pieces of the patterns, many times missing the system itself. As a result, serious problems go unresolved while mainstream "experts" focus on specific events. No matter how educated individuals become, if they cannot escape the confinements of formal thinking, they will be held hostage by unseen patterns. A central dimension of a critical social studies involves learning to discern patterns in the information with which one is confronted. Postformalists must be able to develop this ability in their efforts to sophisticate their abilities as knowledge workers.

a. *Exploring deep patterns and structures*—uncovering the tacit forces, the hidden assumptions that shape perceptions of the world and the forms that the world takes. Postformalists recognize patterns of exclusion or identify social and/or historical structures that are erased from the curriculum of social studies. Without such recognitions, a teacher or student would see a very different, even a reductionistic and fragmented, view of social reality.

b. *Seeing relationships between ostensibly different things*—developing a metaphoric form of cognition that involves the fusion of previously disparate concepts in unanticipated ways. The concept of mind itself may be thought of as a relationship; in postformalism, the patterns of connection become more important than sets of fragmented parts.

c. *Uncovering various levels of interconnection between mind and ecosystem*—revealing the larger patterns of life forces. Indeed, life itself may have less to do with the parts of a living thing than with patterns of information, the relations between or among the parts, the interconnected dance of the living process. Such patterns of life make it virtually impossible to discern where living things end and nonliving things begin.

3. PROCESS—the cultivation of new ways of reading and researching the world that attempt to make sense of both ourselves and contemporary society. The way modernist civilization has developed, with its Cartesian-Newtonian logic and scientific reductionism, has taken its toll on human creativity. All human beings naturally hold the potential for creative thinking processes, but, through their acculturation and especially their education, many men and women have lost such a capacity. Many analysts argue that prehistoric peoples lived a more creative existence than we do now—a shock to our modernocentric systems. They devised not only tools and useful objects but creative ornamental and spiritual articles as well. Unlike many workers and students today, they did not follow a mechanical routine. For prehistoric humans, every day was different, new, and possibly, quite interesting and exciting. The postformal notion of process attempts to recapture that excitement and interest by devising new processes of perceiving the world, new methods of researching. The postformal process attempts to break the mold, to rethink thinking in a way that repositions men and women as active producers, not passive receivers of knowledge. Such a notion of process understands that processes of analysis need to be developed that understand that all information is "in process," a part of a larger process of development. The river that flows by an observer today is a different river than the one observed last year; it is at a different stage in its own process.

    a. *Deconstruction*—seeing the world as a text to be read. Deconstruction can be defined in many ways: a method of reading, an interpretive process, and a philosophical orientation. Postformalists use all three of these definitions since they view the world as full of texts to be deconstructed, to be explored, for unintended meanings. Scholars who understand this dynamic engage in an active process of discerning the multiple meanings embedded in the various aspects of the world and the impossibility of discerning a final understanding.

    b. *Connecting logic and emotion*—engaging in a creative process that stretches the boundaries of consciousness. Such a process sees the unity of logic and emotion and the synergistic possibilities such a connection implies. The process of postformal knowing, therefore, involves emotional as well as cognitive states of mind. As such, emotions are seen as powerful knowing processes that ground cognition.

c. *Non-linear holism*—transcending simplistic notions of the cause-effect process. Cartesian formalism accepts the notion of linear causality in the social world, while postformalism assumes a complex process of reciprocity and holism. Cause-effect rationality, in this view, may involve the modernist propensity for reductionism and its attendant decontextualization.

4. CONTEXTUALIZATION—the appreciation that knowledge can never stand alone or be complete in and of itself. When one abstracts, one takes something away from its context. Of course, this is necessary in everyday life because there is too much information out there to be understood in detail by the mind. If an object of thinking cannot be abstracted, it will be lost in a larger pattern. The postformal thinker is certainly capable of abstraction, but, at the same time, such a thinker refuses to lose sight of the conceptual field, the context that provides separate entities meaning (Raizen & Colvin, 1991). For example, modernist schooling typically has concentrated on teaching students the "what" of school subjects. Life and job experience has traditionally taught us "how" and "why." If deeper levels of understanding are desired, tasks must be learned in the context in which they fit. In light of such a pronouncement, we can begin to see that novice workers are people who possess no specific knowledge of a particular work setting, even though they may come to the situation with everyday knowledge and academic information. Such "greenhorns" become seasoned veterans only after they gain familiarity with specific social, symbolic, encoded, technical, and other types of workplace resources, i.e., the context of the workplace (Raizen, 1989). Thus, postformal researchers become researchers of contexts. As postformal researchers operate, their ability to focus their attention on the contexts in which a piece of data is found becomes second nature. Meaning making is possible only when information is contextualized.

a. *Attending to the setting*—developing a context in which an observation can assume its full meaning. Information derives meaning only in the context created by other information. Cartesian formalism often fails in its reductionism to analyze setting. Extraneous circumstances, so quickly dismissed by modernism, often prove to be the keys to new insights that change our view of education, society, or the cosmos itself. John Dewey (1916) maintained that an individual is a sophisticated thinker to the degree he or she sees an event not as something isolated but in its relation to the larger experience of human beings.

b. *Understanding the subtle interaction of particularity and generalization*—contextualizing generalization in particularity and particularity in generalization. When thinking is captured by the Cartesian obsession with generalization, the nature of the particular is missed when it is treated as a sample of a species or type, i.e., it is not itself, it is a representative. At the same time, the life force, the visceral dynamic that makes the general worth knowing, is supplied by its contextualization by the particular.

c. *The role of power in shaping the way the world is represented*—making sense of the world around us is not as much a product of our own ability to assimilate information as it is the result of the forces of power, discourse, ideology, and hegemony in the larger society. As dominant power insidiously blocks our ability to accommodate, and our ability to recognize exceptions, it undermines our attempt to modify our socially constructed understandings of ourselves and the world. Thus, postformalism develops a power literacy that contributes to our conceptualization of how "what is" came to be. It is a logical extension of critical constructivism.

Using these features of postformalism, social studies teachers can take critical education to its next frontier. A higher order of thinking that provides us new insights into the complex world that confronts us is a central goal of the democratic social studies education promoted in *Getting Beyond the Facts*. Postformalism allows us to escape the malformations of the surface appearances, to get beyond what are labeled "the facts," so we can act boldly and justly. Here rests the challenging and exciting future of critical education, a new mode of cognition that empowers democratic thinking and democratic action. We can start to imagine what we can become.

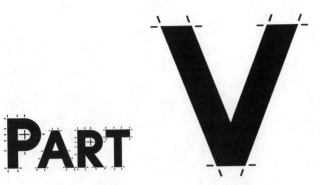

PART V

The Disciplines and the Social Studies

Chapter

The Ubiquitous Method: Inserting Historiography into the History Curriculum*

Every subject has a history, whether it be biology, physics, mathematics, literature, music, art, or education. Thus, history is not simply a body of information but a method, a ubiquitous method, for exploring any subject. Every teacher, therefore, should be a history teacher. Every subject should be approached historically because such an approach grants special insight that no other method provides. To understand one's family background, for example, does not mean that you can list the birthdates of long-deceased relatives and know where they were born. A deeper understanding of one's background involves insight into the origins of one's personal belief system and a comprehension of why these beliefs have been chosen over others. Looking at one's self historically helps locate the origins of moral, aesthetic, and political sensibilities. Moreover, it helps one come to understand the process of identity-formation and constructs a foundation for examining one's biases and prejudices.

Unfortunately, contemporary mainstream social studies does not typically view history as a method. Writing several decades ago, social studies theorist Edgar Wesley criticized the teaching of history in the public schools of his day. Wesley's concerns remain relevant to public school practice in our era:

---

* A version of this article appeared in *Curriculum Review*, XXIV (March/April, 1985) with George Staley, pp 80–83. Reprinted by permission of the publisher.

We see that history is not a simple, unadorned tale, no McGuffey formula for national greatness, no easy story on which psychologists, historians, parents, teachers, and pupils can agree. Being a mass of materials and documents that require infinite reworking it really is not very well adapted to children. Since popular demands, prevailing tradition, and extant laws require that a simple, condensed, abstract, and sketchy précis be prepared for the schools, the historians and educators have done their best to bridge the yawning gap between the complexities of history and the multiplicities of our moral and civic needs (Wronski, 1982, p. 64).

However we interpret Wesley's contention that history is not well adapted to children, his point is clear: History is more than a body of objective facts. It is a "mass of materials and documents," he argues, and the "reworking" or interpretation of this seemingly infinite mound of data cannot be separated from what we call "history." But today, as in Wesley's time, this larger view of history is too infrequently expressed in the social studies, and history is treated as catechism taught as the folk mythology. Even the field's "age of inquiry" failed to shake any sizeable number of social studies teachers from this outlook toward history. After the "fall" of inquiry in the field, the changes in historical outlook often necessitated by the adoption of inquiry methodology several decades ago no longer occur.

IRONCLAD HISTORY: A BODY OF ESSENTIAL FACTS

No subject within the social studies is taught so universally; no subject is so rigid. In the ironclad structure of contemporary technical standards-driven history as a body of essential facts, teachers simply hit one event here and three superficial causes of an event there. Using this approach, little insight into the way human affairs move and evolve is gained by students. The cultural and ideological blinders that restrict this view of history may actually do more harm than good in the long run. The restrictions on the imagination, the literal-mindedness, the oversimplified, reductionistic perspective on cause and effect, and the distortion of the historical process are only a few of the liabilities resulting from the fact-oriented teaching of history. Take, for example, the ethnocentrism so commonly promoted by public school history. Public school history has often refused to view other cultures on their own terms. The necessity of cooperative understandings uniting Americans, history, and the rest of the world has been frequently ignored. Instead of providing an interconnected global perspective for students, American history is presented as an ethnocentric morality tale.

One of the best ways to avoid this ethnocentrism and the simplemindedness that accompanies it is to incorporate historiography into all levels of history teaching. The term, "historiography," is used by historians to denote different concepts. One meaning involves methods of conducting historical research. Another meaning involves the synthesizing of historical information into a historical narrative through the process of interpretation. Such a method is used by professional historians and can be effectively used by social studies teachers and students. Such historiographic interpretation can also be used in teachers' and students' critical examination and comparison of history books and articles. Some historians have referred to this definition of historiography as the study of the study of history. The pursuit of historiography, defined in this manner, forces one to compare perspectives taken by different historians. In this way, the material being studied is reconceptualized since the teacher and student must view it as one of many interpretations, not merely as "the way things were." We will explore further this application of historiography to social studies history teaching later in this chapter.

Edgar Wesley had more to say about this intellectually stifling teaching of American history as unexamined facts. In line with this historiographical approach to teaching history, Wesley argued that history should be used, not taught. Who would think of teaching a course on the content of the dictionary or the encyclopedia? Yet, these are extremely valuable sources of information for the learner. We greatly reduce, Wesley concluded, the effectiveness of history, as well as violate almost all laws of learning when we try to force-feed this almost indigestible potpourri to reluctant eaters. This view of history as a relatively unquestioned set of facts that is force-fed to students seems to be almost an immutable characteristic of many American social studies classes.

Wesley was so discouraged by this seemingly intractable reality that he argued sarcastically that we should abolish history courses, or at least those history courses that look at the subject as a set of unexamined facts. Allen Griffin, another social studies theorist who was a contemporary of Wesley, argued that the only intelligent response to the bits and pieces of information from history is "So what?" Griffin was also discouraged by the prevalence of fact-oriented history teaching in the public schools and argued that history taught in this manner was virtually useless. Griffin went on to argue that, only after the student or teacher asked "So what?"

about historical data, could history actually accomplish anything of value. History's usefulness, he contended, comes from the diligent pursuit of the "so whats" and through reflection on them. Reflection is possible only if individuals identify, or are caused to identify, their beliefs about the matter. Reflection progresses, he continued, as students raise or have raised for them doubts about their beliefs (Engle, 1982).

Asking elementary and secondary students about their perspective on what constitutes history can be quite revealing. Far too often, history is seen as just a course with little relationship to anything outside the course. It consists of isolated facts that lend themselves nicely to an "objective" test. (Indeed, when confronted with an "essay" exam in history, many students bemoan their fate, not so much because they have trouble writing but because they are, all too often, required to put these dull facts into interesting writing—and are downgraded when they have little success.) Furthermore, history is viewed as a national phenomenon that usually consists of politics with an occasional financial panic tossed in. As a result, local history is generally not considered real history (though there are occasional courses in state histories) nor is information that would fall under the categories of intellectual or social history. The notion that history could possibly constitute more than just political and military facts is generally rejected by students with a few social studies courses in their pasts. This is not at all surprising when history, as viewed by the students, is a course that exists only to test one's ability to memorize facts for the test. The "good" history student is the one who memorizes minutiae, not the one who makes connections between the materials in the course and those encounters in the lived world. To say that the concepts of interpretation, historical continuity, and historiography are sometimes alien ideas in the teaching of history to elementary and secondary students is, at best, understatement.

HISTORICAL QUESTIONS IN THE HELL OF FRAGMENTED HISTORY TEACHING

Further discussions with social studies students reveal important insights into the process of historical questioning. Essentially, there are two aspects of the questioning: 1) the questions that teachers ask the students about history; and 2) the questions students themselves ask about history. The questions nonconceptual teachers usually ask concerning the field of history are convergent: Who did this? What year did it take place? and What are the reasons for this event? The questions the students ask about the field of history are, as could be expected, convergent too. This provides us with insights about the way we are taught and how we think. It also provides a good contrast between the way students think while in public school history courses and how they think once they are away from the mind-set perpetuated by these courses. Once students are out of that context, they often not only overcome the "one right answer" syndrome, but they also begin to change the nature of their questions. In addition to convergent questions, the students begin to ask how and why questions: Why did the Texans fight the Mexicans at the Alamo? How did people live before telephones? central heat? indoor plumbing? Why did people settle Mississippi? These types of questions are the ones which ultimately move historians to become historians, and they should be the types of questions around which elementary and secondary history programs are constructed.

It is unfortunate that many history teachers do not, intentionally or otherwise, encourage divergent questioning. As a result, students are not challenged to connect events, to examine the continuity between events, or even to make much sense out of the jumble of facts they receive. Far too many students come out of history courses so unfamiliar with divergent questioning in the field of history that they would deny such questioning is a part of history at all. When faced with divergent questions, students often seek refuge in the history they know, i.e., history of the convergent question and the right answer. Indeed, it bears repeating: When students are removed from the context of the modernist school, they begin to ask divergent questions. Students operating in the cognitive conventions of everyday life seem to think on a higher level than that of traditional schooling.

It is, therefore, difficult to understand how the use of convergent questioning, accompanied by the memorization of bits of historical data, helps students gain insight into the development of America, especially when the data is mythological and ungrounded. It is not surprising that such questioning and memorization do not engender a social and political consciousness. The expectation that students will emerge from the series of elementary and secondary history classes with civic understandings and democratic skills is naïve at best. Too often the purpose of much mainstream history teaching is to produce an unreflective, even fascist, loyalty to the nation state. When history is not taught in an epistemologically complex manner, "facts" are not subjected to critical analysis, and methods of historical knowledge production are not examined, social studies becomes a force for stupidification. When students learn that they have been mislead by history texts and text-bound teachers, they react with anger and cynicism. "Why did they feel the need to mislead me?" students ask as they explore professional historical depictions of previously studied eras or conduct primary research themselves.

The tendency for history to be taught as a series of unrelated facts is exacerbated by standardized tests and technical, top-down-imposed standards. Even teachers who encourage interpretation, reflection, and exploration of the historical process are pressured into teaching history as isolated facts by the tyranny of the tests and standards. Because the tests and standards require a certain body of information to be learned, they exclude the most valuable historical experiences from the social studies curriculum. Fragmented, content-driven history programs often run students through a series of memorizations, barring them from a deeper exploration into an event or a period of history. Excluded from such experiences on the basis that they take too much time, students fail to learn how to understand the flow of a stream of events, construct a compelling picture of life in a specific historical era, or conceptualize the complex and subtle nature of social, cultural, political, and economic change. These are the very reasons we study history in the first place.

When teachers propose to examine a historical figure or an event or theme in detail, administrators and supervisors often hold the specter of the standards test above teachers' heads, asking them if they want to be responsible for students' poor performance on it. Under political pressure to produce good test scores, administrators and supervisors sometimes have little time to concern themselves with the issues of meaningful historical scholarship. They have little time to promote reflection, for they must move on to the next fact covered by the test. They must insist that teachers deliver a precise set of facts and request a precise set of responses from students. The behavioral belief that students learn only what the teacher intends for them to learn is a distortion of learning theory. In the eyes of the social studies teachers and supervisors who accept this belief, there is a one-to-one correspondence between teachers' stimulus and student response. It seems apparent that student study of history often produces totally unintended results. The unintended messages that students pick up from the teaching of fact-oriented, top-down, standards-based history is an example of this process. As important as the bogus historical data or civic attitudes that programs sometimes try to inculcate are the unintended patterns of thinking and the perspective toward learning with which many students leave the history classroom.

THE ESCAPE FROM HISTORY HELL: DEVELOPING CRITICAL ALTERNATIVES

How, then, do we provide workable alternative strategies for the teaching of history to critical democratic social studies teachers? And once presented, how do we keep them from falling back on familiar patterns of fact memorization that are often rewarded by standards driven social studies? The first step is that teachers of history must unite in their opposition to the tyranny of the positivist perspective that dictates that history, like all content areas, must be taught as a series of measurable facts and as information that falls into neat and narrow boundaries. For our counter-Cartesian resistance to succeed, it must have public support. Therefore, teachers of history must develop better public relations and explain to and show the public the problems of fragmented, positivist methods of "teaching" history. Obviously, the "You were taught history all wrong" approach courts disaster. However, the public is generally unaware of the value of history as a process, and so, democratic teachers of history must educate the public. If people are to understand that history is a method and should be taught as such, they must accept that it is a method of gathering insight into whatever topic is being studied. As Cicero put it: "To remain ignorant of things that happened before you were born is to remain a child." History, then, is the broadest intellectual means of becoming educated, of developing a critical consciousness.

Again, history can be taught as a method of inquiry into any subject, be it America, nuclear physics, or music. It is a method of organizing information, attitudes, and opinions in ways that transcend chronology and afford us the opportunity to go beyond history as a discrete body of information. Teaching history as a method is one of the most important goals of a history class, for the method can be applied to other content areas as well as outside of school. Indeed, visiting history as a method makes history a means of making meaning, of interpreting the world and one's relation to it. Further, can we really have a sophisticated understanding of a subject unless we have a grasp of its historical development? For example, can we teach grammar as anything more than a set of rules to be memorized unless we understand its evolution? Wouldn't it be more meaningful, if not more interesting, to begin secondary school chemistry historically rather than with memorization of the periodic table? For many people in the U.S., American Indians existed only at the time of the Pilgrims and later as a barrier to the development of the West in the late 1800s. The neglect Native Americans now suffer is, no doubt, a result of a lack of historical understanding on the part of most U.S. citizens. Grammar, chemistry, American Indian history, and all school subjects did not just appear; they have a context, and understanding this context is the key to understanding the subject and its expression in everyday life. Such a history is the basis of the postformal notion of etymology and thus holds profound cognitive consequences.

Critical social studies teachers need to become historical scholars-in-residence in the schools. Much like the artist-in-the-schools programs that have helped expose teachers and students alike to the value and benefits of art, so, too, could a historian-in-the-schools program help establish the teaching of history as a ubiquitous method. The historian would be a scholar, steeped in historical methodology and other knowledge production strategies in the bricolage, who possessed the research skills needed by teachers to explore the history of their disciplines. The historian-in-residence could help teachers develop historical programs in biology, math, or computer science. With ever increasing technological concerns in the schools, such a person would provide an unusual and interesting role, as well as a much needed academic one.

In addition to viewing history as a method and a part of every discipline, the development of historical interpretation should be one of the most important benefits to be derived from critical complex elementary and secondary history programs. Teachers of history can profit from the application of historiography in their classes. Historiography examines how different historians in different eras have viewed the same historical events. This outlook is certainly valuable to the professional education of historians. It teaches them about the different schools of historical thought and provides them a better understanding of the problems which confront all historians. It grants professional historians a perspective on the conflicts that have traditionally divided the discipline and the ideologies that shape the way historians view the past. Knowing these biases and ideological predispositions, historians are better prepared to see the past in greater epistemological complexity.

But this historiographical perspective is important not only to professional historians. It can provide many benefits for history students at all levels—even those who have no intention of becoming professional historians. First, historiography grants insight into the fact that history is a point of view. What we study is not static but is determined by the concerns of the present and the ideological frames of the observer. The value of this insight is that it evokes critical thought and skepticism about what we read and hear concerning historical issues. It allows students and teachers to rise above official information and explore a topic within a larger hermeneutical horizon. Such a critical historiographical perspective precludes an unthinking acceptance of the "facts" that social studies teachers are provided by standards and the tests that measure them. In other words, it grants a more sophisticated ability to evaluate sources.

Secondly, it provides a critical perspective on how to study history. The historical writings of a period take on far more complexity when we understand that how the historian views the past tells us as much about him or her and his or her era as it tells us about the historical event in question.

Thirdly, it requires a higher level of cognition from the student since he or she is forced to examine and distinguish different schools of thought. This can become a compelling introspective experience as students must determine why certain schools of thought are more appealing to them than others.

Fourthly, it brings history to life. Examining the past historiographically removes the distinction between past and present. No longer is the past a remote, unapproachable realm of isolated events. Because historians of the past and present continue a dialogue with one another about the meaning of events, the voices of the past are still alive. The arguments of interpretation are not relegated only to past events but apply to the interpretation of present events, to everyday life. Contemporary occurrences are seen as outgrowths of past events and are viewed in the context of past interpretations. Students who become involved in this timeless dialogue will catch on to the excitement of thinking, interpreting, and exploring various intellectual terrains.

This historiographical view of elementary, secondary, and even university history will certainly stimulate some interesting classroom approaches. A teacher operating from this perspective might collect copies of history textbooks used in a school district over the past several decades. Students could compare interpretations and analyze what concerns of the authors motivated changes in the coverage of events. Students could examine the difference in the books used by themselves and their parents. Examining the changes in history textbooks over the past decades could yield important insights into the changing role of minorities and women in American social and political life. It could grant insight into the impact of certain events, such as Vietnam, Watergate, the Iran hostage crisis, the Gulf War, and the conflict in Kosovo. The historiographical perspective is not applicable only in the first two weeks of a history course: It is an omnipresent outlook that it can (and should) be used in every lesson a history teacher prepares.

One of the consistent desires of far too many public school history programs is that for order, so much so that order often takes precedence over thinking. Clearly, there is a need for a form of conceptual order because ordering helps individuals find patterns in the chaos that surrounds them. In this sense, order is the freedom from chaos and the go-ahead for constructing increasingly complex conceptual relationships. But the order created by the way many history courses are organized is a pseudo-order, a regulatory regimentation, that falls into the trap of assuming that a history lesson is ordered if it is arranged chronologically. Historical data arranged chronologically presents an inert story. There is nothing else to be done, for it is already arranged, it is already ordered, and only needs to be learned (i.e., memorized for the fragmented standards test). We know that events that occur concurrently and/or in progression may not seem to have anything to do with each other. The key to historical interpretation—making sense out of history—is to find connections between events. What was the relationship between the Falklands War between Argentina and Great Britain in 1982 and Israel's subsequent invasion of Lebanon? What connections can be made among the defeat of Germany in World War I, U.S. economic policies of the late 1930s, and the attack on Pearl Harbor in 1941? The NAFTA agreements of the 1990s and the protests against the World Trade Organization in 2000?

Instead of challenging students to analyze history as exemplified by the above questions, we all too often settle for the inculcation of a superficially examined set of facts governed by a false sense of order. We want the students to know that some brave men died fighting at the Alamo for Texas independence in 1836. Why these men did so (other than the general notion that good Americans fight for freedom) and the connections between the events surrounding the Alamo and the Mexican War a decade later remain essentially unexamined. Instead of teaching and encouraging a historiographic view, we settle for the safe teaching of a textbook that is passed off as "truth." A historiographical perspective would allow for the rejection of the false sense of order and for the opening of history to critical interpretive analysis.

Given the reality of how much mainstream history is taught, the real excitement and adventure of history and historical investigation is lost. The opportunity to play historical detective is rarely provided to students. And why should it be, when students are rewarded, not for exploring history, but for absorbing information? Furthermore, not only are the professional possibilities of being a historian denigrated because of "grim" job prospects, but most of the elements that move individuals to be professional (or amateur) historians are usually excluded from the contemporary history curriculum. Generally speaking, the motivation for those students who do become historians comes from outside the school or from an individual teacher, rather than from a history course. While this is unfortunate, the real tragedy is that most students never experience the critical consciousness that comes from historically based thinking and the civic insight that accompanies it.

Chapter 21

Social Psychoanalysis in the Social Studies: Critical Theory and Historiography

Because of the fact that, for most of its existence, the Institute for Social Research in Frankfurt had no historian closely associated with its activities, analysts of the Frankfurt School have often ignored the historiographical concerns of critical theory. This is unfortunate because, in the writings of Horkheimer, Adorno, Marcuse, and Habermas (not to mention the scores of scholars who view themselves within the critical tradition), there exist numerous historiographical references. This chapter attempts to explore a few dimensions of the relationship between critical theory and historiography, especially the connection between historical research and psychoanalysis.

GROUNDING A POSTSTRUCTURALIST PSYCHOANALYSIS

Within the critical theoretical tradition, this connection between social research and Freudian psychoanalysis is quite explicit. The traditional critical theorist's appropriation of Freud's concerns with the unconscious, irrationality, repression, feeling, and sexuality and their important relation to everyday social life is central to understanding the purposes of the Frankfurt School. The Frankfurt School critical theorists understood the complex ways that the unconscious and the irrational shape human consciousness and social behavior. If we are serious about developing a critical complex social studies, then an awareness of the psychoanalytical and its relation to consciousness construction, politics, and social behavior is essential.

Any force that shapes agency (our ability to act in the world) in a manner that is contradictory to the ways in which we ourselves think of an experience is important, even if the notion of self is not as stable and knowable as early psychoanalysts assumed. Indeed, it is psychoanalysis that allows us to view the formation of identity from unique vantage points not attainable via other methodologies. In such a procedure, analysts often discern the unconscious processes that create resistance to progressive change and induce self-destructive behavior. Psychoanalysis offers hope to democratic social studies educators concerned with social justice and the related attempt to democratize intelligence as it explores the possibilities of human potential. When psychoanalysis takes into account the Deweyan, the Vygotskian (the work of Russian psychologist Lev Vygotsky and his cognitive theories) and, more recently, the postmodernist rejection of Freud's separation of the psychic from the social realm, it becomes a powerful tool in cognitive and educational psychology and, thus, in social studies education (Alford, 1993; Henriques et al., 1984; Russell, 1993).

In connection with psychoanalysis, I use the term, "depth psychology," an admittedly old-fashioned term, to emphasize the political aspect of historiography and a critical social studies. Depth psychology, with its implication of getting beneath the illusion of surface appearances, focuses directly on the nature of personality development and its relation to creativity, artistic endeavor, and morality. No cognitive/psychological theory worthy of inclusion in a critical democratic social studies can ignore these issues and their relationship to learning, motivation, school performance, and the nature of the teaching process. In addition, a depth psychology, aware of the insights gleaned from an epistemology of complexity, can motivate interest in the way an individual subjectively experiences social, cultural, political, and educational structures. In this context, public issues can be viewed at the private level, and modernist boundaries between the political (external) and personal (internal) can be erased. Post-Cartesian social theory's concerns with identity, difference, and power can be directed to the broad notion of psychological studies by way of the interests of depth psychology (Samuels, 1993). In this reconceptualized context, the democratic work of a critical social studies can never be the same.

Thus, in the name of emancipation and a critical democracy, critical social studies educators and critical psychologists call for an analysis of such issues in relation to educational practice. As we begin to grasp the importance of a socially situated unconsciousness in the production of identity and in the learning process connected to it, practitioners gain vital insight into the ways education might be reconfigured. In this context critical democratic social studies educators are quick to note that their appreciations of psychoanalysis and depth psychology are cautious and very selective. Following the lead of many feminist psychoanalysts, they employ only those aspects of the tradition that are conscious of the problematic nature of defining psychic health as conformity to dominant cultural norms. Taking their cue from feminist theory, such social studies educators understand the patriarchal inscriptions of traditional psychoanalysis and struggle to avoid the hegemonic landmines hidden in the field. To the post-Cartesian social studies educator, psychoanalysis and depth psychology possess progressive features that, in conjunction with a complex epistemological awareness, can be used to create a more just and better-educated world, a resacralized society where human beings are studied and appreciated in terms of their unique individual and social abilities and hard-to-quantify talents (Ventura, 1994; Elliot, 1994; Henriques et al., 1984).

Thus, the epistemologically complex vision of psychoanalysis is a poststructuralist psychoanalysis—poststructuralist in the sense that it reveals the problems embedded in the sciences emerging from modernity and the "universal structures" it constructs (Block, 1995). As poststructuralist psychoanalysis makes use of the subversive aspects of the psychoanalytical tradition, it presents a view of humans quite different than the modernist psychological portrait. In the process it challenges the modernist erasure of feeling, valuing, and caring in contemporary Western societies and attempts to rethink such features in light of power and its construction of consciousness. In this context, the poststructuralist impulse challenges Freud's positioning of the pleasure principle in opposition to the reality principle. In many ways, poststructuralist psychoanalysts argue, such an oppositional construction places Freudianism squarely within the boundaries of Western logocentrism, with its structures of rationality over irrationality, masculinity over femininity, civilization over primitivism, logic over emotion, and play as separate from work.

From the poststructuralist perspective, therefore, the psychoanalytic tradition is complicit in the regulatory objectives of modernist science. In its effort to produce a healthy (read conformist) population, traditional psychoanalysis has, in the same manner as its modernist brother, educational psychology, set out to repress desire. Poststructuralist psychoanalysis has often embraced unconscious desire as a positive feature with the social revolutionary potential to unfasten the hegemonic straitjacket of modernist psychology. For example, in this configuration, play and work are not incompatible activities. Poststructuralism admonishes the discipline of psychology to accept the undesirability of what it is trying to accomplish (Henriques et al., 1984; Elliot, 1994). Psychology must also understand that its rationalistic views of being and its faith in an unexamined rationality are ill-suited for an everyday life in hyperreality, riddled and destabilized by affective intensities and powerful forces of libidinal desire. Humbled by the poststructuralist critique, traditional psychoanalysis timidly looks into the mirror of self-reflection and begins to discern the relationship between suppressed desire and political power, the affiliation between the fear of passion and cultural reproduction. These understandings hold profound consequences for students of social studies.

Obviously, in this context, any use of the psychoanalytical tradition in historical research and a critical social studies must be highly selective. I am highly sensitive to traditional Freudianism's privileging of the familial positioning of the father and the notion of penis envy. I reject traditional psychoanalysis's attribution of psychological differences between men and women to biological causation, with such a position's accompanying assumption that women's subordination is inevitable. This so-called Anglo-Saxon interpretation of Freudian psychoanalysis has long connected the unconscious to the biological needs of men and women. Such interpreters employed behavioristic and positivistic science to prove their deterministic assertions (Henriques et al., 1984). In addition, the postructuralist psychoanalysis used here also understands and refuses to participate in the hierarchical power relations that characterize the relationship between analyst and analysand (the individual being analyzed). The material produced by psychoanalysis is not the property of analysts but is accessible to all parties (Young, 1990).

Too rapid a dismissal of psychoanalysis for the reasons delineated here will miss the democratic and emancipatory possibilities still offered by a reconceptualized psychoanalysis. Poststructuralist psychoanalysis provides social studies educators and historians an unparalleled insight into the hidden content of symbolic expression: repressed life history. The meaning or significance of a patient's actions can be better understood in terms of the latent and unconscious content that moves him or her. Successful interpretations that lead to therapy can be formulated only by uncovering the salient unconscious factors. Therapy proceeds by making these unconscious factors known to the patient and understood by the patient. These understandings inform both a critical democratic social studies pedagogy and a critical historiography. Such post-Cartesian insights help move social studies education, historical research, and psychoanalysis itself beyond their modernist tendencies to be used as methods of adjusting individuals to existing power structures.

Poststructuralist psychoanalysis, with its concern with semiotics, signification, and the construction of interpretation, lays a grounding for a critical form of social research and pedagogical practice. Thus, psychoanalysis has traveled from the individual analysand to a social psychoanalysis concerned with the analysis of both the individual and the society at large. Interpretations in the psychoanalysis of individuals can be developed only within the framework provided by a general theory of neurosis. Similarly, the social researcher/cultural worker, employing a psychoanalytic theoretical structure, generates interpretations in the context of a general theory of social pathology, e.g., a hegemonic patriarchy, an unregulated free market, White supremacy. When the psychoanalytic theoretical structure is injected with a dose of this poststructuralist solution, our work collides with the project of traditional psychology. Instead of the rational subject of modernist psychology, poststructuralist psychoanalysis pays homage to human irrationality: the subversion of will by desire, the multiple and contradictory ways we experience and understand ourselves, the death of a unitary subject in light of our newfound awareness of unconscious processes, and the ambiguous reconnection of affect and cognition.

As social psychoanalysts take their cue from a poststructuralist model of psychoanalysis that adamantly refuses to isolate the individual from the social domain, they no longer fear the emergence of a fragmented self stalking the postmodern hyperreality. The bridge that connects the individual psyche to the social is found in Freud's emphasis of signification. Jacques Lacan, for example, recognized this relationship and based much of his interpretive work upon it (Henriques et al., 1984; Dews, 1987). As individual psyche and the social domain are considered in terms of one another, social psychoanalysts seek to unravel psychic and social constructions within a political context that supports the struggle for critical democracy, social justice, antiracism, and antisexism (Mouffe, 1988). Such a struggle dictates that power blocs and their role in the establishment of hegemonic relations be exposed. Such exposé constitutes a central feature of social psychoanalysis

CONNECTING CRITICAL THEORY AND PSYCHOANALYSIS

This concern with hegemony and power turns the social psychoanalyst's attention to the discourse of critical theory. Like critical theory, social psychoanalysis assumes that the surface appearances of society hide dynamic structures that produce malformations—individual psychoses for the psychoanalysts, social distortions for the critical theorists. Both psychoanalysts and critical theorists seek to address these malformations. Both psychoanalysts and critical theorists emphasize the role of reflexivity and self-awareness—childhood memory and etymological understanding of pathology for the analysand and historical interrogation, subversion of "the given," and the production of countermemory for the social psychoanalyst. In light of the post-Cartesian challenge to any ahistorical, transcendental, or self-authenticating version of truth, social psychoanalysts do not expect their labor to produce a final unilinear historical explanation or the end of history. Emerging from this postmodern rendezvous with critical theory is a critical or resistance form of postmodernism that serves to ground social theory as a transformative and interventionist strategy. Thus, social psychoanalysis is shaped by a poststructuralist model of psychoanalysis, informed by this post-Cartesian contingency and catalyzed by the passion of critical theory (Gibson, 1986; Kincheloe & McLaren, 2000; Zavarzadeh & Morton, 1991).

Given these theoretical dynamics, social psychoanalysts begin to analyze the sociopolitical and epistemological implications of poststructuralist psychoanalytical views of the psychological process that induce individuals to resist change, to reproduce patterns of action that undermine their well-being, and to link the unconscious to the formulation of changes in one's personal situation. Each one of these individual psychological processes conjures an analogue on a larger social terrain. For example, a pedagogy that operates as a form of social psychoanalysis endeavors to recover memory and history in a manner that psychologically permits men and women to reenter the public sphere in personally meaningful and socially committed ways. Social pathologies that have been internalized can be understood by the social actors themselves, thus setting the stage for human agency in not only the rewriting but the remaking of history (Kincheloe & Pinar, 1991). As Paulo Freire (1985) puts it: We must see ourselves as the subjects of history even if we cannot totally escape being its objects.

THE CRITICAL, THE PSYCHOANALYTICAL, AND THE HISTORICAL

The sense that is described as critical is rooted in the historical sense. Our attention to history makes critical consciousness possible (Giroux, 1997). Marcuse (1964) explained this idea in his delineation of two-dimensional thought: as the appearance and essence of "what is" and "what ought to be." We interrogate the dialectic between "is" and "ought," Marcuse argued, through the medium of history. The critical analyst refuses to surrender to immediate facts, fixed images, or the tendency to identify an entity with its function. Instead, he or she begins with the thoroughly historical task of examining the factors that separate the 'is" from the "ought."

Thus, critical theory views history as a force for demystification, i.e., a force that sheds light on the hidden contradictions of societies. In concert with its demystifying function, critical analysts believe that history can illustrate that something else is possible, that rational change is conceivable (Zinn, 1984). Paulo Freire (1985) creatively clarifies this point by observing the differences between the animals and humans. Unlike humans, animals are simply in the universe, unable to objectify either themselves or nature. Thus, animals live a life outside of time; they have no chance of confronting reality or stepping outside of it. Humans, on the other hand, possess the capacity for a historical sense. They can go beyond reality and transcend mere being in the world. They can, Freire argues, "add to the life they have the existence which they make" (p. 68). Because of their temporal understanding and the transcendence it allows, men and women can transform, decide, and create. They can reflect on the domains of their existence and question their relationship to the world; they can experience the dialectic between determinism and freedom. Only creatures who can ponder the fact that they are socially determined are empowered to free themselves. Historical consciousness extends this type of reflection and thus serves as human beings' most accessible force of emancipation.

Critical analysis, therefore, desires a deeper reading of the word and, for that matter, the world. Historical consciousness serves as a force that allows for this deeper reading, for this ability to distinguish essence from appearance. As Freire (1985) advises us, "there is no 'here' relative to a 'there' that is not connected to a 'now,' a 'before,' and an 'after'" (pp. 70–71). Thus, humans must understand what came before in order to comprehend the here and now. To understand themselves, men and women must grasp their own biographies. To change (or emancipate) themselves and/or the world, humans must connect past injustice to present suffering; they must fathom the mind-set of their ancestors in order to expose the forces that have created present absurdities.

Henry Giroux (1988) writes of historical inquiry as a model for constituting the radical potential of memory. Maxine Greene (1984) argues that educational history addresses the sometimes desperate efforts of humans to select and maintain that which they deem a proper human way of life. Educational history considers that which is worthy of conservation in a sea of change, where it determines what is worthy of note in ages past. The historian may find that what he or she considers worthy of note in the past is precisely the opposite of that which educators of the past found worthy of conservation. Indeed, Greene concludes, that which educational historians find to be inappropriate may be the very values and attitudes that have been frozen into our heritage. The historian is unavoidably rendered an interpreter, with all the value choices that accompany the role. Care must be taken to seek those epistemological organizing principles, social values, and ideas that form the framework of our historical interpretations. As we seek a critical democratic way of life through our historical investigations, the radical potential of memory moves toward fulfillment.

Reiterating the theme of this chapter, critical historiography can be viewed as a form of social psychoanalysis. Critical theorist Jurgen Habermas (1970) considers Freudian psychoanalysis a model for a critical science, for it is only psychoanalysis, he argues, that serves as an example of a science incorporating a methodical process of self-reflection. When psychoanalysis recognizes the presence of neurotic symptoms disruptive of a subject's speech, actions, and nonverbal behavior, it transcends the procedures of traditional hermeneutics. The world of surface meanings and appearances has been penetrated by the psychoanalyst, as he or she attempts to bring to the patient's consciousness that which had been previously repressed.

Habermas (1973) sees Freudian psychoanalysis, with its concern with the construction of interpretations, as an important basis for historical research and as an important element in the construction of a philosophy of history. Interpretations in psychoanalysis can only be developed within the context provided by a general theory of neurosis. In a similar vein, the historian, employing a psychoanalytic theoretical structure, develops his or her interpretation in the context of a general theory of society. Indeed, critical theorists argue, this is the case with all historians, whether they are conscious of their theoretical assumptions or not. Without such consciousness, the historian is unaware of the unexamined assumptions, values, and forces that guide his or her historical interpretations. Using the general theory of neurosis not as an authoritative guide but as a reference point, the psychoanalyst begins to understand neurosis as the consequence of a series of developments that result in what is called second nature. Second nature, as described by Freud, refers to that part of the psyche constructed by long-unexamined historical forces. To the individual it appears both rational and natural. The psychoanalyst reconstructs the life history of the patient and the understanding that emerges serves to deconstruct the once impenetrable second nature. Obviously, gaining an understanding of this second nature is a central goal of a democratic social studies.

Thus, critical theory seeks to unravel history in order to achieve the goal of emancipation. Using psychoanalysis, critical theoretical interrogations move beyond traditional history's attempt to interpret historical actors' accounts of their perceptions of themselves and their realities. The actor accounts must be subjected to critical analysis, for they contain formulations that are deemed to be misunderstood by the actors themselves because of social distortion and repression. Thus, using the benchmark of its general social theory, critical historiography seeks to trace the causal connections between ideology and the development of specific societies (Held, 1980).

Once such connections are established, the distortions internalized by individuals can be understood by social actors themselves, and human agency in the making of history can be enhanced. According to Habermas, historical determinism is transcended as individuals come to be more than mere objects who passively observe the inevitable execution of historical laws. Human beings emerge as active agents who, because of their awareness of historical forces and the effects of such forces on individuals, help shape the future expression of these historical forces. In this emancipatory context, critical theory refuses to deemphasize the importance of human intentions and the power of humans as creative, meaning-seeking actors. Freire (1985) is keenly concerned with the possibility of human agency, arguing that history is not a mythical entity outside of, and superior to, human beings; it does not capriciously command them from above. Such a fatalistic outlook suffocates and ultimately kills us. We must, he concludes, see ourselves as the subjects of history, even if we cannot totally escape being its objects.

GETTING BEHIND THE CURTAIN OF IDEOLOGY

Critical historiography as social psychoanalysis thus attempts to subvert the given facts by interrogating them historically. Marcuse (1964) argued that the tendency to make the existing activities and social relationships appear rational and natural (the process of reification) is the product of forgetting. Remembrance moves us toward emancipation by defeating suffering and pursuing joy. Indeed, he concluded, it changes the world, moving us toward a new form of revolution that celebrates the aesthetic and the psychic health of the free individual. As the psychoanalyst attempts to remedy the mystified self-understandings of the analysand, the critical historiographer sees myth deconstruction as an important step toward social progress. Such an attempt, just like the effort of the psychoanalyst to confront patients with the complex forces that helped shape their psyches, is often thwarted by the success of reification in postmodern societies. The power of second nature on the social level is undeniable: History is frozen and seen as undoubtedly rational (Marcuse, 1964; Jacoby, 1975). Until free people invalidate the myths and conceive of the possibilities offered by emancipation, slim is the possibility of critical self-direction on the individual and social levels. The less historically and socially contextualized our understanding of self-production, the more it seems that individuals and society are governed by rational and intractable natural laws (Marcuse, 1955, 1960).

In the same manner that the psychoanalyst uncovers clues in the everyday language of the analysand that will lead to an understanding of the origins of a patient's pathology, the critical historian uncovers the historical antecedents in the communication of social actors, both past and present. This hidden dimension of meaning opens new windows on the process of historical change, since it uncovers the rule of society over its language. Language analysis thus becomes a primary source for historical research. Marcuse (1964) argued that we must "go beyond" the facts and acquire some critical distance from the language that is commonly used and, on the surface, appears too innocuous. This idea is central to the raison d'etre of *Getting Beyond the Facts*.

Everyday experience, Marcuse wrote, takes place before a curtain which conceals the events that often help direct phenomena. Behind the curtain rest the forces of our sociopsychological production. The charge of the critical democratic historian is to get behind the curtain so that he or she is not misled by the deceit of appearance. Once acquainted with the world behind Marcuse's curtain, we travel beyond our one-dimensional assumptions about humans as entities who are moved merely by the dictates of reason and common sense. The critical historian begins to view historical actors as subjects and objects in the complex historical struggle of individuals with nature and society. The focus of historical analysis is directed not only at the strata of societal development but also to the levels of metatheory, individual action, and, importantly, the *Lebenswelt* (life-world). In educational history, which is especially focused on the life of the mind, on ideas, and on the evaluation of thinking, this historical concern with the Lebenswelt takes on additional relevance.

Cartesian scientifically rational knowledge production and modes of social education have not served to nurture the development of a critical historical consciousness. Critical theory has traditionally pointed the finger of blame for this ahistorical, reifying celebration of "what is" at positivism. Never neat and easily characterized, positivism, as defined by critical theory, transcends its categorization as merely an epistemological position. As it moves into the political and psychological realms, positivism exerts a powerful influence on social and educational reality. Such a positivist rationality, critical theorists argue, ultimately quashes humane concerns, and, based on the assumption that it has access to scientifically produced truth, justifies a mind-set that promotes the domination of experts over individuals (Keat, 1981; Kincheloe, 1993, 1995).

When critical theorists address the distortions that produce social and individual pathologies, they point to positivism's instrumental/technical rationality as one of the prime agents of deformity. Positivism congratulates itself as a transhistorical position. It doesn't matter when or where scientific knowledge is produced; if the rules are followed, it is "true." The domain of theory and the realm of practice are deemed to be historically neutral, since positivists proclaim a value neutrality. Such a stance elicits the charge from critical theory that positivists have fallen prey to the fallacy of objectivism. Possessing no mechanism for reflecting on its own presuppositions, positivism, out of necessity, falls into an uncritical support of the status quo. History is irrelevant as a tool for critical analysis when "fact" is separated from its historical context. The physical scientific method is celebrated, while a more rational and historically based mode of thinking is neglected (Giroux, 1997). The positivistic code of the empirical a priori is inviolable: The individual is given the facts and not the factors behind them. Thus, he or she is forced to comfort himself or herself with a mere understanding of the surface, the appearance (Marcuse, 1964).

BACK TO COMPLEXITY: CRITICAL PSYCHOANALYTIC HISTORY REJECTS REDUCTIONISM

All social science attempts to discern how a specific institution or social order achieved its present form. The task of a critical historical analysis, critical theorists argue, cannot be accomplished without the utilization of a social psychoanalytical perspective. Devoid of this perspective, traditional interpretive models possess no mechanism for explaining the complex dynamics of historical change. Often ignoring structural conflict, the traditional interpretive model seeks to explain away endemic contradictions within a society. From such a perspective, therefore, historical change is only possible when forces outside the society exert serious pressure (e.g., war, worldwide economic collapse, natural disaster, etc.) (Fay, 1975).

The social contradictions of complex postmodern societies, so important to critical historiography, are overlooked by noncritical approaches. The repression of human instincts is connected to factors external to the individual—social factors that have been shaped by specific historical conditions (second nature, petrified history). Therefore, critical historiography as social psychoanalysis avoids reductionism by studying the sufferings and needs of historical actors within the framework of specific structural conflicts in the past and present social order (Jacoby, 1975). It offers "quasi-causal" explanations of the contradictions and complexities—quasi-causal in the sense that human consciousness serves as an intermediary between the determining antecedent force and the subsequent action (Fay, 1975). Studying the process of dehumanization in modern industrial societies, Marcuse (1964) focused on instrumental/technical rationality as an example of structural conflict. While individuals relished the material benefits of technical enterprise, they were "mutilated" spiritually by the rationality it produced. The critical historian is ordained to interrogate the roots of instrumental/technical rationality. The exposure of the genesis and influence of such a basic structural conflict within Marcuse's industrialized society and our hyper-real society is emancipatory because it unfreezes the status quo, recontextualizes the particular, and restores human possibility (Adorno & Horkheimer, 1972).

Reflecting Marcuse's appropriation of Freud's historical concern, critical theorists have consistently attended to the dialectic of the particular and the universal. The particular (the individual) is profoundly influenced by the universal (the society). This realization is revolutionary in that it strips away the illusion of the purely autonomous individual. Indeed, this was the threat that psychoanalysis posed to conventional thought when it revealed the often hidden power of society over the individual. As Max Horkheimer wrote, "Psychoanalysis discovers the historical dynamics of society in the microcosm of the monad, as it were, in the mental conflicts of the individual" (Jacoby, 1975, p. 34). Because of this, Marcuse (1964) concluded that psychoanalysis can "break the reification in which human relations are petrified" (p. 181).

When social analysts fail to examine the historical dimensions of ordinary language, Marcuse argued, we leave unexposed the way the universal affects the particular. The mind, he continued, atrophies, the contradictions of the larger society are forgotten, and the individual is viewed in isolation from the universal. Indeed, Marcuse maintained, without an understanding of historical context, the "Happy Consciousness" reigns unchallenged. This Happy Consciousness fails to question the belief that the real is rational, for no conception of its genesis is sought. The productive apparatus of society holds the master key to the safe that stores appropriate thought and action. Thought and action are appropriate in the sense that they support the productive apparatus. Individual autonomy is surrendered to the authority of the logic of the industrial machine (or, in our case, the representations of the hyperreal), that assumes not only an officially sanctioned rationality but an aura of moral authority (Marcuse, 1964).

Critical theory holds that the psychoanalytical perspective is essential to historiography and the social sciences in that it demonstrates the ways in which humans are deindividualized by the society. The process of this deindividualization not only mutilates the individual but even quashes the attempt to expose those unconscious factors fueled by larger social contradictions and complexities that profoundly influence the actual formation of the individual. Critical theory fights the positivism that has resulted from, and at the same time led, Western people's struggle to dominate the natural world. Thus, critical theory in its struggle against positivism seeks to discover critical self-understanding. History becomes the mechanism that humans employ to seek self-knowledge as well as a deep awareness of the origins of existing sociopolitical conventions (Jacoby, 1975).

Such understanding embodies the possibility of humans transcending the reified "natural" world and attaining self-consciousness. Armed with such a critical consciousness, individuals are better prepared to analyze their social worlds and those features about them that give rise to frustrations for themselves and their brothers and sisters. Eschewing the relativism that limits much of history and interpretive social science, critical historiography boldly announces its emancipatory social vision. Invoking the power of psychoanalysis, historiography, from the critical perspective, celebrates human freedom and, in the process, works toward the improvement of the human condition. Critical democratic social studies teachers can make use of such history in their everyday lessons.

Chapter 22

Teaching a Living History for Social Justice: Subjugated Meaning in the Social Studies

The concept of knowledge worker developed throughout *Getting Beyond the Facts* is central to the teaching of history in the critical democratic social studies of the twenty-first century. A critical history emerges at the point where knowledge work and social justice intersect. In this context, social studies teachers dig into the repressed memories and excluded pasts of the marginalized. As Haroon Kharem, of Brooklyn College, asks, "How can you understand America without a knowledge of the nation's history of White racism?" To Haroon's question, I simply answer, "You can't." Yet the inclusion of such a topic in mainstream social studies curricula is typically viewed as a wild, imprudent effort. Critical democratic social studies teachers maintain that such historical study constitutes the heart of the history curriculum.

The kind of history curriculum an uncritical social studies has advocated refuses to recognize culture as a terrain of struggle. The relationship between knowledge and power is ignored, while concern with domination is buried alongside other skeletons of the past. The attempt to win the consent of the governed is used in the effort to diffuse the social conflict that inevitably emerges from domination. Of course, the creation of a one-dimensional national interest is one strategy employed to win the consent of the people—a national interest, it must be added, that often excludes Black, Native American, Latino, female and other minority communities. For example, the dominant definition of the historical classics in music, art and literature that forms the cultural basis of the nation consistently excludes the contributions of non-White, non-European men and most women. The underlying message of such a definition implies that these "other" people are not a part of their country's cultural heritage; they are outside the national interest. Framed in egalitarian rhetoric while excluding the histories of different communities, the struggle for consent masks the reality of a society stratified along race, gender, and class lines (Carby, 1992; Staples, 1984).

The surface harmony heralded by the media, the government, and social studies is merely an image in the minds of those individuals who are shielded by privilege from the injustice experienced by dominated peoples. Such a pseudoharmony idealizes the future as it covers up the historical forces that have structured the present disharmony that it denies (Giroux, 1988). The governed will not deliver their consent if the presence of the conflict becomes too obvious, too overbearing. In the U.S., where the economic disparity between White and non-White is great and continues to grow, the appeal to national unity is heard more frequently. This chapter maintains that any critical democratic social studies must be grounded on rigorous historical scholarship that explores not only excluded race, class and gender histories but also the construction of the public memory about both subjugated and dominant cultural groups. Too often, many of the history curricula I have observed have been taught by teachers not conversant with the discourse of Western historiography. The critical emancipatory project cannot be accomplished outside the grounding such familiarity provides.

THE MAINSTREAM HISTORY CURRICULUM IN THE TWENTY-FIRST CENTURY

The conservative impulse that shapes much contemporary social studies history teaching is quite uncomfortable with the preceding concerns. Conservatives do not attempt to hide their position that non-White and female history, especially the history of racial and gender conflict and oppression, should not be emphasized in the curriculum. Conservative spokesperson Russell Kirk, for example, has argued unabashedly that the purpose of education is to lift a minority student out of his or her subculture rather than immerse him or her in the "trivialities" of ethnic history. What is to be gained by Black studies? What is to be learned by women's studies? Native American studies? Latino/a studies? Answering his own question, Kirk argues that the only advantage derived from these curricular studies is that a student might possibly find a job somewhere as a professor in these studies (Brittan & Maynard, 1984). Thus, the fact that the conquered and oppressed are not remembered is justified in that their memory is not marketable in postmodern technocapitalism. Official history grows even more amnesiac with regard to Black people, and the past and present come to be seen as the inevitable triumph of the deserving.

The European experience is assumed to be universally applicable, the only valid historical experience. This is the idea that tacitly permeated E. D. Hirsch's *Cultural Literacy* in the late 1980s. No account is taken of the historiographical idea that history cannot be relayed by a single method, that the differences in experience between non-European and European cultures necessitate methodological alterations, not to mention different purposes for usurping history in the first place (Dussel, 1981; Harrison, 1985). The result of such perspectives serves to exclude non-European history from the social studies curriculum. This does not mean that these histories are not mentioned. Indeed, one finds more coverage of them in the texts of the twenty-first century than in the 1950s. Nevertheless, the nature of the coverage is so superficial, so decontextualized, so devoid of conflict, that the essence of these experiences is concealed even as educators boast of progress in the area. By the use of one designated day per year or celebratory bulletin boards and "ethnic" meals, many social studies educators assume they are meeting the needs of multiculturalism. When non-White history is taught without a critical edge, students gain little insight into the problems facing different peoples in their culture's history and how these problems affected history in general. Black history, for instance, has often been represented in the social studies curriculum as a set of isolated events: slaves as bit players in the larger portrayal of the Civil War; brief "personality profiles" of Sojourner Truth; Booker T. Washington as a "credit to this race", George Washington Carver and the peanut; Martin Luther King Jr., as the one-dimensional leader of a decontextualized Civil Rights movement now relegated to the past, c. 1955 – c. 1970. The Black history taught in mainstream social studies has not really induced students to ask the question: What does it mean to be an individual of African descent?

Indeed, the perfunctory manner in which Black history has been included in the curriculum has often served as an attempt to defuse the rising tide of Black student consciousness in school settings (Brittan & Maynard, 1984). This uncritical co-option of Black history has allowed educational leaders to point with pride to the diversity dimension of their curriculum, while, at the same time, maintaining a static view of the purposes of social studies in general. Pasted on to the social studies curriculum in a marginal manner, Black history is separated from the larger conversation about the curriculum and thus exerts no effect upon it. The "knowledge" transmitted in schools is untouched by a consciousness of Black history.

Women's history is similarly taught. The mainstream "inclusive" chronicles of the past acknowledge the contributions of certain women, many of whom were seen as supplementary to the history being made by males. Florence Nightingale, Clara Barton, Betsy Ross, and even Harriet Tubman, are added to the curriculum as "stick-ons," reminders that these people also contributed, at least marginally. I recently interviewed several graduate and undergraduate teacher education classes about the history of Rosa Parks and the desegregation of Montgomery's buses. Without exception, the story began something like, "Rosa was tired from a long day at work and didn't want to move all the way to the back of the bus." No one mentioned that Parks was deeply involved in the Civil Rights movement and that her actions on that day in Montgomery, Alabama, were planned by the movement. Describing Parks as "tired" devalues the entire purpose of the civil action and her commitment to social justice.

Non-White, non-male and lower-class history must be integrated into the social studies curriculum on two fronts: 1) to transcend the supplementary, add-on role; and 2) to be studied as areas in their own right. History of non-Whites and females as only integrated aspects of the social studies history curriculum would undermine the attempt to devise Black, Latino, indigenous, female-oriented conceptual frameworks and epistemologies (Sleeter and Grant, 1988). Sulayman Nyang and Abdulai Vandi (1980), for example, provide an excellent example of how an understanding of Black history would affect the way social studies educators teach the European Age of Exploration in the fifteenth and sixteenth centuries. Traditionally, the era has been taught uncritically as an age of heroes whose names were to be memorized along with their "discoveries." Nyang and Vandi place the "discoveries" in broader historical context, examining the assumptions of the Europeans about themselves and other peoples and the effects of European "heroics" on Africans and Asians. Not only do the authors examine the specifics of the Age of Exploration, but they trace the effects of the era on the lives of Europeans, Africans, Asians and colonized peoples.

Bringing a new and additional perspective to bear on the Age of Discovery changes the entire tenor of the pedagogical act. The rote-based memorization of the "discoveries" of Columbus, Cortez, Balboa, de Gama et al. would give way to a thematic conceptualization of the reasons for European expansionism and the effect of such actions on African, Asian, and indigenous peoples. The traditional curricular preoccupation with Europe would expand into a study of non-European cultures. The view of the Age of Exploration as an isolated historical event would be replaced by an understanding of the connections between the past and the present, especially the European past and the African diasporic present. The study of the Age of Exploration would lead naturally into an examination of colonialism and its effects on the daily events of the twenty-first century. Thus, questions generated by critical subjugated histories would fundamentally change what social studies educators and standardized test makers have labeled basic knowledge about Western civilization and U.S. history.

WHITEWASHING THE HISTORICAL FENCE

Multiple histories will not only uncover new dimensions of many experiences but also reveal new ways of seeing dominant culture and dominant social studies education. Having been situated in a state of oppression for so long, these experiences may point the way to more sophisticated definitions of social theory and ethical authority. Oppressed groups often gain unique insights into the forces that move history. They comprehend the culture of their oppressors better than do the oppressors themselves. Such subjugated insights may dramatically alter that which we refer to as knowledge. Yet, social studies continues to teach multiple histories uncritically: Units of study are added on to existing curricula that are otherwise unaltered. The uncritical presentation of slavery or stories from the "homeland" often estranges students from their history more than it connects them. Such material is taught in lieu of thematic connections between past and present or the development of a sense of the problems that have faced non-Whites. Writing of her own public school experience, bell hooks (1981) describes this detachment: "We are taught to love the system that oppressed us."

Noncritical mainstream education has confused traditionalism with a critical conception of tradition. Distinguishing between the two concepts, Enrique Dussel (1976) argues that traditionalism ends with superficial comprehension. Superficial traditionalism does indeed transmit something, but what it tells conceals more than it reveals. It dwells on the surface, thus hiding the critical dimension, inner nature and lived experience. To be critical in a historical context means to "de-present" the present; that is, to take the mundane, hold it up to the light and look at it from another angle. Critically grounded tradition never lets history slip by unquestioned. It requires that we really test and interrogate what tradition transmits, to uncover what has been concealed in the obvious. For example, Black people know they are African descendents, but the important point is to know what that means. It is one thing to know that African Americans gained educational opportunities in the last portion of the nineteenth and the first part of the twentieth century; it is another idea entirely to understand what the dominant culture perceived the purpose of that education to be.

Social studies textbooks inform students, for example, that America, from the beginning was a melting pot, a land without great conflict. No history books, bell hooks (1981) writes, mentioned racial imperialism. The minds of Americans were filled with romantic notions of the New World, the American dream, America as the land where all the races lived together as one. Fearful of dangerous traditions and the reality of oppression and conflict, many history textbook publishers and curriculum developers do not believe that students need to understand the role of racism in America over the past four centuries. With their emphasis on national unity, spokespeople, such as William Bennett and Diane Ravitch, contend that emphasis on matters such as race and culture are inappropriate. We should concentrate less on racial concerns in the contemporary curriculum, they maintain, and focus our attention on the great facts of American history; that is, a sanitized, "White"-washed view of America, the "greatest" nation in history.

Ravitch's and Bennett's perspectives are not unlike the positions taken by mainstream curriculum developers and social educators since the origins of public schools. A survey of contemporary social studies texts reveals that the word "racism" does not appear in their indexes. When this central theme of the African American experience is not raised, serious political consequences result. Indeed, any complex treatment of racism in American history would need to focus on the variety of forms it takes at different historical moments. Racism is not a fixed principle but a contradictory phenomenon that is constantly changing its form in relation to the alterations of wide political and economic structures (Solomos et al., 1982; Hale-Benson, 1986). No American social studies textbook, for example, examines the history of the northern urban African American experience.

As a result, no textbook studies the evolution of institutional racism and its dramatic impact on northern Black communities. If the question of racism is raised, it is viewed in a Southern slavery or Jim Crow context where it was mandated by law and quite overt. Such was not the case in the North. Left without historical explanations of the nature of racism that developed in the urban, industrialized North, social studies students have no conceptual experience that might help them understand why Blacks in Chicago could not gain the same employment and educational opportunities as immigrants from Poland. An understanding of the Black experience in the labor markets of the North is critical in postmodern America, where children of immigrants from Europe ask: "We worked hard and succeeded in America, why didn't Blacks?" Thus, as James Anderson (1986) concludes, it is easy for such students to buy into popular theories of Black social pathology and blame the Black victim of racism for the difference in status between African Americans and White immigrants in the urban North.

Most social studies history texts simply remove racial studies from any notion of power, a strategy that serves to hide the social relations of domination in which racism is situated. A central function of non-White and women's history as a component of the social studies must involve their ability to expose naïve notions about the nature of racism and sexism, including the belief that they are simply attitudes that need to be changed. Such treatment of racism and sexism perpetuates a cultural blindness that submerges the recognition of the social relations of the lived world. Historical myths of progress, such as the success of racial integration, women's rights, and the conquest of prejudices, eclipse the power relationships that sustain institutional racism and reproduce inequality in the very classrooms that point out the decline of prejudice (Carby, 1980, 1982; Harrison, 1985). Although social studies curricular reformation has often concerned itself with the removal of race and gender stereotyping from history textbooks or with the artifacts produced in specific cultural sites, such as arts, religion, music, dance, and food, a decline in racial and gender oppression has not followed.

DEVELOPING A CRITICAL HISTORICAL CONSCIOUSNESS

Here is where non-White and women's history intervenes; here is where it plays a particularly critical role in the effort to develop a critical consciousness. The histories of racism, sexism, and classism reveal tendencies for virus-like mutations. In the past 50 years, the dominant form of expression has moved from individual "-isms," involving overt acts by individual Whites towards individual non-Whites, to institutional racism that takes the form of public policies and socioeconomic arrangements that deny non-Whites access to legal, medical, or educational facilities. Institutional racism, of course, is particularly insidious because it perpetuates policies that are promoted as racially neutral but exert a discriminatory impact.

A critical racial history reveals these mutations, their geneses, and their contextual development. Such revelations set the stage for the deconstruction of the meanings embedded in words and phrases such as "merit," "quality education," "reverse discrimination," "tuition tax credits," "bad neighborhoods," "at-risk students," "family values" and "law and order." Proceeding from these understandings, we come to realize that people are not just viewed in terms of stereotypes but also in relationship to their power and status (Brittan & Maynard, 1984; Piliawsky, 1984; Bowser, 1985). Thus, inequality is not simply a matter of prejudice, a cultural phenomenon; it is also grounded in the way certain groups are economically and politically located in history.

Understanding this political-economic location of marginalized groups, this evolution of prejudice, this critical tradition, permits those who are historically conscious to move closer to an awareness of non-White and female visions, philosophies, and pedagogies. Subjugated peoples have to establish their own visions—visions that stand in stark contrast to the worldviews assumed by those established in the current centers of power. The ultimate power of any history is in its truth telling. As history is removed from the afternoon shadows cast by the dominant culture, its truth telling reshapes the present as it creates new visions of the future. The historiographical assumption embedded in this concept is that the future is somehow imprinted in the past (Holt, 1986). It is not just the subjugated consciousness that stands to be remolded but dominant consciousness as well. The possibility offered by critical subjugated history confronts teachers with the question of what constitutes official knowledge (Inglis, 1985). If successful, a critical democratic social studies will force history teachers, history curriculum developers, and, it is hoped, the public to ask where does knowledge come from, who certifies it, and what its political impact involves.

Michel Foucault's notion of subjugated knowledges helps us to theorize the possible curricular roles of non-White and female history. Foucault would resurrect these subjugated knowledges: 1) history that has been buried or disguised, typically a history of subjugation, conflict, and oppression lost in a dominant theoretical framework or wiped out by a triumphant history of ideas; and 2) knowledges that have been disqualified as inferior to the dominant definitions of scientificity, knowledge regarded as primitive by mainstream intellectuals (Foucault, 1980). The knowledges of the culturally different fall into this latter meaning, since Western intellectuals have traditionally viewed non-Western epistemologies as illogical, and not worthy of serious philosophical analysis. One theme runs through both meanings: the historical consciousness of conflict. Foucault admonishes the dominant culture to end its suppression of the role of conflict in history, and in discourse, a role that is suppressed in a variety of contexts, the mainstream curriculum included. Foucault used the term genealogy to describe the process of remembering and incorporating these memories of subjugated knowledges, conflict, and the dimensions of power they reveal into active contemporary struggles (Welch, 1991).

Foucault's genealogy is reminiscent of Herbert Marcuse's concept of "dereification," which implied a certain type of remembering. Something extraordinarily important had been forgotten in the contemporary world, Marcuse argued. What had to be retrieved were the human origins of a socially constructed world that had been buried by industrialization and the power of Enlightenment rationality (Jay, 1982). Foucault's genealogy picks up where Marcuse left off. Specifying the nature of excluded contents and meanings, Foucault prepares us for the strategic struggle between the subjugated and the dominant knowledges.

He begins with the realization that the insurrection of subjugated knowledges exists among the oppressed, as in his study of prisons and prisoners. The insurrection is not something that dominant intellectuals can theorize into existence; historians simply acknowledge its reality. Obviously, women's and non-White knowledges are prime examples of

Foucault's notion of subjugated knowledges. No intellectual systematically theorized it; it was already there. W.E.B. DuBois (1973) recognized its existence decades prior to Foucault. To understand ourselves as Black people, he wrote in 1946, we must understand African history and social development—one of the most sophisticated world views, he added, the planet has witnessed. I often refer to DuBois' notion in my classes as the "genius of Africanism."

How might a social studies teacher build his or her practice on the foundation provided by such understandings and theoretical insights? A social studies grounded on an understanding of a history of subjugated knowledge would be aware of the way schools are structured around specific silences and omissions (Giroux, 1988). Teachers would thus seek to incorporate subjugated knowledge by forging links with those marginalized communities—not just the dominant culture's definition of the "successful" elements of those communities, but a variety of groups and subgroups within them. The diverse resources to be found in each community open the school to a variety of community traditions, histories, and cultures discredited within the culture of the school.

The stories, the worldviews, the music, the politics, the humor, the art, of the marginalized community become a central part of everyday school life, never viewed in isolation or as supplements to the "real work" of the school but always in the context of the social curriculum. How do these knowledges, teachers would ask, fit with the dominant knowledge? What dynamics are at work in their interrelationship? The attempt to answer such questions lays the foundation for a critical social studies curriculum, an education that takes the non-White and female experience seriously. The dominant curriculum, with its nonproblematic, standardized definitions of knowledge and its standardized tests, has no room for such activities. It is too busy being accountable to the standards. The isolation from community that results eventually sets up adversarial relationships between teachers and non-White parents, citizens, and political leaders.

Social studies teachers, informed by Foucault's notion of subjugated knowledges, thus rewrite history in their classrooms, but not in the sense of a totalitarian regime (China's official account of the Tiananmen massacre, as an example) that manufacturers a pseudohistory to control its people. This critical rewriting of history involves the inclusion of subjugated knowledges and the new perspectives such countermemories provide. E. P. Thompson, in *The Making of the English Working Class*, alludes to this process of historical rewriting when he describes the task of the labor leaders in the nineteenth century who were struggling to cope with the problems of an industrializing Britain. They had to write a new past, Thompson tells his readers, create forms of unprecedented political organization, and draw upon this new history to invent class traditions from a largely invisible past. There is something pedagogically important here, something that provides a peek at the subtle and complex ways history influences education and political practice.

Nineteenth-century labor leaders took the subjugated historical experience of the working class and theorized it into knowledge—a knowledge that affected the consciousness and pedagogical and political practice of those who grasped it. A solidarity between those who understood the new knowledge was forged and, thereby, a community of learning was established (Inglis, 1985). The subjugated history, the countermemory of the English working class, like the historical experience of African Americans, was not just "dead old history". Within it were found the origins of the problems, the debates, the oppression of the present. This is what happens when the oppressed draw upon their subjugated knowledges and speak for themselves. Insurrections of subjugated knowledges elicit critical interpretations of educational and school codes, symbols and texts, institutional structures of public education, and the possibility of an educational praxis built on the wisdom gleaned from these recognitions (Welch, 1991). The history taught in the critical democratic social studies classroom always draws upon the insurrection of these subjugated knowledges.

REPRESSED MEMORY: CUTTING THE CORD BETWEEN PAST AND PRESENT

Critical subjugated history, in its social psychoanalytical format, is concerned with repressed memory, subjugated knowledge, and the influence of such repression on the life of the present. The power of the memory of repression is nowhere better represented than in the African diasporic experience. Memory finds itself intimately connected to the present since its cultivation helps to liberate the knowledges of peoples long separated from their pasts. With oppressed groups, memory engenders consciousness that leads to a panoply of possible futures. Black historians must draw upon its power in the attempt to secure a place in the public discourse about education.

Thus, once the often eclipsed relationship between past and present is recognized, the tryst between history and politics can be exposed. History is a discourse that exists in a dialectical relationship with political thought (Kaye, 1987). If such a relationship seems paradoxical or dangerous, it is because we often hold such a narrow view of politics. In the popular sense of the term, "politics" typically refers to public office-seeking at the least and the great public issues at the most. If the definition is expanded to include the larger moral and ethical dimensions of power sharing in a society, the relationship between history and politics is rendered less threatening. In the dialectical interplay between history and politics (and education), the way one makes sense of the past is essential in the determination of what political (or educational) perspective one will view as realistic or socially responsible (White, 1987). Indeed, some would argue that all political and educational reasoning is basically a form of historical argument (Popular Memory Group, 1982).

Thus, history, no matter who writes it, is never disinterested. Disinterested history is a luxury only dominant groups can afford. When W.E.B. DuBois (1973) viewed the past, he saw a useful chronicle of methods employed by his Black ancestors to fight slavery and oppression—methods, he believed, that could be put to use in present struggles against racial tyranny. The blueprints for the Black future, he theorized, must be built on a base of problems, dreams, and frustrations. They would not appear out of thin air or be based exclusively on the experience of others. Echoing this theme, Maulana Karenga (1982) argued almost 40 years later that African American history is a reflection not only of what Black people have done but of what they can do. The Black past holds out possibilities because it serves the political function of destabilizing the existing order by revealing its social construction and thus its bogus suprahistorical character.

This critical democratic social studies notion of historical memory confronts mainstream academics and teachers with a profound problem emerging from the Eurocentric, objectivist view of historiography. Historians have long wrung their hands over the relationship between past and present. Obviously, many professional historians would find the concept of critical historical memory incompatible with their idea of disinterested scholarship. Pure scholarship, modernist objectivists would argue, is best served by a consistent resistance to the attempt to compare historical events to the present. Tell the story as it was, many write, and stay away from too much theory. Uncomfortable with the perceived distortion of a politically engaged history, such historians urge their colleagues to understand the past on its own ground, according to the criteria of its own time.

If we are to pursue critical history as subjugated memory, democratic social studies teachers must confront these questions and carefully analyze the nature of the past-present relationship. Objectivist historians are correct when they point to the often dishonorable heritage that has attempted to appropriate the past for some undesirable end. In many hands, history has become little more than a repository of relevant anecdotes, moralist admonitions, and precedents to be invoked at will by jurists and politicians. The intent of critical history is not to reduce the project of history to an immediate political utility, in the sense that specific civics lessons with step-by-step instructions for social improvement can be drawn from historical scholarship. Reagan, Bush, Buchanan, Limbaugh, Gingrich, Thatcher, and the New Right serve as excellent examples of how the conception of immediate utility eventuates in the abuse of history (Kaye, 1987).

A critical subjugated history attempts to move the dialogue between memory and the present to a more subtle level. This is a realm where, admittedly, history is used, but where its use involves the acquisition of critical insight into existing situations and a sensitivity to the values historically embedded within these present realities. Such a task inevitably evokes charges of presentism. The admonition to avoid presentist history is at best a negative injunction, failing even to bestow insight into the attempt to ascertain what a particular segment of the past was like. It does not recognize the fact that the historian's knowledge and experience of the present is necessary to his or her understanding of the past. The appreciation of a historical form rests on recognition of the interplay between past and present. Indeed, the past can be understood only insofar as it has continued to live in the present (White, 1987).

History as subjugated memory eschews antiquarianism. As French historian Marc Bloch, a victim of the holocaust, wrote during the Second World War, antiquarians revere buildings and institutions and romanticize the past, but historians are citizens of the here and now who love life. Following Bloch's imperative, historians must avoid the production of past images for passive consumption only by other historians. Historians' knowledge is necessary to our attempt to understand the workings of social, psychological, and educational processes and their subtle interrelationships. The historian's approach to his or her task, however, must always be informed by dedication to accuracy and infused with a larger social purpose.

Historians, more than other scholars, must be aware of the consequences of historical ignorance and amnesia. Our postmodern unconsciousness of history does not free us from the past, but, to the contrary, traps us in the snare of an unconscious destiny. When the past is forgotten, its power over the present is hidden from view. We are victimized by an amnesia that makes "what is" seem as if "it had to be." Contrary to what antiquarians might argue, historians will be judged by the contributions they make in putting their knowledge of the past to work in the attempt to understand the present and to shape the future. The point is so obvious that it might not be worth stressing, except for the fact that historians have worked so diligently to deny it.

Critical subjugated history forces us to confront two questions: 1) What is the role of critical historians as transmitters of culture? and 2) What is the role of historians in the larger society? These two questions involve the concept of memory, both in a social and an individual sense. To answer these questions, historians must explore the role that memory and historical knowledge play in our lives. The word "memory" directs the attention of historians away from an exclusive concern with the past and towards a concern with the past-present relationship (Popular Memory Group, 1982). Memory, unlike history, has a verb form—to remember. Because the past lives in the present—and, certainly, in the minds of people who live in the present—public memory becomes a focus of political struggle. How it is approached by historians as well as by other social actors is intrinsically a political act. How we remember matters because it informs our existence in the present and our vision of the future. Yet, because of their commitment to particular notions of objectivity and methods of verification, memory has always proven to be a difficult concept for historians to confront.

What does it mean to remember history? What must we do with memories of such history to make them active and alive rather than mere antiques or quaint curiosities? One of the social roles of any historian is to peddle the idea that memory is a vital resource in political life, in social action, or in social education. Memory counters the oppressive "presence" of early twenty-first century life because it helps us to make sense of the nature and changeability of our current conditions. Memory is the means by which we gain self-consciousness about the genesis of our own commonsense beliefs, derived as they are from our social and cultural milieu (Popular Memory Group, 1982). This self-consciousness applies not only to individuals but to institutions as well. The collective memory of educators, for example, aids understanding of a shared social reality that underlies perception of purpose. In other words, it matters if we forget, for example, John Dewey or the race, class, and gender-influenced origin of public schooling, the historical justifications for vocational education, or the origins of social studies as a discipline.

What makes it matter so much is that the relationship between memory and history is so fractured in the twenty-first century. The repair of this fracture must be a central role for critical historians concerned with the world of the present. Our audiences must be confronted not only with the past but with what has happened to the memory of it. Educational leaders and teachers can benefit from an understanding of the phenomenon of historical disengagement that has destroyed our memories of how curricula were developed and why schools have assumed their present forms. Critical democratic social studies educators must reunite memory and history in order to address the ideological distortions that daily confront us in various expressions of popular culture. Power wielders have never had much access to the reshaping of public memory. Blacks, Latinos, women, working-class people and indigenous peoples must constantly monitor the ways their pasts are inserted into the collective historical (un)consciousness of Western societies.

Christopher Lasch writes of history that remembers and history that arises from the need to forget (Kaye, 1987). Historians need to concern themselves with exposing the functional dimension of this need to forget. When the bloodstains are bleached out of the historical record, established power is justified and shored up. The production of what might be called dominant memory is a central historical task. When dominant memory serves to structure consent and build alliances in the functioning of formal politics, the power of memory is revealed (Popular Memory Group, 1982). Such power is illustrated by the American public's memory of the United States' relations with Iran. Most Americans remember only angry Iranians chanting anti-American slogans in the streets of Tehran, a crazed Ayatollah preaching martyrdom, and hostages torn away from their families.

Not included in the dominant memory are images of the CIA working to overthrow the government of Iranian Premier Mohammed Mossedegh in 1953 and replacing it with the friendly Pahlavi Dynasty represented by the young Shah. The structuring of such memories makes a difference. The power of memory in education is revealed by the rewriting of history of the Educational Testing Service to exclude the eugenicist origins of, and influence on, what passes as a value-neutral, objective testing service (Owen & Doerr, 1999). The form that public memory takes is always a struggle between imperializing and localizing powers. Critical democratic social studies teachers must be informed historical scholars, capable of filling in the omissions and offering a sense of possibility to oppressed and dominant groups.

The possibility that critical history holds does not involve the presentation of past heroics, resistances, and dreams for simple imitation. The past cannot be repeated; present circumstances are unique and will not allow such a tack. The mere repetition of a past formula is bogus. The possibility of a critical social studies curriculum rests in its fresh restatement for each new age and new generation. This, obviously, is no panacea; it simply immerses students in the vital flow, the white water of tradition. In the process, they come to see the possibilities for liberation in the everyday stream of events. Because history does not lead automatically to our finding the right strategy for the present, several other steps of emancipatory socioethical analysis must be pursued if individuals are to come to a reflective sense of what they are to do.

These steps, Beverly Harrison (1985) writes, include the delineation of our solidarities and loyalties. Every political and curricular stance is influenced by the solidarities and loyalties to groups it aims to serve. Rebecca Chopp agrees, arguing that, since there are no purely individual categories for meaning, freedom, or reason, solidarity forms the basis for ideological critique and historiographical theory. Solidarity with marginalized and oppressed groups forms the cornerstone of history, and the critical social studies curriculum holds little meaning outside the bounds of such solidarity (Chopp, 1986).

Drawing upon the insights of Chopp and Harrison, critical social studies educators have come to realize that insight into oppressed history alone does not provide a pedagogy sufficient for the emancipatory task. An emancipatory pedagogy must begin with critical traditions, confirm them as subjugated knowledges, and interrogate them in order to understand their relationship to present realities and mutated forms of racism, sexism and other oppressions. A critical subjugated history becomes a starting point for curriculum theorizing about what students and others need to learn in addition to their own cultural, racial, gender, and class experiences; that is, the relationship between dominant and subjugated knowledges. William Pinar (1988) clarifies the issue when he writes, "After self-revelation, the question becomes, what do I make of what is revealed?" (p. 272) All people are more than just their history, their experiences, what they have been conditioned to be. In other words, once a critical multicultural curriculum, with its new histories and new voices is laid bare, what are we to make of this knowledge? How are we to connect it to our own lives and the lives of others?

CONSTRUCTING A LIVING HISTORY IN THE SOCIAL STUDIES: ESCAPING EUROCENTRISM

Once we understand mainstream social studies' tendency to use narrow guidelines to exclude non-White, lower-socioeconomic class, and women's experiences, how do critical historians begin the process of curriculum development in both school and cultural locations? Western societies have been, are now, and always will be Eurocentric, Cartesian modernists proclaim. Concluding that nothing about such a position is racist, conservatives such as E. D. Hirsch maintain that the Eurocentric nature of America was intact by 1776. What about the cultural exchanges that have occurred in the U.S. before and after 1776? Hirsch conveniently ignores the important contributions to the national culture by a potpourri of immigrants from all corners of the globe, not to mention the indigenous peoples who lived in American before the arrival of the Europeans. Critical democratic social studies, at this point, works to devise a curriculum that connects these historical understandings to the lives of individuals from both dominant and subordinate groups.

Joyce King and Carolyn Mitchell (1995), in their book *Black Mothers to Sons: Juxtaposing African American Literature with Social Practice*, provide profound insights into ways of shaping the historically contextualized subjugated (in this case, Afrocentric) social studies curriculum. Concerned with the personal experiences of Black mothers with their sons, King and Mitchell brought Black mothers together for a group conversation where they discussed, compared, and analyzed their lived worlds in the light of vignettes from African American literature. Using literature as a mirror for life and, thus, a generative pedagogical activity, rubbed against the grain of traditional Eurocentric literacy criticism, with its privileging of art/literature as an aesthetic not a political dynamic.

Here, literature was not being used as an aesthetic but as an evocative device in the sociopolitical context of the Black culture. What King and Mitchell were developing in this process was an innovative research methodology into the Black experience that held profound implications for social studies. When Black literature was examined vis-à-vis social practice, the authors found a valuable strategy to enlighten educators about the vicissitudes of Black life and the false and misleading nature of popular stereotypes of Black mothers and Black families.

King and Mitchell were concerned with providing a setting where the literary encounter evoked a group conversation about the relevant topics . As researchers, King and Mitchell made no attempt to cultivate detachment, seeking instead personal interaction with the participants. Drawing upon the method, critical social studies educators use their historical and power-related understandings to ground this coming together of students, teachers, and members of the community in exploring the meaning of such concepts in their lives. Critical teachers work to help students gain self-knowledge through the awareness of the social origins of their mutual emotions and traumas.

Using King and Mitchell's mothers as a model, the critical groups identify shared problems and work to solve them. This "research for change" model is central to a critical social studies and can be used to enable conversations among a variety of groups about many different topics. As a means of examining how individuals and groups receive knowledge, the method engages group members in a process of rewriting knowledge. One can imagine many possibilities for deploying the method in the critical social studies context, including group analysis of film and TV representations of African Americans or the methods by which academic knowledge about Blacks and other oppressed groups is produced.

What King and Mitchell are proposing involves a form of paradigmatic analysis—an examination of knowledge production—in this case, a Eurocentric knowledge production about individuals of African heritage. As we have discussed in our concept of an epistemology of complexity, modernist Eurocentric forms of epistemology separate spirit and emotion from reason and intellect, meanwhile promoting the superiority of reason and intellect. The Eurocentric epistemology posits that the knowledge emerging from its cultural assumptions is universal, neutral, and objective. King and Mitchell's Afrocentric paradigmatic analysis claims, however, that such knowledge tacitly reflects a Eurocentric world view and covertly reifies the status quo. An epistemology and research methodology constructed by the dominant powers within a society sees the world from that dominant vantage point. From this perspective, Blacks and other marginalized groups are often objectified as members of subcultures who don't share dominant values.

Eurocentric ways of seeing produce an epistemological power that induces individuals to acquiesce to modernist criteria for judging what is of worth in human experience. This epistemological colonialism moved Europeans across the centuries to see themselves as producers and purveyors of truth. Through their science and rationality, they often came to think that they possessed the solutions to all earthly (and sometimes unearthly) problems. As agents of truth, Europeans were able to justify a variety of crimes against humanity, especially non-White humanity (Dion-Buffalo & Mohawk, 1992). It is the effects of this Eurocentric one-truth epistemology that King and Mitchell's method seeks to analyze. Obviously, such analysis is central to a critical democratic social studies.

The core of the critical social studies curriculum involves the effort to understand the world as seen from the margins, the marginalized. Some have referred to this dynamic as decentering the center, viewing subjugated experience as well as whiteness from an outsider's vantage point. The pedagogical implications of such a move are dramatic when multiple accounts replace the "Truth." In the light of the ways Black, Latino, Asian and indigenous lives are misrepresented in both academia and the media, such a curriculum is profoundly needed by non-White students with understandably low self-esteem, not to mention students from the dominant culture whose anger towards the marginalized grows daily in postmodernity. A curriculum that sees from the margins operates differently than the dominant social studies curriculum, starting, for example, a study of race in the United States not with slavery but with the pre-fifteenth-century civilizations in West Africa. Such an approach tells a different story since it frames the African American struggle as one to regain its original strength, not as a story of a traditionally weak, enslaved people trying to develop a sense of dignity. One doesn't find such an approach in the top-down standards-driven history curriculum.

The critical social studies curriculum of the marginalized does not attempt merely to replace Eurocentrism with Afrocentrism or androcentrism with gynocentrism. Proponents do maintain, however, that the study of various marginalized peoples should be emphasized because they have been ignored or distorted. They also contend that dominant groups, such as White people, should be viewed from other angles, from non-Eurocentric epistemological assumptions. Such analysis does not mean that we simply demonize whiteness; it does mean that we treasure subjugated ways of knowing. Subjugated stories become a valuable resource to be used to build a better future for individuals from diverse groups, a collective future based on the principles of communitarianism, power sharing and social justice.

With these understandings, a critical history might start with a study of Mexican Americans, for example, before the Mexican War in 1846— the point where many curricula begin their study. Such a critical curriculum would investigate what was occurring in Mexico before the U.S. conquered the northern half of the nation. It would also appreciate that, from a Mexican and/or Native American perspective, the study of Mexican Americans would include gaining a familiarity with the ancient Aztec and Mayan civilizations. In the Anglocentric U.S. history curriculum the study of the conditions in England that led to the Pilgrims' migration is commonplace. Such is not the case with non-White American immigrants (West, 1993; Sleeter & Grant, 1994).

A social studies curriculum that valued marginalized perspectives would search for new ways of seeing in a variety of pedagogical locales. It is a basic premise of historiography that historical analyses of the past often tell readers as much about the time in which they were authored as about the epoch they chronicle. Joel Taxel (1994) points out that teachers must be aware of these dynamics in children's literature, and maintains that a comparative reading of books such as Yates' *Amos Fortune, Free Man* (1950), Hamilton's *Anthony Burns: The Defeat and Triumph of a Fugitive Slave* (1988) and Lyons's *Letters from a Slave Girl: The Story of Harriet Jacobs* (1992) provides a unique insight into changing White perspectives towards African Americans. Indeed, these books are probably more important in this way than they are as studies of slaves' lives.

In a similar vein, Toni Morrison explores racial points of view in literature, analyzing the racial imagination of White mainstream authors and readers. In this context, she exposes the ways the dominant power of whiteness exercises its hegemony in literature, film, and various forms of popular culture. Such hegemonic dynamics induce readers to accept the unjust social status quo, the exclusions of academic disciplines, and the social studies curriculum as it stands. Indeed, the dominant racial imagination is built into the production and organization of knowledge itself (King & Mitchell, 1995). These racialized dynamics provide us further insight into our epistemology of complexity. Understanding the social and historical world in a more complex manner always involves seeing it from the diverse perspectives of differing race, class, and gender groups. Critical historians and social studies educators are always impressed with what profound insights turn up when they are involved in studies of this type.

CONCEPTUALIZING A CRITICAL SUBJUGATED HISTORY IN THE SOCIAL STUDIES: THE INTERSECTION OF AFROCENTRISM AND CRITICAL THEORY

When we use marginalized perspectives as a key ingredient in a critical historical and social studies curriculum, by definition, we study ways of improving the lives of oppressed peoples. Both critical theory and Afrocentrism, though from different cultural traditions, agree on that social educational objective and are willing to work tirelessly to achieve it. Both theoretical positions have much to learn from one another, although in my position as a privileged White analyst, I make no attempt to teach African Americans who claim Afrocentric credentials how critical perspectives can extend the Afrocentric project. This is not my role. The development of Afrocentrism is a Black concern at this historical juncture. The purpose here is simply to point out the ways the theories converge in a manner that informs a critical social studies education. Afrocentrism provides a unique challenge to social studies curricula that hide their Eurocentric ideological features. In this context, Afrocentrism understands the intimate connection between the economic and social stresses that afflict Black communities in Western societies and the crises of knowledge and human meaning that subvert the culture's ability and/or willingness to respond to the chaos.

The drums of Black protest and pain sound loudly in the music of young rappers and reggae artists who provide Afrocentrism with its most audible oppositional voice. Such forms of protest are revered by many non-White (and White) youths and are virtually ignored, except for efforts to curb the music's obscenity or violent expressions, by the dominant culture and mainstream education. Such Afrocentric protests are validated by critical scholars of Black economics who ground their scholarship on the concept of "market failure," or the inability of free-market economies to provide the goods, services, or capital needed by the Black community. This critical theory of Black economics goes on to maintain that a lack of material well-being among individuals and groups within the economy exerts negative economic and cultural consequences for the society as a whole.

Thus, all members of society, not just Blacks, benefit from the eco-nomic development and vitalization of the Black community. Critical social studies teachers learn more from young rappers, Afrocentrists, critical Black economists and many other marginalized voices than just a chronicle of misery. They gain insight from such voices into ways of producing critical scholars who become wielders of oppositional power and cultural workers who upset the stasis of economic, political, and educational systems that have rested comfortably despite the omnipres-ence of glaring racial inequality. In these ways, they gain unique per-spectives into modes of teaching that take seriously the knowledge of the marginalized.

A critical social studies informed by Afrocentrism gains the omi-nous realization that, in the first decade of the twenty-first century, edu-cation cannot be separated from Black survival. As they elicit group reaction to various Black texts, King and Mitchell (1995) refer to the psychic holocaust faced by Black people, young Black males in particu-lar. A critical social studies cannot ignore contemporary media repre-sentations of Black men as animalistic and criminal and their psychological effects on Black males themselves. The unfair political and economic realities Black men face in contemporary American soci-ety cannot be separated from the violence, anger, and destructiveness often turned upon themselves. Like King and Mitchell's cadre of Black mothers of Black sons, critical social studies educators worry about the safety of young Black men. In an era when young Black men in some areas are twice as likely to end up in prison as in college, Black male sur-vival becomes a serious question.

Because of the severity of the social environment young Black men must negotiate, King, Mitchell and the Black mothers understand that lessons must sometimes be taught harshly, albeit lovingly. Critical social studies learns from this dynamic, since it provides a power literacy that helps students gain insight into the ways the world works in reality instead of the sanitized version depicted in mainstream social studies textbooks and Disney movies. A social studies that teaches Black males the nature of racism and provides maps of the socioeconomic terrain is far more valu-able for our threatened Black sons than a pedagogy of denial.

Such a critical curriculum pulls no punches when it studies racial codes embodied in concepts such as "good neighborhoods," "quality edu-cation," and the Los Angeles judicial and law enforcement's use of NHI (no humans involved) to refer to young urban Black males. While it is unfortunate that we must tell our young Black male students and other marginalized students that they must "be better" intellectually and ethically than their White middle/upper-middle class peers if they want to escape poverty and its accompanying danger, it is nonetheless a necessity. Such cold revelations must always be accompanied by affirmations of the brilliance of the African diasporic tradition, the genius of Africanism, and the profound knowledge and talents young Black men bring with them to social studies classrooms.

A CRITICAL DEMOCRATIC SOCIAL STUDIES AFFIRMS THE GENIUS OF AFRICANISM

As a critical democratic social studies explores the degradation of Africanness in Western societies, it concurrently looks at the genius of things African for the purpose of providing affirmational experiences for Black students. Critical social studies educators want children of African descent (and children from other cultural/racial backgrounds as well) to understand African history, philosophy and culture. In the spirituality and communitarianism expressed through its art, storytelling, and lived culture, the African tradition affirms both individuality and collectivity. The brilliance of Black men and women in the disaporic historical tradition involved their ability to avoid nihilism in spite of the despair of their enslaved position.

Through their cultural constructions of meaning, feeling, and love, they created a psychic armor that protected them from the hopelessness and cruelty of slavery and oppression. Such armor remained in place from the seventeenth century to the 1970s, when it began to disintegrate. Despite the trials and tribulations of Black life, Black suicide rates in the U.S. were the lowest of any group. By the 1990s young Black Americans' suicide rate was the highest of any ethnic group. Critical social studies educators, drawing upon the knowledge of the Afrocentric tradition, want to understand the psychological power of Black ancestors to deal with inequality and oppression as one portion of a larger strategy of social transformation (Hall, 1992; West, 1992, 1993; King & Mitchell, 1995; Gresson, 1995).

In addition to Stuart Hall's (1992) three unique features of the African diasporic tradition—style, music, and the use of the body (each of which deserves volumes of analysis)—the Black academic/literary tradition can help individuals to survive and make sense of their lives. The chills and tears I have seen elicited in class by Paul Laurence Dunbar's "The Haunted Oak," with its overwhelming take on the history of violence against Black men in the United States, has opened pathways to liberation from the meaningless and violence of oppression. From the perspective of the hanging tree, Dunbar writes of the emotions elicited by the innumerable lynchings of Black innocents. The charismatic power of haunted oaks, autobiographies of figures such as Malcolm X, and stories by authors such as Ralph Ellison, Toni Morrison, Alice Walker, Richard Wright, Claude Brown and Zora Neale Hurston have changed the lives of many Black males. Interestingly, prison journals often speak of the magic of such literature. Obviously, such literature should be found in social studies curricula as well as prison libraries.

The social studies curriculum of Black affirmation is a Black studies program that overtly forges connections between academia and everyday Black life, and Black cultural production. Drawing upon the collective Black experience in life, history, and literature, the curriculum induces students to reexamine their lives from an Afrocentric perspective. The knowledge produced in this reflective activity can provide basic understandings needed to transform Western culture. Such a critical Black social studies pays special attention to the cultural production of Black youth: rap, reggae, hip-hop etc. Houston Baker, Jr. (1993) maintains that reggae, for example, has extended Black studies to the young. Understanding the role of reggae and rap artists as public intellectuals, Baker describes his use of rap to gain pedagogical entrée to a group of poor, racially and ethnically diverse British secondary students.

Describing Shakespeare's *Henry V* using rap—"a cold dissing, def con man, tougher-than-leather and smoother-than-ice, an artisan of words"—Baker took students on a pedagogical journey back and forth between *Henry V* and Public Enemy's "Don't Believe the Hype." In this context, a cultural hybridity was developed that affirmed Black racial identities and cultural production, while at the same time teaching a valuable traditional lesson in the Eurocentric canon. It is important to note in this context that a critical democratic social studies, in its embrace of the margins, makes no effort to exclude and degrade all that is Eurocentric. In Baker's case, Afrocentricity was used as a vehicle for the exploration of the traditional canon. Neither Baker nor I would always use Black cultural production to get to a European concept. Often, we would explore the Afrocentric for its own intrinsic merit as a way to get to another Afrocentric point (King & Mitchell, 1995). There are times to escape Eurocentrism in a critical social studies, and there are times to study it.

Drawing on the Black experience induces social studies teachers and other cultural workers to address the Black aesthetic. Such a perspective turns everyday life into aesthetic objects of perception; in such a context, people, lived activities, tragedies, and celebrations can all be viewed in a moral, political, and ethical context. The symbolic realm is connected to lived reality in a manner that helps to construct a new consciousness. I have referred to this elsewhere as postformal thinking (Kincheloe & Steinberg, 1993; Kincheloe, Steinberg & Hinchey, 1999; Kincheloe, Steinberg, & Villaverde, 1999; Kincheloe, 1995). The Black aesthetic provides the possibility for a pedagogy of affirmation of students of African descent.

As the metaphor of jazz is introduced as a curricular principle, Black and White students are drawn into African ways of seeing and being. Jazz, as it is used here, is not only a musical form but an approach to life, with its improvisational flexibility and resistance to the positivist certainty of either/or epistemologies. A jazz epistemology can be used to signify an epistemology of complexity. Like a jazz pianist, the improviser operates both individually and in concert with the group. Indeed, the pianist's individuality catalyses the creative tension within the group, leading it to previously unimagined accomplishments. No other culture has produced a musical or aesthetic form comparable to jazz—another example of the genius of Africanism.

This jazz motif is employed in Afrocentric pedagogies, curriculum development, and research strategies. Just as jazz musicians play a split second before the beat and tease the note as an unstable sonic frequency, teachers and other cultural workers develop new takes on old assumptions. Thus, what has been called the "tragic magic" of jazz becomes an omnipresent dynamic within the Afrocentric imperative and its production of a scholarly method that is grounded on an understanding of oppressed people's pain and frustration. Critical social studies teachers understand that merely teaching students a Black history concerned with great Black people and their accomplishments is insufficient in the quest for affirmation. A key aspect of the pedagogy of affirmation involves the ability of students both to understand and to act on a set of ever evolving moral, ethical, and scholarly principles. The tragic magic of jazz is directly connected to Black pain and anguish. So is the curriculum of affirmation because it induces children and young adults to identify and make sense of the pain they confront daily in the nihilism that surrounds them. As they come to understand their pain, oppressed students are nurtured in the effort to express their understandings creatively and therapeutically (Jafa, 1992; Nightingale, 1993; West, 1993).

AS I WALK THROUGH THE VALLEY OF THE SHADOW OF DEATH: SOCIAL STUDIES, RAP, AND THE BLACK AESTHETIC

Black resistance to the right-wing resurgence and what Aaron Gresson (1995) has termed the recovery of White supremacy has emerged in the past couple of decades not as much in the academic and political spheres but in popular cultural expressions such as Black literature, Black film, Black music videos, and, especially, rap. The Black aesthetic fueled this counterhegemonic cultural moment, as rappers responded to the pain of racism in a variety of creative ways. A critical social studies curriculum of affirmation takes these cultural expressions very seriously, studying and learning from them insights into the issues they address, as well as the experiences that shaped the lives of the individuals who produced them.

Emerging from the economic crisis of young African Americans in New York in the 1970s, rap addressed the vilification of Black youth. Bringing together the language skills of Black ministers and the African polyrhythmic tradition, rap uses Black rage to construct a new popular cultural art form. Cornel West (1993) believes that rap is the first step on the way to something great, because it strives to create a social vision of a better future. Always contradictory, rap's sometime violent misogyny and homophobia cannot be excused. As we listen to or interpret rap, social studies educators must not fall into an all-or-nothing glorification or romanticization. Cultural workers can comfortably point out the contradictions of rap, since they encourage those around them always to listen with a critical ear (Nightingale, 1993; Gray, 1995).

In many ways, it can be claimed that the most compelling and politically conscious expressions of the Black aesthetic in the last two decades have come from rap. Truly a Black art form, rap cannot be easily "covered" (appropriated) by White musicians—the careers of Vanilla Ice and Eminem being no exceptions. The urban blackness of the form seems to necessitate a style accessible mainly to African American youth—a quality that undermines its acceptance as a serious musical form. As with other popular cultural forms, the power of rap involves its ability to construct fields of interest that are connected to affective dynamics such as desire and anger. Critical social studies educators know that the understanding of the way rap (and other forms of popular culture) constructs fields of interest is extremely important. Anyone who teaches young people should possess an awareness of rap that can be deployed at many different times for many different reasons. Too often, I talk to social studies teachers and teacher educators who dismiss rap and its cultural/pedagogical importance. Such educators are often the ones who possess little visceral identification with the pain and hopelessness experienced by many of their Black students.

The positive sites of rap are full of energy, and sometimes rage, but are always concerned with injustice. The obscenity of White male corporate profit-taking, for example, is a common political theme in a genre that relentlessly pursues the wrongs of the state. As a source of racial pride and a condemnation of racism, rap negotiates gangsta rage with stop-the-violence appeals. Within the rap cosmos, there are works devoted to the rights of Black women, opposed to child abuse and rape, dedicated to teaching an Afrocentric curriculum, critical of police officers who don't respect the rights of individuals etc. Indeed, rap is a form of social education. While the types of rap continue to expand, almost all of them maintain their connection to the Black aesthetic (Baker, 1993; Gray, 1995).

Rap and the Black aesthetic are examples of the sources social studies teachers can study in a critically reconceptualized social studies curriculum. Obviously, students of African descent can profit from the study of such alternative sources, but I want students and individuals from all backgrounds to understand the issues raised by rappers and their relationship to the production of well-educated, well-informed, and civically courageous people. Critical social studies, with its historical contextualization, power literacy, social vision, pedagogical imagination, and commitment to democracy and justice, can contribute to the formulation of new educational and political spheres in the dangerous new times Western societies and the U.S. face in the twenty-first century. With these ideas in mind, the teaching of history and social studies in general can never be the same.

Chapter 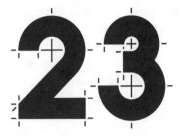 23

"Free Enterprise" as High School Economics: Confronting the Victory of the Market

As previously discussed, the last 30 years of American political history have witnessed an unprecedented alliance between religious conservatives in the Christian Right and corporate wielders of power touting the free enterprise system and a laissez-faire, neoclassical version of economic theory. New Right fundamentalists painted a Sunday-school morality play, depicting liberals in the 1960s as the demons whose ungodly permissiveness initiated the moral, spiritual, educational, and, ultimately, economic decline of America. Confident, divinely sanctioned ministers made the Puritan dream fashionable again, as they parroted John Winthrop's famous metaphor of America as a "city on the hill, a shining beacon" of Christian morality to a corrupt Old World. Although Brooks Brothers-clad corporate leaders found the evangelical crowd a little gauche and a bit embarrassing in their zeal, they nevertheless welcomed them into a political alliance that would change the social, political, and economic face of America. The fact that the evangelicals were political allies, business leaders reasoned, did not require their admittance to exclusive country clubs; we can be close, they thought, but not all *that* close (Grossberg, 1992; Hursh & Ross, 2000).

Though the road has been sometimes rocky, the conservative alliance has stayed together well enough to dictate the public political and economic conversation into the first decade of the twenty-first century. The role of free enterprise economics in this coalition and its impact on the social studies has been profound and in many situations even bizarre. In one of the first expressions of what would come to be known as the Christian Right, Alice Moore, the wife of a fundamentalist Protestant minister in Kanawha County, West Virginia, led a group of concerned citizens in a textbook protest. In 1974 the group successfully rid the Kanawha County schools of what were considered to be liberal and immoral textbooks and served as a model for similar protests and political protests around the nation.

During the heat of the controversy, Moore stated that she wanted literature prohibited from the schools that "encouraged skepticism" in the family unit, which, she said, comes from the marriage of a man and a woman, belief in God, the American political system, the laws and legal system of the nation and the state, the history of America as "the record of one of the noblest civilizations which ever existed," respect for other people's property, the need for study of the traditional rules of grammar, and *the free enterprise economic system*. To this day, Moore represents a significant number of people who rank the inculcation of an uncritical version of free enterprise as co-equal with the teaching of Christian morality and the "basic academic skills." Moore and her fellow crusaders were the emerging Moral Majority's educational vanguard. They have been exerting an influence on social studies curricula ever since. This curricula has reframed the nature of the educational conversation about the teaching of history, geography, government, and in relation to the concerns of this chapter—economics.

NAME CHANGES, IDEOLOGICAL CHANGES: FROM ECONOMICS TO THE FREE ENTERPRISE SYSTEM

Beginning in the years immediately following the Kanawha County textbook controversy and picking up steam with the founding in the late 1970s of the Moral Majority and in 1980 with the election of Ronald Reagan, conservative forces in various communities worked to change the name and objectives of the teaching of economics at the secondary level. The old half-year "economics" class quickly morphed into a class entitled, "the free enterprise system." Obviously, there is nothing wrong with a detailed study of the American economic system. Something is problematic, however, when the courses are offered in an uncritical, indoctrinating manner. Alice Moore observed that one of the goals of the John Dewey-oriented educational establishment has been to make students open-minded on moral, religious, political, and economic matters. In the eyes of Moore and her followers, this open-mindedness was described as subversion: "Anti-American, anti-Christian, depressing, and negative humanism." Free enterprise courses meet Moore's and the Christian Right's goals, in that they carefully avoid the cultivation of analytical activities involving the analysis of competing points of view.

The free enterprise economics courses I examined were designed for a totalitarian school system, since they emphasized the acquisition of predetermined content, taught in a teacher-centered classroom. Social studies goals of critical thinking and problem solving were not important in the classroom where economic "truths" were passed along, without analysis, for student memorization. Rarely were students encouraged to develop skills that helped them distinguish between statements that were factual reports or value judgments. This antidemocratic economics discouraged questions concerning the person or organization responsible for the material presented. Evaluation of the purpose of information was not important. Little attention was given to methods of gathering or organizing data. The manner in which the student acquired knowledge, an important concern of a critical social studies, was irrelevant in most free enterprise classrooms. As a part of the larger right-wing reeducation project, the free enterprise curriculum played an important ideological role in shaping the American consciousness.

In the classrooms I observed, indoctrination of the students into an unquestioned belief in the virtues of the free enterprise system was the central goal. "I believe in indoctrinating our children," Alice Moore proclaimed. Social studies exists to create patriotism, she told me in an interview, and that means teaching respect for free enterprise economics. "If that means indoctrination, then so be it." During a high school social studies teacher-community conference where I served as a consultant, one principal told an agreeable group of community leaders, i.e. successful business people, about the virtues of his school's new free enterprise economics classes. The classes, he said, teach our young people that free enterprise economics is the best economic system in the world and engender a respectful attitude toward our community's business people. When a contumacious college social studies professor—me—raised the point that such a course might fall into the category of indoctrination, the principal, much to the delight of his audience, contended that, when it came to economics, he saw "nothing wrong with a little indoctrination." During my own secondary social studies teaching experience, I encountered great difficulty structuring open inquiry lessons in economics after students emerged from the indoctrination of free enterprise classes. Each year, during my unit on socialism, I found that critical analysis was rendered virtually impossible by students who had been taught to equate a controlled economic system with everything from atheism to old-fashioned evil. Certainly, my teaching of the topic brought me under the suspicion of being an agent of the great Communist conspiracy.

VOX ELIGERE, VOX DEI: CERTIFYING POWER

The articulate opinions of the economically advantaged are often taught as truth in the high school free enterprise classroom. The voice of the advantaged, regularly given access to television, radio, and the press, is much louder than the words of the economically disadvantaged, who, especially in these days of the free market, are generally ignored. As I studied the free enterprise classes, I wanted to know who furnished the expensive curriculum materials I observed. Certainly, it was not the welfare mothers of the South Bronx. The materials were furnished by large corporations and by local businesses. It is the successful local business leader who serves as the guest speaker in the free enterprise class, not the unsuccessful businessperson or spokesperson for the local janitors' union. During my days as a secondary teacher, I listened patiently to many local entrepreneurs speak to large groups of social studies students. At their mildest, the community-resources people extolled the virtues of positive thinking and pointed to the sure success awaiting those willing to work. The most virulent condemned the welfare loafers living in taxpayer-provided opulence with their Cadillacs, color TVs, and liquor. Not once was a community person with an alternative viewpoint invited, nor was there ever a presentation that offered an economic debate between proponents of diverse economic positions. Even while I taught on an Indian reservation in the poorest county in the U.S., I never witnessed a free enterprise program in which proponents of different economic viewpoints participated. It is a testimony to the power of the voice of economic advantage that on a reservation with 75% unemployment, young American Indian high school students emerge from free enterprise economics classes filled with free market theory and ready to accept an elimination of government job training programs as the only path to a sound economy.

Regardless of whether I observed the free enterprise classes in the North, South, East, or West or in the inner city, suburbs, or backwoods, free enterprise economics taught that people-oriented services of governments, such as public education, aid to the cities, unemployment benefits, health care, housing programs, or environmental and safety regulations, are devoid of merit and serve only to stifle the national economic machine. I watched high school economics teachers in the free enterprise class repeatedly transmit such theory as fact. The following economic myths were often overtly included or were implicit in the classes. Not once did I hear any of them qualified or challenged. One can discern in the myths the intersection of free enterprise theory with a positivist epistemology.

1. UNRESTRAINED ECONOMIC GROWTH IS AN UNMITIGATED BLESSING. Embedded within this myth is the Western Cartesian idea of progress, which, in its single-mindedness, fails to appreciate the disastrous consequences it produces. Pollution, industrial waste, dangerous radiation, and a cancer epidemic constitute only a few of the problems created by unrestrained economic growth.

2. THE FREE MARKET IS THE BEST MODEL FOR ORGANIZING SOCIAL LIFE. This myth contends that the operation of the free market involves a group of self-directed individuals selecting from a wide range of options those things they most want. It is this situation that represents the modernist utopia of personal freedom. The point missed, of course, is that the freedom assumed in the model does not exist in reality. Individuals are constantly constrained by the oppression resulting from power asymmetries of various sorts.

3. ALL OF THE IMPORTANT SOCIAL VALUES SHAPED BY THE FREE MARKET ARE MEASURABLE AND QUANTIFIABLE. Economic growth expressed in terms of GNP or leading market indicators becomes the ultimate measure of social well-being.

4. POLITICAL AND ECONOMIC DECISIONS ARE MADE ONLY IN RATIONAL AND DISPASSIONATE WAYS. In the context created by this myth, emotion becomes a manifestation of weakness and rationality a sign of strength. Using the critique of modernist positivism, we can understand that the definition of "rational" is inscribed with power and

political self-interest, so that those who dominate can define their position as rational and that of those who oppose them as irrational. By following the "objective" dictates of the free market, for example, economists, corporate leaders, and political functionaries are assumed to make rational, disinterested, scientific decisions about governance. The fact that a wide range of subjective assumptions about the economic, social, and political cosmos are implicit in such scientific rationality is never mentioned.

5. SCIENCE AND TECHNOLOGY LAY THE FOUNDATION FOR THE GOOD LIFE. Examining this type of economics education, one would never know about the intense debates surrounding science and technology and their social impact. The continuing dominance of science and technology in the pursuit of a positivist utopia is simply not problematized in free enterprise economics classes. The critique of scientific modernism and the technocratic mind-set is not a part of the conversation.

6. BIOLOGY AND PSYCHOLOGY, IN PARTICULAR, PROVIDE A VERIFIABLE PICTURE OF HUMAN BEINGS THAT CAN BE USED TO PROVIDE ORDER AND PROMOTE THE GOOD SOCIETY. One of the great ironies of modernity is that the same science that promised human emancipation and freedom has been deployed for purposes of control and manipulation. Biology and psychology are used to justify forms of rationality that undermine human freedom in a variety of economic organizations.

JESUS WAS AN ADVOCATE OF FREE MARKET CAPITALISM: DEVELOPING GOD'S ECONOMICS

A social studies student sitting through these free enterprise classes would rarely hear of the existence of poor people in our society. It is heresy in these golden days of the free market to intimate that there may be times when the interests of rich people and poor people are in opposition. Teaching about different economic systems is a mere guise, Alice Moore and her allies contend, of generating class hatred. Studies of poverty, she implies, are usually undertaken to promote anti-American socialism. Jerry Falwell sees direct correlation between his fundamentalist Christianity, free enterprise economics, and the socialistic influences that operate in the schools. In his opinion, laissez-faire economics is clearly outlined in the *Book of Proverbs*. In his Liberty Baptist College (now Liberty University) in Lynchburg, Virginia, free enterprise economics is taught with a zealous vengeance. A student of social studies education, Frances Fitzgerald (1981), described her observation of a college social studies class where students asked, laughingly, if there were really ever people who believed in socialism. The professor answered, "Fourier, Blanqui," and then, on the board, wrote, "Thesis, antithesis, synthesis." He later added, in response to a student who asked who these people were, that they represented the dictatorship of the proletariat. FitzGerald's observation of the social studies classes at Liberty Baptist College sounds hauntingly familiar to my observations of free enterprise high school classes around the country:

> At the Liberty Baptist School, students are protected both from information and from most logical processes. There is no formal ban on logic, but since analytical reasoning might lead to skepticism . . . it is simply not encouraged except in disciplines like engineering, where it could be expected to yield a single correct answer. . . . In anything resembling human affairs, the intellectual discipline consists of moving word-sticks and word facts from one pile to another with the minimum coefficient of friction. (p. 17)

The Christian Liberty Academy in Prospect, Illinois, was founded in part to oppose the creeping socialism of the public school curriculum. Founder Paul Lindstrom, an advocate of the views of the Moral Right, demands that his students learn strict morality and free enterprise economics from kindergarten to the twelfth grade. In their high school economics classes, students are subjected to lessons advocating a return to the gold standard—on biblical authority. The teachers quote Isaiah 1:22 to support their case. "Thy silver has become dross, thy wine mixed with water."

Obviously, most neoclassical economic theorists do not condone the bizarre Christo-economics of the fundamentalist colleges or the most simplistic high school free enterprise classes. Still, both sophisticated and simplistic advocates grant little attention to the problems of the economically disadvantaged. The high school economics student is rarely exposed to the idea that the free market attack on public services can be viewed as an assault on the living standard of the poor. Students are not only shielded from a diversity of economic opinion but are denied any background in the economic arguments of the past. Filled with free market axioms, students in these new economics classes are not encouraged to ask: How did we get here? As Neil Postman (1979, 1995) has contended, nothing should be introduced to students before the teacher is prepared to grant the student some historical perspective. Without this foundation, the classroom activity becomes degraded into a shallow study of a topic that really does not qualify as a critical analysis because no one knows what went on before. As a result, little critical thinking takes place, for students have little opportunity to trace the development of ideas and assess the impact of specific events on that development.

Corporate Outlets:
Economics in the Key of Management

Since American business often sponsors the preparation of curriculum guides for the free enterprise class, the materials rarely project the corporations in an unfavorable light. In the simplistic economic world presented by the curriculum guides, the free market exists and must be protected from encroachment from various enemies. Seldom is heard a dissenting view from the business-of-America-is-business perspective of the teacher guides. Perish the argument that the greatest historical force against the free market is the postmodern corporation. The contemporary conglomerate, the dissenting argument goes, has great price-setting discretion. Through advertising and its control of information, it has gained the power to influence the taste and ideology of consumers. Corporations in the contemporary era can organize their supplies of raw materials. In these ways, they destroy the freedom of the market—a task corporations feel they must accomplish given the magnitude of their investment. This is a viewpoint not found in the curriculum guides and, in the twenty-first century, seldom heard in most high school economics classrooms.

High school economics courses must examine economics problems critically, asking hard, challenging questions instead of spouting corporate clichés. Teachers must avoid the flagrant ideological oversimplifications of the business-oriented, free enterprise curriculum guides. Contrary to the pronouncements of the teachers' guides, Mobil Oil and the locally owned hardware store are not governed by identical economic forces. Critical democratic high school economics teachers must recruit resource people from diverse economic sectors. The problems stemming from the bias of the modern free enterprise classroom will not be addressed by simplistic presentation of a dissenting viewpoint. But given the dominance of indoctrination-oriented economics classes, it is important for social studies teachers and students to understand that there are competing viewpoints. A short critical historicization of the economic reeducation of Americans is in order.

CONTEXTUALIZING THE ECONOMIC CHANGES OF THE LAST QUARTER OF THE TWENTIETH CENTURY

Fordist Foundations

The economic foundations of twentieth-century life were established in its second decade, when Henry Ford introduced his five-dollar, eight-hour day at his automobile assembly line in Dearborn, Michigan. Drawing on the rationalism of modernism, Fordist production procedures became the highest expression of modernism and the lowest expression of worker dignity. Ford's four production principles were: 1) the standardization of products; 2) the development of special-purpose machinery to be used in the construction of each separate model; 3) the fragmentation of tasks into their component parts, and task assignments developed around the time-motion principles proposed by Frederick W. Taylor; and 4) the replacment of static model assembly by the flow line, in that, instead of workers working around the static product, the product (the car) flowed past the workers on a flow line. Ford, of course, was not the originator of mass production and assembly lines. There are examples of such methods in use as early as the eighteenth century, but Ford was the first to bring the forms of modern industrial organization together with higher wages for workers (Harvey, 1989; Murray, 1992).

What made Ford's project unique was the totality of his scheme. Ford wanted to create a new type of worker and *human*—not just the human as efficient worker but also the human as efficient consumer. *Homo economicus/consumerus* would live, work, and consume in a new society, a modern, rationalized world. Writing from one of Mussolini's prisons, Antonio Gramsci recognized Fordism as a new "mode of living and thinking and feeling life" (Harvey, 1989, p. 126). So total was Ford's system that, in 1916, concerned that workers would not learn how to consume properly, Ford sent a division of social workers into the homes of his workers to teach them morality, proper family life, and the characteristics of "rational shopping." Fordism became synonymous with scientific forms of regulation associated with modernism (Grossberg, 1992).

Thus, Fordism became not only a mode of economic production but also a means of social and political regulation of the American population. In other words, Fordism represented a grand compromise: Though labor maintained some say in collective bargaining, social security benefits, and the minimum wage, it held on to these rights in return for acceptance of Fordist production strategies and corporate schemes to boost productivity and work discipline. The grand compromise was grounded on the faith that, if wage increases were linked to increased productivity, profits were sure to increase. Business and labor were partners in a common economic struggle. Government would serve as a bow-tied referee to protect, in theory, each institution from the excessive power and the low blows of the other.

It is not hard to see how schools were involved in the grand compromise. The spirit of the Fordist view of humans as efficient workers and efficient consumers is quite apparent in the history of twentieth-century American education. Only three years after the opening of Ford's Dearborn, Michigan plant in 1914, David Snedden and Charles Prosser (education's efficiency proponents) helped Congress pass the Smith-Hughes Vocational Education Act—the highest expression of modernist educational efficiency or educational Fordism. The study of teaching and teacher education after 1914 reflects this Fordist spirit. Students and lessons were reduced to standardized units, teacher methodology became a special-purpose technology designed to efficiently facilitate the education production process, knowledge was fragmented into discrete parts, learning was reduced to a technical problem, and students flowed by the teacher in an assembly line sort of process, with teachers dispensing knowledge here and measuring it there, making sure each child met the "quality standards" dictated by the "production managers" in developmental psychology. This theory of economic production and the view of human beings it promoted had profound consequences for a variety of American institutions.

Crumbling Fordist Foundations

As the Fordist compromise began to break down, observers saw not simply an economic decline but a decline of a way of life as well. Fordism, as the economic expression of modernism carried the torch of Western civilization, since it reflected the modernist faith in progress, technological development, and rationality. These very elements, and the arrangements of the Fordist economy based on them, undermined the supremacy of the American economy. The decline of Fordism signaled a decline in the post-Enlightenment faith in rationality as a panacea. As American products became shoddier and shoddier, as profits from planned obsolescence rose, and as students emerged from schools seeming to understand less and less about the world, the evidence of decline mounted (Borgmann, 1992; Bellah et al., 1991).

As the recession of 1973 destroyed the stable environment for corporate profits established by Fordism, the transition to a new regime of production and mode of social regulation began. Many economists locate the beginnings of the end of Fordism in the mid-1960s, with the rise of the Western European and Japanese economies, the displacement of American workers as a result of the success of Fordist rationalization and automation strategies, the decline in corporate productivity and profitability, and the beginning of an inflationary trend. Fordism's ability to contain the contradictions of capitalism weakened during this period, as the inflexibility of American economic arrangements became more apparent. In long-term, large-scale, fixed-capital investments in systems of mass production, inflexibility undermined attempts to adjust to new designs necessary in changing consumer markets.

In labor markets and contracts, inflexibility subverted attempts to reform workplaces with new forms of worker deployment. As Social Security, pension rights, and other entitlements expanded, government revenue collection was thwarted by a stagnant economy. The only avenue of flexibility led to a change in monetary policy that involved printing money at an accelerated rate to keep the economy stable. Thus began the inflationary spiral that ended the postwar boom. All of these specific rigidities were fastened to a configuration of political power that united big labor, big capital, and big government in the embrace of a set of narrow vested interests that undermined the productive capacity of the national economy (Harvey, 1989).

As the oil crisis exacerbated the serious recession of 1973, the ability of American capitalism to extend the consumerist dream to a citizenry with sky-high aspirations was thwarted. No longer did even middle-class Americans believe that their economic lives were destined to improve. The 1970s and 1980s witnessed a series of attempts at economic restructuring in an effort to respond to the collapse of Fordism. These restructuring efforts represented the first manifestations of an emerging economic paradigm shift. Even with the evidence of an economic crisis, the American middle class did not perceive any dramatic economic change until the 1980s. Indeed, even in the mid-1980s, a majority of Americans saw the changes as a moral breakdown and loss of American economic, political, and military hegemony in the world. The "American decline" was framed as a question of will that could be addressed by a renewal of nationalism and military preparedness.

This conservative response to the decline set the tone for policy making on a variety of fronts—political, military, educational, and economic. Committed to economic policy with faith in the wisdom of the market, the conservatives attacked the liberal Fordist compromise, with its embrace of the welfare state. As they attempted to dismantle the welfare state's safety net for the disadvantaged, conservatives in the 1970s, 1980s, and 1990s redefined freedom in economic terms. Freedom, they argued, implies the right to compete and fail, more an entrepreneurial liberty than a civil liberty. With the conservatives in power, the state abandoned its Fordist role as the Great Mediator of competing interest groups and unabashedly embraced corporate interests and need for profits. At the same time, conservatives were winning their political victories, many businesses were desperately seeking to escape the confines of Fordist inflexibility in the workplace. This work would lay the foundation for post-Fordism.

The Dawning of Post-Fordism

Moving from assembly line production to flexible accumulation, post-Fordist business and industry began to rethink their methods of economic production and social and political regulation. Increasing their rates of innovation, centralizing ownership, and advancing the autonomy of banks and financial agencies, the flexible specialists of the new economy of banks and financial agencies have changed the face of consumption. Business and industry in this new paradigm are shaped to respond to markets rather than regulate them. Innovative managers speak of their companies as a cadre of learners who monitor the market, research patterns of taste, and dissect the nature of style. Management builds economic SWAT teams rather than a bulky police force, since they think of economies of scope rather than economies of scale. Production is based on limited runs, reducing costly reliance on large inventories. Such a strategy requires high-tech, flexible machinery and workers as learners who change duties with each alteration in consumer demand. Business time is permanently altered, since the period between design, manufacture, and sales is contracted. The media-saturated hyperreality of the twenty-first century demands the hyperadaptability of procedure (Harvey, 1989; Lather, 1991; Grossberg, 1995; Block, 1990). This emerging post-Fordist regime of economic production is one dimension of a larger postmodern condition of hyperreality.

Hegemony in Post-Fordism

In this post-Fordist era of dynamic flexibility of the workplace, or, as Doug Kellner (1991) puts it, "techno-capitalism," traditional forms of industrial and corporate power are magnified. Faced by increasing pressure to compete internationally, corporate leaders seek new ways to maximize profits, including organizational and technological change to sophisticated procedures for labor control. Indeed, the post-Fordist discourse of America's international economic competition constructs a justification for manipulation and the winning of hegemonic consent of students and workers. If America is not to be economically surpassed by the developing economies of disciplined and authoritarian Asia, the justification goes, we must cultivate more social obedience and commonness of purpose and less democracy and liberty.

Uncritical social education becomes one more aspect of the attempt to win the consent of workers in accepting their tenuous role in the post-Fordist global economy of the New World Order. Academic and vocational education, workplace training, the mobilization of worker affect, involving, at least with men, the cultivation of a masculine work ethic— macho identification with the image of the "hard workin' man," company loyalty, and work as a patriotic act—all combine to produce worker cooperation with corporate interest. These forms of regulation of students and laborers, when supplemented by the pronouncements of mass media, religious fundamentalism, and various branches of government, make for powerful forms of worker hegemony (Simon, Dippo, & Schenke, 1991).

The post-Fordist shaping of a consenting student and worker identity, of course, can be found in many venues. In a feminine context, the work of Linda Valli (1988) has been helpful in uncovering the nature of the regulation of young women students and workers in business education experiences. The students she observed were being trained for clerical jobs in offices and, in the process, were learning about the technology of the contemporary office and its relation to the production of goods and services. Because office education students are almost always young women, Valli found significant information related to identity pro-duction vis-à-vis gender relations. Students were convinced that they already possessed the simplistic abilities the office needed, as no class time was used to improve office-related skills. The office was presented as a naturally low-skill workplace that is impervious to change. Working-class women, the course implied, must simply adjust their lives to these necessary realities, for contestation and resistance would be senseless and futile. Valli concludes that such social educational experience con-tributes to the extension of these young women's identity as subordinate and dependent individuals.

Valli's girls were being conditioned to passivity—an act with pro-found but hidden social and political implications. Rewarded for uncrit-ical acceptance of the unjust arrangements of the status quo, the students came to realize that critical thought and analysis have no place in work education. "Thinking" in Valli's office education program is compensat-ed for the degree to which it reflects the ideology of mainstream courtesy, and marked by a conception of resistance as distasteful and unladylike. Thus, a form of politically passive conformity is cultivated that views good work education students and teachers as obedient to externally imposed ways of thinking and rules that demand the construction of "safe" female identities. Unless they are able to develop oppositional readings to the patriarchal ideology of the office education program or the hidden curriculum of the workplace (which some of the young women are able to do), these students will not be the type of employees who challenge the nature of corporate control. Critical democratic social studies educators have an obligation to alert such students to the harm such a social education can do to them.

Contrary to the celebratory pronouncements of prophets of technoc-racy that a better day is a comin' in a technocapitalist, post-Fordist econ-omy, the status of workers is more precarious than ever. The dawn of the post-Fordist age has been marked by a blatant redistribution of wealth, offensives against labor unions, caps on the minimum wage, adoption of exploitative labor practices, such as the utilization of part-time and third world labor (usually women and minorities), reestablishment of patriar-chal sweatshops and domestic piecework, and extensive use of subcon-tracting. Such policies have undermined the stability of the middle class because an ever-increasing percentage of new jobs are low-wage. A grow-ing number of people are marginal to the workforce, inasmuch as they accept contingent employment in jobs with few benefits and no assurance of security. As post-Fordist changes have moved workers from industrial and agricultural jobs to service and information employment, many men and women have watched their middle-class status disappear. Workers with jobs in the industrial sector have been displaced by new technologies, computerization, and automation. These "deindustrialization" strategies affected middle-level and semiskilled jobs ($9–$12-an-hour jobs, in particular), resulting in further economic bipolarization (Grossberg, 1992; Rumberger, 1984; Kellner, 1991).

Despite these realities, most of the public and economics education conversation about post-Fordist changes is couched in very positive terms. Skill upgrading of work is the order of the day, many economists and educators write. Although skill upgrading is no doubt occurring in some industries, the total economic picture cannot be framed so positively, given the widening disparity of wealth and opportunity. School leaders call for an education to prepare future workers for the high-tech workplace, but research reveals that only a small core of workers will need such skills. Indeed, the way present workplaces are arranged in America, only about one of ten positions has been arranged to require high-skill workers. Deskilling is still the order of the day (Kincheloe, 1999).

Hard Times for the Poor

The economic changes that occurred with the breakdown of Fordism and the advent of post-Fordism in the early 1970s were devastating for some groups but exerted virtually no impact on others. For example, the per capita income of families under age 30 dropped 27 percent between 1973 and 1986—the same decline experienced by the same demographic group between 1929 and 1932 in the Great Depression. During the 1973–1986 period, older, more affluent families actually experienced an increase in income. Because the drop occurred gradually over a thirteen-year period and affected individuals with less power and media access, it was hidden from the public consciousness.

After 1973, the worldwide economic changes, coupled with the growing power of the conservatives, began to undermine government spending on the needs of the public sector. As revenues fell, taxes were lowered, thus producing a unique situation in contemporary industrialized societies: private affluence and public squalor. America's urban communities suffered a decrease in funding that produced environmental negligence, untidy and unsafe parks, dangerous playgrounds, deteriorated public housing, underfunded public transportation, and inadequate social services. Europeans were shocked by the absence of publicly funded planning strategies to shape urban growth and revitalize inner cities in the U.S. Poor individuals (especially the young poor) grew poorer and their numbers swelled because of this economic decline, with its accompanying inflation and the right-wing undermining of tax revenues from the corporations and the wealthy. In human terms, this meant job disruption, marital stress, and family disintegration, resulting in the growth of single-parent families.

After 1973, America changed dramatically. The most disturbing aspect of that change involved the radical redistribution of wealth in American society. By the middle of the 1980s, the chasm between the rich and the poor expanded to a point unseen for almost 50 years. Income for the poorest 20% of the nation dropped 5.2%; at the same time, the wealthiest 20% recorded take-home pay increases of 32.5%. The income of the richest 1% of Americans increased 87 percent! In 1950, U.S. corporations paid 26% of all local, state, and federal taxes. By 1990, they were paying only 8%. If the corporate tax rate had remained steady over those 40 years between 1950 and 1990, then the local, state, and federal governments would have received more than an extra $13 trillion! What is shocking about these figures and the disparity they represent is not that the conservatives accomplished their mission so quickly; the jolting reality is that a majority of middle-class and low-income Americans accepted it without dissent. The acceptance of this reshuffling of the economic deck, this cardshark New Deal, may constitute one of the greatest hegemonic acts, one of the most successful feats of social education ever perpetrated (Coontz, 1992; Bellah et al., 1991; Grossberg, 1992). The free enterprise economics courses were simply the miniscule tip of a gigantic right-wing reeducation iceberg.

Because of "selective attention" to the economic decline, middle-class Americans did not perceive the existence of an economic crisis until the 1992 elections, and, even then, they were confused about its consequences and its causes. Facilitated by an increasing conservative influence on the production of public knowledge, many Americans (especially voting Americans) came to conceptualize the economic problems as a loss of American military, political, and economic leadership in the world (Grossberg, 1992). Caused by the decline of traditional values, this economic regression was seen more as a problem of national "man-

hood" and international domination than as a problem of economic justice and even economic survival.

Fanned by the embarrassment of the oil embargo in 1973 and the
Iranian hostage crisis in 1979–1981, many Americans latched on to
Ronald Reagan's nostalgic portrait of the way America used to be and
should be once again. The politics of nostalgia, with its return to *Little
House on the Prairie* and *Happy Days* images, evoked emotional responses
from Americans who believed the nation was unjustly under siege. What
the hell did we do to deserve the Iranian hostage crisis? they asked,
unaware and uninformed by the mainstream media of U.S. complicity in
the overthrow of democratic government in Iran. The key themes—
going back to the basics and an assertive militaristic foreign policy—
pushed by Reagan, George Bush, and Dan Quayle were supported by
many Americans and blessed by a lapdog, uncritical media.

The new conservatives were extremely successful in breaking up the
old New Deal political economic coalition, of farmers, union members,
and urban ethnic voters. After the Fordist prosperity of the 1950s and
1960s, the members of the coalition no longer identified with being the
allies of the dispossessed. By the 1970s, they were persuaded to align their
interests with the affluent. By the 1980s and 1990s, the children of the
old coalition members, spurred by right-wing, free market glorifications
of greed and individualism, had become unwilling to empathize with the
sorry predicament of the poor. As the rich grew richer and the children's
finances continued to deteriorate, their parent's picture of the truly needy
faded into images of welfare loafers and lowlife cheats. The right-wing
amoebas had absorbed another group that should have been concerned
with the growing disparity of wealth. By the mid-1980s, however, the
existence of economic and political inequality raised few eyebrows. The
language of "traditional values" was being used to condemn those who
fell outside the mainstream (e.g., the non-White poor, advocates of
women's rights, gays and lesbians, and so on). The New Right was firmly in power, and social and economic policy was conceived under a new
set of free market-based rules. The victory of the free market comforted
those on the conservative side of the postmodern divide.

Those rules typically involved the neoclassical economic theory and
its allegiance to the freedom of the market promoted as God's economics
by Alice Moore and subsequent Moral Right proponents. Despite its
moral protestations neoclassicism holds that anything under free market
conditions that turns a profit is permissible and that state regulation is

the bugaboo of economic progress. Specifically, the right-wing economic rules involved the following: 1) the privatization of governmental service agencies; 2) the reallocation of wealth from the poor to the rich; and 3) the establishment of a free market philosophy that promotes individualism, self-help, human resource management, and consumerism, in lieu of ethical values in the public sphere. The game *Monopoly* emerged as a prototype for public life as market maximizers became paragons of success. Economics assumed the status of a total science that explained all human questions, all mysteries of life.

One interesting exception to the belief in the unfettered market has involved the realm of the "defense" economy or "Pentagon socialism." Despite protestations of the virtues of privatization and free markets, right-wing leaders have advocated and voted for battleships and weapons systems that even military leaders do not want—all for the purpose of maintaining jobs and economic health in local economies. Market politics, despite contradictions, and the politics of nostalgia have produced a virtual revolution in American ways of seeing the world: an economic reeducation. Although Bill Clinton's victories in 1992 and 1996 exposed some of the frayed edges of the conservative movement, Clinton's campaigns and presidency illustrated a tendency not to counter right-wing ideologies but to appropriate them. The conservative deployment of the decline of family values as a smokescreen to block public view of the poverty caused by neoclassical economics has yet to be challenged by liberal politicians and educators.

BALANCING THE ECONOMICS CURRICULUM IN THE SOCIAL STUDIES

Many social analysts, myself included, find it amazing how infrequently students are exposed to discourses critical of free market economics. In the eyes of many students and other Americans the economic debate is over: The market won. Why are we even discussing this? The disparity of wealth that exists in the first decade of the twenty-first century within the U.S. and around the world demands the attention of economics/social studies educators. These conditions demand an economic vision, a way of conceptualizing the economy that will bring hope to the lives of poor Americans and poor people around the planet. The two dominant economic visions of the last century are not sufficient. Marxist-Leninist socialism has been a tragic failure; but (and this makes Americans very uncomfortable) multinational corporate capitalism has also manifested fundamental flaws. In significantly different ways, the power elites that direct these systems escape the control of citizens. Indeed, the poisonous effect of these structures on the natural and the social world undermines their viability as economic and social systems in the twenty-first century (Wirth, 1983; Gabbard, 2000).

The get-it-while-you-can ethic of laissez-faire capitalism is too insensitive for the needs of a fragile democracy, the mental health of individuals, economic justice, and an overcrowded planet. Such an economic system transmits its values to all aspects of the society, undermining our ability to make meaning, to make sense of our lives, and to construct a humane vision for our future. A critical democratic social studies asserts there has to be an alternative to doctrinaire state socialism and unbridled free enterprise. There have to be choices other than the Leninist bureaucratic nightmare and the hyperindividualist, socially irresponsible, market capitalism now in ascendancy. Critical democratic social studies educators can provide balance to both the in-school and out-of-school social/economic curriculum by simply questioning the possibility of a better way.

In their questioning of the common economic wisdom of the contemporary era, critical democratic social studies teachers point out that neoclassical economics has gradually subverted many traditional concerns. Undermining the contributions by many religious traditions, social activists, and civic organizations to a "moral" language, neoclassical economics provides a moral code for modernists: self-interest. In this cult of the free market, economists maintain that economic analysis can be deployed not only to determine a strategy, such as whether to increase overhead costs for the 2004 fiscal year, but also in all types of decision-making situations.

Thus, the message is proclaimed that marriage is less about love than about a matter of supply and demand within the market for spouses. Suicide occurs when people find their "total lifetime utility" falling to zero. In other words, from this perspective, all human behavior can be perceived from an economic vantage point, no matter how related it may be to altruism, emotion, love, or compassion (Bellah et al., 1991). Many political and educational leaders, who find their philosophical roots in this neoclassical tradition, have attempted to analyze schooling as merely a function of the laws of the marketplace. Attempting to privatize schools in line with their market philosophy, such leaders undermine the human dimensions of the educational act while diminishing the importance of democracy in the public space (Giroux, 1993).

Assuming that individuals always act rationally to maximize their self-interest, the neoclassicists present a model of a self-regulating market that harmonizes the demands of production, labor, and capital. Supply and demand will regulate prices so that all human and material resources are used in an efficient manner. The market is all-knowing, neoclassical economists claim, and, as a result, possesses the ability to adjust to dramatic changes. For example, technological innovation automates a process of production to the point that 80 percent of the workers are laid off. Always working to restore equilibrium, the market will provide a solution, according to the theorists.

As the cost (potential wages) of the displaced labor declines and the profits of the automated industry increase, a situation is created where an enterprising entrepreneur will rehire the unemployed workers in a firm producing a different product. But what is wrong with this picture? Unfortunately, this simple neoclassical model works best when the skill levels of workers are low. If workplaces possessed high-skill jobs, it would be difficult for laborers to quickly adjust to disruptions. When an industry declines and loses positions, neoclassicists assume that displaced workers will be able to find work quickly because there are so few job-specific skills that would keep, say, sales clerks from adapting to computer jobs (Block, 1990).

Like other modernist Cartesian expressions, neoclassical economics possesses a tendency for decontextualization. When analyzing economic issues, neoclassicists argue that such topics can be separated from the spheres of politics and culture. Just as an educational psychologist who is measuring IQ ignores the context in which a student was raised, neoclassical economists deal only with variables that are internal to the economy. As economics is stripped from its social and political context, it is also extracted from a moral context (Nooteboom, 1991). The prevailing rhetoric of economic battle—the appeal to win the economic war with the other nations of the planet—reveals the emptiness of the neoclassical conversation. Such advocates seem unable to grasp the concept that economic thinking might want to address the provision of joint sustainable prosperity for human beings and that the production of winners and losers seems to miss the point (Chesneaux, 1992; O'Sullivan, 1999). When a local government in an isolated rural area chooses to keep the only grocery store in the district open despite its persistent unprofitability, it has, according to the high priests of neoclassicism, broken the Intergalactic Federation's Prime Directive: "Thou Shalt Not Interfere with the Free Function of the Market." Let the fact that local residents would either have to starve or move be damned. Hunger or cultural disruption are not *economic* issues, after all, free marketers proclaim.

Some advocates of neoclassical economics take their case even further, contending that an unhindered market in babies would resolve troubles concerning unwanted pregnancies, teenage mothers, and surrogate mothers. If women could sell their babies on the open market and baby prices were publicized in the same manner that winter wheat futures were quoted, the free market would quickly solve the problem. Americans always seem shocked when the French and other foreigners refer to our economic system as *le capitalism sauvage*, or "savage capitalism" (Bellah et al., 1991, p. 91). Unfortunately, in many social studies classes, teachers and students cannot speak these words; they are taboo. Such silent censorship cannot continue in a democratic society that supposedly values freedom of speech and discussion of issues. We must demand the right to examine the problems that plague our economic system and the resulting effects on poor people's lives.

Social studies educators must demand the right to discuss and debate who benefits from these neoclassical forms of unregulated capitalism. Critics of the free market argue that, instead of offering opportunity for all, they provide an ideological curtain that hides the free market's tendency to bestow its greatest benefits on those already in possession of wealth and power (Richmond, 1986). Free market capitalism creates a climate that justifies the privileged few's view of reality. Market forces and competition are presented in this construction of the world as cherubs and angels who joyously but silently work to create a harmony between supply and demand, wages and prices, and goods and services. The free market never worked this way, even in the nineteenth century. It certainly does not work this way in the twenty-first century, with multinational corporations powerful enough to sway governments and control markets, government obsession with military spending and the maintenance of the defense sector of the economy, and the formation of economic communities and oil cartels. No local economy is free from larger influences that undermine free trade and equal competition. The neoclassical market model does not account for these intervening factors. Despite all appearances to the contrary, neoclassicists operate in a simple universe: a fantasyland that exists only at Disney World.

A critical democratic social studies is vitally concerned with these issues, these questions of the social, political, cultural, and moral dimensions of economics. In this context, the field of economic sociology is especially important for our purposes as social studies educators. Economic sociology refuses to allow proponents of neoclassicism to get by with their socially decontextualized portrait of economics. Arguing that economic activity is continuously shaped by cultural factors, these scholars provide example after example of the influence of noneconomic background factors in economic affairs. The type of work deemed appropriate for different social groups, for instance, is not simply an economic issue. Because of particular social assumptions, Black men in the early twentieth century worked as train porters. The free market did not dictate such a reality. Women were assigned to low-status clerical jobs near the end of the nineteenth century, replacing men whose status as clerks had been quite high. Again, the market did not dictate this development. How do individuals weigh the value of more money versus more leisure? What factors determine the decision of a graduate student to pursue or not pursue a doctorate instead of stopping with a master's degree? Obviously, economic factors are not the only variables at work in these situations (Block, 1990).

The folly of reductionist economic explanations of daily affairs is obvious. A man wants to buy a book on the relationship between education and the economy at a corporate-owned chain bookstore. He picks up a copy of Richard Brosio's *The Radical Democratic Critique of Capitalist Education* for $39.95. A salesman notices his choice and says, "Why Brosio for $40? We have a special on books on economics and education." The buyer responds, "But I wanted a book that questions everyday assumptions about economics and schooling." The salesman picks up a new edition of neoclassicist Milton Freidman's *Free to Choose*. "But, sir, this one is our Red, White, and Blue Light special. It's a hot value at only $9.99. You'll save $30. Come, look at our other economics and education volumes. They're conveniently arranged by cost." Another customer interrupts the salesman: "I'd like a book on postmodern architecture in the $11 range." Economic considerations do not dictate all decisions concerning consumption.

This facetious example illustrates the larger point: Critical democratic social studies educators cannot ignore the social and moral context of economic affairs. This larger point becomes especially serious when we find that neoclassicists view labor markets just like any other commodity market. The fact that the labor market is occupied by living beings with feelings and emotional concerns is irrelevant. Such human factors are quickly dismissed in the neoclassicist mind-set because it is not people themselves who are an "input" in the process of production but one of their qualities. What matters about human beings in the free market is not their sacred spirit, but their capacity to do work. The most basic concern of critical democratic social studies educators, our students, are stripped of their humanity and reduced to merely another factor in the production process (Block, 1990).

"IT'S A GREAT TIME TO LIVE IN AMERICA": THE ERASURE OF THE ECONOMICALLY DISPOSSESSED

By the turn of the new century, the free market, and cheap labor economic policies pushed by corporate leaders were producing record profits and unprecedented salary increases for upper management. Of course, a painfully small percentage of this money made its way into the hands of low-paid workers and poor people in general. Numerous corporations incorporated superlative celebrations of their good times into their advertisements, attempting to convince people that this was the best of times. "Is this a great time or what?" companies reminded Americans, ignoring issues of worker unemployment, underemployment, and stress derived from living with a precarious job and an uncertain future. Both Republicans and Democrats took credit for this corporate success, celebrated the globalized high-tech future, and said much too little about the growing disparity of wealth within the U.S. and around the world. All that Americans needed to prosper in this future techtopia was a little retraining and high standardized test scores. The public conversation about the future of democracy and global justice and sustainability was limited to small groups and was ignored by the news media.

Before pulling back, the stock market produced phenomenal wealth for those with money to invest, but certainly not for the poor. Such wealth production was presented as "proof" of the superiority of the unbridled market, or, as some argued, the benefits of cheap labor to short-term corporate profits. "But employment has increased in this economic upswing," corporate apologists respond to our skepticism. Only because, we answer, of stagnant wages and increased part-time, no-benefit jobs. The power of corporate information control revealed itself yet again, when some workers cheered the rising stock market as a sign of their increased chance for prosperity.

Some workers bought into the neoclassical economic wisdom that any increase in their wages was bad for the stock market and thus bad for future prosperity. So powerful was the stock market-induced optimism of some workers that they overspent their earnings, pushing consumer debt to unprecedented heights. The rising stock market, they reasoned, would enable them to earn the money to pay off these debts. Many workers believed this even at a time when corporations were gutting employee pension plans. Riding on the Teflon magic carpet of illusory prosperity, government did little to protect workers from the global forces lurking in the shadows of the future.

These ominous shadows will grow bigger and darker if the free market policies now pervasively taught and justified in free enterprise and other social studies classes continue to rule the economic sector. Corporate and political leaders will find it more and more difficult to maintain the illusion of prosperity with people around the world suffering as much as they do. Even in the "best of times," defined by rising corporate profits and record-setting stock prices, few high-paid, high-skill jobs have been created. Indeed, the last decade has marked a watershed in American economic history: increased profits and business prosperity accompanied by minimal job creation, especially good job creation.

This watershed is characterized by a basic change in the relationship between capital and labor, for any semblance of the old Fordist compromise that crumbled in the early 1970s has been erased. Contemporary corporate leaders do not even feel compelled to speak a language of concern for their workers' well-being. Another aspect of the watershed involves the institutionalization of labor competition among Japan, Western Europe, and the United States. Such competition will induce corporations to operate at an accelerating intensity, with a need for greater speed and flexibility and lower overheads—all of which exert negative pressures on workers' interests.

When growing numbers of elite workers, willing to work for less, from developing countries such as India, China, and Malaysia are added to the competition from Europe and Japan, the problems faced by twenty-first-century American workers will intensify. Many economists portray this competitive future as a good thing, as a creative process of capitalism shedding its worn-out skin and emerging triumphant from the metamorphosis. Critical social studies educators, however, are too aware of the fact that the benefits of the change go to the managers, while low-wage workers, left in the wake, struggle to rebound from declining wages and life disruptions. The American public's consciousness of these looming realities has been forestalled by millions of women entering the service workforce to provide families with two incomes. Still, a pessimism about the future is creeping up on American workers, expressed in their worry about their children's economic future. Deep in the recesses of the American subconscious, a knowledge of these dire future possibilities resides. For the time being, most men and women would like to forget about it, and their political representatives are all too happy to oblige their continuing repression of this harsh reality (Rifkin, 1995; Wolman & Colamosca, 1997; Carlson, 1997).

TROUBLE ON THE HORIZON

Though we would rarely know it from free enterprise classes, among specific groups in American culture, evidence is emerging that the virtue of unbridled global capitalism is being questioned. Labor leaders such as John Sweeney and Dennis Rivera—students taking free enterprise classes have no idea who they are—and many of the workers they represent do not accept the globalized free market notion that only short-term corporate profits matter. The Teamsters' strike against United Parcel Service (UPS) in August 1997 illustrated the moral backlash of working Americans toward inhumane economic policies of globalized corporations. The Teamsters saw their strike as a direct attack on the corporate free market politics of lowering labor costs. Over 128,000 Teamsters work part-time for UPS, receiving low wages and no benefits. Most part-timers hold down two or more jobs, and 10,000 Teamsters work more than thirty-five hours per week for UPS under part-time contracts.

Reflecting the actions of hundreds of other U.S. corporations, UPS hired primarily contingent workers; since 1993, over four out of five new hires have been part-time. Such dramatic cutbacks in labor costs might have been more understandable if the company were losing money and near bankruptcy, but UPS was setting new records for one-year profit margins. In 1996, for example, the company made a $1.1 billion profit. To maintain such record profit levels, many U.S. corporations are banding together to develop trade strategies for controlling labor and public opinion. The Employer Group is an organization dedicated to keeping worker wages under $8 per hour by recruiting workers living in poverty from East Asia and Mexico, by soliciting charitable and other nonprofit agencies to run low-cost day care centers for working mothers, and by building cheap dormitories for low-wage workers, just as in the nineteenth-century, firms built so-called company housing for miners and other workers. In the first decade of the twenty-first century, the exploitative practices of management many thought were the product of a bygone era are back with a vengeance (Slaughter, 1997; Seymour, 1997, Wolman & Colamosca, 1997).

Critical democratic social studies educators and labor advocates were heartened by the speed of UPS's concession to several of the Teamsters' demands. Despite corporate media coverage that for the most part denied the validity of labor's concerns with downsizing and part-time job growth, many Americans understood the Teamsters' arguments. The strike stands as an important moment in contemporary labor history because it articulated for a wide audience the underside of the dynamically flexible post-Fordist free market economy. Other events hailing the underside of contemporary globalized capitalism involved the protests against corporate-directed free market policies around the world in Seattle and Washington, D.C. in 2000. It was fascinating to watch TV news coverage of the protests, as angry newspeople vehemently denied their complicity with these corporate forces. The protests indicated that the debate about economic policy is far from over and the coming decade will witness many objectors to the forced orthodoxy of unbridled market capitalism. Social studies teachers are obliged to follow this debate carefully.

LOVE IN THE RUINS: HOPE IN DESPAIR

Smart governmental intervention, progressive unions, third-sector civil programs, integrated vocational and academic programs, and a critical economics education that is uncensored and takes nothing for granted offer hope for the future. I am encouraged by the development of new economics education programs that address the realities delineated in this chapter. For example, the Labor in the Schools Committee of the California Federation of Teachers (CFT) has developed a program about work entitled, "The Yummy Pizza Company." The project puts students to work in the pizza business, introducing them to everyday forms of worker exploitation in a free market economy. Confronted with workplace problems, students explore ways that unions might help mitigate the effects of the market. Given the procorporate information environment in which student consciousness is formed, young people are often shocked to discover the restrictions employees encounter in the workplace. The Yummy Pizza Company helps students understand that the U.S. Constitution protects individuals from government but not from employers. For most students, this is a profound and shocking revelation (Hiber, 1997).

Economics programs of this sort, of course, are a rarity in the corporate-influenced schools of the twenty-first century. Critical democratic social studies educators understand that simulation games like this could be used as a fun way to engage students in an alternative view of the effects of a free market economy. Critical democratic social studies educators are dedicated to integrating social, historical, and philosophical concerns and questions into the study of economics. Like other subject domains conceived within an epistemology of complexity, economics does not exist in isolation from other forces. Any social studies interested in the furthering of democracy will have to confront the power-saturated anti-democratic features of an unbridled free enterprise system. The present repression of such dynamics in U.S. elementary and secondary social studies programs is unacceptable in a free society.

Chapter  24

Geography in Trouble: A Diagnosis of a Sick Discipline*

Geography is a discipline in serious trouble. An important cause of some of geography's problems is the relative absence of philosophic inquiry into the nature of the discipline's roles in the educational process. As with other dimensions of the elementary and secondary social studies curriculum, few analysts have asked, Why should we teach geography? Why has geography been taught the way it has? Where did the geography curriculum originate? Into this unquestioning school climate, more and more teachers fresh from teacher education programs enter, practically oblivious to geographical content and unaware of past uses of geography in the larger educational process.

GEOGRAPHY ON LIFE SUPPORT

Geography will not be saved as a discipline by the development of "slicker" teaching strategies. Teachers trained to plug in new methods to existing mind-sets and curricular structures will not rescue the discipline from the forces working against it. The geography malaise is just one of many educational problems that could profit from a critical democratic analy-

* A version of this article appeared in *The Social Studies*, LXXV (July/August, 1984), pp. 141–144. I would like to thank my friend, Joe Greene, for his help on this chapter. Reprinted by permission of the publisher.

sis. Revitalization may come from increased speculation into the basic purposes for geography's inclusion in the curriculum. The field can certainly benefit from a careful examination of the contention that the essence of the discipline concerns its ability to portray the relationship between the physical world and social, political, historical, cultural, and economic events. The analysis of these topics provides a context that gives meaning to a discussion of how to teach geography. Outside this context, methodological debate is often meaningless and new teaching methods are developed in virtual isolation; such strategies have little relevance for teacher and students and usually do little to place the learning process in a broader social and educational context. As many have perceptively argued, a theory of instruction implemented outside the context of a theory of education will yield a few positive results.

Geography has for years experienced serious problems in elementary and secondary schools. Recently, the discipline has also run into trouble on the college level. In the last few decades, geography major's enrollments in college have fallen with little hope for a reversal of the trend in the near future. Geography departments at the University of Michigan and the University of Pittsburgh have actually disbanded. Geographers in universities around the country were particularly disturbed by the Michigan action because it set a precedent for administrators in an era of right-wing cuts in the higher education budget. Geography departments may be near the top of administrative hit lists, as it has become quite obvious that geographers have little political clout within university political hierarchies. Even now, only one-half of American colleges offer geography courses, and the majority of those institutions who do have only limited course offerings.

While the end of the world for college geographers may not be imminent, geography professors must, at the very least, do a better job of selling their discipline. The popularization of geography, however, has become increasingly difficult in the last couple of decades because of the Cartesian fragmentation and specialization of the field. Some argue that this specialization has destroyed the cohesive core of the discipline. As a result, the ability of geographers to work together has been undermined. The inability to work together has subverted geographers' attempts for disciplinary survival and their efforts to utilize geographic knowledge for the solution of human problems. Indeed, geographers find themselves increasingly isolated and misunderstood in both academia and society at large.

In light of this specialization, elementary and secondary geography has become even more alienated from the work of the academicians. A close relationship with academic geography is necessary for the vitality of the subject in the elementary and secondary schools, but a close working arrangement provides a valuable service for academicians as well, for it forces them to think in terms of the applicability of their knowledge. It is healthy for university and research geographers to address the process of dispensing their knowledge to popular and nontechnical audiences. Undoubtedly, unchecked and unexamined specialization in academic geography limits the dissemination of the discipline's perspectives in the public schools. In fact, geography has often become so specialized that professors often have trouble clarifying the focus of the discipline for the public and clearing up misconceptions that exist. One geographer reported that a non-geographer colleague on his college faculty wanted to know what geographers do now that all continents have been discovered.

Richard L. Morrill, professor of geography at the University of Washington and past president of the Association of American Geographers, argues that geographers must increase their efforts to inform the public about the purview of the discipline. On its fundamental level, Morrill contends, geography assumes that: location matters; there are reasons why places are different; knowledge of how territory is organized and changes is a key problem in science and in society; and physical environment influences human settlement, behavior, and development (Scully, 1982).

Few lay people, not even former secondary geography students, are aware of Morrill's basic geographic issues. Based on their experiences in the elementary and secondary schools, many people associate geographers with those teachers who forced them to memorize state capitals. As two professors from Middlebury College put it: The public often has the "sense that the geographer's intellectual curiosity emanates from photographs of naked people in *National Geographic*" (Scully, 1982, p. 1). Such a statement implies a public resentment concerning what goes on in the geography classroom. Classroom experiences in geography are rarely viewed positively; conversations with students and former students about elementary and secondary geography tend to be laced with words like dull, boring, deadening, stifling, simplistic, and impractical. What is going on in elementary and secondary classrooms? A survey of geographic education literature grants little insight into actual classroom practice. A researcher will find some curricular surveys, but few educators have examined the analytical and cognitive process required, and teaching strategies utilized, in elementary and secondary geography. My own study of numerous elementary and secondary geography classes throughout the U.S. has been very revealing.

FACTS ABOUT FLAX

Public school geography instruction is plagued by what one might describe as the "flax mentality." Geography classroom observations seem inevitably to run into lessons on that nemesis of cotton: flax. Wherever it rears its ugly head, the flax mentality suggests rote memorization of facts taught in conceptual isolation. The larger issues of geography are neglected while components such as map location, topography, and agricultural products are cursorily examined. No connections between these components are explored, for such exploration is not deemed relevant to the ultimate goal of "covering" the book or curriculum guide. While many teachers resent the stifling influences of the flax mentality, many of them are nevertheless trapped by it. In teaching about geography education in my social studies methods classes, I have found many good students to be uncomfortable with methods that transcend the traditional public school study of physical geography and map work. Their definition of geography is often so narrowed by school practice that they refuse to accept cultural and human elements of the discipline as "real" geography.

Geography teaching that has fallen victim to the flax mentality excludes itself from the study of geographic problems. It stifles attempts to open up the classroom to any method that transcends rote memorization in the name of finishing the book or covering all the necessary information. It rules out the possibility of devising geography projects that allow students to apply geographic knowledge in a meaningful context. The flax mentality precludes attempts to make geography interdisciplinary—an essential element in geography's utility in the elementary and secondary school. There are an infinite number of ways to get beyond flax. One way could involve introducing high school students to metaphysical speculation via the fifth century B.C. Greek geographical scholar Herodotus. Herodotus was a historian, philosopher, and cartographer, and he can be studied from the perspectives of all of those disciplines. Some interesting insights emerge when students search for connections between the maps, the world view, and the cosmology of Herodotus. What better symbol for the interdisciplinary nature of secondary geography? An examination of Herodotus by a secondary geography class could make the interdisciplinary connection between philosophy, history, and geography, thus placing geographical perceptions in a meaningful relationship with historical events. Tracing the philosophical thought of Herodotus, students could recognize the subjectivity of map making, as they analyzed the intricate connections between maps, politics, epistemology, and cosmology.

Instead, map work too often takes place in conceptual isolation. High school geography has no need to focus only on the detailed skills of the cartographer. Such practice should certainly be open to highly motivated high school students, but it is generally the domain of only upper level college or graduate students in geography. Map study in the elementary and secondary school should be viewed as a means to an end, a tool used in pursuit of a higher purpose. The purpose may involve solving a problem or directing a student to an interest in or an understanding of the spatial and temporal aspects of a historical event or a contemporary situation. Maps hold special mystique for many students and can accordingly be used in countless creative ways to lead students down new conceptual pathways.

No Questions of Purpose Allowed in Here

In my teaching and supervising experiences, I've seen very few public school geography instructors grapple with normative or speculative questions concerning their field. Those special teachers who have dealt with such questions often feel isolated and alienated from peers who consider their concerns as alternately unimportant or threatening. Present practice at its worst provides the student little more than a mental foundation of physical geographic knowledge that may someday make certain places vaguely recognizable. The typically required map work and state capital memorization contribute little to individual emancipation or critical social education. Present geographic instruction certainly cannot be classified as successful democratic citizenship education nor does it serve to enhance problem solving or critical thinking skills. By encouraging geography teachers to confront questions of purpose, philosophically informed critical social studies educators can contribute much to the health of the field. Unfortunately, however, questions of larger purpose are viewed with such hostility by positivistic educational leaders that such analysis is barred from the classroom. This is unfortunate because all educators, especially geography teachers, can benefit from a healthy analysis of the purposes of their discipline. And no one subjected geography to a more rigorous examination of purpose than did John Dewey.

In the heyday of progressivism, many teachers were aware of Dewey's analysis of geography's curricular role. Today, however, it is rare to find an elementary or secondary geography teacher who is familiar with Dewey's perspective on geography, inasmuch as he is ignored in many colleges of education. Exposure to Dewey's view of geography may be a thought-provoking, even unique, experience for the modern geography teacher. Dewey maintained that only geography supplies a subject matter that gives background and intellectual perspective to what might otherwise be "narrow personal actions or mere forms of technical skill" (Dewey, 1916, p. 210). Every time, he argued, that students learn to improve their ability to place their lives in the context of time and space, their lives gain in meaning. Thus, ordinary experiences become not merely happenings in temporal isolation but events with an enduring substance. In Dewey's geography, knowledge is entered into as an immediate activity, which in turn is placed in a temporal and spatial context. In classic Deweyan terms, geography then becomes a living experience.

From Dewey's perspective, geography's curricular role involves its ability to relate physical geographical facts to social events and then to illustrate the consequences of this relationship. With such connections in mind, Dewey accepted the definition of geography as an account of the earth as the human home—a definition that successful geography teachers need to keep in mind. When the bonds between physical geographical data and social events come apart, then geography becomes merely a conglomeration of isolated bits of information. And it is precisely this situation that has been the case in both Dewey's time and the present. At the foundation of this state of affairs is found the absence of serious speculation about the larger objectives of geography. As Dewey (1916) characterized the teaching of the discipline:

> It appears as a veritable rag-bag of intellectual odds and ends: the height of a mountain here, the course of a river there, the quantity of shingles produced in this town, the tonnage of shipping in that, the boundary of a country, the capital of a state. (p. 211)

AN EXAMPLE: TEACHING HIGH SCHOOL STUDENTS A GEOGRAPHY OF AFRICA

As a high school geography teacher in Tennessee, I taught a tenth grade world geography course. Because of the students' misconceptions, stereotypes, and lack of knowledge about Africa, I developed a nine-week course on the continent. The logic and goals of the geography unit may help us better understand the nature of a critical democratic geography education. To produce my lessons, I compared the larger concerns of a geography curriculum with my critical democratic social studies goals and some specific concerns I had with the study of Africa. The intersection of these three dynamics helped me construct a loose framework for the unit that would conceptually support, but not dictate, classroom activities. I wanted to leave as much room as possible for informed improvisation on my part as well as student input and direction.

My view of the larger goals of geography involved six main concepts:

1. The ability to use and produce maps and other geographical artifacts to help in obtaining data about humans and their relationships to the places they live.
2. The development of knowledge about places, especially their physical and human dimensions and the ways they experience change.
3. An appreciation of the ways that natural processes influence the natural environmental systems that support life on earth.
4. An understanding of human activities, especially their expression in economic, political, cultural, and social spheres, and their relationship to place.
5. An awareness of the importance of natural resources, their cultural meanings, changing uses, and modes of distribution.
6. The capacity to apply a geographical knowledge of people, places, and environments in order to create better, more just and sustainable places for humans to live.

Taking these issues and connecting them to the goals of a critical education, I was ready to think about the main themes of a geography of Africa. Here is a updated version of the African geographical issues with which I wanted the students to engage:

African Geographical Themes

1. Africa, the place
   a. Regions
   b. The peoples and the place
   c. Traditional cultures
   d. Political, economic, and social systems
2. Africa and European colonialism
   a. The nature and effects of colonialism
   b. Racism
   c. Shattered social and political structures—loss of cultural identity
   d. Nationalism in an African context
   e. Resulting ethnic conflicts
3. Africa in a globalized context
   a. Wealthy countries of the northern hemisphere and the countries of the southern hemisphere
   b. Eurocentric economic development
   c. Appropriate technological development
   d. Indigeneity
      i. The power of indigenous knowledge
      ii. Indigenous knowledge meets Western modernism—global localism
   e. Quest for pan-Africanism
4. Poverty in Africa—origins and consequences
   a. Western conquest
   b. Overpopulation
   c. Disease
   d. Environmental damage
   e. Political instability and civil unrest
   f. War

Student study groups can be formed around these four main concerns. In addition to studying the different regions of the continent (Arab Northern Africa, Western Africa, Equatorial Africa, East Africa, and Southern Africa), students could analyze print and Internet sources concerning these themes. Based on their readings and discussion, students could present information and construct handbooks concerning these thematic issues in Africa. Although they would learn physical locations and political demarcations, their knowledge of Africa would not consist of a body of isolated facts but a constellation of interrelated themes that not only would give them insight into African affairs but would help them form a conceptual basis for viewing the rest of the world as well. It is work like this that will revitalize the study of geography in the elementary and secondary schools.

Chapter  25

Educational Studies as a Component of the Social Studies Curriculum*

A study that would be relevant to the lives of social studies students involves the examination of education as a social force. Such studies could be easily incorporated into the social studies curriculum. What is important here is the development of an awareness of the study of education as a social, cultural, and political force and the insight that such an awareness brings. The study of education as a social force within a social studies context may bring about a new dimension of student understanding. Not only does such study allow students to view education as a social force, but it grants students new insight into the effect of that social force on their own lives. Educational studies forces students to address questions of purpose and value concerning the student's personal role in education: Why am I in school? What is this institution trying to do with me? How am I different because of school? Is there a set of values promoted by school? Have I accepted this set of school values? Such questions allow students to put some conceptual distance between themselves and school and to analyze the relationship. Such a process is beneficial because it grants the student the ability to consider the role school plays or could play in her or her life.

* A version of this article appeared in *High School Journal*, LXIX (October–November, 1985), pp. 187–196; I would like to thank Dr. Catherine Lugg for her contributions to this chapter. Reprinted by permission of the publisher.

Constructing Student Self-Reflection in the Social Study of Education

Students are rarely encouraged to be introspective about their role as students. We rarely consider, as did John Dewey, the school experience to be intrinsically important. Educators infrequently consider the student years as a legitimate portion of one's life. As Dewey (1916) put it:

> Our tendency to take immaturity as a mere lack, and growth as something which fills the gap between the immature and the mature is due to regarding childhood comparatively, instead of intrinsically. We treat it simply as a privation because we are measuring it by adulthood as a fixed standard. This fixes attention upon what the child has not, and will not have till he becomes a man (p. 42).

Childhood and school are usually viewed as preparation for some future goal. This outlook denigrates the importance of immediate experience and treats it as merely something to get through. Not only is school regarded as training for some future goal, but it is not regarded as part of the society that surrounds the child. As Dewey (1973) put it, students "should learn as much as possible about the nature which surrounds them and about the society in which they live" (p. 272). School is the nature that surrounds the child and it is the society in which he or she lives. In the process of exploring the society through the school students begin to explore themselves and the forces that have molded them.

The student's motivation is drawn from the relevance and intrinsic appeal of the process, not through fear of external coercion. In this spirit, Dewey (1916) maintained that "since a democratic society repudiates the principle of external authority, it must find a substitute in voluntary disposition and interest; these can only be created by education" (p. 87). One way to realize Dewey's ideal of creating this self-motivation is through the study of school and the analysis of the relationship of the child to the school. In the lived world of actual classroom practice, however, schools often repudiate the democratic values that they claim to promote. Thus, the school becomes a working democratic microcosm marked by both successes and failures in its attempt to apply democratic principles. The critical democratic social studies teacher can take advantage of this inconsistency, since the failure of the school reflects the larger problems of democracy.

In their study of schooling as a social force, students would have the opportunity to study the curriculum, goals, and purposes of the institution. This need not be a subject taught and studied in isolation; rather, it could be part of an American studies program in which students examine how American education reflects American society and American values. Students could take what they know about American societal values, add what they believe to be the purposes of schooling, and from these design and construct a model school system reflecting the students' ideas. During a project such as this, administrators, supervisors, educational scholars, and other teachers could be brought in to discuss and/or explain school objectives and the meaning of education. This dialogue and the resulting student school system model could serve, among other purposes, to expand student knowledge about the institution that takes up a good part of their day, to expose educators to student opinions, and to bring about a schoolwide discussion of the purposes and goals of schooling.

Unfortunately, one of the last places a person would go to hear a discussion of the purpose of education would be to a public school. The possibility of going to a public school to hear students offer an alternative to the present system (perhaps aided and abetted by some administrators and teachers) is almost incomprehensible. In short, discussion of the topic in many schools is taboo. This is certainly one of the major problems of the schools: Purposes and objectives are rarely examined, let alone rethought. Such a conversation should be a central component of any curriculum.

When such a discussion takes place, it is rarely dynamic, spontaneous, or open-ended. Indeed, it is usually a very limited analysis with very specific prearranged outcomes as mandated by some program. That is, before approval and/or funding, a program (or idea) must have specific goals outlined, and objectives must be stated in concise behavioral terms. Of course, then, the goals relate directly to the program (or idea) at hand and rarely beyond. Thus, most discussions about education are tied to specific programs, ideas, or problems rather than a broader sense of educational purpose. Given this, it is unlikely that in school much emphasis will be given to creative or critical inquiry into the role of education in society and its impact on individual consciousness.

USING EDUCATIONAL HISTORY TO PROMOTE REFLECTION IN THE SOCIAL STUDIES CLASSROOM

In a critical educational context concerned with the purposes of schooling, an examination of the founding of the public schools in the U.S. might be in order. Many Americans have been taught a rather simplistic morality tale about the founding of the first public school system in the U.S. in Massachusetts in the 1840s. When I first studied the common school movement I was amazed by the reductionistic, decontextualized account of Horace Mann setting up a school system to teach Massachusetts citizens the academic skills necessary to good citizenship in a democracy. Given my concerns with power and its role in shaping social, cultural, economic, and political events, I was motivated to study the social context in which Mann's work took place. There had to be more to the story. Imagine the discussions and debates about the purpose and effects of schooling that the following historical description of the origins of American public education would elicit among students:

No public system of schools was established in the U.S. at the time of the American Revolution or in the period following it. Though a few influential figures such as Thomas Jefferson supported public schools, little popular interest existed. In a rural, agricultural society, no larger social, political, or economic purpose catalyzed public support of education. Within a few industrializing northeastern states in the 1830s, a heated and divisive discussion about public education emerged. The forces opposing public tax-supported schooling continued to win legislative victories until Horace Mann appeared on the Massachusetts political scene. The debate in Massachusetts and the ways Mann generated support for the schools reveals much about the purposes of education. Mann's crusade relied more on social, political, and economic justifications for public education than on the intrinsic value of academic learning.

In 1837, the Massachusetts legislature appointed Mann its first secretary of the state board of education, a post he held until 1848. Mann went quickly to work, crusading for common schools (Nasaw, 1979). With only a small budget to aid his efforts, Mann attracted support through the sheer force of his personality and a compelling series of annual reports. In fact, educators now consider his campaign for the common school a sort of one-man religious crusade. Mann may have rejected his childhood Calvinism, but he definitely believed in the redemption of society through a system of public schools (Perkinson,

1991). In pursuing his quest, he traveled more than 500 miles, much of it on horseback, visiting local schools and reassuring communities that the state sought only to stimulate local efforts, not replace them (Tyack & Hansot, 1982).

Nevertheless, a financial panic that swept across the country in 1837 increased American fears of mob rule. Unemployment escalated as workers were laid off in massive numbers for the first time in American history. The overwhelming economic distress exacerbated the violence between Protestant and Roman Catholic street gangs, and it swept through the cities of the Northeast. Mann had witnessed one bloody uprising in Boston and blamed the violence on the lack of general education. In the spirit of the modernist Enlightenment, he prescribed reason:

> The mobs, the riots, the burnings, the lynchings, perpetrated by the men of the present day, are perpetrated because of their vicious and defective education. We see and feel the ravages of their tiger passions now, when they are full grown; but it was years ago when they were whelped and suckled. And so too, if we are derelict in our duty in this matter, our children in their turn will suffer. If we permit the vulture's eggs to be hatched, it will then be too late to take care of the lambs. (Karier, 1986, p. 60)

Mann's widely promulgated belief that public schools could build social stability resonated with many Americans. According to Mann's vision, the schools would train children in the ways of industry and thrift, and, through intensive social interaction, children would learn to respect each other. Mann believed that only a common school, where children of all backgrounds could be educated side by side, could lay the foundation for social stability. He saw such schools as the panacea for society's ills (Perkinson, 1991).

To be sure, strong conservative elements of social regulation of the poor in particular informed Horace Mann's educational vision. He believed, for example, in molding children into proper Americans. "Men are cast-iron," he wrote, "but children are wax. Strength expended upon the latter may be effectual, which would make no impression upon the former" (Spring, 1994, p. 67). One crucial element of this molding was "moral education," which included the use of the King James Version of *The Bible*. The "common school" would be a Christian institution, for many nineteenth-century Americans equated morality with Protestant Christianity. Yet, in deference to constitutional (and more importantly, political) dictates, the public school would also be nondenominational, but certainly not Catholic, Jewish, Muslim, or non-Christian. Bible verses would be read, supposedly without doctrinal bias.

This reliance upon the Bible infuriated Catholics and some of the more orthodox Protestants, who perceived Mann's vague and generalized Protestantism as a ploy to gain Protestant political support for the publicly funded schools without alienating any specific Protestant denomination. His was a direct appeal to a "nativism" growing in the country and beginning to dominate the Whig party (Bennett, 1995). The overtly Protestant nature of the public schools was also a means of regulating the growing numbers of Catholic children, ensuring that those who attended the common schools would be exposed to the common tenets of the Protestant faiths (Tyack & Hasnot, 1982; Karier, 1986).

As yet another means of ensuring that the common schools would regulate their charges, Mann insisted that no "controversial" subjects be studied. He worried that any political, social or economic controversy explored within the schoolhouse would eventually undermine political support for the schools themselves (Karier, 1986; Spring, 1994). So, by design, the common school offered a bland curriculum; children absorbed watered-down subject matter in the name of preserving political (and financial) support for their schools, and teachers could not freely explore "contemporary issues."

This "common" education gained support from many industrial interests, who paid a significant portion of the early school taxes. They recognized the common school as an efficient means of maintaining a skilled and docile labor pool, soon the very buttress of capitalism (Tyack & Hansot, 1982). School taxes became a sort of property insurance, a way of preserving the power of corporate capital (Nasaw, 1979). Immigrants would be educated and assimilated, and radical (that is to say, "foreign") ideas regarding the rights of labor would be extinguished. A common school would ensure that children were properly prepared for the needs of industry. Efforts to understand the origins of state-supported public education in America cannot succeed without a thorough appreciation of these industrial, political, and economic needs, and to discuss the impact of economic forces on American schooling we must now backtrack a bit.

Before the Industrial Revolution that began in the United States in the 1820s, 19 of every 20 Americans lived and worked on a farm. Rural dwellers needed practical agricultural knowledge to make a living; reading and writing could be taught in the home after work. After the 1820s, with the beginnings of the Industrial Revolution, many Americans, especially the new urban dwellers, began to sense that the country was changing. At first, Massachusetts was influenced by the socioeconomic effects of industrialization more than any other state, and the economic changes there would create the context for Mann's great idea: the first state-supported compulsory school system in America.

Industrialists found it difficult to adapt agrarian males to the demands of unskilled factory work. Consequently, New England mill owners hired women, children, and the inmates of charitable institutions as laborers. When Irish Catholics began to emigrate in larger numbers, industrialists hired them to replace American-born workers. They soon saw the value in developing "proper" industrial attitudes among both the immigrants and future generations of Americans. This realization led them naturally to consider the role of schools in "attitude adjustment." Thus, the industrialists' support of public education did not reflect a concern for either an empowered, educated citizenry or the economic welfare of American citizens. It reflected the industrialists' economic self-interest, and specifically, a pool of workers with attitudes conducive to industrial productivity and profits for owners of the factories.

Social studies teachers and students should understand this point so as to appreciate the fact that schools pursue more than just academic goals. All educational decisions are also political decisions, since they concern questions of power and its distribution among different interest groups. Americans often have difficulty understanding the dynamics of political questions. Too often we restrict the adjective "political" to the sphere of political parties, candidates, and elections, and we thereby miss the power-related aspects of politics. As a result, we could miss the significance of the political dimensions of Horace Mann's common school crusade and its relevance for contemporary teachers and social studies students. Engaging questions of power with the understanding that power elites possess inordinate influence in the shaping of school policy can help social studies students appreciate how schools work, as well as helping them understand their personal roles in the larger, sociopolitically driven educational process.

Mann worked hard to sell the public schools to his Massachusetts contemporaries. In his conversations with powerful industrialists and business leaders in his home state, he addressed their fear of social disharmony. Made anxious by the growing dissatisfaction of workers with the tedium, danger, long hours, and low pay of industrial jobs, factory owners sought ways to ensure social stability and order. When Mann talked of schools producing a "common core of values," the industrialists inferred that such values would support and promote industrial development. The common schools, Mann said, would turn out factory workers who were docile, easily administered and likely to avoid strikes and working-class violence. Schooling would reduce the poor people's hostility toward the wealthy. These implications were music to the ears of industrial leaders, far more concerned, as they were, with orderly and docile workers than with well-educated and inventive workers, particularly with those workers already discussing "working men's associations" designed to protect their interests against the power of factory owners. One finds a fear of worker organization or revolt perpetually preoccupying the minds of factory owners.

An important question for social studies teachers and students arises in this context: Where in a mid-nineteenth century Massachusetts textile mill would a worker need to exercise creativity or employ a refined ability to analyze and interpret? As far as the owners were concerned, such traits could lead only to labor trouble. As with most educational reform initiatives, the political dimension of the common school movement involved its alliance with monied interests. Although Mann's vision of public schooling went far beyond providing malleable workers, the movement would never have succeeded had the commercial banking and manufacturing interests not believed that schools would yield long-term financial benefits.

The key element in the political coalition that brought universal, compulsory, state-supported education to America was the expectation among the power elite that public schools would inculcate a core of values that would prepare students to accept the inherent indignities of industrial life. The obvious questions that emerge for teachers and students in this educational study involve whether schools still reflect the social, political, and economic concerns of power elites. Social studies teachers may ask: Am I a pawn of dominant power as I teach history, political science, sociology, and economics? Students may ask: Is my consciousness being shaped to view the world in ways that support the interests of power brokers? Such questions are necessary in a critical democratic social studies, and such an educational study provides an excellent way to raise them.

EDUCATIONAL STUDIES IN THE VARIOUS SOCIAL STUDIES DISCIPLINES

Such studies would provide a more textured picture of social processes to social studies students inasmuch as education reflects social values. Educational studies would further help students understand the role of school in society as well as the conflicting historical roles of schools in America. Equally important is the point that educational studies would add new dimensions to every social studies discipline. As a part of history courses, for instance, the origins and growth of public schooling in America would shed light on the development of American society and could take history courses out of the all too common military-oriented drum and trumpet chronology that plagues them. Furthermore, the manner in which society views the role of education and the manner in which society defines an educated person offers insight into the differences between various historical eras.

The role of education in economic development would also be an important topic of study in an economics course. Economics teachers could choose to study a myriad of specific education-related topics. For instance, teachers and students could study the role of education in the formulation of economic policy, especially the role of education in Third World economies. Or the topic of study could involve the training of the workforce and the debate over the methods and purposes of such training, e.g., Is it education's responsibility to provide a workforce that is inculcated with the "proper" attitudes of docility and respect for authority? Indeed, economics classes could study education as a growth industry in an era of privatization and chart any similarities/differences between it and such industries as steel and automobile manufacturing or Internet commerce.

In sociology courses, educational studies could provide an excellent laboratory for the examination of sociological theories. Classes could explore the effects of social class on school development and student performance, the relationship between education and social attitudes, who succeeds or fails in school and why, and similar areas. Additionally, students (and teachers) could gain a better understanding of both education and society by attempting to understand who goes into teaching, who the administrators are, and what school does and doesn't do in the name of social regulation.

Finally, there are few better ways of introducing students to cross-cultural analysis than by examining how people in other societies are educated. Not only will this provide students with cross cultural understanding, it would also offer yet another way of encouraging students to examine critically their own educational experience.

As well as achieving these and other goals in specific disciplines, the inclusion of educational studies in these areas would provide students with new perspectives. Also, students who can understand that education is much more than inculcation of facts and "essential" knowledge and who can question why knowledge is taught in certain ways are bound to become more thoughtful and critical students. Of course, the recognition that the present organization of school is not the only way education can and does take place is liberating and, therefore, a potentially threatening concept. Many teachers and administrators may be threatened by such a study of education because it would encourage serious discussion about education objectives and could ultimately alter the very foundations of the system. But if social studies is to be a dynamic, critical, and democratic experience, the fear of this threat must be transcended, and, more importantly, educators must not be frightened by the prospect of disagreeing with one another on educational goals and purposes. The inclusion of educational studies in the social studies curriculum is one of the ways educators will eventually overcome this fear. Indeed, stimulating substantive discussion about what is being done in schools, as well as how much philosophical diversity is tolerated, will result in strengthening the educational system as a democratic institution.

Educational studies as part of the social studies curriculum can do even more. It is one of the best ways to break down the false dichotomy between the so-called real world and school—something many students have known all along, despite continually being admonished, "What till you get into the real world. . . ." Students know there is nothing unreal about facing a tough test or having a 10-page paper due the day after tomorrow. Unfortunately, this widely held idea that school is somehow not a part of the real world only serves to isolate the schools from the lived world, to send contradictory messages to students, and to degrade the value of critical democratic scholarly work. Because of this, educators are missing the ideal opportunity to study school as another component of everyday life that is inseparable from the larger concerns of the social studies curriculum.

Chapter

Cultural Studies in
the Social Studies

As I have maintained throughout this book, social studies education takes on a different tenor in a postmodern, hyperreal world where information is controlled by private interests with the economic power to constantly pound their self-serving messages into our collective consciousness. In such a dramatically different social circumstance, social studies educators must develop new abilities to study and assess such a change of social climate and seek new ways to apply the findings of such studies to their pedagogies

Critical democratic social studies teachers, concerned with social justice, egalitarianism, higher orders of cognition, and new modes of being human, are especially in need of such skills and abilities. Mutating and strengthening formations of power in hyperreality threaten such goals and have already contributed profoundly to the weakening of U.S. democracy itself. Cultural studies is a field of study that provides social studies educators with new ways of addressing these concerns. Many of the approaches to social studies employed in *Getting Beyond the Facts* find their origins in the field of cultural studies.

DEFINING CULTURAL STUDIES

Cultural studies is an interdisciplinary, transdisciplinary, and sometimes counter disciplinary field that functions within the dynamics of competing definitions of culture. Unlike traditional humanistic studies, cultural studies questions the equation of culture with high culture; instead, cultural studies asserts that myriad expressions of cultural production should be analyzed in relation to other cultural dynamics and social and historical structures. Such a position commits cultural studies to a potpourri of artistic, religious, political, economic, and communicative activities. In this context, it is important to note that while cultural studies is associated with the study of popular culture, it is not primarily about popular culture. Cultural studies interests are much broader and generally tend to involve the production and nature of the rules of inclusivity and exclusivity that guide academic evaluation. In particular, cultural studies looks at the way these rules shape and are shaped by relations of power. Again, these cultural studies dynamics permeate *Getting Beyond the Facts*.

NOT ONE THING, BUT NOT JUST ANYTHING

The preceding is as specific a definition as cultural studies scholars will provide. Cultural studies, many have argued, is not one thing; it perseveres as a multidimensional and fragmented constellation of disciplines that addresses a variety of questions. By no means is its future predictable or subject to the control of our ideological perspective. Concurrently, while the attempt to specify the nature of cultural studies for all temporal and spatial contexts is ill-founded if not impossible, cultural studies is not just anything. Indeed, it can be argued that work in cultural studies examines cultural practices from a perspective that positions them in relation to the dynamics of power. Such a characteristic implies that scholarship in the field will on some level grapple with the interrelationship between cultural production and historical forces.

ENGAGING THE DISCIPLINES

Advocates of cultural studies believe that the study of culture is fragmented among a variety of disciplines (sociology, anthropology, history, literary studies, communications, etc.) to the point that communication between scholars in undermined. This is a fragmentary dynamic that has always adversely affected the work of the social studies. Scholarship has become so isolated that scholars work in private, focusing on narrow areas, rarely analyzing the way one's isolated work fits into a larger whole. Producing knowledge that is so specialized, scholars often have little concern with the meaning of knowledge produced, its application, or its possible effect. Cultural studies attempts to overcome this fragmentation by highlighting culture as a living process that shapes the way we live, view ourselves, and understand the world around us. By adopting cultural studies' overtly multidisciplinary approach, scholars can study larger social issues, such as race, class, gender, sexuality, ethnicity, immigration, and pedagogy from unique perspectives and theoretical positions. As students of cultural studies question the dominant ways of seeing that evolve around the "normal science" of disciplines, they free themselves from the self-validating redundancies that limit insight and chain them to familiar explanations.

CONFRONTING NEW FORMS OF KNOWLEDGE PRODUCTION

Cultural studies advocates argue that the development of mass media has changed the old rules of how culture operates. The Media have become sufficiently powerful to produce both new ways of seeing the world and new meanings for lives and work. Media produce and validate that data described as knowledge. Thus, media shape identities and self-images. It is safe to say that our lifetimes have witnessed a major transformation in how knowledge is produced. If this is true, cultural studies proponents argue, we should expand the types of issues we study in school in general and social studies in particular. For example, while we should, of course, continue to study books and print as academic artifacts, we should also begin to study the values that aural and visual media produce, market, and distribute in TV, radio, film, CDs, computer networks, advertising images, etc. A major transformation has taken place in cultural epistemologies, and, as of yet, academic disciplines have been unequipped to account for such change. Cultural studies has positioned itself as a social force determined to confront these systemic changes and their implications for the purposes of academic institutions.

Confronting a Global Future:
The Move to the Margins

Education is just beginning to appreciate the range of issues foregrounded by technological innovation and globalization. In this context, globalization involves not only the integration of financial systems, the mobilization of planetary communication networks, and the reconfiguration of labor/management systems; it also entails confrontation with new constellations of racial and cultural diversity. While developments such as virtual reality and digital technologies will raise ethical issues unimaginable in the present, issues of diversity will demand attention to questions of social justice that have been repressed in the last three decades. Globalization creates a social context where Western culture can no longer simply be positioned as the paragon of civilization. Non-Western cultures and other marginalized groups have revolted against this exclusionary practice, demanding that their voices and histories be acknowledged. The growth of visual and print media and their impact on all phases of intellectual and artistic life has shifted attention from the traditional study of Western culture to global concerns such as ecology, technology, colonialism, and their manifestations in the omnipresent popular culture.

Advocates of cultural studies contend it is at this point that traditional academic disciplinary configurations fail to engage the educational implications of these cultural, social, and political developments. The "normal science" of the university revolves around the attempt to transmit Western truths from one generation to another. These structured exclusions make it difficult for educators to address the diverse narratives and insights of marginalized cultural groups. Cultural studies proponents maintain that studies of this marginalized culture can provide insights into the study of the culture in question, the study of culture in general, and the study of Western culture in particular—insights often neglected by traditional inquiries into the Western canon. Indeed, life at the margins, when examined at the micro-level of everyday life, can produce a form of analysis that engages popular texts as cultural commodities and sociopolitical documents. These primary sources open "stargates" into new forms of academic work, new dimensions of scholarly interpretation.

CULTURAL STUDIES AS CONTEXT PROVIDER: EXPANDING THE BOUNDARIES OF SOCIAL ANALYSIS

Cultural studies is concerned with its application to the world existing outside the academy. Proponents maintain that the project of cultural studies is to address the most urgent social questions of the day in the most rigorous intellectual manner available. Thus, the everyday concerns of cultural studies are contextually bound. Indeed, the work of the inter-disciplinary discipline is constantly being articulated and rearticulated around new social, cultural, and political conditions. Its engagement with the ever evolving historical context subverts any tendency on the part of cultural studies scholars to become complacent about the field's contributions both inside and outside the academy. So important is this notion of context that some scholars maintain that the primary role of cultural studies involves providing insight into new and ever changing contexts. To conceive cultural studies as radical conceptualism or a theory of context making speaks directly to the field's contribution to the reconceptualization of social analysis.

Radical contextualism implies that the knowledge produced and transmitted by scholars can never stand alone or be complete in and of itself. When one abstracts, he or she takes something away from its context. Of course, such reductionism is necessary in everyday life because there is too much information out there to be understood in detail by the mind. If an object of thinking cannot be abstracted, it will be lost in a larger pattern. Radical contextualism is certainly capable of abstraction, but, at the same time, it refuses to lose sight of the conceptual field, the context that provides separate entities meaning. For example, traditional education, social studies included, has often concentrated on teaching students the "what" of the scholarly disciplines. Life and job experience have traditionally taught us "how" and "why." Data (the "what") is best learned in the context of the "how" and "why." Thus, academic knowledge may best be learned in a situated context, inasmuch as the information connects to the social dynamics of the present. John Dewey understood this point a century ago in his work on social education. If deeper levels of understanding are desired, tasks must be learned in the context in which they fit. In light of such a pronouncement, we can begin to see that the immature scholar is one who possesses no specific knowledge of a particular sociocultural setting, even though he or she may come to the situation with rigorous academic information. Such scholars become seasoned veterans only after they gain familiarity with specific social, symbolic, encoded, technical, and other types of analytical resources, i.e., the context of the lived world. Critical social studies educators must understand this concept if they are to develop an emancipatory pedagogy.

From an analytical perspective, therefore, cultural studies pushes scholars to push beyond the limits of what we already know. For example, we already understand that particular practices reproduce forms of racism and sexism—an important but yet insufficient social understanding. Cultural studies scholars insist that such understandings provide only a starting place for academic analysis. How does, for example, this production of racism and sexism engage in particular contexts with specific individuals to shape political struggles, individual identities, and the role that education plays in the lives of students? It is to engage this form of specific analysis that motivates cultural studies' engagement with the popular, the everyday, and the particularistic. These domains produce not merely unusual texts to be analyzed, but they constitute the stage on which political struggle is played out in the first decade of the twenty-first century.

CONNECTING CULTURAL STUDIES TO THE SOCIAL STUDIES

The analytical dynamics created by cultural studies constructs a unique meta conversation with social studies educators about what they are doing and their impact on the lives of individuals included in their pedagogical orbit. Cultural studies traces its beginnings to the field of education, adult education in particular. Raymond Williams, one of the architects of the field, developed ideas that would help map the concerns of cultural studies when he was an adult educator, integrating academic knowledge into the lived context of working students. Such a context created a cultured dynamic that served to expand the use and meaning of the term "pedagogy." As an amalgam of lived processes that highlights the ways individuals define themselves and their relation to the world, pedagogy moves beyond its identification with only the techniques and methodologies of teaching. In this expanded domain, pedagogy explores identity formation, power, and knowledge production in the context of curriculum content, classroom strategies, evaluation, and teaching purposes. Cultural studies helps social studies teachers and teacher educators ask questions about what knowledge is of most worth, what it means to know something, and in what ways students and teachers are shaped by the world around them.

Cultural studies facilitates the efforts of social studies educators to provide insight into the cultural production of contemporary youth. Locating students in history, exploring their personal experience, and analyzing the cultural engagements in which they invest, is a pedagogical activity cultural studies is well-equipped to undertake. Questions of youth desire, so often misunderstood by mainstream social studies teachers and teacher educators, fit into this same context, as cultural studies analyzes the private terrain of affect, feeling, and pleasure that takes place outside traditional disciplinary structures grounded on reason and rationality. The interaction of this private domain of feeling and desire with the "certified" knowledge of schooling provides a window of entry to students of cultural studies and pedagogy. It is at this point that the study of popular culture and youth culture finds relevance in teaching and teacher education. Here is the cultural space where student identity takes shape and student knowledge is constructed. Understanding this cultural space and the various ways young people encounter it, students of education move to a new dimension of pedagogical insight (Giroux & Simon, 1989; Giroux, 1994, 1997).

CULTURAL STUDIES IN EDUCATION: THE IMPORTANCE OF CULTURAL PEDAGOGY AND SELF-PRODUCTION

In an electronic hyperreality, with an increased importance of representation, signification, and the inscription of meaning on everyday items, power blocs hold new and expanded forms of power. Those who have access to visual, audio, and print media have used these technologies to expand their influence from global locales to the realm of inner consciousness. In this context, cultural studies is fascinated with the ways that electronic forms of communication shape the political and ideological meaning of art, human bodies, consumer products, and other physical objectives. It becomes apparent in this context why cultural studies has emerged as such an important academic movement over the last few decades. The discourse of cultural studies has sought to theorize the ways power and ideology work through everyday life and popular culture to produce meaning, create knowledge, channel desire, and construct subjectivity. In a pedagogical domain, cultural studies analyzes social practices that use visual images, sound, bodily movement, and other representational dynamics to redefine ways of seeing/being.

While educational and social scholars who are involved with the work of cultural studies are undoubtedly committed to the academic domain of schools and universities, such educators are also concerned with cultural pedagogy. Cultural pedagogy involves education and acculturation that take place at a variety of cultural locations, including, but not limited to, formal educational institutions. Cultural studies scholars extend our notion of cultural pedagogy, focusing their attention on the complex interactions of power, knowledge, identity, and learning. Thus, in a cultural studies-influenced social studies education, a better understanding of the process of identity formation is possible. A cultural studies appreciation of cultural pedagogy knows that, in hyperreality, human subjectivity is always shifting and reconstituting itself (meaning that the self is more bombarded than ever by sociopolitical and ideological influences). Thus, as we become more aware of this sociohistorical, ideological construction of self, a space opens where social studies scholars can begin to question and access these constitutive dynamics. Of course, identifying the nature of power is a necessary step in any critical effort to gain self-empowerment, but mere identification is not enough. As cultural studies moves us to the micro level of reception of power and hegemonic ideology by an individual, we examine not only the dynamics of reception but the process of ideological production, the reconstruction of the self in this context.

Students of cultural studies and education pursue their analysis of cultural pedagogy and self-formation in the workings of contemporary corporate ideological production. Studying Reebok advertising, for example, cultural studies scholars focus on the impact of such communications on American youth. Understanding the changes electronic media has made on the consciousness of youth, Reebok promoters address a new corps of young people, flattened of affect and depth and constituted by a set of unconnected signifiers. These changes in youth identity are as much (maybe more) influenced by affective as rational dynamics. Cultural studies scholars see this shift from ideology as simply a rational force to ideology as both a rational and affective force as a dramatic break between modernist and postmodernist notions of ideology. Thus, contemporary cultural pedagogy in its postmodern guise dispenses social meanings and shapes identities more like a maelstrom than an engineering diagram. Electronic media in hyperreality promote a form of ideology by erasure, meaning that, through the fragmentation and decontextualization of current events, little interpretation emerges that challenges the status quo.

Existing disparities and policies are legitimated when disturbing events or negative effects of the world as it is are left out of the headline news capsules and attention-grabbing pictures. While dominant ideology obviously operates in the media, social institutions, and the state, a critical cultural studies understanding of the concept focuses our attention on the ways these macrodynamics play out in everyday life. How does hegemonic ideology undermine individuals' attempts to live their lives in a worthy and secure manner? How does it undermine healthy self-concepts and a sense of empowerment and possibility? As critical democratic social studies educators with a sense of the way hegemonic ideology works ask such questions, they know that power wielders never possess the capability to fix meanings, to shape identities once and for all (Fiske, 1994; Kellner, 1990; Grossberg, 1995; Clegg, 1989). These cultural studies inquiries are central social studies questions for those interested in understanding the sociocultural baggage students bring to school and the ideological forces they must encounter daily.

CULTURAL STUDIES AND MEDIA PEDAGOGY

Students of cultural studies understand that cultural pedagogies don't simply impose particular forms of meaning or ways of looking at the world on people. Cultural pedagogies produce meaning and various social phenomena. Included in this productive dynamic of power, hegemonic ideology is the media's production of identities, role models, and ideals. Such a productive process transcends some simple form of indoctrination, in that it promotes an active form of negotiation between audiences and media producers. The significance of this negotiation process involves the sophistication of our understanding that television, film, music, video games, and CD-ROMs do not have a direct, consistent, nonmediated ideological effect on audiences. Power elites are not sufficiently unified themselves, inasmuch as they constantly unite, divide, and reunite around particular issues to produce ideological messages via the media that are unified and coordinated. Critical cultural studies scholars, therefore, look at media as a discourse for analysis, not as a behavioral event structuring a stimulus-response relationship between producer and audience. In this context, the outcome of media messages in terms of viewer perception cannot be predetermined, even though producers and sponsors of media operate as part of a larger ideological apparatus of the dominant culture. Media images are double-edged, dependent upon audience interpretation, and capable of being deployed in ways unimagined by producers, advertisers, and network programmers. Think of Mattel's Barbie in this context. With a GI Joe voice, Barbie does not simply reproduce patriarchal representations of femininity. It's just more complex than that. Ideology, thus, can be challenged, read in counterhegemonic ways, and employed to promote progressive and egalitarian social change. Media holds no guarantee that it will elicit the effects it desires (Tomlinson, 1991; Aronowitz, 1993; Rand, 1995).

In this context, students of cultural and media pedagogy study various influences of contemporary electronic culture. Disney movies, for example, are able to project themselves as innocent texts that occupy a cultural plane transcending the need for cultural analysis. Cultural studies scholars expose the pedagogical dimensions of such movies, connecting them directly to issues of identity formation, democracy, and social justice. According to such scholars, Disney (not unlike other studios) produces films that reflect and shape American politics, U.S. domestic and global policies, and even the national character. Despite such profound sociopolitical influence, many individuals, unexposed to the analysis of cultural pedagogy in general or media literacy in particular, see Disney only in the isolated context of entertainment. Such a perspective only intensifies hyperreality's threat to democracy, because it represses the multidimensional pedagogical and political dynamics at work in Disney films. It is in contexts like this that cultural studies analysis becomes so important to democratic and educational concerns, since it positions the popular as an object of serious ideological examination (Giroux, 1997).

Cultural studies analysis reveals that Disney films, movies in general, television programs, advertisements, music, and other manifestations of popular culture are not simply products but ideas about the political structure and the values that surround them. Such ideas are the grist of the hegemonic ideology of hyperreality because they covertly contribute to the ways individuals make sense of their race, class, gender, vocational, and civic roles in the culture. In such a context, media provide maps of cultural intelligibility, and ideologically saturated representations of the meanings of the cultural forms that are found in everyday life (Lull, 1995).

CULTURAL STUDIES AND YOUNG PEOPLE IN HYPERREALITY

Cultural studies scholars believe that the realm of popular culture is the most powerful educational force in contemporary America. Critical democratic social studies educators must understand these dynamics in order to gain an important voice in the cultural pedagogical conversation. Without an understanding of cultural pedagogy's role in the shaping of individual identity—youth identity in particular—the role social studies teachers play in the lives of their students will continue to fade. Why do so many of our students feel that life is incomprehensible and devoid of meaning? What does it mean, critical social studies teachers wonder, when young people are unable to describe their moods, their affective affiliation to the society around them? Meanings provided to young people by mainstream institutions often do little to help them deal with their affective complexity, their difficulty negotiating the rift between meaning and affect.

In this new context, traditional social studies knowledge and educational expectations seem as anachronistic as a ditto machine. It is not that learning ways of rational thought and making sense of the world are unimportant, but traditional social studies knowledge and educational expectations have little to offer students about making sense of the way they feel, the way their affective lives are shaped. In no way am I arguing that a cultural studies informed analysis of the production of youth in hyperreality demands some "touchy-feely," "let's get in touch with our feelings" educational superficiality. What is needed in this context is a rigorous analysis of the interrelationship between pedagogy, popular culture, meaning making, and youth subjectivity. In an era marked by youth depression, violence, and suicide, such appreciations become extremely important, even life saving. Pessimism about the future, with its concomitant feelings that no one can make a difference, is the common sense of hyperreality's youth (Grossberg, 1992). If affective production can be shaped to reflect these perspectives, then it can be reshaped to lay the groundwork for optimism, passionate commitment, and transformative educational and sociopolitical activity. In these ways, cultural studies adds a dimension to the work of social studies education unfilled by any other subdiscipline.

By studying, for example, the popular culture consumed by young people and their reactions to it over the last several years, I have gained insight into the lives of contemporary youth, typically not addressed in the social studies literature. As I have analyzed these dynamics, I have come to understand the ways that contemporary culture shapes youth subjectivity in ways unimaginable fifty years ago. Familial alienation, for example, provides a context for understanding young people's increasing retreat into their own subcultures. As I studied the *Home Alone* movies of the early 1990s, I found that a central subtheme of the movies involved Macauley Culkin's character's (Kevin) absolute lack of need for parental figures. Alone, he shops with newspaper coupons, protects his family's house, and defends himself against the thugs who attempt to rob him.

All of this is not unusual in the films of John Hughes, whose children and teenagers rule a cosmos where youth culture is the only one that matters. Like Kevin's parents who leave him behind in both *Home Alone* and *Home Alone 2: Lost in New York*, Hughes' mothers and fathers are starkly absent. Since World War II, youth has consistently become more and more separated from adulthood. As early as the 1950s, young people were beginning to convince their parents that adults were losing their ability to shape the culture in which their children lived, and thus, losing control of their sons and daughters. Academic study of young people in the last half of the twentieth century, as it focused attention on youth as "the problem," was shaped by this fear. Viewing the dominant culture and adult values as unproblematic, mainstream scholars have often seen conflict between young people and their parents as evidence of youth dysfunctionality. This functionalist perspective grounded on order insists that youth be instructed to follow directions and that schools maintain the equilibrium of the status quo (Paul, 1994; Lewis, 1992; Griffin, 1993; Polakow, 1992; Kincheloe, 1996).

Corporations of various types have been quick to pick up on the social placement of youth as a separate cultural category, a distinct market demographic. From toy manufacturers to fast food marketers to movie producers, American businesspeople have worked to exploit the youth market. Such entrepreneurs adeptly recognized that liberal notions of youth as naive innocents who should watch only "quality" movies and TV and play with only educational toys missed the growing worldliness of young people. Young people in the first decade of the twenty-first century are not naive and passive media viewers. As advertisers and marketers have learned, youth are active, analytical viewers who many times make their own meanings of media texts. In this context, corporate analysts began to recognize that youth felt oppressed by the middle-class view of them as innocents in need of protection. Drawing upon young people's discomfort, corporate producers began to market to a more "adult" group of young people. By the late 1960s, youth TV and advertising were grounded in this premise; movies followed closely behind. Such productions dismissed the restraint, discipline, and old-fashioned viewpoint that youth should be under the strict control and supervision of parents. Indeed, the new entrepreneurs, in recognizing youth as a distinct phase of life, identified a covert and subversive youth culture and proceeded to feed it, i.e., to colonize it for their own purposes.

A social analyst does not have to search too far to find that young people's enthusiasm for particular TV shows, movies, music, and foods isolates them from their parents. Tapping into this isolation, young people transform it into a source of power—they know of an entire world unfamiliar to their parents. A covert youth culture existed throughout the twentieth century on playgrounds, and in the streets and schools. In the past, however, such a culture was produced by young people and propagated by youth interaction. The youth culture of hyperreality, however, is created by corporate marketers and dispersed by TV and movies in the hopes of inducing young people to consume. As they adeptly undermine middle-class parents' obsession with achievement and success, advertisers and moviemakers connect the subversive youth culture to their products. The theme permeates cultural texts as diverse as McDonald's hamburger advertisements to youth movies. While touting family values as the overt theme of many of their commercials of the last two decades, McDonald's, for example, has tapped into the subversive youth culture by subtextual references to adult unfamiliarity with contemporary children and youth cultural literacy. In many McDonald's and other corporate commercials, young people make adult ignorance or lack of cool the basis for many of their jokes.

CULTURAL STUDIES AND THE "NEW EDUCATION" OF YOUTH

Alienated from their parents' world and absorbed in a world of TV, movies, video games, CD-ROMs, popular music, the Internet and other aspects of popular culture, postmodern young people have access to a world of information unprecedented in human history. It is here, not in school social studies, where young people find out about the world. Students of cultural studies understand that, with their access to these media, youth have gained an adult-like (not necessarily a well-informed) view of the world. Children in this context are likely to watch Mickey Mouse on the Disney Channel for a few minutes and a gang rape of a fifteen-year-old high school girl on Cinemax for the next half hour. Cultural studies scholars often understand that traditional notions of childhood as a time of sequential learning about the world don't work in a hyperreality saturated with sophisticated but power-driven views of reality. When a hotel porter asks Kevin McAlister in *Home Alone 2* if he knows how the TV in his hotel room works, Kevin replied, "I'm ten years old. TV's my life." The point is well taken, and, as a consciousness-dominating, full-disclosure medium, TV provides everyone—60-year-old adults to 8-year-old children with the same data. As postmodern children gain unrestricted knowledge about things once kept secret from nonadults, the mystique of adults as revered keepers of secrets about the world begins to disintegrate. No longer do the elders know more than children about the experience of youth. Given the social and technological changes, they often know less, for example, about video games, computers, TV programs, and so forth. Thus, the authority of adulthood is undermined, as kids' generational experience takes on a character of its own.

The social impact of such a phenomenon is profound on many levels. A subversive kinderculture is created where kids, through their attention to child-targeted programming and commercials, know something that mom and dad don't. This corporate-directed kinderculture provides kids with a body of knowledge adults don't possess, while children's access to adult themes on TV at least makes them conversant with marital, sexual, business-related, criminal, violent, and other traditionally restricted issues (Steinberg & Kincheloe, 1997). When combined with observations of families collapsing, the dynamics of the struggle of a single mother to support her family, parents involved in the "singles" scene, and postdivorce imposition of adult-like chores, children's TV experience provides a full-scale immersion into grown-up culture.

In the context of childhood education, the postmodern experience of being a kid represents a cultural earthquake. The traditional social studies curriculum of the third grade is determined not only by what vocabulary and concepts are "developmentally appropriate" but by what content is judged to be commensurate with third-grade experience in the lived world (Lipsky & Abrams, 1994; Postman, 1994). Hyperreality explodes traditional notions of curriculum development. Third graders can discuss the relationship between women's self-image and the nature of their sexual behavior. When teachers and the culture of school treat such children as if they know nothing of the adult world, the kids come to find school hopelessly archaic, out of touch with the times. This is why the postmodern subversive kinderculture always views school with a knowing wink and a smirk. How quaint school must look to our postmodern children! Critical social studies teachers take this understanding to heart as they contemplate their professional role.

At this point the importance of cultural studies as an important aspect of social studies asserts itself. What are social studies educators to make of this cultural pedagogy, the youth identities that are formed around it, and the knowledge it produces and transmits to young people? What is the role of the social studies curriculum in these changing cultural conditions? Does it maintain itself unchanged, a rock of stability in the chaos of hyperreality, or does it accommodate to the cultural changes, redefining its role in a new era? These are a few of the foundational questions raised by cultural studies. They hold dramatic implications for the future of social studies education.

Chapter  27

Civics in the Social Studies: Critical Democratic Citizenship Education in a Corporatized Hyperreality

Civics is central to the social studies. Picking up on many themes developed throughout *Getting Beyond the Facts*, this chapter will explore in more depth some of the basic concerns of a critical democratic civics in the social, cultural, political, and economic climate of the twenty-first century. It is amazing that so few states require civics teaching as part of the curriculum in American schools. Throughout the twentieth century, social studies educators from a variety of ideological positions spoke of the centrality of civics in any social studies program (Steinberg, 2000). But, the social fragmentation of American life since the mid-twentieth century, the depoliticization and dislocations of the postmodern condition, and educators' lack of interest in citizenship education have pushed civics to the back burner and made public life much more difficult in contemporary American society. Both students and teachers are disconnected from social and political institutions. It is in this disturbing context that democratic social studies teachers must promote a critical civics (Davis & Fernlund, 1995; Parker, 1997b; Stanley, 2000).

No NEUTRALITY HERE:
THE COMMITMENTS OF A CRITICAL DEMOCRATIC CIVICS

My call for a critical democratic civics is grounded in a concern with the health of democracy in the contemporary U.S. In this emergency context I want to make the commitments of a critical democratic civics education very clear. Such a curricular concept is dedicated to the creation of a politically and power-literate society whose citizens are capable of reestablishing a working democratic system. Such citizens are committed to social and economic justice and are adept knowledge workers who strive to make the world a better place to live. They possess an understanding of the context and goals of political commitment. These are not the type of citizens who band together around one political issue but are those who possess a larger understanding that frames and contextualizes their positions on a variety of issues and concerns.

The critical citizens imagined here develop a coherent system of public values and norms in light of which they are able to view contemporary affairs. Using such a critical democratic system of political meaning, they are able to criticize certain practices and embrace other public actions. In this way they can make affective investments in the pursuit of particular social and political goals worth struggling to achieve. Unapologetically, a critical democratic civics operates to protect the oppressed from exploitive power wielders, to intervene on the side of the subjugated. In this context it openly works to bring together exploited individuals who should be working together to fight oppression. Specifically, social studies educators are dedicated to a critical civics struggle to show poor Whites and non-Whites the political interests they share.

When power shifts and culture changes as much as it has over the last few decades, critical analysts maintain that changes in civic strategies and governance are necessary. Political freedom has been jeopardized by the concentration of economic power, as hierarchies have intensified and inequality has been exacerbated. In relation to their understanding power, inequality, the changing nature of work within society, the corporate control of information, and the dominant (safe) ideologies promoted in mainstream social studies and schools in general, critical democratic civics teachers generate a vision of political activism. In addition, they develop a corresponding vision of a just and practical government for a new sociopolitical era. Do not confuse—as many often do—this political activism with a form of party politics. We are referring to larger issues of democracy, not throwing our support to one political party or another. The rest of this chapter connects a critical civics education to the possibilities inherent in a new post-Cartesian politics.

A CRITICAL NEW POLITICS FOR AN ANTI-DEMOCRATRIC ERA

A regressive modernist view of government, like Cartesian-Newtonian thought in general, fragments our perspective and forces us to see government simply as a discrete political dynamic. Government in a more critical perspective is viewed as part of a larger political, economic, social, technological, informational, and ethical context. Perceiving this complex context allows observers to understand that a decontextualized government that sees itself functioning only in a political sphere cannot address the forces that shape it in contemporary society. The concentration of economic power by corporations over the last 20 years, for example, has dramatically changed the way governments operate. Without the benefit of this economic context and the reforms that a knowledge of it necessitates, government would soon become as superfluous as socks on a rooster. To avoid such a reality, critical civics educators argue that a new social contract is needed that explicitly addresses the ways concentrated economic power undermines political freedom. That contract would specify limits to the economic inequality that a democratic society can tolerate (Freeman & Gilbert, 1992; Reich, 1995).

American government in the twenty-first century has lost sight of the fact that when the poor fail, everyone will eventually pay for it. Thus, social justice is not merely a moral question but a pragmatic strategy for survival. Government's modernist predisposition for scientific rationalism removes political leaders and bureaucratic functionaries from the suffering of the poor and their feelings of marginalization. Governmental efficiency does not address the sense of injustice felt by the marginalized. When the marginalized speak of their hurt and their emotions, they cannot understand why no one in policymaking positions listens. Policy experts, who speak about economics with the authority of science, do not perceive the relevance of the emotional pronouncements of the dispossessed to the subject. When, for example, members of the Justice for Janitors campaign testify about their plight, government economists, operating on a different epistemological set of assumptions, see only uninformed individuals emotionally clouding the relevant issues at hand.

The economists are blind to the connection between their policies and the economic difficulties that groups like the janitors must face daily. Operating outside the rationalistic discourse of positivistic political economics, the janitors, their neighbors, and their families' recognize the experts' blindness—their "rational irrationality."

A central feature of the dominant power bloc's ability to dominate those who fall outside its boundaries involves its ability to use scientific rationality over human emotions. The understanding of this epistemological dynamic, this rational irrationality, is, of course, a central feature of a critical social studies curriculum. In the governmental context, this understanding grounds a critical vision of government; it opens the possibility of developing new forms of thinking that help us transcend the limitations of rationalism. This new form of thinking would help critical civics students see through corporate attempts to mystify them about the politics of self-interest. Corporate leaders and their political allies have been able to convince many individuals that democratic political and economic change is not in their best interest. Whereas conservatives attempt to mystify Americans, especially those from the working class, about democratic reform, liberals tend to focus their reforms on the techniques of government, in the process avoiding fundamental questions of power and its equitable distribution. A prerequisite for the creation of a renewed public sphere, a critical civics is an exposure and disruption of existing power relations.

That path is difficult, there is no doubt. But those committed to a critical vision of government have no choice; they must take the path of maximum resistance, the path that contributes to the nurturance and cultivation of democracy. Such critical citizens must make sure that government collects a fair share of taxes from corporations, enforces laws regulating corporate pollution, protects American jobs from exploitive use of foreign labor, provides health care and health insurance for those who need it, and helps the unemployed find good work. Critical civics educators and their allies in other social spheres understand that a democratic government has numerous means of helping establish a more equal social order.

Contrary to the well-publicized pronouncements of right-wing commentators, the use of such mechanisms will not constitute an attempt to "legislate equality." What such spokespersons fail to realize is that leveling access and weeding out impediments to social mobility is merely an effort to address a flagrantly unfair system. Policies such as these do not constitute a move to provide special advantage but are designed merely to lessen many of the disadvantages poor and other marginalized peoples face daily. A critically grounded government can adjust fiscal policy, taxation, support of research and development, and regulation of collective bargaining, to mention only a few strategies for democracy (Gee, Hull, & Lankshear, 1996; Kallick, 1996)

Advocates of a critical civics are well aware of the potential for governmental tyranny. They know that governmental promises have often turned into nightmares and that public institutions often regulate individuals far more than they contribute to their emancipation. In order to address such political dysfunction, critical civics educators must understand the unexamined belief structures on which it rests. In this regard, we can begin to rethink government, both in its organization and its function. In our critical vision, government works hard to establish and maintain an economic democracy with as little bureaucracy and personal regulation as possible. No one here is advocating some form of blind faith in our reliance on big government, as calls for egalitarian reforms are often represented by right-wing operatives.

We know too much about the pathology of bureaucracy to fall into that trap. In the public conversation about American politics, it is rarely noted that the growth of government in the twentieth century did not take place in a social and historical vacuum. Governmental growth was a response to the growth of corporate power in the industrial era and the unprecedented problems such expansion caused. Small-business owners and farmers were unable to compete with emerging megafirms; monopolies tortured consumers with price fixing; labor lost the power to bargain effectively with its corporate bosses; and intoxicated by their growing power, megacompanies lost interest in consumer and worker health and safety. Such dynamics reflect the indifference of uncontested power wielders.

A NEW CIVICS, A NEW POLITICS IN A CRITICAL DEMOCRATIC SOCIAL STUDIES

The creation of a powerful government as a countervailing force to corporate power was a logical move in the 1930s. And in the power-balancing act created in the Fordist compromise that responded to that need, big government achieved some modest successes in mitigating the impact of disparate wealth. But, of course, big government became, like other hierarchies of administration, more and more bureaucratic in its organizational culture, a situation which resulted in rational irrationalities. When the public became sufficiently fed up with the dysfunctionality of government bureaucracy in the 1970s, corporate leaders took advantage of the impulse and manipulated it to their own ends. Instead of calling for a reform of government bureaucracy and inefficiency in its role as countervailing force to corporate power, corporate leaders and their allies convinced many Americans that neither government nor its countervailing power function were needed. Thus, reference to the all-too-real problem of bureaucratic pathology became a front for a much larger corporate agenda: the end of government interference in its affairs and the termination of attempts to mitigate the growing disparity of wealth (Bowles, Gordon, & Weisskopf, 1990; Wirth, 1983; Ferguson, 1984).

For social studies educators who promote the critical vision of government, the question thus becomes this: How can we create the political power to counter the expanding domination of corporations without the bureaucratic side effects the organizational structure of such an entity tends to produce? In many ways, this may be the most important political question of our era. The concern with bureaucratic government should induce us to strengthen the democratic nature of the state, not destroy it. Maybe, government has something to learn from the more progressive aspects of post-Fordism's organizational strategies. If government understood these features, it would move away from mass-produced administration to a more flexible and decentralized state. Public services in this model would abandon centralized and standardized forms of delivery and focus attention on differentiated, contextually relevant goals. The counterbureaucratic critical governmental vision would embrace a true notion of localism, not the pseudolocalism of post-Fordist megacorporations that paint a "ma-and-pa" facade on their franchises. Indeed, the critical vision holds that government would be big enough to thwart the oppression of corporations but smart enough to perform its tasks humanely.

Many argue that the time has come for a progressive government to relegate many of its functions to other, nongovernmental organizations. However, that proposal is dangerous and must be addressed very carefully. Critical educators and cultural workers need to study this question carefully before dismissing or including the proposal in their critical vision of government. Liberalism has undoubtedly been too single-minded in its reliance on government and, in the process, has ignored the reformist possibilities of other social sectors. Leaders of the women's movement understood this dynamic when they urged women to politicize the personal; democratizing power in personal relationships was not the province of government.

Addressing such personal issues was the concern of men and women and groups in what might be termed "civil society." Women therefore did not push for passage of laws legally forcing men to change diapers and wash dishes. Instead, they sought a variety of social influences, including small groups that aided those who wanted change and educational groups that called attention to problematic forms of masculinity and patriarchal structures. In this context, such civil society efforts would be supported by governmental actions requiring equal pay for equal work, preventing sexual harassment in the workplaces, and increasing educational opportunities for girls in school (Murray, 1992; Gee, Hull, & Lankshear, 1996; Kallick, 1996).

The lesson to be learned from this example is that a socially concerned government is needed but is not to be relied upon to carry out all aspects of social action. Thus, critical civics educators must carefully distinguish between rhetoric that advocates action in civil society for the purpose of shutting down government's role of countering excessive corporate power and discourse that envisions a creative and progressive synergy between government and civil groups. Obviously, the point made here is that civil organizations, such as unions, can play an important role in the quest for social and economic justice, egalitarian institutions, and a critical democratic social studies education.

The possibilities raised by government, education, unions, and other civil organizations working together for such goals are exciting. I have no problem with including an active civil society working with the help of state agencies in our critical civics. If carefully planned, the civil agencies could help rebuild civil life by aiding the poor, extending health care, constructing affordable housing, cleaning up the environment, and helping with education for work. Part of this careful planning would involve the engagement of government support for these supplemental social actions from the civil sector.

The role of civil organizations becomes especially vital given the social, economic, and political changes wrought internationally by the globalized economy and its multinational corporations. The same forces that undermine the well-being of Americans are insidiously operating throughout the world. Americans, either with or without the help of government, must connect their democratic and justice-related interests with people with similar concerns in other countries. Working together, unions, educational organizations, and other civil groups can demand specific standards of behavior from multinational corporations. As we know, the post-Fordist economy pays no allegiance to national boundaries, and as a result, transgovernmental organizations are needed to police the transgressions. Critical civics educators can connect with and help construct these transgovernmental organizations, so they and their students can learn and benefit from the knowledge gained in the effort to monitor and limit the irresponsible behavior of the multinational megacorporations (Moberg, December 16, 1996; Kallick, 1996; Rifkin, 1995; Greider, 1992).

THE FADING PUBLIC POLITICAL DOMAIN: ADDRESSING THE DISSOLUTION OF AMERICAN DEMOCRACY

Electoral politics in the first decade of the twenty-first century is a sham in the ways it attempts to hide the way government actually works from citizens. Of course, this circumstance holds dramatic implications for social studies in general and critical civics education in particular. The sacred values that Americans have associated with democracy are crumbling, as power shifts from the many to the few. Government now responds less to popular will and more to narrow financial interests and influential elites. New alignments of power interests decimate the democratic expectations of a public that grows increasingly jaded and cynical. Interestingly, despite the dramatic breakdown in democracy over the last decades of the twentieth century, the form and veneer of democratic government has stayed the same.

The only change in the format of American electoral politics over the last 30 years has been that more money is spent by and for candidates than ever before. Amazingly, the way American government and civics are taught in elementary and secondary social studies, despite such dramatic changes in the function of democracy, is indistinguishable from such classes of the 1950s. "Now, class, the three branches of government are the executive, legislative, and judicial branches; a bill becomes law by . . ." Such decontextualized teaching conveys a misleading impression of how government works in contemporary America.

A critical civics asks questions left unexplored in most government classes: Why do some groups shape the government's process of decision making, while others have little voice? Why, critical civics educators ask, do monied interests consistently gain government support for their needs, while the vast majority of people are ignored? In building a construct of the world that helps social studies students place themselves socially, critical civics educators describe an American democracy that is a struggle for power, not between citizens but between organized economic interests. How can unorganized working people, weak unions, or small civil organizations compete with corporations or coalitions of corporations that employ teams of lawyers and lobbyists, fund political parties, political action committees, and even TV shows? (The McLaughlin Group, for example, is a corporate-friendly weekly news program funded by General Electric.) The impact of such investments places corporate concerns on the government's front burner, moving the individual needs of citizens off the stove.

The public perception that monied interests control government through bribery misses the subtle way influence is typically peddled. Corporate money employs lawyers and lobbyists with connections. Their job is often to build relationships between corporate leaders with particular needs and government functionaries. Indeed, many of the lawyers and lobbyists are former—many of them high-ranking—governmental officials. Their job is to put the corporate leaders in touch with the government operatives who can help them. Such real-life issues are rarely addressed in mainstream social studies classes. What a disservice this does students who want to make civic contributions.

What do the corporate financiers get for their purchased influence? Generally speaking, the answer involves the passage of legislation tailored to maximize the financial well-being of corporate management, and this pay-off is often referred to as corporate welfare, or welfare for the rich. In 1993, the federal government, for instance, provided $104 billion in direct payments and tax breaks to American multinational corporations. The Sunkist food company received almost $18 million for the promotion of its orange juice. Farming conglomerates collectively received over $29 billion that same year. McDonald's received $456,000 to tout its Chicken McNuggets. Mining, timber, pharmaceutical, and many other types of corporations are annual beneficiaries of such government handouts.

Another bargain corporations get for their money is velvet-glove treatment for corporate or white-collar crime. 62% of Fortune 500 corporations have been involved in one or more significant illegalities;

42% have been found guilty of two or more corrupt activities; 15% have been convicted in five or more cases (Greider, 1992). Corporate influence allows major offending companies to avoid the penalties most working Americans would suffer. Ordinary Americans who are criminals are prohibited from engaging in politics; corporate convicts continue to play dominating roles in the political process. No wonder Senator John McCain's modest proposals for campaign reform in the 2000 Republican primary struck such a nerve with individuals familiar with these power-driven realities.

Corporate lawyers have slyly won legal rulings that consider corporations as organizations the same as people under the law. This means that corporations as a legal entity, not individual corporate leaders, are liable for corporate criminal activity. Since you cannot imprison a corporation and corporate leaders are shielded from prosecution, corporations literally get away with murder and continue to operate with little more than a slap on the wrist. The million-dollar-plus salaries corporations pay their lawyers are lucrative financial investments, since their legal henchmen use their expertise to pervert legislation designed to protect labor unions and workers so as to serve corporate objectives. In fact, laws passed several decades ago to protect the interests of the weakest members of American society are now used daily to undermine the needs of the poor and protect corporations from legal penalties for their sociopathic actions.

Such disparity of treatment insults the concept of equal protection under the law, since it pounds another nail into the coffin of democracy. Without a civic faith in the connections between the governed and the government, the country will descend into a civil chaos that produces more Tim McVeighs, White militias, and violent antigovernment movements of all stripes. The role of the critical civics educator is to reveal these injustices and threats to democracy but also to channel the outrage and cynicism of citizens into democratically affirming and socially responsible actions (Greider, 1992; Bowles, Gordon, & Wiesskopf, 1990; Rifkin, 1995; Schwartz, 1994).

The Need for a Critical Global Civics: Privatization Around the World

The decline of democracy and the decline of government in general is exacerbated by the globalization of the economy and the evolution of powerful national corporations into superpowerful multinational corporations. The multinationals are so powerful that they have subverted the capacity of governments to protect their citizens. Leaders of multinational corporations are now able to bypass established political institutions, among them tax laws, commercial regulations, employment policies, and environmental statutes. Nation-states no longer have the power to regulate their democratic economic spheres as they did even 20 years ago. Given the powerful role of megacorporations, national governments grow more and more reluctant to protect their domestic markets. So far, no governmental strategy has been developed to respond to the profound changes wrought by the power reconfigurations of globalization. Asian, African, and Latin American governments are collapsing, as multinational corporations vie with indigenous people's movements and informal economics to fill the political and economic vacuums created.

The hand of government grows weaker as the invisible hand of the market strengthens in this era of globalization and privatization. Private corporations are better suited to the new electronic world, the privatization argument goes, than traditional governments. Not being connected to any specific geographical place, they can cope with the supersonic pace of global market forces. With their post-Fordist dynamic flexibility, they can move markets quickly from one continent to another, in the process, shaping the commercial and political priorities of all countries they encounter. Thus, governments are adrift and on the retreat in the face of the march of privatization. A critical civics must attend to this expanding crisis of government and carefully delineate a new, globally conscious, justice-directed, democratic, and creative mission for the nation-state. Without a critical vision of government for the new globalized world, privatization is likely to create untenable conditions in the short run for the poor and working people and, in the long run, for everyone (Barnet & Cavanagh, 1994; Aronowitz & DiFazio, 1994; Rifkin, 1995).

The wealthy can protect themselves to a large degree from the deterioration of the public space by withdrawing into their secure and self-sufficient fortresses. Working people and the poor, however, must suffer the brunt of such deterioration because they have no place to which they can retreat. Without an interruption in the march of privatization and the decline of government, more and more individuals will find themselves unemployed or underemployed, sinking ever deeper into an intractable underclass. They will engage in an informal economy to survive, bartering and trading for food. Many will turn to theft, crime, drug dealing, and prostitution to get by.

At one level, talk of privatization may be misleading, since it implies a boundary between the public sector and the private sector that has faded away in the last few years. Because of the overwhelming influence corporations exert on national, state, and local governments, it is hard to delineate exactly where the public ends and the private begins. This blurring of the private and public that comes under the umbrella of privatization is seen in the new business-operated schools with curricula, of course, that discourage questioning the path of the new privatized world and its sacred icons of deregulation, consumerism, competition, and individualization or, more accurately, customization. The highest expression of the communications revolution is the privatized battering of eyes and ears with inducements to consume.

So pervasive and compelling are these advertisements that six-year-olds know more about beer than democracy. Using the neoclassical language of the free market and privatization, the power derived from controlling the global media empire, and their inordinate influence on governments domestic and foreign, megacorporations are becoming the emperors of the twenty-first century (Reich, 1995; Rifkin, 1995; Gee, Hull, & Lankshear, 1996; Barnet & Cavanagh, 1994). If not the emperors, corporations are at least the most important civics teachers of the twenty-first century.

Ford Motor Company's economy, for example, is already bigger than that of Saudi Arabia or Norway. The yearly sales of Philip Morris are larger than New Zealand's annual gross domestic product. Such statistics are interesting but mean little if they are not accompanied by the understanding that the balance of power in global politics has moved from public territorial governments to nomadic private companies. The national state is being supplanted by the meta-state—a coalition of multinational corporations and their allies in national governments, international trade organizations, and education. These multinational corporation-led coalitions are the first secular organizations to plan and operate on a global level. Amazingly, little of the planning and organizational work of the corporate meta-state deals with the questions raised here concerning the deteriorating public space, the growing disparity of wealth, and the teaching of civics.

It seems of little importance to the new emperors that the profit needs of the multinationals are forcing governments to nullify protective labor codes and other securities for poor and working people. In this new context, employers in nations around the world are enabled to pay lower wages and to import cheap, undocumented workers. Thus, the disparity of wealth grows both between rich and poor countries and within rich and poor countries. In light of globalization's creation of the meta-state, there no longer exists a discrete entity called the U.S. workplace; we now have a global workplace. Such issues are central to the ability of civic educators and their students to make sense of the forces that shape the political economy in general and civic consciousness in particular. These understandings are central to the critical civics curriculum (Smart, 1992; Aronowitz & DiFazio, 1994).

LEFT WITHOUT A CLUE: THE EMERGENCE OF A NEW FORM OF GOVERNMENT

Often, when I observe middle school civics teachers lecturing their students about how a bill becomes law, never referring to lobbyists and economic power wielders' role in the process, I wonder about the future of participatory democracy. If students are to learn how power actually operates and how governing takes place in a privatized twenty-first century, they will have to unlearn the fairy-tale civics lessons they learn in many schools. To help these students, workers and other people around the world understand the merging role of these multinational corporations, it may be appropriate to characterize such organizations as a new form of government—corporate government. That designation removes megacompanies from the shadowy realm in which they operate and exposes their function for precisely what it is. Along with their allies in public government, the media, and education, corporations form a private governmental system.

Such a system, via its technopower, regulates its worldwide empire more effectively than any previous form of governance. This ultimate privatization, or rule by private government, holds far more power over people's lives than "public government," because it dictates terms of employment and controls people's livelihood. As this corporate governmental system shapes individuals' ability to make a living, it exacts a degree of subservience that public government could never equal. Corporate governments' ability to punish economically is a more powerful tool of domination than the laws deployed by public government. Dismissal from one's job can take place without warning and can be just as personally devastating as a prison term or even capital punishment. When the effects of dismissal from a job are studied, we find that getting fired often causes the untimely death of a worker—a form of death penalty by the economic government.

The social understanding we have of our governmental system has been skewed by the corporate government's ability to blame socioeconomic problems on the public government. Often, workers, who themselves have been laid off by corporate downsizing or deindustrialization, speak of getting "government off our backs," blaming the corporate action on public government. They often vote for candidates who promise to reduce the size of government and get government out of business affairs, not knowing that they are helping exacerbate the tyranny of an unregulated corporate government. Using this "get government off our backs" mantra, corporations, since the late 1970s, have steadily gained the power to govern and, as a result, make more money. Attempts to make life better for working people become more and more difficult as citizens and elected officials continue to turn power over to the corporate emperors. Despite the picture painted by business leaders and their political allies, public government experienced a decline in power over the last decades of the twentieth century. By the first decade of the twenty-first century, fewer decisions that shape our lives are made through the traditional political process.

An important development that has served to strengthen this corporate government involves the defection of middle- and high-ranking government officials to corporate payrolls. From different presidential administrations, members of the Treasury Department, including legislative counsel and assistant secretaries, Energy Department lawyers, the chair of the Joint Chiefs of Staff, and even former attorney generals of the United States now work for big business. Their job is to influence the decisions their former departments make in a manner that benefits their corporate bosses, and there is no doubt that corporations get what they pay for in this respect. With these functionaries in place and buoyed by the heady freedom of action provided by deregulation, the corporate government is a post-Fordist version of the old urban political machine. Differing in scale and power—there are hundreds of corporate "private" political machines in operation—the corporate government is less attentive to its constituency than the old party machine, since it teaches, leads, and dictates without the accountability sometimes forced on the machines by elections.

This politics of corporatism, armed with IRS technopower, claims, like other governments, to look out for various constituencies in need of protection. It is not public government, corporate government maintains, that speaks for workers but the humane corporation; in other words, your corporation, my McDonald's, "do it all for you." In addition to the broad category of citizens, corporations speak for consumers, stockholders, the world of business in general, and Americans and their interests around the planet. Policies that are beneficial for us, corporate spokespeople maintain, are good for the masses. When particular groups oppose the needs of the corporate government, the myth tells us, they are hurting millions of Americans. Corporate welfare for the rich, for example, is justified on the basis that its real beneficiaries are the "little guys" that such funding allows the corporate government to help.

Because of their unparalleled access to the public via control of the various media, corporations provide appealing and simplistic explanations for complex socioeconomic problems. Do answers such as "big government," a "failure of personal responsibility," the "waning of the work ethic," "rock and rap music," "schools not teaching values," and "welfare loafers" sound familiar? These are the "correct answers" to the civics tests provided by omnipresent corporate civics teachers. What we need, in addition to less public government, corporate government's philosophers conclude, is a positivist intelligentsia that issues indisputable edicts based on management science, neoclassical economics, evolutionary biology, and behavioral theory. By the way, from the perspective of corporate government's educational experts, such an intelligentsia can make use of these disciplines to build a good philosophy of privatized civics education. A critical civics appreciates the fatal limitations of such a pedagogy of regulation.

In light of the power and tyrannical behavior of corporate government, those Americans who have placed such great faith in "the new day of freedom coming," when the public government is to be rendered sufficiently insignificant, are in for profound disappointment. Although their freedom to shop at Wal-Mart may well remain intact in the future, a wide variety of traditional political freedoms, such as having a voice in the making of political policies, will have vanished. The protections citizens enjoy from public government were guaranteed by the Constitution, but no similar document exists to limit corporate government. Indeed, there are no institutions to provide checks and balances in the privatization of government. Unless critical citizens act, nothing will impede the penetration of market values into all phases of human life from romantic relationships to corporate education. In this context, the term "free market" is used as a signifier designed to disguise the coercive process that devalues people and their well-being, as corporate leaders pursue policies that ultimately enhance their profit margins (Reich, 1995; Greider, 1992; Schwartz, 1994).

NOWHERE TO RUN:
THE CORRUPTION OF AMERICAN POLITICAL PARTIES

When push comes to shove in contemporary American politics, neither political party, Republican or Democrat, is willing to challenge corporate government. Both are far too invested in it, too ensnared in its tentacles to resist it. Most important, both parties are too addicted to corporate money to stray too far away. Thus, Americans find themselves in a peculiar situation: Their two major political parties operate in the grasp of the corporate government. Corporate leaders and their political allies in the public government and the media perpetuate the myth that the views expressed by the Republicans and Democrats represent the full spectrum of political opinion. Thus, it is easy to dismiss opinions such as the ones presented here; in the pseudo-universe of civic perspectives, they simply do not exist.

The way to understand the difference between the Republicans and Democrats is to look at their corporate clients, or, as some analysts describe them, their investors. Ideological differences do not divide contemporary political parties; the needs of their clients do. At most, parties serve as mediating agencies between different corporations and not between individuals with differing political viewpoints. In fact, many of the most important issues of American politics involve conflicts between these investors and their Republican and Democratic gladiators. Such corporate control of the political agenda degrades the democratic process and the parties that claim to operate on particular civic principles. At the same time, it undermines the interests of citizens and all those who fall outside the inner circle of corporate management. Republicans have been comfortable with corporate coziness for decades. Often involved with commerce, Republicans have found it easy to view voters as consumers. Their job as politicians, they came to believe, was to identify what voters think and feel and to then adjust their political advertising to those thoughts and feelings. Since Republicans represented the monied interests, no one was particularly surprised when Republicans provided increasing support to the corporate government.

The Democratic Party's sellout was a different matter. Known and identified at one time as the party of average people, the Democrats have grown closer and closer to corporations and their money. By the close of the 1980s, the Democrats were, in reality, the party of corporate lawyers. Such political operatives rotate in and out of private and government jobs and have replaced the old networks of local party leaders, who decades ago formed the basis of the party. When political analysts argue that Democratic liberalism is dead, they are unwittingly referring to the fact that liberal operatives made a devil's pact with corporate money: They could not take corporate money and defy the rule of the free market. Liberals have few ideas because they, like the Republicans, have laid down their arms in deference to neoclassical economics and corporate rule.

The Democrats have particularly courted high-tech corporate moneylenders, winning friends in Silicon Valley and other high-tech corridors. One of the starkest examples of the Democrat's corporate coitus involved their support of corporate raider Frank Lorenzo's attempt to crush the labor unions at Eastern Airlines. Hiring a host of Democratic Party lawyers and influence peddlers to negate the influence of the machinists', pilots', and flight attendants' unions, Lorenzo fought these unions with the help of Democratic "friends of labor." Lorenzo was forced into mediation and eventually lost the airline, but the support generated in the Democratic Party for such a flagrant enemy of labor held profound implications (Cooper, May 27, 1996; Greider, 1992; Reich, 1995).

That forces in the Democratic Party could support Lorenzo illustrated the power of the corporate government in the most unlikely places. With the victory of Bill Clinton in the wake of these capitulations, it comes as no surprise that the New Democrats have consistently supported the freedom of multinational corporations to move, regardless of the consequences for workers in America and around the world. In his two administrations, Clinton never promoted workers' interests to the point that his party's Wall Street supporters might balk. Indeed, it never struck Clinton as a problem that average worker wages were 13% lower by the end of the 1990s than they were in 1973. The Democratic collaborators of the first decade of the twenty-fist century are cavalier about the fact that one of three contemporary workers is unemployed, underemployed, or stuck in the peripheral workforce with no benefits or protections. No wonder so many Americans, working-class Americans in particular, are fed up with both political parties. So far has the Democratic Party strayed from its New Deal concern for the well-being of the poor that only about one in ten Americans identifies it as the party of the average person. How do critical civics educators tell their economically marginalized students that, in the existing political configuration, they have no one to represent their needs?

The corporate government fears the anger that permeates the electorate. Such discontent could lead to an abrupt seismic shift in the political landscape that could express itself in a frightening fascist extremism or, more positively, in a progressive politics that transcends senile liberalism and Social Darwinist conservatism. Many critical analysts have recently advocated formation of an American Labor Party, maybe one that, at least in the short run, would not run a slate of candidates but would campaign for public awareness of the political dynamics discussed here. Many union leaders have endorsed that idea, hoping to devise a way to respond to the corporate government's wildly successful efforts to divide workers around issues of gun control, race, and abortion.

We keep giving the Democratic Party money, union leaders complain, and they kick us down. A little time passes, they continue, and we reward them with more money. A labor party could learn from the ridiculous behavior of the existing political parties that spend hundreds of millions of dollars on vacuous TV advertisements but virtually nothing on grassroots organizing. If political money were spent on developing methods of responding to people rather than manipulating them, citizens would soon understand that the purpose of the party was not simply to win elections but to serve their civic needs. The present operations of the Republicans and the Democrats make it hard for Americans to imagine such a political reality (Bacon, April 1, July 8, 1996; Pollin, 1996; Kallick, 1996; Cooper, April 8, 1996).

The political dysfunctions described here call for new forms of action, new types of civic education. So far, few Americans have objected to forms of education that overtly promote partisan corporate interests. Even traditional high-school economics, as previously argued, has been pressured by business leaders to redesign itself as free enterprise economics, characterized by crass celebrations of neoclassical economics and an unregulated market. Business-operated vocational programs teach future workers little more than compliance to management demands and positive (passive) attitudes. To argue for a critical civics that provides another perspective on what might be democratic is in part an effort to balance a curriculum dominated by the ideologies and economic interests of the corporate government. Since public government no longer works like the model taught in school, critical democratic social studies educators teach an alternative civics that helps future citizens understand the demands of citizenship along the postmodern divide. The corporate government has used its power to saturate the society with what many label as a hegemonic picture of the world. A hegemonic portrait attempts to win citizens' consent to a way of seeing their lives and reality that works to the advantage of those in positions of power.

Despite the fact that the corporate-taught privatized civics is a form of indoctrination, the critical civics proposed here refuses to indoctrinate its perspectives. It does not pass off its belief structures as truth. Despite this protest, many will view such an overtly political form of civics as a manifestation of indoctrination. Such a charge confuses the development of a civic vision with the pedagogy that is used in conjunction with it. Critical social studies educators who teach a critical civics, argue that they can admit their own political commitments while teaching their students to act on the democratic principles of learning to make their own choices and acting on their own beliefs. A major difference separates a corporate privatized civics from the critical civics education presented here. Critical civics teachers always alert their students to the fact that a particular view of the political world is being provided.

Also, students in a critical civics class understand that they are free to agree or disagree with the critical perspective. Their success in the class does not hinge on their acceptance of the point of view of the teacher. They are asked simply to understand the perspective and engage with it in a profound way. Education, especially civics education, is never neutral. Indeed, when we attempt to remain neutral, like many churches in Nazi Germany, we support the prevailing power structure. Recognition of the political implications of thinking suggests that teachers should take a position and make it understandable to their students. However (and critical social studies teachers are very clear about this), teachers' political commitments do not grant them the right to impose these positions on their students. It is important to emphasize this point: It is not the critical civics teachers described here who are guilty of indoctrination; it is the "neutral" corporate civics teachers who never tell their students that they are providing them with a point of view.

Such information producers/teachers simply pass off a view of the superiority of a corporate government (not even using such a term) as the truth. When such corporate advocates promote the notion that all words and deeds that oppose the dominant political ideology of the day are forms of educational indoctrination, they forget how everyday experience is constructed in a sociopolitical context marked by an inequitable distribution of power. To refuse to name the structural sources of human suffering and exploitation or the forces that subvert democracy is not a neutral position, In fact, such a stance subjectively supports oppression and the power relations that sustain it. The mainstream argument that any oppositional way of seeing represents an imposition of one's views on somebody else is similar to the nineteenth-century ruling-class idea that raising one's voice, struggling politically, or engaging in social criticism violated a gentlemanly code of civility (Giroux, 1988). Who's indoctrinating whom? In the name of neutrality, the corporatist mainstream promotes particular forms of decontextualized thinking. Here lies the irony of civic objectivity.

As part of their objective lessons on contemporary government, corporate civics pass along what critical social studies educators view as "an anti-democratic map of political reality." The power of this oppressive map of civic reality is difficult to overestimate (Reich, 1995). A misleading map of reality is being promoted when individuals are induced to buy into a worldview that proposes that public government will not allow businesses and corporations the freedom to act in ways that would improve the lives of workers and consumers; when any growth of public government is seen as bad and any growth of corporations is good; when non-Whites and women are portrayed as having all the advantages and, because of affirmative action, are thriving while White men are suffering; when unions are described as outdated and as doing nothing but impeding the efficient operations of corporations; and when education that teaches the necessity of an unregulated market and worker compliance to management is viewed as nonpolitical, but a critical civics education is seen as political. The success of such promotion has left us with a lack of civic knowledge that undermines our ability to make sense of the macrostructures of which we are a part. Critical civics helps social studies students make sense of the larger social context and of their place in it, because it teaches them the hidden rules and assumptions that permeate the invisible social organism.

In a recent book on vocational education, *How Do We Tell the Workers? The Socioeconomic Foundations of Work and Vocational Education*, I wrote about how a corporate-directed form of vocational education taught workers a civic education grounded on passivity and acceptance of a corporate view of the workplace. Present forms of vocational education, unfortunately, too often avoid the issues raised by a critical civics. When young women are educated for office work, for example, technical knowledge about office equipment and material processing takes precedence.

Issues of social relations, the role of the work in the larger structure of the corporation, safety, worker rights, pay, unions, or the personal effects of new technology are not deemed a part of the vocational curriculum. A vocational program built around an awareness of our critical civics would promote a metaconsciousness of the purposes of vocational education and school in general. With the rise of corporate government and its social and educational influence, an awareness of the objectives of a vocational program becomes more and more important. Students need to understand whose interests are being served by the curriculum, as well as the way the program views their own personal role in the enterprise. Questions concerning this massive corporate power and its ability to quash inquiry into the actual results of vocational programs are infrequently asked in the enterprise of vocational education.

If having power involves learning to act in one's own behalf, few vocational students study power. Corporate government attempts to train its workers to be passive in civics but active in the pursuit of corporate values. It is fascinating to observe this post-Fordist schizophrenia in operation, as future workers are encouraged ad nauseum to use their minds, take chances, show initiative, ask questions, and break away from the chains of tradition—but not in relation to questions of worker rights and justice. Corporate leaders covertly induce workers, worker-trainees, and vocational students to do just the opposite in these domains.

In the corporate mind-set, the idea of empowered worker-citizens who ask questions of democracy and insist on good work is not a pleasant thought. In order to keep such a civic empowerment process from occurring, corporations monitor vocational programs and spend millions of dollars on TV and other media to promote countermessages. Even without the conscious hegemonic messages promoted by corporations, TV as a communications medium seems to undermine the interest of

younger viewers in the political sphere. This has added to the depoliticization process. Political participation has remained relatively stable
among citizens who came of age before TV, but it has fallen precipitously among younger people. Research on younger workers indicates that
political reporting seems remote and nonsensical to them, and, as a
result, they quickly lose interest in it.

If TV has taught these viewers to be hip and cynical about the mediated world it presents, then such hip cynicism reaches its apex in young
viewers' perspectives toward the political domain. Such perspectives
position them as remote and impotent in relation to the political cosmos.
Citizenship thus becomes a concept that simply fails to connect with
everyday life. No one profits from such civic alienation more than corporate government. This circumstance enables it to continue its transference of power from the public to the private with minimal
interference. As corporations colonize the concept of empowerment, the
term's connection with the political sphere is frayed. Empowerment in
this corporate discourse becomes a privatized notion, revolving around
the freedom to consume and to work within wider boundaries of creativity. Just as long as the empowered creative work contributes to an
increase in productivity and short-term profit margins, workers can be as
empowered as they want to be. In the lexicon of the post-Fordist corporate government: Enjoy the benefits of the Brave New Empowered
World! A critical civics in this bizarre dimension becomes far more difficult to teach, but far more necessary.

Critical civics in a vocational educational setting is both a pedagogy
and a political vision that struggles to provide vocational students and
workers with an understanding of the social, economic, political, philosophical, and ethical context in which labor and schooling for it takes
place. A critical civics for workers attempts to counter the confusion created by corporate messages and the crazy-quilt media civics taught on
TV. In a hyperreality marked by confusion and a loss of meaning, critical
civics attempts to make sense of the socioeconomic and political world.
In order to accomplish this difficult feat, the invisible must be made visible. For example, a central feature of any critical vocational teacher's
civics curriculum would involve the recognition of the market's influence
on vocational education.

Indeed, this observation may form the basis of any critical civics program for future workers. This understanding can serve as a springboard to
an analysis of the impact of twenty-first-century global economics on the

work lives of vocational students. In this context, teachers induce students to question the ways public and corporate governmental decisions shape their work futures: Will students be able to gain steady, long-terms jobs? Will they be able to achieve economic security? Will they have access to career advancement and financial mobility? Will the attainment of good work be possible? How as worker-citizens can they help shape political and economic policies to benefit themselves and their fellow workers around the world (Valli, 1988; Reich, 1995; Schwartz, 1994; Lakes, 1994a; Simon, Dippo, & Schenke, 1991).

DIRTYING OUR HANDS: ENGAGING IN POLITICAL WORK

With these understandings of the insidiousness of corporate civics in mind, critical civics demands that students be introduced to the messy everyday world of politics. As unpleasant and distasteful as the media has convinced us to consider this realm, work within it is noble, patriotic, and necessary. Critical civic work in this realm means reaching across racial, class, and gender boundaries and forming alliances with people who are in some way different from oneself in the pursuit of common goals. Such critical civics work involves humbly engaging in dialogue about values and visions and their application in the complexity and ambiguity of everyday life. The work of critical citizenship requires a fidelity to the principles of social and economic justice and a commitment to marginalized individuals that is so strong it can overcome the divisive issues that separate us from one another. Middle- and upper-middle-class "experts" must refrain at all costs from "leading" such a movement and speaking for their lower-status allies. Such agents must develop the ability to work with exploited people in a way that is permeated with a genuine humility.

For all the cynicism that the political and economic events of the last several decades have generated in all of us, we can make a difference. Nothing shocks the unresponsive Congress as much as seeing several of their colleagues defeated in their reelection bids by a popular movement of organized people. Just because public government now takes a back seat to corporate government does not mean that the situation is irreversible. The monied interests have always feared movements that speak in terms of democracy and egalitarianism. Critical democratic social studies educators must confront these contemporary monied interests that have subverted the notion of a government by the people and build coalitions of friends of democracy. Such friends might include a united worldwide labor movement, indigenous peoples movements, environmental movements, women's movements, and ethnic justice movements, all of which can interrupt the smooth operations of the international corporate government. The future of democracy in the U.S. and around the world is intimately connected with the success of our critical civics.

Chapter  28

Teaching Government in a Critical Social Studies: Building a Political Vision

An understanding of the role of government in society is a central feature of any social studies program. This chapter provides social studies teachers with a critical democratic vision of government as it relates to social justice, economic justice, egalitarianism, the politics of knowledge, and the reconstruction of community. In the twenty-first century U.S., there is widespread confusion about the role of government, especially in light of corporate government's domination of the public conversation about the issue.

Looking back on the election of 2000 and the 36 days of confusion, anger, misinformation, and manipulation, the American people gained new insights into the effects of "confusion about the role of government" and civic illiteracy. Millions of Americans watched as talking heads on CNBC, MSNBC, and CNN explained the basic workings of the electoral college and state and federal election laws. Many Americans, for the first time, became aware of the anti-democratic origins of the electoral college and the role of private money in public elections. The degree of the general publics' lack of knowledge and lack of involvement in the governmental/political processes and their effects was brought home to many people. The need for a political vision and a deep, complex understanding of the role of government in everyday life became highlighted by the electoral debacle. In this context, critical social studies educators ask four crucial questions about government as they build a critical political vision:

1. What should the role of government be in a democratic society?
2. Given the changes brought about by the dramatic expansion of corporate power and free market capitalism, what new roles must government play in the twenty-first century?
3. How can social studies educators and cultural workers promote sustainable economic growth and socio-political justice through the development of progressive government and innovative nongovernmental political organizations?
4. How do these political dynamics relate to the rethinking of social studies education in the first decade of the twenty-first century?

GOVERNMENT AS PUBLIC GUARDIAN: ADDRESSING THE SOCIAL TOXINS OF PROFIT SEEKING

The political vision delineated here is acutely aware of the intersection and inseparability of the cultural, economic, and political domains. Contrary to previous political perspectives, a critical vision of government refuses to separate government from these diverse domains. In this way, the factors that affect government and public perceptions of government can be more adequately addressed. A progressive government dedicated to socioeconomic justice guards the society from the negative effects of private profit-seeking activity.

The market has historically never done well in setting a national economic development strategy. It pushes and pulls the economy in conflicting directions, often in ways that undermine long term goals; it has failed to provide even a minimal degree of financial security, adopting a cavalier attitude about its tendency to dismiss workers without warning and pay them wages as low as possible; it has never displayed an interest in mitigating the unequal distribution of income and economic and political power it promotes; it has consistently been unwilling to address undemocratic, authoritarian workplaces; and it has addressed its own environmental destruction only under legal pressure (Pollin & Cockburn, 1991). Without the help of a concerned public government, citizens will be hard pressed to mitigate the social damage caused by the free market's historical neglect of these issues.

For these reasons, many progressive economists have argued that measurements of the GNP, indicating the nation's total economic production, should be supplemented by a figure called the gross national cost (GNC). Subtracting the GNC from the GNP would give Americans a far more revealing picture of the operation and status of the political economy. The GNC would report on the depletion of natural resources, pollution, crime and violence, the welfare of children, the state of inequality, the psychological well-being of citizens, and the degree of waste of human talents. Health costs, the unmeasurable price of human suffering from cancer and other diseases, and cleanup monies could be calculated as part of the socioeconomic liability of environmental pollution.

Such debits far exceed the costs of investments in preventive measures. The short-term, quarterly profit-driven mind-set of government by the free market has prevented the implementation of such ethical and economically efficient policies. Similar preventative long-term strategies could both save money and prevent human suffering in all of the categories delineated. Phenomenal savings in governmental, corporate/business, and individual expenditures could be realized by a society free to pursue such farsighted initiatives. Crime alone, *Business Week* has estimated, costs Americans $425 billion annually. The corporate lobby's successful thwarting of measures to prevent these costly problems is one of the greatest assaults on the public well-being in American history (Reich, 1995).

A critical vision of government demands that whether they want to or not, private firms must operate for the public good. That approach could be implemented not simply through government regulation but also by a cadre of knowledgeable, empowered employees who demand managerial fidelity to a core of responsible socioeconomic goals. Such critical workers would understand that the old ideological maxim, "What's good for General Motors is good for America" is not, nor ever has been, true. They would appreciate the fact that this sort of concept is especially untrue in the twenty-first century because of corporate management's elevation of profit maximization over objectives such as productivity, efficiency, and quality of product or service. The pursuit of short-term profit even takes precedence over the development of the company or over longstanding commitments to employees and communities.

Profit making in a world of predatory capital characterized by the buying and selling of companies is separated from all traditional business activities—even from production itself. A fictitious case study serves as a good example of such practices: Although the public relations department issues saccharine New Age proclamations stating that Acme Enterprises is all about personal freedom and the unfettered human spirit, the company is actually dedicated to the enhancement of short-term profits. Even the father of the owner of Acme Enterprises, who managed the firm when it called itself Acme Thimbles, maintained that his company's goal was to make good thimbles for a profit. We are referring to a difference of emphasis, but a very important difference of emphasis.

The difference between the old Acme Thimbles and the new Acme Enterprises shows up in shifts in management personnel: The former consisted of people primarily involved in production; the latter, of individuals primarily concerned with finance. In Acme Enterprises, finance people close down their 150-year-old plant in Factoryville, Massachusetts, and buy a chain of fast-food pork restaurants called The Speedy Pig. They have demonstrated on numerous occasions their lack of interest in thimble production and their willingness to sacrifice Acme's future for a high-profit quarterly report. Managerial salaries have increased 82% during a five-year period in which profits increased only 4% and worker wages dropped 3%. The few old-timers from Acme Thimble who are left in upper- and middle-management are shocked by the fact that the company's expenditures on research and development is 30% less than it was in 1969. The harmful social side effects of profit seeking at Acme are not difficult to uncover.

Thousands of actual corporations now operate in America in a manner similar to the fictitious Acme. In such companies, loyalty to employees and communities is a lost virtue; in the lexicon of managers, loyalty is a quality that inhibits the dynamic flexibility needed to maintain acceptable quarterly profit margins. The side effects of this value structure are disastrous for the nation's social fabric, not to mention for the lives of the individual employees and particular communities. Corporate leaders and their political representatives have become adept at hiding their culpability from the public and even from those directly affected by such moral shallowness. Deftly using the organization as a form of camouflage, corporations operate on a daily basis to avoid responsibility for their antisocial behavior. The job description of corporate lawyers involves devising creative new strategies to avoid liability for a plethora of public transgressions. A critical democratically responsible government understands these realities and works to address them in a way that allows workers and communities to benefit (Block, 1990; Schwartz, 1994; Reich, 1995).

GOVERNMENT AND THE POLITICS OF ANTISOCIAL CORPORATISM

Corporations, like other human inventions, are social constructions and therefore can be reconstructed by human action. The profit-generating antisocial corporation of the contemporary era is not the only possible model of a corporation. Critical social studies educators understand that we can devise a new type of corporation that is employee operated, democratic, wealth generating, and socially responsible. Indeed, there is no inherent conflict between profitability and the pursuit of critical social goals. It is not economic heresy, though it may be represented as such, to argue that government should have as much say about corporate moves to another location as baseball owners have about a proposed move of the Montreal Expos to Washington, D.C. The owners ask whether the move is good for baseball. Likewise, government could ask whether the move is good for the country. In addition to the problems created in the lives of employees and in the stability of communities by migrating corporations, the efficiency of corporations is grounded in the stability of social relationships. Frequent migrations and corporate raidings undermine such relationships and the smooth operations they encourage.

To mitigate the damage caused by these post-Fordist capital migrations and by the orgy of buying and selling of corporations that has occurred over the last two decades, a progressive government develops criteria of regulation. Policies emerging from such criteria are designed to discourage cities and counties from luring firms from other locations with low taxes, low wages, and cheap public services. When such migrations take place, no new jobs are created and opportunities for economic mobility are temporary at best. A worker can be sure that the jobs at the new plant will last only as long as it takes management to find a new location with even cheaper taxes, wages, and social services. Government policies must prevent migrating corporations from turning communities into revolving doors that waste valuable ecological and human resources in their attempt to induce firms to locate for a few short years.

These socioeconomic dynamics are typically overlooked by state and local economic development officials, whose reports are almost always limited to the number of jobs created when a new industry moves into an area. The nature of the wage and skill level of the jobs and the infrastructure and tax costs to the community are not relevant questions. There are numerous examples of local communities in poor regions actually rejecting high-skill, high-pay jobs out of fear that their presence might force other employers in the area to raise wages. Such "rational irrationality" must be ended by requiring corporations to prove the positive impact of a move in terms of creating new jobs and promoting good work in the new community (Aronowitz & DiFazio, 1994; Block, 1990; Falk & Lyson, 1988). Compare these types of analyses with the fragmented, stupidifying memory work that takes place in many standards-driven social studies government course.

A New Political Economic Bill of Rights

Charles Reich (1995) has argued that in light of present political economic realities, the time has come to take another look at President Franklin Roosevelt's new social contract, first broadcast in January 1944. Informed by Roosevelt's principles, critical democratic social studies educators might want to offer a new bill of rights for the consideration of the American people. Such a delineation of rights would be primarily designed to protect Americans from the inordinate power that corporations have amassed via new technologies and media over the last few decades. As a set of amendments to the Constitution, the political economics Bill of Rights would be grounded on the assumption that political rights and individual liberty cannot exist without economic security and freedom from what I have called corporate government. All Americans in the twenty-first century should possess:

Amendment 1.   The right to good work in the nation's workplaces.

Amendment 2.   The right to monetary compensation for work sufficient to provide adequate food, clothing, and recreation.

Amendment 3.   The right (for farmers and agricultural workers) to raise and sell their products at a return that will provide them and their families with a decent standard of living.

Amendment 4.   The right of every family to an adequate home and medical care.

Amendment 5.   The right to protection from the economic hardships of old age, sickness, accident, and unemployment.

Amendment 6.   The right to educational opportunity.

Amendment 7.   The right to live in a healthy natural environment.

Amendment 8.   The right to protection from racial, ethnic, or sexual discrimination.

Amendment 9.   The right to live in freedom from monopolies, foreign or domestic, is guaranteed by:
  A.   The denial of corporations' right to claim status as individual "persons" under the Fourteenth Amendment.
  B.   The denial of corporations' right to control the political process or public communications.
  C.   The denial of corporations' right to move from one community to another, domestic or foreign, without adequate compensation for the abandoned workers and community and proof that the new community and workers will benefit from the relocation. In corporate moves to foreign countries, the same proof of benefit is required: Workers must be paid a livable wage, environmental standards must be maintained, and communities must benefit.

Amendment 10.   The right to enjoy the benefits of citizenship in the workplace, which includes freedom of speech; freedom to choose one's private style of life; freedom from search and intrusive surveillance; freedom from termination without fair treatment and the spirit of due process; freedom of religion, including the right to wear religious clothing on the job despite employer uniform requirements (Reich, 1995).

Amendment 11.   The right to special considerations because of gender-related social demands. The right of protection from sexual harassment. The right to corporate help with day care and reasonable family leave.

Amendment 12.   The unabridged right to unionization.

CENTRAL TO THE POLITICAL VISION—
A NATIONAL INDUSTRIAL POLICY

A study of the political economic history of the twentieth century indicates to those concerned with socioeconomic justice that neither the free market nor central governmental planning is adequate as a principle for organizing and regulating the economic sphere. A hybrid system focused on particular democratic social and economic goals seems to provide a more pragmatic answer to the economic problems that have plagued industrialized and postindustrial societies. The twenty-first century demands a national industrial policy that addresses those domains in which historical experience indicates the free market has performed poorly: the formulation of a national economic development strategy; the provision of a minimal level of economic security; the production of a fair distribution of wealth and political power; and the protection of the environment. Without such planning, the free market unleashes economic forces that tend to swing between prosperity and poverty—boom today, bust tomorrow. Without a national industrial policy, we witness corporate migrations to Third World locales that leave many U.S. communities and workers economically devastated. Critical social studies educators understand the socioeconomic and political dynamics that necessitate a coordinated national economic policy.

What might such a policy do? A plan of this sort would encourage coordination of activities at the national, state, and local levels to gain a fair apportionment of job opportunities across urban and rural, prosperous and depressed regions. Programs would be developed to maintain existing industrial production, facilitate the opening of new firms, and attract growing industries that help upgrade the skills and wages of particular labor markets. In particular, an industrial policy would reject myopic state and local practices of providing increasingly expensive incentives to attract migratory companies to a particular locale. A basic tenet of such a policy would involve supporting activities that raise the standard of living for working people and increase their participation in the daily affairs of the workplace.

Contrary to the convoluted theories of trickle-down economics, plans that reduce unequal income levels and social inequality actually do stimulate spending, increase demand, and result in job creation. Right-wing opponents of such a commonsense industrial policy argue that the United States could not afford a plan with such radical democratic objectives. New expenditures would be required by such a policy, but they could easily be financed by reducing existing governmentally funded corporate welfare provided to firms without requirements to produce socially beneficial outcomes. Closing corporate tax loopholes provided by political cronies would generate another source of funding, as would an increased sales tax on luxury products and services.

In light of the antiworker, antiunion, and anticommunity policies pursued by the corporate government over the last two decades, the only industrial policy that will work must involve the effort to promote political economic justice and higher wages around the world. Of course, such a task is daunting, since governments in the industrialized world would have to coordinate policies designed to promote higher standards of living for workers, not only with one another but also with impoverished nations that fear being shut out of the possibility of prosperity. The struggle for justice is always difficult, but the struggle projected to a global dimension is even more overwhelming. The understanding we have gained of the globalization process leaves critical social studies educators no choice: For the struggle for justice to win on the local level, it must be fought in the global, the national, and the local arenas.

No matter how hard one local area may push for such desirable goals as higher wages for workers to create an incentive for productivity growth and increased investment in high-productivity and high-skills jobs, the process is undermined when economically disadvantaged areas negotiate independently to undercut labor and other operating costs. Without (inter)national coordination around such issues, successful labor negotiations and progress toward political economic justice can be wiped out in an instant (Pollin & Cockburn, 1991; Block, 1990; Falk & Lyson, 1988; Pollin, 1996; Bowles, Gordon, & Weisskopf, 1990; Greider, 1992).

With protection against capricious capital migrations of this type, worker-owned cooperatives can be established. Under the provisions of an industrial policy dedicated to power-sharing and higher wages, such co-ops could borrow low-interest start-up funds now routinely denied them. With a friendly climate for worker co-ops, critical educators could direct more and more of their curricula to the analysis of information necessary to such endeavors. For workers who hold jobs that are not self-directed and are labor intensive and physically difficult, a democratic national industrial policy would relegate special compensation for unpleasant but socially necessary jobs. That move would be one aspect of a larger effort to reduce the hierarchical division between intellectual and manual labor. Contrary to the pronouncements of mainstream psychology, the difference in the cognitive abilities of people who perform intellectual versus manual labor is not very significant. This appreciation is central to a plethora of political, moral, and educational policies in our critical vision of government, economics, and schooling. This is one reason why our postformal psychology is so important.

In addition, a national industrial policy advocated by critical social studies educators sees through the illusions of free trade policies so popular with contemporary Western neoliberal governments. According to the theory, freeing trade by lifting barriers to international commerce allows each nation to focus on products and services in which they hold a competitive advantage. In this way, all commodities are produced efficiently at the lowest cost, which benefits consumers around the world. When obstacles are presented to free trade, advocates maintain, customers must pay a surcharge that, in effect, subsidizes inefficiency. Like other celebrations of the free market, free trade is based on a view of a world that does not exist in globalized, corporatized reality.

All nations employ numerous strategies to protect their industries: tariffs, quotas, and subsidies, to name but a few. Japan, for example, used "dumping" policies—the protection of domestic enterprises by permitting them to sell their products to foreign consumers below prices prevailing in Japanese domestic markets—to establish a beachhead in the United States and other foreign markets. Soon, the beachhead evolved into total market domination. That industrial policy worked brilliantly, of course, to move Japan into an unprecedented economic position (Aronowitz & DiFazio, 1994; Bowles, Gordon, & Weisskopf, 1990; Bluestone & Bluestone, 1992).

Most nations in the world watched the United States gain world dominance in the production and selling of military hardware through its national policy of subsidizing its defense industries. Learning an important lesson, many nations focused a similar industrial policy on the subsidization of their commercial products. Various nations funded research and development costs for machine-tool industries, semiconductors, supercomputers, high-definition TV, and various industrial materials. By holding on to the fantasy world of free trade, the United States allows Japan, Germany, and other nations to gain an edge in commercial product innovation. Such neglect not only hurts the United States in a purely self-interested economic nationalist sense, but it allows the balance of wealth in the world to grow more disparate by discouraging international coordination of industrial policies. A democratic global industrial policy would not only provide grants and loans to innovative producers but also to firms that employ disadvantaged groups, both domestic and foreign. This policy would also reverse the decline in government-funded basic research. Our democratic industrial policy would focus increased funding of basic research on sustainable and equitable development, with issues of race, class, and gender equity constantly directing its moral compass.

Conservative opponents of a democratic national industrial policy would have us believe that such a governmental role in economic affairs is unprecedented and somehow anti-American. Governmental intervention of the type discussed here is as old as America itself. Although such policies have never been planned and coordinated around long-term socioeconomic visions, government in the nineteenth century promoted economic development via right-of-way grants to private railroad companies and protected struggling industries by way of high tariffs. Throughout the twentieth century, government funded infrastructural needs, such as highways, and subsidized research and development in industries, such as synthetic rubber and integrated circuits.

Curiously, throughout American economic history, zealous fidelity to the rule of the free market has been set aside in times of need. When Japanese computer chips began to undermine American domination of the market, for example, the sacred competition of unimpeded free enterprise was abandoned. IBM negotiated a cooperation agreement with its domestic competitors and successfully petitioned the federal government for research and development funds. Despite all of the rhetorical glorification of the unfettered free enterprise system by the leaders of Chrysler, the company survives in the twenty-first century only because of its bailout by the federal government through an ad hoc national industrial policy. Who among these free market evangelicals is complaining?

Of course, any industrial policy that facilitates the production of wealth in a context centered around the pursuit of socioeconomic justice must address the moral obligations of corporations in the globalized political economy. The corporate oligarchy must be dethroned and called to social accountability. Such a process must be delicately handled, for the rights of free speech in a democratic society apply to potentates of concentrated technopower as well as to the disenfranchised. A critical socioeconomic political vision does not imply the need for a "palace cleaning," with a denial of civic rights for selected groups. Simply put, this vision necessitates applying the obligations of citizenship to corporations in the same manner they are applied to individual men and women.

As delineated in the political economic Bill of Rights, corporate abuses must be identified and addressed. A democratic national industrial policy, for example, would question granting corporate tax credits to companies undermining the quality of products and reducing the number of jobs. This policy would ask corporations to at least share the costs of remedying the social, economic, and environmental problems their policies precipitated. A democratic policy would carefully scrutinize the provision of state, local, and federal governmental subsidies and incentives to firms that failed to live up to their social obligations to their communities.

The free market orgy of deregulation that has dominated the last two decades has failed, but as a society, we have yet to pay the full costs of such failure. Although corporate leaders have benefited from this politics of deregulation, the suffering it causes the poor and racially marginalized continues to escalate. In the shadow of the free market, thousands of small businesses have failed, many workers have lost both jobs and hope, and the quality of public services has disintegrated. The privatization process encouraged by deregulation has been unable to offer affordable housing, support services such as day care, and education. One of the most profound tragedies of this voodoo economic process has been the dismantling of the public sphere.

Interestingly, as Aronowitz and DiFazio (1994) have astutely pointed out, the deregulation steamroller has been most consistently applied to corporate efforts to undermine the position of workers. Under the mantle of deregulation, corporate leaders have contracted jobs, closed long-operating and even profitable factories, broken unions, and undermined workers' health and pension plans. A society that allows such destructive operations to proceed unimpeded has fallen victim to a form of ideological fundamentalism in which fidelity to a free market orthodoxy takes precedence over good sense. A democratic national industrial policy can help restore our sense of values and humanity (Lakes, 1994b; Falk & Lyson, 1988; Greider, 1992).

A critical social studies education can be tied directly to this industrial policy by linking educational programs to our moral vision in general and to job creation and targeted unemployment opportunity in particular (Samper & Lakes, 1994). Students would not be ideologically adjusted to the needs of corporations but would come to understand the socioeconomic context into which they operate. Social studies teacher understanding of a vision of social justice, good work, democratic social policies, and an (inter)national industrial policy are only a few of the pieces necessary to any effort to move the study of government beyond a low-level form of ideological indoctrination.

I am convinced by my decades of observations of students deemed academically incapable that many of them respond enthusiastically and competently to an education that connects them to the realities of the lived world. Once they appreciate both the personal and the social benefits of such integrated, visionary, and pragmatic learning, they will, like most people, avail themselves of it. Thus, the purpose of a critical democratic social studies emerges yet again: The key dynamic to the success of such a process involves the ability of social studies educators to help students understand the democratic vision, and make sense of the bombardment of unconnected information that confuses them. Without this ingredient, all of the brilliant reforms that the most gifted among us can imagine will fail miserably.

DEVISING CRITICAL DEMOCRATIC GOVERNMENTAL POLICIES

Investing in People and Their Needs

As social studies educators sophisticate their democratic social vision, they come to understand that, by denying government's role in the economy, the free market has cut off short-term governmental investments in people who pay long-term dividends. Thus, the logic of the quarterly balance sheet induces policymakers to cut social spending, since the costs resulting from socioeconomic inequality and the social conflict it produces consume nearly one-half of the wealth produced in the United States. The recognition of this phenomenal reality should ground every political and educational discussion that takes place. But, like so many other contemporary social understandings, one is hard pressed to hear reference to it in the public political conversation.

American politics, unfortunately, has operated for the last 30 years as if such real-life side effects of socioeconomic injustice did not exist—as if people could, year after year, generation after generation, operate outside the boundaries of hope and not be in some way damaged by the process. In the perverted logic of the free market, social investments in people, especially the most hopeless among us, were slashed while corporate welfare to the rich grew. Under the banner of getting government off our backs, corporate social obligations were lifted while new regulations on the poor were developed without hesitation: workfare, Ritalin for control of hard-to-teach poor children, new prisons for drug dealers and users, more severe penalties for cheap crack-cocaine convictions than for powder cocaine, war measures against illegal immigrants and denial of education and social services for their children, and armed guards in poor urban high schools, to name only a few.

Governmental investments in education, health, child welfare, transportation, and other social categories have now been neglected for a generation. Not only are such programs helpful to targeted individuals, especially if they are decentralized, locally administered, and personally operated, but the new jobs created by them are distributed in productive sectors of the economy. Many Americans presently hold down two or three jobs, working much of their time to maintain a home and raise their children. Investments in publicly financed privately owned homes and multiple-dwelling rental housing would dramatically improve the lives of millions of Americans.

Currently, such people are held captive by real-estate market fluctuations that have dramatically slashed their home equities and have much too often led to their eviction. There is simply no reason that the mercurial free market should be allowed to destroy individuals' economic security when a national housing plan could be easily formulated. In this regard, poor people with children are also penalized by the absence of public childcare services. No one should be surprised to learn that half the income of many struggling workers is absorbed by mortgage or rent payments and childcare. The decline of the public sector is often viewed by Americans as not having human consequences, but nothing could be further from reality (Coontz, 1992; Pollin, 1996; Aronowitz, 1992).

Jobs

The socioeconomic and political changes fueled by the globalized economy and all of the forces it has unleashed have led to the firing of millions of workers around the world. Despite temporary fluctuations, the rising unemployment rate has fanned worker anger across continents, and projections indicate the problem will only get worse. If such predictions are only partly correct, hundreds of millions of people will find themselves in a position where their talents and energies will be deemed unnecessary and irrelevant. If we do not make plans and develop (inter)national strategies to avoid such a future scenario, the world may find itself steadily plunging into an era of chaos and lawlessness.

A key justification for any critical democratic industrial policy involves not only its moral imperative but a crassly pragmatic need to avoid the possibility of such a stark and frightening Mad Max future. Conservatives and liberals have consistently ignored the reality of the job market, not to mention the projections concerning the depressing effects of globalization and the automation that accompanies it. This reaction has served to downplay the impact of deindustrialization and the nearly six million jobs it has destroyed in the last fifteen years. The conservative and liberal dismissal of the consequences of such realities were well illustrated by their shared belief that new high-tech jobs would fill the gaps in employment left by the globalization process.

The free market cannot generate enough jobs—high-skill, high-paid positions in particular—to make up for accelerating losses. Since the growth in high-skill jobs has slowed, a national job-creation policy is badly needed. A governmental policy, creating jobs that are grounded on the principles of good work, and distributed democratically by reducing the number of hours in the workweek to 35, and redistributing overtime, can help delay the social upheavals of mass unemployment and poverty. Since the 1960s, scores of federal job training programs have been developed and run haphazardly by groups of private businesspeople with little governmental supervision.

Unconnected to a larger, coherent job policy such programs, from CETA to Job Training Partnership Act (JTPA) and beyond, have served as little more than a welfare program for business. Learning from the failures of the past, a government-directed job policy could be grounded in the needed repair of America's infrastructure: road, railroad, and bridge building and repair; construction of waste disposal plants; cleanup of toxic and nuclear wastes; construction of the new housing mentioned earlier; and renovation of public libraries and schools. Such work would continue for decades, given the $5 to $6 trillion long-term costs of this undertaking (Weisman, 1991; Murray, 1992; Bovard, 1987; Melman & Dumas, 1990).

A corps of skilled, unionized workers, organized around a larger international social and political vision, could be employed for these and other socially valuable tasks. Contrary to conservative objections, such work would not be characterized as meaningless jobs designed merely to keep people busy. Unless job creation is tied directly to specific socially necessary tasks, we face the same question that dogged President Clinton's job retraining proposals for high-tech work: Retraining for what high-tech jobs? Where are they? Department of Labor studies indicate that fewer than one in five retrained workers in the 1990s found new jobs at even 80% of their previous salaries. Our democratic job policy is based on the assumption that everyone should benefit from productivity increases derived from technological innovations in information, communications, and industrial machinery. Various forms of compensation can be devised in this context for those who have lost their jobs as a result of these advances. The formulation of smart, creative, socially beneficent, individually rewarding compensation is a central concern of this chapter and the critical vision that guides us.

Corporate policies that dispose of good jobs and undermine communities, as I have consistently argued, must be carefully examined in light of the goals of a national economic plan and a democratic job policy. When corporations move, the plan would induce them to negotiate the provisions of such migration with unions, local communities, and governmental agencies at the local, state, and national levels. Joining with AFL-CIO proposals, the plan focuses much attention on the plight of workers displaced in these corporate migrations as well as on first-time workers and the problems they face as they enter the workforce. As far as these young workers are concerned, free market advocates have fought for years for the enactment of a "training wage" below the minimum wage for inexperienced workers.

Such a provision would create a profit bonanza for many corporate managers, who would hire such youth and fire them at the end of their so-called training period. Thus, labor costs could be saved, but at the expense of older workers, whose wages are used to support their families. A progressive jobs policy would support a flexible minimum wage that takes into account a variety of factors, including the portability of the job, the area of the country and the prevailing wage rates that exist, and the nature of the employee: Is that employee a middle-class teenage part-time worker or one of the millions of workers trying to raise a family on an inadequate income (Falk & Lyson, 1988; Rifkin, 1995; Roberts & Wozniak, 1994)?

Worker Safety

Since Congress passed the Occupational Safety and Health Care Act in 1970, almost 250,000 workers have been killed on the job, and 2 million have died from workplace-generated diseases. Other workers—1.5 million of them—have been permanently disabled as a result of workplace accidents. Yet, the most amazing statistic regarding worker safety tells us that only a handful of companies have ever been prosecuted for on-the-job safety violations. Not only do workers continue to die en masse, but they are killed in the most horrible ways: suffocated by trench cave-ins, electrocuted while working on power lines, blown to bits by explosions in mines and refineries, minced into pieces in cutting machines, burned to death in iron and steel factory fires. In many ways, these types of deaths may be preferable to the long-term suffering caused by death from black lung, brown lung, cancer, or chemical and radiation poisoning. The point is clear: The lax enforcement of OSHA rules has failed to encourage corporate leaders to adopt policies that place the value of worker safety over short-term profits.

American society has demonstrated a lack of interest in issues of worker safety. An accident, for example, that kills several workers attracts little attention in the news and is quickly forgotten. When a construction worker is killed when scaffolding collapses on a high-rise project, people shake their heads and proclaim that the worker understood the risk that went along with the job. Even though OSHA demands a safe workplace, many observers ascribe accidents to the will of God, even when owners are negligent in addressing safety factors. When corporate executives are killed, the news media deliver long obituaries and a series of connected stories about the loss, the tragedy. The difference in news coverage and public concern is connected to a central concern of a critical social studies: class bias. This culture, simply put, cares more about the lives of the rich than about those of the poor. And the perspective is not new; throughout American history, the workplace has always been unsafe. The litany of U.S. workplace tragedies is overwhelming, with its descriptions of thousands killed in mine explosions, of seven hundred deaths in the construction of one tunnel, of hundreds dead in one factory fire after another.

Employers understand that it is cheaper to buy insurance and defer costs to workers and consumers than to actually make their workplaces safer. With the dawning of the age of fast, dynamically flexible post-

Fordist capitalism, the quickened operating pace typically translates into reduced safety and health concerns for workers. "We'll give you your money back if the pizza is not at your door in 30 minutes," Breakneck Pizza executives announce, as their delivery drivers crash into unlucky pedestrians and immovable barricades. Attempts to increase and enforce employer penalties for workplace safety infractions have been successfully crushed by the corporate lobby.

Emasculated during the Reagan-Bush era, OSHA only holds a small fraction of the resources necessary to inspect the nation's 7 million workplaces. OSHA, operating under the auspices of the corporate government, has adopted industry's own Milquetoast health and safety guidelines as its own. When technical help is needed, the office seeks the advice of the business-run National Safety Council. Of course, such meager regulation allows the massacre of U.S. workers to continue and corporate leaders to rest comfortably in their exemption from criminal responsibility for negligence. The only "good" aspect of such lax policies I can imagine is that, with the further deterioration of workplace safety and health standards, U.S. corporations will have less incentive to move to Malaysia and exploit workers there.

Taxes

The basis of a critically reconceptualized federal tax policy would be grounded on the effort to reward good citizenship and to promote social and economic justice. Fair taxes that redistributed just 1% of the income of America's most wealthy 5% could help lift one million people out of poverty. A 1% increase on only the upper 2% of America's wealthiest people would enable the nation to double federal spending on education and still have $20 billion left over. But instead of moving in this type of just direction, tax policy over the last 20 years has worked to redistribute wealth from the poor and working class to the rich. The tax proposals of President George W. Bush take these redistributive tendencies to a new extreme.

The tax breaks and loopholes for corporations and their wealthy owners have been appropriated from the so-called socioeconomic safety net for the needy. Such corporate-designed breaks and loopholes work to subsidize the political campaigning of the most wealthy and powerful political voices in the world. Firms and their political action coalitions receive tax write-offs for the production and dissemination of self-interested propaganda. Under this arrangement, General Motors can deduct the cost of flying its executives and lobbyists to Washington to lobby against workplace safety legislation, whereas workers have to finance their own trips to tell lawmakers about injuries or diseases caused by unsafe workplaces.

When a billion-dollar corporation (one of the few social organizations that can afford the costs of prime-time TV advertising) finds its political activities tax deductible at the same time an individual citizen's attempt to gain a voice in the public conversation is not, critical social studies teachers understand that the spirit of participatory democratic has been snuffed out. An essential aspect of a democratic national industrial policy would expose the Never-Never Land fiction that corporate lobbying and "educational" activities are not political—not political because they are not tied directly to political elections. The cultural changes brought about by contemporary electronically mediated culture have moved much of the process of political consciousness construction outside of the realm of electoral politics. For this and other reasons, a critical democratic study of government can no longer focus simply on the economic and political realms and ignore the cultural domain: in this case, popular culture and the analysis of TV.

In the past, it was assumed that economic and political processes were the domains to study in order to understand the "real world" of politics. To understand the governmental sphere, we have to grasp the processes by which cultural practices shape the way human beings understand issues such as government tax policy and the role various organizations play in creating cultural meanings about such practices. Such an appreciation ties the development of political and economic consciousness directly to the realm of cultural pedagogy, where knowledge and values are produced and transmitted and where identity is formed (du Gay et al., 1997).

A national industrial policy would eliminate governmental subsidies for corporate political activity. The corporate government's transformation of tax laws into elaborate corporate giveaways would end. A democratic tax policy would not offer tax credits for the political activity of those most able to pay, but for those least able—wage workers and ordinary citizens. Any individual who wanted to engage politically would be granted a tax credit of several hundred dollars. Political deductions for several hundred dollars' worth of contributions to election campaigns or political educational efforts would be a part of a democratic tax plan designed to stimulate national and state political organizations to refocus their energies toward neglected citizens and workers instead of megacorporations.

Another aspect of the use of taxes to stimulate individual grassroots efforts to engage in political or civic activity involves the rebuilding of nongovernmental organizations dedicated to the improvement of communities. To fund such positive work, a wide variety of analysts have called for a so-called value-added tax (VAT), a tax that is levied on consumption rather than on income. If small businesses and the consumption of basic necessities such as food, clothing, medicine and medical care, and housing under a certain cost are exempted from such a tax, the VAT holds great possibility as a revenue generator for civic activities.

The tax could be specifically targeted to finance responses to particular problems emerging from the inequities resulting from globalization. We might consider, for example, a VAT on all computers, information, and telecommunications services and products. Revenues collected from this would be used to pay for education and job creation needed in the transition of workers, whose jobs were consumed by the technological revolution, into new vocations—maybe even, nongovernmental civic activity. To avoid regressive deployments of such a VAT, nonprofit organizations, such as schools and humanitarian or philanthropic institutions, would be exempted from it. Charles Reich (1995) has estimated that Americans spend more than $340 billion a year on entertainment and recreation: videotapes, VCRs, cellular phones, home computers, boats, personal airplanes, amusement parks, toys, sporting equipment, movies, live entertainment, and gambling. If a VAT were levied on these expenditures and on corporate advertising, enough money could be raised to subsidize political education and to help the poorest among us achieve a better life.

Current tax policies, corporate tax breaks in particular, are resistant to such socially beneficial and democratic uses. Justifications are often mere smoke screens for crass corporate greed. Tax cuts for General Electric (among hundreds of other firms) allowed the company to reduce taxes on its $6.5 billion profits between 1981–1983 from $330 million a year to a minus figure of $90 million. The corporation received a net cash payment from the government of $283 million. The smoke screen justification for the tax cuts that in only a few years saved GE $1.3 billion (and even more in the long run) was that such revenues would allow the corporation to create thousands of new jobs. Of course, this was not to be the case. In an orgy of downsizing, GE, during this period, laid off 50,000 workers. Other companies followed this pattern, using their new job-creation monies to build cheaper factories, hire less expensive workers in foreign nations, and acquire new firms to add to their corporate assets. It was with the help of this tax cut that GE purchased the National Broadcasting Corporation (NBC) (Greider, 1992).

KNOWLEDGE AND THE FUTURE OF DEMOCRACY: IN THE POSTMODERN CONDITION, GOVERNMENT RUNS ON INFORMATION DEPLOYMENT

In the political realm of the twenty-first century, the production of knowledge and scientific and intellectual work in general has been steadily appropriated by corporations. In this process, knowledge has been captured and deployed in an effort to protect corporations against their critics and produce technological innovations that raise quarterly profit margins. This development, if not challenged, holds ominous implications for the future of democracy. Such a politics of knowledge silences citizens who do not have the fiscal resources to produce data at the same level as do corporations. How do individual citizens answer a corporation that produces a score of expert-generated empirical studies— heavily biased though they may be—that "prove" the corporate claim that the pollutants they dumped in the water supply did not cause miscarriages and deformed babies? Citizens do not typically speak the modernist language of the expert; nor should they. As an excellent example of the power of modernist science, expert empiricism silences the language of lived experience, of pain and suffering.

To make the often-heard argument that the American people are narcissistic and ill-informed is to miss the epistemological dynamics at work in contemporary culture. The public is not ignorant because it does not understand the scientific rationalism of political and social elites. Indeed, its suspicion of such a politics of knowledge illustrates the people's intuition about the irrationality of modernist rationalism. With the decline of political parties in the United States, no powerful group exists to help the people produce information that would lend credence to their intuitions. In some countries, such knowledge production is a primary function of political parties, but not in the United States. Even the knowledge production that takes place in the twenty-first century American university has been curtailed by governmental budget cuts, making a higher and higher percentage of the information generated in higher education corporate-sponsored. It is highly ironic that, just at the time when knowledge work has become more important to the commer-

cial sphere, university budgets are being slashed, despite rising enrollments and overburdened faculty researchers.

There is nothing complex about the politics of knowledge in contemporary university systems. Scholars are often hired to turn out policy
ideas for political debate that support the interests of their corporate
benefactors. These scholarly data producers deliver their information to
corporate lobbyists and lawyers, who then use the ideas to influence public opinion and legislative decisions. The corporate seizure of information and its political effects have taught the American public a hard
lesson: Scientifically produced knowledge is never objective. Such data
emerge from particular questions, motivated by particular interests and
needs, in specific circumstances. In other words, many scholars are for
sale, and the only players wealthy enough to consistently participate in
this knowledge game are the corporations.

One of the most important ways corporations have operated in this
context is by sponsoring ostensibly neutral think tanks (Wolman &
Colamosca, 1997). The American Enterprise Institute (AEI), for example, once viewed as a reactionary little right-wing organization, began in
the late 1970s to pick up wealthy sponsors who liked its probusiness message: AT&T, $125,000; Chase Manhattan Bank, $171,000; Chevron,
$95,000; Citicorp, $100,000; Exxon, $130,000; GE, $65,000; GM,
$100,000, to name only a few. By the late 1990s, AEI had become a
major force in American politics. Scores of the other corporate-fed think
tanks produce data that support specific business-related political projects: the Heritage Foundation, the Cato Institute, the Hudson Institute,
the Hoover Institute, the Progress and Freedom Foundation, the
Manhattan Institute, the Competitive Enterprise Institute, and so on.
These are some of the most important social studies knowledge producers in the twenty-first century. Not only does their research produce
knowledge deployed in a cultural pedagogy of government, but information they produce also finds its way into the social studies textbooks at all
levels of education (Greider, 1992).

Social studies teachers and students need to know that democracy
has been taken captive by corporate knowledge producers, and that government agencies designed to help curb corporate abuses are now operated by corporations themselves. For example, the Bureau of Mines is run
by the coal industry. Such realities remove teachers, students, and other
citizens from access to relevant information, from an understanding of
how the political process actually works. In this context, political action

by citizens, when it occurs, is often reduced to single-issue oppositional tactics. A polluting corporation with unfair labor practices may be confronted and even successfully deferred, but long-term political action that addresses larger systemic problems is more difficult to generate in this unfair knowledge context. Likewise, the needs of workers squeezed in the globalized economy are erased from the public conversation and from the social studies classroom. It is amazing in the twenty-first century that the struggles and hardships of workers around the world do not make it onto the national news or the national political agenda. Such erasure allows a large percentage of Americans to believe that poverty is caused by poor people, and not by corporate leaders, who, in alliance with one another, set wage structures.

IS DEMOCRACY A THING OF THE PAST? CRITICAL CONCEPTIONS OF GOVERNMENT

A social studies education that fails to teach the ability to engage in knowledge work, while passing along archaic notions of the functioning of government in a social, cultural, and economic vacuum is unacceptable. Is it possible for critical democratic social studies teachers to delineate a vision of government that inspires students and other citizens, and helps them make socially beneficial use of their talents and abilities, even if such activities take place outside of the traditional boundaries of what we call the public and private sectors? When asked, most people value the concept of community service. The success of programs such as Habitat for Humanity is testimony to the prevalence of this social value. Critical democratic social studies educators believe that this common value of community service can be used to help mobilize a social and educational movement to redesign the money-saturated political system described here.

Politically speaking, Americans in the twenty-first century are in a bad mood. Angry at the failure of bureaucratic government to respond efficiently to their needs, they are suspicious of any governmental program. Convinced by the corporate media that big government exercises its evil exclusively in the areas of placing senseless bureaucratic regulations on good corporate citizens and throwing away tax dollars on the poor, these angry citizens sometimes end up exacerbating the problems they face. They are often not aware of the fact that the social agencies benefiting the most from big government, as it is now constituted, are the megacorporations. It will take tremendous effort on the part of a variety of cultural workers to counter the corporate information blitz that has planted these perspectives in the minds of so many.

One way to begin the important work of talking back to the corporations and their well-financed political puppets is to find common areas of agreement with conservative critics of government. On one level, their critique of bureaucracy is on target, but the problem is that they condemn only governmental bureaucracy, leaving corporate bureaucracy intact. The nonpublic and nonprivate third sector (civil sector) discussed here would be grounded on an understanding of the failure of centralized bureaucracies and dedicated to a decentralization of some of the socially beneficent tasks assumed over the last six or seven decades by centralized government.

Great caution must be taken in any discussion of this civil sector. The advocacy of support for such a sector cannot dismiss the necessity of public government as a countervailing force to corporate power. We are not talking about (the elder) George Bush's "thousand points of light," that he and other politicians have cynically used to refute and dismantle government's role as a protector of individuals from the ravages of the free market. Republican and some Democratic politicians have used third-sector rhetoric as a device to covertly promote a free market economy in which industry is deregulated, corporate taxes are lowered, and social services and entitlements for the poor are eliminated.

Thus, the use of this third civil sector is important and can accomplish much, but it can never take the place of government. It is just one of a variety of strategies we can use to promote a critical social studies education connected to a socially and economically just political vision. Finances for the civil sector would not just magically appear. Governments of local, state, and national varieties would have to help finance social and educational agencies who were devising locally conceived and administered programs. Many third-sector programs, therefore, would provide humane and personal ways of implementing the social dreams of those who take democracy seriously. Such third-sector activity would not be entirely altruistic, however. Individuals reeling from the economic (and thus psychological) effects of the deindustrialization of globalism would connect with nongovernmental organizations out of self-interest, as well as out of concern for their futures. Only with grassroots local organizations connected to national and international coordinating agencies can economically displaced individuals survive globalized capital migration and the automation that accompanies it.

Critical democratic social studies educators must connect with these non-government organizations, which have sprung up over the last few decades at the local, national, and international levels around opposition to such macrodynamics as the harmful effects of modernity or such micro-dynamics as the destruction of a particular forest. A civil international order is developing. Critical social studies educators and other cultural workers must develop the insight to devise ways of working in cooperation with it that contribute to the social good. As the civil sector works to rebuild local communities, social studies students could participate in third-sector practicums that could not only teach them a variety of practical skills but could involve them in civic activities and political action.

Individuals displaced by globalization could earn a living both through working on beneficial community projects and by teaching social studies students the civic skills they have acquired in their previous life experiences. Social studies educators could help build networks of people with particular academic skills who could be called upon to use these abilities in a wide variety of civic and educational projects. Housing projects for the poor, economic development projects, environmental projects, public information projects, and justice-related projects could be developed in ways that integrated civic, academic, and research-based action. As social studies students connect and work with NGOs that reject the free market ideology that has allowed for the creation of multinational corporate tyrants as well as the dead-end politics of unquestioned nationalism, they would learn the skills of a new politics.

I still find it difficult to comprehend that these types of issues are dismissed from the teaching of government in the twenty-first century. This is why I devote such a large portion of a book on social studies education to the study of research and knowledge work in the social, cultural, economic, political, historical, geographical, and cultural studies domain. Those of us concerned with political education in an era of corporatized depoliticization must provide students and our social studies colleagues with alternatives to the information produced by power wielders. The future of democratic government and public education demands that we understand and act on these dynamics. Indeed, we must get beyond the power-generated "facts" in order to pursue the goals of a critical rigorous education, egalitarianism, social justice, and new ways of being human.

References

Abercrombie, N. (1994). Authority and consumer society. In R. Keat, N. Whiteley, & N. Abercrombie (Eds.), *The authority of the consumer*. New York: Routledge.

Adler, S. (1991). Forming a critical pedagogy in the social studies methods class: The use of imaginative literature. In B. Tabuchinick & K. Zeichner (Eds.), *Issues and practices in inquiry-oriented teacher education*. New York: Falmer.

Adorno, T., & Horkheimer, M. (1972). *Dialectic of enlightenment*. Trans. John Cumming. New York: Herder & Herder.

Airaksinen, T. (1992). The rhetoric of domination. In T. Wartenberg (Ed.), *Rethinking power*. Albany, New York: SUNY Press.

Airhihenbuwa, C. (1995). *Health and culture: Beyond the Western paradigm*. Thousand Oaks, CA: Sage Publications.

Alcoff, L. (1995). Mestizo identity. In N. Zack (Ed.), *American mixed race: The culture of microdiversity*. Lanham, MD: Rowman & Littlefield.

Alford, C. (1993). Introduction to the special issue on political psychology and political theory. *Political Psychology, 14* (2), 199–208.

Allison, C. (1995). *Present and the past*. New York: Peter Lang

Allison, C. (1998). Okie narratives: Agency and whiteness. In J. Kincheloe, Steinberg, S., Rodriguez, N., Chennault, R. (Eds.), *White reign: Deploying whiteness in America*. New York: St. Martin's.

Altrichter, H., & Posch, P. (1989). Does the "grounded theory" approach offer a guiding paradigm for teacher research? *Cambridge Journal of Education, 19* (1), 21–31.

Alvesson, M., & Willmott, H. (1992). On the idea of emancipation in management and organizational studies. *Academy of Management Review, 17* (3), 432–64.

Amott, T. (1993). *Caught in the crisis: Women and the U.S. economy today.* New York: Monthly Review Press.

Amott, T., & Matthaei, J. (1991). *Race, gender, and work: A multicultural economic history of women in the U.S.* Boston: South End Press.

Anderson, E. (1987). Gender as a variable in teacher thinking. In R. Thomas (Ed.), *Higher order thinking: Definition, meaning and instructional approaches.* Washington, DC: Home Economics Education Association.

Anderson, J. (1986). Secondary school history textbooks and the treatment of black history. In D. Hine (Ed.), *The state of African American History: Past, present and future.* Baton Rouge, LA: LSU Press.

Apffel-Marglin, F. (1995). "Development or decolonization in the Andeas?" *Interculture: International journal of intercultural and transdisciplinary research, 28* (6), pp. 3–17.

Apple, M. (1983). Curricular form and the logic of technical control. In M. Apple & L. Weis (Eds.), *Ideology and practice in schooling.* Philadelphia: Temple University Press.

Aronowitz, S. (1983). The relativity of theory. *The Village Voice, 27,* 60.

Aronowitz, S. (1988). *Science as power: Discourse and ideology in modern society.* Minneapolis, MN: University of Minnesota Press.

Aronowitz, S. (1989). The new conservative discourse. In H. Holtz et al. (Eds.), *Education and the American dream.* Granby, MA: Bergin & Garvey.

Aronowitz, S. (1992). *The politics of identity: Class, culture and social movements.* New York: Routledge.

Aronowitz, S. (1993). *Roll over Beethoven: The return of cultural strife.* Hanover, NH: Wesleyan University Press.

Aronowitz, S. (1996). The politics of science wars. In A. Ross (Ed.), *Science wars.* Durham, NC: Duke University Press.

Aronowitz, S., & DiFazio, W. (1994). *The jobless future: Sci-tech and the dogma of work.* Minneapolis, MN: University of Minnesota Press.

Aronowitz, S., & Giroux, H. (1985). *Education under siege.* South Hadley, MA: Bergin & Garvey.

Aronowitz, S., & Giroux, H. (1991). *Post-modern education: Politics, culture, and social criticism.* Minneapolis: University of Minnesota Press.

Ashcroft, B., Griffiths, G., & Tiffin, H. (Eds.). (1995). *The post-colonial studies reader.* New York: Routledge.

Ashley, D. (1991). Playing with the pieces: The fragmentation of social theory. In P. Wexler (Ed.), *Critical theory now.* New York: Falmer.

Astman, J. (1984). Special education as a moral enterprise. *Learning Disability Quarterly*, 7 (4), 299–308.

Astronomical instruments. (1999). <http://www.scinet.org.uk/database /physics/Instruments/p00827c.html>.

Atkinson, P., & Hammersley, M. (1994). Ethnography and participant observation. In N. Denzin & Y. Lincoln (Eds.), *Handbook of qualitative research*. Thousand Oaks, CA: Sage.

Ayers, W. (1992). Disturbances from the field: Recovering the voice of the early childhood teacher. In S. Kessler & B. Swadener (Eds.), *Reconceptualizing the early childhood curriculum*. New York: Teachers College Press.

Bacon, D. (1996, April 1). For a labor economy. *The Nation*, 262 (13), 14.

Bacon, D. (1996, July 8). Will the labor party work? *The Nation*, 263 (2), 22–24.

Baker, H. (1993). *Rap: Black studies and the academy*. Chicago: University of Chicago Press.

Bakhtin, M. (1981). *The dialogic imagination*. Trans. Caryl Emerson & Michael Holquist. Austin: University of Texas Press.

Baldwin, E. (1987). Theory vs. ideology in the practice of teacher education. *Journal of Teacher Education*, 38, 16–19.

Ball, T. (1992). New faces of power. In T. Wartenberg (Ed.), *Rethinking power*. Albany, NY: SUNY Press.

Banfield, B. (1991). Honoring cultural diversity and building on its strengths: A case for national action. In L. Wolfe (Ed.), *Women, work, and the role of education*. Boulder, CO: Westview Press.

Barnet, R., & Cavanagh, J. (1994). *Global dreams: Imperial corporations and the new world order*. New York: Simon & Schuster.

Barrett, G. (1985). *Thinking, knowledge, and writing: A critical examination of the learning process in schools*. Paper presented to the International Writing Convention, University of East Anglia, Norwich.

Barrow, R. (1984). *Giving teaching back to teachers*. Totowa, NJ: Barnes & Noble Books.

Bartolomé, L. (1998). *The misteaching of academic discourses: The politics of language in the classroom*. Boulder, CO: Westview.

Beck, U. (1992). *Risk society: Towards a new modernity*. M. Ritter (Trans.). London: Sage.

Becker, H. (1989). Tricks of the trade. *Studies in Symbolic Interaction*, 10, 481–490.

Beed, C. (1991). Philosophy of science and contemporary economics: An overview. *Journal of Post-Keynesian Economics*, 13 (4), 459–494.

Behn, W. et al. (1976). School is bad: Work is worse. In M. Carnoy & H. Levin (Eds.), *The limits of educational reform*. New York: David McKay Company.

Belenky, M., Clinchy, B., Goldberger, N., & Tarule, J. (1986). *Women's ways of knowing: The development of self, voice, and mind*. New York: Basic Books.

Bell, D., & Valentine, G. (1997). *Consuming geography: We are what we eat.* New York: Routledge.

Bellah, R. et al. (1991). *The good society.* New York: Vintage Books.

Benhabib, S., & Cornell, D. (1987). *Feminism as critique.* Minneapolis, MN: University of Minnesota Press.

Bennett, D. (1995). *The party of fear: The American far right from nativism to the militia movement.* New York: Vintage.

Bennett, W. (1987). *First lessons: A report on elementary education in America.* Washington, DC: U.S. Government Printing Office.

Benson, G. (1989). Epistemology and the science curriculum. *Journal of Curriculum Studies, 21* (4), 329–344.

Berger, A. (1995). *Cultural criticism: A primer of key concepts.* Thousand Oaks, CA: Sage.

Berry, K. (1998). Nurturing the imagination of resistance: Young adults as creators of knowledge. In J. Kincheloe & S. Steinberg (Eds.), *Unauthorized methods: Strategies for critical teaching.* New York: Routledge.

Bersani, L. (1995). Loving men. In M. Berger, B. Wallis, and S. Watson (Eds.), *Constructing masculinity.* New York: Routledge.

Bertman, S. (1998). *Hyperculture: The human cost of speed.* Westport, CT: Praeger.

Besag, F. (1986a). String after the wind. *American Behavioral Scientist, 30* (1), 15–22.

Besag, F. (1986b). Reality and research. *American Behavioral Scientist, 30* (1), 6–14.

Birch, C. (1992). The postmodern challenge to biology. In C. Jencks (Ed.), *The post-modern reader.* New York: St. Martin's Press.

Bizzell, P. (1991). Power, authority, and critical pedagogy. *Journal of Basic Writing, 10* (2), 54–70.

Block, A. (1995). *Occupied reading: Critical foundations for an ecological theory.* New York: Garland.

Block, F. (1990). *Postindustrial possibilities: A critique of economic discourse.* Berkeley: University of California.

Bluestone, B., & Bluestone, I. (1992). *Negotiating the future: A labor perspective on American business.* New York: Basic Books.

Bly, R. (1990). *Iron John.* New York: Addison-Wesley.

Bogdan, R., & Biklen, S. (1982). *Qualitative research for education: An introduction to theory and methods.* Boston: Allyn & Bacon.

Bohm, D., & Edwards, M. (1991). *Changing consciousness.* San Francisco: Harper.

Bohm, D., & Peat, F. (1987). *Science, order, and creativity.* New York: Bantam Books.

Bookchin, M. (1995). *The philosophy of social ecology: Essays on dialectical naturalism* (2nd ed.). Montreal: Black Rose Books.

Borgmann, A. (1992). *Crossing the postmodern divide.* Chicago: University of Chicago Press.

Bottomore, T. (1984). *The Frankfurt School*. London: Tavistock.

Bovard, J. (1987). "The failure of federal job training programs." *USA Today,* 116, pp. 12–17.

Bowers, C. (1982, Summer). The reproduction of technological consciousness: Locating the ideological foundations of a radical pedagogy. *Teachers College Record, 83* (4), 529–557.

Bowers, C., & Flinders, D. (1990). *Responsive teaching: An ecological approach to classroom patterns of language, culture, and thought.* New York: Teachers College Press.

Bowles, S. & Gintis, H. (1976) *Schooling in capitalist America: Educational reform and the contradictions of economic life.* New York: Basic.

Bowles, S., Gordon, D., & Weisskopf, T. (1990). *After the wasteland: A democratic economics for the year 2000.* Armonk, NY: M. E. Sharp.

Bowser, B. (1985). Race relations in the 1980s: The case of the United States. *Journal of Black Studies, 15* (4), 307–324.

Bracy, G. (1987). Measurement-driven instruction: Catchy phrase, dangerous practice. *Phi Delta Kappan, 68* (9), 683–686.

Brady, H., & Barth, J. (1995). The social studies movement. *Social Education, 59* (4), 208–210.

Briggs, J., & Peat, F. (1989). *Looking glass universe: The emerging science of wholeness.* New York: Touchstone.

Brittan, A., & Maynard, M. (1984). *Sexism, racism, and oppression.* New York: Basil Blackwell.

Britzman, D. (1991). *Practice makes practice: A critical study of learning to teach.* Albany, NY: State University of New York Press.

Britzman, D., & Pitt, A. (1996). On refusing one's place: The ditchdigger's dream. In J. Kincheloe, S. Steinberg, & A. Gresson (Eds.), *Measured lies: The bell curve examined.* New York: St. Martin's Press.

Brooks, M. (1984). A constructivist approach to staff development. *Educational Leadership, 32,* 23–27.

Brosio, R. (1994). *The radical democratic critique of capitalist education.* New York: Peter Lang.

Brown, R. (1993). "Cultural representation and ideological domination." *Social Forces, 71* (3), pp. 657–676.

Bullough, R., & Gitlin, A. (1991). Educative communities and the development of the reflective practitioner. In R. Tabachnick & K. Zeichner (Eds.), *Issues and practices in inquiry-oriented teacher education.* New York: Falmer Press.

Butler, J. (1990). *Gender trouble: Feminism and the subversion of identity.* New York: Routledge.

Butler, M. (1998). Negotiating place: The importance of children's realities. In J. Kincheloe & S. Steinberg (Eds.), *Students as researchers: Creating classrooms that matter.* London: Falmer Press.

Cadenhead, K. (1985). Is substantive change in teacher education possible? *Journal of Teacher Education, 36,* 17–21.

Cannella, G. (1997). *Deconstructing early childhood education: Social justice and revolution.* New York: Peter Lang.

Cannella, G. (1999). Postformal thought as critique, reconceptualization, and possibility for teacher education reform. In J. Kincheloe, S. Steinberg, & L. Villaverde (Eds.), *Rethinking intelligence: Confronting psychological assumptions about teaching and learning.* New York: Routledge.

Capra, F. (1982). *The turning point: Science, society, and the rising culture.* New York: Simon & Schuster.

Capra, F. (1996). *The web of life: A new scientific understanding of living systems.* New York: Anchor Books.

Capra, F., Steindl-Rast, D., & Matus, T. (1992). *Belonging to the universe: New thinking about God and nature.* New York: Penguin.

Carby, H. (1980). Multi-culture. *Screen Education, 34,* 62–70.

Carby, H. (1982). Schooling in Babylon. In Centre for Contemporary Cultural Studies (Ed.), *The empire strikes back: Race and racism in 70s Britain.* London: Hutchinson.

Carby, H. (1992). The multicultural wars. In G. Dent (Ed.), *Black popular culture.* Seattle: Bay Press.

Carlson, D. (1991). *Alternative discourses in multicultural education: Towards a critical reconstruction of a curricular field.* Paper presented to the Bergamo Conference on Curriculum Theory and Classroom Practice, Dayton, Ohio.

Carlson, D. (1997). *Making progress: Education and culture in new times.* New York: Teachers College Press.

Carlson, D., & Apple, M. (Eds.). (1998). *Power/knowledge/pedagogy: The meaning of democratic education in unsettling times.* Boulder, CO: Westview.

Carr, W., & Kemmis, S. (1986). *Becoming critical.* Philadelphia: The Falmer Press.

Carson, T., & Sumara, D. (1997). *Action research as a living practice.* New York: Peter Lang.

Carspecken, P. (1996). *Critical ethnography in educational research: A theoretical and practical guide.* New York: Routledge.

Carspecken, P. (1999). *Four scenes for posing the question of meaning and other essays in critical philosophy and critical methodology.* New York: Peter Lang.

Cary, R. (1996). I.Q. as commodity: The "new" economics of intelligence. In J. Kincheloe, S. Steinberg, & A. Gresson (Eds.), *Measured lies: The bell curve examined.* New York: St. Martin's.

Cary, R. (1999). *Critical art pedagogy: Foundations for postmodern art education.* New York: Garland.

Chamberlin, G. (1974). Phenomenological methodology and understanding education. In D. Denton (Ed.), *Existentialism and phenomenology in education.* New York: Teachers College Press.

Champagne, J. (1996). Homo academicus. In P. Smith (Ed.), *Boys: Masculinities in contemporary culture*. Boulder, CO: Westview.

Cherryholmes, C. (1988). *Power and criticism: Poststructural investigations in education*. New York: Teachers College Press.

Chesneaux, J. (1992). *Brave modern world. The prospects for survival*. New York: Thames & Hudson.

Chopp, R. (1986). *The praxis of suffering*. Maryknoll, NY: Orbis Books.

Clark, C. (1987). *Asking the right questions about teacher preparation: Contributions of research on teacher thinking*. Occasional paper number 110. East Lansing, MI: Michigan State University, Institute for Research on Teaching.

Clarke, E., & Henson, M. (1996). Hot damme! Reflections on gay publicity. In P. Smith (Ed.), *Boys: Masculinites in contemporary culture*. Boulder, CO: Westview.

Clatterbaugh, K. (1997). *Contemporary perspectives on masculinity: Men, women, and politics in modern society*. Boulder, CO: Westview.

Clegg, S. (1989). *Frameworks of power*. Newbury Park, CA: Sage.

Clifford, J. (1992). Traveling cultures. In L. Grossberg, C. Nelson, & P. Treichler (Eds.), *Cultural studies*. New York: Routledge.

Clough, P. (1994). The hybrid criticism of patriarchy: Rereading Kate Millett's sexual politics. *The Sociological Quarterly, 35* (3), 473–486.

Clough, P. (1998). *The ends of ethnography: From realism to social criticism*. New York: Peter Lang.

Coben, D. (1998). *Radical heroes: Gramsci, Freire and the politics of adult education*. New York: Garland.

Codd, J. (1984). Introduction. In J. Codd (Ed.), *Philosophy, common sense, and action in educational administrations*. Victoria, Australia: Deakin University Press.

Collins, P. (1990). *Black feminist thought: Knowledge, consciousness, and the politics of empowerment*. New York: Routledge.

Combs, A., & Holland, M. (1990). *Synchronicity: Science, myth, and the trickster*. New York: Paragon House.

Connell, R. (1995). *Masculinities*. Berkeley, CA: University of California.

Connelly, F., & Ben-Peretz, M. (1980). Teachers' roles in the using and doing of research and curriculum development. *Journal of Curriculum Studies, 12* (2), 95–107.

Coontz, S. (1992). *The way we never were: American families and the nostalgia trap*. New York: Basic Books.

Cooper, D. (1994). Productive, relational, and everywhere? Conceptualizing power and resistance within Foucauldian feminism. *Sociology, 28* (2), 435–454.

Cooper, M. (1996, April 8). Harley riding, picket-walking socialism haunts Decatur. *The Nation, 262* (14), 21–25.

Cooper, M. (1996, May 27). Class war @ Silicon Valley: Disposable workers in the new economy. *The Nation, 262* (21), 11–16.

Cooper, M. (1998, March 23). General Pinochet still rules: Twenty-five years after Allende—an anti-memoir. *The Nation, 266* (10), 11–23.

Courteney, R. (1988). *No one way of being: A study of the practical knowledge of elementary arts teachers.* Toronto: MGS Publications.

Cruickshank, D. (1987). *Reflective teaching: The preparation of students of teaching.* Reston, Virginia: Association of Teacher Educators.

Cuban, L. (1984). *How teachers taught.* New York: Longman.

Culler, J. (1981). *The pursuit of signs: Semiotics, literature, deconstruction.* Ithaca, NY: Cornell University Press.

Culler, J. (1982). *On deconstruction: Theory and criticism after structuralism.* Ithaca, NY: Cornell University Press.

Darder, A. (1991). *Culture and power in the classroom.* Westport, CT: Bergin & Garvey.

Davis, J., & Fernlund, P. (1995). Civics: If not, why not? *The Social Studies, 86* (2), 56–59.

Deetz, S. (1993). *Corporations, the media, industry, and society: Ethical imperatives and responsibilities.* Paper presented to the International Communication Association, Washington, DC.

Dei, G. (1994). *Creating reality and understanding: The relevance of indigenous African world views.* Paper presented to the Comparative and International Education Society, San Diego, California.

Dench, G. (1996). *Transforming men: Changing patterns of dependency and dominance in gender relations.* New Brunswick, NJ: Transaction Publishers.

Denzin, N. (1989). Reading *Tender Mercies:* Two interpretations. *Sociological Quarterly, 30,* 37–57.

Denzin, N. (1992). *Symbolic interactionism and cultural studies. The politics of interpretation.* Cambridge, MA: Blackwell.

Denzin, N. (2000). The art and politics of interpretation. In N. Denzin & Y. Lincoln (Eds.), *Handbook of qualitative research.* Thousand Oaks, CA: Sage Publications.

Denzin, N., & Lincoln, Y. (2000). Introduction: Entering the field of qualitative research. In N. Denzin & Y. Lincoln (Eds.), *Handbook of qualitative research.* Thousand Oaks, CA: Sage.

Denzin, N., & Lincoln, Y. (2000). (Eds.) *Handbook of qualitative research.* Thousand Oaks, CA: Sage.

Dewey, J. (1916). *Democracy and education.* New York: The Free Press.

Dewey, J. (1973). *Lectures in China, 1919-1920.* Honolulu, HI: University Press of Hawaii

Dews, P. (1987). *Logics of disintegration: Post-structuralist thought and the claims of critical theory.* New York: Verso.

DeYoung, A. (1989). *Economics and American education.* New York: Longman.

Dickens, D., & Fontana, A. (1994). Postmodernism in the social sciences. In D. Dickens & A. Fontana (Eds.), *Postmodernism and social inquiry*. New York: Guilford.

Dion–Buffalo, Y., & Mohawk, J. (1992). Thoughts from an autochthonous center: Postmodernism and cultural studies. *Akwe:kon Journal, 9* (4), 16–21.

Dionne, Jr., E. (1991). *Why Americans hate politics*. New York: Simon & Schuster.

Dobrin, R. (1987). The nature of causality and reality: A reconciliation of the ideas of Einstein and Bohr in the light of Eastern thought. In D. Ryan (Ed.), *Einstein and the humanities*. New York: Greenwood Press.

Doll, W. (1989). Foundations for a post-modern curriculum. *Journal of Curriculum Studies, 21* (3), 243–253.

Doll, W. (1993). *A post-modern perspective on curriculum*. New York: Teachers College Press.

Donald, J. (1993). The natural man the virtuous woman: Reproducing citizens. In C. Jenks (Ed.), *Cultural reproduction*. New York: Routledge.

Donmoyer, R. (1985). The rescue from relativism: Two failed attempts and an alternative strategy. *Educational Researcher, 14.*

Dowell, P. (1996). *Book reviews, 22* (3), 49–51.

Doyle, W. (1977). Paradigms for research on teacher effectiveness. *Review of Research in Education, 5,* 163–198.

Dubino, J. (1993). The Cinderella complex: Romance fiction, patriarchy, and capitalism. *Journal of Popular Culture, 27* (3), 103–118.

DuBois, W. (1973). The education of black people: Ten critiques, 1906–1960. In H. Aptheker (Ed.), *Monthly review press*. New York.

DuGay, P., et al. (1997). *Doing cultural studies: The story of the Sony Walkman*. London: Sage Publications.

Duke, D. (1979). Environmental influences on classroom management. In D. Duke (Ed.), *Classroom management. Seventy-eighth yearbook of the National Society for the Study of Education*. Chicago: University of Chicago Press.

During, S. (1994). Introduction. In S. During (Ed.), *The cultural studies reader*. New York: Routledge.

Dussel, E. (1981). *A history of the church in Latin America*. Grand Rapids, MI: William B. Eerdmans.

Dussell, E. (1976). *History and the theology of liberation*. Maryknoll, NY: Orbis.

Ebert, T. (1988). The romance of patriarchy: Ideology, subjectivity, and post-modern feminist cultural theory. *Cultural Critique, 10,* 19–57.

Einstein on Spacetime. (1998). <http://webplaza.pt.lu/public/fklaess/html/spacetime.html>.

Eisner, E. (1984). Can educational research inform educational practice. *Phi Delta Kappan, 65* (7), 447–452.

Elliot, A. (1994). *Psychoanalytic theory: An introduction*. Cambridge, MA: Blackwell.

Elliott, J. (1989a). *Studying the school curriculum through insider research.* Paper presented to the International Conference on School-Based Innovations: Looking Forward to the 1990s, Hong Kong.

Elliott, J. (1989b). *Action-research and the emergence of teacher appraisal in the United Kingdom.* Paper presented to the American Educational Research Association, San Francisco.

Ellis, J. (1998). Interpretive inquiry as student research. In S. Steinberg & J. Kincheloe (Eds.), *Students as researchers: Creating classrooms that matter.* London: Falmer.

Ellwood, D. (1988). *Poor support: Poverty in the American family.* New York: Basic Books.

Engle, S. (1982). Alan Griffin: 1907–1964. *Journal of Thought, 17,* 50–57.

Evans, J. (1997). *Relativity and black holes.* <http://www.physics.gmu.edu/classinfo/astr228/coursenotes/In_ch19.htm>.

Falk, W., & Lyson, T. (1988). *High tech, low tech, no tech: Recent industrial and occupational change in the South.* Albany, NY: SUNY Press.

Fay, B. (1975). *Social theory and political practice.* London: George Allen & Unwin.

Fee, E. (1982). Is feminism a threat to scientific objectivity? *International Journal of Women's Studies, 4* (4), 378–392.

Fehr, D. (1993). *Dogs playing cards: Powerbrokers of prejudice in education, art, and culture.* New York: Peter Lang.

Feinberg, W. (1989). Foundationism and recent critiques of education. *Educational Theory, 39* (2), 133–138.

Ferguson, K. (1984). *The feminist case against bureaucracy.* Philadelphia: Temple University Press.

Ferguson, K. (1993). *The man question: Visions of subjectivity in feminist theory.* Berkeley, CA: University of California Press.

Ferguson, M. (1980). *The Aquarian conspiracy: Personal and social transformation in our time.* Los Angeles: J. P. Tarcher, Inc.

Fetterman, D. (1988). Qualitative approaches to evaluating education. *Educational researcher, 17,* 8, pp. 17–23.

Feuer, J. (1995). *Seeing through the eighties: Television and Reaganism.* Durham, NC: Duke University Press.

Fine, M. (1988). Sexuality, schooling, and adolescent females: The missing discourse of desire. *Harvard Educational Review, 58* (1), 29–53.

Fine, M. (1993). Sexuality, schooling, and adolescent females: The missing discourse of desire. In M. Fine & L. Weis (Eds.), *Beyond silenced voices: Class, race, and gender in United States schools.* Albany, NY: SUNY Press.

Fine, M., Weis, L., Powell, L., & Wong, L. (1997). *Off white: Readings on race, power, and society.* New York: Routledge.

Finn, C. (1982). A call for quality education. *American Education, 108,* 28–34.

Fiske, D., & Shweder, R. (1986). *Metatheory in social science: Pluralisms and subjectivities.* Chicago: University of Chicago Press.

Fiske, J. (1993). *Power plays, power works.* New York: Verso.

Fiske, J. (1994). *Media matters: Everyday culture and political change.* Minneapolis, MN: University of Minnesota Press.

Fitzgerald, F. (1979). *America revised.* New York: Random House.

Fitzgerald, F. (1981). *Fire in the lake.* New York: Macmillan.

Flax, J. (1990). Postmodernism and gender relations in feminist theory. In L. Nicholson (Ed.), *Feminism/postmodernism.* New York: Routledge.

Floden, R., & Klinzing, H. (1990). What can research on teacher thinking contribute to teacher preparation? A second opinion. *Educational Researcher, 19* (5), 15–20.

Fontana, A. (1994). Ethnographic trends in the postmodern era. In D. Dickens & A. Fontana (Eds.), *Postmodernism and social inquiry.* New York: Guilford Press.

Fosnot, C. (1988). *The dance of education.* Paper presented to the Annual Conference of the Association for Educational Communication and Technology, New Orleans.

Foucault, M. (1980). *Power/knowledge: Selected interviews and other writings.* New York: Pantheon.

Fowler, G. (1984). *Philosophical assumptions and contemporary research perspectives.* Paper presented to the Speech Communication Association, Chicago.

Fox-Genovese, E. (1988). *Within the plantation household: Black and white women of the old south.* Chapel Hill, NC: University of North Carolina.

Frankel, B. (1986). Two extremes on the commitment continuum. In D. Fiske & R. Shweder (Eds.), *Metatheory in social science: Pluralisms and subjectivities.* Chicago: University of Chicago Press.

Frankenberg, R. (1993). *The social construction of whiteness: White women, race matters.* Minneapolis, MN: University of Minnesota Press.

Freeman, R., & Gilbert, D. (1992). Business, ethics and society: A critical agenda. *Business and Society, 31* (1), 9–17.

Freire, P. (1970). *Pedagogy of the oppressed.* New York: Herder & Herder.

Freire, P. (1985). *The politics of education: Culture, power, and liberation.* South Hadley, MA: Bergin & Garvey.

Freire, P., & Faundez, A. (1989). *Learning to question: A pedagogy of liberation.* New York: Continuum.

Freire, P., & Shor, I. (1987). *A pedagogy for liberation: Dialogues on transforming education.* South Hadley, MA: Bergin & Garvey.

Fried, R. (1995). *The passionate teacher: A practical guide.* Boston: Beacon Press.

Frye, C. (1987). Einstein and African religion and philosophy: The hermetic parallel. In D. Ryan (Ed.), *Einstein and the humanities.* New York: Greenwood Press.

Gabbard, D. (Ed.). (2000). *Knowledge and power in the global economy: Politics and the rhetoric of school reform.* Mahwah, NJ: Lawrence Erlbaum.

Gadamer, H. (1975). Truth and method. In G. Barden & J. Cumming (Eds.), New York: Seabury Press.

Gadamer, H. (1989). *Truth and method.* Trans. J. Weinsheimer & D. Marshall. New York: Crossroads.

Gaines, D. (1990). *Teenage wasteland: Suburbia's dead end kinds.* New York: Harper Perennial.

Gallagher, S. (1992). *Hermeneutics and education.* Albany, NY: SUNY Press.

Galston, W. (1991, December 2). Home alone: What our policymakers should know about our children. *The New Republic,* 40–44.

Gardner, H. (1983). *Frames of mind: A theory of multiple intelligences.* New York: Basic Books.

Gardner, H. (1991). *The unschooled mind: How children think and how schools should teach.* New York: Basic Books.

Garrison, J. (1988). Democracy, scientific knowledge, and teacher empowerment. *Teachers College Record, 89* (4), 487–504.

Garrison, J. (1989, Summer). The role of postpositivistic philosophy of science in the renewal of vocational education research. *Journal of Vocational Education, 14* (3), 39–51.

Gee, J., Hull, G., & Lankshear, C. (1996). *The new work order: Behind the language of the new capitalism.* Boulder, CO: Westview.

Gergen, K. (1991). *The saturated self: Dilemmas of identity in contemporary life.* New York: Basic Books.

Gibson, R. (1984). *Structuralism and education.* London: Hodder & Stroughton.

Gibson, R. (1986). *Critical theory and education.* London: Hodder & Stroughton.

Giroux, H. (1981). *Ideology, culture, and the process of schooling.* Philadelphia: Temple University Press.

Giroux, H. (1987). Introduction: Literacy and the pedagogy of political empowerment. In P. Freire & D. Macedo (Eds.), *Literacy: Reading the word and the world* (p. 16). South Hadley, MA: Bergin & Garvey.

Giroux, H. (1988). *Schooling and the struggle for public life.* Minneapolis: University of Minnesota Press.

Giroux, H. (1991). Introduction: Modernism, postmodernism, and feminism: Rethinking the boundaries of educational discourse. In H. Giroux (Ed.), *Postmodernism, feminism, and cultural politics: Redrawing educational boundaries.* Albany, NY: State University of New York Press.

Giroux, H. (1992). *Border crossings: Cultural workers and the politics of education.* New York: Routledge.

Giroux, H. (1993). *Living dangerously: Multiculturalism and the politics of difference.* New York: Peter Lang.

Giroux, H. (1994). *Disturbing pleasures: Learning popular culture.* New York: Routledge.

Giroux, H. (1997). *Pedagogy and the politics of hope: Theory, culture, and schooling.* Boulder, CO: Westview.

Giroux, H., & McLaren, P. (1988). Teacher education and the politics of democratic reform. In H. Giroux (Ed.), *Teachers as intellectuals: Toward a critical pedagogy of learning.* Granby, MA: Bergin & Garvey.

Giroux, H., & McLaren, P. (1989). Introduction: Schooling, cultural politics, and the struggle for democracy. In H. Giroux & P. McLaren (Eds.), *Critical pedagogy, the state, and cultural struggle.* Albany, NY: State University of New York Press.

Giroux, H., & McLaren, P. (1989). Language, schooling, and subjectivity: Beyond a pedagogy of reproduction and resistance. In K. Borman, P. Swami, & L. Wagstaff (Eds.), *Contemporary issues in U.S. education.* Norwood, NJ: Ablex Publishing Corporation.

Giroux, H., & McLaren, P. (1991). "Language, schooling, and subjectivity: Beyond a pedagogy of reproduction and resistance." In K. Borman, P. Swami, & L. Wagstaff (Eds.), *Contemporary issues in U.S. education.* Norwood, NJ: Ablex Publishing.

Giroux, H., & Simon, R. (1989). Popular culture as a pedagogy of pleasure and meaning. In H. Giroux & R. Simon (Eds.), *Popular culture: Schooling and everyday life.* Granby, MA: Bergin & Garvey.

Gitlin, A. (1983). School structure and teachers' work. In M. Apple & L. Weis (Eds.), *Ideology and practice in schooling* (pp. 193–212). Philadelphia: Temple University Press.

Goldman, R. (1992). *Reading ads socially.* New York: Routledge.

Goldman, R., & Papson, S. (1994). The postmodernism that failed. In D. Dickens & A. Fontana (Eds.), *Postmodernism and social inquiry.* New York: Guilford Press.

Goldman, R., & Papson, S. (1996). *Sign wars: The cluttered landscape of advertising.* New York: Guilford.

Goodlad, J. (1988). Studying the education of educators: Values-driven inquiry. *Phi Delta Kappan, 70* (2), 105–111.

Goodman, J. (1986). *Constructing a practical philosophy of teaching: A study of preservice teachers' professional prospectives.* Paper presented to the American Educational Research Association, San Francisco.

Goodson, I. (1997). *The changing curriculum: Studies in social construction.* New York: Peter Lang.

Goodson, I., & Mangan, J. (1996). Exploring alternative perspectives in educational research. *Interchange, 27* (1), 41–59.

Gordon, E., Miller, F., & Rollock, D. (Eds.). (1990). Coping with communicentric bias in knowledge production in the social sciences. *Educational Researcher, 19* (3), 14–19.

Gore, J. (1993). *The struggle for pedagogies: Critical and feminist discourses as regimes of truth.* New York: Routledge.

Goudlner, A. (1976). *The dialectic of ideology and technology.* New York: Oxford University Press.

Gramsci, A. (1988). *An Antonio Gramsci reader.* New York: Schocken Books.

Gravitational radiation. (1998). <http://zebu.uoregon.edu/~imamura/122/jan12/gw.html>.

Gray, H. (1995). *Watching race: Television and the struggle for "blackness."* Minneapolis: University of Minnesota Press.

Greene, M. (1975). Curriculum and consciousness. In W. Pinar (Ed.), *Curriculum theorizing: The reconceptualists.* Berkeley: McCutchan Publishing Company.

Greene, M. (1984). The professional significance of history and education. In R. Sherman (Ed.), *Understanding history of education* (pp. 70–71). Cambridge, MA: Schenkman Publishing Company.

Greene, M. (1987). *Some notes on Bloom: Toward a new Bloomsalem.* Paper presented to the Institute on Education and the Economy, Teachers College, Columbia University, New York.

Greene, M. (1988). *The dialectic of freedom.* New York: Teachers College Press.

Greene, M. (1995). *Releasing the imagination: Essays on education, the arts, and social change.* San Francisco: Jossey Bass.

Greider, W. (1992). *Who will tell the people? The betrayal of American democracy.* New York: Touchstone.

Gresson, A. (1995). *The recovery of race in America.* Minneapolis, MN: University of Minnesota Press.

Gresson, A. (1997). Professional wrestling and youth culture: Teasing, taunting, and the containment of civility. In J. Kincheloe & S. Steinberg (Eds.), *Kinderculture: Corporate constructions of childhood.* Boulder, CO: Westview.

Gresson, A. (2000). *America's atonement.* New York: Peter Lang.

Griffin, C. (1985). *Typical girls? Young women from school to the job market.* London: Routledge & Kegan Paul.

Griffin, C. (1993). *Representations of youth: The study of youth and adolescence in Britain and America.* Cambridge, MA: Polity Press.

Grimmett, P., Erickson, G., MacKinnon, A., & Riecken, T. (1990). Reflective practice in teacher education. In R. Clift, W. Houston, & M. Pugach (Eds.), *Encouraging reflective practice in education: An analysis of issues and programs.* New York: Teachers College Press.

Grondin, J. (1994). *Introduction to philosophical hermeneutics.* New Haven, CT: Yale University Press.

Gross, A., & Keith, W. (Eds.). (1997). *Rhetorical hermeneutics: Invention and interpretation in the age of science.* Albany, NY: State University of New York Press.

Grossberg, L. (1992). *We gotta get out of this place.* New York: Routledge.

Grossberg, L. (1994). Is anybody listening? Does anybody care? On the state of rock. In. A. Ross & T. Rose (Eds.), *Microphone fiends: Youth music, youth culture* (pp. 41–58). New York: Routledge.

Grossberg, L. (1995). What's in a name (one more time)? *Taboo: The Journal of Culture and Education, 1,* 1–37.

Grumet, M. (1988). *Bitter milk: Women and teaching.* New Haven: Yale University Press.

Grumet, M. (1992). The curriculum: What are the basics and are we teaching them? In J. Kincheloe & S. Steinberg, (Eds.), *Thirteen questions: Reframing education's conversation.* New York: Peter Lang.

Habermas, J. (1970). *Knowledge and human interests.* Translated by J. Shapiro. London: Heinemann.

Habermas, J. (1973). *Theory and practice.* Trans. by J. Viertel. Boston: Beacon Press.

Habermas, J. (1974). *Theory and practice.* Trans. by J. Viertel. London: Heinemann.

Haggerson, N. (2000). *Expanding curriculum research and understanding: A mythopoetic perspective.* New York: Peter Lang.

Hale-Benson, J. (1986). *Black children: Their roots, culture, and learning styles.* Baltimore: The Johns Hopkins University Press.

Hall, S. (1992). What is this "black" in black popular culture? In G. Dent (Ed.), *Black popular culture.* Seattle, WA: Bay Press.

Hall, S. (Ed.). (1997). *Representation: Cultural representations and signifying practices.* Thousand Oaks, CA: Sage.

Hammersley, M., & Atkinson, P. (1983). *Ethnography: Principles in practice.* New York: Tavistock Publications.

Haraway, D. (1991). *Simians, cyborgs, and women.* New York: Routledge.

Harding, S. (1986). *The science question in feminism.* Ithaca, NY: Cornell University Press.

Harding, S. (1996). Science is "good to think with." In A. Ross (Ed.), *Science wars.* Durham, NC: Duke University Press.

Harris, K. (1984). Philosophers of education: Detached spectators or political practitioners. In J. Codd (Ed.), *Philosophy, common sense, and action in educational administration.* Victoria, Australia: Deakin University Press.

Harrison, B. (1985). *Making the connections: Essays in feminist social ethics.* Boston: Beacon Press.

Harvey, D. (1989). *The condition of postmodernity.* Cambridge, MA: Basil Blackwell.

Hauser, K. (1992). Unlearning patriarchy: Personal development in Marge Piercy's *Fly Away Home. Feminist Review, 42,* 33–42.

Haymes, S. (1995). Educational reform: What have been the effects of the attempts to improve education over the last decade? In J. Kincheloe & S. Steinberg (Eds.), *Thirteen questions: Reframing education's conversation*. New York: Peter Lang.

Hebdige, D. (1989). *Hiding in the light*. New York: Routledge.

Hedley, M. (1994). The presentation of gendered conflict in popular movies: Affective stereotypes, cultural sentiments, and men's motivation. *Sex Roles, 31* (11/12), 721–740.

Hekman, S. (1990). *Gender and knowledge: Elements of a postmodern feminism*. Boston: Northeastern University Press.

Held, D. (1980). *Introduction to critical theory: Horkheimer to Habermas*. London: Hutchinson.

Heller, A. *A theory of history*. London: Routledge & Kegan Paul.

Henriques, J. et al. (1984). *Changing the subject*. New York: Methuen.

Herrnstein, R., & Murray, C. (1994). *The bell curve: Intelligence and class structure in American life*. New York: The Free Press.

Hess, D. (1995). *Science and technology in a multicultural world: The cultural politics of facts and artifacts*. New York: Columbia University Press.

Hiber, A. (1997, August 11). See Dick strike. Strike, Dick, strike. *The Nation, 21* (19), 10.

Hicks, E. (1999). *Ninety-five languages and seven forms of intelligence*. New York: Peter Lang.

Hinchey, P. (1998). *Finding freedom in the classroom: A practical introduction to critical theory*. New York: Peter Lang.

Hirsch, E. D. (1987). *Cultural literacy*. Boston: Houghton Mifflin.

Hodge, R., & Kress, G. (1988). *Social semiotics*. Ithaca, NY: Cornell University Press.

Holstein, J. & J. Gubrium (1994). "Phenomenology, ethnomethodology, and interpretive practice. " In N. Denzin & Y. Lincoln (Eds.), *Handbook of qualitative research*. Thousand Oaks, CA: Sage Publications.

Holt, T. (1986). Whither now and why? In D. Hine (Ed.), *The state of African American history: Past, present, and future*. Baton Rouge, LA: LSU Press.

hooks, b. (1981). *Ain't I a woman? Black women and feminism*. Boston: South End Press.

hooks, b. (1989). *Talking back*. Boston: South End Press.

hooks, b. (1994). *Outlaw culture: Resisting representations*. New York: Routledge.

Horkheimer, M. (1972). *Critical theory*. New York: Seabury.

Horton, M., & Friere, P. (1990). *We make the road by walking: Conversations on education and social change*. Philadelphia: Temple University Press.

Howe, K. (1985). Two dogmas of educational research. *Educational Researcher, 14*, 10–18.

Hultgren, F. (1987). Critical thinking: Phenomenological and critical foundations. In R. Thomas (Ed.), *Higher-order thinking: Definition, meaning and instructional approaches*. Washington, DC: Home Economics Education Association.

Hursh, D., & Ross, E. (2000). *Democratic social education: Social studies for social change*. New York: Falmer Press.

Husserl, E. (1970). *The crisis of European sciences and transcendental phenomenology: An introduction to phenomenology*. Evanston, IL: Northwestern University Press.

Hutcheon, B. (1989). *The politics of postmodernism*. New York: Routledge.

Hutcheon, L. (1988). *A poetics of postmodernism*. New York: Routledge.

Inglis, F. (1985). *The management of ignorance: A political theory of the curriculum*. New York: Basil Blackwell.

Jacoby, R. (1975). *Social amnesia*. Boston: Beacon Press.

Jafa, A. (1992). 69. In G. Dent (Ed.), *Black popular culture* (pp. 249–254).

Jaggar, A. (1983). *Feminist politics and human nature*. Totowa, NJ: Rowman & Allanheld.

Jardine, D. (1998). *To dwell with a boundless heart: Essays in curriculum theory, hermeneutics, and the ecological imagination*. New York: Peter Lang.

Jay, M. (1973). *The dialectical imagination: A history of the Frankfurt School and the Institute of Social Research, 1923-1950*. Boston: Little, Brown, & Company.

Jay, M. (1982). Anamnestic totalization. *Theory and Society, 7*, 110–117.

Jayaratne, T. (1982). The value of quantitative methodology for feminist research. In G. Bowles & R. Klein (Eds.), *Theories of women's studies*. Boston: Routledge & Kegan Paul.

Jegede, O. (1994). African cultural perspectives and the teaching of science. In J. Soloman & G. Aikenhead (Eds.), *STS education: International perspectives on reform*. New York: Teachers College Press.

Jenks, C. (1993). The necessity of tradition: Sociology or the postmodern? In C. Jenks (Ed.), *Cultural reproduction*. New York: Routledge.

Jennings, J. (1992). Blacks, politics, and the human service crisis. In J. Jennings (Ed.), *Race, politics, and economic development: Community perspectives*. New York: Verso.

Jipson, J., & Paley, N. (1997). *Daredevil research: Recreating and analytic practice*. New York: Peter Lang.

Johnson, A. (1999). Teaching as sacrament. In J. Kincheloe, S. Steinberg, & L. Villaverde (Eds.), *Rethinking intelligence: Confronting psychological assumptions about teaching and learning*. New York: Routledge.

Johnson, C. (1996). Does capitalism really patriarchy? Some old issues reconsidered. *Women's Studies International Forum, 19* (3), 193–202.

Johnson, W. (1991). Model programs prepare women for skilled trades. In L. Wolfe (Ed.), *Women, work, and school: Occupational segregation and the role of education*. Boulder, CO: Westview.

Jonasdottir, A. (1994). *Why women are oppressed*. Philadelphia: Temple University Press.

Jones, M. (1992). The black underclass as systemic phenomenon. In J. Jennings (Ed.), *Race, politics, and economic development: Community perspectives*. New York: Verso.

Jones, N., & Cooper, M. (1987). *Teacher effectiveness and education: A case of incompatibility*. Paper presented to the American Educational Research Association, Washington, DC.

Jordan, J. (1985). *On call: Political essays*. Boston: South End Press.

Kallick, D. (1996, November 11). Left turn ahead. *The Nation, 263* (15), 22–24.

Kaltsounis, T. (1997). Multicultural education and citizenship education at the crossroads: Searching for common ground. *The Social Studies, 88* (1), 18–22.

Kamii, C. (1981). Teachers' autonomy and scientific training. *Young Children, 31*, 5–14.

Karenga, M. (1982). *Introduction to black studies*. Los Angeles: Kawaida Publications.

Karier, C. (1986). *The individual, society, and education: A history of American educational ideas* (2nd ed.). Urbana, IL: University of Illinois Press.

Kaufman, B. (1978). Piaget, Marx, and the political ideology of schooling. *Journal of Curriculum Studies, 10* (1), 19–44.

Kaye, H. (1987). The use and abuse of the past: The new right and the crisis of history. *Socialist Register*, 332–365.

Keat, R. (1981). *The politics of social theory: Habermas, Freud, and the critique of positivism*. Chicago: The University of Chicago Press.

Keat, R. (1994). Skepticism, authority, and the market. In R. Keat, N. Whiteley, & N. Abercrombie (Eds.), *The authority of the consumer*. New York: Routledge.

Keating, A. (1995). Interrogating "whiteness," (de)constructing "race." *College English, 57* (8), 901–918.

Kegan, R. (1982). *The evolving self: Problem and process in human development*. Cambridge, MA: Harvard University Press.

Kellner, D. (1989). *Critical theory, Marxism, and modernity*. Baltimore: Johns Hopkins University Press.

Kellner, D. (1990). *Television and the crisis of democracy*. Boulder, CO: Westview.

Kellner, D. (1991). Reading images critically: Toward a postmodern pedagogy. In H. Giroux (Ed.), *Postmodernism, feminism, and cultural politics: Redrawing educational boundaries*. Albany, NY: State University of New York Press.

Kellner, D. (1995). *Media culture: Cultural studies, identity and politics between the modern and the postmodern*. New York: Routledge.

Kelly, L. (1996). "When does the speaking profit us? Reflection on the challenges of developing feminist perspectives on abuse and violence by women." In M. Hester, L. Kelly & J. Radford (Eds.), *Women, violence, and male power*. Bristol, PA: Open University Press.

Kemmis, S. et al. (Eds.). (1982). *The action research reader*. Geelong, Victoria: Deakin University Press.

Kimball, R. (1990). *Tenured radicals: How politics has corrupted our higher education*. New York: Harper & Row.

Kincheloe, J. (1990). Meta-analysis, memory, and the politics of the past: Historical method, curriculum, and social responsibility. *Social Science Record, 27* (2), 31–39.

Kincheloe, J. (1991). *Teachers as researchers: Qualitative paths to empowerment*. New York: Falmer.

Kincheloe, J. (1993). *Toward a critical politics of teacher thinking: Mapping the postmodern*. Westport, CT: Bergin & Garvey.

Kincheloe, J. (1995). *Toil and trouble: Good work, smart workers, and the integration of academic and vocational education*. New York: Peter Lang.

Kincheloe, J. (1996). The new childhood: *Home Alone* as a way of life. *Cultural Studies, 1*, 221–240.

Kincheloe, J. (1999). *How do we tell the workers? The socio-economic foundations of work and vocational education*. Boulder, CO: Westview.

Kincheloe, J. (2001). *The sign of the burger: McDonald's and the culture of power*. Philadelphia: Temple University Press.

Kincheloe, J., & McLaren, P. (2000). Rethinking critical theory and qualitative research. In N. Denzin & Y. Lincoln (Eds.), *Handbook of qualitative research*. Thousand Oaks, CA: Sage.

Kincheloe, J., & Pinar, W. (1991). *Curriculum as social psychoanlysis: Essays on the significance of place*. Albany, NY: SUNY Press.

Kincheloe, J., & Steinberg, S. (1993). A tentative description of postformal thinking: The critical confrontation with cognitive theory. *Harvard Educational Review, 63* (3), 296–320.

Kincheloe, J., & Steinberg, S. (1997). *Changing multiculturalism*. London: Open University Press.

Kincheloe, J., Slattery, P., & Steinberg, S. (2000). *Contextualizing teaching*. New York: Addison Wesley Longman.

Kincheloe, J., Steinberg, S., & Gresson, A. (Eds.). (1996). *Measured lies: The Bell Curve examined*. New York: St. Martin's Press.

Kincheloe, J., Steinberg, S., & Hinchey, P. (Eds.). (1999). *The postformal reader: Cognition and education*. New York: Falmer.

Kincheloe, J., & Steinberg, S., Rodriguez, N., & Chennault, R. (Eds.) (1998). *White reign: Deploying whiteness in America*. New York: St. Martin's Press.

Kincheloe, J., Steinberg, S., & Tippins, D. (1999). *The stigma of genius: Einstein consciousness, and education*. New York: Peter Lang.

Kincheloe, J., Steinberg, S., & Villaverde, L. (1999). *Rethinking intelligence: Confronting psychological assumptions about teaching and learning*. New York: Routledge.

King, B. (1990). Creating curriculum together: Teachers, students, and collaborative investigation. Paper presented at the American Educational Research Association, Boston, Massachusetts.

King, J. & Mitchell, C. (1995). *Black mothers to sons*. New York: Peter Lang.

Kipnis, L. (1988). Feminism: The political consciousness of postmodernism. In A. Ross (Ed.), *Universal abandon? The politics of postmodernism*. Minneapolis, MN: University of Minnesota Press.

Kitchener, R. (Ed.). (1988). *The worldview of contemporary physics: Does it need a new metaphysics?* Albany, NY: SUNY Press.

Klein, R. (1982). How to do what we want to do: Thoughts about feminist methodology. In G. Bowles & R. Klein (Eds.), *Theories of women's studies*. Boston: Routledge & Kegan Paul.

Kliebard, H. (1987). *The struggle for the American curriculum, 1893-1958*. New York: Routledge.

Kloppenberg, J. (1991). Social theory and the de/reconstruction of agricultural science: Local knowledge for an alternative agriculture. *Rural Sociology, 56* (4), 519–548.

Kneller, G. (1984). *Movements of thought in modern education* (2nd ed.). New York: John Wiley & Sons.

Kogler, H. (1996). *The power of dialogue: Critical hermeneutics after Gadamer and Foucault*. Cambridge, MA: MIT Press.

Kohli, W. (2000). Teaching in the danger zone: Democracy and difference. In D. Hursch & E. Ross (Eds.), *Democratic social education: Social studies for social change*. New York: Falmer.

Koller, A. (1981). *An unknown woman: A journey to self-discovery*. New York: Bantam Books.

Kovel, J. (1981). *The age of desire*. New York: Pantheon Books.

Kovel, J. (1998). Dialect as praxis. *Science and Society, 62* (3), 474–480.

Kramer, D. (1983). Postformal operations? A need for further conceptualization. *Human Development, 26*, 91–105.

Krievis, L. (1998). Creating north. In S. Steinberg & J. Kincheloe (Eds.), *Students as researcher: Creating classrooms that matter*. London: Falmer.

Kristeva, J. (1987). *In the beginning was love*. New York: Columbia University Press.

Kroath, F. (1989). How do teachers change their practical theories? *Cambridge Journal of Education, 19* (1), 59–69.

Lakes, R. (1994a). Critical education for work. In R. Lakes (Ed.), *Critical education for work*. Norwood, NJ: Ablex.

Lakes, R. (1994b). Is this workplace democracy?: Education and labor in postindustrial America. In R. Lakes (Ed.), *Critical education for work: Multidisciplinary approaches*. Norwood, NJ: Ablex.

Lash, S. (1990). *Sociology of postmodernism*. New York: Routledge.

Lather, P. (1986). Research as praxis. *Harvard Educational Review, 56*, 257–277.

Lather, P. (1991). *Getting smart: Feminist research and pedagogy with/in the post-modern.* New York: Routledge.

Lavine, T. (1984). *From Socrates to Sartre: The philosophical quest.* New York: Bantam Books.

Lawler, J. (1975). The Marxian dialectic—dialectic investigations by Bertell Ollman. *Monthly Review, 46* (9), 48–51.

Layton, L. (1994). *Blue Velvet:* A parable of male development. *Screen, 35* (4), 374–393.

Leistyna, P., Woodrum, A., & Sherblom, S. (1996). *Breaking free: The transformative power of critical pedagogy.* Cambridge, MA: Harvard Educational Review.

Leshan, L., & Margeneu, H. (1982). *Einstein's space and Van Gogh's sky: Physical reality and beyond.* New York: Macmillan Publishing Company.

Lesko, N. (1989). *Symbolizing society: Stories, rites, and structure in a Catholic high school.* New York: Falmer.

Levenson, T. (1997). Q: How smart was he. A: (very smart). Unpublished manuscript.

Levins, R. (1998). Dialectics and systems theory. *Science and Society, 62* (3), 375–389.

Lewis, J. (1992). *The road to romance and ruin: Teen films and youth culture.* New York: Routledge.

Lewis, M. (1990). Interrupting patriarchy: Politics, resistance, and transformation in the feminist classroom. *Harvard Educational Review, 60* (4), 467–488.

Lincoln, Y., & Guba, E. (1985). *Naturalistic inquiry.* Beverly Hills, CA: Sage Publications.

Lipsky, D., & Abrams, A. (1994). *Late bloomers, coming of age in today's America: The right place at the wrong time.* New York: Times Books.

Loewen, J. (1995). *Lies my teacher told me.* New York: New Press.

Loewen, J. (1999). *Lies across America: What our historical sites get wrong.* New York: New Press.

Long, D. (1995). Sociology and pedagogy for liberation: Cultivating a dialogue of discernment in our classrooms. *Teaching Sociology, 23,* 321–330.

Lowe, D. (1982). *History of bourgeois perception.* Chicago: University of Chicago Press.

Lugg, C. (1996). *For god and country: Conservatism and American school policy.* New York: Peter Lang.

Lugones, M. (1987). Playfulness, "world"-traveling, and loving perception. *Hypatia, 2* (2), 3–19.

Luke, T. (1991). Touring hyperreality: Critical theory confronts informational society. In P. Wexler (Ed.), *Critical theory now.* New York: Falmer.

Lull, J. (1995). *Media, communications, and culture: A global approach.* New York: Columbia University Press.

Luttrell, W. (1993). Working class women's ways of knowing: Effects of gender, race, and class. In L. Castenell & W. Pinar (Eds.), *Understanding curriculum as a racial text: Representations of identity and difference in education*. Albany, NY: SUNY Press.

Lyotard, J. (1984). *The postmodern condition*. Minneapolis, MN: University of Minnesota Press.

Macedo, D. (1994). *Literacies of power: What Americans are not allowed to know*. Boulder, CO: Westview.

Macmillan, J., & Garrison, J. (1984). Using the "new philosophy of science" in criticizing current research traditions in education. *Educational Researcher, 13*, 15–21.

Madison, G. (1988). *The hermeneutics of postmodernity: Figures and themes*. Bloomington, IN: Indiana University Press.

Maeroff, G. (1988). A blueprint for empowering teachers. *Phi Delta Kappan, 69* (7), 472–477.

Maher, F. & Rathbone, C. (1986). "Teacher education and feminist theory: Some implications for practice." *American Journal of Education, 94* (2), pp. 214–235.

Mahoney, M., & Lyddon, W. (1988). Recent developments in cognitive approaches to counseling and psychotherapy. *The Counseling Psychologist, 16* (2), 190–234.

Mandell, S. (1987). A search for form: Einstein and the poetry of Louis Zukofsky and William Carlos Williams. In D. Ryan (Ed.), *Einstein and the humanities*. Westport, CT: Greenwood Press.

Manning, P., & Cullum-Swan, B. (1994). Narrative, content, and semiotic analysis. In N. Denzin & Y. Lincoln (Eds.), *Handbook of qualitative research*. Thousand Oaks, CA: Sage.

Marcus, G., & Fischer, M. (1986). *Anthropology as cultural critique: An experimental moment in the human sciences*. Chicago: University of Chicago Press.

Marcuse, H. (1955). *Eros and civilization*. Boston: Beacon Press.

Marcuse, H. (1960). *Reason and revolution: Hegel and the rise of social theory*. Boston: Beacon Press.

Marcuse, H. (1964). *One dimensional man*. Boston: Beacon Press.

Marcuse, H. (1978). *The aesthetic dimension*. Boston: Beacon Press.

Mardle, G. (1984). Power, tradition, and change: Educational implications of the thought of Antonio Gramsci. In J. Codd (Ed.), *Philosophy, common sense, and action in educational administration*. Victoria, Australia: Deakin University Press.

Marker, P. (1993). Not only by our words: Connecting the pedagogy of Paulo Freire with the social studies classroom. *Social Science Record, 30* (1), 77–89.

Marshalidis, S. (1997). *Consciousness and education: A process perspective*. <http://faculty.erau.edu/meshalis/consciousness.htm/s>.

Marsick, V. (1989). Examining new paradigms for workplace learning. In C. Coggins (Ed.), *Proceedings of the Annual Adult Education Research Conference,* Madison, Wisconsin, Madison Department of continuing and Vocational Education.

Mathison, S. (2000). Promoting democracy through evaluation. In D. Hursch & E. Ross (Eds.), *Democratic social education: Social studies for social change.* New York: Falmer.

May, W., & Zimpher, N. (1986). An examination of three theoretical perspectives on supervision: Perceptions of preservice field supervision. *Journal of Curriculum and Supervision, 1* (2), 83–99.

McCall, A. (1996). Making a difference: Integrating social problems and social action in the social studies curriculum. *The Social Studies, 84* (5), 203–209.

McCarthy, C., & Apple, M. (1988). Race, class, and gender in American educational research: Toward a nonsynchronous parallelist position. In L. Weis (Ed.), *Class, race, and gender in American education.* Albany, NY: State University of New York Press.

McCarthy, T. (1978). *The critical theory of Jurgen Habermas.* Cambridge, MA: The MIT Press.

McCarthy, T. (1992). The critique of impure reason: Foucault and the Frankfurt School. In T. Wartenberg (Ed.), *Rethinking power.* Albany, NY: SUNY Press.

McKernan, J. (1988). Teacher as researcher: Paradigm and praxis. *Contemporary Education, 59* (3), 154–158.

McLaren, C. (1996). Boys and education in Australia. In C. McLean, M. Carey, & C. White (Eds.), *Men's ways of being.* Boulder, CO: Westview.

McLaren, P. (1989). *Life in schools.* New York: Longman.

McLaren, P. (1991). Decentering culture: Postmodernism, resistance, and critical pedagogy. In N. Wyner (Ed.), *Current perspectives on the culture of schools.* Boston: Bookline Books.

McLaren, P. (1991). Schooling and the postmodern body: Critical pedagogy and the politics of enfleshment. In H. Giroux (Ed.), *Postmodernism, feminism, and cultural politics: Redrawing educational boundaries.* Albany, NY: State University of New York Press.

McLaren, P. (1992a). Literacy research and the postmodern turn: Cautions from the margins. In R. Beach, et al. (Ed.), *Multidisciplinary perspectives on research.* Urbana, IL: National Council of Teachers of English.

McLaren, P. (1992b). Collisions with otherness: "Traveling" theory, post-colonial criticism, and the politics of ethnographic practice—the mission of the wounded ethnographer. *Qualitative Studies in Education, 5* (1), 1–15.

McLaren, P. (1994a). Multiculturalism and the postmodern critique: Toward a pedagogy of resistance and transformation. In H. Giroux & P. McLaren (Eds.), *Between borders: Pedagogy and the politics of cultural studies.* New York: Routledge.

McLaren, P. (1994b). An interview with Heinz Sünker of Germany: Germany today—history and future (or dilemmas, dangers and hopes). *International Journal of Educational Reform, 3* (2), 202–209.

McLaren, P. (1995). *Critical pedagogy and predatory culture: Oppositional politics in a postmodern era.* New York: Routledge.

McLaren, P. (1997). *Revolutionary multiculturalism: Pedagogies of dissent for the new millennium.* Boulder, CO: Westview.

McLaren, P. (2000). *Che Guevara, Paulo Freire, and the pedagogy of revolution.* Lanham, MD: Rowman & Littlefield.

McLaren, P., & Morris, J. (1997). Mighty Morphin Power Rangers: The aesthetics of macho-militaristic justice. In J. Kincheloe & S. Steinberg (Eds.), *Kinderculture.* Boulder, CO: Westview.

McLaren, P., Hammer, R., Reilly, S., & Sholle, D. (1995). *Rethinking media literacy: A critical pedagogy of representation.* New York: Peter Lang.

McLean, C., (1996a). The politics of men's pain. In C. Mclean, M. Carey, & C. White (Eds.), *Men's ways of being.* Boulder, CO: Westview.

McLean, C., (1996b). Boys and education in Australia. In C. Mclean, M. Carey, & C. White (Eds.), *Men's ways of being.* Boulder, CO: Westview.

McLean, C., Carey, M., & White, C. (1996). Introduction. In C. Mclean, M. Carey, & C. White (Eds.), *Men's ways of being.* Boulder, CO: Westview.

McNay, M. (1988). Educational research and the nature of science. *The Educational Forum, 52* (4), 353–362.

Melman, S. & Dumas, L. (April 16, 1990). "Planning for economic conversion." *The Nation, 250* (15), pp. 509, 522–528.

Merleau-Ponty, M. (1962). *Phenomenology of perception.* London: Routledge Kegan Paul.

Merleau-Ponty, M. (1975). *The structure of behavior.* Boston: Beacon Press.

Metzger, E., & Bryant, L. (1993). Portfolio assessment: Pedagogy, power, and the student. *Teaching English in the Two Year College, 20* (4), 279–288.

Mies, M. (1982). Toward a methodology for feminist research. In G. Bowles & R. Klein (Eds.), *Theories of women's studies.* Boston: Routledge & Kegan Paul.

Miller, S., & Hodge, J. (1998). *Phenomenology, hermeneutics, and narrative analysis: Some unfinished methodological business.* Unpublished paper.

Miller, T. (1993). *The well-tempered self: Citizenship, culture, and the postmodern subject.* Baltimore: Johns Hopkins University Press.

Moberg, D. (1996, December 16). Labor as neighbor. *The Nation, 263* (20), 18–21.

Morris, M. (1988). Tooth and claw: Tales of survival and Crocodile Dundee. In A. Ross (Ed.), *Universal abandon? The politics of postmodernism.* Minneapolis, MN: University of Minnesota Press.

Morrow, R. (1991). Critical theory, Gramsci and cultural studies: From structuralism to post-structuralism. In P. Wexler (Ed.), *Critical theory now*. New York: Falmer.

Mosse, G. (1996). *The image of man: The creation of modern masculinity*. New York: Oxford University Press.

Mostern, K. (1994). Decolonization as learning: Practice and pedagogy in Frantz Fanon's revolutionary narrative. In H. Giroux & P. McLaren (Eds.), *Between borders: Pedagogy and the politics of cultural studies*. New York: Routledge.

Mouffe, C. (1988). Radical democracy: Modern or postmodern? In A. Ross (Ed.), *Universal abandon? The politics of postmodernism*. Minneapolis: University of Minnesota Press.

Mullen, C. (1999). Whiteness, cracks, and inkstains: Making cultural identity with Euroamerican preservice teachers. In P. Diamond & C. Mullen (Eds.), *The postmodern educator: Arts-based inquiries and teacher development*. New York: Peter Lang.

Mullin, J. (1994). Feminist theory, feminist pedagogy: The gap between what we say and what we do. *Composition Studies/Freshman English News, 22* (1), 14–24.

Murray, J., & Ozanne, J. (1991). The critical imagination: Emancipatory interests in consumer research. *Journal of Consumer Research, 18* (2), 129–144.

Murray, R. (1992). Fordism and post-Fordism. In C. Jencks (Ed.), *The post-modern reader*. New York: St. Martin's Press.

Musolf, R. (1992). Structure, institutions, power, and ideology: New directions within symbolic interactionism. *The Sociological Quarterly, 33* (2), 171–189.

Myers, L. (1987). The deep structure of culture: Relevance of traditional African culture in contemporary life. *Journal of Black Studies, 18* (1), 72–85.

Nasaw, D. (1979). *Schooled to order: A social history of public schooling in the United States*. New York: Oxford University Press.

National Commission on Excellence in Education. (1983). *A nation at risk: The imperative for educational reform*. Washington, DC: U.S. Government Printing Office.

Nelson, C., Treichler, P., & Grossberg, L. (1992). Cultural studies: An introduction. In C. Nelson, P. Trichler, & L. Grossberg (Eds.), *Cultural studies*. New York: Routledge.

Nieto, S. (1996). *Affirming diversity: The sociopolitical context of multicultural education*. White Plains, NY: Longman.

Nightingale, C. (1993). *On the edge: A history of poor black children and their American dreams*. New York: Basic Books.

Nixon, J. (1981). Postscript. In J. Nixon (Ed.), *A teachers' guide to action research*. London: Grant McIntyre.

Noblit, G. (1984). The prospects of an applied ethnography for education: A sociology of knowledge interpretation. *Educational Evaluation and Policy Analysis, 6* (1), 95–101.

Noblit, G. (1999). *Particularities: Collected essays on ethnography and education.* New York: Peter Lang.

Noffke, S. (2000). Identity, community, and democracy in the new social order. In D. Hursh & E. Ross (Eds.), *Democratic social education: Social studies for social change.* New York: Falmer.

Noffke, S., & Brennan, M. (1991). Student teachers use action research: Issues and examples. In B. Tabachnick & K. Zeichner (Eds.), *Issues and practices in inquiry-oriented teacher education.* New York: Falmer.

Nooteboom, B. (1991). A postmodern philosophy of markets. *International Studies of Management and Organization, 22* (2), 53–76.

Nussbaum, M. (1987). Undemocratic vistas. *New York Review of Books, 34,* 20–26.

Nyang, S., & Vandi, A. (1980). Pan Africanism in world history. In M. Asante & A. Vandi (Eds.), *Contemporary black thought: Alternative analyses in social and behavioral science.* Beverly Hills, CA: Sage Publications.

Ohanian, S. (1985). On stir-and-serve recipes for teaching. *Phi Delta Kappan, 65,* 697–702.

Olesen, V. (1994). Feminisms and models of qualitative research. In N. Denzin & Y. Lincoln (Eds.), *Handbook of qualitative research.* Thousand Oaks, CA: Sage.

Oliver, D., & Gershman, K. (1989). *Education, modernity, and fractured meaning: Toward a process theory of teaching and learning.* Albany, NY: State University of New York Press.

Orteza, Y. M. (1988). Broadening the focus of research in education. *Journal of Research and Development in Education, 22* (1), 23–28.

O'Sullivan, E. (1999). *Transformative learning: Educational vision for the 21st century.* London: Zed.

Owen, D., & Doerr, M. (1999). *None of the above: The truth behind the SATs.* Lanham, MD: Rowman & Littlefield.

Owens, W. (1997). The challenges of teaching social studies methods to preservice elementary teachers. *The Social Studies, 88* (3), 113–120.

Pagano, J. (1990). *Exiles and communities.* Albany, NY: State University of New York Press.

Pang, V., Gay, G., & Stanley, W. (1995). Expanding conceptions of community and civic competencies for a multicultural society. *Theory and Research in Social Education, 23* (4), 302–331.

Parker, W. (1997b). Democracy and difference. *Theory and Research in Social Education, 25* (2), 220–234.

Parker, W. & Jarolimek, J. (1997). *Social studies in elementary education.* Upper Saddle River, NJ: Prentice-Hall.

Patton, P. (1989). Taylor and Foucault on power and freedom. *Political Studies, 37,* 260–276.

Paul, W. (1994). *Laughing screaming: Modern Hollywood horror and comedy.* New York: Columbia University Press.

Peace, A. (1990). Dropping out of sight: Social anthropology encounters postmodernism. *Australian Journal of Anthropology, 1* (1), 18–31.

Peat, F. (1990). *Einstein's moon: Bell's Theorem and the curious quest for quantum reality.* Chicago: Contemporary Books.

Peoria Astronomical Society. (1998). *Beyond the event horizon: An introduction to black holes.* <http://www.astronomical.org/astbook/blkhole.html>.

Perkinson, H. (1991). *The imperfect panacea: American faith in education, 1865-1900.* (3rd ed.) New York: McGraw Hill.

Peters, M., & Lankshear, C. (1994). Education and hermeneutics: A Freiran interpretation. In P. McLaren & C. Lankshear (Eds.), *Politics of liberation: Paths from Freire.* New York: Routledge.

Peters, W., & Amburgey, B. (1982). Teacher intellectual disposition and cognitive classroom verbal reactions. *Journal of Educational Research, 76* (2), 94–99.

Pfeil, F. (1995). *White guys: Studies in postmodern domination and difference.* New York: Verso.

Piliawsky, M. (1984). Racial equality in the United States: From institutionalized racism to 'respectable' racism. *Phylon, 45* (2), 135–143.

Pinar, W. (1975). Currere: Toward reconceptualization. In W. Pinar (Ed.), *Curriculum theorizing: The reconceptialists.* Berkeley: McCutchan Publishing Company.

Pinar, W. (1988). Time, place, and voice: Curriculum theory and the history moment. In W. Pinar (Ed.), *Contemporary curriculum discourses.* Scottsdale, AZ: Garsuch Scarisbrick.

Pinar, W. (1991). Curriculum as social psychoanalysis: On the significance of place. In J. Kincheloe & W. Pinar (Eds.), *Curriculum as social psychoanalysis: Essays on the significance of place.* Albany, NY: State University of New York Press.

Pinar, W. (1994). *Autobiography, politics, and sexuality: Essays in curriculum theory, 1972-1992.* New York: Peter Lang.

Pinar, W. (1998). *Curriculum: Toward new identities.* New York: Garland.

Pinar, W. (1999). *Contemporary curriculum discourses: Twenty years of JCT* (2nd ed.). New York: Peter Lang.

Pinar, W., Reynolds, W., Slattery, P., & Taubman, P. (1995). *Understanding curriculum.* New York: Peter Lang.

Polakow, V. (1992). *The erosion of childhood.* Chicago: University of Chicago Press.

Pollin, R. (1996, September 30). Economics with a human face. *The Nation, 263* (9), 21–23.

Pollin, R., & Cockburn, A. (1991, February 25). The world, the free market, and the left. *The Nation, 252* (7), 224–236.

Ponzio, R. (1985). Can we change content without changing context? *Teacher Education Quarterly, 12* (3), 39–43.

Popenoe, D. (1996). *Life without father.* New York: The Free Press.

Popkewitz, T. (1981). The study of schooling: Paradigms and field-based methodologies in education research and evaluation. In T. Popkewitz & B. Tabachnick (Eds.), *The study of schooling.* New York: Praeger Publishers.

Popkewitz, T. (1987). Organization and power: Teacher education reforms. *Social Education, 39,* 496–500.

Popular Memory Group. (1982). Popular memory: Theory, politics, and method. In Centre for Contemporary Cultural Studies (Eds.), *Making histories: Studies in history-writing and politics.* Minneapolis, MN: University of Minnesota Press.

Porter, A. (1988). Indicators: Objective data or political tool. *Phi Delta Kappan, 69* (7), 503–508.

Postman, N. (1979). *Teaching as a conserving activity.* New York: Delta.

Postman, N. (1985). Critical thinking in an electronic era. *Phi Kappa Phi Journal, 65,* 4–8, 17.

Postman, N. (1989). Learning by story. *The Atlantic, 264* (6), 119–124.

Postman, N. (1994). *The disappearance of childhood.* New York: Vintage Books.

Postman, N. (1995). *The end of education: Redefining the value of school.* New York: Knopf.

Preskill, S. (1991). We can live freedom: The Highlander Folk School as a model for civic education. *Social Science Record, 28* (2), 11–21.

Prettyman, S. (1998). Writing and passing notes: Resistance, identity, and pleasure. In S. Steinberg & J. Kincheloe (Eds.), *Students as researchers: Creating classrooms that matter.* London: Falmer.

Prigogine, I., & Stengers, I. (1984). *Order out of chaos.* New York: Basic Books.

Probyn, E. (1993). True voices and real people: The "problem" of the autobiographical in cultural studies. In V. Blundell, J. Shepherd, & I. Taylor (Eds.), *Relocating cultural studies: Developments in theory and research.* New York: Routledge.

Pruyn, M. (1994). Becoming subjects through critical practice: How students in one elementary classroom critically read and wrote their world. *International Journal of Educational Reform, 3* (1), 37–50.

Puk, T. (1994). Epistemological implications of training social studies teachers: Just who was Christopher Columbus? *The Social Studies, 85* (5), 228–232.

Quantz, R. (1992). On critical ethnography (with some postmodern considerations). In M. LeCompte, W. Millroy, & J. Preissle (Eds.), *The handbook of qualitative research in education* (pp. 447–505). New York: Academic Press.

Radford, J., & Stanko, E. (1996). Violence against women and children: The contradictions of crime control under patriarchy. In M. Hester, L. Kelly, & J. Radford (Eds.), *Women, violence, and male power.* Bristol, PA: Open University Press.

Rains, F. (1998). Is the benign really harmless? Deconstructing some "benign" manifestations of operationalized white privilege. In Kincheloe, J., Steinberg, S., Rodriguez, N., & Chennault, R. (Eds.), *White reign: Deploying whiteness in America.* New York: St. Martin's Press.

Raizen, S. (1989). *Reforming education for work: A cognitive science perspective.* Berkeley, CA: NCRVE.

Raizen, S., & Colvin, R. (1991, December 11). Apprenticeships: A cognitive-science view. *Education Week*, 26.

Ramsay, C. (1996). Male horror: On David Cronenberg. In P. Smith (Ed.), *Boys: Masculinities in contemporary culture.* Boulder, CO: Westview.

Rand, E. (1995). *Barbie's queer accessories.* Durham, NC: Duke University Press.

Rapko, J. (1998). Review of *The power of dialogue: Critical hermeneutics after Gadamer and Foucault. Criticism, 40* (1), 133–138.

Rapping, E. (1994). *Mediations: Forays into the culture and gender wars.* Boston: South End Press.

Rattigan, N., & McManus, T. (1992). Fathers, sons, and brothers: Patriarchy and guilt in 1980s American cinema. *Journal of Popular Film and Television, 20* (1), 15–23.

Reason, P., & Rowan, J. (1981). Issues of validity in new paradigm research. In P. Reason & J. Rowan (Eds.), *Human inquiry.* New York: John Wiley.

Reich, C. (1995). *Opposing the system.* New York: Crown Publishers.

Reinharz, S. (1979). *On becoming a social scientist.* San Francisco: Jossey-Bass.

Reinharz, S. (1982). Experiential analysis: A contribution to feminist research. In G. Bowles & R. Klein (Eds.), *Theories of women's studies.* Boston: Routledge & Kegan Paul.

Reinharz, S. (1992). *Feminist methods in social research.* New York: Oxford University Press.

Reitz, C. (1988). *Bennett, Bloom, and Boyer: Toward a critical discussion.* Paper presented at the Southwest Community Colleges Humanities Association, Kansas City, Missouri.

Reynolds, R. (1987). "Einstein and psychology: The genetic epistemology of relativistic physics." In D. Ryan (Ed.), *Einstein and the humanities.* New York: Greenwood Press.

Richmond, S. (December, 1986). "The white paper, education, and the crafts: An assessment of values." *The Journal of Educational Thought, 20* (3), pp. 143–155.

Rifkin, J. (1995). *The end of work: The decline of the global labor force and the dawn of the post-market era.* New York: Tarchner/Putnam.

Robbins, D. (1991). *The work of Pierre Bourdieu.* Boulder, CO: Westview.

Roberts, M., & Wozniak, R. (1994). *Labor's key role in workplace training.* Washington, DC: AFL-CIO.

Rodriquez, N., & Villaverde, L. (1999). *Dismantling white privilege.* New York: Peter Lang.

Roman, L., & Apple, M. (1990). Is naturalism a move away from positivism? In E. Eisner & A. Peshkin (Eds.), *Qualitative inquiry in education: The continuing debate*. New York: Teachers College Press.

Romanish, B. (1986). Critical thinking and the curriculum: A critique. *The Educational Forum, 51* (1), 45–56.

Rorty, A. (1992). Power and powers: A dialogue between buff and rebuff. In T. Wartenberg (Ed.), *Rethinking power*. Albany, NY: SUNY Press.

Rosen, S. (1987). *Hermeneutics as politics*. New York: Oxford University Press.

Rosenau, P. (1992). *Postmodernism and the social sciences: Insights, inroads, and intrusion*. Princeton, NJ: Princeton University Press.

Ross, A. (1996). Introduction. In A. Ross (Ed.), *Science wars*. Durham, NC: Duke University Press.

Ross, D. (1984). A practical model for conducting action research in public school settings. *Contemporary Education, 55* (2), 113–117.

Ross, E. (1988). *Teacher values and the construction of curriculum*. Paper presented to the American Educational Research Association, New Orleans, Louisiana.

Ross, E. (1997). The struggle for the social studies curriculum. In E. Ross (Ed.), *The social studies curriculum: Purposes, problems, and possibilities*. Albany, NY: SUNY Press.

Ross, E. (2000). Diverting democracy: The curriculum standards movement and social studies education. In D. Hursh & E. Ross (Eds.), *Democratic social studies education: Social studies for social change*. New York: Falmer.

Rubin, L. (1994). *Families on the faultline: America's working class speaks about the family, the economy, race, and ethnicity*. New York: Harper Collins.

Ruddick, J. (1989). *Critical thinking and practitioner research: Have they a place in initial teacher training?* Paper presented to the American Educational Research Association, San Francisco, California.

Rumberger, R. (1984). The growing imbalance between education and work. *Phi Delta Kappan, 65* (5), 342–346.

Russell, D. (1993). Vygotsky, Dewey, and externalism: Beyond the student/discipline dichotomy. *Journal of Advanced Composition, 13* (1), 173–197.

Ryan, K. (1989). Confessions of a teacher educator. In H. Holtz, et al. (Eds.), *Education and the American dream*. Granby, MA: Bergin & Garvey.

Salisbury, J., & Jackson, D. (1996). *Challenging macho values: Practical ways of working with adolescent boys*. Bristol, PA: Falmer.

Samper, M., & Lakes, R. (1994). Work education for the next century: Beyond skills training. In R. Lakes (Ed.), *Critical education for work: Multidisciplinary approaches*. Norwood, NJ: Ablex.

Samuels, A. (1993). *The political psyche*. New York: Routledge.

Schleifer, R., Davis, R., & Mergler, N. (1992). *Culture and cognition: The boundaries of literacy and scientific inquiry*. Ithaca, NY: Cornell University Press.

Scholes, R. (1982). *Semiotics and interpretation*. New Haven, CT: Yale University Press.

Schon, D. (1987). *Educating the reflective practitioner*. San Francisco: Jossey-Bass Publishers.

Schwandt, T. (2000). Three epistemological stances for qualitative inquiry: Interpretivism, hermeneutics, and social constructivism. In N. Denzin & Y. Lincoln (Eds.), *Handbook of qualitative research* (2nd ed.). Thousand Oaks, CA: Sage.

Schwartz, B. (1994). *The costs of living: How market freedom erodes the best things in life*. New York: W. W. Norton.

Schweder, R. & Fiske, D. (1986). "Introduction: Uneasy social science." In D. Fiske & R. Schweder (Eds.), *Metatheory in social science: Pluralisms and subjectivities*. Chicago: University of Chicago Press.

Scully, M. (1982, May 26). Academic geography: Few students, closed departments, fuzzy image. *The Chronicle of Higher Education*, 1, 12.

Sedgwick, E. (1995). Gosh, Boy George, you must be awfully secure in your masculinity! In M. Berger, B. Wallis, & S. Watson (Eds.), *Constructing masculinity*. New York: Routledge.

Selden, S. (1984). Objectivity and ideology in educational research. *Phi Delta Kappan, 66* (4), 281–283.

Semali, L., & Kincheloe, J. (1999). *What is indigenous knowledge? Voices from the academy*. New York: Falmer.

Semali, L., & Pailliotet, A. (1999). *Intermediality: The teacher's handbook of critical media literacy*. Boulder, CO: Westview.

Sengé, P. (1990). *The fifth discipline: The art and practice of the learning organization*. New York: Doubleday.

Seymour, C. (1997, August 11). Low-wage innovations. *In These Times, 21* (19), 18–20.

Shankar, D. (1996). "The epistemology of the indigenous medical knowledge systems of India." *Indigenous Knowledge and Development Moniter, 4* (3), pp. 13–14.

Shapiro, M. (1992). *Reading the postmodern polity: Political theory as textual practice*. Minneapolis, MN: University of Minnesota Press.

Shapiro, S. (1989). Towards a language of educational politics: The struggles for a critical public discourse of education. *Educational Foundations, 3* (3), 79–100.

Sherman, R., Webb, R., & Andrews, S. (1984). Qualitative inquiry: An introduction. *Journal of Thought, 19*, pp. 25–31.

Shiva, V. (1993). *Monocultures of the mind*. London: Zed Books.

Shotter, J. (1993). *Cultural politics of everyday life*. Toronto: University of Toronto Press.

Shweder, R. & Fiske, D. (1986). Introduction: Uneasy social science. In D. Fiske & R. Shweder (Eds.), *Metatheory in social science: Pluralisms and subjectivities.* Chicago: University of Chicago Press.

Sidel, R. (1992). *Women and children last: The plight of poor women in affluent America.* New York: Penguin Books.

Siegel, F. (1986). Is Archie Bunker fit to rule? Or: How Immanueal Kant became one of the founding fathers. *Telos, 69,* 3–29.

Silliman, M. (1990). The closing of the professorial mind: A meditation on Plato and Allan Bloom. *Educational Theory, 40* (1), 147–151.

Simon, R. (1989). Empowerment as a pedagogy of possibility. In H. Holtz, et al. (Eds.), *Education and the American dream.* Granby, CT: Bergin & Garvey.

Simon, R., Dippo, D., & Schenke, A. (1991). *Learning work: A critical pedagogy of work education.* Westport, CT: Bergin & Garvey.

Slattery, P. (1995). *Curriculum development in the postmodern era.* New York: Garland.

Slaughter, J. (1997, August 11). Face-off at UPS. *In These Times, 21* (19), 6–7.

Slaughter, R. (1989). Cultural reconstruction in the post-modern world. *Journal of Curriculum Studies, 3,* 255–270.

Sleeter, C., & Grant, C. (1988). *Making choices for multicultural education.* Columbus, OH: Merrill Publishing Company.

Sleeter, C., & Grant, C. (1994). *Making choices for multicultural education: Five approaches to race, class, and gender* (2nd ed.). New York: Merrill.

Smart, B. (1992). *Modern conditions, postmodern controversies.* New York: Routledge.

Smith, D. (1999). *Pedagon: Interdisciplinary essays in the human sciences, pedagogy, and culture.* New York: Peter Lang.

Smith, G. (1996). Dichotomies in the making of men. In C. McLean, M. Carey, & C. White (Eds.), *Men's ways of being.* Boulder, CO: Westview.

Smith, J. (1983). Quantitative versus qualitative research: An attempt to clarify the issue. *Educational Researcher, 12,* 6–13.

Smith, P. (1989). Pedagogy and the popular-cultural-commodity text. In H. Giroux & R. Simon (Eds.), *Popular culture: Schooling and everyday life.* Granby, MA: Bergin & Garvey.

Smith, P. (1996). Introduction. In P. Smith (Ed.), *Boys: Masculinities in contemporary culture.* Boulder, CO: Westview.

Sobchack, V. (1991). Child/alien/father: Patriarchal crisis and generic exchange. In C. Penley, E. Lyon, L. Spigel, & J. Bergstrom (Eds.), *Close encounters: Film, feminism, and science fiction.* Minneapolis, MN: University of Minnesota Press.

Solomos, J. et al. (1982). The organic crisis of British capitalism and race: The experience of the seventies. In Centre for Contemporary Cultural Studies (Ed.), *The empire strikes back: Race and racism in 70s Britain.* London: Hutchinson.

Soltis, J. (1984). On the nature of educational research. *Educational Research, 13,* 5–10.

Spring, J. (1984, April). Education and the Sony war. *Phi Delta Kappan, 65* (8), 534–537.

Spring, J. (1994). *The American school: 1642–1993.* New York: McGraw Hill.

Stanley, W. (2000). Curriculum and the social order. In D. Hursh & E. Ross (Eds.), *Democratic social education: Social studies for social change.* New York: Falmer.

Staples, R. (1984). Racial ideology and intellectual racism: Blacks in academia. *The Black Scholar, 15* (2), 2–17.

Steinberg, S. (1997). The bitch who has everything. In S. Steinberg & J. Kincheloe (Eds.), *Kinderculture: The corporate construction of childhood.* Boulder, CO: Westview.

Steinberg, S. (2000). The new civics: Teaching for critical empowerment. In D. Hursh & W. Ross (Eds.), *Democratic social education: Social studies for social change.* New York: Falmer.

Steinberg, S., & Kincheloe, J. (1998). *Students as researchers: Creating classrooms that matter.* London:

Steinberg, S., & Kincheloe, J. (Eds.). (1997). *Kinderculture: The corporate construction of childhood.* Boulder, CO: Westview.

Steward, D., & Mickunas, A. (1974). *Exploring phenomenology.* Chicago: American Library Association.

Still right after all these years. (1998). <http://news3.news.wisc.edu/052einstein /frame_drag4.html>.

Sünker, H. (1994a). Are intellectuals the keepers of political culture? Some reflections on politics, morality, and reason. In R. Farnen (Ed.), *Nationalism, ethnicity, and identity: Cross national and comparative perspectives.* New Brunswick, NJ: Transaction Publishers.

Sünker, H. (1994b). Pedagogy and politics: Heydorn's survival through education and it's challenge to contemporary theories of education (Bildung). In S. Miedema, G. Bieste, & W. Wardekke (Eds.), *The politics of human science.* Brussels: VUB Press.

Sünker, H. (1998). Welfare, democracy, and social work. In G. Flosser & H. Otto (Eds.), *Towards more democracy in social services: Models of culture and welfare.* New York: de Gruyter.

Surber, J. (1998). *Culture and critique: An introduction to the critical discourses of cultural studies.* Boulder, CO: Westview.

Swartz, E. (1993). Multicultural education: Disrupting patterns of supremacy in school curricula, practices, and pedagogy. *Journal of Negro Education, 62* (4), 493–506.

Talbot, M. (1986). *Beyond the quantum.* New York: Bantam Books.

Talbot, M. (1991). *The holographic universe.* New York: Harper Collins.

Taussig, M. (1987). *Shamanism, colonialism, and the wildman: A study in terror and healing*. Chicago: University of Chicago Press.

Taxel, J. (1994). Political correctness, cultural politics, and writing for young people. *The New Advocate, 7* (2), 93–108.

Terkel, S. (1972). *Working*. New York: Avon.

Thiele, L. (1986). Foucault's triple murder and the modern development of power. *Canadian Journal of Political Science, 19* (2), 243–260.

Thornton, S. (1997). Matters of methods. *Theory and Research in Social Education, 25* (2), 216–219.

Tomlinson, J. (1991). *Cultural imperialism*. Baltimore: Johns Hopkins University Press.

Tripp, D. (1988). *Teacher journals in collaborative classroom research*. Paper presented to the American Educational Research Association, New Orleans, Louisiana.

Tyack, D., & Hansot, E. (1982). *Managers of virtue: Public school leadership in America, 1829-1980*. Cambridge: Harvard University Press.

Usher, R., & Edwards, R. (1994). *Postmodernism and education*. New York: Routledge.

Valli, L. (1988). Gender identity and the technology of office education. In L. Weis (Ed.), *Class, race, and gender in American education*. Albany, NY: SUNY Press.

Van Hesteran, F. (1986). Counseling research in a different key: The promise of human science perspective. *Canadian Journal of Counseling, 20* (4), 200–234.

Vande Berg, L. (1993). *China Beach*, prime time war in the postfeminist age: An example of patriarchy in a different voice. *Western Journal of Communication, 57,* 349–366.

Vande Berg, O., & Nicholson, S. (1989). *Teacher transformation in the South African context: An action research approach*. Paper presented to the International Conference on School-Based Innovations: Looking forward to the 1990s, Hong Kong.

Vattimo, G. (1994). *Beyond interpretation: The meaning of hermeneutics for philosophy*. Stanford, California: Stanford University Press.

Ventura, M. (1994, July/August). The age of endarkenment. *Utne Reader, 64,* 63–66.

Voloshinov, V. (1973). *Marxism and the philosophy of language*. New York: Seminar Press.

Walby, S. (1989). Theorising patriarchy. *Sociology, 23* (2), 213–234.

Walby, S. (1990). *Theorising patriarchy*. Oxford: Basil Blackwell.

Wallace, M. (1987). A historical review of action research: Some implications for the education of teachers in their managerial role. *Journal of Education for Teaching, 13* (2), 97–115.

Ward, S. (1996). *Reconfiguring truth: Postmodernism, science studies, and the search for a new model of knowledge.* Lanham, MD: Rowman & Littlefield.

Warde, A. (1994). Consumers, identity, and belonging: Reflecting on some theses of Zygmunt Bauman. In R. Keat, N. Whiteley, & N. Abercrombie (Eds.), *The authority of the consumer.* New York: Routledge.

Wartenberg, T. (1992a). Situated social power. In T. Wartenberg (Ed.), *Rethinking power.* Albany, NY: SUNY Press.

Wartenberg, T. (1992b). Introduction. In T. Wartenberg (Ed.), *Rethinking power.* Albany, NY: SUNY Press.

Waters, M. (1989). Patriarchy and viviarchy: An exploration and reconstruction of concepts of masculine domination. *Sociology, 23* (2), 193–211.

Weil, D. (1998). *Towards a critical multi-cultural literacy: Theory and practice for education for liberation.* New York: Peter Lang.

Weil, D. & Anderson, H. (Eds.), (2000). *Perspectives in critical thinking: Essays by teachers in theory and practice.* New York: Peter Lang.

Weiler, K. (1988). *Women teaching for change.* South Hadley, MA: Bergin & Garvey.

Weinstein, D., & Weinstein, M. (1991). Georg Simmel: Sociological flaneur bricoleur. *Theory, Culture, and Society, 8,* 151–168.

Weis, L. (1988). "High schools girls in a de-industrializing economy." In L. Weis (Ed.), *Class, race, and gender in American education.* Albany, NY: Suny Press.

Weisberg, J. (1987). Sex and drugs and Heidegger. *Washington Monthly, 19,* 49–53.

Weisman, J. (1991). "Some economists challenging view that schools hurt competitiveness." *Education Week, 9* (11) (November 13), p. 1, 14–15.

Welch, S. (1991). An ethic of solidarity and difference. In H. Giroux (Ed.), *Postmodernism, feminism, and cultural politics: Redrawing educational boundaries.* Albany, NY: State University of New York Press.

Wertsch, J. (1991). *Voices of the mind: A sociocultural approach to mediated action.* Cambridge, MA: Harvard University Press.

West, C. (1991). *The ethical dimensions of Marxist thought.* New York: Monthly Review Press.

West, C. (1992). Nihilism in black America. In G. Dent (Ed.), *Black popular culture.* Seattle: Bay Press.

West, C. (1993). *Race matters.* Boston: Beacon Press.

Westkott, M. (1982). Women's studies as a strategy for change: Between criticism and vision. In G. Bowles & R. Klein, *Theories of women's studies.* Boston: Routledge & Kegan Paul.

Wexler, P. (1991). Preface. In P. Wexler (Ed.), *Critical theory now.* New York: Falmer.

Wexler, P. (1996). *Holy sparks: Social theory, education and religion.* New York: St. Martin's Press.

Wexler, P. (1997). *Social research in education: Ethnography of being.* Paper presented at the International Conference on The Culture of Schooling, Halle, Germany.

Wexler, P. (2000). *The mystical society: Revitalization in culture, theory, and education.* Boulder, CO: Westview.

White, H. (1978). *Tropics of discourse.* Baltimore: Johns Hopkins University Press.

White, H. (1987). *The content of the form.* Baltimore: Johns Hopkins University Press.

Whitson, J. (1991). *Constitution and curriculum.* New York: Falmer.

Wiggins, G. (1989). A true test: Toward a more authentic and equitable assessment. *Phi Delta Kappan, 70* (9), 703–713.

Willis, P. (1977). *Learning to labour: How working class kids get working class jobs.* Farnborough, England: Saxon House.

Wilson, S. (1977). The use of ethnographic techniques in educational research. *Review of Educational Research, 47* (1), 245–265.

Winegar, R. (1984). *The National Commission on Excellence in Education and the limits of educational reform.* Paper presented to the Southeast Philosophy of Education Society, Mobile, Alabama.

Wirth, A. (1983). *Productive work—in industry and schools.* Lanham, MD: University Press of America.

Wolff, J. (1997). Women in organizations. In S. Clegg & D. Dunkerly (Eds.), *Critical issues in organizations.* London: Routledge Direct Editions.

Wolman, W., & Colamosca, A. (1997). *The Judas economy: The triumph of capital and the betrayal of work.* New York: Addison-Wesley.

Woods, A., & Grant, T. (1998). *Reason in revolt: Marxism and modern science.* <http://easyweb.easynet.co.uk~zac/chapter7.htm>.

Wronski, S. (1982). Edgar Bruce Wesley (1891–1980): His contributions to the past, present and future of the social studies. *Journal of Thought, 17,* 60–74.

Yeager, E., & Wilson, E. (1997). Teaching historical thinking in the social studies methods courses: A case study. *The Social Studies, 83* (3), 121–126.

Yeakey, C. (1987). Critical thought and administrative theory: Conceptual approaches to the study of decision-making. *Planning and Changing, 18* (1), 23–32.

Young, R. (1990). *A critical theory of education: Habermas and our children's future.* New York: Teachers College Press.

Yudice, G. (1995). What's a straight white man to do? In M. Berger, B. Wallis, & S. Watson (Eds.), *Constructing masculinity.* New York: Routledge.

Zavarzadeh, M., & Morton, D. (1991). *Theory, (post)modernity, opposition: An "other" introduction to literacy and cultural theory.* Washington, DC: Maisonneuve Press.

Zeuli, J., & Bachmann, M. (1986). *Implementation of teacher thinking research as curriculum deliberation.* Occasional Paper Number 107. East Lansing: MI State University, Institute for Research on Teaching.

Zinn, H. (1984). What is radical history? In. R. Sherman (Ed.), *Understanding history of education* (2nd ed.) (pp. 101–102). Cambridge, MA: Schenkman Publishing Company.

Zinn, M. (1994). Feminist rethinking from racial-ethnic families. In M. Zinn & B. Dill (Eds.), *Women of color in U.S. society.* Philadelphia: Temple University Press.

Zinn, M., & Dill, B. (1994). Difference and domination. In M. Zinn & B. Dill (Eds.), *Women of color in U.S. society.* Philadelphia: Temple University Press.

Zohar, D. & Marshall, I. (1994). The quantum society: Mind, physics, and a new social vision. New York: Milliam Morrow and Company.

Zunker, V. (1986). *Career counseling: Applied concepts of life planning.* Monterey, CA: Brooks/Cole Publishing.

Index

reductionism 313, 341
Reebok 700
reflective knowledge 271
reflexive awareness 558
Reich, C. 738, 752
Reinharz, S. 521
religious difference 332
religious faith 92
religious fundamentalism 95, 657
Renaissance 60
Republicans 71, 667, 724, 756
resacralization 314, 315
research 13, 14, 16, 78, 122, 141,
    210, 211, 213, 219, 220, 223,
    274, 350, 486, 497, 498, 565,
    572, 596, 757; abilities 273; ana-
    lysts 290; as a political act 498;
    methodology 207; paradigms 260
researchers 143, 224, 234, 272, 362,
    505, 563
resistant, democratic action 134
responsibility 235
revitalization 167
rewriting history 9
rhizomatics 497
Ricardo, Lucy and Ricky 531
Right-Wing
Right-Wing 332; commentators 712;
    curriculum of regulation 339;
    economic rules 662; education
    reforms 330; educational litera-
    ture 343; groups 60; notion of
    Tradition 338; regulatory stories
    332
Ritalin 746
Rivera, D. 669
Rivithead 321
Rodman, D. 80
Roosevelt, F. 738
Rorty, A. 556
Ross, E. W. 44
Ross, B. 620
Ryle, G. 135

Sanders, D. 318
SAT 106
Satanism 519
scholarship 13
school: choice 84; culture 17; curricu-
    lum 130; structure 193
schooling 85
science 217; and scientific research
    469; and technology 650; educa-
    tion/teachers 471, 475, 476, 478,
    479, 485, 486, 487, 492, 502,
    505, 507
Scientific: elite 477; knowledge 105,
    106, 107; management 101,102;
    management of industry 127;
    method 184; pedagogy 101;
    rationality 474; rationality 479;
    research 236, 485; revolution 91,
    313; theory 141; thinking 479
Scientists 484
Scully, D. 85
secondary research 374
secular humanism 7
Selden, S. 213, 560
self-production 303
self-direction 51
self-knowledge 310, 634
self-reflection 360, 472
Semali, L. 313
semiological study 229
semiotic researchers 230
semioticians 228
semiotics 218, 228, 230, 497-498
sense knowledge 105
separateness 238
separation of the knower and the
    known 201
Sergeant Joe Friday 565
sexism 624, 698
sexual revolution 5
Sexual Politics 513
Shakespeare, W. 640
Shell Oil Company 327

Studies in the Postmodern Theory of Education

General Editors
Joe L. Kincheloe & Shirley R. Steinberg

Counterpoints publishes the most compelling and imaginative books being written in education today. Grounded on the theoretical advances in criticalism, feminism, and postmodernism in the last two decades of the twentieth century, Counterpoints engages the meaning of these innovations in various forms of educational expression. Committed to the proposition that theoretical literature should be accessible to a variety of audiences, the series insists that its authors avoid esoteric and jargonistic languages that transform educational scholarship into an elite discourse for the initiated. Scholarly work matters only to the degree it affects consciousness and practice at multiple sites. Counterpoints' editorial policy is based on these principles and the ability of scholars to break new ground, to open new conversations, to go where educators have never gone before.

For additional information about this series or for the submission of manuscripts, please contact:

Joe L. Kincheloe & Shirley R. Steinberg
c/o Peter Lang Publishing, Inc.
275 Seventh Avenue, 28th floor
New York, New York 10001

To order other books in this series, please contact our Customer Service Department:

(800) 770-LANG (within the U.S.)
(212) 647-7706 (outside the U.S.)
(212) 647-7707 FAX

Or browse online by series:
www.peterlangusa.com